Lecture Notes in Computer Science   8285

Commenced Publication in 1973
Founding and Former Series Editors:
Gerhard Goos, Juris Hartmanis, and Jan van Leeuwen

Joanna Kołodziej   Beniamino Di Martino
Domenico Talia   Kaiqi Xiong (Eds.)

Algorithms and Architectures for Parallel Processing

13th International Conference, ICA3PP 2013
Vietri sul Mare, Italy, December 18-20, 2013
Proceedings, Part I

 Springer

Volume Editors

Joanna Kołodziej
Cracow University of Technology, Institute of Computer Science
Cracow, Poland
E-mail: jokolodziej@pk.edu.pl

Beniamino Di Martino
Seconda Università di Napoli, Dipartimento di Ingegneria
Industriale e dell' Informazione
Aversa, Italy
E-mail: beniamino.dimartino@unina.it

Domenico Talia
DIMES and ICAR-CNR, c/o Università della Calabria
Rende, Italy
E-mail: talia@deis.unical.it

Kaiqi Xiong
Rochester Institute of Technology, B. Thomas College
of Computing and Information Sciences
Rochester, NY, USA
E-mail: kxxics@rit.edu

ISSN 0302-9743   e-ISSN 1611-3349
ISBN 978-3-319-03858-2   e-ISBN 978-3-319-03859-9
DOI 10.1007/978-3-319-03859-9

Springer Cham Heidelberg New York Dordrecht London

Library of Congress Control Number: 2013954770
CR Subject Classification (1998): F.2, D.2, D.4, C.2, C.4, H.2, D.3
LNCS Sublibrary: SL 1 – Theoretical Computer Science and General Issues

Typesetting: Camera-ready by author, data conversion by Scientific Publishing Services, Chennai, India

Printed on acid-free paper

Springer is part of Springer Science+Business Media (www.springer.com)

Message from the General Chairs

Welcome to the proceedings of 13th International Conference on Algorithms and Architectures for Parallel Processing (ICA3PP 2013), organized by the Second University of Naples with the support of St. Francis Xavier University. It was our great pleasure to hold ICA3PP 2013 in Vietri sul Mare in Italy. In the past, the ICA3PP 2013 conference series was held in Asia and Australia. This was the second time the conference was held in Europe (the first time being in Cyprus in 2008).

Since its inception, ICA3PP 2013 has aimed to bring together people interested in the many dimensions of algorithms and architectures for parallel processing, encompassing fundamental theoretical approaches, practical experimental projects, and commercial components and systems. ICA3PP 2013 consisted of the main conference and four workshops/symposia. Around 80 paper presentations from 30 countries and keynote sessions by distinguished guest speakers were presented during the three days of the conference.

An international conference of this importance requires the support of many people and organizations as well as the general chairs, whose main responsibility is to coordinate the various tasks carried out with other willing and talented volunteers. First of all, we want to thank Professors Andrzej Gościński, Yi Pan, and Yang Xiang, the Steering Committee chairs, for giving us the opportunity to hold this conference and their guidance in organizing it. We would like to express our appreciation to Professors Laurence T. Yang, Jianhua Ma, and Sazzad Hussain for their great support in the organization.

We would like to also express our special thanks to the Program Chairs Professors Joanna Kołodziej, Kaiqi Xiong, and Domenico Talia, for their hard and excellent work in organizing a very strong Program Committee, an outstanding reviewing process to select high-quality papers from a large number of submissions, and making an excellent conference program. Our special thanks also go to the Workshop Chairs Professors Rocco Aversa and Jun Zhang for their outstanding work in managing the four workshops/symposia, and to the Publicity Chairs Professors Xiaojun Cao, Shui Yu, Al-Sakib Khan Pathan, Carlos Westphall, and Kuan-Ching Li for their valuable work in publicizing the call for papers and the event itself. We are grateful to the workshop/symposia organizers for their professionalism and excellence in organizing the attractive workshops/symposia, and the advisory members and Program Committee members for their great support. We are grateful to the local organizing team, for their extremely hard working, efficient services, and wonderful local arrangements.

Last but not least, we heartily thank all authors for submitting and presenting their high-quality papers to the ICA3PP 2013 main conference and workshops/symposia.

December 2013

Beniamino Di Martino
Albert Y. Zomaya
Christian Engelmann

Message from the ICA3PP 2013 Program Chairs

We are very happy to welcome readers to the proceedings of the 13th International Conference on Algorithms and Architectures for Parallel Processing (ICA3PP 2013) held in Vietri sul Mare, Italy, in December 2013.

ICA3PP 2013 was the 13th event in this series of conferences that is devoted to algorithms and architectures for parallel processing starting from 1995. ICA3PP is now recognized as a main regular scientific venue internationally, covering the different aspects and issues of parallel algorithms and architectures, encompassing fundamental theoretical approaches, practical experimental results, software systems, and product components and applications.

As the use of computing systems has permeated in every aspect of daily life, their scalability, adaptation, and distribution in human environments have become increasingly critical and vital. Specifically, the main areas of the conference include cluster, distributed and parallel systems, and middeware that cover a variety of topics such as big data, multi-core programming and software tools, distributed scheduling and load balancing, high-performance scientific computing, parallel algorithms, parallel architectures, scalable and distributed databases, dependability in distributed and parallel systems, as well as wireless and mobile computing.

ICA3PP 2013 provided a widely known forum for researchers and practitioners from many countries around the world to exchange ideas on improving the computational power and functionality of computing systems through the exploitation of parallel and distributed computing techniques and models.

The ICA3PP 2013 call for papers received a great deal of attention from the computer science community and 90 manuscripts were submitted from 33 countries. These papers were strictly evaluated on the basis of their originality, significance, correctness, relevance, and technical quality. Each paper was reviewed by at least three members of the Program Committee and external reviewers. Based on these evaluations of the papers submitted, 10 distinguished papers and 31 regular papers were selected for presentation at the conference, representing 11% of acceptance for distinguished papers and 34% for regular papers. This book consists of the two parts: distinguished papers and regular papers. All of them are considered as the papers of the main conference tracks.

The success of any conference depends on its authors, reviewers, and organizers. ICA3PP 2013 was no exception. We are grateful to all the authors who submitted their papers and to all the reviewers for their outstanding work in refereeing the papers on a very tight schedule. We relied heavily on a team of volunteers, especially those in Italy, to keep the ICA3PP 2013 wheel turning.

Last but not least, we would also like to take this opportunity to thank the whole LNCS Springer editorial team for their support in the preparation of this publication.

December 2013

Joanna Kołodziej
Domenico Talia
Kaiqi Xiong

Organization

ICA3PP 2013 was organized by the Second University of Naples, Italy, Department of Industrial and Information Engineering, and St. Francis Xavier University, Canada, Department of Computer Science. It was hosted by the Second University of Naples in Vietri sul Mare (Italy) during December 18–20, 2013.

Steering Committee

Andrzej Gościński   Deakin University, Australia
Yi Pan   Georgia State University, USA
Yang Xiang   Deakin University, Australia

Advisory Committee

Minyi Guo   Shanghai Jiao Tong University, China
Ivan Stojmenovic   University of Ottawa, Canada
Koji Nakano   Hiroshima University, Japan

Conference Organizers

General Chairs

Beniamino Di Martino   Second University of Naples, Italy
Albert Y. Zomaya   The University of Sydney, Australia
Christian Engelmann   Oak Ridge National Laboratory, USA

Program Chairs

Joanna Kołodziej   Cracow University of Technology, Poland
Domenico Talia   Università della Calabria, Italy
Kaiqi Xiong   Rochester Institute of Technology, USA

Workshop Chairs

Rocco Aversa   Second University of Naples, Italy
Jun Zhang   Deakin University, Australia

Publicity Chairs

Xiaojun (Matt) Cao   Georgia State University, USA
Shui Yu   Deakin University, Australia

Al-Sakib Khan Pathan International Islamic University of Malaysia,
  Malaysia
Carlos Westphall Federal University of Santa Catarina, Brazil
Kuan-Ching Li Providence University, Taiwan

Web Chair

Sazzad Hussain St. Francis Xavier University, Canada

Technical Editorial Committee

Sazzad Hussain St. Francis Xavier University, Canada
Magdalena Szmajduch Cracow University of Technology, Poland

Local Organization

Pasquale Cantiello Second University of Naples, Italy
Giuseppina Cretella Second University of Naples, Italy
Luca Tasquier Second University of Naples, Italy
Alba Amato Second University of Naples, Italy
Loredana Liccardo Second University of Naples, Italy
Serafina Di Biase Second University of Naples, Italy
Paolo Pariso Second University of Naples, Italy
Angela Brunitto Second University of Naples, Italy
Marco Scialdone Second University of Naples, Italy
Antonio Esposito Second University of Naples, Italy
Vincenzo Reccia Second University of Naples, Italy

Program Committee

Alba Amato Second University of Naples, Italy
Henrique Andrade JP Morgan, USA
Cosimo Anglano Università del Piemonte Orientale, Italy
Ladjel Bellatreche ENSMA, France
Jorge Bernal Bernabe University of Murcia, Spain
Ateet Bhalla Oriental Institute of Science and Technology,
  Bhopal, India
George Bosilca University of Tennessee, USA
Surendra Byna Lawrence Berkeley National Lab, USA
Aleksander Byrski AGH University of Science and Technology,
  Poland
Massimo Cafaro University of Salento, Italy
Pasquale Cantiello Second University of Naples, Italy
Eugenio Cesario ICAR-CNR, Italy
Ruay-Shiung Chang National Dong Hwa University, Taiwan

Dan Chen	University of Geosciences, Wuhan, China
Jing Chen	National Cheng Kung University, Taiwan
Zizhong (Jeffrey) Chen	University of California at Riverside, USA
Carmela Comito	University of Calabria, Italy
Raphal Couturier	University of Franche-Comté, France
Giuseppina Cretella	Second University of Naples, Italy
Gregoire Danoy	University of Luxembourg, Luxembourg
Eugen Dedu	University of Franche-Comté, France
Ciprian Dobre	University Politehnica of Bucharest, Romania
Susan Donohue	College of New Jersey, USA
Bernabe Dorronsoro	University of Lille 1, France
Todd Eavis	Concordia University, Canada
Deborah Falcone	University of Calabria, Italy
Massimo Ficco	Second University of Naples, Italy
Gianluigi Folino	ICAR-CNR, Italy
Agostino Forestiero	ICAR-CNR, Italy
Franco Frattolillo	Universitá del Sannio, Italy
Karl Fuerlinger	Ludwig Maximilians University Munich, Germany
Jose Daniel Garcia	University Carlos III of Madrid, Spain
Harald Gjermundrod	University of Nicosia, Cyprus
Michael Glass	University of Erlangen-Nuremberg, Germany
Rama Govindaraju	Google, USA
Daniel Grzonka	Cracow University of Technology, Poland
Houcine Hassan	University Politecnica de Valencia, Spain
Shi-Jinn Horng	National Taiwan University of Science & Technology, Taiwan
Yo-Ping Huang	National Taipei University of Technology, Taiwan
Mauro Iacono	Second University of Naples, Italy
Shadi Ibrahim	Inria, France
Shuichi Ichikawa	Toyohashi University of Technology, Japan
Hidetsugu Irie	University of Electro-Communications, Japan
Helen Karatza	Aristotle University of Thessaloniki, Greece
Soo-Kyun Kim	PaiChai University, Korea
Agnieszka Krok	Cracow University of Technology, Poland
Edmund Lai	Massey University, New Zealand
Changhoon Lee	Seoul National University of Science and Technology (SeoulTech), Korea
Che-Rung Lee	National Tsing Hua University, Taiwan
Laurent Lefevre	Inria, University of Lyon, France
Keqiu Li	Dalian University of Technology, China
Keqin Li	State University of New York at New Paltz, USA
Loredana Liccardo	Second University of Naples, Italy

Kai Lin	Dalian University of Technology, China
Wei Lu	Keene University, USA
Amit Majumdar	San Diego Supercomputer Center, USA
Tomas Margale	Universitat Autonoma de Barcelona, Spain
Fabrizio Marozzo	University of Calabria, Italy
Stefano Marrone	Second University of Naples, Italy
Alejandro Masrur	TU Chemnitz, Germany
Susumu Matsumae	Saga University, Japan
Francesco Moscato	Second University of Naples, Italy
Esmond Ng	Lawrence Berkeley National Lab, USA
Hirotaka Ono	Kyushu University, Japan
Francesco Palmieri	Second University of Naples, Italy
Zafeirios Papazachos	Aristotle University of Thessaloniki, Greece
Juan Manuel Marn Pérez	University of Murcia, Spain
Dana Petcu	West University of Timisoara, Romania
Ronald Petrlic	University of Paderborn, Germany
Florin Pop	University Politehnica of Bucharest, Romania
Rajeev Raje	Indiana University-Purdue University Indianapolis, USA
Rajiv Ranjan	CSIRO, Canberra, Australia
Etienne Riviere	University of Neuchatel, Switzerland
Francoise Saihan	CNAM, France
Subhash Saini	NASA, USA
Johnatan Pecero Sanchez	University of Luxembourg, Luxembourg
Rafael Santos	National Institute for Space Research, Brazil
Erich Schikuta	University of Vienna, Austria
Edwin Sha	Chongqing University, China
Sachin Shetty	Tennessee State University, USA
Katarzyna Smelcerz	Cracow University of Technology, Poland
Peter Strazdins	Australian National University, Australia
Ching-Lung Su	National Yunlin University of Science and Technology, Taiwan
Anthony Sulistio	High Performance Computing Center Stuttgart (HLRS), Germany
Magdalena Szmajduch	Cracow University of Technology, Poland
Kosuke Takano	Kanagawa Institute of Technology, Japan
Uwe Tangen	Ruhr-Universität Bochum, Germany
Jie Tao	University of Karlsruhe, Germany
Luca Tasquier	Second University of Naples, Italy
Olivier Terzo	Istituto Superiore Mario Boella, Italy
Hiroyuki Tomiyama	Ritsumeikan University, Japan
Tomoaki Tsumura	Nagoya Institute of Technology, Japan
Gennaro Della Vecchia	ICAR-CNR, Italy
Luis Javier Garca Villalba	Universidad Complutense de Madrid (UCM), Spain
Chen Wang	CSIRO ICT Centre, Australia

Table of Contents – Part I

Distinguished Papers

Regular Papers

Table of Contents – Part II

Part II: International Workshop on Big Data Computing (BDC 2013)

Part III: International Workshop on Trusted Information in Big Data (TIBiDa 2013)

Part IV: Cloud-assisted Smart Cyber-Physical Systems (C-SmartCPS 2013)

Clustering and Change Detection in Multiple Streaming Time Series

Antonio Balzanella and Rosanna Verde

Second University of Naples, Dep. of Political Sciences
{Antonio.balzanella,Rosanna.verde}@unina2.it

Abstract. In recent years, Data Stream Mining (DSM) has received a lot of attention due to the increasing number of applicative contexts which generate temporally ordered, fast changing, and potentially infinite data. To deal with such data, learning techniques require to satisfy several computational and storage constraints so that new and specific methods have to be developed. In this paper we introduce a new strategy for dealing with the problem of streaming time series clustering. The method allows to detect a partition of the streams over a user chosen time period and to discover evolutions in proximity relations. We show that it is possible to reach these aims, performing the clustering of temporally non overlapping data batches arriving on-line and then running a suitable clustering algorithm on a dissimilarity matrix updated using the outputs of the local clustering. Through an application on real and simulated data, we will show that this method provides results comparable to algorithms for stored data.

Keywords: Time series data streams, Clustering, Change detection.

1 Introduction

A growing number of applicative fields is generating huge amounts of temporal data. We can take, for instance, data generated by real-time trade surveillance systems for security fraud and money laundering, communication networks, power consumption measurement, dynamic tracing of stock fluctuations, internet traffic, industry production processes, scientific and engineering experiments, remote sensors. In these contexts, data are sequences of values or events obtained through repeated measurements over time.

Traditional learning techniques for temporal data have their reference in temporal data mining and time series analysis literature [22], however new challenges emerge when data are collected on-line, fast changing, massive, and potentially infinite.

Data stream mining [25] is the recent research field which aims at developing new methods for the analysis of such kind of data.

Algorithms for data stream mining should meet a set of stringent design criteria[14]: i) time required for processing the incoming observations has to be small and constant, ii) memory requirements have to be reduced with reference to the amount of data to be processed, iii) algorithms have to perform only

J. Kołodziej et al. (Eds.): ICA3PP 2013, Part I, LNCS 8285, pp. 1–14, 2013.

one scan of the data iv) knowledge about data should be available at any point in time or on user demand.

In order to deal with these requirements, the analysis of stream data is, often, performed using synopses, which are data structures storing summaries of the incoming data. The general idea is to update and/or generate synopsis data structures every time a new element or a batch of elements is collected and then, to extract the knowledge starting from the summaries rather than directly from the observations.

This mode of processing data enforces a trade-off between the accuracy of the data mining techniques and the computational and storage constraints. Thus, one of the challenges is to develop effective and space-time efficient synopses which allow to provide a good approximation of the results of data analysis techniques for stocked data.

Several kinds of synopses have been developed for data stream processing: sampling based on the reservoir sampling algorithm [24][2], on line histogram construction [13], wavelets as data stream synopsis [16], sketches, which are small-space summaries for a distribution vector (e.g., histogram) based on using randomized linear projections of the underlying data vectors [12][15], finally, techniques aiming at representing streaming time series into reduced space[20][3].

Data stream mining methods use synopses for performing, on-line or off-line, usual data mining tasks such as frequent pattern mining, association rules detection, classification, clustering.

In this paper, we focus on a specific clustering problem. We propose a new strategy able to detect a partition of a set of streams into clusters and a representation of the clusters through suitable prototype functions.

In data stream framework, the clustering aims at dealing with two different challenges. The first is to analyze a single univariate or multivariate data stream with the objective to reveal a partition of the observations it is composed of. The second is to analyze multiple data streams generated by several sources (for example sensor networks) to find (and make available at any time), a partition of streams which behave similarly through time.

The latter is the topic of this paper and is usually referred to as *clustering of time series data streams* since it considers each data stream as a univariate time series of potentially infinite size, which acquires, on-line, new observations.

Due to the constraints in data stream analysis, clustering of time series data streams is strongly differentiated by the batch clustering of time series. In particular, it needs to satisfy several specific requirements: it has to be possible to recover the clustering structure of a user chosen time interval without performing a further pass on data; summaries should be recorded on-line in order to get an overview of the monitored phenomenon over time; algorithms should still support the addition of new streams during the monitoring process and adapt the clustering to the new available information.

A further important issue is to take into account the evolution of data and the consequent, possible, change in the proximity relations among the streams. The evolution in the proximities impacts on the clustering structure which should be updated to reflect the new condition. Moreover, it is desirable to detect this change in order to provide a suitable alert, useful for decision support.

In order to satisfy these requirements, we introduce a new strategy for clustering temporally ordered data streams, based on discovering a global partitioning of the streams starting from the clustering of local batches of data.

The proposed method is based on performing the clustering of incoming data batches to provide, as output, a set of locally representative profiles and to allow the updating of a proximity matrix which records the dissimilarities among the streams. The overall partition of the streams is then obtained through a suitable clustering algorithm on the on-line updated proximity matrix. This strategy allows to discover evolutions of the data streams through an appropriate measure which monitors the changes in proximity relations.

We will still show that this approach supports the possibility of recovering the partition of the streams in a time interval chosen by the user, introducing a tilted windows method which stores recent information at a finer granularity level and outdated data at a courser level of detail.

It is interesting to note that our proposal is not based on some specific technique for preprocessing the incoming data in order to reduce the dimensionality and/or to deal with noise or missing items. In addition the clustering method will not make reference to a specific dissimilarity measure for comparing the streams. This allows to generalize our proposal to a high range of streaming time series clustering problems, where a suitable representation of data and an appropriate distance measure can be chosen according to the applicative context that must be analyzed.

The paper is organized as follows. Section 2 presents some of the main existing proposals for data streams clustering. Section 3 introduces the details of our strategy. In Section 4 the proposed strategy is evaluated on real data. Finally, Section 5 closes the paper.

2   State of Art

The data stream clustering problem has been widely dealt with in recent years. Several proposals ([17] [1]) address the challenge of the clustering of the observations of univariate or multivariate data streams (a wide review is available in [18]). The clustering of multiple data streams, which is the challenge of this paper, is a more recent topic. Interesting proposals have been introduced in [5][6][23] The first one is an extension, to the data stream framework, of the *k-means* algorithm for time series. The main drawback of this strategy is the inability to deal with evolving data streams. This is because the final data partition only depends from the data of the most recent window. Moreover it does not allow to interrogate for the clustering structure over user defined time intervals.

The second proposal, named Clustering On Demand (COD), is based on performing an on-line scan of the data for dimensionality reduction using a multi resolution approach based on wavelet transformation or on piecewise linear regression. The reduced time series are indexed by suitable hierarchies which are

Table 1. Main notations

Notation	Description	Notation	Description
Y	Set of n streams	P	Partition of the set of streams Y
Y_i	Single streaming time series	P^w	Partition of the data framed by the window w
w	Windows on data	L^w	Set of prototypes of the local partition P^w
s	Size of each window	C	Number of clusters of each local partition P^w
Y_i^w	Subset of the stream Y_i	A^w $[a^w(i,m)]$	= Matrix storing the dissimilarities among the streams

processed, off-line, by a suitable clustering algorithm which retrieves the partitioning structure of the streams. Although this method is able to deal with evolving data streams, its main drawback is that it is only effective when data can be appropriately represented using the wavelet transformation or the piecewise linear regression. In addition it does not manage the addition of new data streams.

The third mentioned approach is a top-down strategy named Online Divisive-Agglomerative Clustering (ODAC) where a hierarchy is built according to a dissimilarity measure based on the correlation among the streams. The proposed divisive approach incrementally updates the distance among the streams and executes a procedure for splitting the clusters on the basis of the comparison between the diameter of each cluster and a threshold obtained using Hoeffding bounds. In order to deal with evolution in data, ODAC provides a criterion to aggregate the leafs still based on the clusters diameters and Hoeffding bounds.

3   Clustering Algorithm for Multiple Data Streams

Let $Y = \{Y_1, ..., Y_i, ..., Y_n\}$ be a set of n streams $Y_i = \{(y_1, t_1), ..., (y_j, t_j), ...,\}$ made by real valued ordered observations on a discrete time grid $T = \{t_1, ..., t_j, ...\} \subseteq \Re$.

The objective is to get a partition P of Y in a predefined number C of homogeneous clusters C_k with $k = 1, ..., C$. We propose a new strategy based on Dynamic Clustering Algorithm (DCA) that according to the classic schema in [10][11] optimizes a measure of best fitting between the clusters of streams and the way to represent them.

We perform the partitioning of data in two main phases which we distinguish in an $on-line$ and in an $off-line$ phase.

In the on-line phase, the incoming data are split into non overlapping windows and then a partitioning of the subsequences in each window is achieved. The outputs of this on-line clustering process are: the prototypes of the clusters of the partitions associated to each window and the proximities among the subsequences of the several streams. This proximity measures are recorded in a proximity matrix which is updated with the new proximities at each clustering process performed on the set of subsequences in each window.

The on-line phase is then stopped at a certain time τ, which corresponds to a number of processed windows set apriori or on demand by the user. A global partitioning of the streams recorded until the stopping of the on-line clustering is then performed, off-line, using the DCLUST algorithm on dissimilarity matrix [11]. In particular, we consider in input the proximity matrix which contains information about the proximities between the pairs of subsequences as updated at each on-line clustering.

Repeating this off-line phase for different intervals of time in which the on-line process is stopped, it is possible to discover changes in the structure of clustering that corresponds to changes in the behavior of the subsequences along time.

3.1   On-line Partitioning Process on Subsequences

According to the introduced clustering schema, the first step consists in splitting the incoming parallel streams into non overlapping windows, where each window $w = 1, \ldots, \infty$, is an ordered subset of T having size s which frames a subset $Y_i^w = \{y_j, \ldots, y_{j+s}\}$ of Y_i called subsequence.

A Dynamic Cluster Algorithm (DCA) [10][9] is then performed on the subsequences $Y_1^w, \ldots, Y_i^w, \ldots, Y_n^w$ of the current window by looking for P^* among all the partitions P_C of Y^w in C classes and L^* among all the representations spaces L_C of the partition of Y^w in C classes, such that is minimized a measure Δ of fitting between L and P:

$$\Delta(P^*, L^*) = Min\{\Delta(P, L)/P \in P_C, L \in L_C\}$$

The definition of the algorithm is performed according to two main functions:

- g: the *representation function* allowing to associate to each partition $P \in P_C$ of the $Y_i^w \in Y^w$ in C classes C_k ($k = 1, \ldots, C$) an element of the representation space of the classes, herein indicated as $L : g(P) = L$, and
- f: the *allocation function* allowing to associate to each $g_k \in L$ a partition $P : f(L) = P$.

The first function concerns the representation structure L for the classes $\{C_1, \ldots, C_k\} \in P$. Our proposal is based on a description of the classes again in terms of subsequences, so that we choose to represent the clusters by profiles of the subsequences belonging to the clusters, here called prototypes, here denoted as $L^w = (g_1^w, \ldots, g_k^w, \ldots, g_K^w)$ for the cluster C_k^w (with $k = 1, \ldots, C$) of each partition P^w of the set Y^w (for each window w).

The definition of the *allocation function* f allows to assign a subsequence Y_i^w to a cluster C_k^w according to its similarity with the prototype g_k^w.

Given a suitable distance function $d(\cdot)$, the criterion $\Delta(P^w, L^w)$ optimized in DCA is usually defined as the sum of the measures $d(Y_i^w, g_k^w)$ of fitting between each subsequence Y_i^w in a cluster $C_k^w \in P^w$ and the prototypes g_k^w, expressed as:

$$\Delta(P^w, L^w) = \sum_{k=1}^{K} \sum_{Y_i^w \in C_k^w} d(Y_i^w, g_k^w) \tag{1}$$

The DCA algorithm used for carrying out the partition P^w and the related prototypes in L^w can be synthesized, in our context, by the following steps:

1. *Initialization*: Fixed a number C of clusters in which partition the set Y^w, detect a random partition $P^w = \{C_1^w, \ldots, C_k^w, \ldots, C_C^w\}$
2. *Representation step*: For $k = 1, \ldots, C$, detect the prototype
   $g_k^w = argmin(\sum_{Y_i^w \in C_k^w} d(Y_i^w, g_k^w))$
3. *Allocation step*: For $i = 1, \ldots, n$ allocate the subsequence Y_i^w to the cluster C_k^w such that $d(Y_i^w, g_k^w) < d(Y_i^w, g_{k'}^w)$ with $k \neq k'$

Steps 2 and 3 are repeated until the convergence to a stationary point.

Whenever the chosen distance function is the Euclidean distance, the algorithm is equivalent to the well known *K-means* algorithm where the prototypes are the average of subsequences in each local cluster.

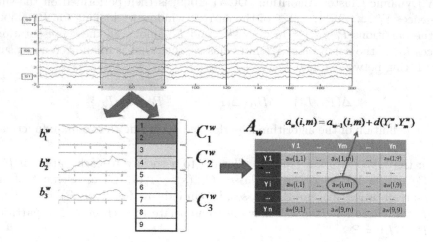

Fig. 1. On-line steps

On-line Proximity Matrix Updating. The outputs of the Dynamic Clustering Algorithm on the subsequences of each window are the *prototypes* of several clusters of local partition P^w that are the syntheses of the behavior of the streams at time periods corresponding to the size of the windows. iven the nature of the data and the limit in the time executionThe computation of the proximities between each pair of subsequences is prohibitive from a computational point of view taking into account the arriving frequency of the streams. Thus, in order to obtain information about the proximities between couples of subsequences we introduce a proximity matrix which records, for each partition of the subsequences in a window, the status of the proximities between the couples Y_i^w and Y_m^w ($\forall i, m = 1, \ldots, n$) in the cells $a^w(i, m)$ (with $i, m = 1, \ldots, n$) of the matrix $A^w = [a^w(i, m)]$, having denoted with A^w the status of the matrix A at the time corresponding to the processing of the window w.

In [4] we proposed to assign to the cells $a^w(i, m)$ and $a^w(m, i)$ the value 1 if Y_i^w and Y_m^w belong to the same cluster; the value 0 if the subsequences belong to different clusters. Updating the matrix A with values 0 or 1 (for all the pair $i, m = 1, \ldots, n$) at each partition of the local window, at a certain time the matrix A stores in each cell $a^w(i, m)$ the number of times each couple of streams is allocated to the same cluster of a local partition P^w. Even if the matrix A for a large number of windows approximates a matrix of similarities, it does not take into account any information about the internal cohesion of the clusters or the heterogeneity among streams belonging to different clusters.

In order to introduce more information in this proximity matrix, always respecting the computational constraints, we introduce a new approach based on updating the dissimilarities rather than the similarities among the streams.

According to this new strategy, the dissimilarities $d(Y_i^w, Y_m^w)$ between the couples Y_i^w, Y_m^w (with $i, m = 1, \ldots, n$) are computed as follows:

If $Y_i^w, Y_m^w \in C_k^w$, $d(Y_i^w, Y_m^w)$ is equal to $W_k^w = \frac{\sum_{Y_i^w \in C_k^w} d(Y_i^w; g_k^w)}{|C_k^w|}$ that is the average distance of the subsequences Y_i^w in a cluster C_k^w to the correspondent prototype g_k^w; It is worth noting that $W_k^w = \frac{\sum_{i, m \in C_k^w} d(Y_i^w; Y_m^w)}{|C_k^w| \cdot |C_k^w - 1|}$ when the prototypes g_k^w (for $k = 1, \ldots, C$) of the C clusters of the local partition P^w are the average profiles of the subsequences belonging to the several clusters and $d(.)$ is the Euclidean distance.

If $(Y_i^w \in C_k^w) \wedge (Y_m^w \in C_l^w)$ (with $k \neq l = 1, \ldots, C$), the dissimilarity value is $D_{i,l} = d(Y_i^w; g_l^w)$ that is the distance of a subsequence Y_i^w, belonging to the cluster C_k^w to the prototype g_l^w of a cluster C_l^w at which Y_m^w belongs.

We note that for the subsequences in the same cluster, the cell $a^w(i, m)$ is updated with the same value W_k^w while, for couples of streams belonging to different clusters, the cell $a^w(i, m)$ is updated with a different value $D_{i,k}$ depending on the distance of the stream Y_i^w to the prototype g_k^w of the cluster C_k^w at which Y_m^w belongs.

In synthesis, for each partition P^w of the subsequences in a window w, the cells of A are updated as follows:

$a^w(i, m) = a^{w-1}(i, m) + W_k^w$ if $Y_i^w, Y_m^w \in C_k^w$

$a^w(i, m) = a^{w-1}(i, m) + D_{i,l}$ if $Y_i^w \in C_k^w$ and $Y_m^w \in C_l^w$

3.2 Off-Line Partitioning through the Dynamic Clustering Algorithm for Dissimilarity Tables

In order to obtain a global partition P from the stored results of the local partition P^w we propose to use the Dynamic Clustering Algorithm on a Dissimilarity Table ($DCLUST$) [11] on the proximity matrix A^w. In such a way the criterion optimized for obtaining the partition P is consistent with the criterion optimized in the clustering of each local batch of data.

The aim of the *DCLUST* is to partition a set of elements into a fixed number of homogeneous classes (that we can choose to be equal or not equal to the number of clusters of each local partition) on the basis of the proximities between pairs of elements. The optimized criterion is based on the sum of the dissimilarities between elements belonging to the same cluster. Because the dissimilarities between pair of streams (Y_i and Y_m) are the values in the cells $a^w(i,m)$ of A^w, the DCA criterion can be expressed as:

$$\Delta(P,L) = \sum_{k=1}^{C} \sum_{i,m \in C_k} a^w(i,m) \tag{2}$$

According to the schema of DCLUST, the prototypes of the clusters corresponds to the streams Y_{m^*}: $m^* = argmin_m(\sum_{i \in C_k} a^w(i,m))$ with $Y_m \in C_k$ (for $k = 1, \ldots, C$).

The DCLUST algorithm schema is the following:

1. *Initialization*: The initial vector of prototypes, L contains random elements of S
2. *Allocation step*: A stream Y_i is allocated to the cluster C_k if $a^w(i,m) < a^w(i,j)$ with Y_m the prototype of C_k and Y_j the prototype of C_l (for all $k, l = 1, \ldots, C$)
3. *Representation step*: For each $k = 1, \ldots, C$, the prototype Y_m representing the class C_k is the stream $Y_{m^*} \in C_k$

Steps 2 and 3 are repeated until convergence.

It is easy to prove that the DCLUST on the dissimilarity matrix A, choosing as prototypes of the clusters the elements (streams) to the minimum distance from the other elements of the clusters, converges to a stationary value.

3.3   A Tilted Time Frame Approach for Detecting a Partitioning of the Streams over Defined Time Intervals

An important feature of the matrix A^w is that it satisfies the additive property:

Let $t_1, t_2 \in T$ be two time stamps and A_{t_1} and A_{t_2} be the corresponding dissimilarity matrices. The dissimilarity matrix in the interval $t_2 - t_1$ is $A_{\Delta t_1, t_2} = A_{t_2} - A_{t_1}$.

If the matrix A^w is stored at every update, it should be possible to recover the dissimilarities among the flows of data for every temporal interval. However, due to the storage constraints imposed by the data stream framework this is not possible and only a set of time stamps has to be selected for storing the proximities. With this aim, we introduce a tilted windows schema which aims at storing recent information at a fine scale and long-term information at a coarse scale.

There are several possible ways to design a tilted time frame. Here we recall the natural tilted time frame model and the logarithmic tilted time frame model.

In the natural tilted time frame model, the time frame is structured in multiple granularity based on the natural or usual time scale: the most recent 4 quarters (15 minutes), followed by the last 24 hours, then 31 days, and then 12 months.

The second model is the logarithmic tilted time frame model, where the time frame is structured in multiple granularities according to a logarithmic scale. If the most recent time stamp stores the proximities until the current time, the remaining slots for recording the proximity matrix correspond to $1, 2, 4, 8, 16, 32, \ldots$ windows ago.

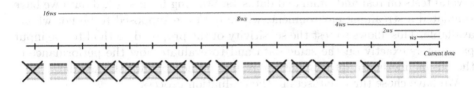

Fig. 2. Tilted time frame model

Though any tilted time frame model can be used in the proposed strategy, we will adopt the logarithmic schema which can be realized by simply deleting the non required matrices as shown in fig.2.

Change Detection. As previously stated, an important requirement for streaming time series clustering is the capability to monitor the evolution in proximity relations among the streams over time.

Starting from the on-line updated matrix A and recalling the additive property which allows to discover the proximities in a user chosen time period, we introduce two measures to understand, respectively, the overall and the pairwise change in the proximities among the streams in two temporal intervals $\Delta t' = [t_1, t_2]$ and $\Delta t'' = [t_3, t_4]$.

The first measure is referred to as *Structural Change* (SC) and is based on the Frobenius norm:

$$SC_{\Delta t', \Delta t''} = \left\| \frac{A_{\Delta t'}}{b_{\Delta t'}} - \frac{A_{\Delta t''}}{b_{\Delta t''}} \right\|_2 \tag{3}$$

where:
$A_{\Delta t'}$ and $A_{\Delta t''}$ are the proximity matrices computed for the time intervals $[t_1, t_2]$ and $[t_3, t_4]$;
$b_{\Delta t'}$ and $b_{\Delta t''}$ are the number of windows in $[t_1, t_2]$ and $[t_3, t_4]$;

The second measure which is referred to as pairwise change (PC), returns a matrix storing, in each cell, the strength of the change in pairwise proximity relations:

$$PC_{\Delta t', \Delta t''} = \left| \frac{A_{\Delta t'}}{b_{\Delta t'}} - \frac{A_{\Delta t''}}{b_{\Delta t''}} \right| \tag{4}$$

The pairwise change measure is computed by taking into account the difference between the dissimilarities at the two time periods normalized by the number of windows included in each of them in order to adapt to the different size of $\Delta t'$ and $\Delta t''$.

4   Experimental Results

In order to evaluate the performance of the proposed strategy we have run several tests on real and simulated datasets. Starting from stocked data we have simulated a streaming environment, where data are supposed to be not wholly available. This allows to test the sensitivity of the proposed method to the input parameters exactly on the same data and to evaluate how the performance of the on-line method approximates the results of methods for stocked data.

We have chose three datasets in the evaluation process:

The first is made by 76 highly evolving time series, downloaded from Yahoo finance where the observations are the daily closing price of several random chosen stocks. Each time series is made by 4000 observations.

The second is made by 179 highly evolving time series which collect daily electricity supply at several locations in Australia. Each time series is made by 3288 observations.

The third is a simulated dataset consisting in $n = 100$ time series each having 6,000 observations. The streams are generated according to two clusters. At the time stamp $t = 3000$ (in the middle of the series generation), we simulate a change in the proximities by changing the parameters of the equations used to generate the data. Especially for $t < 3000$, the data partition is $P' = \{Y_1, \ldots, Y_{50}\} \{Y_{51}, \ldots, Y_{100}\}$ while for $t > 3000$, the streams partition becomes: $P'' = \{Y_1, \ldots, Y_{25}, Y_{76}, \ldots, Y_{100}\} \{Y_{26}, \ldots, Y_{75}\}$. Such dataset has been introduced for evaluating the capability to discover changes in proximity relations.

Since one of the aims of the strategies for data stream mining is to produce results which approximate the ones provided by techniques for stocked data, we have compared the results obtained by the proposed method to the well known k-means algorithm performed on stored time series. Such choice is motivated by the common objective of finding a partition of the data, optimizing a criterion of maximum homogeneity of the elements in each cluster in terms of within deviance.

Our tests, have not been extended to existing clustering methods for streaming time series since they share different objectives. In particular, the on-line k-means proposed by Beringer and Hullermeier, in [5], is not able to deal with evolving data streams, while the clustering of time sieries data streams proposed by Rodrigues et al. in [23], is a hierarchical method, finally, the Adaptive Clustering for Multiple Evolving Streams proposed by Bi-Ru Dai et al., in [6] is not focused on giving summaries of incoming data while these are recorded.

We have considered several common indexes to assess the effectiveness of the proposal (See [8][7][19]). The Calinski-Harabasz Index(CH), Davies-Bouldin(DB)

Index and Silhouette Width Criterion(SW), are used as internal validity criteria for evaluating the compactness of clusters and their separation. The Rand index (RI) and the Adjusted Rand index (ARI) are used to measure the consensus between the partition obtained by our proposal and the partition obtained using the k-means.

In order to perform the testing of our procedure, we need to set the size s of each temporal window and the number of clusters C. For the k-means we only need to set the global number of clusters C.

The Euclidean distance is used as dissimilarity function in both the procedures.

According to this choice, the local clustering performed by DCA algorithm on the subsequences in each window, is a k-$means$ where the prototypes are the average profile of the data in a cluster.

Parameter C has been set, for the first and second datasets, running the k-$means$ algorithm using $C = 2, \dots, 8$. For each value of C we have computed the Within Deviance. We have chosen $C = 4$ for the first dataset and $C = 3$ for the second dataset, since these are the values which provide the highest improvement of the clusters homogeneity in terms of Within Deviance.

For the third dataset we have chose $C = 2$ since data have been generated so as to belong to two clusters.

By evaluating, through the mentioned indexes, the partitioning quality for several values of s we can state that the choice of the windows size does not impact on the clusters homogeneity. As a consequence, the choice of the value of such parameter, can be performed according to the kind of required summarization. For example, if we need to detect a set of prototypes for each week of data, we choose a value of the window size which frames the observations in a week.

In our tests, we have used windows made by 30 observations for the first two datasets and 50 for the third one.

In order to compare the clustering performance of the proposed method to the k-means, we show, respectively in table 2 and table 3, the values of the introduced internal and external validity indexes.

Looking at the values of the internal validity indexes, computed for our proposal and for the k-means on stocked data, it emerges that the homogeneity of the clusters and their separation, is quite similar.

Table 2. Internal validity indexes

Dataset	On-line clustering			k-means algorithm		
	DB	CH	SW	DB	CH	SW
Electricity supply	2.104	26.353	0.227	2.172	26.504	0.229
Financial data	1.793	15.291	0.307	1.754	15.594	0.321
Simulated dataset	0.521	5.714	0.857	0.521	5.714	0.857

Table 3. External validity indexes

Dataset	Rand Index	Adjusted Rand Index
Power supply	0.95	0.88
Financial data	0.91	0.86
Simulated dataset	1	1

Moreover, the value of the Rand Index and of the Adjusted Rand Index highlights the strength of the consensus between the obtained partitions.

A further aim of our tests is to evaluate if the proposed strategy is able to discover the time point of the evolution, to measure its strength and to understand which streams have the strongest evolution. To reach this aim we will only refer to the simulated dataset.

We need to set the two time intervals over which the tests are made. We have chosen to perform a dynamic monitoring such that the first time interval $\Delta t' = [t_1, t_2]$ is made by the most recent 150 observations corresponding to three windows of data, while the second time interval $\Delta t'' = [t_3, t_4]$ is made by the previous 150 observations not included in $\Delta t' = [t_1, t_2]$.

The main results for the $SD_{\Delta t', \Delta t''}$ measure are shown in the following figure:

It is possible to note that the the peak in the plot is in correspondence of the middle of the monitoring activity such as expected. Moreover, looking at the following figure which illustrates the values of the $PC_{\Delta t', \Delta t''}$ matrix, it is possible to discover which pairs of streams highlight strong changes in proximity relations at the time point $t = 3000$.

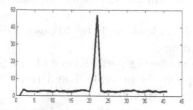

Fig. 3. $SC_{\Delta t', \Delta t''}$ measure over time

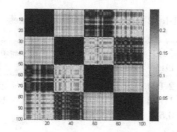

Fig. 4. $PC_{\Delta t', \Delta t''}$ matrix at $t = 3000$

5   Conclusions

In this paper we have introduced a new strategy which deals with two related problems in data stream mining: clustering and change detection. Starting from a set of on-line arriving data streams, we perform the clustering of temporally non overlapping data batches and then we run an appropriate clustering algorithm on a dissimilarity matrix updated using the outputs of the local clustering. The comparison of the dissimilarities at two time stamps allows to discover changes in data.

References

1. Aggarwal, C.C., Han, J., Wang, J., Yu, P.S.: A framework for clustering evolving data streams. In: VLDB 2003: Proceedings of the 29th International Conference on Very Large Data Bases, pp. 81–92. VLDB Endowment (2003)
2. Aggarwal, C.C.: On biased reservoir sampling in the presence of stream evolution. In: VLDB, San Francisco (2001, 2006)
3. Balzanella, A., Irpino, A., Verde, R.: Dimensionality reduction techniques for streaming time series: A new symbolic approach. In: Classification as a Tool for Research. Studies in Classification, Data Analysis, and Knowledge Organization, pp. 381–389. Springer, Heidelberg (2010)
4. Balzanella, A., Lechevallier, Y., Verde, R.: Clustering multiple data streams. New Perspectives in Statistical Modeling and Data Analysis. Springer, Heidelberg (2011)
5. Beringer, J., Hullermeier, E.: Online clustering of parallel data streams. Data and Knowledge Engineering 58(2), 180–204 (2006)
6. Dai, B.-R., Huang, J.-W., Yeh, M.-Y., Chen, M.-S.: Adaptive Clustering for Multiple Evolving Streams. IEEE Transactions On Knowledge And Data Engineering 18(9) (2006)
7. Calinski, R.B., Harabasz, J.: A dendrite method for cluster analysis. Communications in Statistics 3, 1–27 (1974)
8. Davies, D.L., Bouldin, D.W.: Cluster Separation Measure. IEEE Transactions on Pattern Analysis and Machine Intelligence 1(2), 95–104 (1979)
9. De Carvalho, F., Lechevallier, Y., Verde, R.: Clustering methods in symbolic data analysis. In: Classification, Clustering, and Data Mining Applications. Studies in Classification, Data Analysis, and Knowledge Organization, pp. 299–317. Springer, Berlin (2004)
10. Diday, E.: La methode des Nuees dynamiques. Revue de Statistique Appliquee 19(2), 19–34 (1971)
11. Diday, E., Noirhomme-Fraiture, M.: Symbolic Data Analysis and the SODAS Software. Wiley (2008)
12. Flajolet, P., Martin, G.N.: Probabilistic counting. In: SFCS 1983: Proceedings of the 24th Annual Symposium on Foundations of Computer Science, pp. 76–82. IEEE Computer Society, Washington, DC (1983)
13. Gama, J., Pinto, C.: Discretization from Data Streams: applications to Histograms and Data Mining. In: Proceedings of the 2006 ACM Symposium on Applied Computing, pp. 662–667 (2006)
14. Ganguly, A.R., Gama, J., Omitaomu, O.A., Gaber, M.M., Vatsavai, R.R.: Knowledge discovery from sensor data. CRC Press (2009)

15. Greenwald, M., Sanjeev, K.: Space-efficient online computation of quantile summaries. SIGMOD Rec. 30(2), 58–66 (2001)
16. Guha, S., Harb, B.: Wavelet synopsis for data streams: minimizing non-euclidean error. In: KDD, pp. 88–97 (2005)
17. Guha, S., Meyerson, A., Mishra, N., Motwani, R.: Clustering Data Streams: Theory and practice. IEEE Transactions on Knowledge and Data Engineering 15(3), 515–528 (2003)
18. Kavitha, V., Punithavalli, M.: Clustering Time Series Data Stream - A Literature Survey. International Journal of Computer Science and Information Security, IJCSIS 8(1) (April 2010) ISSN 1947-5500
19. Hubert, L., Arabie, P.: Comparing partitions. Journal of Classification, 193–218 (1985)
20. Camerra, A., Palpanas, T., Shieh, J., Keogh, E.: iSAX 2.0: Indexing and Mining One Billion Time Series. In: ICDM 2010 (2010)
21. Laxman, S., Sastrya, P.S.: A Survey of temporal data mining. SADHANA, Academy Proceedings in Engineering Sciences 31(2), 173–198 (2006)
22. Mitsa, T.: Temporal Data Mining. CRC Press (2010) ISBN:9781420089769
23. Rodriguess, P.P., Pedroso, J.P.: Hierarchical Clustering of Time Series Data Streams. IEEE Transactions on Knowledge and Data Engineering 20(5) (2008)
24. Vitter, J.S.: Random sampling with a reservoir. ACM Trans. Math. Softw. 11, 37–57 (1985)
25. Yu, P.S., Wang, H., Han, J.: Mining Data Streams. In: Maimon, O., Rokach, L. (eds.) The Data Mining and Knowledge Discovery Handbook 2005. Springer (2005)

Lightweight Identification of Captured Memory for Software Transactional Memory⋆

Fernando Miguel Carvalho[1,2] and João Cachopo[2]

[1] DEETC, ISEL/Polytechnic Institute of Lisbon, Portugal
mcarvalho@cc.isel.ipl.pt
[2] INESC-ID Lisboa / Instituto Superior Técnico, Universidade de Lisboa, Portugal
joao.cachopo@ist.utl.pt

Abstract. Software Transactional Memory (STM) implementations typically instrument each memory access within transactions with a call to an STM barrier to ensure the correctness of the transactions. Compared to simple memory accesses, STM barriers are complex operations that add significant overhead to transactions doing many memory accesses. Thus, whereas STMs have shown good results for micro-benchmarks, where transactions are small, they often show poor performance on real-world–sized benchmarks, where transactions are more coarse-grained and, therefore, encompass more memory accesses.

In this paper, we propose a new runtime technique for lightweight identification of captured memory—LICM—for which no STM barriers are needed. Our technique is independent of the specific STM design and can be used by any STM implemented in a managed environment. We implemented it on the Deuce STM Framework, for three different STMs, and tested it across a variety of benchmarks.

Using our technique to remove useless barriers, we improved the performance of all baseline STMs for most benchmarks, with speedups of up to 27 times. Most importantly, we were able to improve the performance of some of the benchmarks, when using an STM, to values close to or better than the performance of the best lock-based approaches.

Keywords: Software Transactional Memory, Runtime Optimizations.

1 Introduction

Some researchers (e.g. [6]) question the usefulness of Software Transactional Memory (STM), because most STM implementations fail to demonstrate applicability to real-world problems: In many cases, the performance of an STM on a real-world–sized benchmark is significantly lower than the sequential version of the benchmark, or even than the version using coarse-grain locks. The loss of performance is often attributed to the *over-instrumentation* [19] made on these

---

⋆ This work was supported by national funds through FCT, both under project PEst-OE/EEI/LA0021/2013 and under project PTDC/EIA-EIA/108240/2008 (the Ru-LAM project).

J. Kołodziej et al. (Eds.): ICA3PP 2013, Part I, LNCS 8285, pp. 15–29, 2013.

benchmarks by overzealous STM compilers that protect each and every memory access with a barrier that calls back to the STM runtime.

Thus, several researchers proposed optimization techniques to elide useless barriers—for instance, to elide barriers when accessing transaction local memory. The most effective proposals (e.g. [2], [5], [13] and [19]) decompose the STM's API in heterogeneous parts that allow the programmer to convey application-level information about the behavior of the memory locations to the instrumentation engine. Yet, this approach contrasts with one of the main advantages of an STM, which is to provide a transparent synchronization API, meaning that programmers just need to specify which operations are atomic, without knowing which data is accessed within those operations. That is the approach used by Deuce STM [14], an STM framework for the Java environment.

Afek et al. [1] added to Deuce STM a static analysis technique to enable compile-time optimizations that avoid instrumentation of memory accesses in several situations, including to transaction local memory. Yet, this approach does not accomplish the performance improvements shown by solutions based on heterogeneous APIs that were also proposed to Deuce STM [5]. In fact, static compiler analysis is often imprecise and conservative, and thus cannot remove all unnecessary barriers, because program modules are dynamically loaded, for example, and it is impossible to perform whole program compiler analysis. However, we argue that automatic approaches that keep the transparency of the STM API are better suited to the overall goal of STMs. So, in this paper, we propose to tackle this problem and find a technique based on runtime analysis that automatically and efficiently elide STM barriers for transaction local memory.

Our work is based on the proposal of Dragojevic et al. [8], which introduces the concept of *captured memory* as memory allocated inside a transaction that cannot *escape* (i.e., is *captured* by) its allocating transaction. Captured memory corresponds to newly allocated objects that did not exist before the beginning of their allocating transaction and that, therefore, are held within the transaction until its successful commit. They use the term *capture analysis* (similar to *escape* analysis) to refer to a compile- or runtime-time algorithm that determines whether a memory location is captured by a transaction or not.

Given the lack of demonstrable effectiveness of the static compiler analysis [1], here we are interested in exploring the proposal of Dragojevic et al. [8] for *runtime capture analysis*, adapt it to a managed runtime environment and make it more efficient. More specifically, the main contributions of this paper are:

- A new runtime technique for lightweight identification of captured memory—LICM—for managed environments that is independent of the underlying STM design (Section 3). Our approach is surprisingly simple, yet effective, being up to 5 times faster than the *filtering* algorithm proposed by [8] (which we briefly introduce in Section 2.2).
- We implemented the LICM in Deuce STM, which already includes some optimization techniques in its original implementation (Section 2.1). Our implementation uses a new infrastructure of enhancement transformations,

which is described in Section 4. By providing an implementation of our proposal within Deuce STM, we were able to test it with a variety of baseline STM algorithms, namely, LSA [16], TL2 [7], and JVSTM [10].

– We performed extensive experimental tests for a wide variety of benchmarks (Section 5), including real-world–sized benchmarks that are known for being specially challenging for STMs. The goal of these tests was not only to evaluate the performance of our proposal, but, more importantly, to assess the usefulness of the runtime capture analysis, thus completing the analysis of [8] about how many of the memory accesses are to captured locations. Besides the STAMP [4], we also analyze the STMBench7 [12], and the JWormBench [5], which were not included in [8].

– For the first time, in some of the more challenging benchmarks, the LICM makes STM's performance competitive with the best fine-grained lock-based approaches. Moreover, given its lightweight nature, it has almost no overhead when the benchmark presents no opportunities for optimizations.

In Section 6, we discuss related work on optimization techniques for STMs. Finally, in Section 7, we conclude and discuss some future work.

2 Past Solutions for Compiler Over-Instrumentation

A naive STM compiler translates every memory access inside a transaction into a read or a write barrier, which typically require orders of magnitude more machine cycles than a simple memory access. So, whereas the approach taken by STM compilers ensures the correctness of the whole application, it also degrades its performance significantly. In this section, we present an overview on past solutions to elide useless STM barriers.

2.1 Deuce STM Optimizations

Deuce STM is a Java-based STM framework that provides a bytecode instrumentation engine implemented with ASM [3]. Its two major goals are: (1) to be able to integrate the implementation of any synchronization technique, and, in particular, different STMs; and (2) to provide a transparent synchronization API, meaning that a programmer using it just needs to be concerned with the identification of the methods that should execute atomically. For this purpose, the programmer marks those methods with an @Atomic annotation and the Deuce's engine automatically synchronizes their execution using a synchronization technique that is defined by the programmer in a class that implements the Context interface (for more detailed information about Deuce STM see [14]).

During instrumentation, Deuce STM can perform two optimizations to suppress useless STM barriers. First, Deuce STM does not instrument accesses to final fields, as they cannot be modified after creation. This optimization avoids the use of STM barriers when accessing immutable fields, provided that they were correctly identified in the application code.

Second, programmers may exclude some classes from being transformed by specifying the names of the classes to be excluded via a runtime parameter (org.deuce.exclude). This approach, however, reduces the transparency of the Deuce API. Moreover, it has some limitations: It does not work with arrays, nor can it be used when the same class has both instances that are shared and instances that are not shared across the transaction's boundaries. So, there is no support in the original Deuce STM for identifying objects that are transaction local and it is not feasible to do it through the existent mechanisms.

2.2   Runtime Capture Analysis

Our proposal is based on the work of Dragojevic et al. [8], originally proposed for the Intel C++ STM compiler, but that we adapted to the Deuce STM.

In Algorithm 1, we show the pseudo code for a read and a write barrier in Deuce STM when using runtime capture analysis. In both cases, the barrier first checks whether the object being accessed is captured by the current transaction. If so, it accesses data directly from memory; otherwise, it executes the standard full barrier. As in Deuce STM, object fields are updated in place using the sun.misc.Unsafe pseudo-standard internal library.

Algorithm 1. Read and write barriers when using runtime capture analysis

> in the following, ref is an object, $addr$ is the address of the field accessed on ref, val is the value read/written, and ctx is the transaction's context
1: **function** $onReadAccess(ref, val, addr, ctx)$
2:     **if** $isCaptured(ref, ctx)$ **then**
3:         **return** val ▷ returns the field's value if the object ref is captured by ctx
4:     **else**
5:         **return** $ctx.onReadAccess(ref, val, addr)$ ▷ full STM barrier has to be used
6:     **end if**
7: **end function**

8: **function** $onWriteAccess(ref, val, addr, ctx)$
9:     **if** $isCaptured(ref, ctx)$ **then**
10:        $Unsafe.putInt(ref, addr, val)$ ▷ Updates the field in-place.
11:    **else**
12:        $ctx.onWriteAccess(ref, val, addr)$ ▷ full STM barrier has to be used
13:    **end if**
14: **end function**

The performance of this solution depends on the overhead of the capture analysis, which is made by the isCaptured function. So, if the potential savings from barrier elision outweighs the cost of runtime capture analysis, then the average cost of a barrier in an application will be reduced and the overall performance will be improved.

In the Dragojevic et al's original proposal the capture analysis algorithm was intertwined with the memory management process. The key idea of their algorithm was to compare the address of the accessed object, ref, with the ranges of memory locations allocated by the transaction. To perform this analysis, all transactions must keep a *transaction-local allocation log* for all allocated memory.

So, the performance of the isCaptured function depends on the performance of the search algorithm that needs to lookup the allocation log for a specific address, which ultimately depends on the efficiency of the data structure used to implement the allocation log. In their work, they implemented and tested three different data structures: a search tree, an array, and a *filter* of memory ranges. The search tree allows insertions and removals of memory ranges and search operations to determine if an address belongs to a memory range stored in the tree. The array implementation of the log simply keeps all memory ranges allocated inside a transaction as an unsorted array. Finally, the *filtering* approach uses a hash table as a filter: When a block of memory gets allocated, all memory locations belonging to the block are hashed and the corresponding hash table entries are marked with the exact addresses of the corresponding memory locations; thus, this filtering scheme allows false negatives.

Dragojevic et al's experimental results show similar performance improvements for the three data structures,[1] peaking at 18% for 16 threads and the Vacation benchmark in a low-contention configuration.

On a managed runtime environment with automatic memory management, we do not have readily access to the memory allocation process, so that we can log which memory blocks are allocated by a transaction and, therefore, we cannot implement the capture analysis algorithm based on the search tree or the array data structures. Thus, we adapted the hash table filtering algorithm, replacing it with an IdentityHashMap of the JDK and we logged the references of the objects instantiated by a transaction. In our case, and contrary to the original approach, this implementation does not allow false negatives, which increases the reliability of the capture analysis, but incurs in further overhead to maintain the transaction-local allocation log. Nevertheless, using our implementation with the TL2 STM, we get a performance improvement similar to what was shown in [8]: For a low-contention configuration of the Vacation benchmark, we achieve a performance improvement of 32% at 16 threads (see Figure 1).

3   Lightweight Identification of Captured Memory

Although the implementation of the Dragojevic et al's filtering technique improves the overall performance of Deuce STM, the isCaptured algorithm is still much more expensive than a simple memory access: We have to calculate the System.identityHashCode() for the accessed object and then we have to lookup an hash table for that object.

In fact, even with this runtime capture analysis, Deuce STM still does not perform well in some of the most challenging benchmarks, such as the Vacation [4] or

---

[1] With the hash table performing slightly worse, 5% in the worst case, than the alternatives.

the STMBench7 [12], where transactions are more coarse-grained and, therefore, encompass more memory accesses.

We claim that is, in part, due to the relative high cost of the isCaptured function, and that, if we can lower that cost, we may solve the problem. To see what is the effect of removing all the STM barriers for transaction local memory in these benchmarks, we identified the classes that are instantiated inside a transaction scope, we excluded those classes from being instrumented (in the cases where that was possible without compromising the correctness), and then we measured the speedup obtained.

In Vacation, most of the transaction local objects are arrays and, therefore, we have no easy way to avoid those STM barriers in Deuce STM. On the other hand, in STMBench7 the operations traverse a complex graph of objects by using iterators over the collections that represent the connections in that graph. Typically, these iterators are transaction local and, thus, accessing them using STM barriers adds unnecessary overhead to the STMBench7's operations. To confirm this intuition, we logged the objects instantiated in the scope of a transaction and we also logged the read-set and the write-set for each operation of the STMBench7. Thus, we could identify which barriers access transaction local objects as shown in the results of Table 1. Then, we suppressed those barriers, excluding the whole class definition from being transformed and we measured the speedup for each operation.

Table 1. Barriers suppressed for each STMBench7 operation (r and w denote read and write barrier, respectively) and the corresponding speedup on the operation when we exclude the accessed classes from being instrumented. All classes, except LargeSetImpl, belong to the java.util package.

Operation Id	st1	st2	st3	st4	st5	st6	st7	st8	st9	st10	op1	op2	op3	op4	op5	op6	op7	op8
AbstractList$Itr	w	w	w		w	w	w	w	w	w						w	w	w
AbstractMap$2$1												w	w					
HashMap			rw				rw	rw	rw									
HashMap$Entry			rw				w	w	w									
HashMap$Entry []			rw				w	w	w									
HashSet			w				w	w	w									
LargeSetImpl																		
StringBuilder				rw														
TreeMap$KeyIterator	w					w						w	w					
TreeMap$ValueIterator					w													
""$AscendingSubMap												w	w					
""$EntrySetView												w	w					
""$EntryIterator												w	w					
Speedup TL2	2.5	1.3	6.1	1.1	3.4	2.4	1.4	3.5	4.4	2.9		3.1	3.1			1.7	1.9	1.9

From the results of Table 1, we can observe that there are transaction local objects for almost all of the STMBench7's operations (except for op1, op4 and op5) and the majority of their classes are related to the iterators of the java.util collections, which confirms our expectations that these iterators are transaction local. In the same table we can also observe a large speedup of each operation when we avoid the STM barriers that access those transaction local objects. So, based on these results, we expect that using an efficient capture analysis technique has a great influence on the overall performance of the STMBench7 with Deuce.

In our work, we propose to make the runtime capture analysis algorithm faster by using the following approach: We label objects with unique identifiers of their creating transaction, and then check if the accessing transaction corresponds to that label, in which case we avoid the barriers. For this purpose, every transaction keeps a *fingerprint* that it uses to mark newly allocated objects, representing the objects' *owner* transaction. Thus, the isCaptured algorithm just needs to check if the owner of the accessed object corresponds to the transaction's fingerprint of the executing Context. In this case, it performs an identity comparison between the fingerprint of the accessing transaction and the owner of the accessed object, as shown in Algorithm 2.

Algorithm 2. The LICM algorithm of the isCaptured function

1: **function** $isCaptured(ref, ctx)$
2:      **return** $ref.owner = ctx.fingerprint$
3: **end function**

Every time a new top-level transaction begins, its context gets a new unique fingerprint. So, when a new object is published by the successful commit of its allocating transaction, any previously running or newly created transaction calling the isCaptured method for that object will return false, because their fingerprint cannot be the same as the fingerprint recorded on that object. At the end of the top-level transaction, we do not need to clear the context's fingerprint because a new fingerprint will be produced on the initialization of the next top-level transaction.

The generation of new fingerprints is a delicate process that must be carefully designed to avoid adding unintended overhead to either the Deuce STM engine or the underlying STM. A naive approach to identify each transaction uniquely is to use a global counter, but this approach adds unwanted synchronization among threads that we would like to avoid. In fact, to address this problem, we considered three different options for the generation of the fingerprints: (1) use a global quiescent counter; (2) use a number of type long that is assembled by combining a thread identifier with a per-thread sequence number; and (3) use a newly allocated instance of class Object as a fingerprint. We discarded the first option because we cannot do it simultaneously efficient and without the support of either synchronization or any atomic operation. The other two options have both benefits and costs. The second option avoids memory allocation, but it requires some mechanism to deal with the wraparound of the numbers. On the other hand, the third option avoids rollover and aliasing issues associated with counters, but it imposes additional memory management burden.

Within these options, we chose the third, because it is the simplest approach that solves all the problems as it relies on the garbage collection subsystem to provide uniqueness and the ability to recycle unused fingerprints. Furthermore, we do not expect to see significant differences between the alternatives, given that the fingerprint is created when the transaction starts and corresponds to a very small cost of the entire transaction. According to the results presented in Figure 1, the TL2 enhanced with the LICM technique outperforms the filtering approach and can improve the performance of the baseline STM by 60%—almost twice the speedup achieved with filtering.

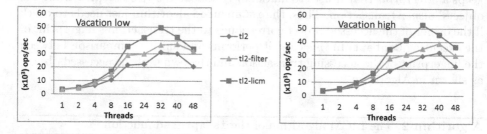

Fig. 1. The throughput for two workloads (low-contention and high-contention) of the Vacation benchmark, when using the TL2 STM. We show results for the baseline STM (*tl2*), for the STM enhanced with the filtering implementation (*tl2-filter*), and for our LICM approach (*tl2-licm*).

4 Extending Deuce STM

There are some transactional optimization techniques, such as the LICM and the multi-versioning used by JVSTM, that require a specific type system distinct from the one provided by the managed environment. Moreover, and in the particular case of the LICM, it also needs to perform additional tasks beyond the standard behaviour provided by the STM barriers. Yet, the original Deuce STM just provides extensibility in terms of the specification of the STM algorithm, but it allows neither the definition of additional behavior orthogonal to all STMs, nor any modification to the standard type system. We extended Deuce STM to support the previous requirements and we followed three major guidelines:[2] (1) to avoid changing the current Deuce STM API; (2) to guarantee retro-compatibility with existing applications and STMs for Deuce; and (3) to provide the ability to enhance any existing STM with the capture analysis technique without requiring either its recompilation or any modification to its source-code.

Extending Deuce STM with the capture analysis technique requires two main changes to the Deuce STM core structures: (1) the `Context` implementation of any STM must keep a fingerprint representing the identity of the transaction in execution and must perform the capture analysis shown in Algorithm 1; and (2) a *transactional class* (i.e., a class whose instances are accessed in a transactional scope) must have an additional field, `owner`, to store the fingerprint of the transaction that instantiates it.

---

[2] This adaptation of Deuce is available at
https://github.com/inesc-id-esw/deucestm/

To support the first feature, we added a new system property, org.deuce.filter that enables the specification of a *filter context*—that is, a class that implements the Context interface and adds some functionality to any existing Context (using the decorator design pattern [11]). The new class ContextFilterCapturedState uses this approach, so that it can be applied to an existing Context of any STM.

To ensure that all transactional objects have a owner field, their classes must inherit, directly or indirectly, from the class CapturedState. To support this feature, we added to the Deuce STM framework a new infrastructure that allows the specification and execution of *enhancers*, which are additional transformations to the standard Deuce instrumentation. These enhancers are instances of classes implementing the interface Enhancer and they may be added to the Deuce engine through the system properties org.deuce.transform.pre and org.deuce.transform.post, depending on whether they should be performed before or after the standard Deuce instrumentation. Moreover, the enhancers may be combined in a chain of transformations, when more than one enhancer is specified in the same *pre* or *post* property.

5   Performance Evaluation

All the tests were performed on a machine with 4 AMD Opteron(tm) 6168 processors, each one with 12 cores, resulting in a total of 48 cores. The JVM version used was the 1.6.0_33-b03, running on Ubuntu with Linux kernel version 2.6.32.

To evaluate the performance of our approach, we used the STMBench7 [12], the STAMP [4], and the JWormBench [5] benchmarks, with the LSA [16], the TL2 [7], and the JVSTM [10] STMs, all implemented in the Deuce STM framework. In all tests we show the results for the baseline STM, for the STM with LICM support (identified by the suffix *-licm*), and for the STM with filtering support (identified by the suffix *-filter*).

Moreover, given that the STMBench7 and the JWormBench benchmarks also have a medium/fine-grained locking synchronization strategy, we also compare the performance of the lock-based approach with the STM-based approach, showing that for certain STMs, using LICM makes the performance of the STM-based approach close to (or better than) the performance of the lock-based approach. In particular, for the STMBench7 and a low number of threads, JVSTM outperforms the medium-lock approach.

5.1   STAMP Benchmarks

STAMP is a benchmark suite that attempts to represent real-world workloads in eight different applications. We tested four STAMP benchmarks: K-Means, Ssca2, Intruder, and Vacation.[3] We ran these benchmarks with the configurations

---

[3] The original implementation of STAMP is available as a C library and these four benchmarks are the only ones available for Java in the public repository of Deuce that are running with correct results.

proposed in [4]: For Vacation Low, "-n 256 -q 90 -u 98 -r 262144 -t 65536"; for Vacation High, "-n 256 -q 90 -u 60 -r 262144 -t 65536"; for Intruder, "-a 10 -l 128 -n 65536 -s 1"; for KMeans, "-m 15 -n 15 -t 0.00001 -i random-n65536-d32-c16.txt"; and for Ssca2, "-s 13 -i 1.0 -u 1.0 -l 13 -p 3".

In Table 2, we show the speedup of each STM with LICM support for 1 thread and for N threads. Note that a speedup higher than 1 means that the performance improved with LICM, whereas a speedup lower than 1 means that performance decreased with LICM. The results in Table 2 show that LICM improves the performance of the baseline STMs for the majority of the evaluated benchmarks and that, when it has no benefits (due to the lack of opportunities for elision of barriers), the imposed overhead is very low.

Table 2. The speedup of each STM with LICM support for 1 thread and N threads. In the latter case we also show, between parentheses, the number of threads that reach the peak of performance, with and without the LICM support, respectively. We emphasise in bold the speedup values that are higher than 1.0.

1 thread	Vacation Low-contention	Vacation High-contention	Intruder	KMeans	Ssca2
LSA	**1.2**	**1.2**	**1.4**	0.9	1.0
TL2	**1.1**	**1.1**	**1.2**	0.9	0.9
JVSTM	**1.1**	**1.1**	**1.2**	1.0	1.0
N threads					
	7.0	**6.0**	**1.7**	1.0	0.9
LSA	(40/8)	(40/12)	(16/8)	(32/32)	(8/8)
	1.6	**1.6**	**1.3**	1.0	1.0
TL2	(32/32)	(32/40)	(16/16)	(12/24)	(8/8)
	1.1	1.0	**1.1**	1.0	1.0
JVSTM	(8/8)	(40/40)	(8/8)	(4/4)	(32/32)

The speedup we observed in Intruder and Vacation agrees with the results of [8], which provide evidence for some opportunities of elision of transaction local barriers. From our analysis, Intruder instantiates an auxiliary linked list and a byte[], whose barriers can be elided with our capture analysis technique. On the other hand, Vacation performs three different kinds of operations, each one including an *initialization* phase and an *execution* phase. In the initialization phase it instantiates several arrays with the arguments that should be parametrized in the operations performed by each transaction. These auxiliary arrays are transaction local and their access barriers can be suppressed through capture analysis.

Although the performance with LICM is similar for LSA and TL2, LSA shows better speedup due to scalability problems verified in the LSA when executed without the LICM—in this case we registered a high rate of aborts due to the eager ownership acquisition approach followed by LSA. For the JVSTM we do not observe the same improvement in performance because, although LICM helps to elide useless barriers for transaction local objects, they still incur in additional metadata that penalizes the corresponding memory accesses (in the case of the TL2 and the LSA, there is no in-place metadata associated with the transactional objects).

According to [8], neither K-Means nor Ssca2 access transaction local memory and, thus, in these cases there are no opportunities for eliding barriers with capture analysis. Our results are consistent with this, but still show that our technique for capture analysis has almost no overhead in performance and it just degrades the performance of up to 10% in the worst case.

5.2   STMBench7 Benchmark

LSA and JVSTM have the best performance in the STMBench7, when compared to TL2, because of their versioning approach, which allows read-only transactions to get a valid snapshot of memory and thus, they always commit successfully. Yet, LSA shows a huge scalability problem when not using capture analysis, due to the overhead of useless STM barriers when accessing transaction local objects. This happens even in the case of the read-dominated workload because most of the read-only operations use write barriers, thereby forcing the transactions to be executed as read-write transactions. The operations are classified as read-only because they do not change shared objects, but they still need to use write barriers (when not using captured analysis) because they change transaction-local objects. When this happens, LSA cannot optimize the execution of read-only transactions. Once the useless barriers are elided with LICM, LSA can already take advantage of read-only transactions and we see that it scales for an increasing number of threads, as depicted in the results of Figure 2.

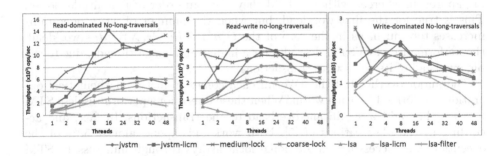

Fig. 2. The STMBench7 throughput for LSA and JVSTM, in the three available workloads, without long traversal operations. For readability reasons we omitted TL2, which is the worst of the STMs.

In the results of Figure 2 we omitted TL2, which is the STM with the worst performance. We can also observe that the performance of *LSA-licm* is between 20% and 80% better than *LSA-filter*, depending on the workload. Even though LSA-licm performs better, its results are still far from the results obtained with JVSTM-licm, which is the most performant STM in the STMBench7. In fact, JVSTM-licm gets better results than the medium-lock synchronization approach for a number of threads lower than 24. In this case, JVSTM benefits from its lock-free commit algorithm and from the lazy ownership acquisition approach, in contrast to the eager approach of the LSA.

5.3   JWormBench Benchmark

In [5], we used the JWormBench benchmark to explore the effects on performance of relaxing the transparency of an STM. To that end, we extended the Deuce API with a couple of annotations that allow programmers to specify that certain objects or arrays should not be transactified. Using this approach, we got an improvement of up to 22-fold in the performance. Now, with our new LICM technique, we got similar results but without having to change the original Deuce API.

There are two major sources of unnecessary STM barriers in the JWorm-Bench: (1) a global immutable matrix containing the world nodes (which cannot be expressed as immutable in Java), and (2) the auxiliary arrays to the worm operations. The first barriers can be suppressed by excluding the class `World` from the instrumentation of Deuce On the other hand, the second barriers will be automatically elided through our LICM technique.

In Figure 3, we show the results obtained for the JWormBench benchmark. TL2 and LSA present the same performance in both workloads of the JWorm-Bench and, so, we show the results for LSA only. In this case *LSA-licm* performs between 2 and 5 times faster than *LSA-filter*. Unlike what happened for the STM-Bench7, LSA with capture analysis is always better than JVSTM in the JWorm-Bench, because these workloads have transactions with a smaller average length and with a lower level of contention. But, most importantly, we can see that both STMs get results close to the results obtained with the fine-grained locking approach, whereas without LICM they were an order of magnitude slower. This is true for the first workload, but when the number of write operations increases too much, as in the case of the $O(n^2), NReads, NWrites$ workload, the performance of JVSTM degrades for a higher number of threads, due to the big overhead of its read-write transactions.

The major overhead of the JWormBench comes from the mathematical operations performed by each worm. When these operations perform useless STM barriers they add a significant overhead to the transactions. In fact, and according to the observations of [5], both workloads spend almost 50% of the execution time accessing transactional local arrays through unnecessary STM barriers. Furthermore, this situation increases too much the average length of the transactions and, therefore, increases the rate of aborted transactions. In those circumstances all STMs incur in huge overheads and substantially decrease the overall throughput.

6   Related Work

Compiler over-instrumentation is one of the main reasons for the STM overheads and an obstacle to the use of STMs in real-world–sized applications. The use of unnecessary barriers on transaction-local memory access has a huge contribution to this behavior and in the past few years several solutions have been proposed to mitigate this problem.

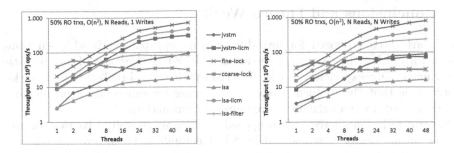

Fig. 3. The JWormBench throughput for LSA, JVSTM, and locks, for two different wokloads. Note that the vertical axes use a logarithmic scale.

One of the first contributions of Harris et al. [13] proposed a direct access STM with a new decomposed interface that is used in the translation of the atomic blocks and is exposed to the compiler, giving new opportunities for optimization. Another approach, proposed by Yoo et al. [19], is to use a new `tm_waiver` annotation to mark a function or block that should not be instrumented by the compiler for memory access—*waivered* code. Likewise, Ni et al. [15] propose that programmers have the responsibility of declaring which functions could avoid the instrumentation through the use of the annotation `tm_pure`. The same approach has been followed in managed runtime environments, such as the work of Beckman et al. [2], which proposes the use of access permissions, via Java annotations, that can be applied to references to affect the behavior of the object pointed by that reference. Carvalho et al. [5] also proposed the use of Java annotations to identify the object fields and arrays that could be accessed directly, avoiding the STM barriers.

Contrary to these approaches that involve the programmer and, thus, reduce the transparency of the STM approach, the work of Riegel et al. [17] propose to tune the behavior of the STM for individual data partitions. Their approach relies on compiler data structure analysis (DSA) to identify the partitions of an application, which may be thread-local or transaction-local. The work of Dragojevic et al. [8] propose a technique for automatic capture analysis. They provide this feature at runtime and also in the compiler using pointer analysis, which determines whether a pointer points to memory allocated inside the current transaction. Similar optimizations also appear in Wang et al. [18], and Eddon and Herlihy [9], which apply fully interprocedural analyses to discover thread-local data.

Our work builds on the work of Dragojevic et al, by proposing a lightweight technique for the runtime identification of captured memory for managed environments. A key aspect for the effectiveness of our approach is that it is performed at runtime (albeit with very low overheads). In contrast with this, Afek et al. [1] integrated static analysis in Deuce STM to eliminate redundant read and write operations in transactional methods, including accesses to transaction local-data. Yet, the results presented in their work are far from the speedups shown with our approach.

7   Conclusions and Future Work

STMs are often criticized for introducing unacceptable overhead when compared with either the sequential version or a lock-based version of any realistic benchmark. Our experience in testing STMs with several realistic benchmarks, however, is that the problem stems from having instrumentation on memory locations that are not actually shared among transactions.

Several techniques have been proposed to elide useless STM barriers in programs automatically instrumented by STM compilers. From our analysis, the main contributions in this field follow three distinct approaches: (1) runtime capture analysis; (2) compiler static analysis to elide redundant operations; and (3) decomposition of the STM APIs to allow programmers to convey the knowledge about which blocks of instructions or memory locations should not be instrumented. The latter approach is more efficient and has shown bigger improvements in the performance of the STMs, but has the inconvenient of reducing the transparency of the STMs APIs. Yet, to the extent of our knowledge, none of the previous solutions demonstrated performance improvements with the same magnitude of the results that we present here for the STMBench7 and Vacation benchmarks.

Our approach can solve one of the major bottlenecks that reduces the performance in many realistic applications and simultaneously preserve the transparency of an STM API, as shown with its implementation in the Deuce STM framework. By adding a minor overhead in memory space to all transactional objects (the reference to its owner), we get a huge speedup in the Vacation and the STMBench7 benchmarks. In fact, for the first time in the case of STM-Bench7, we were able to get better performance with an STM than with the medium-grain lock strategy. Moreover, integrating LICM in a managed runtime may further reduce the overhead of our approach and provide a significant boost in the usage of STMs.

References

1. Afek, Y., Korland, G., Zilberstein, A.: Lowering STM overhead with static analysis. In: Cooper, K., Mellor-Crummey, J., Sarkar, V. (eds.) LCPC 2010. LNCS, vol. 6548, pp. 31–45. Springer, Heidelberg (2011)
2. Beckman, N.E., Kim, Y.P., Stork, S., Aldrich, J.: Reducing STM overhead with access permissions. In: International Workshop on Aliasing, Confinement and Ownership in Object-Oriented Programming, IWACO 2009. ACM (2009)
3. Binder, W., Hulaas, J., Moret, P.: Advanced Java bytecode instrumentation. In: Proceedings of the 5th International Symposium on Principles and Practice of Programming in Java, PPPJ 2007. ACM (2007)
4. Cao Minh, C., Chung, J., Kozyrakis, C., Olukotun, K.: STAMP: Stanford transactional applications for multi-processing. In: IISWC 2008: Proceedings of The IEEE International Symposium on Workload Characterization (2008)
5. Carvalho, F.M., Cachopo, J.: STM with transparent API considered harmful. In: Xiang, Y., Cuzzocrea, A., Hobbs, M., Zhou, W. (eds.) ICA3PP 2011, Part I. LNCS, vol. 7016, pp. 326–337. Springer, Heidelberg (2011)

6. Cascaval, C., Blundell, C., Michael, M., Cain, H.W., Wu, P., Chiras, S., Chatterjee, S.: Software transactional memory: Why is it only a research toy? Queue 6(5) (September 2008)
7. Dice, D., Shalev, O., Shavit, N.N.: Transactional locking II. In: Dolev, S. (ed.) DISC 2006. LNCS, vol. 4167, pp. 194–208. Springer, Heidelberg (2006)
8. Dragojevic, A., Ni, Y., Adl-Tabatabai, A.-R.: Optimizing transactions for captured memory. In: Proceedings of the Twenty-first Annual Symposium on Parallelism in Algorithms and Architectures, SPAA 2009. ACM (2009)
9. Eddon, G., Herlihy, M.P.: Language support and compiler optimizations for STM and transactional boosting. In: Janowski, T., Mohanty, H. (eds.) ICDCIT 2007. LNCS, vol. 4882, pp. 209–224. Springer, Heidelberg (2007)
10. Fernandes, S.M., Cachopo, J.: Lock-free and scalable multi-version software transactional memory. In: Proceedings of the 16th ACM Symposium on Principles and Practice of Parallel Programming, PPoPP 2011. ACM (2011)
11. Gamma, E., Helm, R., Johnson, R.E., Vlissides, J.M.: Design patterns: Abstraction and reuse of object-oriented design. In: Wang, J. (ed.) ECOOP 1993. LNCS, vol. 707, pp. 406–431. Springer, Heidelberg (1993)
12. Guerraoui, R., Kapalka, M., Vitek, J.: STMBench7: A benchmark for software transactional memory. In: Proceedings of the 2nd ACM SIGOPS/EuroSys European Conference on Computer Systems 2007, EuroSys 2007. ACM (2007)
13. Harris, T., Plesko, M., Shinnar, A., Tarditi, D.: Optimizing memory transactions. In: Proceedings of the 2006 ACM SIGPLAN Conference on Programming Language Design and Implementation, PLDI 2006. ACM (2006)
14. Korland, G., Shavit, N., Felber, P.: Noninvasive concudrrency with Java STM. In: Electronic Proceedings of the Workshop on Programmability Issues for Multi-Core Computers. MULTIPROG (March 2010)
15. Ni, Y., Welc, A., Adl-Tabatabai, A., Bach, M., Berkowits, S., Cownie, J., Geva, R., Kozhukow, S., Narayanaswamy, R., Olivier, J., Preis, S., Saha, B., Tal, X., Tian, A.: Design and implementation of transactional constructs for C/C++. In: Proceedings of the 23rd ACM SIGPLAN Conference on Object-oriented Programming Systems Languages and Applications, OOPSLA 2008 (2008)
16. Riegel, T., Felber, P., Fetzer, C.: A lazy snapshot algorithm with eager validation. In: Dolev, S. (ed.) DISC 2006. LNCS, vol. 4167, pp. 284–298. Springer, Heidelberg (2006)
17. Riegel, T., Fetzer, C., Felber, P.: Automatic data partitioning in software transactional memories. In: Proceedings of the Twentieth Annual Symposium on Parallelism in Algorithms and Architectures, SPAA 2008. ACM (2008)
18. Wang, C., Chen, W., Wu, Y., Saha, B., Adl-Tabatabai, A.: Code generation and optimization for transactional memory constructs in an unmanaged language. In: Proceedings of the International Symposium on Code Generation and Optimization, CGO 2007 (2007)
19. Yoo, R.M., Ni, Y., Welc, A., Saha, B., Adl-Tabatabai, A.-R., Lee, H.-H.S.: Kicking the tires of software transactional memory: why the going gets tough. In: Proceedings of the Twentieth Annual Symposium on Parallelism in Algorithms and Architectures, SPAA 2008. ACM (2008)

Layer-Based Scheduling of Parallel Tasks
for Heterogeneous Cluster Platforms

Jörg Dümmler and Gudula Rünger

Technische Universität Chemnitz, Department of Computer Science, 09107 Chemnitz, Germany
{djo,ruenger}@cs.tu-chemnitz.de

Abstract. The programming model of parallel tasks is a suitable programming abstraction for parallel applications running on heterogeneous clusters, which are clusters composed of multiple subclusters. In this model, an application is decomposed into parallel tasks, each of which can be executed on an arbitrary number of processors. The advantage of this programming approach is that each task only needs to be implemented for a homogeneous environment while the complete application can still benefit from the entire performance of the heterogeneous cluster by a concurrent execution of independent parallel tasks on different subclusters. The execution of such an application on a specific platform is controlled by a schedule that maps each parallel task onto a set of processors.

In this article, we propose an algorithm for the scheduling of parallel tasks with precedence constraints on heterogeneous clusters. This algorithm is an extension of a layer-based scheduling approach for homogeneous platforms with an additional phase that assigns the parallel tasks to appropriate subclusters. Three different versions of this additional phase are considered. An experimental evaluation, based on simulation results as well as on measurements with different application benchmarks, shows that the proposed scheduling approach outperforms existing scheduling algorithms in most situations.

1 Introduction

A heterogeneous cluster is a distributed memory platform composed of multiple homogeneous subclusters. Such a platform results from the combination of compute nodes with different processors into a single large cluster or from the combination of the compute resources of different institutions into a grid-like environment. Although applications for these platforms can be developed using a message-passing model such as MPI, this may be tedious from the programmer's point of view and may lead to a poor portability of the application performance, since the heterogeneity of the processors and network links has to be taken into account explicitly. Thus, it is desirable to support the development of large applications for heterogeneous clusters by appropriate high-level programming models and software tools.

Such a programming model is the model of parallel tasks, in which an application is decomposed into a set of parallel tasks each of which can be executed on multiple processors in parallel. There may be data or control dependencies between parallel tasks that enforce an execution of the respective tasks one after another, but independent parallel tasks can be executed concurrently on disjoint subsets of processors. The

J. Kołodziej et al. (Eds.): ICA3PP 2013, Part I, LNCS 8285, pp. 30–43, 2013.

advantage of this approach is that each parallel task can be executed in a homogeneous environment within a single subcluster, while the entire performance of the heterogeneous system is still exploited by running independent tasks concurrently on different subclusters. The execution of the parallel tasks on the subclusters can be managed by a suitable compiler or runtime environment. For example, the CM-task compiler [7] only requires the programmer to provide a high-level specification program defining the structure of the application and implementations of the parallel tasks for a homogeneous environment. Thus, the programmer is completely relieved from dealing with platform heterogeneity.

The execution of a parallel application consisting of parallel tasks requires a schedule that defines the execution order of independent parallel tasks and maps the parallel tasks to subclusters of the heterogeneous target platform. The computation of an optimal schedule that leads to the best application performance is a strongly NP-hard problem. As a consequence, several heuristics have been proposed, including M-HEFT [17], H-CPA [11], and Δ-CTS [16]. These heuristics are based on list scheduling, i.e., in each step the task with the highest priority value is assigned to a set of processors that optimizes a given objective function.

An alternative to this scheduling approach are layer-based scheduling algorithms, which have been used successfully for homogeneous platforms [4]. These algorithms first build layers each of which include only independent parallel tasks, and then schedule the layers one after another. In this article, we extend a layer-based scheduling algorithm [15] to heterogeneous platforms by introducing an additional phase that assigns each parallel task of a given layer to one subcluster of the target platform. For this phase, we propose three different versions that use the sequential execution time, the data parallel execution time, and the mixed parallel execution time of the parallel tasks, respectively. The contributions of this article include the following.

- It presents three layer-based scheduling algorithms for heterogeneous clusters that differ in the assignment of the tasks of a layer to the subclusters of the target platform.
- It includes an experimental evaluation that compares the performance of the proposed algorithms and existing scheduling algorithms using synthetic scheduling problems as well as application benchmarks, which include solvers for ordinary differential equations and flow solvers coming from the NAS Parallel Benchmark suite. The comparison shows that the proposed scheduling approach leads to the best results in most cases.

The article is structured as follows. Section 2 introduces the programming model of parallel tasks and defines the corresponding scheduling problem. The scheduling algorithm for heterogeneous clusters is proposed in Sect. 3. The experimental results are presented in Sect. 4. Section 5 discusses related work and Sect. 6 concludes.

2   Parallel Programming Model

In the programming model of parallel tasks, a parallel application is represented by an annotated directed acyclic graph $G = (V, E)$ called application task graph, see Fig. 1

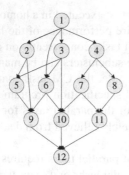
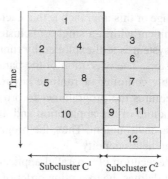

Fig. 1. Representation of an application task graph consisting of 12 parallel tasks $\{1, \ldots, 12\}$ (left) and a corresponding schedule on a heterogeneous system consisting of two subclusters C^1 and C^2 (right)

(left) for an example. The set V of nodes represents the parallel tasks that are assumed to be executable on an arbitrary number of processors. The set E of edges models the data and control dependencies between the parallel tasks. A data dependency $(A, B) \in E$ exists between parallel tasks A and B if A produces output data that is required by B as an input. Such a data dependency may lead to a data redistribution operation at runtime if A and B are executed on different sets of processors or the data distribution of the output of A and the input of B do not match.

The parallel target platform is a heterogeneous cluster composed of c subclusters $C^1, \ldots, C^c$. Each subcluster C^i consists of P^i identical processors that are interconnected by a homogeneous network, $i = 1, \ldots, c$. The computation and communication performance of subcluster C^i is captured by the average execution time t^i_{op} of an arithmetical operation, the network startup time t^i_s and the network byte transfer time t^i_b. The interconnection network between subclusters C^i and C^j is defined by the startup time $t^{(i,j)}_s$ and the byte transfer time $t^{(i,j)}_b$, $1 \leq i, j \leq c, i \neq j$.

The nodes of the application task graph are associated with cost functions that provide an estimate of the execution time of the corresponding parallel task depending on the subcluster and on the number of processors used for the execution. We assume that each parallel task can only be executed by processors belonging to the same subcluster because of two reasons. First, the interconnection network within a subcluster is usually much faster compared to the interconnection between different subclusters. Thus, running a parallel task across multiple subclusters may lead to a large communication overhead caused by the slow interconnection network. Second, parallel tasks are usually implemented for a homogeneous execution environment, i.e., there is no internal load balancing to account for different processor speeds. The runtime estimates for the parallel tasks are represented by functions

$$T^i_{par} : V \times [1, \ldots, P^i] \to \mathbb{R}^+$$

where $T^i_{par}(A, p)$ denotes the execution time of parallel task $A \in V$ executed on p processors of subcluster C^i, $i = 1, \ldots, c$.

The edges of the application task graph are associated with communication costs resulting from data redistribution operations. These costs depend on the amount of data to be transferred between the source and target parallel task as well as the source and target processor sets and specific subclusters. These costs are captured by functions

$$T_{Re}^{(i,j)} : E \times [1, \ldots, P^i] \times [1, \ldots, P^j] \to \mathbb{R}^+$$

where $T_{Re}^{(i,j)}((A, B), p_1, p_2)$ denotes the communication cost between parallel task $A \in V$ executed on p_1 processors of subcluster C^i and parallel task $B \in V$ executed on p_2 processors of subcluster C^j, $i, j = 1, \ldots, c$.

A schedule S assigns each parallel task $A \in V$ a set $PG(A)$ of processors, a subcluster $SC(A)$, and a starting point in time $ST(A)$. The finish time $FT(A)$ for parallel task A can then be computed by

$$FT(A) = ST(A) + T_{par}^{SC(A)}(A, |PG(A)|)$$

where $|PG(A)|$ denotes the number of processors in set $PG(A)$. An illustration of a schedule is given in Fig. 1 (right). A schedule is called *feasible* if it fulfills the following two conditions.

- Before the start of a parallel task all required input data must have been produced by the predecessor tasks and made available on the correct set of processors in the correct data distribution, i.e., if $(A, B) \in E$ then $FT(A) + T_{re}^{(i,j)}((A, B), p_1, p_2) \leq ST(B)$ for all $A, B \in V$ where $i = SC(A)$, $j = SC(B)$, $p_1 = |PG(A)|$ and $p_2 = |PG(B)|$.
- Parallel tasks that have an overlapping execution time interval on the same subcluster have to be executed by disjoint subsets of processors, i.e, if $[ST(A), FT(A)] \cap [ST(B), FT(B)] \neq \emptyset$ and $SC(A) = SC(B)$ then $PG(A) \cap PG(B) = \emptyset$ for all $A, B \in V$.

The *makespan* $C_{max}(S)$ of a schedule S is defined as the maximum finish time of any parallel task in the application, i.e., $C_{max}(S) = \max_{A \in V} FT(A)$. The goal is to determine a feasible schedule with minimum makespan. This scheduling problem is strongly NP hard even for the special case of precedence constraints in the form of chains and a platform consisting of a single subcluster [3].

3   Scheduling Algorithm

In this section, we propose a scheduling algorithm for heterogeneous platforms that uses a layer-based approach, see Alg. 1 for the coarse structure. The algorithm consists of four consecutive phases. The first phase partitions the parallel task graph into layers of independent parallel tasks (lines 1 and 2). Next, each parallel task of a given layer is assigned to one of the c subclusters (line 3). In the third step, a partial schedule is computed for each subcluster considering only the parallel tasks assigned to this subcluster (line 4). Finally, all computed partial schedules are combined into the global schedule taking the data re-distribution costs between layers into account (line 5). In the following, these phases are described in detail.

Algorithm 1. Scheduling algorithm overview

Input   : Parallel task graph $G = (V, E)$; Heterogeneous platform with c subclusters
Output : Schedule S
begin

1   construct shrinked task graph G' from G;
2   decompose G' into l layers $L_1, \ldots, L_l$;
     for $(i = 1, \ldots, l)$ **do**
3   partition L_i into c disjoint subsets $W_{i,1}, \ldots W_{i,c}$;
4   **for** $(j = 1, \ldots, c)$ **do** schedule node set $W_{i,j}$ onto subcluster C^j;
5   build global schedule S;

3.1 Decomposition Phase

The decomposition phase consists of two substeps. First, the algorithm identifies all linear chains of parallel tasks in the input application task graph G and replaces each chain of maximum size with a single node (line 1 of Alg. 1) resulting in the shrinked graph G'. A linear chain is defined as a subgraph of a graph G consisting of at least two nodes with the following properties:

- There exist a unique entry and a unique exit node that precede and succeed, respectively, all other nodes of the linear chain.
- All nodes of the linear chain except the entry node have exactly one predecessor that also belongs to the linear chain.
- All nodes of the linear chain except the exit node have exactly one successor, which is also part of the linear chain.

A linear chain is of maximum size if it is not possible to add more nodes to the chain without violating one of these conditions. The rationale behind this step is to ensure that all tasks of a linear chain are scheduled to the same set of processors and, thus, to avoid expensive data redistribution operations between these parallel tasks.

In the second substep, the decomposition phase builds layers of independent parallel tasks by using a greedy heuristic that runs over the parallel task graph in a breadth first manner and puts as many parallel tasks into a layer as possible. The goal is to construct layers with a maximum number of parallel tasks, since this gives the most flexibility for the next phases of the scheduling algorithm. For example, the task graph from Fig. 1 (left) is decomposed into the five layers $\{1\}$, $\{2,3,4\}$, $\{5,6,7,8\}$, $\{9,10,11\}$, and $\{12\}$.

3.2 Cluster Assignment Phase

The cluster assignment phase is an additional step added to the layer-based scheduling algorithm [15] that is responsible for dealing with the heterogeneity of the platform. The goal of this phase is to assign each parallel task of a given layer to one of the c subclusters in such a way that a minimum execution time for the entire layer results. For this purpose, it tries to assigns more computational work to subclusters with more and faster processors than to subclusters with a low number of processors or slow processors.

Algorithm 2. Assignment of tasks to subclusters.

> **Input** : Layer with k independent parallel tasks $L_i = \{M_1, \ldots, M_k\}$
> **Input** : Heterogeneous platform with c subclusters
> **Output**: Set of tasks $W_{i,j}$ for each subcluster C^j, $j = 1, \ldots, c$
> **begin**
> 1   **for** $(j = 1, \ldots, c)$ **do** initialize $W_{i,j} = \emptyset$;
> 2   sort $\{M_1, \ldots, M_k\}$ such that $T^1_{par}(M_1, 1) \geq \ldots \geq T^1_{par}(M_k, 1)$;
> 3   **for** $(j = 1, \ldots, k)$ **do**
> 4   determine subcluster C^l that minimizes est_load($C^l, W_{i,l} \cup \{M_j\}$);
> 5 $W_{i,l} = W_{i,l} \cup \{M_j\}$;

The general procedure is outlined in Alg. 2. First, the parallel tasks of the layer are sorted according to the sequential execution time on the first subcluster (line 2). This sorting criterion is a rough approximation of the computational complexity of the tasks, which is usually accurate enough to ensure that large tasks are scheduled before small ones. Next, the algorithm considers the parallel tasks of the layer one after another and assigns the currently considered parallel task to the subcluster with the minimum estimated total load (lines 4 and 5). The estimated total load of a subcluster C^l depends on the current parallel task and all parallel tasks that have previously been assigned to C^l, $l = 1, \ldots, c$. In the following, we propose three different definitions of the function est_load leading to three different scheduling algorithms (*H-Layer-SEQ, H-Layer-PAR* and *H-LAYER-MIX*).

Sequential Execution Time (*H-Layer-SEQ*). The first approach uses the sequential execution time of the parallel tasks to estimate the current load of a given subcluster, i.e., for subcluster C^j and a set W of tasks the estimated load is defined as

$$\text{est\_load}_{SEQ}(C^j, W) = \sum_{M \in W} T^j_{par}(M, 1).$$

The advantage of this definition is its low computational complexity. The different processor speeds of the subclusters are taken into account, i.e., a subcluster having faster processors is assigned more work.

Data Parallel Execution Time (*H-Layer-PAR*). An alternative is to use the data parallel execution times for the computation of the estimated load. For subcluster C^j with P^j processors and a set W of tasks the estimated load is defined as

$$\text{est\_load}_{PAR}(C^j, W) = \sum_{M \in W} T^j_{par}(M, P^j).$$

The advantage over the approach based on the sequential execution time is that also scalability effects of the parallel tasks are taken into account.

Mixed Parallel Execution Time (*H-Layer-MIX*). The drawback of the previous two definitions for the estimated load is that they only provide a very rough measure of the individual processors' workload in the final schedule. For example, the function est_load$_{SEQ}$ does not take the number of processors of the subclusters into account. As a result, a small subcluster with fast processors is assigned more work than a large cluster with slow processors. The function est_load$_{PAR}$ ignores the scheduling decisions within the individual subclusters. As a result, the load of a subcluster, which is assigned many parallel tasks with a low scalability is overestimated, because in the final schedule these tasks can run concurrently using only a small number of processors.

Due to these observations, we propose a third version to estimate the workload, which is based on the mixed parallel execution time. It is defined as

$$\texttt{est\_load}_{MIX}(C^j, W) = T_{min}$$

where T_{min} is the makespan of the mixed parallel schedule for the set W of parallel tasks on subcluster C^j as computed by Alg. 3, see Sect. 3.3 for a detailed description. The advantage of this approach is that it usually provides a better load balance between the subclusters than the previous two approaches. The drawback is the high computational complexity, since Alg. 3 has to be executed $k \cdot c$ times for a layer consisting of k parallel tasks. In our experiments we have considered task graphs with layers consisting of up to 256 parallel tasks and the scheduling was still performed in reasonable time.

3.3   Cluster Scheduling Phase

The cluster scheduling phase computes a schedule for a set of independent parallel tasks on a single subcluster, i.e., a homogeneous target environment. The resulting scheduling problem, which is a subproblem of the scheduling for heterogeneous platforms has been addressed by many different algorithms, see [4] for an overview. In the following, we present an algorithm based on list scheduling [15] that yields good results in practice.

The pseudo code of this approach is outlined in Alg. 3. First, the algorithm partitions the set of processors of one subcluster C^j into g disjoint subsets of processors and then assigns each parallel task to one of these subsets. The number g of subsets is selected from all possible values (see the loop in line 2), such that the overall execution time for all parallel tasks is at a minimum. For a specific number g, first g equal-sized subsets of processors are created (line 3). Next, the parallel tasks are sorted with respect to their parallel execution time (line 4) to ensure that large parallel tasks are scheduled first. The scheduling algorithm considers the parallel tasks one after another and assigns each parallel task to the subset of processors that currently has the minimum accumulated execution time (line 6). The accumulated execution time of a subset G_l is defined to be the sum of the parallel execution times of all parallel tasks previously assigned to G_l. After all parallel tasks have been assigned, an iterative group adjustment step is performed to reduce load imbalances between the g processor groups (line 7). This step tries to find two processor groups G_1 and G_2, such that moving one processor from G_1 to G_2 decreases the maximum accumulated execution time of these two groups. This step is repeated as long as such pairs of groups can be found. Afterwards, the total execution time of the entire layer is computed (line 8) and the currently best schedule is updated if applicable (line 9).

Algorithm 3. Scheduling for a single subcluster.

Input : Set of n independent parallel tasks $W_{i,j} = \{M_1, \dots, M_n\}$

Input : Subcluster C^j with P^j processors

Output: Partial Schedule for $W_{i,j}$ on C^j

begin

1 $\quad T_{min} = \sum_{q=1}^n T_{par}^j(M_q, P^j);$

2 $\quad$ **for** $(g = 1, \dots, \min\{P^j, n\})$ **do**

3 $\qquad$ build g disjoint subsets of processors $G = \{G_1, \dots, G_g\}$ of size $p_g = P^j/g;$

4 $\qquad$ sort $\{M_1, \dots, M_n\}$ such that $T_{par}^j(M_1, p_g) \geq \dots \geq T_{par}^j(M_n, p_g);$

5 $\qquad$ **for** $(q = 1, \dots, n)$ **do**

6 $\qquad\quad$ assign M_q to group G_l with the smallest accumulated execution time;

7 $\qquad$ adjust processor group sizes;

8 $\qquad$ $T_a(g) = \max_{1 \leq q \leq g}$ accumulated execution time of $G_q;$

9 $\qquad$ **if** $(T_a(g) < T_{min})$ **then** $T_{min} = T_a(g);$

---

4 Experimental Evaluation

The performance of the proposed scheduling algorithms is evaluated by a comparison with the algorithms H-CPA and S-HCPA [11], M-HEFT1 and M-HEFT2 [17], and Δ-CTS [16]. All algorithms are implemented in the scheduling toolkit SEParAT [5]. We consider synthetic scheduling problems in Subsect. 4.1 as well as application benchmarks running on an existing heterogeneous cluster in Subsect. 4.2.

4.1 Simulation Results

For the simulation, we consider 15360 synthetic task graphs created by the *daggen* graph generation program [2], see Tab. 1 (left) for an overview of the parameters used for the generation. The task graphs consist of 10, 50, 100, and 200 nodes. The shape of the generated graphs is controlled by the parameters width, regularity and density, which define the average number of independent tasks, the variety in the number of independent tasks between layers, and the number of edges, respectively. These parameters can be selected in the range from 0 to 1; we have used four different values (0.1, 0.3, 0.7, 0.9) for each of these parameters. The jump parameter defines the maximum distance between source and target layer of the edges where a value of 1 means that edges exist only between successive layers. We have used jump distances of 1, 2, and 4.

The computational complexity of a task is either $a \cdot n$ (modeling an image processing application), $a \cdot n \log n$ (modeling the sorting of an array), or $a \cdot n^{\frac{3}{2}}$ (modeling a matrix-matrix multiplication). The value n determines the input data size that has been selected with uniform distribution from the interval $[4\,\text{MB}, \dots, 121\,\text{MB}]$, and a is a parameter that has been selected uniformly from the interval $[2^6, \dots, 2^9]$. Four different scenarios are considered: IMAGE (only image processing tasks), SORT (only sorting tasks), MMM (only matrix-matrix multiplication tasks), and MIX (the type of each task is determined randomly). The parallel execution time of the tasks has been modeled using Amdahl's law assuming a non-parallelizable fraction, which has been selected from

Table 1. Parameters for the synthetic task graphs and synthetic heterogeneous platforms

Graph Parameter	Values	Platform Param.	Values
Number of Nodes	{ 10, 50, 100, 200}	Sublusters	{ 2, 4, 8, 16 }
Graph Width	{ 0.1, 0.3, 0.7, 0.9 }	Base GFlops	{ 0.5, 1.0, 2.0 }
Graph Regularity	{ 0.1, 0.3, 0.7, 0.9 }	Heterogeneity	{ 1, 2, 5 }
Graph Density	{ 0.1, 0.3, 0.7, 0.9 }	Machine samples	#5
Jump length	{ 1, 2, 4 }		
Cost Model	{IMAGE, SORT, MMM, MIX}		
Graph samples	#5		
Total graphs	15360	Total machines	180

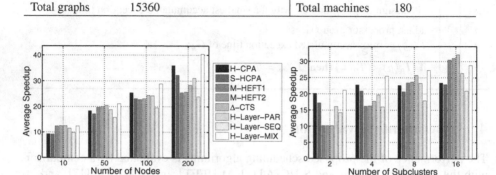

Fig. 2. Computed speedups in the simulation depending on the number of nodes in the task graph (left) and on the number of subclusters (right)

the interval $[0, \ldots, 0.25]$ with uniform distribution. Finally, for each set of different parameters we have created 5 samples.

The synthetic heterogeneous platforms consist of 2, 4, 8, and 16 subclusters where each subcluster has 2^k processors. The parameter k is chosen from the interval $[3, \ldots, 8]$, i.e., each subcluster has between eight and 256 processors. The speed of the processors is selected uniformly from the interval $[g, \ldots, g \cdot h]$ where g is the base GFlops rate and h is the heterogeneity of the platform. We used three different base GFlops rates $(0.5, 1.0, 2.0)$ and three different heterogeneity factors $(1, 2, 5)$. The type of the interconnection is determined at random. For the intra-cluster networks we consider 10, 20, and 40 GBit Infiniband networks, and the inter-cluster connection is either a 1 or a 10 GBit ethernet. 5 sample machines are created for each set of different parameters leading to 180 different platforms, see Tab. 1 (right) for an overview of the parameters.

As a measure for the quality of the computed schedules, we use the speedup over a sequential execution on the fastest processor of the platform. Figure 2 shows the speedups for different numbers of nodes and different numbers of subclusters averaged over all experiments. The results show that *H-Layer-MIX* clearly outperforms *H-Layer-PAR*, which in turn outperforms *H-Layer-SEQ*. The proposed layer-based approach is especially beneficial for large task graphs, since these graphs often have large layers providing more flexibility for the cluster scheduling phase. For small layers, the consecutive scheduling of the layers may result in unused processor time because there are not enough tasks to employ all available subclusters. This is also illustrated by the results for 16 subclusters where the layer-based algorithms have a lower performance than

Table 2. Hardware configuration of the heterogeneous cluster platform used for the experiments

CPU type	CPU clock	Peak Perf.	Nodes	Procs./Node	Cores/Proc.	Total Cores
Intel Xeon 'Westmere'	2.67 GHz	10.67 GFlops	5	2	6	60
AMD Opteron 'Istanbul'	2.1 GHz	8.4 GFlops	1	4	6	24
Intel Xeon 'Clovertown'	2.33 GHz	9.33 GFlops	2	2	4	16
AMD Opteron 'Egypt'	1.8 GHz	3.6 GFlops	4	4	2	32

the two *M-HEFT* algorithms and Δ-*CTS*. This problem can be addressed by using the Move-Blocks algorithm [10], which combines the layers in the final schedule with the goal to minimize the processor idle time. Altogether, the results show that *H-Layer-MIX* delivers the best results in most situations.

4.2   Application Benchmarks

As application benchmarks, we consider flow solvers from the NPB-MZ parallel benchmark suite [20] as well as different solvers for ordinary differential equations (ODEs). The cost functions for the parallel tasks have been obtained by measuring the execution times on the individual subclusters using different numbers of processors and fitting the measured times to an appropriate function prototype.

Hardware Description. The application benchmarks have been executed on a heterogeneous cluster consisting of four subclusters with a total of 132 processor cores, see Tab. 2 for an overview of the hardware configuration. All nodes of the heterogeneous cluster are interconnected with a 10 GBit/s Infiniband network. The MVAPICH2 1.5.1 library has been used to provide MPI support. The application benchmarks have been compiled with the Intel Compiler 12.1 with full optimizations enabled.

NPB-MZ Benchmarks. The NPB-MZ benchmarks [20] include three different solvers (LU-MZ, SP-MZ and BT-MZ) for the solution of flow equations on a three-dimensional discretization mesh partitioned into zones. One time step of these solvers consists of independent computations for each zone followed by a border exchange between neighboring zones. For the purpose of the benchmarks, we use one parallel task for the computations of one zone. The resulting parallel task graph is a sequence of fork-join graphs. For each solver, there are several benchmark classes that differ in the global mesh size and in the number of zones, see Tab. 3 for an overview of the classes used in this article.

The LU-MZ and SP-MZ benchmarks define equal-sized zones leading to an identical number of computations for each parallel task. As a consequence, the major scheduling objective is to assign each subcluster a number of parallel tasks according to its relative computational performance. Within the individual subclusters, Alg. 3 computes equal-sized processor groups. Figure 3 (left) shows the measured performance for the LU-MZ benchmark. *H-Layer-MIX* clearly produces the best schedule for class *B*. For class *C*, the scheduling algorithms Δ-*CTS*, *H-Layer-PAR*, and *H-Layer-MIX* produce similar schedules. The other algorithms are not competitive.

Table 3. NPB-MZ benchmark configuration

Benchmark	Class	Global Mesh	No. of Zones
LU-MZ	B	$304 \times 208 \times 17$	16 equal-sized
LU-MZ	C	$480 \times 320 \times 28$	16 equal-sized
SP-MZ	A	$128 \times 128 \times 16$	16 equal-sized
SP-MZ	B	$304 \times 208 \times 17$	64 equal-sized
SP-MZ	C	$480 \times 320 \times 28$	256 equal-sized
BT-MZ	A	$128 \times 128 \times 16$	16 of varying size
BT-MZ	B	$304 \times 208 \times 17$	64 of varying size
BT-MZ	C	$480 \times 320 \times 28$	256 of varying size

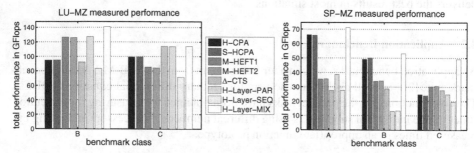

Fig. 3. Performance of different scheduling decisions for the LU-MZ benchmark (left) and the SP-MZ benchmark (right) on the heterogeneous cluster

The results for the SP-MZ benchmark are shown in Fig. 3 (right). The best overall performance is obtained by the algorithms *H-CPA*, *S-HCPA*, and *H-Layer-MIX*. The algorithms *M-HEFT1*, *M-HEFT2* and *Δ-CTS* lead to a significantly lower performance caused by allocating too many processors to the parallel tasks.

The zones of the BT-MZ benchmark have different sizes and, thus, the scheduling algorithms also need to adjust the processor group sizes within the subclusters accordingly. The results for this benchmark are shown in Fig. 4 (left). The performance of the scheduling algorithms varies depending on the benchmark class. The algorithms *H-CPA* and *S-HCPA* lead to a very poor performance for class A, but are competitive for classes B and C. The *M-HEFT* algorithms lead to good results only for classes A and B. The best overall algorithm is *H-Layer-MIX*, since it provides the best performance for classes B and C, while being close to the best for class A.

ODE Benchmarks. The numerical solution of ordinary differential equations (ODEs) can be computed by time stepping methods where each time step computes a fixed number K of approximations that are combined to form an approximation of higher order. Examples for such solvers are the Iterated Runge-Kutta (IRK), the Parallel Adams-Bashforth (PAB), the Parallel-Adams-Bashforth-Moulton (PABM) [19], and the extrapolation (EPOL) methods. The task graphs of the IRK, PAB, and PABM methods consist of a sequence of layers each of which comprising K identical parallel tasks. The task graph of the EPOL method consists of K independent linear chains with different

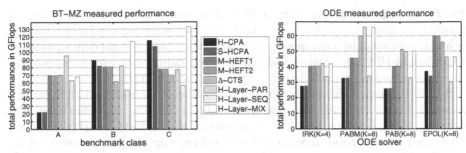

Fig. 4. Performance of the computed schedules for the BT-MZ benchmark (left) and for different ODE solvers (right) as measured on the heterogeneous cluster

lengths and one parallel task that combines the results computed within these chains. For the benchmarks, we use an ODE system that arises from a Galerkin approximation of a Schrödinger-Poisson system.

The results in Fig. 4 (right) show that there are substantial differences in the performance of the parallel ODE solvers and that there is no single best scheduling algorithm. In general, the scheduling algorithms Δ-*CTS*, *H-Layer-PAR*, and *H-Layer-MIX* are best suited for these application benchmarks. *H-Layer-SEQ* leads to a considerably lower performance due to a significant load imbalance between the subclusters.

5   Related Work

There are two major approaches to the scheduling of parallel tasks with precedence constraints on homogeneous target platforms: layer-based approaches and critical-path-based approaches. Critical-path-based approaches consist of two steps: an allocation step that assigns each parallel task a number of processors and a mapping step that assigns specific processors to the parallel tasks and also determines the execution order based on the precedence constraints. These two steps may be independent from each other as in CPA[14], MCPA[1] or MCPA2[9], or may be executed repeatedly in a coupled fashion as in CPR[13] or Loc-MPS[21]. The layer-based approach[15,4] first partitions the parallel task graph into layers of independent tasks and then schedules the resulting layers one after another using a scheduling algorithm for independent tasks. A layer-based approach for the scheduling on multicore clusters with a hierarchically organized interconnection networks has been proposed in[6].

The scheduling of precedence constrained parallel tasks on heterogeneous target platforms usually follows a critical-path-based approach. The algorithms M-HEFT1 and M-HEFT2[17] have been derived from a list-scheduling algorithm for standard sequential tasks[18]. In these algorithms, the parallel platform is modeled as a set of configurations where each configuration consists of a set of identical processors. In each step of the algorithm, an unscheduled parallel task is selected and scheduled to the configuration that minimizes its finish time. The task is selected based on the length of the longest path to an exit node where the length of a path is computed as the sum of the computation and communication costs of the nodes and edges along this path.

H-CPA and S-HCPA[11] are extensions of CPA for heterogeneous cluster platforms. In the allocation step, each parallel task is assigned a number of processors from a virtual homogeneous reference cluster. The subsequent mapping step first translates this reference allocation to allocations on the individual subclusters and then schedules each task to the subcluster that minimizes its completion time. Several improvements of H-CPA and M-HEFT that mainly lead to a better utilization of the execution resources at the expense of a higher makespan have been suggested in [12].

Δ-CTS [16] uses a list-scheduling approach where in each step multiple parallel tasks with a similar priority value are scheduled together. The maximum number of processors for each of these parallel tasks is bounded and the tasks are scheduled, such that a minimum termination time for each group of tasks results. The reasoning behind this approach is to prevent one parallel task to use too many execution resources and thus preventing other independent tasks to be scheduled for a concurrent execution.

MCGAS [8] is a scheduling algorithm for multiple subclusters with a performance guarantee that depends on the exact platform configuration. The processors of different clusters are assumed to have a roughly identical computational performance. The number of processors for each parallel task is computed using a linear program formulation for the discrete time-cost trade-off problem. The mapping to groups of processors is performed by a modified list scheduling approach that restricts the maximum number of processors that may be used for any parallel task.

In contrast to these scheduling algorithms for heterogeneous platforms, we pursue a layer-based scheduling approach. Our approach is an extension of an existing scheduling algorithm for homogeneous platforms to heterogeneous cluster-of-clusters systems.

6 Conclusion

We have considered the scheduling of parallel tasks with precedence constraints on heterogeneous clusters consisting of multiple subclusters. The scheduling uses a layer-based approach, which has shown to be suitable for homogeneous platforms in previous work [15,4]. The extension of this approach to heterogeneous target platforms requires an additional phase that partitions the independent parallel tasks of a given layer into subsets and assigns these subsets to the individual subclusters. For this phase, we have suggested three different heuristics resulting in three different scheduling algorithms. The proposed algorithms encompass *H-Layer-SEQ* that uses the sequential execution time, *H-Layer-PAR* that uses the data parallel execution time, and *H-Layer-MIX* that uses the mixed parallel execution time of the parallel tasks for the assignment onto subclusters. An experimental evaluation using simulation as well as application benchmarks from the NPB-MZ parallel benchmark suite and from the area of solvers for ordinary differential equations has shown that *H-Layer-MIX* outperforms the other two algorithms as well as previously proposed scheduling algorithms in most situations.

References

1. Bansal, S., Kumar, P., Singh, K.: An improved two-step algorithm for task and data parallel scheduling in distributed memory machines. Parallel Comput. 32(10), 759–774 (2006)
2. DAG Generation Program, http://www.loria.fr/~suter/dags.html

3. Du, J., Leung, J.T.: Complexity of Scheduling Parallel Task Systems. SIAM J. Discret. Math. 2(4), 473–487 (1989)
4. Dümmler, J., Kunis, R., Rünger, G.: Layer-Based Scheduling Algorithms for Multiprocessor-Tasks with Precedence Constraints. In: Proc. of the Int. Conf. ParCo 2007. Advances in Parallel Computing, vol. 15, pp. 321–328. IOS Press (2007)
5. Dümmler, J., Kunis, R., Rünger, G.: SEParAT: Scheduling Support Environment for Parallel Application Task Graphs. Cluster Computing 15(3), 223–238 (2012)
6. Dümmler, J., Rauber, T., Rünger, G.: Combined Scheduling and Mapping for Scalable Computing with Parallel Tasks. Scientific Programming 20(1), 45–67 (2012)
7. Dümmler, J., Rauber, T., Rünger, G.: Programming Support and Scheduling for Communicating Parallel Tasks. J. Parallel Distrib. Comput. 73(2), 220–234 (2013)
8. Dutot, P.F., N'Takpe, T., Suter, F., Casanova, H.: Scheduling Parallel Task Graphs on (Almost) Homogeneous Multicluster Platforms. IEEE Trans. Parallel Distrib. Syst. 20(7), 940–952 (2009)
9. Hunold, S.: Low-Cost Tuning of Two-Step Algorithms for Scheduling Mixed-Parallel Applications onto Homogeneous Clusters. In: Proc. of the 10th IEEE/ACM Int. Conf. on Cluster, Cloud and Grid Computing (CCGRID 2010), pp. 253–262. IEEE Computer Society (2010)
10. Kunis, R., Rünger, G.: Optimizing Layer-based Scheduling Algorithms for Parallel Tasks with Dependencies. Concurr. Comput.: Pract. Exper. 23(8), 827–849 (2011)
11. N'Takpé, T., Suter, F.: Critical path and area based scheduling of parallel task graphs on heterogeneous platforms. In: Proc. of the 12th Int. Conf. on Parallel and Distributed Systems (ICPADS 2006), pp. 3–10 (2006)
12. N'Takpé, T., Suter, F., Casanova, H.: A Comparison of Scheduling Approaches for Mixed-Parallel Applications on Heterogeneous Platforms. In: Proc. of the 6th Int. Symp. on Parallel and Distributed Computing (ISPDC 2007), pp. 35–42. IEEE Computer Society (July 2007)
13. Radulescu, A., Nicolescu, C., van Gemund, A., Jonker, P.: CPR: Mixed Task and Data Parallel Scheduling for Distributed Systems. In: Proc. of the 15th Int. Parallel & Distributed Processing Symp. (IPDPS 2001). IEEE (2001)
14. Radulescu, A., van Gemund, A.: A Low-Cost Approach towards Mixed Task and Data Parallel Scheduling. In: Proc. of the Int. Conf. on Parallel Processing (ICPP 2001), pp. 69–76. IEEE (2001)
15. Rauber, T., Rünger, G.: Compiler support for task scheduling in hierarchical execution models. J. Syst. Archit. 45(6-7), 483–503 (1998)
16. Suter, F.: Scheduling Δ-Critical Tasks in Mixed-parallel Applications on a National Grid. In: Proc. of the 8th IEEE/ACM Int. Conf. on Grid Computing (GRID 2007), pp. 2–9. IEEE Computer Society, Washington, DC (2007)
17. Suter, F., Desprez, F., Casanova, H.: From Heterogeneous Task Scheduling to Heterogeneous Mixed Parallel Scheduling. In: Danelutto, M., Vanneschi, M., Laforenza, D. (eds.) Euro-Par 2004. LNCS, vol. 3149, pp. 230–237. Springer, Heidelberg (2004)
18. Topcuouglu, H., Hariri, S., Wu, M.Y.: Performance-Effective and Low-Complexity Task Scheduling for Heterogeneous Computing. IEEE Trans. Parallel Distrib. Syst. 13(3), 260–274 (2002)
19. van der Houwen, P., Messina, E.: Parallel Adams Methods. J. of Comp. and App. Mathematics 101, 153–165 (1999)
20. van der Wijngaart, R., Jin, H.: The NAS Parallel Benchmarks, Multi-Zone Versions. Tech. Rep. NAS-03-010, NASA Ames Research Center (2003)
21. Vydyanathan, N., Krishnamoorthy, S., Sabin, G., Catalyurek, U., Kurc, T., Sadayappan, P., Saltz, J.: An Integrated Approach to Locality-Conscious Processor Allocation and Scheduling of Mixed-Parallel Applications. IEEE Trans. Parallel Distrib. Syst. 20(8), 1158–1172 (2009)

Deadline-Constrained Workflow Scheduling
in Volunteer Computing Systems

Toktam Ghafarian[1] and Bahman Javadi[2]

[1] Department of Computer Engineering
Khayyam Institute of Higher Education, Iran
t.ghafarian@khayyam.ac.ir
[2] School of Computing, Engineering and Mathematics
University of Western Sydney, Australia
b.javadi@uws.edu.au

Abstract. One of the main challenges in volunteer computing systems is scheduling large-scale applications expressed as scientific workflows. This work aims to integrate partitioning scientific workflows and proximity-aware resource provisioning to increase the percentage of workflows that meet the deadline in peer-to-peer based volunteer computing systems. In the partitioning phase, a scientific workflow is partitioned into sub-workflows in order to minimize data dependencies among them. We utilize knowledge-free load balancing policy and proximity of resources to distribute sub-workflows on volunteer resources. Simulation results show that the proposed workflow scheduling system improves the percentage of scientific workflows that meet the deadline with average of 18% under a moderate workload.

Keywords: scientific workflow scheduling, deadline-constrained workflow, Peer-to-peer based volunteer computing systems, proximity-aware scheduling.

1 Introduction

Volunteer computing (VC) systems exploit the idle cycle of distributed resources to run scientific applications such as SETI@home [1], EDGeS@Home [2] and climate-prediction.net [3]. While popular application form in the volunteer computing systems is Bag of Tasks (BoT) applications, there are a number of scientific and engineering applications that are determined by a set of dependent tasks called workflow such as Montage [4], Epigenomics [5], and Sipht [7].

The scheduling problem is assigning the dependent tasks in the workflow on available resources in VC systems. To tackle this problem, we propose a new scheduling algorithm based on our previous work called CycloidGrid [8]. CycloidGrid is a proximity-aware architecture for resource discovery in P2P-based VC systems.

The proposed workflow scheduling system divides workflow into sub-workflows by an algorithm based on tabu search in order to minimize data dependencies among sub-workflows. Then, the resource provisioning phase distributes these sub-workflows onto volunteer resources based on Quality of Service (QoS) constraints in

J. Kołodziej et al. (Eds.): ICA3PP 2013, Part I, LNCS 8285, pp. 44–57, 2013.

terms of its deadline, minimum CPU speed and minimum RAM or hard disk requirements, and proximity of resources. The distribution of sub-workflows onto volunteer resources is done by load balancing policy with an analytical model based on queuing theory that is independent of information of resources and application characteristics. The contributions of our work is summarized as applying a partitioning algorithm to divide scientific workflows into sub-workflows and integration of that with resource provisioning based on QoS constraints and proximity of resources.

The rest of this paper is organized as follows: Section 2 includes related work. Section 3 presents CycloidGrid architecture. Section 4 discusses the proposed deadline-constrained workflow scheduling system. Section 5 describes the performance evaluation of the proposed workflow scheduling system. Conclusions and future works are presented in Section 6.

2   Related Work

There are several studies that investigated workflow scheduling in distributed computing systems. There are some works such as HEFT [10], Min-Min [14], and MaxMin [15] on workflow scheduling problem where they considered a workflow as Directed Acyclic Graph (DAG), and proposed some heuristics to solve it. Also some other works [16, 17] considered partitioning of scientific workflows in the dynamic grids. Our work focuses on partitioning of scientific workflow along with resource provision with regard to QoS constraints, load balancing and proximity of resources.

The use of graph partitioning algorithm for workflow DAG is discussed in some works [18,19,21]. Kalayci et al. [19] proposed a decentralized execution approach for large-scale workflow. They partitioned a workflow into sub-workflows and then assigned them to the peer domain. If each workflow management system on one peer domain detects a problem that affect on QoS constraints, some tasks are migrated to another peer domain. Our work applies partitioning phase, but in the resource provision phase, it considers the load balancing and proximity of resources along with QoS constraints of workflow. Kumar et al. [21] applied graph partitioning algorithm to minimize the data movement during workflow execution. They used multi-constraint graph partitioning algorithm for workflow partitioning in order to distribute tasks evenly in the system with minimization of internodes communication. They focused only on workflow partition phase, while this work focuses on workflow partitioning and resource provisioning.

Lin et al. [20] used graph partitioning method to divide resources into some execution sites in the distributed system, but workflow is not partitioned.

Chen et al. [13] proposed two methods for integration of workflow partitioning problem and resource provisioning. The first method takes into account the resource information in the system to distribute a load in a balanced manner, and the second one used a method based on genetic algorithm for combination of resource selection and job scheduling. The aim of this method is reducing the makespan and resource cost, but it ignores the proximity of resources in resource provisioning phase.

3   CycloidGrid Architecture

CycloidGrid [8] is proximity-aware resource discovery architecture in P2P-based volunteer computing systems. There are three types of node in this architecture called reporting node, host node and client node as it is shown in Figure1.

The reporting node collects the information of resources in the system. CycloidGrid applies decision tree (DT) to classify resources in the system. The attributes used to classify resources are CPU speed, the amount of RAM, available hard disk space, operating system, and processor model. DT has five levels corresponding to each resource attribute and four attribute values are considered for each resource attribute, therefore the resources are classified into 1024 clusters in this DT. Each cluster of DT is assigned to one reporting cluster. A reporting cluster has some reporting nodes that keep the information of resources categorized in this cluster.

The host node executes allocated sub-workflows and it can schedule input workflows assigned to it. The client node imports input workflows into the system and sends them to one of active host node to schedule. This node also keeps the executable code of workflow, input files, intermediate and output results during the execution of workflow. The host nodes and the client nodes are grouped into some host clusters. Therefore, there are two types of clusters in the CycloidGrid. They are called host cluster and reporting cluster. For more information about this architecture, you can refer to [8].

4   The Proposed Deadline-Constrained Workflow Scheduling System

Each workflow application is modeled as a DAG where nodes are tasks of workflow and directed edges show the data dependencies among the tasks. In this graph, a task without any parent tasks is called *entry* task, and a task without any child nodes is called *exit* nodes. Each workflow application is assumed to have some characteristics as follows:

- Number of dependent tasks and the estimated duration of each task.
- Deadline constraint, minimum CPU speed, minimum RAM or hard disk requirements are considered as QoS constraints.

The proposed workflow scheduling system includes workflow partitioning and resource provisioning. The workflow partitioning phase is performed in the client node and it aims to divide a workflow into sub-workflows in order to minimize data dependencies among them. Resource provisioning phase is performed by the host node with cooperation of the reporting nodes in order to submit sub-workflows onto volunteer resources that satisfy QoS constraints of workflow, and it tries to increase the percentage of workflow that meet the deadline constraint.

4.1   Workflow Partitioning

Since each workflow is considered as a DAG, the problem of partitioning workflow can be considered as a graph partitioning problem. It aims to partition a DAG into disjoint subsets of approximately equal size, such that the number of edges whose endpoints are in different subsets is minimized. In other words, the purpose of this phase is partitioning a workflow into sub-workflows such that the sum of data transfer among them is minimized. To do this, we apply a modified version of tabu search partitioning algorithm [24] for partitioning a workflow.

In this partitioning algorithm, at first a workflow is partitioned randomly into k approximate equal size sub-workflows. The tabu search algorithm replaces the current solution (a set of sub-workflows) with a best non-recently visited neighboring solution. This algorithm uses tabu list to forbid the recently visited solutions in order to prevent cycling.

We assume the weight of each sub-workflow is computed as sum of its estimated task computation time. This algorithm is based on two move operators that aid to minimize the sum of cutting edges among sub-workflows. Also, the move operators try to avoid partition imbalance in terms of sub-workflow weight. These two move operators transfer one or two vertex between two sub-workflows. This strategy is based on move gain that shows how much a sub-workflow is improved in terms of cutting edges when a vertex is moved to another sub-workflow.

These two move operators are single-move and double-move. Single-move moves one highest gain vertex to randomly another sub-workflow such that the target sub-workflow is not max weight sub-workflow and its weight is lower than source sub-workflow. Double move chooses two highest gain vertexes. One of these vertexes is moved according to the single-move policy and the other one moves to a sub-workflow that is not equal to max weight sub-workflow and the target sub-workflow of single-move in the first phase. Also its source sub-workflow is not equal to the target sub-workflow of single-move and its target sub-workflow.

The move operators only consider moving a vertex to another sub-workflow if it is adjacent to at least one vertex of this sub-workflow. This policy reduces the number of candidate movements for any iteration. Also these move operators contribute to have balanced sub-workflow in terms of weight along with minimization of sum of data communication time among sub-workflows.

These two moves are done in tabu search algorithm in a token ring way [9]. In this way, one neighborhood search is done on the local optimum generated by the previous one, and this process continues until no improvement is possible. When a vertex is moved from a source sub-workflow to another one, moving back to its source sub-workflow is forbidden for next some iteration. To add diversification to the tabu search, the perturbation mechanism is applied. This step is consisted of selecting a random target sub-workflow except max weight sub-workflow and moving a random vertex from a sub-workflow with its weight is more than target sub-workflow.

4.2   Resource Provisioning Phase

Each workflow application is partitioned into sub-workflows by the tabu search algorithm discussed in Section 4.1 in the client node. Also the client node computes the upward rank of each task in the workflow by HEFT algorithm [10]. The upward rank of each task in the workflow is computed by the following equation:

$$k_{n_i} = C_{n_i} + \max_{n_j \in chidren(n_i)} \left(t_{ij} + k_{n_j} \right) \tag{1}$$

$$k_{n_{exit}} = C_{n_{exit}}$$

Where C_{n_i} is computation time of task n_i and t_{ij} is average communication time between two tasks n_i and n_j. Average communication time is computed based on average network bandwidth.

Figure 1 illustrates the interaction among different nodes in the workflow scheduling system. The client node submits sub-workflows along with the rank of their tasks to the randomly active node in the system (step 1). This node is called *injection* node. The injection node is responsible for resource provisioning of this workflow. At first it sends a request to the subset of reporting nodes (step 2). The selected reporting nodes are chosen by DT in terms of the QoS constraints of workflow. These QoS constraints are minimum CPU speed, minimum RAM or hard disk space. DT specifies the reporting node that contains the resource information satisfy these constraints.

Selected reporting nodes advertise some resources based on QoS constraints and knowledge–free load balancing policy that are discussed in the next section (step 3). The number of advertised resources by one reporting node is equal to the number of sub-workflows. The identifier of these resources along with the weighted rank of CPU speed returns back to the injection node (step 4). As each workflow has deadline constraint, the injection node applies Algorithm 1 to select target resources to run these sub-workflows (step5).

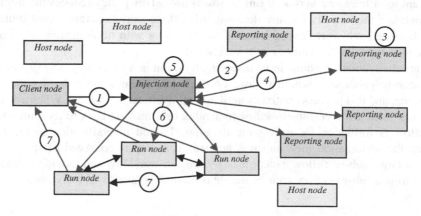

Fig. 1. Interaction among different nodes in the workflow scheduling system

According to Algorithm 1, the injection node finds the resource with maximum rank of CPU speed (lines 1-7) in order to increase the percentage of workflows that meets assigned deadline, then finds the resource with minimum communication delay (lines 8-14) in order to decrease the communication delay to send sub-workflows. If the resource with maximum rank is equal to the resource with minimum communication delay, this resource will be selected (lines 15-18). Otherwise, next minimum communication delay resource is selected until half of resources are examined (lines 19-20). After that, the next resource with maximum rank of CPU speed is selected (line 21). This procedure is continued until the number of target resources is equal to the number of sub-workflows.

Algorithm 1: Selection of target resources for running sub-workflows in the injection node

---

Input: d_i, R_i *are the* rank of CPU speed and communication delay of each advertised resource i respectively, $1 \leq i \leq N$ (*N=number of advertised resources*)
Output: S contains the index of target resources
1. *maxRank* $\leftarrow 0$
2. foreach resource i do
3.   if $(d_i > maxRank)$ then
4.   *maxRank* $\leftarrow d_i$
5.   *maxIndex* $\leftarrow i$
6.   end
7. end
8. *minDelay* $\leftarrow$ *maxvalue*
9. foreach resource i do
10.   if ($R_i < minDelay$) then
11.   *minDelay* $\leftarrow R_i$
12.   *minIndex* $\leftarrow i$
13.   end
14. end
15. if   *maxIndex* == *minIndex* then
16.   Add maxIndex to S
17.   if size(S)== number of sub-workflows return S
18. end
19. else if half of resources are not selected   then
20.   find next minimum communication delay and goto 8
21.   else find next maximum rank and goto 1
22. end

The communication delay R_i in Algorithm1 is equal to the communication delay between the client node and the advertised resource plus the delay between the injection node and the advertised resource. The communication delay between two peers in the system is computed according to our previous work [8] by a network model based on queuing theory. In this analytical model each connection between two peers is modeled by a GI/GI/1 queue. So the communication delay is computed according to the following equation [8]:

$$R = (2S_p) + \left(\frac{\sigma_p^2 \times \lambda_p^2}{2 \times \left((S_p^{-1}) - \lambda_p\right)}\right) + \sum_{i=s+1}^{d} S_{p_i} \tag{2}$$

where,

$$S_p = 0.5 \times \alpha_{net} + F \times \beta_{net} \tag{3}$$

S_p is service time for each connection between two peers, and $\alpha_{net}, \beta_{net}$ are network latencies and the inverse of bandwidth along the link between two adjacent peers by a routing algorithm, respectively. F is a flow size between two peers. σ_p^2, λ_p is a variance and inter-arrival rate of traffic at source peer's queue. Last term in Equation (2) is equal to sum of service time along the route between peer next to the source peer and destination peer.

After target resources are selected by Algorithm1 to run sub-workflows, the sub-workflows are submitted to the target resources (step 6). These resources are called *run nodes* in this phase. In the run node, the tasks of each sub-workflow are ordered by descendent order of upward rank k_{n_i}, and are kept in the priority queue. The ordering of tasks provides a topological order of them and preserves the precedence constraints between them.

To run a sub-workflow, the tasks are selected from the priority queue, if a task is the entry task or the results of all parent tasks are ready, this task will be run and it is deleted from the queue, then its result are sent back to its children, if not, jump over this task and next task is examined. The queue is run in the circular way. Each host node run assigned sub-workflows in increasing order of sum of sub-deadlines. The output results of tasks are transferred between run nodes directly, and also they are kept as backup in the client node (step 7).

Load Balancing Policy. The selection of advertised resources in the reporting nodes is done based on QoS constraints and a load balancing policy [25]. This analytical model is a knowledge-free approach based on routing in parallel queues. In this model, the resource pool in the reporting node is classified into some logical clusters. The resources in one logical cluster have similar processing speed. In this model, the objective function is to find the optimal arrival rate to each logical cluster such that the incoming requests are distributed in the balanced manner among its logical clusters. The optimal arrival rate to each logical cluster j (γ_j) based on this model is computed by the following equation [25]:

$$\gamma_j = \frac{1}{L_j} - \frac{1}{L_j} \times \sqrt{\frac{1 - \lambda^2 \times \sigma^2 + \left(C_{s_j}^2 - 1\right) \times \lambda \times L_j}{1 - \lambda^2 \times \sigma^2 + 2 \times \lambda \times (L_j - z)}} \tag{4}$$

Where L_j is average and $C_{s_j}^2$ is the squared coefficient of variance for service time of sub-workflows on cluster j. λ, σ^2 is the arrival rate and the variance of incoming requests to the reporting node. z is a Lagrange multiplier , a numerical solution based on bisection algorithm is used to search z between its lower and upper bound. Average service time of each sub-workflow is computed by the following equation:

$$L_j = \bar{V} \times \bar{T} \times \frac{U_m}{U_j} \tag{5}$$

Where $\bar{V}$ is average size of sub-workflows and $\bar{T}$ is average execution time of any task in the workflow. The scaling factor for this equation is equal to division of maximum average CPU speed of all logical clusters in the reporting node to average processing speed of this logical cluster.

The dispatch policy in each reporting node among logical clusters based on its optimal arrival rate (γ_j) is Billiard. This dispatch policy is a generalized form of round robin policy and it takes into account the sequence of routing called the billiard sequence [11]. The billiard sequence is generated by the following equation:

$$h_b = \min_{\forall h} \left\{ \frac{X_h + Y_h}{\gamma_h} \right\} \tag{6}$$

Where h_b is a selected logical cluster and X_h, Y_h are n-size vector of integer numbers. X_h is set to 1 for fastest logical cluster and zero for all other logical clusters [12]. Y_h counts the number of requests that sent to each logical cluster. It initializes to zero for all logical clusters queue and increments by 1 for selected one. γ_h is the optimal arrival rate for each logical cluster that is computed by Equation 4.

Deadline Assignment to Workflow. Each workflow has a defined deadline. Deadline assignment to the workflow includes assigning sub-deadline to each task in the workflow. We use slack time to compute the sub-deadline [26]. The slack time of the workflow is amount of extra time for a workflow to increase its critical path and it is finished by its deadline. It is computed by the following equation:

$$SLT(wf) = DL(wf) - CPT(wf) \tag{7}$$

Where $DL(wf)$ is a deadline of the workflow and $CPT(wf)$ is a critical path of the workflow. The critical path is assumed is lower than the deadline in order to complete a workflow by the deadline is possible. The level of each task (l_{n_i}) in the workflow can be computed by the following equation:

$$l_{n_i} = \max_{n_j \in parent(n_i)} l_{n_j} + 1 \tag{8}$$

$$l_{n_{entry}} = 0$$

Slack time of the workflow is divided among all tasks by its level such that a level with more number of tasks and more total run time of tasks gets a larger portion of slack time. The slack time of the level l is computed by the following equation [26]:

$$SLT(l) = SLT(wf) \left[\left(\alpha \times \frac{Num(l)}{Num(wf)} \right) + \left((1 - \alpha) \times \frac{Srt(l)}{Srt(wf)} \right) \right] \tag{9}$$

Where $Num(l)$ and $Num(wf)$ are the number of tasks in level l and workflow wf, respectively. Also, $Srt(l)$ and $Srt(wf)$ are total run time of all tasks in level l and workflow wf, respectively. The $\propto$ parameter is between 0 and 1 in order to change the weight of number of tasks and total run time of all tasks.

The sub-deadline of task n_i (DL_{n_i}) is computed as follows:

$$DL_{n_i} = ls_{n_i} + rt_{n_i} + SLT(l_{n_i}) \tag{10}$$

Where $\left(ls_{n_i}\right)$ is the latest start time of the task and it is computed as follows:

$$ls_{n_i} = \max_{n_j \in parent(n_i)} DL_{n_j} \tag{11}$$

$$ls_{entry} = 0$$

And $\left(rt_{n_i}\right)$ is the task execution time and $SLT(l_{n_i})$ is the slack time of its level.

5   Performance Evaluation

To evaluate the performance of the deadline-constrained workflow scheduling system, CycloidGrid simulator [8] is used. The physical network in CycloidGrid is emulated by the Brite topology generator [12]. The nodes are connected by Waxman model [12], and the bandwidth between two nodes varies from 10Mb/s to 100Mb/s with uniform distribution. The number of resources is equal to 1000 with heterogeneous computing characteristics. The percentage of workflow applications that meet the deadline is the performance metric.

5.1   Workload Model

Various scientific workflow applications are considered to evaluate the performance of the proposed workflow scheduling system. These workflows are an astronomy application (Montage) [4], seismology application (CyberShake) [27] and two bioinformatics applications (Epigenomics [5], and Sipht [7]). These workflows cover a wide range of application domains and a variety of resource requirements. These scientific workflows are generated with 30 tasks by Bharathi et al. [5, 28]. Workflow applications submit to the system by Weibull distribution based on an existing Grid workload model [29]. This distribution with its parameter is listed in Table 1. The QoS constraints for each workflow application is deadline, minimum CPU speed and minimum RAM or hard disk requirement.

The workload is generated for 1 day and 2.5 hours is considered as warm-up to avoid bias before the system steady-state. Each experiment is performed several times by using different workloads and average results are reported. The reported results have coefficient of variance less than $0.01 (CV < 0.01)$. We generate different workload by modifying the first parameter of Weibull distribution (the scale parameter α) as shown in Table 1. Therefore, the number of workflows increase from 8000 (i.e.$\alpha = 11$) to 14000 (i.e.$\alpha = 7$).

The background traffic of Internet and Internet flow size to compute communication delay in the system are followed Weibull distribution and Pareto distribution as shown in Table 1 [6].

Table 1. Input parameters for the workload model

Parameters	Distribution/Value
Workflow inter-arrival time	Weibull ($7 \leq \alpha \leq 11, \beta = 4.25$)
Internet inter-arrival time	Weibull($\alpha = 0.06, \beta = 0.15$)
Internet flow size	Pareto($\alpha = 3, \beta = 1.05$)

5.2 Baseline Policies

We compared proposed scheduling system (Tabu) with two other policies as follows:

- FM: in this strategy, we partition workflow with popular multi-way Fiduccia–Mattheyses [22, 23] graph partitioning algorithm, and then we select run nodes to run-sub-workflows by Algorithm 1.
- Random: in this strategy, the workflow is partitioned into sub-workflows randomly, and run nodes are selected randomly among the advertised resources in the injection node.

However, the baseline policies differ in two ways. The first one is workflow partition algorithm; each of them is based on one partitioning algorithm. The second one is proximity-aware feature. Tabu and FM are proximity-aware and select closer resource to client node and injection node according to Algorithm1; whereas Random selects run nodes from the advertised resources that satisfy QoS constraints randomly.

5.3 Simulation Results

Simulation results show the percentage of workflows that meet the deadline versus the arrival rate for different policies. In these experiments, we assume the system is relatively is static and no peer joins or leaves during the simulation.

Figure 2 shows the percentage of the workflow that meet the deadline for Montage workflow by increasing the arrival rate. In this figure, Tabu surpasses FM and Random policies with improvement factor of 23% and 79%, respectively. Since Montage is an I/O-intensive workflow with few CPU-intensive tasks, so minimization of data dependency between the sub-workflows and a proximity-aware feature has more impact on increasing the percentage of successful workflows in Tabu and FM policies compared to Random policy. When α parameter decreases, the number of workflow in the system is increased; whereas the number of volunteer machine is fixed. So the performance of all policies in meeting the deadline drops off.

Figure 3 presents the experimental results for CyberShake workflow. The improvement factor of Tabu with respect to FM and Random is 14% and 44%, respectively. CyberShake is a data-intensive workflow with large input/output files, so the proximity-aware feature of Tabu and FM shows its impact on the percentage of the successful workflows compared to Random policy.

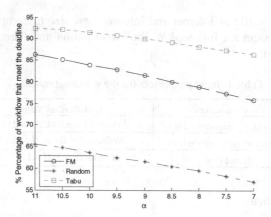

Fig. 2. Percentage of job that meet the deadline for Montage workflow versus arrival rate

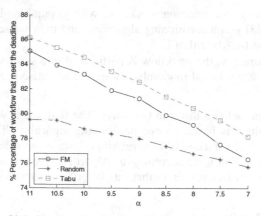

Fig. 3. Percentage of job that meet the deadline for Cybershake workflow versus arrival rate

Figure 4 presents the experimental results for Epigenomics workflow. The improvement factor of Tabu with respect to FM and Random policies are 23% and 49%, respectively. Unlike Montage workflow, Epigenomics is a CPU-intensive workflow with fewer fan-in jobs, so the percentage of the successful workflows with respect to Random is lower than Montage workflow. It shows that the partitioning algorithm has low impact on scheduling of this workflow and other parameters such as load balancing and proximity-awareness has more impact on percentage of successful workflows.

Figure 5 represents the experimental results for Sipht workflow. In this workflow, Tabu improves the percentage of workflows that meet the deadline by 12% compared to FM and 72% with respect to Random. Sipht workflow has many tasks with short run time and a few tasks with long run time. If the run time of tasks is small, the load balancing strategy has little influence on system performance. So, the impact of partitioning algorithm and proximity-awareness is more than load balancing in this workflow. Meanwhile Sipht similar to Epigenomics is primarily a CPU-bound workflow. So, partitioning algorithm and proximity-awareness influence a few on the percentage of successful workflows. Therefore, the percentage of the successful workflows in Sipht in overall is lower than Epigenomics workflow.

The proposed workflow scheduling policy performs better for I/O-intensive and CPU-intensive workflows. In fact, the emphasis of the partitioning algorithm is grouping tasks with more data dependencies in the same sub-workflow, so it lessens the communication delay in I/O-intensive workflows and improves the system performance. Also the knowledge-free load balancing policy influences on the performance of CPU-intensive workflows by distributing the load fairly among the resources in the system.

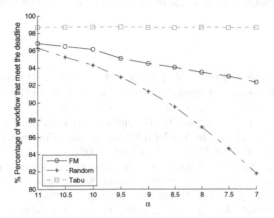

Fig. 4. Percentage of job that meet the deadline for Epigenomics workflow versus arrival rate

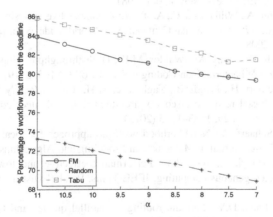

Fig. 5. Percentage of job that meet the deadline for Sipht workflow versus arrival rate

6   Conclusions

In this paper, we proposed a deadline-constrained workflow scheduling system in peer-to-peer based volunteer computing systems. Each workflow has QoS constraints in terms of deadline, minimum CPU speed and minimum RAM or hard disk requirements. We integrate a workflow partitioning with the resource provisioning to increase the percentage of the successful workflows in P2P-based VC systems. We compare the performance of the proposed workflow scheduling system with two other baseline policies. The result of simulations indicate that Tabu policy significantly increase the percentage of workflow that meet the deadline with improvement factor 18%, 61% in average with respect to FM and Random policies.

As part of future work, we will consider other partitioning algorithms to improve partitioning phase for data-intensive workflows. Another interesting extension is using Cloud resources in some of peers. In fact, we can send failed workflows from VC systems to Cloud resources to meet the deadline constraints of this workflow.

References

1. Anderson, D.P., Cobb, J., Korpela, E., Lebofsky, M., Werthimer, D.: SETI@home: An experiment in public-resource computing. Commun. ACM 45, 56–61 (2002)
2. EDGeS@Home project, http://home.edges-grid.eu
3. Christensen, C., Aina, T., Stainforth, D.: The challenge of volunteer computing with lengthy climate model simulation. In: The 1st IEEE International Conference on e-Science and Grid Computing, pp. 8–15. IEEE Press, New York (2005)
4. Berriman, G.B., Deelman, E., et al.: Montage: a grid-enabled engine for delivering custom science grade mosaics on demand. In: 16th Annual Symposium Electronic Imaging Science and Technology, pp. 221–232. SPIE Press, California (2004)
5. Bharathi, S., Chervenak, A., Deelman, E., Mehta, G., Su, M.H., Vahi, K.: Characterization of Scientific Workflows. In: The Third Workshop on Workflows in Support of Large-scale Science, pp. 1–10. IEEE Press, New York (2008)
6. Basher, N., Mahanti, A., Williamson, C., Arlitt, M.: A comparative analysis of web and peer-to-peer traffic. In: The 17th International Conference on World Wide Web, pp. 287–296. ACM Press, New York (2008)
7. Livny, J., Teonadi, H., Livny, M., Waldor, M.K.: High-throughput, kingdom-wide prediction and annotation of bacterial Non-Coding RNAs. PLoS ONE 3, e3197 (2008)
8. Ghafarian, T., Deldari, H., Javadi, B., Yaghmaee, M.H., Buyya, R.: CycloidGrid: A proximity-aware P2P-based resource discovery architecture in volunteer computing systems. Future Gener. Comp. Sy. 29, 1583–1595 (2013)
9. Di Gaspero, L., Schaerf, A.: Neighborhood portfolio approach for local search applied to timetabling problems. Journal of Mathematical Modeling and Algorithms 5, 65–89 (2006)
10. Topcuouglu, H., Hariri, S., Wu, M.Y.: Performance-effective and low-complexity task scheduling for heterogeneous computing. IEEE Trans. Parallel Distrib. Syst. 13, 260–274 (2002)
11. Hordijk, A., der Laan, D.V.: Periodic routing to parallel queues and billiard sequences. Math. Method Oper. Res. 59, 173–192 (2004)
12. Medina, A., Lakhina, A., Matta, I., Byers, J.: BRITE: an approach to universal topology generation. In: IEEE International Symposium on Modeling, Analysis and Simulation of Computer and Telecommunication Systems, pp. 346–353. IEEE Press, New York (2001)
13. Chen, W., Deelman, E.: Integration of workflow partitioning and resource provisioning. In: 12th IEEE/ACM International Symposium on Cluster, Cloud and Grid Computing, pp. 764–768. IEEE Press, New York (2012)

14. Blythe, J., Jain, S., Deelman, E., Gil, Y., Vahi, K., Mandal, A., Kennedy, K.: Task scheduling strategies for workflow-based applications in Grids. In: IEEE/ACM International Symposium on Cluster, Cloud and Grid Computing, pp. 759–767. IEEE Press, New York (2005)

15. Braun, T.D., Siegel, H.J., et al.: A Comparison of eleven static heuristics for mapping a class of independent tasks onto heterogeneous distributed computing systems. J. Parallel Distr. Com. 61, 810–837 (2001)

16. Duan, R., Prodan, R., Fahringer, T.: Run-time Optimization of grid workflow applications. In: 7th IEEE/ACM International Conference on Grid Computing, pp. 33–40. IEEE Press, New York (2005)

17. Wieczorek, M., Prodan, R., Fahringer, T.: Scheduling of scientific workflows in the ASKALON grid environment. SIGMOND Record 34, 56–62 (2005)

18. Dong, F., Akl, S.: Two-phase computation and data scheduling algorithms for workflows in the grid. In: International Conference on Parallel Processing, p. 66. IEEE Press, New York (2007)

19. Kalayci, S., Dasgupta, G., Fong, L., Ezenwoye, O., Sadjadi, S.: Distributed and adaptive execution of condor DAGman workflows. In: The 23rd International Conference on Software Engineering and Knowledge Engineering, pp. 587–590. Knowledge Systems Institute, Illinois (2010)

20. Lin, C., Shih, C., Hsu, C.: Adaptive dynamic scheduling algorithms for mapping ongoing m-tasks to pr 2 grid. J. Inf. Sci. Eng. 26, 2107–2125 (2010)

21. Kumar, S., Das, S., Biswas, R.: Graph partitioning for parallel applications in heterogeneous grid environments. In: International Parallel and Distributed Processing Symposium, pp. 66–72. IEEE Press, New York (2002)

22. Sanchis, L.A.: Multiple-way network partitioning. IEEE Trans. on Computers 38, 62–81 (1989)

23. Sanchis, L.A.: Multiple-way network partitioning with different cost functions. IEEE Trans. on Computers 42, 1500–1504 (1993)

24. Benlic, U., Hao, J.K.: An effective multilevel tabu search approach for balanced graph partitioning. Comput. Oper. Res. 38, 1066–1075 (2010)

25. Ghafarian, T., Deldari, H., Javadi, B., Buyya, R.: A proximity-aware load balancing in peer-to-peer-based volunteer computing systems. J. Supercomput. 65, 797–822 (2013)

26. Malawski, M., Juve, G., Deelman, E., Nabrzyskiz, J.: Cost and Deadline-Constrained Provisioning for Scientific Workflow Ensembles in IaaS Clouds. In: The International Conference on High Performance Computing, Networking, Storage and Analysis, pp. 1–11. IEEE Press, New York (2012)

27. Deelman, E., Callaghan, S., Field, E., Francoeur, H., Graves, R., Gupta, V., Jordan, T.H., Kesselman, C., Maechling, P., Mehta, G., Kaya, D.O., Vahi, K., Zhao, L.: Managing large-scale Workflow Execution from resource provisioning to provenance tracking: the Cyber-Shake example. In: Proceedings of the Second IEEE international Conference on E-Science and Grid Computing, p. 14. IEEE Press, New York (2006)

28. Workflow Generator, https://conflence.pegasus.isi.edu/display/Pegasus/WorkflowGenerator

29. Iosup, A., Sonmez, O., Anoep, S., Epema, D.: The performance of Bags-of-Tasks in large-scale distributed systems. In: The 17th International Symposium on High Performance Distributed Computing, pp. 97–108. ACM Press, New York (2008)

Is Sensor Deployment Using Gaussian Distribution Energy Balanced?

Subir Halder[1,2] and Amrita Ghosal[1,2]

[1] Department of CSE, Dr. B.C. Roy Engineering College, Durgapur, India
[2] Department of CST, Bengal Engineering and Science University, Howrah, India
sub.halder@gmail.com, ghosal_amrita@yahoo.com

Abstract. Energy is one of the scarcest resources in wireless sensor network (WSN). One fundamental way of conserving energy is judicious deployment of sensor nodes within the network area so that energy flow remains balanced throughout the network. Node deployment using Gaussian distribution is a standard practice and is widely acceptable when random deployment is used. Initially, an analysis is done to establish that Gaussian distribution based node deployment is not energy balanced. Standard deviation has been identified as the parameter responsible for energy balancing. A deployment strategy is proposed for energy balancing using customized Gaussian distribution by discretizing the standard deviation. Performance of the deployment scheme is evaluated in terms of energy balance and network lifetime. Simulation results demonstrate that proposed deployment strategy significantly outperforms conventional Gaussian distribution based node deployment scheme in terms of the two performance metrics.

Keywords: Node deployment, Gaussian distribution, Energy hole, Network lifetime, Wireless sensor network.

1 Introduction

Node deployment is a fundamental issue in wireless sensor networks (WSNs) that affects many facets of network operation, including energy management, routing, security, etc. There are broadly two types of deployment categories in WSNs- random deployment and another is deterministic deployment [1]. Random deployment is typically used in physically inaccessible areas e.g., volcanoes, seismic zones etc., where nodes are usually dropped from helicopter [2]. On the other hand, deterministic deployment is preferable in physically accessible areas e.g., target tracking, urban monitoring, soil monitoring etc., where nodes are placed by hand at selected spots prior to network operation [2].

It is well known that lifetime of WSN depends on the node deployment strategy [1], [3]. The reason is that nodes located at one-hop away from the base station/sink have to relay traffic from other nodes, resulting in faster consumption of energy for data reception and retransmission. When such first-hop nodes have exhausted their energy, it is useless even if other nodes may have sufficient residual energy resulting in the phenomenon known as energy hole problem [3]. Therefore, if any part of the

J. Kołodziej et al. (Eds.): ICA3PP 2013, Part I, LNCS 8285, pp. 58–71, 2013.

network is affected by the energy hole problem, the whole network gets affected as uneven consumption of energy leads to premature decrease of network lifetime. To avoid this, care should be taken during node deployment such that energy dissipation in all nodes takes place uniformly ensuring load balancing throughout the network. One solution to address non-uniform dissipation of energy is to deploy varying number of nodes to combat extreme load near the sink. Gaussian distribution [4] is a promising approach that follows non-uniform distribution allowing more number of nodes near the sink.

Many works have been reported that deal with the issue of load balancing to reduce energy hole problem for prolonging network lifetime. All these works have been conducted through different approaches e.g., homogeneous node deployment strategy [3], [4], relay node deployment strategy [5], regulating transmission range [6], data routing algorithm [7] and mobility of nodes [8]. Each type of the above approach have their strengths and limitations. In most of the existing works, the proposed deployment strategies and data routing algorithms have guaranteed the increase of network lifetime by balancing energy. In this work, we concentrate on the solution based on homogeneous node deployment strategy. Different from [4], our goal is further enhancement of network lifetime by deploying nodes using two dimensional Gaussian distribution in circular layered network architecture. In this work, we focus on finding the answer for the following questions-

— Does Gaussian distribution based node deployment technique provides energy balancing?
— If not, what modification is needed to provide energy balancing?

Our main contributions in this paper are as follows:

— We analyzed the method of controlling network lifetime by balancing the energy consumption of all nodes in layered network architecture. It is found that number of nodes and their distribution has significant role in controlling network lifetime.
— We analyzed energy balancing by deploying nodes using Gaussian distribution in layered network architecture and found standard deviation acts as a parameter that controls number of nodes and their deployment in a layer. It is also found that choosing of judicious value of standard deviation for energy balancing is completely heuristic.
— To alleviate the above shortcomings of Gaussian distribution based node deployment, we proposed a customized Gaussian distribution based node deployment strategy.
— Performance of the scheme is evaluated through quantitative analysis. In quantitative analysis both ideal and realistic scenarios are provided for showing the impacts of routing and medium access control (MAC) protocols on the performance of the strategy.

The rest of this paper is organized as follows: In section 2, literature review is elaborated. The system model considered for the present work is described in section 3. Analysis on energy balancing and network lifetime of Gaussian distribution based node deployment is presented followed by the proposed deployment strategy in Section 4. In section 5, simulation results under ideal and more realistic scenarios are provided. Finally the paper is concluded with some mention about the future scope of the work in section 6.

2   Literature Review

The works addressing the solutions of enhancement of network lifetime, mentioned in the previous section has been elaborated in this section.

Wang et al. [4] have given an analytical model for coverage and network lifetime issues of WSNs using two-dimensional Gaussian distribution. The coverage probability in the Gaussian distribution is decided by factors such as distance between the desired point and the centre point, Gaussian standard deviation etc. By controlling the values of the different parameters mentioned above one can get the desired coverage probability and increased network lifetime. Using the proposed deployment algorithm, larger coverage and longer network lifetime is achieved using limited number of sensor nodes. However, authors have not validated whether the proposed deployment algorithm ensures energy balancing or not. Wang et al. [5] have presented an in-depth analysis on the traffic-aware relay node deployment problem considering locations of sensor node and sink are known before hand. Based on the analysis they have developed optimal solution for relay node deployment with single sensor node, both with single and multiple traffic flows. The authors have developed a hybrid algorithm that successfully returns optimal number of relay nodes and their respective locations. The results show that network lifetime achieved by the algorithm is very close to the upper bound of the optimal solution and achieves 6 to 14 times improvement over existing traffic-aware relay node deployment strategies. However, the proposed solution works in continuous domain resulting in fractional number of relay nodes and simple rounding of numbers causing severe performance degradation. Azad and Kamruzzaman [6] have proposed energy balanced transmission range regulation policies for maximizing network lifetime in WSNs. Authors have considered the concentric ring based network architecture where the sink is located at center. Firstly they have analyzed the traffic and energy usage distribution among nodes and found two parameters- ring thickness and hop size responsible for energy balancing. Based on the analysis, they have proposed a transmission range regulation scheme of each node and determined the optimal ring thickness and hop size for maximizing network lifetime. Simulation results show substantial improvements in terms of network lifetime and energy usage distribution over existing policies. However, before implementation of the proposed transmission policies significant computation is required for determining the optimal ring thickness and hop size. Also the scheme requires minimum node density for its implementation. Boukerche et al. [7] have initially studied the problem of energy-balanced data propagation in corona based WSNs both for uniform and non-uniform deployments. The authors have proposed a density based data propagation protocol towards balancing the energy consumption. The basic idea of the proposed protocol is that in each step the node in a corona that holds data on-line calculates the probability of data delivery either by hop-by-hop or direct to the final destination (the sink) based on the density information of the neighbouring coronas. In particular, performance of the proposed density based data propagation protocol is near-optimal for uniform node deployment. However, the proposed data propagation algorithm has better performance under uniform deployment compared to non-uniform deployment. Lin et al. [8] have developed an energy balancing scheme for cellular-topology based clustered WSN using mobile agents. They have designed an energy prediction strategy by means of which mobile agents know about the remaining energy of all sensor nodes. Nodes with less remaining energy communicate through mobile agent and avoid long-distance communication thereby evading uneven energy consumption. The drawback of this work is that high energy consumption is incurred as two kinds of transmission power are adopted- one is the higher transmission power for ensuring inter-cluster communication among mobile agents and the other is the lower transmission power used for intra-cluster communication.

3   The Models

In this section, network model along with some basic assumptions and node deployment model are provided followed by the energy consumption model.

3.1   Network Model

We consider a two dimensional plane (a×a) covered by a set of uniform-width coronas or annuli [3], [4] as shown in Fig. 1. Each such annuli is designated with width r as layer. The sink is located at the centre of the network area. Nodes are placed within the area of a layer where area of layer-i (A_i) is equal to $\pi (2i-1)r^2$ for i=1,2,...,N. Here i=1 indicates the layer nearest to the sink and i=N indicates the layer farthest from the sink.

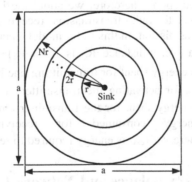

Fig. 1. Layered network architecture

3.2   Assumptions

We assume that deployed nodes are static, homogeneous and battery powered with each node having ε_0 as initial energy while an unlimited amount of energy is set for the sink. We assume clock-driven periodic data gathering applications where sensory data generation rate is proportional to the area (1 sq. unit). Given a unit area, if the data generation rate is ρ bits per second, it means ρ bits/sec of data is transmitted towards the sink. The data is collected by the nodes and sent to the sink through multi-hop communication after a time-interval of 1sec. Each node has the same transmission range R_c and sensing range R_s. The relationship amongst R_c, R_s and r is assumed as $R_c \geq r$ and $2R_s \geq r$. Further, two nodes can reach each other if they are located within their transmission ranges. Without loss of generality, during theoretical analysis an ideal MAC layer with no collisions and retransmissions is assumed for simplicity purpose. For simulations in addition to ideal MAC, we consider a MAC protocol for investigating the impact caused by the MAC protocol to make the assumption realistic.

3.3   Deployment Model

We assume nodes deployed in different layers around the sink using two dimensional Gaussian distribution. We assume the sink is located at (0, 0), therefore, in our case mean value is (0, 0) i.e., standard deviations (σ) for x and y dimensions are equal. Gaussian distribution used for node deployment is given as

$$f(x, y) = \frac{1}{2\pi\sigma^2} e^{-\left(\frac{x^2+y^2}{2\sigma^2}\right)}. \tag{1}$$

3.4   Energy Consumption Model

The energy model specifies the energy consumption by node during various operations such as radio transmission, reception, sensing, and computing. In wireless networks the energy spent for transmission and reception is much greater than the energy spent for sensing or computation. Therefore, we adopt the First Order Radio model [4] considering energy spent for radio transmission, reception and a distance square energy loss for channel transmission. In this radio model, energy consumed by a node for transmitting m-bit data over a distance R_c is $E_{tx}(m, R_c) = m\left(e_{elec} + e_{amp} \times R_c^2\right) = m \times e_t$ where $e_t = e_{elec} + e_{amp} \times R_c^2$ is energy spent for transmitting one bit of data, e_{elec} (e.g., 50 nJ/bit) is the energy spent for activating the transmitter or receiver circuitry, e_{amp} (e.g., 10 pJ/bit/m^2) is the energy spent for the transmitter amplifier to communicate. The corresponding energy consumed for receiving m-bit data is $E_{rx}(m) = m \times e_{elec} = m \times e_r$, where $e_r = e_{elec}$ is energy required to receive one bit of data.

4   Analysis of Energy Balance and Network Lifetime

In this section an analysis on energy balance and network lifetime for a general node deployment strategy are presented. Next analysis on network lifetime is done while nodes are deployed using Gaussian distribution. In both analyses, it is found that certain parameter(s) have significant influence on network lifetime and by controlling the parameter values lifetime can be extended. In presence of several existing definitions of network lifetime and energy balance, the present work considers the following definitions throughout the paper.

Definition 1 (Network Lifetime). We consider network lifetime as the time interval from the beginning of the network operation until the proportion of dead nodes exceeds a certain threshold, which may result in loss of coverage of a certain region, and/or network partitioning. If the energy consumption of each node within layer-i is E_i (same/uniform) and the total number of nodes in layer-i is T_i, the lifetime of a layer-i in the network is $\frac{\varepsilon_0 \times T_i}{T_i \times E_i} = \frac{\varepsilon_0}{E_i}$. From the expression, it is evident that in our case network lifetime is same as the lifetime of a node in layer-i.

Definition 2 (Energy Balance). Balanced energy depletion means that all nodes in the network deplete their energy simultaneously, i.e., the lifetime of all nodes are the same and identical to the corresponding network lifetime. If uniform energy consumption of each sensor node within the same layer is achievable, then balanced energy depletion is achieved if $\frac{\varepsilon_0}{E_i} = \frac{\varepsilon_0}{E_j} \forall i, j, i \neq j$. When balanced energy depletion is achieved, the lifetime of all sensor nodes are same and identical to network lifetime.

We assume that a node transmits data towards sink via shortest path. So, a node in layer-i requires i hops to transmit data to the sink. In a practical scenario, the number of hops may be greater than i hops to reach the sink. The nodes of all the layers except the farthest layer from the sink spend energy transmitting their own sensory data, receiving data from nodes of adjacent layers farther away from the sink and forwarding the received data. Nodes in the farthest layer spend energy only for transmitting their own data. Therefore, the data transmission rate of a node in a layer-i (n_i) is given as

$$n_i = \begin{cases} \dfrac{\rho \times A_i}{T_i} + \dfrac{\sum_{h=i+1}^{N}(\rho \times A_h)}{T_i} & \text{for } i = 1, 2, \ldots, (N-1) \\ \dfrac{\rho \times A_N}{T_N} & \text{for } i = N \end{cases} \qquad (2)$$

The average energy consumption rate (avg ECR) per node for communication (transmission/reception) in a layer-i is computed using the information of n_i (see (2)) as,

$$E_i = \begin{cases} \dfrac{\rho \times A_i}{T_i} e_t + \dfrac{\sum_{h=i+1}^{N}(\rho \times A_h)}{T_i}(e_t + e_r) & \text{for } i = 1, 2, \ldots, (N-1) \\ \dfrac{\rho \times A_N}{T_N} e_t & \text{for } i = N \end{cases} \qquad (3)$$

Energy consumption across the network is balanced [3] when all the nodes of the network exhaust their energy at the same time. So, from Definition 2, the following condition must be satisfied $\frac{\varepsilon_0}{E_1} = \frac{\varepsilon_0}{E_2} = \cdots = \frac{\varepsilon_0}{E_N}$, or, $E_1 = E_2 = \cdots = E_N$.

Now using (3) and replacing the values, we have

$$\left[\frac{\rho \times A_i}{T_i} e_t + \frac{\sum_{h=i+1}^{N}(\rho \times A_h)}{T_i}(e_t + e_r) \right] = \left[\frac{\rho \times A_{i+1}}{T_{i+1}} e_t + \frac{\sum_{h=i+2}^{N}(\rho \times A_h)}{T_{i+1}}(e_t + e_r) \right].$$

Therefore, after simplification and basic transformations, the number of nodes to be deployed in layer-i for balanced energy consumption is given as

$$T_i = \left[\frac{(2i-1)e_t + (e_t + e_r)\sum_{h=i+1}^{N}(2h-1)}{(2i+1)e_t + (e_t + e_r)\sum_{h=i+2}^{N}(2h-1)} \right] T_{i+1}. \qquad (4)$$

Equation (4) implies that for balanced energy consumption, the number of nodes required in a layer nearest to the sink is maximum and it decreases in the layers farther away from the sink i.e., $T_1 > T_2 > \cdots > T_N$. Also (4) implies that one can compute T_i, for i=1,2,...,(N-1), if T_N is known a priori. Here, we argue that T_N can be computed with the help of given network area (a×a), communication range (R_c), and sensing range (R_s) considering complete coverage and connectivity.

After obtaining balanced energy consumption, when nodes are distributed according to (4), the network lifetime can be analytically expressed as

$$
LT_i = \begin{cases} \dfrac{T_i\,\varepsilon_0}{\left[(\rho\times A_i)e_t+(e_t+e_r)\sum_{h=i+1}^{N}(\rho\times A_h)\right]} & \text{for } i=1,2,...,(N-1) \\[4mm] \dfrac{T_N\,\varepsilon_0}{(\rho\times A_N)e_t} & \text{for } i=N \end{cases}
\tag{5}
$$

As we have assumed earlier that the nodes in a layer report data to the sink in minimum hops, therefore the derived network lifetime (see (5)) provides us the upper bound of network lifetime. Also it can be concluded that the upper bound of network lifetime is achievable by controlling the number of nodes in a layer-i i.e., T_i, as given in (4).

4.1   Gaussian Distribution Based Deployment Strategy

According to the proposed Gaussian distribution based node deployment strategy [4], when nodes are deployed in layer-i of a corona based network, the probability is given as

$$
P_i = \begin{cases} e^{-\frac{(i-1)^2 R_c^2}{2\sigma^2}} - e^{-\frac{i^2 R_c^2}{2\sigma^2}} & \text{for } 1 \le i \le (N-1) \\[4mm] e^{-\frac{(N-1)^2 R_c^2}{2\sigma^2}} - e^{-\frac{(N\,r)^2}{2\sigma^2}} & \text{for } i = N \end{cases}
\tag{6}
$$

It is evident from the above equation that any two points in a layer having equal distances from the center-point, have the same deployment probability.

Let us consider T_{tot} number of nodes in the network and T_i' numbers of nodes are deployed in layer-i where nodes are deployed using Gaussian distribution. Using (6), the number of nodes deployed in layer-i is evaluated

$$
T_i' = \begin{cases} T_{tot} \times \left(e^{-\frac{(i-1)^2 R_c^2}{2\sigma^2}} - e^{-\frac{i^2 R_c^2}{2\sigma^2}} \right) & \text{for } 1 \le i \le (N-1) \\[4mm] T_{tot} \times \left(e^{-\frac{(N-1)^2 R_c^2}{2\sigma^2}} - e^{-\frac{(N\,r)^2}{2\sigma^2}} \right) & \text{for } i = N \end{cases}
\tag{7}
$$

The analytical result plotted in Fig. 2 illustrates number of nodes computed (using (7)) and deployed using Gaussian distribution indeed guarantee balanced energy consumption amongst nodes in all layers of the network. The analytical results are plotted considering, similar to [4], two network sizes 5-layer and 8-layer where 800 and 1000 nodes are deployed, respectively. We assume initial energy of each node is 10J, communication range of each node is 20m, standard deviation (σ) is 50 and a unit area generates data at the rate of 1 bit per second.

From Fig. 2(a) it is observed that irrespective of network size, nodes in different layers have different avg ECR per node which ensures that the node deployment strategy is not energy balanced. It is also observed that for 8-layer network the nodes located in layer-3 and 4 have minimum avg ECR per node while nodes located in layer-1 and 7 have maximum. This is due to the fact that number of nodes deployed in layer-1 and 7 are not sufficient to handle the load whereas more than sufficient nodes are deployed in layer-3 and 4 to handle the load. It is the primary reason, according to us, for uneven avg ECR among the nodes in different layers. As the nodes near the sink have maximum avg ECR per node, the lifetime of a node in layers nearer to the sink is minimum compared to the layers farther away from the sink as shown in Fig. 2(b). This indicates that nodes deployed using Gaussian distribution is not energy balanced and hence maximum network lifetime is not achievable.

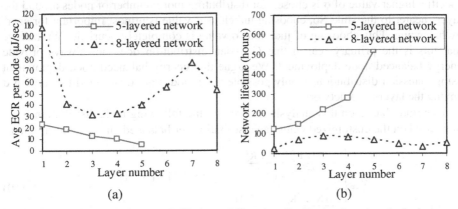

(a)   (b)

Fig. 2. Energy balance and network lifetime of Gaussian distribution based node deployment. (a) Average energy consumption rate per node of a layer for 5-layer and 8-layer network sizes. (b) Network lifetime of a layer for 5-layer and 8-layer network sizes.

4.2 Proposed Customized Gaussian Distribution Based Deployment Strategy

Let us investigate the reason behind the imbalance in energy consumption of a node in a layer when it is deployed using Gaussian distribution. From energy balancing perspective, from Definition 2, the following condition must be satisfied

$$\left[\frac{\rho \times A_i}{T_i'}e_t + \frac{\sum_{h=i+1}^{N}(\rho \times A_h)}{T_i'}(e_t + e_r)\right] = \left[\frac{\rho \times A_{i+1}}{T_{i+1}'}e_t + \frac{\sum_{h=i+2}^{N}(\rho \times A_h)}{T_{i+1}'}(e_t + e_r)\right].$$

Therefore, the integer number of nodes to be deployed in layer-i for balanced energy consumption is given as

$$T_i' = \left\lceil \frac{A_i e_t + (e_t + e_r)\sum_{h=i+1}^{N}A_h}{A_{i+1}e_t + (e_t + e_r)\sum_{h=i+2}^{N}A_h} \right\rceil T_{i+1}'. \tag{8}$$

We argue that the imbalance in energy consumption of a node in layer-i primarily occurs as the number of nodes derived using (7) is not equal or near equal to the number of nodes derived using (8). Therefore, to obtain balanced energy consumption T_i' given in (7) must be equal to the T_i' given in (8), i.e.,

$$T_i' = T_{tot} \times P_i = \left[\frac{A_i e_t + (e_t + e_r) \sum_{h=i+1}^{N} A_h}{A_{i+1} e_t + (e_t + e_r) \sum_{h=i+2}^{N} A_h} \right] T_{i+1}'$$

$$T_{tot} \times e^{-\frac{(i-1)^2 R_c^2}{2\sigma^2}} - e^{-\frac{i^2 R_c^2}{2\sigma^2}} = \left[\frac{A_i e_t + (e_t + e_r) \sum_{h=i+1}^{N} A_h}{A_{i+1} e_t + (e_t + e_r) \sum_{h=i+2}^{N} A_h} \right] T_{i+1}' . \qquad (9)$$

From (9), it is evident that determination of number of nodes $\left(T_i' \right)$ and its distribution primarily depends on the standard deviation (σ) of Gaussian distribution. To be more specific, higher value of σ is chosen for distributing more number of nodes around the layers nearer to the sink. So, choosing judicious σ value is utmost important for energy balancing. This choosing of judicious σ value is completely heuristic. We believe that this is the primary reason that Gaussian distribution does not always provide energy balanced node deployment. We argue that energy balanced node deployment using Gaussian distribution is only possible when nodes are distributed by varying σ among the layers in a network.

Therefore, based on this analysis we propose the following node distribution function based on the customized Gaussian distribution for balanced energy consumption.

$$P_i' = \begin{cases} e^{-\frac{(i-1)^2 R_c^2}{2\sigma_i^2}} - e^{-\frac{i^2 R_c^2}{2\sigma_i^2}} & \text{for } 1 \leq i \leq (N-1) \\ e^{-\frac{(N-1)^2 R_c^2}{2\sigma_N^2}} - e^{-\frac{(N r)^2}{2\sigma_N^2}} & \text{for } i = N \end{cases} \qquad (10)$$

where σ_i^2 is the variance of layer-i for i=1,2,…,N.

Theorem 1. For a given network area, energy balancing takes place amongst nodes when nodes are deployed using customized Gaussian distribution where its variance is given as

$$\sigma_i^2 = \frac{-\frac{R_c^2}{2} \left[(2i-1)^2 - i^4 \frac{T_i}{T_{tot}} \right]}{\left(i^2 \frac{T_i}{T_{tot}} - 2i + 1 \right) \pm \sqrt{\left(2i - i^2 \frac{T_i}{T_{tot}} + 1 \right) + 2 \frac{T_i}{T_{tot}} \left\{ (2i-1)^2 - i^4 \frac{T_i}{T_{tot}} \right\}}} .$$

Proof: It has been shown in (9) that for balanced energy consumption T_i' number of nodes need to be deployed in layer-i. As nodes are to be deployed using customized Gaussian distribution, hence from (9),

$$T_{tot} \times e^{-\frac{(i-1)^2 R_c^2}{2\sigma^2}} - e^{-\frac{i^2 R_c^2}{2\sigma^2}} = \left[\frac{A_i e_t + (e_t + e_r) \sum_{h=i+1}^{N} A_h}{A_{i+1} e_t + (e_t + e_r) \sum_{h=i+2}^{N} A_h} \right] T_{i+1}'$$

$$e^{-\frac{(i-1)^2 R_c^2}{2\sigma^2}} - e^{-\frac{i^2 R_c^2}{2\sigma^2}} = \frac{T_i'}{T_{tot}}.$$

Now expanding the above exponential function as a Taylor series and considering the first three terms for simplicity, we have

$$\left(\frac{R_c^2}{2\sigma^2}\right)^2 \left(\frac{(2i-1)^2}{2} - \frac{i^4 T_i'}{2T_{tot}}\right) + \frac{R_c^2}{2\sigma^2}\left((2i-1) - \frac{i^2 T_i'}{T_{tot}}\right) - \frac{T_i'}{T_{tot}} = 0.$$

The solution of the above equation for positive value of σ^2 is given as

$$\sigma^2 = \frac{\frac{R_c^2}{2}\left[(2i-1)^2 - i^4\frac{T_i}{T_{tot}}\right]}{\left(i^2\frac{T_i}{T_{tot}} - 2i + 1\right) \pm \sqrt{\left(2i - i^2\frac{T_i}{T_{tot}} + 1\right) + 2\frac{T_i}{T_{tot}}\left\{(2i-1)^2 - i^4\frac{T_i}{T_{tot}}\right\}}}.$$

It is evident from the above equation that for each value of i we obtain a value of σ^2 i.e., value of the variance depends on layer number i. Therefore, for balanced energy consumption, nodes are to deployed using customized Gaussian distribution by following the value of variance

$$\sigma_i^2 = \frac{\frac{R_c^2}{2}\left[(2i-1)^2 - i^4\frac{T_i}{T_{tot}}\right]}{\left(i^2\frac{T_i}{T_{tot}} - 2i + 1\right) \pm \sqrt{\left(2i - i^2\frac{T_i}{T_{tot}} + 1\right) + 2\frac{T_i}{T_{tot}}\left\{(2i-1)^2 - i^4\frac{T_i}{T_{tot}}\right\}}}.$$

Finally, we claim that the proposed deployment is feasible. As reported in state-of-the-art work [9], air-dropped deployment in a controllable manner is feasible even in an inaccessible terrain. We propose to compute the desired number of nodes in each part (layer/annuli) of the network offline prior to the actual deployment using (4). At last, the nodes are to be dropped (e.g. from helicopter) using a point (sink) as the center using the proposed customized Gaussian distribution (see (10)).

5   Performance Evaluation

Performance of the present Customized Gaussian Distribution based Node Deployment (CGDND) strategy, reported in the earlier section is measured based on two parameters- energy balancing and network lifetime.

5.1   Simulation Arrangement

For performing the simulation experiments MATLAB (version 7.1) is used. Simulation results of our strategy CGDND are compared with one existing node deployment strategy namely Node Deployment with Gaussian Distribution (NDGD) [4]. For both the schemes, in order to have an integer number of nodes for each layer upper ceil function is employed. Extensive simulation has been performed with a confidence level of 95% and average of 2000 independent runs has been taken while plotting the simulation graphs. The values of transmission range, sensing range and initial energy in each sensor are taken as 20m, 10m and 10J respectively [4]. We conducted the experiments by deploying 800 and 1000 nodes for networks with 5 and 8 layers, respectively. In the simulation experiments, we focus on the following metrics: a) avg ECR per node defined as the average energy spent per node in a layer during the network operation; b) network lifetime as defined in section 3. First metric is useful for determining whether the energy consumption in a network is energy-balanced and second metric is for consequent enhancement of network lifetime. Two sets of experiments are conducted for evaluating the performance of the proposed deployment strategy. One set of experiment measures energy balancing in the network and the last set verifies the enhancement of network lifetime.

5.2   Analytical Results

Shown in Fig. 3 is the analytical result of the number of nodes deployed in each layer for CGDND and NDGD (two different values of σ) strategies using 8-layer network deployed with 1000 nodes. Our primary observation is that except the schemes i.e. NDGD with σ=50 and σ=25, in the strategy CGDND, the number of deployed nodes reduces in layers as the distance of layers from the sink increases fulfilling the objective of deploying more nodes near the sink. It is also observed that NDGD gives more redundant nodes in layer-3 when σ=50 and in layer-2 when σ=25. When nodes are deployed in NDGD using σ=25, it fails to deploy any nodes in layers 6, 7 and 8. All these imply that choosing of judicious value of σ is utmost important for fulfilling the objective of energy balancing.

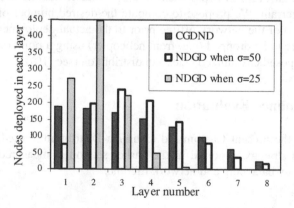

Fig. 3. Nodes deployed in each of the layer when nodes are deployed using CGDND and two variants (σ=50 and σ=25) of NDGD for 8-layer network

5.3   Simulation Results and Discussion

During simulation, we have considered q-switch [3] as routing protocol and funne-ling-MAC [10] as a MAC protocol for realistic scenario. The scenario considered in section 4 for analysis of energy balance and network lifetime is considered as ideal scenario. In q-switch routing the source node always selects one reachable forwardee node with maximum remaining energy in its subsequent inner layer for forwarding data. If there is more than one forwardee node with the same maximum remaining energy, one of them is chosen randomly. The funneling-MAC is a hybrid MAC proto-col where nodes located within layer-2 use TDMA whereas nodes beyond layer-2 use CSMA/CA. Furthermore, we have considered energy consumption rate as 20%, 5% and 2.5% of the energy consumption rate of reception for sensing, idle and sleep mode respectively. In simulation plots scheme names with '(R)' signify performance under realistic scenario and without it under ideal scenario.

5.3.1 Energy Balancing

Figure 4 shows avg ECR per node for different network sizes. We observe that in CGDND, for both ideal and realistic scenarios, the avg ECR per node of a particular network size is constant for all layers and this rate varies with network sizes. Precisely avg ECR per node increases with increase in network size. For example, in case of ideal scenario, avg ECR per node is 13.5 µJ/sec for 5-layer network area whereas for 8-layer network it is 44.16 µJ/sec. Similarly, in realistic scenario, avg ECR per node is 16.1 µJ/sec for 5-layer network whereas for 8-layer network it is 46.73 µJ/sec. In NDGD it is observed that avg ECR per node varies in different layers for a given network size. Also, in NDGD, irrespective of network size, nodes in layer-1 have maximum avg ECR per node and nodes in farthest layer have the lowest avg ECR per node. This justifies our claim that CGDND is relatively more energy balanced com-pared to the competing scheme NDGD.

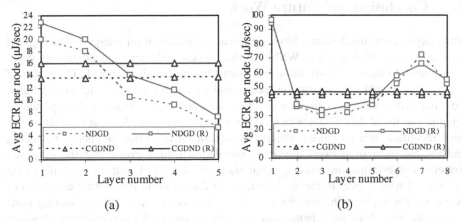

Fig. 4. Average energy consumption rate per node under ideal and realistic scenarios for vari-ous network sizes. (a) 5-layer network. (b) 8-layer network.

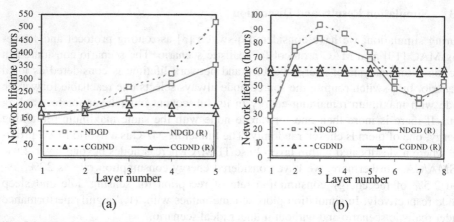

(a)   (b)

Fig. 5. Network lifetime under ideal and realistic scenarios for various network sizes. (a) 5-layer network. (b) 8-layer network.

5.3.2 Network Lifetime

The graphs illustrated in Fig. 5 represent the network lifetime for two different network sizes. It is observed irrespective of the scenarios, that with increase in network size network lifetime decreases e.g., in realistic scenario for 5-layer network it is 172.52 hours whereas for 8-layer network it is 59.44 hours. This is due to the fact that with increase in network size, the nodes in the innermost layer need to relay increased volume of data from the outer layers thereby causing more energy consumption. Moreover, in CGDND the flat nature of the plot ensures that in all the layers, network lifetime terminates in more or less the same time as compared to NDGD. This ensures that energy in CGDND is balanced to a greater extent.

6   Conclusion and Future Work

Node deployment mechanisms have significant implication on energy balancing and prolonging network lifetime in WSNs. In this work a node deployment strategy using a customized Gaussian distribution has been presented and evaluated. The target of the strategy is achieving energy balancing and enhancing network lifetime. Initially, we have analyzed network lifetime of a Gaussian distribution based node deployment scheme and found its efficiency in terms of energy balancing. Standard deviation has been identified as a parameter which has significant influence on energy balancing and enhancement of network lifetime. Simulation results prove that the proposed strategy outperforms an existing Gaussian distribution based node deployment scheme [4] with respect to energy balancing in the network. As a future extension of our work, the deployment strategy may be made more realistic by considering node placement error. Also, the scheme may be analyzed further for improvement considering performance metrics e.g., end-to-end delay, packet loss and throughput.

References

1. Halder, S., Ghosal, A., DasBit, S.: A Pre-determined Node Deployment Strategy to Prolong Network Lifetime in Wireless Sensor Network. Computer Communications 34(11), 1294–1306 (2011)
2. Halder, S., Ghosal, A., Saha, A., DasBit, S.: Energy-Balancing and Lifetime Enhancement of Wireless Sensor Network with Archimedes Spiral. In: Hsu, C.-H., Yang, L.T., Ma, J., Zhu, C. (eds.) UIC 2011. LNCS, vol. 6905, pp. 420–434. Springer, Heidelberg (2011)
3. Wu, X., Chen, G., Das, S.K.: Avoiding Energy Holes in Wireless Sensor Networks with Nonuniform Node Distribution. IEEE Trans. on Parallel and Distributed Systems 19(5), 710–720 (2008)
4. Wang, D., Xie, B., Agrawal, D.P.: Coverage and Lifetime Optimization of Wireless Sensor Networks with Gaussian Distribution. IEEE Trans. on Mobile Computing 7(12), 1444–1458 (2008)
5. Wang, F., Wang, D., Liu, J.: Traffic-Aware Relay Node Deployment: Maximizing Lifetime for Data Collection Wireless Sensor Networks. IEEE Trans. on Parallel and Distributed Systems 22(8), 1415–1423 (2011)
6. Azad, A.K.M., Kamruzzaman, J.: Energy-Balanced Transmission Policies for Wireless Sensor Networks. IEEE Trans. on Mobile Computing 10(7), 927–940 (2011)
7. Boukerche, A., Efstathiou, D., Nikoletseas, S.E., Raptopoulos, C.: Exploiting Limited Density Information Towards Near-optimal Energy Balanced Data Propagation. Computer Communications 35(18), 2187–2200 (2012)
8. Lin, K., Chenb, M., Zeadally, S., Rodrigues, J.J.P.C.: Balancing Energy Consumption with Mobile Agents in Wireless Sensor Networks. Future Generation Computer Systems 28(2), 446–456 (2012)
9. Huang, R., Song, W.Z., Xu, M., Peterson, N., Shirazi, B., LaHusen, R.: Real-World Sensor Network for Long-Term Volcano Monitoring: Design and Findings. IEEE Trans. on Parallel and Distributed Systems 23(2), 321–329 (2012)
10. Ahn, G.S., Miluzzo, E., Campbell, A.T., Hong, S.G., Cuomo, F.: Funneling-MAC: A Localized, Sink-Oriented MAC For Boosting Fidelity in Sensor Networks. In: Proc. of 4th ACM Int'l Conf. on Embedded Network and Sensor System, pp. 293–306 (2006)

Shedder: A Metadata Sharing Management Method across Multi-clusters[*]

Qinfen Hao[1], Qianqian Zhong[2,**], Li Ruan[1,**], Zhenzhong Zhang[2],
and Limin Xiao[1]

[1] State Key Laboratory of Software Development Environment, Beihang University,
Beijing 100191, China
[2] School of Computer Science and Engineering, Beihang University,
Beijing 100191, China
{haoqf,ruanli,xiaolm}@buaa.edu.cn,
{bradyzhong,zzzhang}@cse.buaa.edu.cn

Abstract. With the increase of large number of data, multi-clusters structure has been adopted for data storage. Therefore, the demand for file metadata sharing across global scale clusters is quickly rising. However, today's software can not provide features to reflect these desires well. In this paper, We propose and develop a metadata sharing management method called Shedder. First Shedder can allow customized multi-clusters metadata sharing structure. Next, Shedder can provide highly efficient global synchronization for all clusters. Finally, Shedder allows customized user view generated from global namespace. Our evaluation for Shedder shows that Shedder provides low latency for global synchronization. Dynamic transformation from global namespace to customized user view also has low time cost for different size of workloads.

Keywords: Metadata Sharing, Authorization control, Global synchronization, customized user namespace.

1 Introduction

With the increasing data in single cluster or data center, global storage over the Wide Area Networks (WAN) is inevitable [4]. Management of multiple clusters deployed over the nation or even at the global scale is significant to improve the whole system's accessability. Many research work has proposed methods to

---

[*] This paper is supported by the Hi-tech Research and Development Program of China (863 Program) under Grant No. 2011AA01A205, the National Natural Science Foundation of China under Grant No. 61370059, the National Natural Science Foundation of China under Grant No. 61003015, the Doctoral Fund of Ministry of Education of China under Grant No. 20101102110018, Beijing Natural Science Foundation under Grant No. 4122042 and the fund of the State Key Laboratory of Software Development Environment under Grant No. SKLSDE-2012ZX-23.
[**] Corresponding authors.

J. Kołodziej et al. (Eds.): ICA3PP 2013, Part I, LNCS 8285, pp. 72–86, 2013.

guarantee data locality for low latency I/O operations [6, 7, 11]. On the other hand, many applications or users often only concerns about metadata lookup and not read or write real data frequently like web page indexing. However, few work focuses on file metadata sharing across geographically clusters. Additionally, how to present customized and customized user view from same global namespace for applications to tune lookup performance is also important.

We give an example to illustrate this demand above. Flickr, Facebook and Flipboard have photo sharing or magazine sharing services. They may use multiple clusters to store these data. Their users are used to looking up all newest photo or news information like title, publisher, create time, permission configuration and so on. But eventually they only fetch a small fraction of real photo or news data to view. Therefore, it will spend most of time on metadata sharing across geographically clusters to which different users access. Accelerating metadata lookup will obviously reduce waiting time for refreshing metadata.

Meanwhile, users usually view photos or contents others share with but not expect to change them like Wikipedia. We call this kind of access mode as write once read many [14]. The paper will focus on this scenario to tune the performance of metadata sharing.

In this paper, we propose a method called Shedder to solve problems of metadata sharing management. Firstly, due to various demands of applications, one cluster needs to decide which clusters it will transmit metadata to. That belongs to authorization control and will eventually affect cluster network topology. Shedder supports customized interconnections across multi-clusters to allow various logical network topology. Secondly, as for global metadata synchronization across clusters, original two-phase commit (2PC) protocol [15] has low efficiency especially for our write-once-read-many scenario. Therefore, Shedder uses a modified 2PC protocol to improve metadata reading performance. Thirdly, for each independent cluster, metadata lookup of global namespace is a basic command and unit. But most applications have their own lookup characteristics. Shedder also provides a customized namespace view to each cluster from the same global namespace. We demonstrate that user view generator uses efficient data structure and has high transformation performance.

The rest of this paper is organized as follows: Section 2 describes problem definition and system overview. Section 3 describes authorization control of Shedder. Section 4 elaborates the design of synchronization approach. Section 5 illustrates the design of generation algorithm of customized user view from global namespace. Section 6 shows performance model, simulation experiments and results analysis. Section 7 describes related work and Section 8 concludes this paper.

2 Architecture Overview

2.1 Scenario for Global Storage Clusters

Firstly, we describe a usual scenario that multiple users access the global storage system consisting of multiple clusters shown as Figure 1. User1 expects to look up what files are stored in these clusters, including not only Cluster A but also all other clusters. Meanwhile, User1 would also like to reorganize these metadata and categorize them according to his access characteristics. Thus he can quickly look up information according to the given domain. Moreover, User1 can fetch large amount of files especially small files via reorganized metadata more quickly because paths of these files have been optimized and locating them is faster than that of original file namespace. Likewise, all users may have totally different user view, which though comes from the same global namespace.

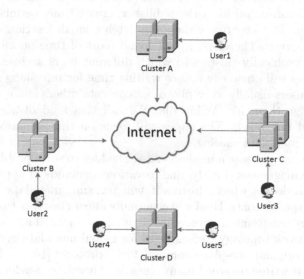

Fig. 1. User access model over WAN

2.2   System Design of Shedder

Our metadata sharing management method Shedder can manage and coordinate clusters of global storage system over the wide area networks, illustrated as Figure 2. It consists of three main components. Authorization control module (simply called AC Module)uses ACL (Access Control List) mechanism to determine what metadata updates can be generated, which clusters can receive updates and which metadata requests, no matter from internal global storage system or from external environment, can be granted. User View Generation is to help clusters finish synchronization of metadata updates and maintain global consistency. Finally, generation algorithm for customized user view is automatically executed after the global synchronization.

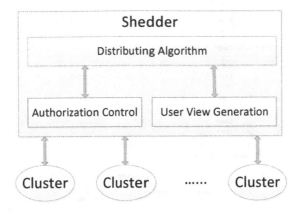

Fig. 2. Architecture Overview for Shedder

3 Authorization Control

Shedder regards underlying clusters as a whole global storage system. Therefore, there are two kinds of access requests needed to be controlled by authorization mechanism.

First is external access requests outside the global storage system. Clusters need to be found by legal users at the same time they need to defend anonymous attacks. Shedder can make sure each cluster always recognizes requests from trusted domains. If requests don't come from allowed positions, cluster will refuse to provide connections or service.

Second kind of access requests attribute to internal communication. Though each cluster has to recognize others' requests inside the global storage system for synchronizing global namespace, that doesn't mean all requests should be approved and executed. Due to different scenarios, relationship between clusters can be complicated and have various pattern, shown as Figure 3. One cluster can choose which clusters can acquire its metadata and namespace. Others that are not granted cannot find one's namespace unless there are some clusters that have received one's metadata willing to transfer these metadata to them. Therefore, Shedder supports a lot of logical network topology for the demands of applications or users.

Also, for every cluster, its authorization configuration information may be changed at running time. The same request can be accepted after refused at the first time or vice versa. Shedder can dynamically adjust its coordination strategy to match the change of authorization configuration information. These can be done by adding special flags to the transfer packets.

Shedder defines what operations for metadata to be considered metadata updates. Users can use these operation primitives to update metadata. AC Module also has whitelists and blacklists from user configurations to limit transmit

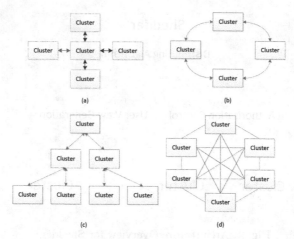

Fig. 3. Customized Logical Network Topology. (a) is a single center topology structure. (b) means ring structure. (c) represents tree topology structure. (d) is a complete graph structure.

of updates. In addition, administrator has power to decide which users from external networks can access Shedder. Then Shedder appoints one cluster as local position for one user to connect according to time delay of WAN access.

4   Global Synchronization

4.1   Synchronization Strategy

Since all clusters are connected and communicated with each other through the Internet, Shedder consider them and the Internet as a big undirected graph. But we don't adopt physical link between routers as edges. Authorization control has determined the topological structure. Imagine that one's metadata information may be transferred to the destination under control of another one, then two logical edges will be formed.

Next, delving into this model carefully we find we are just expecting each cluster to receive metadata updates from its previous nodes in global topology graph. Once it obtains all updates that are newer than that it already has, it will refuse other updates that are older. However, it's difficult to determine whether all clusters have received each cluster's updates, respectively. To solve the issue, we add a timer for every synchronization operation and simply adopt breadth-first distributing approach. When any cluster receives updates, it sends a message back to the sender. The sender will record how many clusters have received updates. In a worst situation, some certain clusters have still not sent feedback to the sender because, for example, the cluster is down and unavailable. So the sender needs to report to Shedder. Shedder will detect whether the cluster is connected. If not, Shedder will remove the cluster out of the global storage system and announce all other clusters to change their global topology graph.

Otherwise Shedder will notice the sender it can assume that cluster has received updates and finish this round of updates transmit, though in fact shedder doesn't assure whether that cluster can eventually receive the updates.

4.2   Modified 2PC Protocol

Shedder allows clusters to change metadata that are originally not theirs. Here we use modified two-phase commit protocol, which not only supports timeout mechanism but also allows commit delay technology.

The former is set to prevent long waiting if certain cluster is suddenly unavailable at voting phase. 2PC protocol containing timeout mechanism is often called three-phase commit protocol. The latter prevent blocking status appearing. Since the real data is only stored in one cluster, we choose this cluster as coordinator. other clusters which have coordinator's metadata are participants. When one cluster changes metadata (in our scenario, it usually can be creating new photos, renaming photos and deleting photos), it sends update request to coordinator. Then coordinator start a voting phase for this request in which it's the same as the original 2PC protocol. If the voting result is refusal, then coordinator notice the request sending participant to cancel the metadata operation. If the result means agreement, at this time the coordinator tells the request sending participant to execute the operation but for other clusters coordinator doesn't notice them. It just caches the voting result in its buffer queue, waiting for next global synchronization to commit them. The reason for this method is that in write-once-read-many scenarios the real data generally can not be modified, and then the change of metadata could be regarded as the change of reference to the data. We only need to maintain the mapping between new reference of same data at each cluster and the local metadata to assure the accuracy of access, without wasting much time to synchronize every incoming metadata update. Hence, through delaying commit phase, we avoids blocking status when waiting commit result. At the same time, because there is only one copy of real data in coordinator, so it can keep the data consistent and can decide the commmit sequence for metadata updates.

5   Generation of Customized User View

5.1   Reorganizing User View from Global Namespace

Assume that all clusters have updated to the common newest version of global namespace at certain time. Multiple users access their local cluster to look up metadata described as Figure 1. However, due to various applications or user demands, they expect to see different user view, shown as Table 1 for example.

Global namespace shows that Cluster A has information of two departments, each of which contains a lot of files. It also owns information of two products each of which consists of multiple software modules. Here assume that Cluster B has the same category compared with Cluster A, though unnecessary. As for Cluster

C and Cluster D, they expect to see different user view since demands from local applications may be totally various. Therefore, we can build a transformation model to maintain mapping from global namespace to local user view while also keeping reverse connections information for users to fetch specific files.

5.2   File Index Model for User View

Since we expect to change the file system view for users to see, we need to reestablish the B-tree index, shown as Figure 4. Usually looking up a file starts from parsing the file path, which means node nearer root is faster to be indexed than that which is farther away from root. On the other hand, we often consider all children nodes of a parent node belong to some certain category according to the parent node's characteristics. Therefore, we can cluster the same category from different clusters into one high level node on the index tree.

Table 1. Global Namespace and Local User Views for Each Cluster. dept means department. * indicates all files in the folder.

(a) Global Namespace

| /ClusterA/{dept1, dept2}/* |
| /ClusterA/{product1, product2}/* |
| /ClusterB/{dept1, dept2}/* |
| /ClusterB/{product1, product2}/* |

(b) User View for Cluster C

| /dept1/{ClusterA, ClusterB}/* |
| /dept2/{ClusterA, ClusterB}/* |
| /ClusterA/{product1, product2}/* |
| /ClusterB/{product1, product2}/* |

(c) User View for Cluster D

| /product1/{ClusterA, ClusterB}/* |
| /product2/{ClusterA, ClusterB}/* |
| /ClusterA/{dept1, dept2}/* |
| /ClusterB/{dept1, dept2}/* |

5.3   Reverse Connections to Find Original Files

As for Shedder, it doesn't synchronize data across clusters. In other words, Shedder doesn't allow replications of files through clusters that not only costs too much bandwidth when files are large but also needs complicated consistency management. To simplify access model for users, Shedder assure that original files are stored only in one cluster where they are created. Hence, Shedder maintains a reverse mapping relationship between local user view and global namespace. If user only looks up metadata, there is no need to access the reverse mapping. Only when user needs to fetch corresponding files can the reverse mapping be accessed.

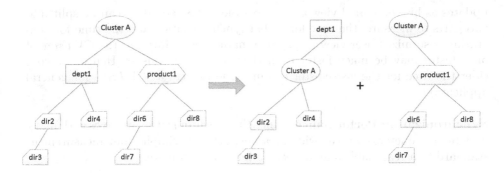

Fig. 4. Transformation for File Index. Assume dept is primary category for users to look up and we ignore specific files as leaves of the tree for simplicity.

5.4   Generation of Customized User View

The default User View is presented regarding cluster domain as category. Shedder provides user view configuration rule for users. When certain directory, let's say LuckyDir, is appointed as category, Shedder starts following procedure to form a new configured user view to users: scan file paths to find LuckyDir, then move cluster domain to the tail of LuckyDir and submit commit. The time complexity of the procedure is various because the order of LuckyDir is higher, the length of path needed to be scanning is shorter. The worst of time complexity is linear.

On the other hand, as for restoration, when we need to fetch the original files, we don't need to move cluster domain again to the original structure. We have made a flag (a soft link) when transformation so that we can take advantage of it to reconstruct the original path. Therefore, the mapping turns out to be a path checking procedure: if the directory of first order is cluster domain, nothing needs to do; otherwise scan the path and if the current directory scanned is a soft link, then ignore it and jump to the next directory till the end.

6   Experiments

6.1   Performance Modeling

To demonstrate our observation on global synchronization and customized user view of global namespace across clusters would be acceptable and feasible, in this section we build cost model for Shedder and present performance analysis for the model. Firstly we propose a formula to represent the time of the whole process in which Shedder works.

$$GVTime = T_{sync} + T_{view} \tag{1}$$

$GVTime$ means the whole process time between the time when one cluster updates its part of metadata and the time when one user can look up these updates as his configured view at the possible fastest speed. It can be split into two parts to measure: the time for global synchronization and the time for generating customized user view from global namespace. However, the $GVTime$ of one cluster may be much faster than that of another cluster. Hence, we consider the time for the last cluster to finish the process as $GVTime$ for general applications.

Synchronization Performance. Since the synchronization involves with many variable parameters over the wide area networks, we simplify our measurement standard to a reasonable and applicable formula as follows.

$$T_{sync} = 2 \times T_{delay} + 2 \times \frac{N_{updates}}{S_{netcard} \times \frac{1}{2 \times (N_{cluster} - 1)}} \tag{2}$$

T_{delay} indicates the transmit delay time from one cluster to another cluster. $N_{updates}$ means the size of metadata updates for specific cluster where any basic metadata operation counts. $S_{netcard}$ represents the transfer rate of network card in one machine. $N_{cluster}$ is the number of clusters that Shedder monitors. Notice when a cluster is transmitting metadata updates to other clusters it is also receiving updates from all other ones, although it is impossible for these updates to be processed at the same time.

Moreover, in our application scenario, users usually expect to look up large number of metadata information. Small number of updates is less meaningful since previous metadata updates stored in local cluster can provide similar results for those batch processing applications. As for large amount of metadata updates, it will cost most of time for Shedder to transmit them instead of network delay. It is very obvious especially when multiple clusters transmit their own updates at the same time. Therefore, the synchronization cost model can be simplified as follows.

$$T_{sync} = k \times \frac{N_{updates}}{V_{transmit}} \tag{3}$$

where k means a constant coefficient, and $V_{transmit}$ is also a constant parameter indicating the transmit rate of metadata updates in one cluster. Here T_{sync} is proportional to $N_{updates}$, which proves that Shedder can synchronize these clusters enough efficiently.

Generation of User View. Traditionally, file namespace would like to use tree model to manage file metadata such as Linux ext3 file system. Considering total memory access for looking up metadata information in Shedder, here we adopt multi-tier, hash mapping structure to organize file namespace, shown as Figure 5.

We build hash table for each level of directories. And each tier is connected with another by hashing mapping of directory name. Assume certain file has h prefix directories, the time of looking up this file is about $O(h)$ (exactly it

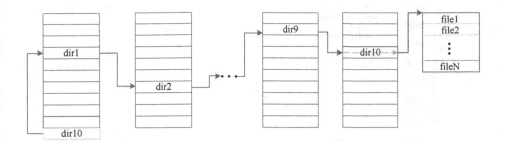

Fig. 5. Structure and Transformation for User View. Multiple files (file1, file2 etc.) are stored in the directory /dir1/dir2/.../dir9/dir10. Through user view transformation by Shedder, dir10 is moved to the top directory.

should be $O(hL_{dir})$ where L_{dir} means the average length of directory name), which means h times of memory access.

As for configuring user view, when we find the specific directory, we can create a new item of it on the top directory and let the new item point to the original top directory as Figure 5 illustrates. In addition, the original position of dir10 will become a soft link that will not be parsed by Shedder. Hence, we totally only need $O(hN_{updates})$ time to generate configured user view.

6.2   Hardware and Software Platforms

Since what we are concerned about is metadata, we deploy three nodes for each cluster to store them. Each machine has two Intel(R) Xeon(R) CPU 5160, DDR 667MHz 4GB of memory, 100GB HDD disk and running 2.6.32-71-kernel x86_64 Ubuntu. These nodes are running with 100Mbps network rate in LAN. For each cluster, we deploy Hadoop-1.0.4 to set up the underlying storage system with JDK 1.7.0_21.

6.3   Synchronization Performance Validation

According to the formula 23, the major two factors determines the rate of synchronization: size of metadata updates and number of clusters belonging to the global storage system. More accurately, not all clusters will receive same updates because of authorization control. So the real size of updates to be transmit will be much smaller. Experiment results are illustrated as follows.

Figure 6 shows synchronization time increase is nearly linear to the increase of number of metadata updates when number of updates is large. Fluctuation appears when number of updates is small. The main reason is when transmit time of metadata updates is comparable to the network delay, the result will be various due to the nondeterminism of network delay. But generally for enough large number of metadata updates Shedder has linear performance to synchronize clusters' global namespace.

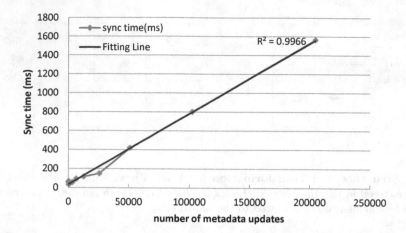

Fig. 6. Cost time with constant cluster numbers. Each metadata operation counts for metadata updates. In experiment we consider creating files as metadata operations since number of files is usually changing more frequently. So the size of each entry of metadata update is about 100B. Sync time means the time when all clusters have received all replies. There are four clusters in total.

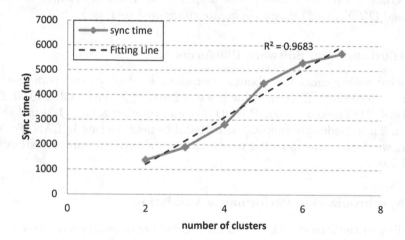

Fig. 7. Cost time with constant metadata updates. Constant number of metadata updates is 100×2^{11}, the size of each of which is about 100B.

Figure 7 illustrates that synchronization time of Shedder is basically proportional to theoretical fitting line, which conforms with Formula 2. Waiting more clusters for reply makes the whole synchronization time longer. But there is also a hidden reason: we use multiple threads to expect to transmit metadata updates at the same time. In fact it is unlikely to send updates concurrently. The operating system only allows one thread to put data into the buffer of network card each time. Therefore, when metadata to be transmit is large enough, the effect of waiting in the queue for writing network buffer will be enlarged.

6.4   Customized User View Generation Performance Validation

Referring to the time complexity of generation method as Section 6.1, we measures the effect of two parameters, number of metadata updates and tier deep of LuckyDir, respectively. In our implementation of Shedder, we support dynamic change of LuckyDir, which needs Shedder to deal with all metadata updates including old and new coming ones. Experiment results are illustrated as follows.

Figure 8 shows that the cost time of generation method is basically linear with the increase of number of updates, which demonstrates our cost model for customized user view is accurate. When one cluster creates 10^6 new files, it only costs about 1.8s to finish dynamic transformation when LuckyDir is at the reasonably 10th tier of directory path. Moreover, Shedder can support dynamic generation of customized user view when multiple clusters expect to join or leave this global storage system since it can process new metadata updates fast enough. That is crucial when certain cluster is unavailable and its metadata information can not be achieved. Other clusters can quickly discard old metadata updates belonging to that cluster to make sure users don't execute invalid operations in future.

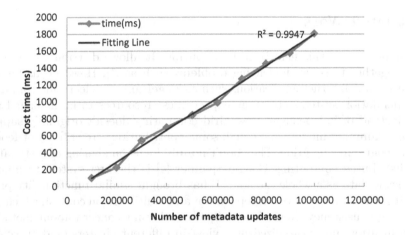

Fig. 8. Transformation cost time with constant LuckyDir. Number of metadata updates has the same definition as Figure 6, the size of each of which is about 100B. Cost time means the whole transformation time from global namespace to configured user view. And LuckyDir lies at the 10th tier of directory path.

From Figure 9 we can find that the cost time increases slowly with the increase of the deep of directory tier. When the tier of LuckyDir changes from 10 to 50, the final cost time only increases about $150ms$. It proves our expectation to be true because the change of directory tier nearly has no effect on computing time for generating user view. Therefore, the small slope of fitting line demonstrate that our cost model for customized user view generation is highly efficient and has low latency.

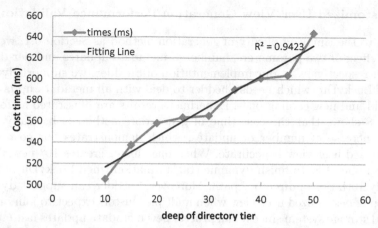

Fig. 9. Cost time with constant metadata updates. Though usually people don't consider directory with too deep level as the LuckyDir, we still measure extensive data to evaluate the performance of Shedder. Cost time has the same meaning as Figure 8. Constant metadata updates are 2×10^5.

7   Related Work

Earliest pioneer in this field is grid computing. It allows distributed resources to get together to solve challenging problems such as [1]. However, as for current important Internet applications such as PageRank [3], electronic commerce recommendation systems etc., they expect these resources to be managed as a whole instead of independent ones. Grid computing doesn't originally support such programming model [2]. Though some contributions [16, 17] adopt federation of geographically grids, They don't mainly focus on sharing of metadata.

In distributed computing, Google Spanner [4] is the first system to manage global scale data as a whole though [11] has brought similar functionality previously. It focuses on synchronous replication and multi-version control, which permit strong consistency. Nevertheless, Spanner doesn't concern about metadata synchronization and customized user view in different clusters or data centers since Google's applications focus more on data instead of metadata. Moreover, Spanner mainly replicates small files globally. For large files, even multi-version control can't guarantee strong consistency and writing performance. Fortunately, [8–10] provide other methods to realize causal consistency. But still, they don't think about customized user view for tuning metadata lookup performance.

In addition, some distributed file systems indeed propose approaches to distribute metadata [5, 6]. Ceph file system provides a pool of metadata servers for high scalability. [12, 13] have similar metadata management through Paxos protocols. However, all clients see a unified view of global namespace, which can not adjust to specific applications' needs. Moreover, the assembly of metadata servers cannot acquire metadata locality and will bring high latency access performance over wide area networks. GPFS v3.5 [7] has proposed a method called

Active File Management (AFM) to allow users to create a given user view of global namespace across GPFS clusters. But real time, dynamic configuration of user view is not supported. Meanwhile, GPFS alternatively caches part of data of other clusters into memory for synchronization, which will bear a big burden when cached data turns big.

8 Conclusion and Future Work

Customized logical network topology, global synchronization and customized user view of global namespace across clusters over the wide area networks is critically desirable for large amount of metadata sharing. Our solution Shedder aims at providing a generic method to define logical network interconnections through authorization control, synchronize file metadata from different clusters and provide customized user view according to users' dynamic configuration. The cost model proposes that Shedder has high performance of synchronization and user view generation. Our experimental evaluations with different workloads and parameters have proven the effectiveness and low latency of Shedder.

Finally, our work has several aspects that can be enhanced in the future. File prefetch can be made when Shedder finds which file metadata user often looks up. According to locality law, it has high probability for the user to fetch these files. File prefetch can obviously improve the whole performance of fetching remote real files. Moreover, usually the used memory storing global namespace is not out of memory boundary because of authorization control (cluster can refuse to receive some metadata updates for saving memory), but as a developing perspective, if we really expect much more metadata updates, a pool of metadata servers at the top of one cluster should be established. These servers store received metadata updates. Then one user fetches what he wants from these servers. This will support concurrent metadata access from large amounts of users.

References

1. SETI@HOME project, http://setiathome.berkeley.edu/
2. Foster, I., Zhao, Y., Raicu, I., Lu, S.: Cloud Computing and Grid Computing 360-Degree Compared. In: Grid Computing Environments Workshop, GCE 2008 (2008)
3. Page, L., Brin, S., Motwani, R., Winograd, T.: The PageRank Citation Ranking: Bringing Order to the Web. Technical Report. Stanford InfoLab
4. Corbett, J.C., Dean, J., Epstein, M., et al.: Spanner: Google's Globally-Distributed Database. In: 10th USENIX Symposium on Operating Systems Design and Implementation, OSDI 2012 (2012)
5. Schmuck, F., Haskin, R.: GPFS: A Shared-Disk File System for Large Computing Clusters. In: Proceedings of the Conference on File and Storage Technologies (FAST 2002), Monterey, CA, January 28-30, pp. 231–244 (2002)
6. Weil, S.A., Brandt, S.A., Miller, E.L., Long, D.D.E.: Ceph: A Scalable, High-Performance Distributed File System. In: OSDI 2006 Proceedings of the 7th Symposium on Operating Systems Design and Implementation, pp. 307–320 (2006)

7. Fadden, S.: An Introduction to GPFS Version 3.5. IBM Systems and Technology Group
8. Lloyd, W., Freedman, M.J., Kaminskyy, M., Andersen, D.G.: Don't Settle for Eventual: Scalable Causal Consistency for Wide-Area Storage with COPS. In: Proceedings of the 23rd ACM Symposium on Operating Systems Principles, SOSP 2011 (2011)
9. Kraska, T., Pang, G., Franklin, M.J., Madden, S., Fekete, A.: MDCC: Multi-data center consistency. In: Proceedings of the 8th ACM European Conference on Computer Systems, EuroSys 2013, pp. 113–126 (2013)
10. Lamport, L.: The part-time parliament. ACM TOCS, 16(2) (1998)
11. Baker, J., Bond, C., Corbett, J.C., Furman, J., Khorlin, A., Larson, J., Leon, J.-M., Li, Y., Lloyd, A., Yushprakh, V.: Megastore: Providing scalable, highly available storage for interactive services. In: CIDR (January 2011)
12. Chang, F., Dean, J., Ghemawat, S., Hsieh, W.C., Wallach, D.A., Burrows, M., Chandra, T., Fikes, A., Gruber, R.E.: Bigtable: A Distributed Storage System for Structured Data. In: OSDI 2006: Seventh Symposium on Operating System Design and Implementation, Seattle, WA (November 2006)
13. Lakshman, A., Malik, P.: Cassandra - A Decentralized Structured Storage System. ACM SIGOPS Operating Systems Review Archive 44(2), 35–40 (2010)
14. Ghemawat, S., Gobioff, H., Leung, S.-T.: The Google File System. In: SOSP 2003, Bolton Landing, New York, USA, October 19-22 (2003)
15. Gray, J.N.: Notes on Database Operating Systems. In: Flynn, M.J., Jones, A.K., Opderbeck, H., Randell, B., Wiehle, H.R., Gray, J.N., Lagally, K., Popek, G.J., Saltzer, J.H. (eds.) Operating Systems. LNCS, vol. 60, pp. 393–481. Springer, Heidelberg (1978)
16. Palmieri, F., Pardi, S.: Towards a federated Metropolitan Area Grid environment: The SCoPE network-aware infrastructure. Future Generation Computer Systems 26(8), 1241–1256 (2010)
17. Esposito, C., Ficco, M., Palmieri, F., Castiglione, A.: Interconnecting Federated Clouds by Using Publish-Subscribe Service. Cluster Computing (2013)

PDB: A Reliability-Driven Data Reconstruction Strategy Based on Popular Data Backup for RAID4 SSD Arrays

Feng Liu[1], Wen Pan[1], Tao Xie[2], Yanyan Gao[1], and Yiming Ouyang[1]

[1] Computer and Information College, Hefei University of Technology, Hefei, P.R. China
{fengliu089,wenwen412,littlek.gao}@gmail.com, oyym@hfut.edu.cn
[2] Computer Science Department, San Diego State University, San Diego, USA
txie@mail.sdsu.edu

Abstract. With the application of MLC (multi-level cell) and TLC (triple-level cell) techniques, the price of NAND flash memory based SSD (solid-state drive) decreases rapidly with increasing capacity. However, these techniques negatively influence the reliability of SSD as they lead to a larger number of raw flash memory errors. When multiple such reliability degraded SSDs organized in a RAID structure SSD failures could occur. Thus, a reliability-aware data reconstruction mechanism that can quickly recover the data of a failed SSD onto a replacement SSD becomes essential. In this paper, we propose a reliability-driven data reconstruction strategy called PDB (Popular Data Backup) for RAID4 and SPD-RAID4 (Splitting Parity Disk - RAID4), a variant of RAID4. PDB collaboratively backups popular data among data SSDs to achieve a shorter "window of vulnerability". Experimental results demonstrate that compared with the traditional SOR (Stripe Oriented Reconstruction) method PDB can shorten reconstruction time up to 31.3%.

1   Introduction

In order to decrease the price and increase the capacity of NAND flash memory based SSD (hereafter, SSD) [1], manufacturers are aggressively pushing flash memory into smaller geometries and letting each flash memory cell store multiple bits by employing either MLC (multi-level cell) or TLC (triple-level cell) technique [2]. Unfortunately, these techniques negatively influence the reliability of SSD as they lead to a larger number of raw flash memory errors compared with SLC (single-level cell) technology, in which each cell stores only one bit. As flash memory density increases, it becomes less reliable for it is more subject to various device and circuit level noises as well as retention errors [2]. Besides, a flash memory cell can only be reprogrammed in a limited number of times (called "program/erase cycles"), after which data can no longer be guaranteed to be correctly written into the cell [1], [3]. These scaling down techniques also substantially reduce the endurance of flash memory. For example, the available P/E (program/erase) cycles of MLC NAND flash memory has dropped from ~10K for 5x nm flash to around ~3K for current 2x nm flash [2].

Since a single SSD cannot satisfy the performance and reliability requirements demanded by data-intensive applications like video processing and bioinformatics, an

J. Kołodziej et al. (Eds.): ICA3PP 2013, Part I, LNCS 8285, pp. 87–100, 2013.

array of SSDs organized in some RAID (Redundant Array of Independent Disk) [4] structures has been proposed to serve such applications [5], [6]. However, when individual SSDs tend to be increasingly unreliable, the reliability of an SSD array becomes a severe problem. In particular, when an SSD fails a data reconstruction mechanism must be able to quickly recover its data onto a replacement SSD so that the length of the reconstruction time (or "window of vulnerability") is sufficiently short [7]. A shorter "window of vulnerability" can alleviate performance degradation caused by data recovery. More importantly, it enhances SSD array reliability by lowering the probability of a subsequent SSD failure during an ongoing data reconstruction process [8], [9]. It is understood that a second SSD failure during a data reconstruction process could cause permanent data loss, which brings enormous economic loss in industry [8]. For instance, 50 percent of companies that lose critical business systems for more than 10 days never recover [8]. Apparently, a reliability-driven data reconstruction strategy that can shrink the "window of vulnerability" for a RAID structured SSD array is much needed. To the best of our knowledge, very little research about SSD array data reconstruction has been reported in the literature.

A RAID4 (block-level striping with dedicated parity) structured SSD array stores parity information on a dedicated SSD drive (i.e., the parity SSD) and distributes data among multiple data SSDs. It can tolerate one drive failure due to data redundancy. Among various RAID formats, RAID4 has not been popular because the dedicated parity drive becomes a performance bottleneck as parity data must be written to it for every block of non-parity data. Nevertheless, we recently proposed a new variant of RAID4 architecture called SPD-RAID4 (Splitting Parity Disk - RAID4) for parallel SSD arrays [10]. It splits the parity SSD into a configurable number of smaller ones. Thus, multiple small capacity parity SSDs can operate in tandem with the data SSDs to achieve a high performance [10]. For example, SPD-RAID4 turns a standard RAID4 array with five 512 GB SSDs (four data SSDs plus one parity SSD) into a new SSD array with four 512 GB data SSDs and two 256 GB parity SSDs. Note that the total cost of the two SSD arrays is almost the same as at the time of this writing the price of a 256 GB Intel SSD is about half of that of a 512 GB Intel SSD [10]. Experimental results from [10] demonstrate that in terms of mean response time SPD-RAID4 outperforms the widely used RAID5 (block-level striping with distributed parity) by up to 20.3%. As a result, in this paper we propose a reliability-driven online data reconstruction strategy called PDB (Popular Data Backup) for SPD-RAID4.

PDB divides each data SSD into a large user zone and a small mirroring zone. While the user zone serves outside user I/O requests, the mirroring zone of a data SSD backups its immediate neighbor data SSD's popular read data in real-time. Assume that an SPD-RAID4 SSD array has four data SSDs (from left to right: S0, S1, S2, and S3). PDB dynamically replicates S0's most popular read data onto S1's mirroring zone. If S0 fails S1 can speed up the data reconstruction process by dumping the replica of S0's most popular data onto a new replacement SSD. Similarly, S2 backups S1's most popular read data. Lastly, S0's mirroring zone is used to backup S3's most popular read data. PDB makes data SSDs help each other in a circular linked list format. Essentially, it is a data reconstruction strategy based on a collaborative popular data real-time backup scheme. PDB exploits the temporal and spatial locality of workloads and dynamically keeps track of the popularity changes of each data region. Section 3 explains the PDB strategy in details.

To evaluate the performance of PDB, we first largely extend a validated single SSD simulator called SSDsim [11] to an SSD array simulator, which can simulate an SSD array in RAID4, RAID5, and SPD-RAID4 formats. Next, PDB and a conventional data reconstruction mechanism named SOR (Stripe-Oriented-Reconstruction) [12] are implemented into the SSD array controller of the simulator. Finally, we use 3 real-world traces to conduct a comprehensive simulation study. Experimental results show that in terms of reconstruction time on RAID4 and SPD-RAID4, PDB outperforms SOR by up to 20.9% and 31.3%, respectively.

The remainder of this paper is organized as follows. Related work and motivation is presented in the next section. We describe the PDB strategy in section 3. In section 4, we evaluate the performance of SOR and PDB based on real-world traces. Section 5 concludes this paper with a summary.

2   Related Work and Motivation

2.1   SSD Basics

An SSD is a data storage device that uses NAND flash memory to store persistent data [1]. Main parts of an SSD include flash controller, internal cache, and flash memory [1]. Flash controller manages the entire SSD including error correction, interface with flash memory, and servicing host requests [1]. The flash memory part of an SSD consists of multiple identical packages. Each package has multiple dies that share one serial I/O bus and common control signals [1]. Each die contains multiple planes with each having thousands of blocks and one data register as an I/O buffer. Each block has multiple pages (e.g., 64 pages in one block). The common size of a page ranges from 2K to 8K. Flash memory offers three basic operations: program or write, read, and erasure [1]. While reads and writes are page-oriented, erasure can be conducted only at block granularity [11]. Flash memory does not allow in-place updates as a write operation can only change bits from 1 to 0 [2]. On the contrary, an erasure operation changes all bits of a block to 1 and a block must be erased before being programmed (written) [2].

2.2   Existing Data Reconstruction Approaches

When a disk fails, a parity-encoding-based RAID-structured disk array can restore to the normal operating mode by successively rebuilding each block of the failed disk onto a replacement drive while continuing to serve I/O requests from users [13]. This process is called data reconstruction or data recovery, which is normally performed by a background process activated in either the host or the disk array controller [13]. Existing data reconstruction approaches are all dedicated to HDDs (hard disk drives). They can be generally divided into three categories: (1) reorganizing data layout [14]; (2) optimizing reconstruction workflow [7], [8], [12], [13], [15], [16], [17]; (3) cache assisted reconstruction [9], [18].

Approaches in the first group improve reconstruction performance by reorganizing the data layout of the replacement disk or parity data units during data recovery [14]. One drawback of these approaches is that changing data layout incurs a high overhead. Mainstream data reconstruction approaches fall in the second category. They can improve disk array reliability and alleviate performance degradation by optimizing reconstruction workflow. SOR (Stripe-Oriented Reconstruction) [12] is one representative approach in this category. SOR creates a set of reconstruction processes associated with stripes so that multiple reconstruction processes can run in parallel.

Since reducing user I/O traffic directed to a degraded RAID set is an effective approach to simultaneously reduce reconstruction time and alleviate user performance degradation, Workout [7] exploits the temporal locality of workloads to reduce user requests during reconstruction. However, its cost is very high as a surrogated RAID set is required to help the degraded disk array. Cache has been widely used in data reconstruction strategies [9], [18]. CORE [3] was developed on top of a hybrid disk array where HDDs and SSDs collaborate to optimize reconstruction.

Our PDB strategy concentrates on SSD array data reconstruction by using an approach completely different from the existing ones. By dividing each data SSD into a large user zone and a small mirroring zone, PDB collaboratively backups immediate neighbor data SSD's popular read data in real-time to significantly reduce reconstruction time, and thus, further enhances the reliability of system.

2.3 SPD-RAID4 Scheme

We recently developed a new SSD data reconstruction strategy called SPD-RAID4 [10], which is a variant of a standard SSD RAID4 structure. To the best of our knowledge, it is the first data reconstruction approach devoted to an SSD array.

SPD-RAID4 splits the parity SSD into a configurable number of smaller ones. It is composed of m data SSDs and n small capacity parity SSDs. In a standard SSD RAID4 array, only one parity SSD undertakes all parity updates, which makes it wear out quickly. This problem can be largely solved in SPD-RAID4 because multiple parity SSDs evenly receive parity updates. In addition, when a request spans across two or more stripes, the parity SSDs can work in parallel, and thus, significantly boosts the SSD array performance. If a data SSD fails, multiple parity SSDs can serve requests in parallel when recovering data in the fault data SSD. Experimental results demonstrate that the performance of SPD-RAID4 is better than that of SSD RAID5 [10]. The scope of this research is to develop a reliability-driven data construction strategy for SPD-RAID4.

2.4 Workload Locality

In many applications, 80% accesses are directed to 20% of the data, a phenomenon that has long been known as Pareto's Principle or "The 80/20 Rule" [19]. It indicates the existence of temporal locality and spatial locality in various workloads. Temporal locality, on the time dimension, refers to the repeated accesses to specific data blocks within relatively small time durations. Spatial locality, on the space dimension, refers to the clustered accesses to data objects within small regions of storage locations within a short timeframe. Previous studies observe that 10% of files accessed on a web server approximately account for 90% of the requests and 90% of the bytes transferred [8]. Such studies also found that 20%-40% of the files are accessed only once for web workloads [8]. The two types of localities have been frequently exploited to boost system performance. PDB also exploits the two access localities. It dynamically tracks each data SSD's popular read data. And then each data SSD backups the most popular read data of its immediate neighbor data SSD in real-time. Although the size of popular data is small, it can serve a large number of user requests.

2.5   Motivation

Modern large capacity SSDs become less reliable due to a spectrum of aggressive scaling down techniques. Meanwhile, RAID-structured SSD arrays are replacing traditional HDD based disk arrays in various data-intensive applications. Thus, the reliability of SSD arrays becomes a critical issue. Especially, when one SSD fails in an SSD array, a reliability-aware data reconstruction approach is desperately needed. Unfortunately, to the best of our knowledge, little research has been done in SSD array data recovery. Motivated by our observations on the facts mentioned above and the insights on workload locality characteristics provided by other researchers, in this paper we propose a new reliability-driven data reconstruction strategy PDB to enhance RAID-structured SSD arrays' reliability during data recovery. PDB achieves reliability enhancement during reconstruction with a minimum performance penalty.

3   The PDB Strategy

3.1   Architecture Overview

Fig. 1 shows the architecture of the PDB strategy on an SPD-RAID4 structured SSD array with 4 identical data SSDs (i.e., SSD0, SSD1, SSD2, SSD3) and 2 parity SSDs (i.e., SSD4, SSD5). The capacity of each parity SSD is a half of a data SSD. SSD0 is in shadow, which indicates that it becomes a failed SSD after running for a while (see Fig. 1). Each data SSD's popular read data is replicated in real-time onto its corresponding immediate neighbor data SSD's mirroring zone in normal mode. For simplicity, the immediate neighbor SSD is named as a buddy SSD. For example, SSD1 is the buddy SSD of SSD0 and SSD0 is the buddy SSD of SSD3 (see Fig. 1). When SSD0 suddenly fails PDB does not need to reconstruct its popular data as it has been stored on SSD1. Rather, PDB simply dumps it to a new replacement SSD, which can save data reconstruction time. Note that the requests that target on the popular data of SSD0 during the data recovery period can be served by SSD1. Obviously, when all SSDs are working correctly, the burden of each data SSD increases because each buddy SSD needs to backup its sponsored data SSD's popular data in real-time. Thus, PDB causes performance degradation when all SSDs are fine. Our experimental results presented in Section 4.2 show that compared with SOR the performance degradation of PDB in normal mode is no larger than 6.8% in terms of mean response time. However, PDB shrinks data reconstruction time by up to 31.3%. We argue that

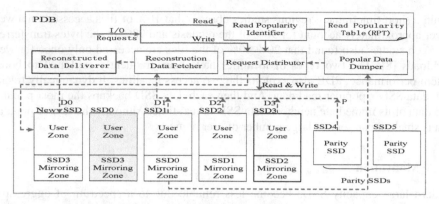

Fig. 1. Architecture overview of PDB

it is worthwhile to trade a slight performance degradation for a substantial improvement in data reconstruction time because PDB noticeably improves SSD array reliability during a data recovery process. The shorter a "window of vulnerability" is, the more reliable an SSD array is.

PDB consists of five key modules: read popularity identifier (RPI), request distributor (RD), popular data dumper (PDD), reconstruction data fetcher (RDF), and reconstructed data deliverer (RDD). The RPI module is responsible for identifying the popular data based on the recent access times of incoming user read requests in normal mode. The RD module directs I/O requests into either a user zone or a user zone and its corresponding mirroring zone. PDD dumps the popular data from the buddy SSD's mirroring zone to a new replacement SSD. Multiple RDFs are launched during reconstruction. Each of them reads one data block or a parity block from a surviving data SSD or a parity SSD. Next, the rebuilt data block D0 can be computed by D0=XOR(D1, D2, D3, P). Finally, RDD writes the reconstructed data D0 onto the replacement SSD.

In the normal mode, when a read request arrives PDB first identifies whether its associated data is popular by consulting the Read Popularity Table (RPT) (see Fig. 1). If it is popular, PDB backups it onto the mirroring zone of the corresponding buddy SSD once it cannot be found in the mirroring zone. If it is unpopular, PDB directly reads it from the right data SSD. Upon receiving a write request, PDB first checks whether it resides in the mirroring zone of the corresponding buddy SSD. If it does, PDB writes it into the right SSD and the mirroring zone of the corresponding buddy SSD simultaneously through the RD module. If not, PDB only writes it onto the right data SSD. When an SSD fails, the entire SSD array enters into the recovery mode. In this mode, when a read request arrives, if it targets on the failed SSD and the data has not been rebuilt onto the replacement SSD, PDB checks whether the data has been stored in the mirroring zone of the failed SSD's buddy SSD. If yes, PDB will directly read it from there, and then, PDD dumps it to the replacement SSD (see Fig. 1). If not, PDB will launch multiple RDF processes to fetch data from surviving SSDs.

For example, in Fig. 1 data blocks D1, D2, D3 and the corresponding parity block P are fetched by 4 RDF processes in parallel from SSD1, SSD2, SSD3, and SSD4, respectively. Note that the 3 data blocks and the parity block P belong to one stripe. After conducting an XOR operation (see Fig. 1), the reconstructed data block D0 will be delivered to the replacement SSD by the RDD module. The replacement SSD now can serve the read request. When a write request that targets on the failed SSD comes, it will be re-directed to the new replacement SSD.

3.2   Key Data Structures and Algorithm

PDB relies on two key data structures RPT and RL (restore list) to identify popular read data and replicate it into corresponding buddy SSD's mirroring zone. Fig. 2 demonstrates their implementation details and the algorithm of restore function is shown as below. PDB evenly divides each user zone into multiple non-overlapping but consecutive logical data regions. Each node in RL represents a data region and keeps track of region information that will be replicated to corresponding buddy SSD. The closer the node towards the head of RL, the more popular it is. The size of each region is equal to the size of a flash memory block (e.g., one flash memory flock has 64 pages and each page is 2 KB). RPT keeps track of the popularity of all logical data regions by using variables: id and $visit\_count$. The id of an incoming read request is calculated by the equation below:

$$id=\text{int}(LPN/block\_size). \tag{1}$$

where LPN is the logic page number of a request and $block\_size$ is set to 64, which is the number of pages in a flash block. Equation (1) indicates that an id contains a block size data region. For example, request LPN 0 to LPN 63 all belong to id 0. The value of $visit\_count$ represents the popularity of a data region. Its value is incremented by 1 when a read request hits the data region. If the value of $visit\_count$ is equal to or greater than the popularity threshold, PDB takes the corresponding data region as a popular region. When the RPT table is full, the least popular data region with the fewest access times will be kicked out to accommodate a new popular data region. Then PDB inserts the corresponding node into RL and write the data in popular region into mirroring zone of indicated buddy SSD.

Data consistency in PDB includes two aspects: (1) The key data structures must be safely stored; (2) The real-time backup data in buddy SSD must be updated timely to guarantee data consistency. Firstly, to prevent the loss of key data structures in the event of a power supply failure or a system crash, PDB stores them in a non-volatile RAM (NVRAM). Since the size of RPT is generally small (1,024 entries with each entry 4 bytes in our experiments), it will not incur significant extra hardware cost. Secondly, the popular read data must be safely stored in corresponding buddy SSD. To ensure the popular data recovered to replacement SSD is not out-of-date, when the corresponding buddy SSD exists identical LPN of a write operation, the backup data must be updated simultaneously to make it always up to date.

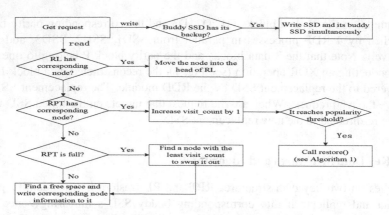

Fig. 2. Workflow of PDB in normal mode

Algorithm 1.

---

restore()
Write data in indicated zone into corresponding buddy SSD and create a node
if restore list does not reach the maximum length **then**
    Directly insert the node into the head of restore list
else
    Delete the node in the queue tail and invalidate data of tail node
end if

3.3   Implementation

The original SSDsim [11] can only simulate a single SSD. We significantly extend it so that SSD RAID4 and SPD-RAID4 are also supported. On this basis, we also implement a baseline reconstruction mechanism SOR and our proposed strategy PDB on both RAID4 and SPD-RAID4. The size of a flash page is set to 2 KB in our experiments. When updating the parity data on the parity sub array, we also employ the round-robin way to write parity data evenly across all parity SSDs.

Once the host sends a request, the RAID controller gets the device number and its LPN as well as the stripe number by a division operation. The mapping from a logical address to a physical address is controlled by FTL (flash translation layer) implemented inside each SSD. When a read request comes, PDB identifies the popularity of corresponding logical data region. Once it is taken as a popular page (we take a page in a popular data region as a popular page), PDB redirects the data to mirroring zone of corresponding buddy SSD while it returns to host at the same time if it has not been in buddy SSD. If the read operation is directed to the failed SSD, PDB checks that whether the indicated data has been stored in corresponding buddy SSD. If it has, PDB directly reads it from corresponding buddy SSD and dumps data in indicated data region to the replacement SDD. Otherwise, RDF and RDD are launched. When the popular data has been successfully dumped, the system can directly respond the subsequent identical requests. Although the size of popular data is small, it can serve a large number of user requests, and thus, significantly reduces reconstruction time.

4   Performance Evaluation

4.1   Experimental Setup

Among existing data reconstruction schemes, SOR is a widely used data recovery mechanism with the lowest overhead. Therefore, we implemented SOR and PDB on both SSD RAID 4 and SPD-RAID4 structures. Our simulator is built based on a validated SSD simulator called SSDsim [11], which is an event-driven, modularly structured, and highly accurate simulator for a single SSD. We added about 2,700 lines of C codes to extend SSDsim to an SSD array simulator and implement the two data reconstruction schemes. The RAID controller fetches a request from a trace file and splits it into multiple sub-requests.

We use three real-world traces [20] to compare the performance of SOR and PDB. The three traces and their characteristics are summarized in Table 1. The three Websearch (hereafter, Web) traces were collected from a machine running a web search engine. The read-dominated Web trace exhibits a strong locality.

The number of data SSDs and parity SSDs are both configurable for SPD-RAID4. We conducted our performance evaluation of the two strategies on SPD-RAID4 with 2 parity SSDs as we found that 2 is the optimal choice of the number of parity SSDs. The default number of data SSDs is 4. The number of RAID4's data SSD is also set to 4 and its parity SSD's capacity is twice of a parity SSD in SPD-RAID4. Due to the limited footprints of traces, the capacity of each data SSD is set to 16 GB in our experiments and the capacity of each parity SSDs in SPD-RAID4 is 8 GB. The capacity of the only parity SSD in RAID4 is 16 GB as well.

4.2   Real-World Trace Experimental Results

In this section, we evaluate the performance of PDB by comparing it with a classical data reconstruction method SOR on both RAID4 and SPD-RAID4 structured SSD arrays. Fig. 3 shows the read, write and overall mean response times of PDB and SOR before data reconstruction in the normal mode. The marks "_R", "_W", and "_O" represent read, write and overall mean response time, respectively. For PDB, the logical data region size is set to 128 KB, which is equal to a flash block size. The goal of this group of experiments is to measure PDB's performance degradation during the normal mode before an SSD failure happens.

Table 1. Real-world traces characteristics

Trace Name	Read Ratio (%)	Avg. Size (KB)	Intensity (reqs./s)	Duration (minute)
Web 1	99.98	15.14	335	52.5
Web 2	99.97	15.07	297	256.6
Web 3	99.98	15.41	16	4543.9

From Fig. 3, we can see that the performance of PDB on both RAID4 and SPD-RAID4 is consistently and slightly worse than that of SOR before reconstruction in the three traces. Compared with SOR, PDB degrades performance in terms of overall mean response time on SPD-RAID4 by 4.7%, 3.8% and 3.1% on the three traces, respectively (see Fig. 3b). Note that the maximum overall performance loss is only 4.7% in Web1 trace case on both RAID4 and SPD-RAID4 structures. The reason for PDB's performance degradation is that it has extra work to do comparing with SOR. In particular, PDB needs to dynamically keep track of popularity changes of read requests and stores popular data in the mirroring zone in real-time, which inevitably increase its burden, and thus, enlarges the mean response time of user requests.

An SSD array enters the data recovery mode after one data SSD fails. To understand the performance and reliability enhancement of PDB during reconstruction, we measure mean response time during reconstruction and reconstruction time in a group of experiments whose results are demonstrated in Fig. 4 and Fig. 5. From Fig. 4a, we can clearly see that in the data recovery mode PDB even performs better in terms of mean response time during reconstruction than SOR in RAID4 format on Web1 and Web2 traces by 13.9% and 2.9%, respectively. It only performs a little bit worse in Web3 trace. However, on SPD-RAID4 structure, PDB only performs better on Web1 trace (see Fig. 4b). Still, on average PDB's performance degradation in data recovery mode is only 2.1% compared with SOR. The almost negligible performance degradation during reconstruction is because that when the reconstruction time

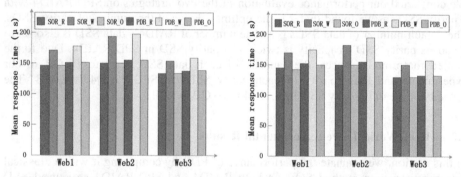

Fig. 3. Performance comparisons before reconstruction on (a) RAID4; (b) SPD-RAID4

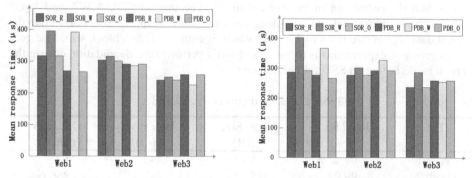

Fig. 4. Performance comparison during reconstruction on (a) RAID4; (b) SPD-RAID4

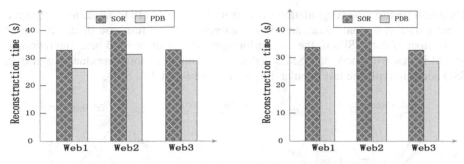

Fig. 5. Reconstruction time on (a) RAID4; (b) SPD-RAID4

decreases (see Fig. 5) the number of reconstruction requests per time unit obviously enlarges, which prolongs the mean response time of user requests. Therefore, the performance of PDB during reconstruction is lowered down.

The reconstruction times of SOR and PDB on RAID4 and SPD-RAID4 are illustrated in Fig. 5. It shows that on both RAID4 and SPD-RAID4 structures the reconstruction time of PDB is consistently less than that of SOR. In case of SPD-RAID4, PDB shrinks reconstruction time by 21.8%, 22% and 13.3% on the three traces, respectively (see Fig. 5b). PDB manifests a similar improvement in reconstruction time in RAID4 scenario (see Fig. 5a). Note that the much shorter reconstruction time shown in Fig. 5 compared with HDD array situations comes from two facts: (1) SSD has a much faster read and write speed than HDD [0]; (2) the footprint of the three traces is relatively small, and thus, the amount of data need to be rebuilt is not large. PDB's improvement in terms of reconstruction time stems from its ability to directly respond popular read requests targeting on the failed SSD from the mirroring zone of its buddy SSD. In this way PDB does not need to launch a standard reconstruction mechanism like SOR does. In addition, all three workloads are read-dominant and have strong locality, which can be effectively exploited by PDB to substantially reduce reconstruction time. Although the stored popular data in a buddy SSD only takes a small percentage of total data amount, a large percentage of requests may access them consecutively due to workload locality explained in Section 2.4. Therefore, PDB can significantly reduce reconstruction time to shrink the "window of vulnerability", and thus, can enhance SSD array reliability. We argue that scarifying slightly in performance in the normal mode to obviously shrink reconstruction time is a good trade- off for modern SSD arrays organized in a RAID structure.

The purpose of our last group of experiments is to study the impacts of the number of data SSDs in an SPD-RAID4 SSD array on the performance of PDB. Several interesting observations can be made from the results shown in Fig. 6. First of all, for all 3 traces, we can see that the performance of both SOR and PDB before reconstruction (i.e., in the normal mode) increases when the number of data SSDs is enlarged. It is easy to understand that with more data SSDs the SSD array can process user requests faster. Next, SOR consistently outperforms the PDB strategy on the three traces when the number of data SSDs is increasing. However, the performance gap between the two strategies shrinks with an increasing number of data SSDs (see Fig. 6), which is true for all 3 traces. Take the Web1 trace for example, the performance difference between the two reduces from 6.8% to 2.9%.

The small performance degradation stems from the fact that PDB needs to backup the popular data in normal mode, and thus, enlarges its mean response time. The larger the number of data SSDs is, the less performance degradation PDB has. The rationale behind is that with more data SSDs and a fixed amount of total workloads each data SSD needs to replicate less popular data for its sponsored data SSD.

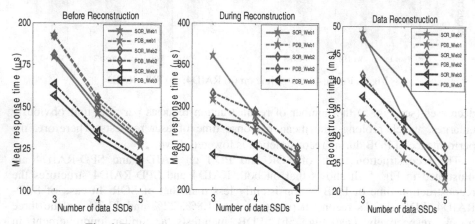

Fig. 6. The impacts of the number of data SSDs on performance

Furthermore, we can see that in the data recovery mode, PDB only performs better when the number of data SSDs is 3 or 4 in Web1 trace. PDB's worse performance during reconstruction is because it gives data reconstruction task a higher priority than processing user requests during reconstruction. Finally, for all 3 workloads and all data SSD numbers, the PDB strategy consistently outperforms the SOR mechanism in reconstruction time (see Fig. 6). When the number of data SSDs increases, the reconstruction times for both SOR and PDB decrease. The reason for the decreased reconstruction time on a larger size SSD array is that fewer user requests arrive on an individual data SSD in the recovery mode, which in turn reduces the reconstruction time. In particular, in Web1 case PDB can shrink the reconstruction time by up to 31.3% when there are 3 data SSDs in a SPD-RAID4 SSD array (see Fig. 6). However, the reconstruction time decreases the most when the number of data SSDs is 4 in the case of Web2 and Web3 traces. It is clear that SOR also lowers down its reconstruction time when the number of data SSDs increases from 3 to 5. More importantly, in Web1 trace, its improvement in terms of reconstruction time becomes more noticeable than that of PDB situation when the number of data SSDs enlarges from 3 to 5. The reason is that the amount of data that need to be rebuilt by SOR reduces faster than PDB.

5   Conclusions

With larger and more affordable yet less reliable SSDs, developing an efficient data reconstruction strategy with reliability-awareness for emerging SSD arrays organized in some RAID structures becomes a critical problem to be solved. Unfortunately, very little research about SSD array data reconstruction has been reported in the literature. To the best of knowledge, this research is the first step towards solving the critical issue. In this paper, we develop and evaluate a novel online data reconstruction strategy called PDB for both conventional RAID4 and SPD-RAID4. The PDB strategy exploits the workload locality, which has been frequently observed in a spectrum of real-world workloads like the three web search traces. It utilizes a collaborative popular data backup mechanism among all data SSDs to largely shrink the "window of vulnerability", and thus, enhances SSD array reliability. Our Experimental results demonstrate that compared with a traditional reconstruction method SOR the PDB strategy can further shorten reconstruction time by up to 31.3% on SPD-RAID4.

PDB, however, in its current format, only applies the popular data backup scheme among all data SSDs. When a parity SSD fails, it still uses a conventional reconstruction method, which is currently used by SOR. The main reason is that parity data generally does not exhibit obvious locality, which makes PDB inefficient. Considering that normally the number of data SSDs is larger than that of parity SSDs, the probability of a data SSD failure is higher than a parity SSD failure. Thus, PDB could enhance SSD array reliability in majority cases. Also, PDB may not work well under write-dominated workloads. One direction of the future of this research is to extend it to incorporate write-dominated. Finally, we only integrate PDB into RAID4 and SPD-RAID4 SSD arrays. In our future work, we are going to integrate it into different RAID architectures such as RAID5.

Acknowledgments. This work is sponsored in part by the U.S. National Science Foundation under grant CNS-(CAREER)-0845105 and Key Technologies R & D Program of Anhui Province (China)-11010202190.

References

1. Agrawal, N., Prabhakaran, V., Wobber, T., Davis, J.D., Manasse, M., Panigrahy, R.: Design Tradeoffs for SSD Performance. In: USENIX Ann. Technical Conference, pp. 57–70. USENIX Association, Berkeley (2008)
2. Cai, Y., Haratsch, E.F., Mutlu, O., Mai, K.: Threshold Voltage Distribution in MLC NAND Flash Memory: Characteristization, Analysis, and Modeling. In: The Conf. on Design, Automation and Test in Europe, EDA Consortium San Jose, pp. 1285–1290 (2013)
3. Xie, T., Sharma, A.: Collaboration-Oriented Data Recovery for Mobile Disk Arrays. In: 29th Int'l Conf. on Distributed Computed Systems, Montreal, pp. 631–638 (June 2009)
4. Patterson, D.A., Gibson, G., Katz, R.H.: A Case for Redundant Arrays for Inexpensive Disks (RAID). In: Boral, H., Larson, P.A. (eds.) 1988 ACM SIGMOD Int'l Conf. on Management of Data, pp. 109–116. ACM, New York (1988)
5. Im, S., Shin, D.: Flash-Aware RAID Techniques for Dependable and High-Performance Flash Memory SSD. J. IEEE Transaction on Computer. 6(1), 80–92 (2011)
6. Lee, Y., Jung, S., Song, Y.H.: FRA: A Flash-aware Redundant Array of Flash Storage Devices. In: 7th IEEE/ACM Int'l Conf. on Hardware/Software Codesign and System Synthesis, pp. 163–172. ACM, New York (2009)

7. Wu, S.Z., Jiang, H., Feng, D., Tian, L., Mao, B.: Workout: I/O Workload Outsourcing for Boosting RAID Reconstruction Performance. In: 7th USENIX Conf. on FAST, pp. 239–252. USENIX Association, Berkeley (2009)

8. Tian, L., Feng, D., Jiang, H., Zhou, K., Zeng, L.F., Chen, J.X., Wang, Z.K., Song, Z.L.: PRO: A Popularity-Based Multi-Threaded Reconstruction Optimization for RAID-Structured Storage Systems. In: 5th USENIX Conf. on FAST, pp. 277–290. USENIX Association, Berkeley (2007)

9. Xie, T., Wang, H.: MICRO: A Multilevel Caching-Based Reconstruction Optimization for Mobile Storage Systems. J. IEEE Transactions on Computers 57(10), 1386–1398 (2008)

10. Pan, W., Liu, F., Xie, T., Gao, Y.Y., Ouyang, Y.M., Chen, T.: SPD-RAID4: Splitting Parity Disk for RAID4 Structured Parallel SSD Arrays. In: 15th Int'l Conf. on High Performance Computing and Communications. IEEE Press, Zhangjiajie (2013)

11. Hu, Y., Jiang, H., Feng, D., Tian, L., Luo, H., Zhang, S.P.: Performance Impact and Interplay of SSD Parallelism through Advanced Commands, Allocation Strategy and Data Granularity. In: Int'l Conf. on Supercomputing, pp. 96–107. ACM, New York (2011)

12. Holland, M.: Online Data Reconstruction in Redundant Disk Arrays. In: PhD Dissertation CMU-CS-94-164, Carnegie Mellon Univ., Pittsburgh (1994)

13. Holland, M., Gibson, G.A., Siewiorek, D.P.: Fast, On-Line Failure Recovery in Redundant Disk Arrays. In: 23rd Ann. Int'l Symp. on Fault-Tolerant Computing, pp. 422–443. IEEE Press, Toulouse (1993)

14. Hou, R.Y., Menon, J., Patt, Y.N.: Balancing I/O Response Time and Disk Rebuild Time in a RAID5 Disk Array. In: 26th Hawaii Int'l Conf. on Systems Sciences, pp. 70–79. IEEE Press, Hawaii (1993)

15. Lee, J.Y.B., Lui, J.C.S.: Automatic Recovery from Disk Failure in Continuous-Media Servers. J. IEEE Transaction on Parallel and Distributed Systems 13(5), 499–515 (2002)

16. Wu, S.Z., Feng, D., Jiang, H., Mao, B., Zeng, L.F., Chen, J.: JOR: A Journal-Guided Reconstruction Optimization for RAID Structured Storage Systems. In: 15th Int'l Conf. on Parallel and Distributed Systems, pp. 609–616. IEEE Press, Shenzhen (2009)

17. Wu, S.Z., Jiang, H., Mao, B.: IDO: Intelligent Data Outsourcing with Improved RAID Reconstruction Performance in Large-Scale Data Centers. In: 26th Int'l Conf. on Large Installation System Administration, pp. 17–32. USENIX Association, San Diego (2012)

18. Wan, S., Cao, Q., Huang, J.Z., Li, S.Y., Li, X., Zhan, S.H., Yu, L., Xie, C.S., He, X.B.: Victim Disk First: An Asymmetric Cache to Boost the Performance of Disk Arrays Under Faulty Conditions. In: USENIX Annual Technical Conference. USENIX Association, Berkeley (2011)

19. Gomez, M.E., Sontonja, V.: Characterizing Temporal Locality in I/O Workload. In: Int'l Symp. on Performance Evaluation of Computer and Telecommunication Systems, San Diego (July 2002)

20. SPC, Storage Performance Council I/O Traces,
http://traces.cs.umass.edu/index.php/Storage/Storage

Load and Thermal-Aware VM Scheduling on the Cloud

Yousri Mhedheb[1], Foued Jrad[1], Jie Tao[1], Jiaqi Zhao[2], Joanna Kołodziej[3],
and Achim Streit[1]

[1] Steinbuch Center for Computing, Karlsruhe Institute of Technology, Germany
{yousri.mhedheb,foued.jrad,jie.tao,achim.streit}@kit.edu
[2] School of Basic Science, Changchun University of Technology, China
scorpiozhao@yahoo.com.cn
[3] Institute of Computer Science, Cracow University of Technology, Poland
jokoldziej@pk.edu.pl

Abstract. Virtualization is one of the key technologies that enable Cloud Computing, a novel computing paradigm aiming at provisioning on-demand computing capacities as services. With the special features of self-service and pay-as-you-use, Cloud Computing is attracting not only personal users but also small and middle enterprises. By running applications on the Cloud, users need not maintain their own servers thus to save administration cost.

Cloud Computing uses a business model meaning that the operation overhead must be a major concern of the Cloud providers. Today, the payment of a data centre on energy may be larger than the overall investment on the computing, storage and network facilities. Therefore, saving energy consumption is a hot topic not only in Cloud Computing but also for other domains.

This work proposes and implements a virtual machine (VM) scheduling mechanism that targets on both load-balancing and temperature-balancing with a final goal of reducing the energy consumption in a Cloud centre. Using the strategy of VM migration it is ensured that none of the physical hosts suffers from either high temperature or over-utilization. The proposed scheduling mechanism has been evaluated on CloudSim, a well-known simulator for Cloud Computing. Initial experimental results show a significant benefit in terms of energy consumption.

Keywords: Cloud Computing, Green Computing, Virtualization, VM Scheduling, Thermal-aware Scheduler, Load Balancing.

1 Introduction

Cloud Computing [16,26] is a novel computing paradigm. It provisions computing capacities, including hardware, software, applications, networks as well as storage, as services with a business model of pay-as-you-use. Its special features lie in that users can access the computing resources via Internet with a thin-client, such as a Web browser, without the interaction of administrators. Additionally, Cloud Computing shows the advantages in elasticity, system management, cost-efficiency, customized environment and on-demand resource provision [23,17]. Therefore, an increasing number of Cloud infrastructures [5,29,18] have been established after the first computing Cloud, the Amazon Elastic Compute Cloud [1].

J. Kołodziej et al. (Eds.): ICA3PP 2013, Part I, LNCS 8285, pp. 101–114, 2013.

Several underlying technologies enable Cloud Computing, where the virtualization technology is especially important because virtual machines are the base for delivering any Cloud services, which are categorized as Infrastructure as a Service (IaaS), Platform as a Service (PaaS) and Software as a Service (IaaS) [16]. Actually, the virtualization approach has been used for 60 years with an initial application of running different binary codes on the expensive hardware in the late 50's. Today, Cloud Computing makes virtualization a hot topic again because it relies on this technology to provide on-demand, elastic computing resources. The virtualization itself has also been developed from simple approach to mature techniques with a standard virtualization layer called hypervisor or virtual machine monitor. This layer is responsible for resource allocation and the virtualization of the processor, the memory and devices.

An important issue in Cloud Computing is the scheduling of virtual machines on physical hosts. A Cloud centre is equipped with several thousands of physical hosts, each of them can host an incoming virtual machine request. A traditional approach of scheduling virtual machines is a kind of FIFO approaches, where all hosts are contained in a list and the first physical machine that matches the requirement of the VM is selected to host the VM.

Scheduling is not a new topic. This issue exists in various scenarios, like task scheduling in parallel and distributed systems [10,24,25,19] and job scheduling in computing Grids [20,11,12]. Researchers have also proposed a number of algorithms, including those targeting on energy consumption. In the field of Cloud Computing, saving energy is especially important because it adopts a business model and the Cloud providers are surely expecting a low operation overhead. Therefore, this work developed a specific algorithm for scheduling the virtual machines on the Cloud. This algorithm first performs an initial scheduling and then inspects the change of workload and temperature on the host. In case of over-loading or over-heating, the VM is migrated to another host, hence to avoid hot spots with respect to load and temperature. We implemented this algorithm on CloudSim [4], a well-known simulation platform for research work in Cloud Computing. The initial experimental results show the feasibility of the developed algorithm, especially in saving energy consumption.

The remainder of the paper is organized as following. Section 2 introduces the related work in energy-aware scheduling algorithms. Section 3 describes the concept of the proposed approach, followed by the implementation details in Section 4. The evaluation results are then depicted in Section 5. The paper concludes in Section 6 with a brief summary and future directions.

2   Related Work

Task scheduling has been a hot topic in various research domains. As a result, a lot of research works have been performed for investigating the scheduling strategies on different systems with features like load-balancing and energy-awareness.

The work described in [27] and [24] exploited Dynamic Voltage Frequency Scaling (DVFS) to implement a power-aware task clustering algorithm for parallel HPC tasks. Authors of [14] also relied on DVFS to schedule independent tasks on a single processor. The work presented in [15] used DVFS to build a hybrid global/local search optimization framework for reducing the energy requirement of multiprocessor system with dynamic workloads.

Authors of [13] applied a thermal-aware strategy based on the RC-Thermal model [21] to reduce the peak temperature of HPC servers under stochastic workloads. The approach in [30] combines both techniques used in [27] and [13] for solving a temperature-aware scheduling problem. For this, the authors implemented an approximation algorithm based on the Lumped RC-Thermal model and DVFS to study the effect of using the thermal constraints on maximizing the performance of tasks running on some CPU architectures.

Concretely on virtualized machines, task scheduling at the high level is actually VM scheduling that handles the allocation of virtual machines to the physical hosts. Over the last years, the topic of VM scheduling has been addressed. The work presented in [8] implemented a guest-aware priority-based scheduling scheme to support latency-sensitive workloads. The proposed scheduling scheme prioritizes the virtual machines to be allocated by using the information about priorities and status of guest-level tasks in each VM. It preferentially selects the VMs that run latency-sensitive applications to be scheduled thus to reduce the response time to the I/O events of latency-sensitive workloads. Authors of [28] proposed a novel VM scheduling algorithm for virtualized heterogonous multicore architectures. The algorithm exploits core performance heterogeneity to optimize the overall system energy efficiency.

The work in [7] proposed a strategy for VM scheduling on the Cloud with load balancing. The scheduling decision is based on the historical information and current state of the system. Authors of [9] proposed a scheduler, which schedules the virtual machines based on the knowledge about the duration of timed instances to optimize the virtual to physical machine assignment. The main goal of this scheduler is to reduce the cumulative machine uptime and thereby save the energy consumption. The work in [2] is also one of the few approaches that deal with energy-aware scheduling of Cloud-based resources. The authors implemented a simulation environment based on CloudSim [4] to evaluate different power-aware scheduling policies for VMs running on a large scale Cloud centre. Furthermore, they showed how the VM migration and VM pining techniques can optimize the load-balancing and the total energy consumption of the datacenter. Our work is similar to this work, however, we combine both power and thermal-aware scheduling policies to reduce the energy consumption. More importantly, we extend this work to support using temperature constraints as new scheduling parameters. The evaluation on CloudSim has shown the improvement of this approach over the existing one in terms of saving energy consumption. The experimental results will be given after the description of the proposed scheduling algorithm and its implementation.

3   The Thermal-Aware VM Scheduling Scheme

Modern processors have a tolerance limit to the on-chip temperature. A higher temperature over this limit (i.e., case temperature) not only increases the energy consumption but also may result in defect in hardware. We designed a novel thermal-aware scheduling scheme in order to avoid the occurrence of this scenario.

The proposed scheduler is called ThaS (Thermal-aware Scheduler). As shown in Figure 1, ThaS implements an interface between the VMM (hypervisor) and the virtual machines in a Cloud centre. It replaces the conventional scheduling algorithm of a hypervisor to map a virtual machine request to a physical machine with consideration of the load and temperature on the hosts. The deployment, such as start, stop, migration, etc., of the virtual machines on the physical host remains the task of the hypervisor. In this way, our scheduler acts as an allocation decision component for the hypervisor.

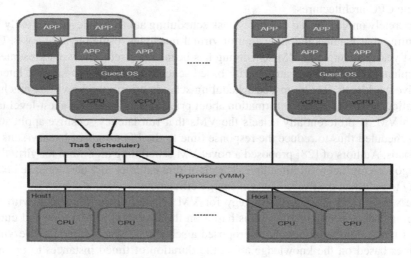

Fig. 1. Software architecture of the Thermal-aware Scheduler

Our thermal-aware scheduling concept is based on several existing strategies, which are applied for the requirement of different scheduling scenarios. These strategies are individually integrated in our framework at the runtime based on the current load and temperature state. The main tasks of our scheduler ThaS are the following:

– **Thermal-Aware Energy-Management:** The first purpose of ThaS is to schedule VMs with respect to the temperature of the processors. Such scheduling strategy needs a temperature model that describes the changes of this parameter as applications (here virtual machines) are running. We applied the lumped RC thermal model for this initial work due to its simplicity. This model is however limited to a single-core processor. Therefore, ThaS supports now only single-core machines. For the next version of ThaS we will adopt the Hotspot [6] tool that models multicore architectures with more accuracy but not more complexity. Hotspot uses an analogy between electrical circuit phenomena and a heat transfer phenomena. The heat flow between the internal CPU chip blocks is modeled by connecting thermal resistors and thermal storage in blocks. The power consumed by each chip (which typically corresponds to a function unit) is modeled by a power source.
– **Power-Aware Energy Management:** For power management we apply DVFS. Since the power consumption depends on the CPU usage, this metric has to be

measured before each VM scheduling step in the whole simulation process in order
to calculate the current consumed energy by the CPU.

– **Migration of Virtual Machines:** Migration or live migration refers to the process
  of moving a running virtual machine or application from one physical machine to
  another. In addition to the machine image, the data storage and network connectivity of the virtual machines have also to be transferred from the source host to the
  destination. The proposed scheduling scheme implements this kind of VM migration and runs the entire migration process transparently to the user. The migration
  contains several steps, including the Push phase, the Stop phase, the Copy phase
  and the Pull phase. The VM migration can take a long time when a VM has a large
  amount of memory. In order to save the unnecessary energy consumption during
  the VM migration, we implemented two strategies in ThaS: i) the Pining strategy
  that allows the allocation of multiple VMs on the same host to free other physical
  hosts; ii) the energy-save-modus strategy that sets the unused hosts (or CPUs) in
  the idle mode.

ThaS decides during the runtime which VM must be running on which host. It works
in the following way: As a starting point a VM request coming from the user is scheduled on a physical host based on the traditional Round-Robin scheme. In order to make
a decision, ThaS calls the thermal model and the power model to acquire all scheduling
parameters including the current CPU temperature, the CPU usage for each host, the
datacenter configuration and the application (VM) requirements. In case that a physical host approaches to the critical temperature (Temperature_threshold) or the critical
CPU utilization value (Utilization_threshold), ThaS looks for another host with better
temperature or load criteria and migrates the running VM from the source host to the
destination host. Therefore, the proposed approach schedules the virtual machines not
only for minimizing the energy consumption but also for load-balancing.

4 ThaS Implementation

In order to verify the concept and to validate the functionality of the proposed scheduling strategies, we implemented a Java-based simulation environment for ThaS. The
prototypical implementation is based on CloudSim [4], a well-known simulator for research work on the Cloud.

An important task of ThaS is to figure out the critical hosts. The following pseudo-
code shows how the scheduler performs this task. As can be seen in the code, the scheduler goes through all the available hosts to find the hosts, whose temperature and CPU
usage exceed the specified thresholds. The detected hosts are then marked as candidates
for VM migration and added to the list MigratingFromHosts. This list is adopted in the
second step as the input list.

```
Input:  HostList , VmList
Output:  MigratingFromHosts
For each host in hostList Do
    If isHostOverThresholdTemperature(host) Then
        overThresholdTempHosts <- add host
    Else
        If isHostOverThresholdUtilization(host) Then
```

```
            overUtilizedHosts <- add host
        Endif
    Endif
Endfor
MigratingFromHosts <- overThresholdTempHosts+overUtilizedHosts
Return MigratingFromHosts
```

In the second step, the list of critical hosts, which has been created by the scheduler in the first step, is processed again for finding for VMs running on them. These virtual machines are the concrete migration candidates. The candidate VMs are then sorted by their CPU usage. The VMs with minimal CPU usage have higher priority of migration in order not to bring high workload on the target host, thus to avoid further migrations. For the same reason the scheduler must also ensure that the temperature on the target host does not exceed the threshold. At the end of processing, this scheduling step creates a list VMstoMigrateList that contains all VMs, which are the actual migration candidates.

```
Input: MigratingFromHosts
Output: VMstoMigrateList
For each host in MigratingFromHosts Do
    While true Do
    vm <- getVmtoMigrate(host)
    If vm = Null Then
    break
    Endif
    VMstoMigrateList <- add vm
    host <- deallocate vm
    If !(isHostOverThresholdTemperature(host) &&
        isHostOverThresholdUtilisation(host)) Then
    break
    Endif
    Endwhile
Endfor
Return VMstoMigrateList
```

The last step of the VM migration process is to find an appropriate target host for hosting the migration candidates in the list created in the last step. Here, the workload requirements (e.g., needed resources) have to be taken into account. Our scheduler first observes the temperature on the destination host. If this temperature is below the threshold value (Temperature_threshold) and the requirement of the VM is fulfilled, the observed host is selected as the target host. In case that several target hosts are found, the one with the minimum energy consumption is chosen for hosting the VM to be migrated.

```
Input: MigratingFromHosts, vmstoMigrateList
Output: MigrationMap
MigrationMap <- null
vmstoMigrateList.SortDecreasingCPUUtilisation
For each vm in vmstoMigrateList Do
    allocatedHost<- null
    minPower<- Max
    For each host not in MigratingFromHost DO
        If host has enough resources for vm Then
            power <- estimatePower(host,vm)
        Endif
        If host switchedOff && host overUtilizedAfterAlloc ||
            overThresholdTemparureAfterAlloc (power)
            Then continue
        Endif
        If power < minPower Then
```

```
            allocatedHost <- host
            minPower <- power
       Endif
       If allocatedHost != NULL Then
            allocate vm to allocatedHost
       Endif
     Endfor
     MigrationMap <- add (vm, allocatedHost)
   Endfor
   Return migrationMap
```

To further improve the scheduling efficiency in terms of energy consumption, a reallocation of VMs is designed in the proposed scheduler. This scheme concerns the hosts that are underutilized. In case that the CPU usage of a physical host is below the minimal value, the VMs on it are migrated to other hosts. The underutilized hosts are then set in the sleep mode for the purpose of saving energy. The idle hosts are not candidates of destination host for VM migration.

5   Experimental Results

5.1   Simulation Setup

As mentioned above, the prototype of the scheduler is implemented on top of CloudSim, which models large datacenters provisioning computing infrastructures as services. CloudSim implements a view of infinite computing resources. This feature is important for us to evaluate the proposed thermal-aware scheduling algorithms on a large virtualized datacenter infrastructure. In contrast, validation on a real Cloud infrastructure will be extremely difficult for performing different experiments in order to examine the full functionality of the implemented scheduler and the impact of the scheduling strategies.

The simulation duration was set to one day with a scheduling interval of five minutes in the simulation. In addition, a workload of 50 cloudlets (applications) was modeled, each with a CPU core and a computational requirement of 2500 MIPS.

In order to calculate the CPU temperature at a specific timestamp, our thermal model requires the current performance and consumed power of the processors. The later is determined using a power model. The power consumption of computing resources in a datacenter is mainly determined by the total consumed CPU, memory, disk, and cooling power. It has been shown that the power consumption of a server can be described exactly by a linear relationship between the power consumption and CPU utilization (u), even if Dynamic Voltage and Frequency Scaling (DVFS) is employed. An idle server usually uses 70% of the maximum power consumption [3].

Table 1 lists all setup parameters applied in the simulation based tests. The first block in the table shows the thermal constants for the lumped RC thermal model. The values in the table are typical values of a single core CPU obtained from [6].

We configured CloudSim for a datacenter with 50 diverse hosts, each of them composing half of the HP ProLiant G4 servers. The other half is modeled as the HP ProLiant G5 servers. The characteristics of the servers are given in the second block of Table 1. The frequency of each core on the HP ProLiant G4 Server is 1860 MIPS and for the HP ProLiant G5 Server the value is 2660 MIPS. Each server is modeled with a connection of 1 GB/s bandwidth. The corresponding power model used by each server is gathered

Table 1. The experimental setups

	Thermal Parameter	Value	Unit
Thermal Constants	Initiale CPU Temperatur (T_{init})	318	Kelvin
	Ambiente Temperatur (T_{amb})	308	Kelvin
	Case Temperatur (T_{case})	353	Kelvin
	Thermal Capacity (C_{th})	340	Joule/Kelvin
	Thermal Resistance (R_{th})	0.34	Kelvin/Watt
Simulated physical machines	Server Host Type	HP_Proliant_G4	HP_Proliant_G5
	Host_MIPS	1860	2660
	Host_Cores	1	1
	Host_RAM [MB]	2048	4096
	Host_BW [Gbit/s]	1	1
	Host_Storage [TB]	1	1
Virtual machine configuration	VM Type	VM_MIPS	VM_RAM [MB]
	1	500	613
	2	1000	1740
	3	2000	1740
	4	2500	870
	VM_Cores	VM_BW [Mbit/s]	VM_Size [GB]
	1	100	2.5

from SpecPower08 [22]. The simulation of less powerful CPUs is advantageous for a better evaluation of the effect of the VM migration because few workload is required to result in the overload of a server.

The last block of Table 1 gives the properties of the four modeled VM types with the assumption that all VMs are running on single core machines. As shown in the table, we use different VMs with various values in MIPS and RAM to model real scenarios. The bandwith and VM size for all simulated virtual machines are set as 100 Mbit/s and 2.5 GB individually.

The implemented scheduler relies on two thresholds for migration decisions, one is the Temperature_threshold and the other is the Utilization_threshold. In order to have a simulation-based evaluation applicable, it is important to perform experiments with workload traces of a real system. The simulation experiments [2] have demonstrated that energy consumption from a CPU utilization rate of 90% rises very quickly. Therefore we have chosen a value of 0.9 as the Utilization_threshold. If the CPU utilization reaches this threshold, the VMs running on it may be migrated to another host with lower CPU usage. The selection of the Temperature_threshold is not as easy as the Utilization_threshold. In the following subsection we demonstrate how we achieved an optimal threshold of 343 Kelvin with a trade-off between power consumption and SLA violation.

5.2 Simulation Results

The first experiment was performed for studying the impact of the Temperature_threshold. Figure 2 demonstrates the experimental results. The upper picture in the figure depicts the impact on the energy consumption and the middle one shows the resulted number of migrations by different thresholds, while the lower figure depicts the impact of the threshold on the Service Level Agreement (SLA) violations. The thresholds range from 333 to 360, as presented in the x-axis. The SLA violation metric represents the percentage of unallocated CPU performance relative to the total requested performance in the workloads.

Observing all three diagrams, it can be seen that the lines can be divided into four areas with different impact values, as marked in the upper diagram. In the first area, i.e., the Temperature_threshold between 333K (initial temperature) and 335K, the energy consumption remains constant and its value is 52 KWh per day. Our ThaS scheduler only decides to migrate the VMs when the temperature of the source host has reached the Temperature_threshold. If a VM should be migrated there must be a destination host with a CPU temperature below the threshold. Because, logically, all hosts have a temperature above the Temperature_threshold, our scheduler does not find any target host on which the VMs can be migrated. Hence, there is no VM migration in this area, as shown in the middle diagram. The scheduler has also no influence at all (see the lower diagram), which leads to increased and constant energy consumption and no SLA violations.

In the second region ($335K <$ Temperature_threshold $< 340K$) the effectiveness of the scheduler can be seen clearly. In contrast to the first area, the scheduler finds now hosts with temperatures below the threshold Temperature_threshold. These hosts are selected by the scheduler as the target hosts for VM migration. The number of target hosts increases as the threshold Temperature_threshold being enlarged, because with a higher threshold there must be more hosts whose temperature is below the threshold. As a result, also more VM migrations are performed as depicted in the middle diagram. As any VM migration causes a modeled CPU performance degradation of 10%, the percentage of SLA violations increases with a large number of migrations. Overall, the second area shows that i) The scheduler starts VM migration only from a certain Temperature_threshold (here 335 K); ii) The higher the threshold value for the temperature is, the more target hosts are available as candidates for VM migrations.

In the third area ($340Kelvin <$ Temperature_threshold $< 353Kelvin$), the variation of the Temperature_threshold has no influence on the power consumption any more since the number of the destination hosts ($host temperature <$ Temperature_threshold) remains constant in this region. Correspondingly the number of migrations is nearly not changed. This results in a nearly constant power consumption and SLA violation percentage.

In the fourth area ($Temperature\_threshold > 353Kelvin$) the energy consumption is reduced slightly. The reason for this is that the scheduler sets all hosts with CPU temperature over the case temperature (T_case=353 Kelvin) in the sleep mode. It moves away all running VMs on these hosts and then puts the hosts in the idle status. This mechanism results in a small reduction of energy consumption. However, a higher SLA violation is resulted, as can be seen in the lower picture, due to the fact that not all user requirements can be fulfilled with a few numbers of active hosts.

To summarize the results in Figure 2: the number of VM migrations significantly depends on the value of the Temperature_threshold; the energy consumption remains

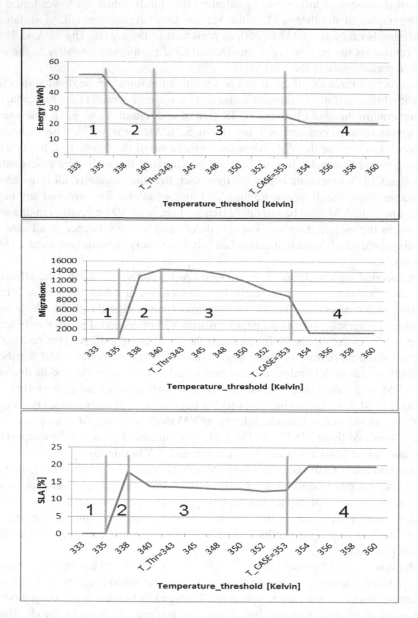

Fig. 2. The impact of Temperature_threshold on the energy consumption (upper diagram), the number of migrations (middle diagram) and the SLA violation (lower diagram)

high when no migration is possible and only after a certain threshold with the temperature VM migration is performed, which leads to a reduction of energy consumption; when the case temperature (T_case) is reached most hosts are put into sleep mode, which affects the CPU Utilization_threshold that in turn leads to a low number of VM migrations.

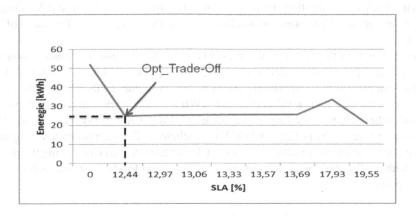

Fig. 3. Optimal trade-off for the Temperature_threshold

Our goal in thermal-aware scheduling is to minimize both the energy consumption and the SLA violation as possible. Therefore, we try in the selection of threshold values (Temperature_threshold and Utilization_threshold) to take a trade-off, where the energy consumption and the SLA violation shall both remain at a minimum. From the previous simulation results, we have observed that the third area of the different waveforms is the optimum range and the threshold value for the temperature shall be chosen from this field.

In order to give a more clear view about this optimal threshold of temperature, we created another diagram containing the energy consumption and the SLA violation. Figure 3 depicts this graph. Observing the graph in the figure, it can be seen that there is a point where both the energy and the SLA violation are low. This point (threshold 343 Kelvin) is exactly the optimal threshold we are looking for. Hence, we selected 343 Kelvin as the optimum value of the Temperature_threshold for our experiments.

To further examine the efficiency of the implemented scheduler, we compared the results of our ThaS scheme with three other scheduling schemes. The first one is Non_power_aware, which was implemented without consideration of the CPU usage. It reflects the energy consumption in a datacenter with full CPU power.

The second scheme is DVFS. It schedules tasks on basis of the CPU voltage and frequency. It relies on the information from the CPU performance and power model to set the priorities for the VM placement. No migration is performed by the DVFS scheduling. The energy consumption is calculated as a function of the CPU usage and is regulated automatically and dynamically based on DVFS.

The last scheme is Power_aware_ThrMu [2]. This scheduling algorithm focuses on minimizing the CPU usage by setting up physical hosts in the idle mode. It migrates the running VMs of a host with CPU usage over a threshold to other hosts. We choose a Utilization_threshold of 0.9 for this scheme.

In contrast, our scheduling algorithm ThaS performs VM migration based not only on the CPU usage but also on the CPU temperature. Here, we adopted the lumped RC thermal model for computing the temperature. The two thresholds in the VM migration are set with the Utilization_threshold of 0.9 and the Temperature_threshold of 343 Kelvin.

Figure 4 depicts the result of the experiment, where the energy consumption was measured during a single simulation run with all four algorithms. Comparing ThaS with the other scheduling algorithms, it can be observed that ThaS achieves the lowest energy consumption with a value of 25.64 KWh per day, while the energy consumption with other schemes are Non_power_aware of 150.68 KWh, DVFS of 52.98 KWh and Power_aware_ThrMu of 28.9 KWh. We conclude: i) The support of VM migration mechanisms is required for efficiently using Cloud resources. ii) Combining the power-aware with the thermal-aware scheduling strategies provides the best results for energy consumption.

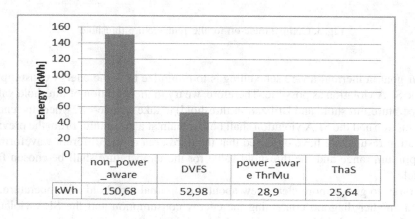

Fig. 4. Comparison of ThaS with other scheduling schemes

6 Conclusions

Scheduling is a hot topic in different scientific domains, including distributed systems, peer-to-peer environments, High Performance Computing as well as Cloud Computing. In Cloud Computing the scheduling problem concerns majorly the scheduling of virtual machines on a physical host. In this paper we propose and implement a load-aware and thermal-aware scheduling mechanism that is capable of preventing the occurrence of over-loaded or over-heated physical machines hence balancing the entire system. The validation results show the benefit of the developed mechanism in terms of energy consumption.

This is our initial work in the research field of energy issues in Cloud centers. The proposed mechanism achieves a reduction of power consumption but we still need a better algorithm for finding the best location to host a virtual machine towards the lowest energy consumption in the complete system. We are currently studying vision cognitive algorithms, which are usually used for solving global optimization problems, and will apply them to schedule the virtual machines on the Cloud. Furthermore, we will improve the accuracy of our thermal model to support multi-core CPU architectures used by current Cloud infrastructures.

References

1. Amazon Elastic Compute Cloud, http://aws.amazon.com/ec2/
2. Beloglazov, A., Buyya, R.: Optimal Online Deterministic Algorithms and Adaptive Heuristic for Energy and Performance Efficient Dynamic Consolidation of Virtual Machines in Cloud Datacenters. Concurrency and Computation: Practice and Experience 24(3), 1397–1420 (2012)
3. Beloglazov, A., Buyya, R.: Adaptive threshold-based approach for energy-efficient consolidation of virtual machines in cloud data centers. In: Proceedings of the 8th International Workshop on Middleware for Grids, Clouds and e-Science (2010)
4. Calheiros, R.N., Ranjan, R., Beloglazov, A., De Rose, C.A.F., Buyya, R.: CloudSim: A Toolkit for Modeling and Simulation of Cloud Comp uting Environments and Evaluation of Resource Provisioning Algorithms. Software: Practice and Experience 41(1), 23–50 (2011)
5. Google App Engine, http://code.google.com/appengine/
6. Hotspot, http://lava.cs.virginia.edu/HotSpot/
7. Hu, J., Gu, J., Sun, G., Zhao, T.: A Scheduling Strategy on Load Balancing of Virtual Machine Resources in Cloud Computing Environment. In: Proceedings of the International Symposium on Parallel Architectures, Algorithms and Programming, pp. 89–96 (2010)
8. Kim, D.-S., Kim, H., Jeon, M., Seo, E., Lee, J.: Guest-Aware Priority-Based Virtual Machine Scheduling for Highly Consolidated Server. In: Luque, E., Margalef, T., Benítez, D. (eds.) Euro-Par 2008. LNCS, vol. 5168, pp. 285–294. Springer, Heidelberg (2008)
9. Knauth, T., Fetzer, C.: Energy-aware scheduling for infrastructure clouds. In: Proceedings of the IEEE International Conference on Cloud Computing Technology and Science, pp. 58–65 (2012)
10. Kolodziej, J., Khan, S., Wang, L., Byrski, A., Nasro, M., Madani, S.: Hierarchical Genetic-based Grid Scheduling with Energy Optimization. In: Cluster Coimputing (2013), doi:10.1007/s10586-012-0226-7
11. Kolodziej, J., Khan, S., Wang, L., Kisiel-Dorohinicki, M., Madani, S.: Security, Energy, and Performance-aware Resource Allocation Mechanisms for Computational Grids. In: Future Generation Computer Systems (2012), doi:10.1016/j.future.2012.09.009
12. Kolodziej, J., Khan, S., Wang, L., Zomaya, A.: Energy Efficient Genetic-Based Schedulers in Computational Grids. In: Concurrency and Computation: Practice & Experience (2013), doi:10.1002/cpe.2839
13. Lin, S., Qiu, M.: Thermal-Aware Scheduling for Peak Temperature Reduction with Stochastic Workloads. In: Proceedins of IEEE/ACM RTAS WIP, pp. 53–56 (April 2010)
14. Manzak, A., Chakrabarti, C.: Variable voltage task scheduling algorithms for minimizing energy/power. IEEE Transactions on Very Large Scale Integration System 11(2), 270–276 (2003)

15. Martin, S., Flautner, K., Mudge, T., Blaauw, D.: Combined dynamic voltage scaling and adaptive body biasing for lower power microprocessors under dynamic workloads. In: Proceedings of the 2002 IEEE/ACM International Conference on Computer-aided Design, pp. 721–725 (2002)
16. Mell, P., Grance, T.: The NIST Definition of Cloud Computing, http://csrc.nist.gov/publications/drafts/800-145/Draft-SP-800-145_cloud-definition.pdf
17. Menzel, M., Ranjan, R.: CloudGenius: Decision Support for Web Service Cloud Migration. In: Proceedings of the International ACM Conference on World Wide Web (WWW 2012), Lyon, France (April 2012)
18. The Rackspace Open Cloud, http://www.rackspace.com/cloud/
19. Ranjan, R., Buyya, R., Harwood, A.: A Case for Cooperative and Incentive Based Coupling of Distributed Clusters. In: Proceedings of the 7th IEEE International Conference on Cluster Computing (Cluster 2005), Boston, Massachusetts, USA, pp. 1–11 (September 2005)
20. Ranjan, R., Harwood, A., Buyya, R.: A SLA-Based Coordinated Super scheduling Scheme and Performance for Computational Grids. In: Proceedings of the 8th IEEE International Conference on Cluster Computing (Cluster 2006), Barcelona, Spain, pp. 1–8 (September 2006)
21. Skadron, K., Abdelzaher, T., Stan, M.R.: Control-theoretic techniques and thermal-rc modeling for accurate and localized dynamic thermal management. In: Proceedings of the 8th International Symposium on High-Performance Computer Architecture, HPCA 2002, p. 17. IEEE Computer Society, Washington, DC (2002)
22. SpecPower08, http://www.spec.org
23. Wang, L., Khan, S.: Review of performance metrics for green data centers: a taxonomy study. The Journal of Supercomputing 63(3), 639–656 (2013)
24. Wang, L., Khan, S., Chen, D., Kolodziej, J., Ranjan, R., Xu, C., Zomaya, A.: Energy-aware parallel task scheduling in a cluster. Future Generation Computer Systems 29(7), 1661–1670 (2013)
25. Wang, L., Khan, S., Dayal, J.: Thermal aware workload placement with task-temperature profiles in a data center. The Journal of Supercomputing 61(3), 780–803 (2012)
26. Wang, L., Laszewski, G., Younge, A., He, X., Kunze, M., Tao, J., Fu, C.: Cloud Computing: a Perspective Study. New Generation Computing 28(2), 137–146 (2010)
27. Wang, L., Tao, J., von Laszewski, G., Chen, D.: Power Aware Scheduling for Parallel Tasks via Task Clustering. In: Proceedings of the IEEE 16th International Conference on Parallel and Distributed Systems, ICPADS (2010)
28. Wang, Y., Wang, X., Chen, Y.: Energy-efficient virtual machine scheduling in performance-asymmetric multi-core architectures. In: Proceedings of the 8th International Conference on Network and Service Management and 2012 Workshop on Systems Virtualiztion Management, pp. 288–294 (2012)
29. Windows Azure Platform, http://www.microsoft.com/windowsazure
30. Zhang, S., Chatha, K.S.: Approximation Algorithm for the Temperature-aware Scheduling Problem. In: Proceedins of IEEE/ACM International Conference on Computer-Aided Design, pp. 281–288 (November 2007)

Optimistic Concurrency Control for Energy Efficiency in the Wireless Environment

Kamal Solamain, Matthew Brook, Gary Ushaw, and Graham Morgan

School of Computing Science, Newcastle University, Newcastle-upon-Tyne, UK

Abstract. The ubiquity of smart portable devices has led to concurrency control for the mobile network becoming an area of growing concern. Conventional optimistic concurrency control techniques require retries of failed or disputed transactions, which place additional drain on the energy consumption of both the network and the smart device. We present a Distributed Later Validation Earlier Write Optimistic Concurrency Control (DLVEW) algorithm to efficiently handle transactions running on the server side without disturbing transactions running on clients. Our simulation shows an increase in throughput and reduction in both the response time and the number of missed deadlines of transactions. The corresponding reduction in contentious transactions needing to be restarted leads to a lower power cost for the network as a whole.

1 Introduction

Smartphone applications are placing greater demands on energy resources. Millions of smartphones and tablet devices are being used for more complex tasks, so the power consumption of the servers and network is increasing, and the battery recharge life of each phone or tablet is becoming shorter. An algorithm which reduces the energy cost of a transaction between a client (i.e. the phone) and the server will multiply to a significant energy saving across all devices in use. In particular, if the number of failed transactions due to contention can be reduced, thereby lowering the number of times a transaction must be repeated, then the overall power consumption will also be reduced.

Many applications require an asymmetrical channel whereby the frequency of read transactions requested by the client is significantly higher than the number of write transactions. Taking the example of a stock trading application; there are far more transactions involving a read-only checking of stock prices, compared to the number of transactions involving a sale or other event requiring an update transaction (i.e. users typically check far more share prices than they buy shares). A common implementation of this type of application involves the use of a broadcast disk protocol [1], whereby the database is repeatedly broadcast to the clients in its entirety. This approach means that there is no requirement for the client to send a read request to the server; the client simply waits for the requested piece of data to appear in the cycled transmission, and the server does not have to respond to individual client requests to send data. Clearly this greatly reduces the amount of traffic on the network, and the amount of requests

J. Kołodziej et al. (Eds.): ICA3PP 2013, Part I, LNCS 8285, pp. 115–128, 2013.

which the server must process. This type of approach is particularly useful when a relatively small database must be read by many clients.

Earlier studies on transaction processing in wireless environments were focused on read-only transactions [2] [3] [4]. Update transactions must also be considered. Optimistic Concurrency Control (OCC) is a well-understood solution for this type of situation [5]. However these protocols tend to involve heavy use of the network in both directions to request and validate read transactions, which renders the approach less applicable to mobile networks [2] due to limited uplink bandwidth and battery life. In [6] Lee proposed a variant of the OCC algorithm suitable for a broadcast environment known as forward and backward optimistic concurrency control (FBOCC). This algorithm performs partial backward validation [7] against committed transactions at the beginning of every broadcast cycle at mobile clients. It also performs forward validation [7] against concurrently running transactions at the server (including both server transactions and update mobile transactions).

In this paper we develop a DLVEW algorithm for broadcast disk which is more efficient at handling concurrently running transactions at the server without disturbing transactions running on the client. We achieve this by changing the ordering of the validate step at the server so that it takes place after the write step (conventionally it occurs before writing). In [8] we showed that this approach is applicable as optimistic concurrency control on resource-constrained devices such as smart-phones. We now extend this work to the broadcast disk model for mobile network applications that require significantly more read transactions than write transactions. Our results show that, with this technique, the number of client-server transactions which miss their deadline due to concurrency issues is reduced. The non-intuitive ordering of the validation phase, combined with the requirement of a rerun policy, improves efficiency while reducing the energy consumption of the network.

2   Background and Related Work

2.1   Broadcast Disk and Optimistic Concurrency Control

Many studies have proposed transmitting data over wireless networks using data broadcasting techniques [9] [10]. The broadcast disk protocol continuously broadcasts all data objects in the database. Clients view this broadcast as a disk, accessing required data as it is broadcast. The number of mobile devices does not affect their access time (as it is read-only). This approach makes conventional concurrency control techniques inapplicable [2]. E.g. using locking techniques could lead to swamping the server with lock requests. Similarly for timestamp based techniques, communication between clients and the server is needed for every read operation to keep track of both read and write timestamp; this can be unwieldy in broadcast environments. Conventional OCC [5] cannot be directly applied to mobile transaction processing because of the communications which consume the limited uplink bandwidth and battery power [6].

The optimistic concurrency control approach using a three-phased transaction execution consisting of read, validate and write (RVW) phases was described in [5]. During the read phase of a transaction, clients access data without restriction and make their own local copy of this data. If any writes are required, they are made to the client's local copy before the validation phase is entered. The validation phase ensures that any changes a client has made locally can be satisfied globally. Other executing transactions are considered to determine whether the write requests made locally can be satisfied without invalidating the overall read-write schedule. If the write requests are valid then the transaction moves onto the write phase and the local changes are committed to the persistent store at the server. Otherwise, the transaction must abort and restart.

Harder [7] proposed two schemes for the validation phase: Backward Oriented Optimistic Concurrency Control (BOCC) and Forward Oriented Optimistic Concurrency Control (FOCC). BOCC operates by comparing the read set of a validating transaction with the write sets of all currently executing transactions that have finished the read phase before the validating transaction. If a conflict is identified then the validating transaction must be aborted and restarted in its entirety. FOCC, on the other hand, is based on comparing the write set of the validating transaction with the read sets of all currently executing transactions that have yet to finish the read phase. When a conflict is found, FOCC provides a degree of flexibility in that a number of resolution policies are possible. It is this flexibility in resolution policy which has made FOCC the focus of further works [11]. However, aborting validating transactions is expensive because such transactions have used resources and completed execution. The Never Abort Validating transactions (NAV) strategy ensures that these resources will not be wasted by guaranteeing that the validating transaction commits [12]. However, a major drawback of FOCC is that concurrent transactions have to be blocked in their read phase while validating transactions are executing the validation and write phase in a critical section.

Virtual execution [13] involves pre-fetching data which will be required for a subsequent rerun of an aborted transaction. The approach enables transactions that are known to be in conflict to continue execution and complete the read phase, in order to pre-fetch the data that will be required for the subsequent rerun. Significant performance gains can be made when allowing the transaction to rerun using the pre-fetched data, due to access invariance. There is typically no disk I/O overhead required for the transaction during rerun. Significantly, battery power savings can be gained by deploying such a technique on mobile devices [14]. However, the issue of consistency arises for a transaction that operates using pre-fetched data as some of the pre-fetched data may have since been modified.

Lee has proposed a variant of the OCC algorithm called forward and backward optimistic concurrency control (FBOCC) [6]. FBOCC is a concurrency control algorithm suitable for mobile transactions in wireless broadcast environments. It consists of two validation stages. Partial backward validation is performed at clients between the write set of committed transactions at the server and the read set of running transactions at the client at the beginning of every data cycle. This includes both read-only transactions and update transactions. Any conflicted transaction will be aborted. Successfully validated read-only mobile transactions will proceed to commit locally. Successfully validated mobile updated transactions are sent to the server to be validated globally. Forward validation is performed at the server between the write set of validating transactions and the read set of running transactions. This includes transactions generated and executed at the server, and update transactions which are sent for validation by clients to the server. Server conflicted transactions will be aborted. Conflicted update transactions will be aborted and will restart at the client. Update transactions must perform final partial backward validation at the server before starting forward validation. This final validation is needed in case of existing update transactions committed at the server since the last backward validation performed at the client. FBOCC is designed to minimize the use of the uplink channel in two ways: validation of read-only transactions locally at clients (these constitute the majority of mobile transactions); and early validating and aborting update transactions locally at clients, which makes update transactions more likely to pass the validation and write phases at the server.

2.2   Real-Time Requirements and Phase Ordering

The LVEW algorithm [8] [14] changes the order of the traditional RVW phases. The write phase now follows the read phase with validation occurring after the write is complete. In addition to the reordering of the phases the algorithm makes use of a rerun policy. Transactions are rolled back using in-memory data derived from retaining a buffer that records the writes of committing transactions and the reads of uncommitted transactions. Moving the validation phase ensures the nearest to expiring transaction (i.e. the closest to reaching its deadline) is afforded priority to commit. Also, there is no need to block concurrently running transactions during the write and validation phases. This promotes real-time efficiency and allows greater determinism. Writes become visible to transactions in the read phase earlier, affording more likelihood of reading up-to-date data.

In [14] we made two observations when considering real-time requirements. Firstly, transactions that enter rerun execute quicker than those in their initial run (as there is likely to be no disk access). Secondly, the validation phase presents a degree of non-determinism with respect to how long it will take (i.e. we can't predict how many transactions require validation). Reruns can occur multiple times with minimal hindrance to transaction deadlines, as they execute with no disk latency. It would therefore be advantageous to keep transactions in rerun until we can deterministically say that, when a transaction leaves rerun, it will complete and meet its deadline, irrelevant of the delay imposed by the validation step. This would provide prioritization of rerun transactions without the concern for non-deterministic latency during the validation phase.

In [8] we applied this thinking to concurrent transactions on the shared resources of a smart device. The use of a virtual execution enabled OCC coupled with the reordering of the validation and write phases allowed for an overall improvement in performance. When transactions are in a rerun state we can off-set their validation until after the write phase of a transaction. The first benefit of this approach is that writes may become visible to transactions in the read phase earlier, affording more likelihood of reading up-to-date data. Secondly, overall blocking may be reduced, as in the original OCC protocols, transactions in the read phase will need to be blocked as a transaction commits changes to the database (to prevent out of date reads from the database). Such blocking would not be required, as out of date reads will be caught by the later validation step.

2.3   Energy Efficiency

An important objective of much of the work on concurrency control for mobile networks is to reduce the energy consumption, especially the battery life of the mobile devices. Much of the literature makes the point that conventional OCC techniques are less suited to mobile applications for this reason [6] [11] [15]. Accessing a conventional hard disk drive is expensive in terms of power usage, as the disk must attain read speed, and the appropriate data sector be found. Even solid state drives are significantly more expensive to access compared to local memory. Consequently reducing the number of times that a disk is accessed will reduce the energy consumed. Clearly a reduction in the frequency of transactions that must be rerun will reduce the amount of disk accesses which must be instigated, leading to a reduction in the energy usage. In general, it is better to perform execution at the fixed server, rather than at a mobile client [16]; this thinking can also be applied to concurrency resolution. Any energy saving achieved at the mobile device must be offset against the additional energy cost caused by any increase in communication over the network [17]. A protocol based on broadcast disk, which reduces the amount of validation messages going back and forth between clients and server, appears to meet this constraint.

2.4   Contribution

The background described in this section leads to the contribution made by this paper. Whereas previous work [18] [19] has described developments for the broadcast disk protocol which improve the client performance, we concentrate on the behaviour at the server. Our improvements are compatible with that existing work on client efficiency. We describe a new optimistic concurrency control algorithm suitable for a wireless broadcast environment in which the write phase occurs before the validation phase at the server. This approach has shown improvement in overall system throughput and the likelihood that transactions complete within their specified deadline.

We also deploy a rerun policy at the client. This reduces the access cost in the read phase when a transaction is aborted; this consequently reduces the battery usage in the mobile device. Additionally we show a reduction of the effect of the conflict increase rate on transaction results due to the increase of throughput rate at the server. Our work allows a server to resolve more contention, and therefore increases mobile devices' performance, while reducing the energy cost due to retrying failed or conflicted transactions.

3 Protocol

We describe a read-write-validation approach to optimistic concurrency control for energy efficiency of transaction processing in a wireless broadcast disk environment. We also present pseudo-code to describe the algorithms execution. Our protocol builds on the FBOCC protocol proposed in [6] by performing a LVEW algorithm for validation at the server. The algorithm is performed in two stages.

3.1 Partial Backward Validation at Mobile Clients

All running transactions at clients (i.e. both the read-only transactions and update transactions) are validated at the beginning of every broadcast cycle by performing backward validation with the write set of committed transactions at the server. Conflicted transactions are marked for rerun, but continue execution until the end of the read phase in order to pre-fetch all read set data to memory [13]. When a conflicted transaction reaches the end of the read phase, we update the conflicted data objects in memory and rerun without accessing the persistent store. Optimistic concurrency control performs better if transactions are allowed to reach the end of their read phase before being aborted [20]. This is intuitive, as transactions that have been aborted early have not retrieved all the required data for the rerun phase. Rerun policy has a significant impact in saving battery power consumption in resource-constrained clients such as mobile devices [18] [14]. Not conflicted read-only transactions can proceed and commit locally at the client. Not conflicted update transactions will be sent to the server in order to be validated globally.

Pseudo-code for partial backward validation is presented as follows:

Algorithm 3.1. PARTIALBACKWARDVALIDATION(T_m)

$$\textbf{if } (C_i \cap RS(T_m)) \neq 0$$

$$\textbf{then} \begin{cases} \textbf{for } \text{ each } O_k \text{ in } (C_i \cap RS(T_m)) \Big\{ \textbf{ do } \text{update } O_k \text{ in } CS(T_m) \\ \textbf{if } T_m \text{ is in initial run} \\ \quad \textbf{then } \text{mark } T_m \text{ for rerun} \\ \quad \textbf{else } \begin{cases} \text{update } T_m \text{ with } CS(T_m) \\ \text{rerun } T_m \end{cases} \end{cases}$$

$$\textbf{else } \text{store the data in } C_i$$

T_m is the transaction generated at the client. ControlInfo(C_i) os the set of data items which was updated. Conflicted Set (CS) given $CS(T_m)$, this contains the updated values from C_i and T_m has been found to conflict with. Each item (O_k) in $CS(T_m)$ is cached until $RS(T_m)$ can be updated with these updated values. We choose to cache these values rather than directly update the read set of T_m

so as to make it clear that the calculations (writes) would not be automatically updated if we chose to update $RS(T_m)$ directly. $RS(T_m)$ can be updated when T_m has finished the initial run or, if it is in rerun, when it is aborted. Upon updating, $CS(T_m)$ is discarded.

We assume that a transaction which is executing in the read phase reads the required data and performs any necessary computation. Similarly, a transaction which is in the commit phase will update any values that were written to during its read phase. The scheduler will handle rerunning transactions that have been marked for rerun, along with the process of updating the read sets for conflicting transactions.

3.2 LVEW and Final Validation at the Server

One of the transactions which are ready to commit will be chosen to enter the write phase by the scheduler. We employ an earliest deadline policy to give priority to transactions that are closest to deadline expiration. Once this transaction has completed the write phase, it performs forward validation against all concurrently running transactions at the server [8] [14]. This includes locally generated transactions and update transactions that have been received from clients for global validation. Any locally generated conflicted transactions will be marked for rerun. They will continue executing until the end of the read phase in the first run as described previously. Conflicted update mobile transactions will be aborted and rerun again at the client. When a validating transaction finishes the write and validation phases, the write set will be broadcast in the next broadcast cycle with the control information table. This information is used for partial backward validation at clients to keep mobile transactions consistent. However, update transactions have to perform final backward validation with any possibly committed transactions after the update transaction has finished partial validation at the client, and before starting LVEW validation at the server [18] [6]. The results of this validation (commit or abort) will also be included in the information table as acknowledgment to the mobile client for further actions.

3.3 Justifying Read-Write-Validate

This approach fundamentally changes the order of the traditional transactional phases as introduced in [5]. The write phase now follows the read phase with the validation phase now occurring after the write phase. Both the write and validation phases are collectively considered a single critical section, so only one transaction is allowed to be executing in either of these phases (adopted widely and described originally in [5]). We use a forward validation strategy in combination with a No Sacrifice policy [15] that guarantees a transaction entering the critical section will commit. This means that transactions which conflict with the validating transaction must be aborted. We choose to employ a rerun policy so that transactions in their initial run will continue to the end of the read phase before being rerun.

By combining the write and validation phases into a single critical section, the ordering of transactions becomes trivial as we can guarantee system correctness based on serializability criteria in either scheme. However, without using forward validation coupled with a No Sacrifice policy, it would be more costly to employ a RWV ordering. Without these mechanisms, if a validating transaction is aborted, it would be expensive to undo the changes made during the write. This would also result in an increased number of conflicts due to any transactions that have accessed the same data having to be aborted or rerun. With the addition of a rerun policy we see further performance improvements when combined with a RWV ordering.

Real-time transactional databases need to handle transactions with timing constraints in the form of deadlines. Upon arrival, a transaction must be processed in a timely fashion to ensure that the changes made during the read phase are successfully committed to the database before a deadline is reached. Factors such as system contention have a direct impact on satisfying transactional deadlines. Such factors occur during validation. Therefore in the traditional OCC phase ordering the validation step introduces a degree of non-determinism with regards to how long writes will take to become visible in the database (delaying entry to the write phase). The validation phase is required to ensure system correctness with regards to transactions that are still executing, rather than providing a direct benefit to the validating transaction itself. If the write phase is brought before the validation phase then we remove the non-deterministic timing constraints of the validation phase allowing the transaction to commit sooner. Consistency is still maintained in a virtual execution environment as the validation phase will detect transactions that are in conflict during rerun stages.

By altering the phase ordering we also remove a degree of blocking present in the original FOCC based on read-validate-write ordering (RVW). Under RVW a transaction executing in the read phase will eventually have to be blocked to allow a transaction in the critical section to complete. If any of these read-phase transactions which do not conflict with the validating transaction are allowed continuing execution, they may potentially enter a conflicted state. This will arise if a future value is read by a transaction in the read phase that is shared with the write set of a committing transaction. There will be ambiguity as to which value would have been read (the one written by the committing transaction or the old value). In essence, this undetected conflicted transaction will read inconsistent data that the validating transaction will have modified during the write phase. As a result, all concurrently running transactions must be blocked to allow the validating transaction to commit. Any newly arriving transactions will also be blocked from entering the read phase during this time to avoid further conflict. By employing a read-write-validate (RWV) ordering, we no longer have to block any transaction from progressing (we do not consider the transactions waiting to enter the critical section as being blocked). Having completed the write phase, a validating transaction will only need to validate against transactions that were active while the validating transaction was writing. These active transactions may have read data that has now been updated. Any newly arriving transactions (those arriving while a transaction is validating) cannot conflict with the validating transaction, as the data they read will have already been updated.

Pseudo-code for LVEW and final validation using the same notation explained in the section on partial backward validation is presented as follows:

Algorithm 3.2. SERVERVALIDATION(T_v)

comment: 1 Final backward validation:

for each T_i (i = 1...n) $\begin{cases} \textbf{if } (RS(T_v) \cap WS(T_i) \neq 0) \\ \quad \textbf{then return} \text{ (fail)} \end{cases}$

comment: 2 Write:

Commit $WS(T_v)$ to database
$C_i = C_i \cup WS(T_v)$

comment: 3 Forward validation:

for each T_j (j = 1...n) $\begin{cases} \textbf{if } (WS(T_v) \cap RS(T_j) \neq 0) \\ \quad \textbf{then abort } T_j \end{cases}$

Our approach is orthogonal to the back-off method [18] and the OCC for broadcast disks scheme [19]. That is to say, both of these approaches can be combined with our work.

4   Simulation and Results

We describe the simulation model which we have used to demonstrate our protocol, providing a brief overview of the structure of the model and the parameters that were used. We then discuss the results by comparing the performance of our simulated model with the a simulation of the original protocol FBOCC [6].

4.1   Simulation Environment

We have developed a simulation model that is based on the model presented in [6] [18] [19]. We have increased the transaction arrival rate at the server by a factor of 100 to a figure representative of current applications. The model was also extended slightly in order to accommodate the rerun of transactions and the format of our LVEW validation protocol, for meaningful comparison. The model investigates different performance characteristics of our protocol versus FBOCC combined with virtual execution. We present a range of results which highlight the performance benefits of LVEW validation using a virtual execution policy. The simulation model consists of a server, a client, and the broadcast disk structure. Only one client was used in our simulation, to provide direct comparison to the existing work; the work is built upon broadcast disk implementations where the read transaction is carried out entirely on the client (so the number of clients is irrelevant), and mobile update transactions are relatively rare. The

Table 1. Parameters used in the simulation experiments

Parameter	Value
Server	
Transaction length	8
Read operation probability	0.5
Disk access time	1000
Transaction arrival rate	1 per 20000 to 1 per 1667
Concurrency control protocol	OCC with LVEW
Priority scheduling	Earliest deadline first
Client	
Transaction length	4
Read operation probability	0.5
Fraction of read only transactions	0.75
Minimum slack factor	2 (uniformly distributed)
Maximum slack factor	8 (uniformly distributed)
Mean inter-operation delay	65536
Mean inter-transaction delay	131072

server executes the server transactions based on conventional FV and LVEW algorithms. The deadline of transactions is calculated by the following formula:

Deadline = arrival Time + uniform (Minimum Slack factor, Maximum Slack factor) * execution time

Execution time is estimated using the values of transaction length, CPU time and disk access (mean inter-operation delay in mobile transaction). Table 1 shows the parameters which were used during the simulation experiments. The time unit is in bit-time, which is the time to transmit a single bit. For a broadcast bandwidth of 64 kbps, 1 M bit-time is equivalent to approximately 15s.

4.2   Simulation Results

Due to the real-time nature of the application domain, our experiments focus on measuring the miss rate percentage, which is the percentage of transactions missing their deadlines. Another performance metric is the throughput which is strongly connected to miss rate; throughput is the number of transactions committed per time unit. Figures 1-3 show the throughput, average response time and miss rate of server transactions. Figures 4-7 show the throughput and miss rate of clients transactions. In each graph we present the results of two protocols: DLVEW and FBOCC.

Figure 1 shows the throughput for an increasing rate of transactions. We define throughput as the number of committed transactions, with the commit occurring at the end of the write phase for both phase orderings. All protocols share a common progression; of particular interest is the point that is reached in both sets of data where contention is too high and the throughput starts to degrade. The number of transactions which miss their deadline (fig 3) is also impacting the throughput, as these transactions are aborted and will never

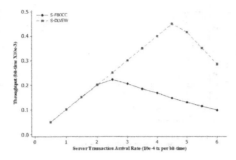

Fig. 1. Throughput at the server

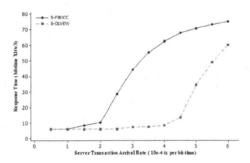

Fig. 2. Response time at the server

commit. As the rate increases, the number of late transactions increases and so the throughput falls.

Figure 2 shows the average response time for an increasing rate of transactions. The response time is only included for transactions that successfully commit. As the rate increases, the transaction response time increases due to high contention. We see that, between 1 and $6*(10^{-4})$ transactions per bit-time, the LV approach has a lower response time than FV. This indicates that the cost of the validation phase does not affect the transactions commit time in our approach. The response time stabilizes after 80000 bit-time due to the deadline assignment; only transactions that have a sufficiently large deadline will be able to commit. Regardless of the benefits of our protocol, at this level of contention, transactions expire during the initial run in the read phase.

Figure 3 shows the percentage of transactions which miss their deadline. For each protocol, as the rate increases, the percentage of missed deadlines also increases. Between 2 and $6*(10^{-4})$ transactions per bit-time, the LV approach has a lower miss rate than FV. With a high level of system contention, transactions experience longer delays in accessing the disk and the CPU. This results in transactions being more likely to miss the deadline during the initial run and never entering rerun.

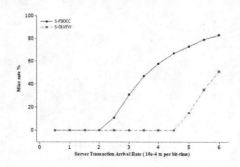

Fig. 3. Miss rate at the server

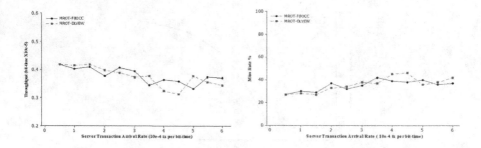

Fig. 4. Throughput and miss rate of read only transactions at clients

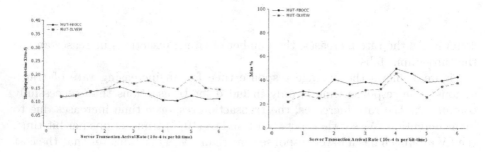

Fig. 5. Throughput and miss rate of update transactions at clients

Figure 4 shows the miss rate and throughput of mobile read only transactions. The figures demonstrate that both protocols generate similar results. This result was expected because read only transactions execute and commit locally in the client.

Figure 5 shows the miss rate and throughput of update mobile transactions. Figure 5a illustrates that the throughput of both protocols is similar when contention at the server is low. The LV protocol demonstrates higher throughput whenever the server transaction arrival rate has increased. Figure 5b shows that the miss rate of the LV protocol is always lower than the miss rate of the FV protocol in all contentions, which is convenient for real-time mobile applications.

5 Conclusions

In [8] we identified the possibility that, in combination with virtual execution, a performance improvement could be made by allowing the write phase to be accomplished before the validation phase . In [8] [14] we explored this idea in the context of multiple applications running concurrently on a resource-constrained device. We showed that, not only does this reversal maintain correctness, it also brings performance benefits. This is particularly evident for real-time systems. In this paper we deploy our approach to further develop forward backward optimistic concurrency control for mobile transactions in the wireless environment.

We have developed a simulation of this technique (using an appropriate simulation as used by earlier works in the area) in order to demonstrate the performance. We have then benchmarked the results from these tests against the original FBOCC approach combined with a virtual execution model. We have shown that our approach significantly improves both the throughput and the miss rate of the overall system when compared to the original technique. We have simulated 100x more frequent transaction arrivals than the previous works, to reflect the modern usage of the technology.

Our seemingly counter-intuitive idea of changing the phase order to read-write-validate, combined with virtual execution, requires significantly fewer accesses of the server data, and completely eliminates blocking transactions at the read phase. This leads to resolving more contention by a more able server, and therefore increases mobile devices performance, while reducing the energy cost due to retrying failed or conflicted transactions.

References

1. Acharya, S., Alonso, R., Franklin, M., Zdonik, S.: Broadcast disks: data management for asymmetric communication environments. ACM SIGMOD Record 24, 199–210 (1995)
2. Shanmugasundaram, J., Nithrakashyap, A., Sivasankaran, R., Ramamritham, K.: Efficient concurrency control for broadcast environments. ACM SIGMOD Record 28(2), 85–96 (1999)
3. Pitoura, E., Chrysanthis, P.K.: Scalable processing of read-only transactions in broadcast push. In: Proceedings of 19th IEEE International Conference on Distributed Computing Systems, pp. 432–439. IEEE (1999)
4. Barbará, D.: Certification reports: supporting transactions in wireless systems. In: Proceedings of the 17th International Conference on Distributed Computing Systems, pp. 466–473. IEEE (1997)
5. Kung, H.T., Robinson, J.T.: On optimistic methods for concurrency control. ACM Transactions on Database Systems (TODS) 6, 213–226 (1981)
6. Lee, V.C.S., Lam, K.W., Kuo, T.W.: Efficient validation of mobile transactions in wireless environments. Journal of Systems and Software 69(1-2), 183–193 (2004)

7. Härder, T.: Observations on optimistic concurrency control schemes. Information Systems 9(2), 111–120 (1984)
8. Solaiman, K., Brook, M., Ushaw, G., Morgan, G.: A read-write-validate approach to optimistic concurrency control for energy efficiency of resource-constrained systems. In: Proceedings of the 9th International Wireless Communications and Mobile Computing Conference. IEEE (2013)
9. Juran, J., Hurson, A., Vijaykrishnan, N., Kim, S.: Data organization and retrieval on parallel air channels: Performance and energy issues. Wireless Networks 10(2), 183–195 (2004)
10. Lee, V.C., Lam, K.W., Son, S.H., Chan, E.Y.: On transaction processing with partial validation and timestamp ordering in mobile broadcast environments. IEEE Transactions on Computers 51(10), 1196–1211 (2002)
11. Lee, J.: Precise serialization for optimistic concurrency control. Data & Knowledge Engineering 29(2), 163–178 (1999)
12. Huang, J., Stankovic, J.: Concurrency control in real-time database systems: Optimistic scheme vs. two-phase locking. Univ. of Messachusetts, COINS Technical Report, 90–66 (1990)
13. Franaszek, P.A., Robinson, J.T., Thomasian, A.: Access invariance and its use in high contention environments. In: Proceedings of Sixth International Conference on Data Engineering, pp. 47–55. IEEE (1990)
14. Solaiman, K., Morgan, G.: Later validation/earlier write: Concurrency control for resource-constrained systems with real-time properties. In: 2011 30th IEEE Symposium on Reliable Distributed Systems Workshops (SRDSW), pp. 9–12. IEEE (2011)
15. Lee, J.: Concurrency control algorithms for real-time database systems. PhD thesis, Citeseer (1994)
16. Kumar Madria, S., Mohania, M., Bhowmick, S.S., Bhargava, B.: Mobile data and transaction management. Information Sciences 141(3), 279–309 (2002)
17. Miettinen, A.P., Nurminen, J.K.: Energy efficiency of mobile clients in cloud computing. In: Proceedings of the 2nd USENIX Conference on Hot Topics in Cloud Computing, p. 4. USENIX Association (2010)
18. Park, S., Jung, S.: An energy-efficient mobile transaction processing method using random back-off in wireless broadcast environments. Journal of Systems and Software 82(12), 2012–2022 (2009)
19. Jung, S., Choi, K.: A concurrency control scheme for mobile transactions in broadcast disk environments. Data & Knowledge Engineering 68(10), 926–945 (2009)
20. Yu, P.S., Dias, D.M.: Analysis of hybrid concurrency control schemes for a high data contention environment. IEEE Transactions on Software Engineering 18(2), 118–129 (1992)

POIGEM: A Programming-Oriented Instruction Level GPU Energy Model for CUDA Program

Qi Zhao, Hailong Yang, Zhongzhi Luan, and Depei Qian

Sino-German Joint Software Institute,
Department of Computer Science and Engineering,
Beihang University, No.37, Xuanyuan Road, Beijing 100191, China
{qi.zhao,hailong.yang,zhongzhi.luan,depei.qian}@jsi.buaa.edu.cn

Abstract. GPU architectures tend to be increasingly important in multi-core era nowadays due to their formidable computational horsepower. With the assistant of effective programming paradigms as CUDA, GPUs are widely adopted to accelerate scientific applications. Meanwhile, the surging energy consumption by GPUs becomes a major challenge to both GPU architects and programmers. In addition to the efforts designing energy efficient GPU architecture, comprehensive understanding on how programming affects the energy consumption of GPU application is also indispensable from the programmer perspective.

In this paper, we present a programming-oriented PTX instruction level energy model to provide programmers the ability of predicting the energy consumption of their program. Distinct from previous models which require hardware performance counters or architectural simulations, our model relies on the PTX instruction of a CUDA program which is not only portable but also accurate. With the selected PTX instructions based on empirical study, we apply linear regression to build the GPU energy model. One appealing advantage of our model is that it does not require any instrumentation or profiling of the GPU application during execution. Actually, our model is able to advise the programmers step by step to illustrate how their way of programming impacts the final energy consumption, especially at the stage of hacking the codes. Our model is evaluated on NVIDIA GeForce GTX 470 with Rodinia benchmark suites. The results show the accuracy of our model is promising with average prediction error below 3.7%. With the help of our GPU energy model, the programmers are gaining valuable insights to improve the energy efficiency of the application.

Keywords: Programming-oriented, Instruction level, Energy prediction, CUDA.

1 Introduction

With the rapid development of CMOS technology and the increase of the number of transistors on chips as the Moore's Law dictates, the energy consumption of chip is rising up simultaneously. Such unsustainable energy consumption hinders the further elevation of the chip performance. What's worse, with power

J. Kołodziej et al. (Eds.): ICA3PP 2013, Part I, LNCS 8285, pp. 129–142, 2013.

densities doubling every 18-24 months as shown in Figure 1 and large-scale HPC systems and datacenter continuing to increase in scale, the energy consumed by these facilities becomes dominant and contributes a significant portion of the entire operational cost. Meanwhile, graphics processing units (GPUs) have been widely used in HPC systems and modern heterogenous datacenter. Nowadays, the prominent computing horse power of GPUs grants them dramatically higher performance than their CPU counterpart. Consequently, GPUs are pervasively utilized to accelerate a wide variety of scientific applications [1]. This trend has been promoted with the recent advancements in programming paradigms as CUDA [2], which greatly simplify the way to exploit the tremendous computation capacity of GPUs for general purpose applications. However, while delivering substantial computation power with a large number of processor cores and abundant memory bandwidth, GPUs have consumed considerable energy at the same time. Therefore, it is important to take the factor of energy efficiency into consideration when programming GPU applications. Specifically, comprehensive understanding on how programming affects the energy consumption of GPU applications is missing and how to optimize GPU applications to achieve higher energy efficiency still remains a challenge.

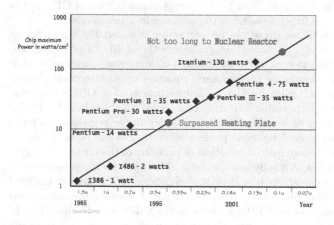

Fig. 1. Moore's Law for power consumption [3]

Although it is indispensable to acquire the ability to measure GPU power consumption accurately before further investigating the energy issues, existing approaches to GPU power measurement are quite deficient. Since the current GPUs are not equipped with internal power sensors, the GPU power is either observed from a separate power meter or deduced from the probed voltage and current on the GPUs. Such approaches require additional hardware devices and are not practical solutions, whereas software approaches to estimate the power consumption are still in the early stages, which could not provide accurate power prediction for GPU applications due to its coarse granularity. Moreover, the existing approaches primarily rely on performance profiling and cannot provide any insight on energy consumption from programming perspective.

CUDA, proposed by NVIDIA, is a widely accepted programming paradigm for general purpose computing in both academia and industry. Thus it would be representative to understand the energy consumption of GPUs in terms of CUDA program. In particular, how CUDA program impacts the GPU energy consumption from the way it is designed and implemented. However, in order to systematically analyze and quantify this impact, it is necessary to study at the finest level - the instruction level. In this paper, we proposed a programming-oriented energy model to predict the energy consumption of CUDA program at the instruction level. Using this model, we can derive the energy consumption of a specific CUDA program more accurately and conveniently. Furthermore, our model can be incorporated into CUDA integrated development environment which provides the programmers with insights on how much energy their program consumes while they are programming simultaneously. Unlike the previous power model that estimates the GPU power consumption at coarse granularity as Hong [4], our model applies statistical method to correlate the instruction information with power consumption of CUDA program. Compared to Hong's model, our model is built with instructions strongly correlated to the energy consumption, which significantly improves the accuracy of the model. In contrast to [5][6], our model does not require performance profiling yet derives the energy consumption of CUDA program with the instructions composing the program.

In sum, our work makes the following contributions:

1. We present a practical approach to measure energy consumption of single CUDA PTX instructions accurately which lays the foundations for building our energy model.
2. We propose an instruction level energy model to predict energy consumption of CUDA programs for programmers. Our model not only accurately predicts the energy consumption of CUDA programs, but also enables energy-aware GPU programming.
3. The evaluation with Rodinia benchmarks show that our model achieves 3.699% average prediction error. The results demonstrate our model is capable to facilitate programmers aware of energy consumption of the their codes while they are programming.

2   Challenge

2.1   Measurement Granularity

In terms of model accuracy, the first thing that we have to consider carefully is the granularity. The granularity of the measurement directly affect the difficulty of building our model and the accuracy of our model. Fine-grained model, which requires fine-grained measurement, are theoretically accurate for energy prediction but hard to implement, while a coarse-grained model has a simple building process but may lead to low prediction accuracy. As we have known, CUDA program code impacts the energy consumption at various levels. The design of system software, the actual application source code, and the process of translation into machine instructions - all of these determine the energy consumption of the CUDA program. For CUDA program, the kernel codes are first compiled into PTX [7]codes, which is associated with different PTX instructions, and then the PTX codes are compiled by *ptxas* tool into cubin format which is a kind of binary format that can be loaded into GPU directly. However, it is not directly exposed to programmers [8]. Therefore, in order to systematically analyze and quantify this cost, we decide to build our energy consumption model at the PTX instruction level.

2.2 Model Accuracy

The model accuracy is the most important criterion for evaluating the energy model, and how to guarantee the model accuracy is the second challenge to us. We should first design fine measurement approach to guarantee the accuracy of the measurement of the energy consumption of single PTX instructions. Secondly we need to choose a model which is capable to depict relation between the instruction and energy consumption.

2.3 Execution Reliance

Most of the existing GPU power models [4][5][6][9][10][11] rely on GPU simulator or performance profiling. Such requirement prohibits them acquire energy consumption of GPU program during the stage of the programming. Moreover, such power models are incapable of providing programmers effective and valuable guidances on energy-efficient optimizing. The major reason for this drawback is all of them need the complete program that can actually run on hardware. To this end, our model, based on PTX instruction level energy analysis, provides the capacity of predicting program at any time of programming. Therefore, making programmers aware of the energy consumption of their program even if not completed yet become reality. Furthermore, it would allow programmers to refactor application logic to eliminate energy hotspots in the first place and thus might help programmers to make their programs more energy-efficient.

3   Measurement Approach

3.1 Hardware Environment

Our hardware environment for measurement contains a computer with an Nvidia GeForce GTX 470 GPU which consists of 448 SPs and 1280MB GDDR5 DRAM. The computer also contains an Intel Pentium Dual E2180 2-core processor, 2GB RAM and a 250GB SCSI hard drive. The operating system is Ubuntu-11.04 with CUDA driver 4.2 installed. As it shows in Figure 2, in order to measure the energy consumption precisely, we used two power supplies, one separated ATX power supply to power the GPU card and the other for the rest of the

Fig. 2. The hardware environment in our experiments for measurement and evaluation

computer including CPU, motherboard and etc. Moreover, we put an external power meter between the GPU card power supply and the 220V AC wall outlet which could measure the power of the GPU directly [12]. Our power meter is Everfine PF9805 and the instrumental precision of measurement time is 0.3s.

3.2 Microbenchmark

There are massive instructions within CUDA PTX ISA as shown in Table 1. In order to model the energy consumption of CUDA program, we choose the instruction subset which strongly impacts the application energy consumption. As we focus on accelerating scientific computing, not graphical computing, our target instructions are selected from the computing aspect shown in Table 1. The GPU computation can be briefly divided into two parts: arithmetic process and memory access. In detail, integer arithmetic instructions, floating-point instructions, comparison and selection instructions and logic and shift instructions are attributed to the first part. The second part includes data movement and conversion instructions. Control flow instructions, although not captured by the previous two parts, contribute negligible energy consumption in a GPU program, thus not evaluated in this study. In addition, the rest instructions in Table 1 are seldom explored in scientific computing, therefore, there are excluded from our GPU energy model.

The fundamental idea is to collect the statistics of the energy consumption of every single instruction running on one SP. Therefore, we design an algorithm for building the synthetic microbenchmark for every instruction. Each microbenchmark has a loop that repeats one instruction running on all SPs simultaneously for a certain time period which should be long enough for us to measure the total energy consumption. For most of the instructions, we could use Algorithm 1 with the inline PTX assembly [13] to build microbenchmark.

As line 5-7 in Algorithm 1 show, the instruction that being measured could be written into one single statement without any other extra instructions and then run repeatedly by using for loop statement. However, just running this

Table 1. List of instructions in parallel thread execution (PTX) ISA

Category	Instructions	Selection
Integer Arithmetic Instructions	add, sub, mul, mad, sad, div, rem, abs, neg, min, max, popc, clz, bfind, brev, bfe, bfi	√
Extended-Precision Integer Arithmetic Instructions	add.cc, addc, sub.cc, subc, mad.cc, madc	
Floating-Point Instructions	add, sub, mul, fma, mad, div, abs, neg, min, max, rcp, sqrt, rsqrt, sin, cos, lg2, ex2	√
Comparison and Selection Instructions	set, setp, selp, slct	√
Logic and Shift Instructions	and, or, xor, not, cnot, shl, shr	√
Data Movement and Conversion Instructions	mov, prmt, ld, ldu, st, prefetch, isspacep, cvta, cvt	√
Texture Instructions	tex, tld4, txq	
Surface Instructions	suld, sust, sured, suq	
Control Flow Instructions	{ }, @, bra, call, ret, exit	
Parallel Synchronization and Communication Instructions	bar, membar, atom, red, vote	
Video Instructions	vadd, vadd2, vadd4, vsub, vsub2...	
Scalar Video Instructions	vadd, vsub, vabsdiff, vmin, vmax...	
SIMD Video Instructions	vadd2, vadd4, vsub2, vsub4, vavrg2...	
Miscellaneous Instructions	trap, brkpt, pmevent	

could not avoid the overhead brought by the for loop. Every time when execute the "add.U32" statement, there will be an increase of "m" and the comparison between "m" and 10000000. So we design a method to eliminate this impurity. Taking the Algorithm 1 as an example, we should first run it and record the power statistics from power meter. After that, we rewrite the code by repeating line 6 twice in the body of the "for" loop. We run it again and receive a new record from power meter. This time the "for" loop will repeat the "add.U32" instruction for 20000000 times. As a result, the difference between two energy consumption measurement results are purely the energy consumption of running "add.U32" for 10000000 times. At last, divided by repeating times(10000000) and the number of SPs in GPU, the result should be the energy consumption of executing "add.U32" on one SP for one time.

Nevertheless, some instructions cannot be written in this way due to their own characteristics and the limitation of inline PTX assembly like "slct". We just need do few changes on Algorithm 1 to implement those special microbenchmarks like Algorithm 2. Moreover, we use the same mechanism as we use with Algorithm 1 stated above to obtain the energy consumption of executing one single instruction on one SP for one time.

Algorithm 1. Sample kernel of using inline PTX assembly in microbenchmarks

Input:
    Two set of arrays, A_n, B_n;
Output:
    The sum of the two input arrays, C_n;
1: Initialize n, the index for SP to find target in array
2: $asm(".reg\ .U32\ t1\ (t2\ \&\ t3);")$
3: $asm("ld.global.U32\ t1, [\%0];"\ ::\ "r"\ (\&A[n]));$
4: $asm("ld.global.U32\ t2, [\%0];"\ ::\ "r"\ (\&B[n]));$
5: **for** "$m < 10000000$" **do**
6:     $asm("add.U32\ t3, t1,\ t2;"\ ::);$
7: **end for**
8: $asm("mov.U32\%0, t3;"\ :\ "=r"(C[n]));$
9: **return** C_n;

Algorithm 2. Sample kernel of **NOT** using inline PTX assembly in microbenchmarks

Input:
    Two set of arrays, A_n, B_n, C_n, D_n;
Output:
    The sum of the two input arrays, D_n;
1: Initialize n, the index for SP to find target in array
2: **for** "$m < 10000000$" **do**
3:     $D[n] = (C[n] \geqslant 0)?A[n] : B[n];$
4: **end for**
5: **return** D_n;

3.3   Single Instruction Energy Consumption

We build all the microbenchmarks for every single instructions that we select shown in Table 1 and implement our measurement on the real machine introduced in Section 3.1. Each microbenchmark run for multiple times and we take the average as our results. The measurement for each microbenchmark is processed as the following steps: 1) Start the metering program on power meter and recording instantaneous power. 2) Run the microbenchmark. 3) Wait a few seconds after the microbenchmark finishes and then stop the metering program. In this way we could obtain an instantaneous power profile on the whole running process of the microbenchmark.

Taking the Figure 3 for example, Y axis stands for instantaneous power and X axis stands for time so that the area of the shadow is the energy consumed on GPU by running the microbenchmark. Nevertheless, there is a fixed base power consumption of GPU as the blue bold line shows in Figure 3, the area of the shadow eliminating the fixed power consumption is the pure energy consumption of the microbenchmark. Divided by the repeated times of the instruction that the microbenchmark stressed on and the amount number of the core in use, we

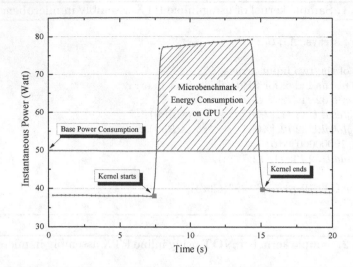

Fig. 3. The instantaneous power of running microbenchmarks

can get the final result of one instruction. Finally, Table 2 shows the results of all the instructions that we selected to build the model.

4   Energy Model

4.1   PTX Instruction Count

In order to collect the PTX instruction statistics of a CUDA program which is further used to build our model, CUDA compilation is leveraged to generate the PTX instructions. In short, CUDA compilation process works as follows: the program is separated by the CUDA front end (*cudafe*), into C/C++ host code and the *.gpu* device code. Depending on the value of the -code option to *nvcc*, this device code is further translated by the UCDA compilers/assemblers into CUDA binary (*cubin*) and intermediate PTX code. Hence, we could collect the execution times of every instruction in CUDA program by analysing the intermediate PTX code produced during the compilation process.

4.2   Linear Regression

Linear regression is a standard technique to model the correlation between independent variables and a dependent variable by assuming linearity between the variables. We attempted to derive a linear model where independent variables are based on PTX instruction statistics of a kernel execution, and the dependent variable is the energy consumption of the kernel.

In Section 2, we have discussed that the granularity of our model is at PTX instruction level. Currently, we should choose the independent variables for our

Table 2. The energy consumption of single PTX instrcutions. The unit of Energy is $10^{-9} J$.

Instruction	Energy	Instruction	Energy	Instruction	Energy
abs(float)	2.716	bfe	257.9	or	2.203
add(float)	2.115	bfi	0.1306	selp	3.941
cos	7.612	bfind	31.94	shl	2.692
div(float)	3.323	brev	81.26	shr	3.265
ex	1.555	clz	1.232	slct	7.836
fma	6.246	div(int)	8.099	xor	4.382
lg	0.8598	mad	3.646	cvt	0.9422
max(float)	0.8063	max(int)	2.844	cvta	0.3221
min(float)	0.8404	min(int)	21.50	mov	0.4955
mul(float)	2.136	mul(int)	2.880	prefetch	1.043
neg(float)	2.036	neg(int)	2.744	prmt	0.4728
rcp	2.339	popc	3.372	st	0.7243
rsqrt	2.443	rem	7.580	ldu	0.5344
sin	6.116	sad	3.104	ld	0.4748
sqrt	1.999	sub(int)	2.150	isspacep	0.6938
sub(float)	2.174	and	2.547	cnot	2.630
abs(int)	4.077	add(int)	4.556	not	2.133

model. As we already know, different PTX instruction stresses different parts of GPU and we have already split the PTX instructions into two groups in Section 3: arithmetic process and memory access. So we let these two groups to be the independent variables of our model. Besides, we should also add the base power consumption, caused by electrical circle, heat and so on, into our model.

Specifically for our energy model, let E be the energy consumption of CUDA program and $\alpha_{i,j}$ $(1 \leqslant i \leqslant n, 1 \leqslant j \leqslant m)$ be the energy consumption of single PTX instruction, where n, m denote the number of the instruction on computation and memory respectively. Meanwhile, let $c_{i,j}$ $(1 \leqslant i \leqslant n, 1 \leqslant j \leqslant m)$ be the number of each instruction occurring in CUDA kernel program and T be the number of the threads the CUDA kernel uses. We derive a model as:

$$E = k_1 T \sum_{i=1}^{n} \alpha_i c_i + k_2 T \sum_{j=1}^{m} \alpha_j c_j + \beta t \tag{1}$$

where k_1, k_2 denotes the contribution of the arithmetic process part and memory access part instructions to the energy consumption of the whole CUDA kernel program. β is the base power consumption which is a constant parameter and t is the execution time of the program.

Refering to the execution time, our model uses the predicted time to predict the energy consumption. We use a precise GPU analytical timing model [14] to predict the execution time. In this timing model, the total execution time of a GPGPU application is calculated with one of Equations 2, 3, and 4 based on the number of running threads, MWP, and CWP in the application. MWP represents the number of memory requests that can be serviced concurrently and CWP represents the number of warps that can finish one computational period during one memory access period. N is the number of running warps. Mem_L is the average memory latency. Mem_cycles is the processor waiting cycles for memory operations. Comp_cycles is the execution time of all instructions. Repw is the number of times that each SM needs to repeat the same set of computation.

$Case1:$ $If\,(MWP\ is\ N\ warps\ per\ SM)\ and\ (CWP\ is\ N\ warps\ per\ SM)$

$$\left(Mem\_cycles + Comp\_cycles + \frac{Comp\_cycles}{\#Mem\_insts} \times (MWP - 1)\right)(\#Repw)$$

(2)

$Case2:$ $If\,(CWP \geqslant MWP)\ or\ (Comp\_cycles > Mem\_cycles)$

$$\left(Mem\_cycles \times \frac{N}{MWP} + \frac{Comp\_cycles}{\#Mem\_insts} \times (MWP - 1)\right)(\#Repw)$$

(3)

$Case3:$ $If\,(MWP > CWP)$

$$(Mem\_L + Comp\_cycles \times N)\,(\#Repw)$$

(4)

5 Evaluation

5.1 Model Training

To obtain the model parameters, we design a set of synthetic benchmarks that combine mixed PTX instructions. Each benchmark has several loops that repeat a certain mixed set of instructions. To be noted, all these synthetic benchmarks should cover all the instructions in PTX instruction set while keep themselves differing from one another. Consequently, it guarantees that the samples are scattered uniformly within the solution space and maintain as much variance as possible, which further improves the accuracy of the model. Here we used 15 synthetic benchmarks for model training. The final regression model is shown as Equation 5.

$$E = 0.734 \times T \sum_{i=1}^{n} \alpha_i c_i + 1.224 \times T \sum_{j=1}^{m} \alpha_j c_j + 50 \times t$$

(5)

For linear regression analysis, R Square measures the proportion of the variability in the dependent variable about the origin explained by regression. The R Square of our regression is 0.81 which indicates the data and our model fit well. The value of the test of significance for our model is less than 0.05 which implies our linear regression model is effective. The values of the test of significance for two independent variables are both less than 0.05 so that we can consider that the two independent variables have significant effects on the dependent variable.

5.2   Energy Prediction

To evaluate the accuracy of our model, we select 16 representative benchmarks from Rodinia benchmark suite [15]. Considering the execution time of some benchmarks are extraordinary short, even shorter than the measurement precision of the power meter we used, we write a simple script to run each program continuously and repeatedly for a certain times to prolong the execution time. Meanwhile, with the energy consumption of executing one instruction on one core for one time, we could easily calculate the energy consumption of the benchmarks above. At last, we evaluate the prediction accuracy by comparing the predicted energy consumption with the measured energy consumption.

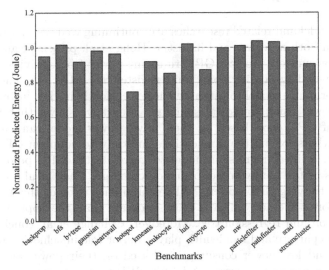

Fig. 4. The normalized predicted energy consumption of Rodinia benchmarks

As shown in figure 4, the predicted energy consumption of these benchmarks are normalized to their measurements. The distance of the bar away from the 1.0 line in Y axis is the relative error of each prediction. The relative error distributes from 0.18% to 9.46% except three of them (hotspot, leukocyte, myocyte) exceed 10%. The average relative error of those below 10% is 3.699%. For GPU programmers, the prediction given by the model is accurate enough to comprehend the energy consumption.

The relative error of hotspot benchmark is 25.373% while 14.664% for leukocyte and 12.655% for myocyte. The reasons why these relative errors exceed 10% are probably as following analysis. Hotspot benchmark contains a series of iteration which are difficult to determine the exact number of each type of instruction executed on GPU. The other reason is hotspot contains codes of multiple data transformation between GPU memory and CPU memory which may has a side effect on the energy consumption. Those operations may increase the energy consumption on GPU while not increase the execution time of benchmark. Leukocyte and myocyte suffer from the similar problems causing the relative error exceeding 10%.

Some of the benchmarks have a substantially low prediction error. For gaussian, nn and srad, their prediction errors are only 1.781%, 0.185% and 0.180% respectively. Mostly because their code structures are similar enough to our model's and their predicted execution time are more precise than the other benchmarks because of the characteristics of the execution time prediction model we used. In sum, our model is well trained and provides accurate energy prediction ability for GPU programmers.

6   Related Work

GPU power model and related researches are continuing to draw more and more attention from both academia and industry. Hong et al. presented an empirical model which accurately predicts GPU run-time power from activities of single components including floating point unit, register file, ALU, etc. They rely on an early performance model to estimate the execution behavior, instead of predicting the power using statistical samples. They have shown that throttling the number of GPU cores based on their novel power model can save energy. In [6], the authors extend the applications in study to common GPGPU kernels and build a linear regression model to correlate the GPU power and the measurements of the hardware performance counters. Chen et al. designed an approach for studying GPU power [9]. Their approach extends the model using the random forest method which is more accurate than the approaches using linear regression and regression tree. Moreover, Collange et al. concluded that memory access pattern and bandwidth play a major role in achieving both good performance and low power consumption based on their power measurement [16]. Pool et al. present an energy model for GPU that is based on the amount and type of work performed in various parts of the unit while their model are typically adequate for graphical applications [17]. Ma et al. presented an SVR regression model to predict the dynamic power consumption of a GPU with the counters from perfkit while their model is more suitable for graphics applications as well [10]. However, the researches done by Rofouei et al. [18] and Huang et al. [19] advocated the use of GPUs for general purpose computing from an energy standpoint, pointing out that though they require more power, their higher speeds reduce overall energy. Luo et al. proposed an execution time prediction model and an energy consumption model to help programmers have a better insight into the performance and energy-saving bottleneck of parallel applications on GPU architectures [11].

Our GPU power model at instruction level was inspired by Vivek Tiwari's work [20]. In their paper, they described an alternative measurement based on instruction level power analysis approach that provides an accurate and practical way to quantify the power cost of software. Although their research focused on software running on CPU, the way of thinking energy problems and the method of solving the problems are also useful for GPU architecture.

7 Conclusion and Future Work

In this paper, we presented a programming-oriented energy model based on the PTX instruction level energy analysis of CUDA programs. Unlike the existing model, our model leveraged the PTX instructions of the CUDA program as input and gave the energy consumption of that program as output in order to provide GPU programmers the insight of their program from energy aspect. In addition, we could apply the ability of predicting the energy consumption of CUDA program at creation time which enables programmer to refactor application logic to eliminate energy hotspots in the first place aiming at making their programs more energy-efficient. The experimental results showed that our model was effective to predict the energy consumption of CUDA programs.

Nevertheless, our paper still has several deficiencies that we eagerly want to solve them in the future. First is that we ignored to include the influence of the GPU analytical timing model into our consideration during our whole establishment of energy model. Although the timing model we used is precise and well established in Hong's paper [14], we should analyse the influence to verify how much suitable this timing model is for our energy model. The other one is the resolvent for divergence which is caused by input-dependent code fragments during counting the exact number of instructions of PTX code. In our model, we are indeed disable to eliminate such divergence now. However, in the future, our preliminary solution is analysing such code fragment separately. We will explicitly indicate the relationship between the energy and the input scale.

Moreover, our model also needs to be improved from multiple aspects. First, we should realize the ability of predicting energy consumption of code segment that cannot be compiled into PTX code, such as the code of a single function, the code of a single statement and etc. With such ability, the programmer is provided with more insight on CUDA program, for which they become aware of which part of their code is energy efficient and vice verse. They might know which part of their code is energy-efficient and which are not. Furthermore, programming suggestions could be supplemented to guide the programmers optimizing their code for better energy efficiency. Secondly we may extend our model to support the heterogonies system. Our model could predict the energy consumption of CUDA kernel program running on GPU card so far. As CUDA program contains non-kernel part which runs on CPU counterpart, the implementation of this extension could improve the widely adoption of our model.

Acknowledgment. This work was partially supported by the National Science Foundation of China under the grant No.61133004, National High Technology Research and Development Program ("863" Program) of China under the grant No.2012AA010902.

References

1. Owens, J.D., Houston, M., Luebke, D., Green, S., Stone, J.E., Phillips, J.C.: Gpu computing. Proceedings of the IEEE 96(5), 879–899 (2008)
2. Kirk, D.: Nvidia cuda software and gpu parallel computing architecture. In: ISMM, vol. 7, pp. 103–104 (2007)

3. Hsu, C.-H., Feng, W.-C.: A power-aware run-time system for high-performance computing. In: Proceedings of the 2005 ACM/IEEE Conference on Supercomputing, p. 1. IEEE Computer Society (2005)

4. Hong, S., Kim, H.: An integrated gpu power and performance model. In: ISCA 2010. ACM (2010)

5. Chen, J., Li, B., Zhang, Y., Peng, L., Peir, J.-K.: Tree structured analysis on gpu power study. In: ICCD 2011. IEEE (2011)

6. Nagasaka, H., Maruyama, N., Nukada, A., Endo, T., Matsuoka, S.: Statistical power modeling of gpu kernels using performance counters. In: Green Computing Conference (2010)

7. NVIDIA Compute. Ptx: Parallel thread execution isa version 2.3, 1 (2010), Dostopno na: http://developer.download.nvidia.com/compute/cuda/3

8. NVIDIA Compute. CUDA Compiler Driver NVCC (2013)

9. Chen, J., Li, B., Zhang, Y., Peng, L., Peir, J.-k.: Statistical gpu power analysis using tree-based methods. In: 2011 International Green Computing Conference and Workshops (IGCC), pp. 1–6. IEEE (2011)

10. Ma, X., Dong, M., Zhong, L., Deng, Z.: Statistical power consumption analysis and modeling for gpu-based computing. In: Proceeding of ACM SOSP Workshop on Power Aware Computing and Systems, HotPower (2009)

11. Luo, C., Suda, R.: A performance and energy consumption analytical model for gpu. In: 2011 IEEE Ninth International Conference on Dependable, Autonomic and Secure Computing (DASC), pp. 658–665. IEEE (2011)

12. Ma, K., Li, X., Chen, W., Zhang, C., Wang, X.: Greengpu: A holistic approach to energy efficiency in gpu-cpu heterogeneous architectures. In: 2012 41st International Conference on Parallel Processing (ICPP), pp. 48–57. IEEE (2012)

13. NVIDIA Compute. Using Inline PTX Assembly in CUDA (2013)

14. Hong, S., Kim, H.: An analytical model for a gpu architecture with memory-level and thread-level parallelism awareness. ACM SIGARCH Computer Architecture News 37, 152–163 (2009)

15. Che, S., Boyer, M., Meng, J., Tarjan, D., Sheaffer, J.W., Lee, S.-H., Skadron, K.: Rodinia: A benchmark suite for heterogeneous computing. In: IEEE International Symposium on Workload Characterization, IISWC 2009, pp. 44–54. IEEE (2009)

16. Collange, S., Defour, D., Tisserand, A.: Power consumption of GPUs from a software perspective. In: Allen, G., Nabrzyski, J., Seidel, E., van Albada, G.D., Dongarra, J., Sloot, P.M.A. (eds.) ICCS 2009, Part I. LNCS, vol. 5544, pp. 914–923. Springer, Heidelberg (2009)

17. Pool, J., Lastra, A., Singh, M.: An energy model for graphics processing units. In: 2010 IEEE International Conference on Computer Design (ICCD), pp. 409–416. IEEE (2010)

18. Rofouei, M., Stathopoulos, T., Ryffel, S., Kaiser, W., Sarrafzadeh, M.: Energy-aware high performance computing with graphic processing units. In: Workshop on Power Aware Computing and System (2008)

19. Huang, S., Xiao, S., Feng, W.-c.: On the energy efficiency of graphics processing units for scientific computing. In: IEEE International Symposium on Parallel & Distributed Processing, IPDPS 2009, pp. 1–8. IEEE (2009)

20. Tiwari, V., Malik, S., Wolfe, A., Lee, M.T.-C.: Instruction level power analysis and optimization of software. In: Technologies for Wireless Computing, pp. 139–154. Springer (1996)

PastryGridCP: A Decentralized Rollback-Recovery Protocol for Desktop Grid Systems

Heithem Abbes and Thouraya Louati

LaTICE Research Lab., ESSTT, Université de Tunis
5 Avenue Taha Hussein, BP, 56, Bâb Manara, Tunis, Tunisie
heithem.abbes@esstt.rnu.tn, thouraya.louati@gmail.com

Abstract. Desktop Grids are composed of several thousands of resources. They are characterized by high volatility of resources, due to voluntary disconnections or failures. This could affect the proper termination of applications execution. PastryGrid is a decentralized system which manages desktop grid resources and user applications over a fully decentralized P2P network. In this paper we present PastryGridCP: our rollback-recovery protocol, which is based on checkpoints designed for the decentralized Desktop Grid system PastryGrid. It provides fault tolerance for grid applications and ensures the termination of the execution of applications in a transparent way to users. We have conducted out experimentations on 110 nodes of Grid'5000. Obtained results validate our protocol and improve the performance of applications.

Keywords: Desktop Grid, fault tolerance, rollback-recovery, checkpoints, decentralization, Grid'5000.

1 Introduction

Today's personal computers are powerful but, most of the time, a large proportion of their computational power is left unused. A desktop grid exploits the idle CPU cycles from the desktop machines and puts it to work solving scientific problems. These systems are designed to provide to scientists with low cost, readily available computing resource, to solve important scientific problems. Researchers are using desktop grids to simulate protein folding *Folding@home* and model climate change *Climateprediction.net*. A large majority of volunteer computing projects are based on BOINC.

However, desktop grids have some limitations as the high volatility of its computing resources. They may join and leave the system at any time, especially during a problem resolution. The users of the desktop grid should get the result of their applications, so, ensuring proper termination of the applications running on a large number of volatile resources is a real challenge.

PastryGrid [1] is a decentralized system which manages desktop grid resources and user applications over a fully decentralized P2P network, Pastry overlay [2].

J. Kołodziej et al. (Eds.): ICA3PP 2013, Part I, LNCS 8285, pp. 143–152, 2013.

To tolerate nodes volatility, the services of PastryGrid have been passively replicated [3]. Consequently to a failure, PastryGrid restarts failure tasks on new nodes from the beginning. Then, hours of computing become completely useless. On the one hand, there is a waste of resources and on the other hand, the termination of the execution of applications is compromised, especially applications composed of long running tasks.

To handle failures, we have integrated to PastryGrid a rollback-recovery protocol based on checkpoints. Our protocol, named PastryGridCP, is able, by interacting with the grid services of PastryGrid, to manage checkpoints in a decentralized manner and to restart automatically applications having a failure.

This paper is organized as follows. Sect. 2 discusses the related work. Sect. 3 outlines the architecture of PastryGrid. Sect. 4 presents PastryGridCP. Sect. 5 describes the results from the performance evaluation of our protocol. Finally, Sect. 6 gives conclusions and future work.

2   Related Work

In this section, we present an overview of some desktop grid systems. We specify whether they have established a rollback-recovery protocol or they have restricted to a reallocation of tasks with a restart from the beginning.

BOINC [4] is a platform for global computing which allows running bag of tasks applications. To tolerate voluntary disconnections or failures, it uses the application level checkpointing through the use of its API to instrument applications and to specify checkpoint triggering time. All the checkpoints are stored locally in the node. However, this approach presents a clear limitation. Following a failure, if this node reconnects within a *time-out*, it will continue its calculations from these checkpoints, otherwise the local checkpoint will not be available and becomes useless. Furthermore, the server will distribute the task to another node to restart from the beginning.

Condor [5] is a distributed system for high throughput computing. Its architecture is centralized; it is composed of a central manager and computing nodes. Condor supports distributed applications with dependencies between tasks. It uses the user level checkpointing through the use of its checkpoint library. All checkpoints are stored on one server (centralized storage).

There are several other centralized desktop grid systems such XtremWeb [6], Entropia [7] and decentralized as Vigne [8], OurGrid [9], OrganicGrid [10], Cohesion [11], CCOF [12], Alchemi [13], GPU [14]. These systems have not yet established a rollback-recovery protocol, if a node fails, they restart failed tasks from the beginning.

3   Overview of PastryGrid

3.1   Architecture

PastryGrid [15] is based on structured peer-to-peer overlay *Pastry*. A DHT "Distributed Hash Table" is built on top of this overlay to manage entities composing PastryGrid distributed services. The principal service of PastryGrid is the RDV *"Rendez-Vous point"* which represents the data storage service. Pastry-Grid supports bag of independent tasks applications and workflow applications. A workflow application is the succession of several modules. A module is a set of tasks, using the same binary file and, generally, different input files. Tasks of the same module can be executed in parallel. The relations between modules are often time dependencies, a task of a module has to use the results of a task of a previous module and must wait until it will be completed to start.

To deal with the volatility of desktop grid resources, PastryGrid uses a fault tolerant system to ensure the availability of the RDV. In fact, if the user wants to retrieve results of its applications, it's necessary that the RDV is always available. Passive replication is used to make the RDV highly available, that is ensured by PAST [16]. It ensures k copies of the state of a node. To tolerate the failure of nodes executing tasks, PastryGrid adopts another strategy because replication becomes expensive if applied to all nodes. A service called FTC "Fault Tolerance Component", highly available, is created dynamically for each application. It supervises tasks. Following a failure, it affects failed tasks to new nodes to restart from the beginning. PastryGrid does not have a rollback-recovery protocol.

4   PastryGridCP: Our Rollback-Recovery Protocol

4.1   Features of PastryGridCP

To ensure the termination of the execution of applications on a wide number of volatile resources, following a failure, applications must restart from a check-point. This is the purpose of our rollback-recovery protocol, PastryGridCP, de-signed for the desktop grid system PastryGrid. Our protocol provides a solution to the volatility as well as the size of the desktop grids. It is transparent to applications and users ensuring the following three criteria:

- *Transparency to Applications:* Our protocol is based on a checkpointing ap-proach transparent for applications, including those that were not designed to tolerate faults.
- *Simplicity of Use:* The user should not worry about managing consequences of failure of its application that can be distributed over a large number of resources in the grid. Thus, our protocol provides a solution that guarantees a high level of transparency: managing the checkpoints and restarting auto-matically failed applications without user intervention.
- *Scalability:* Desktop grids are composed of several thousand of resources. They allow to run many applications which are composed of multiple tasks. Our rollback-recovery protocol must therefore scale well, this means that it must provide good performance even for large applications. Thus, it should not rely on a centralized architecture and must manage and save checkpoints in a decentralized manner. In fact, there are three types of backup: local, shared and distributed. For the checkpoints saved *locally* on the node, as is the case for the BOINC system, the limit here is that the checkpoints, saved locally, will

be lost when the node disconnects. For the **shared backup**, the checkpoints of all applications are stored on a server, as is the case for the Condor system. The major drawback here is that the server can become a bottleneck that leads to a single point of failure in the system. The third solution is the **distributed backup**, the checkpoints are stored in a distributed manner. The most appropriate backup for our context is the distributed backup.

Table 1 presents a comparison of our rollback-recovery and those of BOINC and Condor in terms of application model, transparency, management of checkpoints and type of storage.

Table 1. Comparing the rollback-recovery in desktop grid systems

System	Application model	Transparency	Managing checkpoints	Storage
BOINC	Bag of tasks	No	Yes	Local
Condor	Workflow	No	No	Centralized
PastryGridCP	BoTs and Workflow	Yes	Yes	Decentralized

4.2   Architecture of PastryGridCP

Our rollback-recovery protocol PastryGridCP deals with bag of independent tasks and workflow applications.

Architecture. The approach of saving the state of a process that ensures transparency to the applications and to users is the system level checkpointing. For PastryGridCP we have chosen BLCR [17] "Berkeley Lab Checkpoint/Restart", which is currently the most used solution at system level. Thus, each node of the grid has BLCR. Without user intervention, our protocol manages checkpoints generated by the backup after saving the state of each process. Following a failure, it takes over the automatic restart of failed applications.

Management of Checkpoints. The management of checkpoints is not addressed in the desktop grid systems. As is the case for the Condor system, it is the responsibility of the user to do this task. To ensure simplicity, our protocol discharges the user of this task, and takes over the management of checkpoints. Pastry-GridCP uses the data storage service of PastryGrid, the RDV, for persistent and stable storage of checkpoints. The RDV is highly available and accessible from all nodes of the grid throughout the execution. This service can ensure high availability of checkpoints due to the passive duplication (as mentioned before). A RDV is created for each application, thus it ensures the decentralization of the storage. In fact, the checkpoints of various applications will be distributed across all nodes in the system: checkpoints of an application will be stored on a node which is different from those of other applications. This will avoid to associate the storage space to a central node.

Restart Application after a Failure. Restart an application following a failure requires, firstly, to find available resources that match the application requirements and secondly, to locate the data needed to the restart and make them available on the new selected nodes:

- PastryGridCP must find new nodes to replace failed nodes. Therefore, it relies on the FTC service of PastryGrid to find available nodes which are able to restart failed tasks. This can be done by comparing the performance criteria of the tasks, already described in the job submission description file, with machine characteristics which are described in the machine description file.
- Our protocol takes over the location of data needed to the restart by contacting the appropriate RDV and then makes them available on selected nodes to restart. The data needed to restart a task include: the binary file, the checkpoint, data files (inputs) and the description file of the task.

Scalability. Given the size of desktop grids, the number of users and the number of applications running on the grid, a centralized architecture that would put constraints on a central point could limit the scalability of our protocol. Therefore, on the one hand, we have avoided a centralized backup, a single server which stores all the checkpoints of all applications. On the other hand, we have avoided that a server orchestrates applications processes to notify them to do the backup. Each process saves its state independently of other processes and also to prevent concurrent access to the data storage point.

Interface for PastryGrid Users. For a better quality of service, we offer the user/ administrator the opportunity to describe his checkpoint in the description file of the application. This file defines tasks and associated needs in terms of resources. We rely on the definition proposed by the "Open Grid Forum" OGF. The OGF introduced the concept of Job Checkpointing. It is an *XML* file composed of three tags. For the ***LevelCheckpoint***, this tag has three possible values: system level checkpointing, application level checkpointing and user level checkpointing. The default value is the system level approach. For the ***ProtcolManagement***, this tag allows, firstly, whether it is the simple protocol, dedicated for applications such as bag of tasks and workflow, coordinated protocol or uncoordinated protocol for applications which communicate frequently by exchanging messages. Secondly, the user must specify the frequency of checkpoints. For the ***FileManagement***, this tag is used to specify the number of duplicates of a checkpoint.

Operation of the Protocol. Our rollback-recovery protocol deals with bag of tasks and workflow applications. In fact, during the normal execution of the application, periodically, a checkpointing is triggered. Eventually, the checkpoints are sent to the appropriate RDV. Following a failure, the application restarts from a checkpoint. This requires finding appropriate resources and retrieving the checkpoints to continue the execution of the application. Saving a checkpoint of an application, such as bag of independent tasks and workflow, means saving data needed to restart each of its tasks. For workflow applications (parallel applications loosely coupled), we do not save the state of communication channels as is the case for tightly coupled parallel applications. Communication between tasks, in a workflow, does not create dependencies between them.

5   Experimental Evaluation

5.1   Experimental Setup

To validate our protocol, we performed out experiments on Grid'5000, an experimental testbed for distributed computing that federates ten sites in France. We used 110 nodes of the Graphene and Griffon clusters from the Nancy site. Graphene and Griffon nodes are equipped with a quadcore Intel Xeon (respectively X3440 processor x86_64 CPU, 2.53 GHz and L5420 processor x86_64 CPU, 2.5 GHz), 16 GB of RAM and local disk storage of 320 GB. They are interconnected with Gigabit Ethernet (measured 117.5 MB/s for TCP sockets with MTU = 1500 B with a latency of 0.1 ms).

We have chosen the system level approach BLCR which is sufficiently completed to save the state of a process. For our experiments, we have equipped all compute nodes by blcr-0.8.2 while the operating system is a Debian Linux distribution. All nodes have PastryGrid. The new version, including our rollback-recovery protocol PastryGridCP, is available on SourceForge [18]. The prototype of PastryGrid is fully coded in Java. It uses the open-source implementation FreePastry of Pastry to create an overlay network of nodes and to implement hash tables manipulation functionalities.

We are targeting applications such as bag of independent tasks and workflow. Each task receives an input and generates an output. The dependencies between tasks are managed at the job submission description file "Application.xml". Our test applications are workflows (distributed applications, over many nodes, with dependencies between tasks). For our experiments, the number of parallel tasks varies from 10 to 60 and the duration of each task is about 120 seconds. The total duration of all the experiments is 24 hours. PastryGridCP depends on several parameters which are the frequency of checkpoints and their eventual sending to RDV. We set these parameters as follows: the time between two periodic checkpoints is set to 2 seconds and the time between two sending to the RDV is set to 20 seconds. We have chosen both values 2 and 20 seconds because this constitutes a worst case scenario for the system overhead.

5.2   Experimental Evaluation of Execution without Failure

We study in this section, the overhead generated by our protocol, PastryGridCP, during the execution without failure. There are two overheads to analyze: the overhead in terms of storage and the overhead in terms of performance.

The Overhead in Terms of Storage: Given an application composed of several tasks, our protocol can generate a large number of checkpoints. To avoid this overhead, for each new checkpointing, the old checkpoint is overwritten and replaced by the new one. In addition, we have implemented a pull approach to remove obsolete checkpoints.

The Overhead in Terms of Performance: Some rollback-recovery techniques, such as [5] and [19], proceed as follows: each time a checkpointing is triggered, they require to stop running the application, make a checkpointing and restart the application from the last checkpoint. This will have a significant impact on application performance and will generate an overhead compared to an execution without a checkpointing strategy. This overhead evolves according to the frequency of checkpoints.

In PastryGridCP, we have avoided interrupting the execution of the application at the moment of the checkpointing process. The checkpointing is performed in parallel with the execution of tasks. Our strategy works well for bag of tasks and workflow applications (our test applications). But, for tightly coupled parallel applications, it cannot be done in a safe way while the process executes because it could lead to an inconsistency. Our strategy avoids an overhead in terms of performance.

Fig. 1 illustrates a comparison of the performances of applications with and without PastryGridCP. Obtained results depict executions of applications with tasks ranging from 10 to 60. The graph called "PG without CKPT" represents the performance of applications without PastryGridCP and "PG with CKPT" represents the performance of applications with PastryGridCP. Each experiment has been performed twice and we plot the mean measurements.

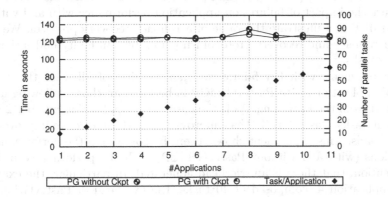

Fig. 1. Applications performance with and without the protocol PastryGridCP

The first result is that checkpoints are effectively on nodes running tasks as well as on the RDV of each application. The results show, by comparing the two curves, that PastryGridCP does not delay applications and does not penalize their performance. We note that our protocol has no impact on application performance during execution without failure. We deduce that whatever the frequency of checkpoints, the overhead in terms of performance is negligible. The results of this experiment show also the scalability of our protocol. By increasing the number of tasks from 10 to 60, PastryGridCP has good performance for applications. This is due to its decentralized approach for managing checkpoint data that allows to take over many tasks and to provide greater scalability.

5.3   Experimental Evaluation by Injecting Faults

We study in this section, the behavior of PastryGridCP facing to failures. We mainly focus our analysis on the performance when restarting after a failure.

Performance: It is interesting to have a good tradeoff between applications performances during execution without failure and those on restart. The performance during execution without failure depends of the overhead generated by PastryGridCP on application performance when running without failure. As we have already mentionned, it is negligible. The performance of restarting after a failure includes the time needed to deal with the consequences of failure: the time required to retrieve the data needed to restart and the time required to restart. To inject faults in a random manner, we create probabilistic scenarios (choosing randomly a percentage of distinct Worker-Nodes and inject the fault progressively on those nodes). We haven't injected the fault on RDV and FTC because our goal is to study the behavior of the Worker-Nodes.

We have established two scenarios with different percentages of failures: 20%, 50%. These scenarios allow to analyze the behavior of PastryGrid facing failures when the failure rate is low (20%, 22 failed nodes) (see Fig. 2, left part) and high (50%, 55 failed nodes) (see Fig. 2, right part). We want, through these scenarios, to measure the impact of failures on application performance with and without PastryGridCP and illustrate the value of a rollback-recovery protocol. We note that, our rollback and recovery protocol isn't used by non faulty nodes that are executing tasks.

The experiment, with low failure rate, shows, first of all, that the performance of applications with PastryGridCP is better than those, following a failure, restart from the beginning. As is the case of the application number 2 composed of 20 tasks, PastryGridCP has improved its performance, an improvement of 100 seconds. This experiment shows, then, by comparing the performance of applications (with and without PastryGridCP) with the performance in fault free execution, that there is an overhead generated. In particular, the example of the application 4, composed of 40 tasks, the overhead of PastryGridCP is about 50 seconds and without the protocol the overhead is about 125. Similarly, for the experiment with a high failure rate, our protocol improves the performance of applications. As is the case of the application number 5, composed of 40 tasks, has an improvement of 188 seconds compared to a recovery from the beginning.

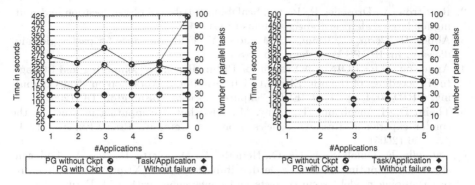

Fig. 2. Behavior of PastryGrid by injecting 20% and 50% of failures

6   Conclusions and Future Works

We have presented our rollback-recovery protocol PastryGridCP, for the desktop grid system PastryGrid, based on checkpointing and DHT distribution of checkpoint data. Our protocol ensures the termination of the execution of applications in spite of failures. It offers a solution to the volatility and the size of the desktop grids. In fact, it does not rely on a centralized architecture which limits its scalability. The approach is decentralized and is performed concurrently to the application execution implying very low overhead. Furthermore, it allows the distribution of checkpoints across multiple data storage services and it ensures the high availability of checkpoints. The experimental results show that whatever the failure rate is low or high, PastryGridCP could improve the performance of applications and reduce the overhead of the recovery from the beginning.

In our future works, we plan to manage dynamically the frequency of checkpoints to reduce the storage overhead. In the present work, this frequency is chosen by the user when he submits the application. This parameter may influence the behavior of the protocol. On the one hand, with a fewer checkpoints, we risk losing the computation in case of a failure between two checkpoints. On the other hand, with a lot of checkpoints, we could generate an important storage overhead at run time. We note that this overhead is generated only at run time. After the termination of the application, each node removes automatically obsolete checkpoints as soon as it finishes running tasks successfully. This parameter should be adapted according to the frequency of failure of nodes. It is interesting to take into account the stability parameter of each node based on the historical connection times. This allows then, to compare the stability time of the node with the duration of the task and make better decisions by setting optimal periods inter-checkpoints.

References

1. Abbes, H., Cérin, C., Jemni, M.: PastryGrid: decentralisation of the execution of distributed applications in desktop grid. In: MGC 2008, pp. 1–6 (2008)

2. Rowstron, A., Druschel, P.: Pastry: Scalable, distributed object location and routing for large-scale peer-to-peer systems (2001)
3. Abbes, H., Cérin, C., Jemni, M., Missaoui, Y.: Fault tolerance for pastrygrid middleware. In: IPDPS Workshops, pp. 1–8 (2010)
4. Anderson, D.P.: BOINC: A System for Public-Resource Computing and Storage. In: Proceedings of the 5th IEEE/ACM International Workshop on Grid Computing, GRID 2004, pp. 4–10. IEEE Computer Society, Washington, DC (2004)
5. Thain, D., Tannenbaum, T., Livny, M.: Distributed computing in practice: the condor experience. Research articles. Concurr. Comput.: Pract. Exper. 17(2-4), 323–356 (2005)
6. Cappello, F., Djilali, S., Fedak, G., Hérault, T., Magniette, F., Néri, V., Lodygensky, O.: Computing on large-scale distributed systems: XtremWeb architecture, programming models, security, tests and convergence with grid. Future Generation Comp. Syst. 21(3), 417–437 (2005)
7. Chien, A., Calder, B., Elbert, S., Bhatia, K.: Entropia: architecture and performance of an enterprise desktop grid system. J. Parallel Distrib. Comput. 63(5), 597–610 (2003)
8. Rilling, L.: Vigne: Towards a self-healing grid operating system. In: Nagel, W.E., Walter, W.V., Lehner, W. (eds.) Euro-Par 2006. LNCS, vol. 4128, pp. 437–447. Springer, Heidelberg (2006)
9. Cirne, W., Vilar Brasileiro, F., Andrade, N., Costa, L., Andrade, A., Novaes, R., Mowbray, M.: Labs of the World, Unite!!! J. Grid Comput. 4(3), 225–246 (2006)
10. Chakravarti, A.J., Baumgartner, G., Lauria, M.: The organic grid: self-organizing computation on a peer-to-peer network. Trans. Sys. Man Cyber. Part A 35(3), 373–384 (2005)
11. Schulz, S., Blochinger, W., Held, M., Dangelmayr, C.: COHESION - A microkernel based Desktop Grid platform for irregular task-parallel applications. Future Gener. Comput. Syst. 24(5), 354–370 (2008)
12. Zhou, D., Lo, V.: Cluster Computing on the Fly: Resource Discovery in a Cycle Sharing Peer-to-Peer System. In: IEEE Intl. Workshop on Global and Peer-to-Peer Computing, pp. 66–73 (2004)
13. Luther, A., Buyya, R., Ranjan, R., Venugopal, S.: Alchemi: A.NET-based Enterprise Grid Computing System. In: 6th International Conference on Internet Computing (ICOMP 2005), Las Vegas (2005)
14. Mengotti, T.: GPU, a Framework for Distributed Computing over Gnutella. Master's thesis, ETH Zuerich, Switzerland (2004)
15. Abbes, H., Cérin, C., Jemni, M.: A decentralized and fault-tolerant Desktop Grid system for distributed applications. Concurrency and Computation: Practice and Experience 22(3), 261–277 (2010)
16. Rowstron, A., Druschel, P.: Storage management and caching in PAST, a large-scale, persistent peer-to-peer storage utility. In: Proc. of the 18th ACM Symp. on Operating Systems Principles, pp. 188–201. ACM, New York (2001)
17. Duell, J.: The design and implementation of Berkeley Labs linux Checkpoint/Restart. Technical report (2003)
18. PastryGrid Source Code (May 2013), http://sourceforge.net/projects/pastrygrid/
19. Mehnert-Spahn, J., Ropars, T., Schoettner, M., Morin, C.: The architecture of the xtreemOS grid checkpointing service. In: Sips, H., Epema, D., Lin, H.-X. (eds.) Euro-Par 2009. LNCS, vol. 5704, pp. 429–441. Springer, Heidelberg (2009)

Improving Continuation-Powered Method-Level Speculation for JVM Applications*

Ivo Anjo and João Cachopo

ESW
INESC-ID Lisboa/Instituto Superior Técnico/Universidade de Lisboa
Rua Alves Redol 9, 1000-029 Lisboa, Portugal
{ivo.anjo,joao.cachopo}@ist.utl.pt

Abstract. Most applications running on the Java Virtual Machine (JVM) make extensive use of dynamic object-oriented programming features such as inheritance, polymorphism, and encapsulation. This makes them very hard or even impossible to analyze statically, defeating most of the automatic parallelization research done so far for traditional compute-heavy scientific applications.

In this paper, we propose and evaluate multiple extensions to the JaSPEx-MLS framework, a speculative parallelization framework that is aimed at irregular applications. This framework works atop a modified JVM and employs Method-Level Speculation (MLS), a task-identification technique that is better suited for irregular applications. Our custom JVM is a modified version of the OpenJDK Hotspot VM that was extended with support for first-class continuations, while still inheriting Hotspot's high-performance features such as just-in-time compilation, adaptive optimization, state-of-the-art garbage collection, and support for the latest Java versions. JaSPEx-MLS automatically modifies applications to use Software Transactional Memory (STM) and to allow the spawn and synchronization of speculative tasks in a scheme similar to Fork/Join parallelism. Speculative execution is supported by our novel relaxed STM model, which is tightly coupled with our framework and includes support for integrating with Futures.

We present novel techniques for improving MLS runtime task extraction and coordination, describe our implementation of those techniques onto JaSPEx-MLS, and present experimental results showing their impact on both reducing speculative execution overheads and extracting further parallelism from sequential applications.

Keywords: Speculative Parallelization, Method-Level Speculation, Fork/Join Parallelism, First-Class Continuations, OpenJDK Hotspot JVM.

* This work was supported by national funds through FCT – Fundaç ão para a Ciência e a Tecnologia, both under project PEst-OE/EEI/LA0021/2013 and under project PTDC/EIA-EIA/108240/2008 (the RuLAM project).

J. Kołodziej et al. (Eds.): ICA3PP 2013, Part I, LNCS 8285, pp. 153–165, 2013.

1 Introduction

With multicore processors reaching near-ubiquity in the computing market, it becomes ever more important for applications to take advantage of all the available parallel execution resources of modern computers.

Because retrofitting concurrency onto existing applications is usually a hard and error-prone task, an enticing alternative is the usage of automatic parallelization. Parallelizing compilers [2] attempt to automatically extract concurrency by proving that parts of a sequential application can be safely executed in parallel. The problem is that they fail to parallelize many irregular applications [6,9] that employ dynamic data structures, loops with complex dependences and control flows, and other abstractions, which are very hard or even impossible to analyze. Thread-Level Speculation (TLS) systems [8,11,15] attempt to work around this issue by optimistically running parts of the application in parallel, even if the TLS system is not able to statically prove that there will be no dependences. Instead, correctness is dynamically ensured at runtime, by validating now-parallel operations during or after their execution.

In previous work [1], we proposed the JaSPEx-MLS speculative parallelization framework, which employs Method-Level Speculation (MLS), a technique that uses method calls as speculative task spawn points [3,9,11,18], combined with Software Transactional Memory (STM) for buffering and tracking the speculative program state, and supported by first-class continuations. In that work, our main focus was on the code modifications needed for safe speculative execution of Java bytecode, while at the same time minimizing the runtime overheads imposed by our custom STM, but we left some open issues that limited the amount of parallelism our framework was able to extract — our runtime thread management and coordination/result fetching model was very simple, and as it relied on waiting between tasks, an unbalanced speculative task selection could easily lead to system underuse, as most tasks would spend considerable time stopped while waiting for results from other tasks.

In this paper, we tackle our previously open issues with multiple novel techniques for MLS runtime task extraction and coordination that rely on state transfer and buffering using continuations. We build upon our previous work by:

- Extending existing experimental support for continuations in the OpenJDK Hotspot JVM to better fit the use-cases of MLS parallelization (Section 3);
- Exploring how continuations can be used to implement MLS in the JaSPEx-MLS framework (Section 4.2);
- Presenting a technique that allows the thread pool to buffer tasks for execution, while still preserving correctness and avoiding deadlocks (Section 4.3);
- Proposing a novel *task freeze* technique where we allow threads that host speculative tasks to be reused instead of blocking by *freezing* tasks for later resume, possibly by another thread (Section 4.4);
- Introducing an extension to our custom software transactional memory model for allowing STM-assisted return value prediction (Section 4.5);
- Evaluating the impact of the proposed techniques in extracting parallelism and reducing speculative execution overheads (Section 5).

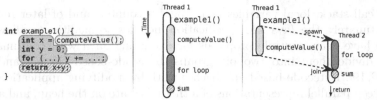

Fig. 1. Execution of `example1()` method when run normally (center) and parallelized with MLS (right). Note that `computeValue()` is executed in the normal program order (at the start of `example1()`); the `for loop` is executed speculatively.

2 Method-Level Speculation

Method-level speculation (MLS) is a speculative parallelization strategy first discussed in the context of Java in [3], and shown to be a promising source for parallelism by [9, 11, 18]. This technique works by speculatively executing the code following the return of a method call in parallel with the method call itself.

MLS shares many similarities with the Fork/Join (F/J) model, which was also recently introduced into the Java platform with the Java Fork/Join framework [7]. The MLS spawn operation works similarly to the fork operation, but with an important distinction. In the MLS model the new task spawned (forked) starts executing the code following the spawn point, and the method itself is executed as part of the previously existing task, whereas in the F/J model the reverse happens: a new task is created to execute the method call being forked, and the code following the fork is the one executed as part of the previously existing task — note that this distinction is in the models themselves, regardless of the runtime strategies chosen for execution. For both F/J and MLS, the join operation is similar, and serves to synchronize a pair of tasks where one needs to obtain the result of another's computation. In addition, the F/J framework targets parallel algorithms, where tasks have simpler and less strict ordering semantics than those required of an MLS system.

An example of method-level speculation is shown in Figure 1. When the `computeValue()` method call is reached, the current thread (`T1`) begins executing it, while at the same time triggering the spawn of the speculative execution (by `T2`) of the code following the return of that method.

In this example, both the original parent thread and the speculative child thread have to join to produce the result of the method. If the value of the variable `x` was never used, it would be possible to speculate past the return of `example1()`, and continue the execution of the method that invoked it. Alternatively, even if `x`'s value is needed to proceed with the execution, we can employ return value prediction to guess a probable value of `x`, as discussed in Section 4.5.

3 First-Class Continuations on the JVM

First-class continuations allow an application to have control over its own control flow: they allow the current program execution state to be saved, and later resumed. Mapping it to the Java platform means having a way of saving a thread's call stack, local variables and program counter, and of later restoring it. Unfortunately, the Java VM specification includes no facilities to allow this.

There have been multiple proposals for extending Java with continuations. We can divide them into two big groups: bytecode-based [10, 13] and VM-based [16, 19]. Bytecode-based approaches work by modifying application bytecode to keep parallel representations of a thread's state on the heap, and also by modifying methods so that the entire call stack can be rebuilt from the parallel representation. Although this approach is successful and works with any JVM, it suffers from very large overheads, which unfortunately are always present, even if the application never actually tries to capture or resume any continuation.

The other approach — VM-based continuations — works by modifying the JVM, adding hooks that allow access to the VM's internal representation of threads. Usually, with such an implementation, there are no extra overheads when continuations are not being used, but it is non-portable and VM-specific.

To support our framework, we looked into VM-based continuation implementations that worked atop the OpenJDK Hotspot JVM, as it is one of the highest performing and most used production VMs. To obtain our continuation-supporting VM, we extended the work by Hiroshi [19]: this implementation provided continuations aimed at web servers, where the state of a web interaction was kept inside a continuation between each request/response pair from the same client. This meant that when a continuation was created at the end of each web interaction, the thread state that was saved would no longer be needed until the next request from that client, so the continuation implementation would also, during the capture operation, clear the existing state and reset the thread to a clean state ready to serve the next client. It also meant that each continuation could only be resumed at most once, as it was expected that at the end of each interaction a new one would be created.

Our custom JVM extended this work by removing its restrictions: our implementation allows the same continuation to be resumed multiple times, and it is optimized so that capturing a continuation also preserves the state of the thread, allowing execution to proceed immediately after a continuation is captured. While the latter could be simulated with added overhead, the support for resuming a continuation multiple times is essential for JaSPEx-MLS's use of continuations, as explored in Section 4.2. Finally, several internal VM design choices lead to native methods not being allowed in a call stack being captured, and because Hotspot's reflective invocation API is built using native code, we developed our own VM-agnostic alternative reflective invocation system that relies on runtime bytecode generation, allowing our framework to combine the use of reflection and continuations.

4   Runtime Extensions to the JaSPEx-MLS Framework

In this section, we will start with a brief introduction of the JaSPEx-MLS framework (Section 4.1) and how continuations are used to implement MLS (Section 4.2). We then present our hybrid technique for safely allowing the buffering of speculative tasks, while still avoiding deadlocks (Section 4.3), followed by our novel *task freeze* technique that enables thread reuse (Section 4.4). Finally, we describe an extension to our STM model that adds support for STM-assisted return value prediction (Section 4.5).

4.1   The JaSPEx-MLS Parallelization Framework

JaSPEx-MLS [1] is a software-based speculative parallelization framework employing Method-Level Speculation that provides both a Java classloader that modifies application code as it is requested by the virtual machine, and a runtime Java library that orchestrates speculative execution. The framework is implemented in Java, and modifications to applications are done via bytecode rewriting. It also depends on having a VM with continuation support, which is provided by a modified version of the OpenJDK Hotspot VM (Section 3).

The JaSPEx-MLS classloader (introduced in more detail in [1]) is responsible for, whenever a class is requested by the application, preparing its code for speculative parallelization, consisting of four main steps: (1) transactification, (2) dealing with non-transactional operations, (3) task spawn point injection, and (4) modifications to support Futures.

The classloader first transactifies applications by modifying their code to use our low-overhead software transactional memory, which is designed to be type-specific and easily inlined by the VM. The transformation process then adds hooks to deal with non-transactional operations, such as calls to native code and to some JVM services: Whenever application code is running speculatively, and a non-transactional operation is to be executed, we ensure the safety of the operation by synchronizing with earlier (in the original program order) speculative tasks, aborting the current task if needed. In addition, there is limited support for automatic transactification of JDK classes, and we have implemented alternative transactionally-friendly versions of commonly used operations.

Our classloader decides where to insert speculative task spawn points by first performing local analysis of a method's control flow. We use this information to avoid creating both overly small and too many tasks; optionally this process can also be augmented by information from an automatic profiling pass. Each selected spawn point corresponds to a normal method call, which is morphed into a call to the JaSPEx-MLS runtime library that returns a `Future` as a replacement for the original method's return value. This future, similarly to the ones employed in the Java Fork/Join framework, allows the speculative task to obtain the result of its parent task's computation, corresponding to the execution of the original method call. As the original application being parallelized has no references to futures, and Java bytecode is typed, our classloader needs to perform various code modifications to adapt the original code to the use of futures.

After the prepared classes are loaded by the classloader into the VM, control is transferred to the runtime orchestration library, which becomes responsible for coordinating speculative tasks, and for parallelizing the application while still respecting the original sequential program semantics — even in the presence of non-transactional operations. The runtime library is also responsible for starting,

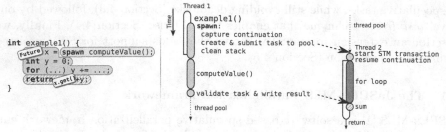

Fig. 2. Runtime view of Figure 1's `example1()` task creation and execution

maintaining, and validating the STM transactions that allow tasks to perform speculative reads and writes to the program heap. Speculative work is submitted to a thread pool, which we attempt to keep busy at all times, as described in further detail in the following sections.

4.2 Mapping MLS to Continuations

As described in Section 2, under the MLS model, we change method calls into speculation spawn points. For instance, in Figure 2, we transform the invocation of the `computeValue()` method into a spawn point for a new task that will speculatively execute the code following the `spawn` instruction.

This is where the support for first-class continuations enters: JaSPEx-MLS captures a continuation representing the current thread's state — program counter, local variables, method arguments, and all pending invocations in the stack — and attaches it to the newly created speculative task. It then cleans the current call stack, throwing it away, as it will not be needed after the method is completed, and proceeds to execute the `computeValue()` method. Note that doing the inverse would also be possible: schedule the execution of `computeValue()` on another thread, along with the current active task and transaction, and continue executing the `for loop` in the current thread. The problem with this alternative approach is that it can easily lead to delays in executing code earlier in the program order, while devoting more resources to code that is more speculative.

Whenever a speculative task is picked up by a thread, it starts a new STM transaction, and resumes the previously captured continuation. Execution jumps to the spawn operation that replaced the `computeValue()` method, where a `Future` is returned representing the return value for the method, and the (speculative) execution begins.

Each continuation may be resumed up to two times: The first resume happens when a task first executes speculatively, while the second may happen if, after the first execution, validation of the STM transaction fails and the task is re-executed.

4.3   Thread Pool Buffering

After a new speculative task is created, it is submitted for execution to the JaSPEx-MLS thread pool, which is based on Java's `ThreadPoolExecutor` API. In our original design [1], the thread pool did not buffer tasks, instead allocating a limited number of threads based on the number of available CPUs, and accepted new tasks only when there were idle threads. This design was chosen to avoid possible deadlocks: Because our model allows tasks to be spawned in any order, task spawning becomes unpredictable; when combined with the fact that tasks may need to block while waiting for other tasks to finish their work, task buffering becomes prone to deadlocking, as it is possible for all the available threads in the thread pool to be blocked while waiting for results from a task that is still in the queue waiting to be executed. By disallowing buffering, we guarantee that at least one of the threads in the system is making progress, as it is hosting the oldest task in the system — which will never need to wait.

As benchmarking revealed that task buffering, when it did not cause any issues, was more efficient than direct hand-overs to the thread pool, we developed a hybrid technique that starts by using buffering, but augments it with monitoring the thread pool for deadlocks, and allows fallback to the earlier task hand-over scheme if needed. To detect deadlocks, a dedicated thread periodically polls the state of the thread pool queue: As any given task is queued at most once, if the same task sits at the head of the pool for some amount of time — we expect most tasks to execute in sub-second times — we check the state of all the threads. If all threads in the pool are in the waiting state, it means that the system is probably deadlocked. As such, we fallback to the earlier scheme without buffering, and temporarily create more threads to execute the remaining buffered tasks. This approach combines the best of both task queuing modes: it maintains correctness for all applications while providing increased performance to those where buffering causes no issues.

Note that if, when a task is submitted, the pool is full, the spawn is aborted. This happens in both pool queuing modes, either when the pool is fully busy, or when the buffer is full.

4.4   Task Freeze

During speculative execution, a task may need to access the result from another speculative task. If the other task has not yet finished its computation, the current task must wait until the value becomes available. A similar case occurs when a task is about to execute a non-transactional operation: the task needs to wait until it becomes the oldest task in the system. In both cases, the threads hosting the waiting tasks are still considered as busy, and are unavailable for executing other tasks, thus leaving the machine's parallel resources underused.

A possible approach to solve this issue would be thread reuse, which unfortunately is not straightforward in our model: If a thread picks up a more recent task for execution, and the new task ends up depending on the older task to finish, the system becomes deadlocked — unable to ever finish the new task or to switch back to executing the previous one.

To safely support thread reuse, we again rely on our extended JVM with support for continuations. Whenever a thread executing a task would block waiting for its parent task to finish, instead we *freeze* the task, by saving both a continuation containing the current state of the task and the currently active STM transaction. This frozen task is associated with its parent task, which will be responsible for finishing the task's work after its own. This allows the thread previously hosting the task to be returned to the thread pool, where it can safely proceed to work on other tasks, instead of blocking, as before.

The *thaw* operation happens when, after finishing its work, the parent task discovers a frozen child task waiting to be finished. As the parent task is finished, the thread directly switches to working on the child task without needing to return to the thread pool — the child's continuation is resumed, its STM transaction is validated, and execution proceeds from where the freeze left off. Note that it is possible for a queue of frozen tasks to form, and a parent may have to thaw several children, always directly switching between them without returning to the thread pool.

Because capturing continuations adds some overhead, we have further identified and optimized a common use case where we can avoid the need for continuations. Whenever a child task is able to complete its work, but needs to wait for its parent to finish before it can validate and commit its own speculative state changes to the global program state — as it does not know if it read something that will be later changed by one of its parent tasks — we can use a simpler freeze. As the child task is finished with its work, there is no state on the stack that needs preserving, and in this case the freeze operation consists only in saving the STM transaction, avoiding an unneeded capture/resume cycle.

4.5   Return Value Prediction

One of the biggest challenges in the MLS model is dealing with operations that work on the return values of methods that have yet to finish executing. Our framework represents the return values of these methods with Futures, and our modifications to the application code allow futures to be written both to local variables and also to the heap, via special collaboration with our STM implementation. But the previous options are only useful if the value from the method call is not read immediately. Otherwise, no useful work would be done in parallel: a speculative task spawned to run the code following a method call would immediately stall waiting for the result from its parent task. In our previous work, whenever the JaSPEx-MLS classloader detected that this would happen, it declined to inject the spawn operation that would create a new task.

A possible solution to this issue lies with the use of Return Value Prediction (RVP) [5, 12]. The idea of RVP is that whenever a task would stall waiting for a returned value to be produced by another task, we guess a probable value for the computation, and continue executing the task using this assumption — we speculate on the returned value from a task.

We have implemented RVP in JaSPEx-MLS as a novel extension to our STM model: Whenever a prediction is produced, we register it with our STM as a

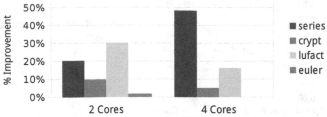

Fig. 3. Improvement obtained by the new JaSPEx-MLS extensions, relative to benchmark executions using JaSPEx-MLS but with the new extensions disabled, for multiple benchmarks from the JGF

read of a specially reserved memory location. This memory location is unique for each task from which we obtain a prediction: It is possible for a speculative task to obtain multiple predictions corresponding to values from multiple other tasks. When a task finishes and produces the final return value, it writes it to the special memory location. When later the task that read the prediction attempts to commit, the memory location hosting the prediction is checked as part of read-set validation. If the prediction was correct, its value will be seen as valid by the STM, otherwise the speculative task is aborted and re-executed.

We support multiple prediction strategies (as proposed in other works [5,12]), and update predictors during transaction commit operations. As an option, when RVP is being employed, the JaSPEx-MLS classloader can be configured to inject code to spawn speculations even when the value is immediately consumed.

5   Experimental Results

In this Section, we present preliminary experimental results obtained with the JaSPEx-MLS framework. We tested our prototype on an Intel Core i7 4770 computer with 16GB of RAM, running Ubuntu Linux 13.10 (snapshot) 64-bit, with hyperthreading disabled, and our modified OpenJDK VM.

We tested several JVM benchmarks from the Java Grande Forum (JGF) benchmark suite.[1] The chosen benchmarks are single-threaded, and no modifications to their source code were made. We present results with two and four processor cores enabled in the machine. To test with two cores, we locked the VM process to only two cores of the quad-core machine.

We first characterize the performance of the new techniques proposed in this work for the framework by comparing the benchmark execution performance to a version of JaSPEx-MLS where their usage was disabled. The results of this testing are presented in Figure 3. For the `series` benchmark, the new features improved performance noticeably. Interestingly, freezing tasks only improved performance when combined with the task buffering changes; combining freezing with the simpler no-buffering pool actually regressed performance, showing that task submission to the pool was indeed a bottleneck in our system. Both `crypt` and `lufact` show modest gains with 4 cores. Finally, `euler` was not able to

---

[1] http://www.epcc.ed.ac.uk/research/java-grande

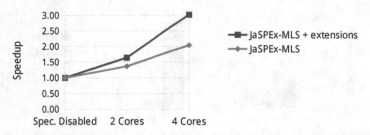

Fig. 4. Speedup of the `series` benchmark, when compared to the original sequential version's runtimes, both with the new extensions enabled and disabled

improve from the new features, but it was also not negatively impacted either. Not shown are the `fft` benchmark as it behaved similarly to crypt, and both `sor` and `sparsematmult` because no useful spawn points where injected.

Figure 4 compares the actual speedup obtained in the `series` benchmark, when compared to the original sequential version's runtime, when running JaSPEx-MLS both with and without the new extensions. Compared to our previous work [1], we see improved scaling in the `series` benchmark, hitting a speedup of 3.03x with 4 cores. The remaining benchmarks were omitted, as even with the new extensions they are not yet able to surpass the original version's performance, as they still need improvements to task selection and scheduling. For all the benchmarks tested, the baseline execution with the code modifications active but where no speculations are ever spawned reveals up to 3% overhead when compared to the original unmodified versions, showing that the optimizations done by the virtual machine are able to almost nullify the added overheads, making non-speculative code execution perform at production VM speeds, while still ready for speculative execution and for capturing continuations.

6   Related Work

Because executing code transactionally can impose very large overheads, recent TLS proposals, similarly to JaSPEx-MLS, try to optimize the transactification and transactional model as much as possible: In SpLIP [8], a speculation system that targets mostly-parallel loops, the authors propose avoiding performance pitfalls present on other software TLS proposals by having speculations commit their work in parallel, and using in-place updates. Fastpath [15] is also aimed at extracting parallelism from loops using speculation. This system distinguishes between the thread running in program order, and other speculative threads: The lead thread always commits its work, and has minimal overhead, whereas speculative threads suffer from higher overheads and may abort. The current JaSPEx-MLS relaxed STM model is very similar to the Fastpath value-based algorithm, the biggest differences being our support for futures and RVP.

Rountev et al. [14] studied the parallelism available on multiple Java sequential benchmarks, and propose that parallelization be broken into two steps: (1) the modification of a sequential program into a sequential concurrently-friendly program; and (2) the parallelization itself. They also introduce a new technique to help identify parallelism-inhibiting memory accesses.

Hu et al. [5] studied the importance of return value prediction to MLS and similar speculative schemes, showing that RVP could provide clear performance advantages by simulating the execution of multiple benchmarks on a specially modified Java VM. Pickett [12] also studied multiple predictors and proposed a hybrid design that dynamically chooses the best predictors for a given call site.

The idea of using futures in Java coupled with speculative execution was also explored in a different context by Welc et al. [17]: In their work on safe futures for Java, the authors extend Java with support for futures that are guaranteed to respect serial execution semantics. In contrast with our automatic approach, to use safe futures, programmers need to manually change their code to employ futures instead of normal method calls, including solving cases where the return value from a method is consumed or written immediately. JCilk [4] is a Java-based language for parallel programming that provides a programming style very similar to Fork/Join. It extends Java with three new keywords, and includes very detailed and strict semantics for exception handling, aborting of side computations, and other interactions between threads that try to minimize the complexity of reasoning about them. Similarly to the safe futures, programmers also need to manually prepare their program for execution using JCilk.

SableSpMT [11] is a Java MLS-based automatic parallelization framework. Like JaSPEx-MLS, it performs RVP, but unlike our approach, a simpler task spawn model is used: Although the main thread is allowed to spawn multiple speculative tasks, the tasks themselves cannot spawn further speculative tasks — nested speculation is not allowed. SableSpMT is based a modified SableVM virtual machine, which unfortunately includes only an interpreter and a very simple garbage collection algorithm. In contrast with SableSpMT, JaSPEx-MLS fully supports nested speculation, and in our system the garbage collector works normally, whereas in SableSpMT it invalidates all running speculations.

7   Conclusions and Future Work

In this paper, we have presented multiple novel techniques for improving MLS runtimes. These techniques were developed as part of our ongoing work on the creation of the JaSPEx-MLS software-based speculative parallelization framework, which aims to parallelize irregular Java/JVM applications automatically.

We started by introducing our extensions to previous experimental work that added first-class continuations to the OpenJDK Hotspot JVM — we removed several restrictions and further optimized the implementation for our use-cases. We analyzed the issues underlying both the safe buffering of speculative tasks for execution, where we proposed an hybrid scheme with a dynamic deadlock detector, and thread reuse via *task freezing*, allowing blocked threads to be freed up for safely executing other tasks. We also described our STM-assisted return value prediction support, which allows a task to continue execution by obtaining (possibly multiple) predictions from other concurrently executing speculative tasks that have not yet finished.

Evaluation of our techniques shows that they improve our MLS runtime, allowing a decrease in overheads and enabling us to unlock further latent parallelism, improving the speedup obtained in the tested benchmarks.

In the future, we intend to work on improving the runtime management of tasks by adding a task scheduler, and also to improve our automatic profiling pass so that unprofitable speculations are more aggressively culled.

References

1. Anjo, I., Cachopo, J.: A software-based method-level speculation framework for the java platform. In: Kasahara, H., Kimura, K. (eds.) LCPC 2012. LNCS, vol. 7760, pp. 205–219. Springer, Heidelberg (2013)
2. Blume, W., Doallo, R., Eigenmann, R., Grout, J., Hoeflinger, J., Lawrence, T.: Parallel programming with Polaris. Computer 29(12), 78–82 (1996)
3. Chen, M., Olukotun, K.: Exploiting method-level parallelism in single-threaded Java programs. In: 7th International Conference on Parallel Architectures and Compilation Techniques (PACT-1998), pp. 176–184. IEEE (1998)
4. Danaher, J., Lee, I., Leiserson, C.: The jcilk language for multithreaded computing. In: OOPSLA 2005 Workshop on Synchronization and Concurrency in Object-Oriented Languages, SCOOL (2005)
5. Hu, S., Bhargava, R., et al.: The role of return value prediction in exploiting speculative method-level parallelism. Journal of Instruction-Level Parallelism 5(1) (2003)
6. Lam, M., Wilson, R.: Limits of control flow on parallelism. ACM SIGARCH Computer Architecture News 20(2), 46–57 (1992)
7. Lea, D.: A Java fork/join framework. In: Proceedings of the ACM 2000 Conference on Java Grande, pp. 36–43. ACM (2000)
8. Oancea, C., Mycroft, A., Harris, T.: A lightweight in-place implementation for software thread-level speculation. In: Proceedings of the 21st Annual Symposium on Parallelism in Algorithms and Architectures (SPAA 2009), pp. 223–232. ACM Press (2009)
9. Oplinger, J., Heine, D., Lam, M.: In search of speculative thread-level parallelism. In: 8th International Conference on Parallel Architectures and Compilation Techniques (PACT 1999), pp. 303–313. IEEE (1999)
10. Ortega-Ruiz, J., et al.: Continuation-based mobile agent migration (2010)
11. Pickett, C.J.F., Verbrugge, C.: Software thread level speculation for the java language and virtual machine environment. In: Ayguadé, E., Baumgartner, G., Ramanujam, J., Sadayappan, P. (eds.) LCPC 2005. LNCS, vol. 4339, pp. 304–318. Springer, Heidelberg (2006)
12. Pickett, C.J.F., Verbrugge, C.: Return value prediction in a Java virtual machine. In: Proceedings of the 2nd Value-Prediction and Value-Based Optimization Workshop (VPW2), pp. 40–47 (2004)
13. RIFE Team: RIFE : Web continuations (2006)
14. Rountev, A., Van Valkenburgh, K., Yan, D., Sadayappan, P.: Understanding parallelism-inhibiting dependences in sequential Java programs. In: International Conference on Software Maintenance (ICSM 2010), pp. 1–9. IEEE (2010)
15. Spear, M.F., Kelsey, K., Bai, T., Dalessandro, L., Scott, M.L., Ding, C., Wu, P.: Fastpath speculative parallelization. In: Gao, G.R., Pollock, L.L., Cavazos, J., Li, X. (eds.) LCPC 2009. LNCS, vol. 5898, pp. 338–352. Springer, Heidelberg (2010)

16. Stadler, L., Wimmer, C., Würthinger, T., Mössenböck, H., Rose, J.: Lazy continuations for Java virtual machines. In: 7th International Conference on Principles and Practice of Programming in Java (PPPJ 2009), pp. 143–152. ACM Press (2009)
17. Welc, A., Jagannathan, S., Hosking, A.: Safe futures for Java. ACM SIGPLAN Notices 40(10), 439–453 (2005)
18. Whaley, J., Kozyrakis, C.: Heuristics for profile-driven method-level speculative parallelization. In: Proceedings of the 2005 International Conference on Parallel Processing (ICPP 2005), pp. 147–156. IEEE Computer Society (2005)
19. Yamauchi, H.: Continuations in servers. In: JVM Language Summit 2010 (2010)

Applicability of the (m,k)-firm Approach for the QoS Enhancement in Distributed RTDBMS

Malek Ben Salem[1], Fehima Achour[1], Emna Bouazizi[1], Rafik Bouaziz[1], and Claude Duvallet[2]

[1] MIRACL Laboratory, Higher Institute of Computer Science and Multimedia, Sfax University, Tunisia
{mal.bensalem,fehima.achour,emna.bouazizi,Raf.Bouaziz}@gmail.com
[2] LITIS, Université du Havre, 25 rue Philippe Lebon, BP 540, F-76058, Le Havre Cedex, France
claude.duvallet@gmail.com

Abstract. Many real-time applications are geographically distributed and have to use large amounts of real-time data. Using DRTDBMS[1] is increasingly needed to better manage the large amount of real-time data. In order to take into account unpredictable workload, Quality of Service (QoS) based approaches are the most appropriate. In the particular case of distributed applications, it is necessary to consider the problems of load balancing for user transactions between different sites. Feedback Scheduling approaches can adapt to unpredictable workload variations. In this paper, we propose to apply a (m,k)-firm approach to schedule user transactions in a distributed feedback scheduling architecture. We also show that our approach can significantly improve the performance of existing approaches by increasing the number of transactions that meet their deadlines while maintaining the DRTDBMS in a stable state.

1 Introduction

Currently, many applications use distributed computing, real-time processing and require, in addition, the management of large amount of data. Thus, DRTDBMS are increasingly needed to satisfy these applications since they are designed to manage, in both, large volumes of distributed data and real-time constraints of transactions. DRTDBMS include a set of nodes connected via communication networks for transaction processing, where data and transactions are totally distributed.

DRTDBMS are greatly exposed to unpredictable workload, caused by user transactions arriving at varying frequencies, and then to an unbalanced distribution of this workload between nodes. This leads to instability periods in which the system becomes overloaded. During overloading periods, there is a lack of DRTDBMS resources, so that transactions greatly miss their deadlines.

---

[1] Distributed Real-Time Database Management Systems.

J. Kołodziej et al. (Eds.): ICA3PP 2013, Part I, LNCS 8285, pp. 166–175, 2013.
© Springer International Publishing Switzerland 2013

Therefore, it is essential to keep the system in a stable state in order to guarantee a better QoS. To control system's instability periods, approaches based on feedback control real-time scheduling theory and allowing to handle imprecise computation are proposed [13][14]. Furthermore, Wei et al. [3] proposed an algorithm for QoS guarantees in DRTDBMS based on a distributed feedback control scheduling architecture (DFCSA).

In this paper, our objective is to enhance QoS in DRTDBMS by maximizing the number of transactions which meet their deadlines, while maintaining a robust DRTDBMS behaviour facing instability periods. Our approach consists of extending the DFCSA by applying the (m,k)-firm approach to user transactions, which consists of decomposing each one of them into mandatory sub-transactions and other optional. Thus, mandatory ones have to be executed on time, however, optional ones are executed only if there is enough time before reaching the transaction's deadline. In such a way, we relax the atomicity property of transactions, which imposes that a transaction is either performed in its entirety or not at all. Indeed, in DRTDBMS, imprecise results provided on time are more preferred than exact results provided late.

The remaining of the paper is organized as follows. In Section 2, we present existing architecture on which our work is based. Section 3 describes our proposed approach for QoS guarantees in DRTDBMS. Our work is evaluated according to a set of simulation results in Section 4. We conclude the paper, in Section 5, by briefly discussing our approach and by presenting our future work.

2   Related Work

In this section, we describe our distributed real-time database model by presenting data and transaction models, and defining the basic performance metric we consider. Similarly, we present the QoS management architecture proposed in [3], on which we based our work. We finish by giving an overview of the previous work in which the (m,k)-firm approach is used for the QoS enhancement.

2.1   Data Model

In our data model, we consider a main memory database in which we have real-time and non real-time data. Real-time data are sensor data from physical world, and are updated periodically to reflect accurately the real world state. Each real-time data object has a *validity interval* beyond which it becomes useless, and a *timestamp* indicating the last observation of the real world state. Non real-time data are those found in conventional databases and that do not change dynamically with time.

In a DRTDBMS, using data replication increases the data availability at different sites. Then, it significantly helps transactions to meet their time requirements [3]. Data could be either fully or partially replicated. The full replication consists of replication of all data to all sites in the distributed system. However, in the partial replication, only the portion of the most accessed data items in the database are replicated but not necessary to all sites.

2.2 Transaction Model

In our model, we consider firm deadline transactions [11], where if a transaction misses its deadline, it will be aborted and becomes useless for the system. Transactions are divided into update and user transactions according to the type of their accessed data items. Update transactions are executed periodically, in order to refresh real-time data objects. They update, likewise, real-time data replicas. We consider that each update transaction consists of one sub-transaction, having always a write operation. User transactions are aperiodic. We consider that each one consists of a set of sub-transactions. Then, each sub-transaction is composed of a set of read operations on both real-time and non real-time data objects, and of write operations on only non real-time data objects.

In distributed real-time databases, we distinguish local transactions from global transactions [5] according to the location of their required data items. Local transaction is the one requiring data that are entirely stored at the same site. And so, it seems that it will be totally executed at this same site. Global transaction is the one requiring reference to data at one or more distant site. Then, it is distributed so that it runs at one or more than a site (other than its local site). It should be noted that when dealing with DRTDBMS models that are based on a load balancing technique, a transaction may have all of its required data at its local site, but it is then distributed in order to alleviate the overload situation of that site.

2.3 Performance Metric

The main performance metric, we consider in our model, is the *Success Ratio* (*SR*). It is a QoS parameter which measures the percentage of transactions that meet their deadlines. It is defined as follows:

$$SR = 100 \times \frac{\#timely}{\#timely + \#tardy}(\%). \tag{1}$$

where *#timely* and *#tardy* represent, respectively, the number of transactions that have met and missed their deadlines.

2.4 QoS Management in DRTDBMS

The QoS is increasingly important for evaluating the performance of a DRT-DBMS, in which the system performance depends on the workload distribution. In [3], Wei et al. proposed an architecture using feedback-based global load balancers and local feedback controllers. This architecture, called DFCSA, on which we base our work, aims a load balancing between system nodes and an efficient management of transactions workload fluctuations. In what follows, we describe briefly the basic components of the DFCSA.

The *admission controller* is used to regulate the system workload in order to prevent its overloading, by referring to the estimated CPU utilization and the target utilization set point of the system. The *transaction manager* handles the transactions' execution. It consists of a concurrency controller (CC), a freshness manager (FM), a data manager (DM) and a replica manager (RM). The CC solves accessing data conflicts appearing between transactions using the 2PL-HP (Two Phase Locking High Priority) [1] protocol. The FM checks the data freshness and blocks an user transaction if the accessed data item is stale. The DM has to update real-time data replicas, and the RM handles data replicas using a replication control protocol.

At each sampling period, the *local monitor* samples the system performance data, by referring to statistics about transactions' execution which it retrieves from the transaction manager. Measured values belong to the feedback control loop and are, then, reported to the local controller. The *local controller* includes the local utilization controller and the local miss ratio controller, which generate, respectively, the local miss ratio and the local utilization control signals, based on the received values and on the system reference parameters, according to which this controller sets the system target utilization to be considered at the next sampling period. The *scheduler* is used to schedule transactions according to the EDF (Earliest Deadline First) algorithm [2]. The *global load balancer* collaborates with its corresponding at other nodes, by exchanging their system performance data, in order to ensure the system load balancing, which is guaranteed by transferring transactions from highly overloaded nodes to less overloaded nodes. The amount of workload to be transferred is controlled by the LTF (load transferring factor) of each node.

2.5   The (m,k)-firm Approach in Literature

The (m,k)-firm approach was initially introduced for periodic tasks in real-time systems [6], in order to relax strict real-time constraints. It has also been adapted to transactions in real-time databases, aiming to decrease the number of missed deadlines [15][8]. In DRTDBMS, a distributed $\binom{m}{k}$-firm real-time transactions model has been proposed in [16]. It consists of decomposing each transaction T_i into k_i sub-transactions, among which m_i are mandatory and the others are optional. Mandatory sub-transactions are distinguished from optional according to their weights, i.e., the m_i mandatory sub-transactions are those having the highest weights. To handle $\binom{m}{k}$-firm transactions, the authors defined in [7][16] a new commit protocol and a new concurrency control protocol. The commit process of $\binom{m}{k}$-firm transactions is based on committing at least the m successfully executed mandatory sub-transactions if there is no time to wait for the execution of optional sub-transactions. For the concurrency control, there is a consideration of both (m,k)-firm and temporal constraints of transactions.

3   Applicability of the (m,k)-firm Approach on the DFCSA for QoS Enhancement in DRTDBMS

Our approach consists of applying the (m,k)-firm approach for user transactions in the distributed feedback-based architecture DFCSA [3], for QoS enhancement in DRTDBMS. Our approach, called *(m,k)-Firm-User-DFCSA* is then an extension of the conventional DFCSA. It involves both the admission control, the concurrency control and the commit process of transactions, by adapting their functioning to take into account the (m,k)-firm constraints of user transactions. In following sections, we describe new functioning principles of these components. Our challenge is to increase the number of transactions that meet their deadlines while maintaining a robust system's behaviour, face to unpredictable workloads induced by user transactions. The general outline of our approach architecture is shown in Fig. 1. Compared to the conventional DFCSA, it is distinguished by the *(m,k)-Firm-User admission controller* and the *(m,k)-Firm-User concurrency controller* as shown in Fig. 1, and by the *(m,k)-Firm-User commit process* even it does not appear in this figure. We note that we proceed with a full data replication policy of real-time data as in [3].

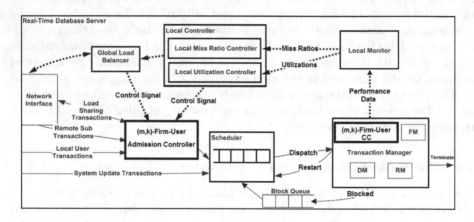

Fig. 1. The (m,k)-Firm-User-DFCSA

3.1   The (m,k)-firm Constraints Model for User Transactions

In our approach, each user transaction T_i ($i \in [1..n]$) submitted to the system is decomposed into a set of sub-transactions. We denote by k_i, the number of sub-transactions of T_i. Distinguishing mandatory sub-transactions from optional ones is based on the criticality of data required by transactions. For example, in an air traffic control system and from a meteorological perspective, data like strength and trajectory of the wind are considered as more critical than data like the moisture rate in the air. Indeed, each sub-transaction ST_{ij} ($j \in [1..k_i]$) consists of a set of operations, each of which accesses a precise data item having a specific criticality. Thus, each operation accessing a critical data item is considered as critical, too. An importance level IL_{ij} is then assigned to ST_{ij}, that we defined as follows:

$$IL_{ij} = \frac{Number\ of\ critical\ operations\ of\ ST_{ij}}{Total\ number\ of\ operations\ of\ ST_{ij}}. \tag{2}$$

Accordingly, the m_i mandatory sub-transactions of T_i are those having high-est importance levels. Considering the $\frac{m}{k}$ ratio parameter that should be fixed, in advance, by the DBA (Database Administrator). Then, the value of m_i is determined as follows:

$$m_i = \frac{m}{k} \times k_i. \tag{3}$$

3.2 The (m,k)-Firm-User Admission Controller

The admission controller of user transactions in the conventional DFCSA oper-ates in a binary way in order to respect the atomicity property of transactions, so that either it accepts a transaction with all of its operations or it totally rejects it. In our approach, we propose an admission controller, called *(m,k)-Firm-User ad-mission controller* (cf. Fig. 1), that takes into account the (m,k)-firm constraints defined for user transactions, aiming to relax the strict decision of the classical one of the DFCSA. The *(m,k)-Firm-User admission controller* attempts to al-low more user transactions to be admitted in the system, while ensuring their execution before their deadlines. Therefore, it tolerates the partial admission of a transaction, in which only its mandatory sub-transactions are admitted, if it is not possible to accept it in its entirety during overloading periods.

At each node, when admitting an user transaction T_i, the *(m,k)-Firm-User admission controller* relies on both QoS parameters belonging to the feedback loop, in order to inquire about the system state, and the (m_i,k_i)-firm constraints of T_i. In fact, it is based on the *estimated CPU utilization* and on the target utilization value, adjusted by the local controller, to decide whether the current transaction will be totally or partially accepted in the system, or even rejected. We note that transactions are rejected in case the *estimated CPU utilization* is higher than *the target utilization* [3], given that such case reflects a system's overload. Therefore, for each T_i, the estimated execution time of its k_i sub-transactions is initially credited to the *estimated CPU utilization*. Then, the *(m,k)-Firm-User admission controller* checks if, according to the new value, T_i may be accepted in the system. Otherwise, it checks again if the system is able to accept T_i by reducing its execution time, when only considering its m_i mandatory sub-transactions. If even the partial admission of T_i is impossible, it will be totally rejected. The admission controller has also to check whether T_i may be terminated before reaching its deadline or not, according to its arrival date and its execution time. With the *(m,k)-Firm-User admission controller*, T_i has more opportunities to enter the system, given that it can be accepted if it is possible to terminate, at least, its m_i mandatory sub-transactions before its deadline.

3.3 The (m,k)-Firm-User Concurrency Controller

In the *(m,k)-Firm-User-DFCSA*, we propose a specific concurrency controller, called *(m,k)-Firm-User concurrency controller* (cf. Fig. 1), that consider (m,k)-firm constraints of user transactions. Via this new concurrency controller, we aim to ensure that the admission of optional sub-transactions does not lead to overload the system when considering data access conflicts. In our approach, the use of the $\binom{m}{k}$-firm CC protocol, proposed in [7] for $\binom{m}{k}$-firm transactions concurrency control, is appropriate in case of conflicts between user transactions having (m,k)-firm constraints. However, in our (m,k)-firm constraints model, we proceed with sub-transactions importance levels rather than weights. This slight adjustment is then considered in the protocol that we call *Adapted-$\binom{m}{k}$-firm CC* and that operates as follows. Considering a sub-transaction ST_r that requests a lock on a data item d, and a sub-transaction ST_h that holds a lock on this same d, where ST_r and ST_h do not belong to the same transaction. In order to decide which one will get access to d, the *Adapted-$\binom{m}{k}$-firm CC* checks, at first, if there is no risk that ST_r's deadline expires by waiting for ST_h to finish its execution. In this case, ST_r is inserted into the block queue of the data d, and ST_h continues executing. Otherwise, if ST_r and ST_h are of different labels, the mandatory one get access to d. Else, if ST_r and ST_h are either both mandatory or both optional, transactions' deadlines are considered, so that the one having the earliest deadline will get the lock on d. If even their deadlines are equal, so:

- if ST_r and ST_h are mandatory, the one having the greater $\frac{m}{k}$ ratio will get access to d, given that its vital part is more important.
- if ST_r and ST_h are optional, the one having the greater importance level will get the lock on d.

In the *(m,k)-Firm-User-DFCSA*, the *Adapted-$\binom{m}{k}$-firm CC* cannot be used for resolving conflicts between user and update transactions, given that they haven't the same characteristics. Thereby, we proposed the *(m,k)-firm-2PL-HP* protocol, which is adapting the 2PL-HP protocol to take into account (m,k)-firm constraints of user transactions. Within this protocol, each update transaction is considered as composed of only one mandatory sub-transaction. Hence, if the conflicting sub-transaction is optional, the *(m,k)-firm-2PL-HP* protocol prioritize the update transaction. Otherwise, the highest priority will be assigned to the transaction having the earliest deadline as in the conventional 2PL-HP.

3.4   The (m,k)-Firm-User Commit Method

In a DRTDBMS, a transaction commits only if all of its sub-transactions commit. However, with the commit method we proposed in the *(m,k)-Firm-User-DFCSA*, that we called *(m,k)-Firm-User commit method*, an user transaction T_i can commit if, at least, its m_i mandatory sub-transactions commit. Furthermore, in our commit method, and following the PROMPT protocol principle [10], we allow transactions to borrow non-committed data. This aims to reduce the blocking time of transactions, caused by the inaccessibility of data held by transactions waiting for committing, and give them more opportunities to meet their deadlines. By this way, we relaxed the isolation property of transactions, which imposes that the result of a transaction, that have not yet finished its execution, should be invisible for other transactions. However, the lending data process in our approach is controlled, so that it can only be performed by mandatory sub-transactions, considering that the optional ones can be ignored when committing a transaction.

4   Simulations and Results

In this section, we aim to evaluate the QoS performance provided by the proposed *(m,k)-Firm-User-DFCSA*, based on simulation results.

4.1   Simulation Principle

We have evaluated our approach according to a set of simulation experiments, where a set of parameters have been varied. Each simulation result represents the average of 10 simulations. The system parameters for simulations are shown in Table 1. We note that real-time data are fully replicated at each node. Transactions are scheduled according to the EDF algorithm, which prioritize the transaction having the earliest deadline. For resolving conflicts between transactions, we use the (m,k)-Firm-User concurrency controller which consider the (m,k)-firm constraints defined to user transactions. Distributed transactions are committed according to the (m,k)-Firm-User commit method. The parameter settings of user transactions are summarized in Table 2. We note that arrival times of these transactions are generated according to the "Poisson" process. In the set of our experiments, we varied the value of the $\frac{m}{k}$ ratio, in order to show the effect of either increasing or decreasing the number of mandatory sub-transactions for each user transaction. In our experiments results, we only consider user transactions.

Table 1. System parameter settings

Parameter	Value
Simulation time (ms)	3000
Number of nodes	8
Number of real-time data	20/node
Number of classic data	1000/node
Real-time data validity (ms)	[500, 1000]
MDE value	[2, 5]

Table 2. User transactions parameters

Parameter	Value
Number of sub-transactions	[2,4]
Number of write operations	2
Number of read operations	[0,2]
Write operation time (ms)	2
Read operation time (ms)	1
Slack factor	10
Remote data ratio	20%
$\frac{m}{k}$ ratio	[0.5, 0.7]

4.2   Results and Discussions

By referring to Fig. 2, we can assert that the conventional DFCSA yields the lowest number of successful user transactions, compared to the result provided by the *(m,k)-Firm-User-DFCSA*. This remains true, whatsoever in case 1) the

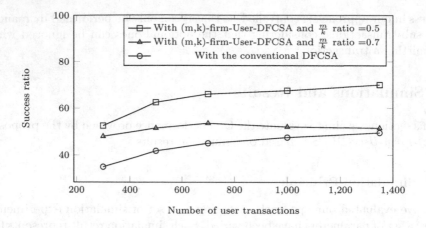

Fig. 2. Simulation results for user transactions

$\frac{m}{k}$ ratio is equal to 0.5 or 2) when it is equal to 0.7. We can also notice that the best result is provided in case 1), where the performance gain is for about 20%. This is because that in case 2), more of mandatory sub-transactions are required to be executed than in case 1), which tolerates the reject of more optional sub-transactions. Thus, we can say that the number of successful user transactions increases by reducing the number of mandatory sub-transactions, that is by reducing the value of the $\frac{m}{k}$ ratio. This allows more of user transactions to be successfully executed, given that with the *(m,k)-Firm-User concurrency controller*, conflicts are resolved in favour of mandatory sub-transactions. In addition, with the *(m,k)-Firm-User commit method*, we have less requirements to validate a user transaction, given that it can be committed if at least its *m* mandatory sub-transactions are successfully executed. Then we can say that, with the *(m,k)-Firm-User-DFCSA*, transactions are executed under good conditions having more opportunity to be successfully terminated before their deadlines.

5   Conclusion and Future Work

In this paper, we have presented the *(m,k)-Firm-User-DFCSA* for QoS enhancement in DRTDBMS. In our work, we have applied the (m,k)-firm approach to user transactions, then we have proposed specific admission control, concurrency control and commit process to manage these transactions while considering their newly-defined (m,k)-firm constraints. Experimental results confirmed the benefit of the proposed approach on increasing the number of transactions which meet their deadlines, even in the presence of unpredictable workload. Furthermore, we can say that the minimal QoS is guaranteed when executing only mandatory sub-transactions, and then, the more optional sub-transactions are executed, the more the QoS is enhanced.

We plan to extend this work in several ways. We will propose to apply the (m,k)-firm approach on update transactions combined with the *(m,k)-Firm-User-DFCSA*, aiming to allow for more transactions to meet their deadlines without affecting the data freshness.

References

1. Abbott, R.K., Garcia-Molina, H.: Scheduling Real-Time Transactions: A Performance Evaluation. ACM Trans. Database Syst. 17, 513–560 (1992)
2. Liu, C.L., Layland, J.W.: Scheduling Algorithms for Multiprogramming in a Hard-Real-Time Environment. J. ACM 20, 46–61 (1973)
3. Wei, Y., Son, S.H., Stankovic, J.A., Kang, K.D.: QoS Management in Replicated Real Time Databases. In: 24th IEEE International Real-Time Systems Symposium, pp. 86–97. IEEE Computer Society, Washington (2003)
4. Pu, C., Leff, A.: Replica Control in Distributed Systems: An Asynchronous Approach. In: ACM SIGMOD International Conference on Management of Data, pp. 377–386. ACM Press, Denver (1991)
5. Haj Said, S., Sadeg, B., Ayeb, B., Amanton, L.: The DLR-ORECOP Real-time Replication Control Protocol. In: 12th IEEE International Conference on Emerging Technologies and Factory Automation, pp. 1–8. IEEE, Palma de Mallorca (2009)
6. Ramanathan, P., Hamdaoui, M.: A Dynamic Priority Assignment Technique for Streams with (m,k)-firm Deadlines. IEEE Trans. Comput. 44, 1443–1451 (1995)
7. Haubert, J., Sadeg, B., Amanton, L.: Relaxing the Real-Time Constraints in Distributed Real-Time Database Management Systems. In: 10th Int.Conf. on Real-Time and Embedded Computing Systems and Applications, pp. 647–661. Springer, Gothenburg (2004)
8. Bouazizi, E., Duvallet, C.: Utilisation des Contraintes (m,k)-firm pour la Gestion de la QdS dans les SGBD Temps Réel. In: INFORSID, Lille, pp. 95–110 (2011)
9. Haubert, J., Sadeg, B., Amanton, L.: Reducing the blocking time in weighted real-time distributed transaction management. In: 3rd IEEE International Symposium on Signal Processing and Information Technology, pp. 584–587 (2003)
10. Haritsa, J.R., Ramamritham, K.: The PROMPT Real-Time Commit Protocol. IEEE Trans. Parallel Distrib. Syst. 11, 160–181 (2000)
11. Xiong, M., Ramamritham, K.: Deriving Deadlines and Periods for Real-Time Update Transactions. IEEE Trans. Comput. 53, 567–583 (2004)
12. Kang, K.-D., Son, S.H., Stankovic, J.A., Abdelzaher, T.F.: A QoS-Sensitive Approach for Timeliness and Freshness Guarantees in Real-Time Databases. In: 14th Euromicro Conference on Real-Time Systems, pp. 203–212. IEEE Computer Society, Vienna (2002)
13. Amirijoo, M., Hansson, J., Son, S.H.: Specification and Management of QoS in Real-Time Databases Supporting Imprecise Computations. IEEE Trans. Comput. 55, 304–319 (2006)
14. Lu, C.: Feedback Control Real-Time Scheduling. PhD thesis, University of Virginia (2001)
15. Haubert, J., Amanton, L., Sadeg, B., Mammeri, Z.: Admission Control for Relaxed Real-Time Transactions. In: IEEE Int. Computer Systems and Information Technology Conference, pp. 328–334 (2005)
16. Haubert, J., Sadeg, B., Amanton, L.: $\binom{m}{k}$-firm real-time distributed transactions. In: 16th WIP Euromicro Conference on Real-Time Systems, pp. 61–65 (2004)

A Parallel Distributed System for Gene Expression Profiling Based on Clustering Ensemble and Distributed Optimization

Zakaria Benmounah and Mohamed Batouche

Computer Science Department, College of NTIC, Constantine University 2,
25000 Constantine, Algeria
{zbenmounah,mcbatouche}@gmail.com

Abstract. With the development of microarray technology, it is possible now to study and measure the expression profiles of thousands of genes simultaneously which can lead to identify subgroup of specific disease or extract hidden relationships between genes. One computational method often used to this end is clustering. In this paper, we propose a parallel distributed system for gene expression profiling (PDS-GEF) which provides a useful basis for individualized treatment of a certain disease such as Cancer. The proposed approach is based on two major techniques: the GIM (Generalized Island Model) and clustering ensemble. GIMs are used to generate good quality clusterings which are refined by a consensus function to get a high quality clustering. PDS-GEF system is implemented using Matlab®'s PCT (Parallel Computing Toolbox™) which runs on a desktop computer, and tested on 34 different publicly available gene expression data sets. The obtained results compete with and even outperform existing methods.

1   Introduction

During the last decade, biomedical research has undergone changes which have transformed the development towards automation and at the same time the treatment has led to an increase in speed and high throughput [1]. One of the emergent technologies following this development which is considered as a platform for various applications is Microarrays technology. The latter assesses the expression patterns of thousands of genes at one time, and helps to identify appropriate targets for therapeutic intervention and discovery of new disease subclasses. Microarray has three major classes [2]: class comparison, class prediction and class discovery. The first involves finding differences in expression levels between predefined groups of samples. The second class involves identifying the class membership of a sample based on its gene expression profile. The third class involves analyzing a given set of gene expression profiles with the goal to understand the mechanisms underlying a disease by discovering subgroups of genes that share common features. A computational method often used for class discovery is clustering which aims at dividing the data points (genes) into groups (clusters) using similarity measures, such

J. Kołodziej et al. (Eds.): ICA3PP 2013, Part I, LNCS 8285, pp. 176–185, 2013.

as Correlation or Euclidean distance [3, 4]. The notion of "cluster" cannot be precisely defined [5] which is one of the reasons that explains the wide range of clustering algorithms proposed in the literature to solve the problem of gene expression profiling [6, 7, 8].

When facing clustering algorithm for gene expression, selecting the best clustering method with the correct parameter values is not an easy task in most cases. Users may not be capable of introducing the precise parameter value. Therefore a small change on the input parameter may impact the output result. Also if not properly handled, noisy genes data may degrade significantly the quality of the results. The frequently used method to overcome these limitations is clustering ensemble. It takes as an input a set of clusterings generated by different algorithms [9], or by the same algorithm using different parameters [10], and provides as an output a better quality final clustering [11, 12].

In this paper, we propose a parallel distributed system for gene expression profiling (PDS-GEF) dedicated for class discovery which provides a useful basis for individualized treatment of a certain disease such as Cancer. The proposed approach is based on two major techniques: the GIM (Generalized Island Model) and clustering ensemble. GIMs are composed of many metaheuristics (particle swarm optimization, ant colony optimization, artificial bee colony, genetic algorithm ...) performing in parallel and cooperating by using a migration operator. They are used to generate good quality clusterings which are refined by a consensus function to get a high quality clustering. PDS-GEF system is implemented using Matlab's PCT (Parallel Computing Toolbox) which runs on a desktop computer, and is tested on 34 different publicly available gene expression data sets.

The rest of the paper is organized as follows. In section 2, we present the background and related works. Sections 3 and 4 are dedicated to the description and the implementation of the proposed approach for gene expression profiling. In section 5, we present the experimental results obtained by using publicly available data sets. Finally, conclusions and future work are drawn.

2   Background and Related Work

Before a formal description of our approach, we briefly introduce the principle of the two used methods namely generalized island model and clustering ensemble.

2.1   Generalized Island Model

The Generalized Island Model (GIM) [13] is as an approach that can be applied to a broad class of optimization algorithms. The study of the effect of this generalized model distribution was performed on several well-known population based clustering metaheuristics which include: the differential evolution (DE) [14], Genetic Algorithms (GA) [15], search for harmony (HS) [16], artificial bees' colony (ABC) [17], particle swarm optimization (PSO) [18], ant colony optimization (ACO) [19]. The GIM has been proposed in order to improve the diversity of solutions. It enables to efficiently distribute algorithms across multiple processors. A new operator called the migration operator can improve the overall performance of algorithms. Informally, this operator has both the role to select individuals in the current island to be sent to other islands, as well as to potentially introduce individuals outside the local population.

2.2   Clustering Ensemble

Cluster ensemble is made up of two steps: Generation and Consensus Function [20] (see figure 1). In the following, we describe these two steps.

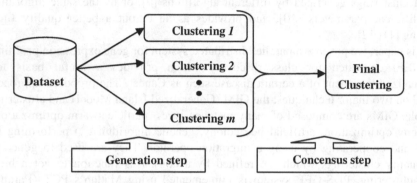

Fig. 1. Diagram of the general process of cluster ensemble [20]

Generation Step. Is the first step of the cluster ensemble. Given a data set, it generates a collection of clustering solutions. For best performance, it is necessary to apply the most appropriate method so that the combined result will bring considerable changes in the outcome of the second step.

Consensus Function. Is the main step of the clustering ensemble. It combines the clustering solutions of the ensemble and produces a best clustering as the final output. There are two main consensus function approaches: objects co-occurrence and median partition. Ensemble clustering has been shown to be NP-complete [21].

Many algorithms have been developed in this field [20]. COMUSA finds the true number of final clusters but it requires an exact parameter [22]. EAC, COMUSA, and CSPA may not reveal the relationship between clusters [23]. Although HGPA is very fast, however cannot handle large data with noise [9]. LCE needs a lot of computation [24]. GCC Genetic methods suffer from long execution times [25]. In the domain of clustering ensemble, determining crossover, chromosome encoding, mutation, and the fitness function are not immediate. DICLEANS outperforms all algorithms cited above in time execution and clusters quality, it uses minimum spanning tree as the input where each vertex represents an input cluster and each vertex represents the intercluster similarity [26].

3   The Proposed Approach

In this section, the main aspects of our proposed approach are considered. The proposed approach is two-level architecture (see figure 2). The first stage is composed of various configurations of GIM. The second stage consists in consensus clustering technique which will take as input the good clusterings solutions obtained in the first stage and generates a high quality clustering.

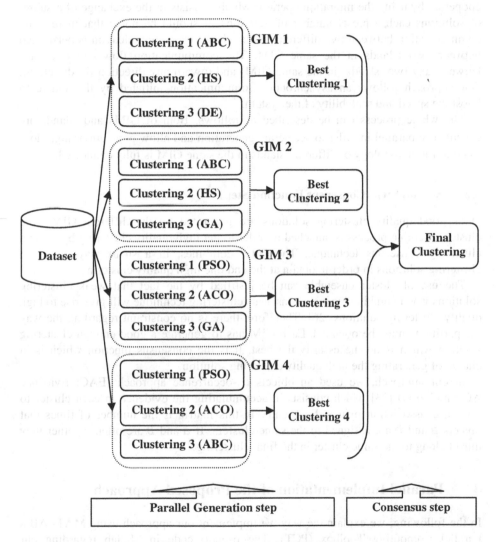

Fig. 2. Architecture of the PDS-GEF system

3.1   First Level (Parallel Generation Step)

In our system, we use four GIMs including each three islands representing instances of existing clustering algorithms based optimization selected among the following list: DE (Differential Evolution), PSO (Particle Swarm Optimization), HS (Harmony Search), GA (Genetic Algorithm), and ABC (Artificial Bee Colony). All the selected algorithms are population based.

Inside one GIM, optimization algorithms (Metaheuristics) work in parallel and cooperate by using the migration operator which consists in the exchange of a subset of solutions each a preset number of iterations. It should be noted that there is no communication between two different GIMs. However, communication is performed between two islands in the same GIM. The communication flow can circulates between any two islands (in the same GIM) and toward any direction (bi-direction). Our approach follows an asynchronous communication initiated by the source to boost the speed and scalability of the system.

The whole process can be described as follows. Both of GIMs and islands are executed in parallel in order to accelerate generation and allow population migration. The migration topology of different islands in the same GIM is fully connected.

3.2   Second Step (Consensus Function Step)

Once good quality clustering solutions are generated by the different GIMs, the cluster ensemble process is launched in order to get high quality clustering by using a clustering consensus technique. The latter combines, in a smart way, a set of clustering solutions in order to obtain at the end one high quality clustering.

The use of cluster ensemble can be justified by the fact that weak clustering solutions when combined using a consensus clustering technique will give rise to high quality clustering solutions [26]. Therefore, there is no constraint regarding the way the partitions must be obtained. Each GIM has to generate a good enough clustering solution which is not necessarily the best. It is the consensus function which is in charge of generating the high quality clustering solution.

In our approach, we used an objects co-occurrence approach (EAC: Evidence ACcumulation) [23] which consists in accumulating the evidence in each cluster to form a coassociation matrix. Each entry in this matrix is the number of times that objects a and b are assigned to the same clusters. If a and b are often together they must belong to the same cluster in the final clustering.

4   Parallel Implementation of the Proposed Approach

In the following, we explain the way we implement our approach using MATLAB's Parallel Computing Toolbox (PCT). The pseudo code in Matlab regarding our approach can be summarized as follows:

```
Program: PDS-GEF
  input: gene expression data sets
  Matlabpool(12);
  spmd
    switch labindex % the identifier of each Island
      case 1:  apply Island (1)  algorithm;⎫
      case 2:  apply Island (2)  algorithm;⎬ % GIM 1
      case 3:  apply Island (3)  algorithm;⎭
      case 4:  apply Island (4)  algorithm;⎫
      case 5:  apply Island (5)  algorithm;⎬ % GIM 2
      case 6:  apply Island (6)  algorithm;⎭
      case 7:  apply Island (7)  algorithm;⎫
      case 8:  apply Island (8)  algorithm;⎬ % GIM 3
      case 9:  apply Island (9)  algorithm;⎭
      case 10: apply Island (10) algorithm;⎫
      case 11: apply Island (11) algorithm;⎬ % GIM 4
      case 12: apply Island (12) algorithm;⎭
    end % switch
  end % spmd
  BestClustering ← EAC (BestClusterings); % consensus
  Matlabpool close;
  output: BestClustering; % final result
end.
```

Our proposed system is composed of 12 parallel cooperating islands algorithms. The pseudo code of the Island algorithm:

```
algorithm: Island(id)
  input: id % identification number
  P  % initial population
  S  % selection strategy
  R  % recombination policy
  Ai % optimization algorithm
  Ui % number of iteration in Ai
  initalize P; % initialize population
  while !stop_criterion
    P'← Ai(P, Ui);   % new population
    M ← S(P');        % selection policy
    labSend M;        % send selected solutions
    M'←labReceive;    % receive migrant solutions
    P''← R(P', M');  % recombination policy
    P ← P'';          % update current population
  end % while
end.
```

In each island, a metaheuristic (GA, PSO, ACO, HS, DE, ABC) is deployed to carry out the clustering generation process. Its dynamic can be described as follows. Initially, the metaheuristic is launched with randomly generated population P. After ui iterations, a set M of solutions, chosen using a selection policy S to undergo migration, is broadcasted to all neighboring islands. Once all selected solutions sent by neighboring islands are received, a recombination policy R is used to form the new population. This process is repeated until a stopping criterion is reached. labSend and labReceive are two functions in Matlab's parallel computing toolbox used for communication purposes.

5   Experimental Results

To assess the performance of our system, we tested our approach on 34 different publicly available gene expression data sets having the proprieties shown in table 1.

Table 1. Description of used gene expression datasets [27]

Dataset Name	Array Type	Tissue	Total samples	Num classes	Total Genes	Selected # of Genes
Bladder carcinoma	Affymetrix	Bladder	40	3	7129	1203
Breast Cancer	Affymetrix	Breast	49	2	7129	1198
Breast-Colon tumors	Affymetrix	Breast, Colon	104	2	22283	182
Carcinomas	Affymetrix	Multi-tissue	174	10	12533	1571
Central nervous system-1	Affymetrix	Brain	34	2	7129	857
Central nervous system-2	Affymetrix	Brain	42	5	7129	1379
Endometrial cancer	D-Channel	Endometrium	42	4	8872	1771
Glioblastoma multiforme	D-Channel	Brain	37	3	24192	1411
Gliomagenesis	D-Channel	Brain	50	3	41472	1739
Gliomas-1	Affymetrix	Brain	50	4	12625	1377
Gliomas-2	Affymetrix	Brain	28	2	12625	1070
Gliomas-3	Affymetrix	Brain	22	2	12625	1152
Hepatocellular carcinoma	D-Channel	Liver	178	2	22699	85
Leukemia-1	Affymetrix	Bone Marrow	248	2	12625	2526
Leukemia-2	Affymetrix	Bone Marrow	248	6	12625	2526
Leukemia-3	Affymetrix	Blood	72	2	12582	1081
Leukemia-4	Affymetrix	Blood	72	3	12582	2194
Leukemia-5	Affymetrix	Bone Marrow	72	2	7129	1877
Leukemia-6	Affymetrix	Bone Marrow	72	3	7129	1877
Lung tumor-1	Affymetrix	Lung	203	5	12600	1543
Lung tumor-2	D-Channel	Lung	66	4	24192	4553
Lymphoma-1	D-Channel	Blood	42	2	4022	1095
Lymphoma-2	D-Channel	Blood	62	3	4022	2093
Lymphoma-3	Affymetrix	Blood	77	2	7129	798
Melanoma	D-Channel	Skin	38	2	8067	2201
Mesothelioma	Affymetrix	Lung	181	2	12533	1626
Multi-tissue	Affymetrix	Multi-tissue	190	14	16063	1363
Prostate cancer-1	D-Channel	Prostate	104	5	20000	2315
Prostate cancer-2	D-Channel	Prostate	92	4	20000	1288
Prostate cancer-3	D-Channel	Prostate	69	3	42640	1625
Prostate cancer-4	D-Channel	Prostate	110	4	42640	2496
Prostate cancer-5	Affymetrix	Prostate	102	2	12600	339
Round blue-cell tumor	D-Channel	Multi-tissue	83	4	6567	1069
Serrated carcinomas	Affymetrix	Colon	37	2	22883	2202

Array Type refers to the type of microarray used in the experiment. There are two types namely Affymetrix and Double Channel. Tissue indicates the tissue from where the samples were taken. Total samples is the number of conditions used in the experiment and it represents the dimensional of data. Num of Classes is the optimal number of groups (clusters) expected after the data has been clustered. Total genes is the number of genes present in the experiment. Selected # of Genes is the data set is large and a lot of information corresponds to genes not showing any interesting changes during the experiment. Filtering allows to find the interesting genes and passes over genes with expression profiles that do not show anything of interest.

Table 2. Number of Clusters on Gene Expression Data Sets

Data Set	True Cluster	DiCLEANS	Our approach
Bladder carcinoma	3	2	3
Breast Cancer	2	2	2
Breast-Colon tumors	2	2	4
Carcinomas	10	6	6
Central nervous system-1	2	2	3
Central nervous system-2	5	4	4
Endometrial cancer	4	4	4
Glioblastoma multiforme	3	2	2
Gliomagenesis	3	2	4
Gliomas-1	4	4	3
Gliomas-2	2	2	5
Gliomas-3	2	2	2
Hepatocellular carcinoma	2	3	2
Leukemia-1	2	2	2
Leukemia-2	6	3	5
Leukemia-3	2	2	3
Leukemia-4	3	3	3
Leukemia-5	2	2	2
Leukemia-6	3	3	2
Lung tumor-1	5	3	4
Lung tumor-2	4	2	2
Lymphoma-1	2	2	2
Lymphoma-2	3	2	2
Lymphoma-3	2	3	2
Melanoma	2	2	2
Mesothelioma	2	2	2
Multi-tissue	14	5	6
Prostate cancer-1	5	5	7
Prostate cancer-2	4	5	2
Prostate cancer-3	3	2	2
Prostate cancer-4	4	5	3
Prostate cancer-5	2	6	2
Round blue-cell tumor	4	5	2
Serrated carcinomas	2	2	2

The data sets used in our approach are filtered from non significant genes. We compared our results with the expected optimal number of classes and also with a recent developed consensus function called DiCLEANS (Divisive Clustering Ensemble with Automatic Cluster Number) [26]. The experimental results show that our approach competes with and even outperforms DiCLEANS in some cases as shown in table 2.

6   Conclusion and Future Work

In this work, we proposed a parallel distributed system for gene expression profiling PDS-GEF dedicated to class discovery using microarrays technology. It combines mainly two major techniques namely distributed optimization and clustering ensemble. The parallel distributed optimization techniques are used for generating good quality cluster solutions which are combined to get high quality clustering by exploiting a consensus function namely EAC technique. The proposed approach is implemented using Matlab's PCT (Parallel Computing Toolbox) which runs on a desktop machine. The parallelism allows dealing with the huge amount of data inherent to bioinformatics. The conducted experiments on real data sets have led to very encouraging results.

There are many ways to improve the performance of the system and the quality of the resulting clustering. The use of MATLAB Distributed Computing Server, GPU and cluster of GPUs will certainly improve the performance of the system. The application of other consensus functions like DiCLEANS or those based on median partition would also enhance the quality of the resulting clustering yielding to a better diagnosis.

References

1. Jens, S., Kerstin, B., Anette, J., Jvrg, D.H., Philipp, A.: Microarray Technology as a Universal Tool for High-Throughput Analysis of Biological Systems. Combinatorial Chemistry & High Throughput Screening 9, 365–380 (2006)
2. Tarca, A.L., Roberto, R., Sorin, D.: Analysis of microarray experiments of gene expression profiling. American Journal of Obstetrics and Gynecology 195, 373–388 (2006)
3. Aach, J., Rindone, W., George, M.S.: Systematic management and analysis of yeast gene expression data. Genome Research 10, 431–445 (2000)
4. Bethin, K.E., Nagai, Y., Sladek, R., Asada, M., Sadovsky, Y., Hudson, T.J., et al.: Microarray analysis of uterine gene expression in mouse and human pregnancy. Mol. Endocrinol. 17, 1454–1469 (2003)
5. Vladimir, E.C.: Why so many clustering algorithms. Sigkdd Explorations 4, 65–75 (2002)
6. Daxin, J., Chun, T., Aidong, Z.: Cluster Analysis for Gene Expression Data: A Survey. IEEE Transaction on Knowledge And Data Engineering 16, 1370–1386 (2004)
7. Kerr, G., Ruskin, H.J., Crane, M., Doolan, P.: Techniques for clustering gene expression data. Computer in Biology and Medecine 38, 283–293 (2008)
8. Harun, P., Burak, E., Andy, D.P., Çertin, Y.: Clustering of high throughput gene expression data. Computer & Operation Research 39, 3046–3061 (2012)

9. Strehl, A., Ghost, J.: Cluster A Knowledge Reuse Framework for combining Mutiple Partitions. J. Machine Learning Research 3, 583–617 (2002)
10. Fred, A., Jain, A.: Combining Multiple Clusterings Using Evidence Accumulation. IEEE Transaction Pattern Analysis and Machine Intelligence 27, 835–850 (2005)
11. Strehl, A., Ghosh, J.: Cluster: Cluster Ensembles - A Knowledge Reuse Framework for Combining Multiple Partitions. J. Machine Learning Research. 3, 583–617 (2002)
12. Mimaroglu, S., Erdil, E.: Obtaining Better Quality Final Clustering by Merging a Collection of Clusterings. Bioinformatics 26, 2645–2646 (2010)
13. Izzo, D., Ruciński, M., Biscani, F.: The Generalized Island Model. In: Fernandez de Vega, F., Hidalgo Pérez, J.I., Lanchares, J. (eds.) Parallel Architectures & Bioinspired Algorithms. SCI, vol. 415, pp. 151–170. Springer, Heidelberg (2012)
14. Ravi, V., Aggarwal, N., Chauhan, N.: Differential Evolution Based Fuzzy Clustering. In: Panigrahi, B.K., Das, S., Suganthan, P.N., Dash, S.S. (eds.) SEMCCO 2010. LNCS, vol. 6466, pp. 38–45. Springer, Heidelberg (2010)
15. Sheikh, R.H., Raghuwanshi, M.M., Jaiswal, A.N.: Genetic Algorithm Based Clustering: A Survey. Emerging Trends in Engineering and Technology 8, 314–319 (2008)
16. Alia, O.M., Al-Betar, M.A., Mandava, R., Khader, A.T.: Data Clustering Using Harmony Search Algorithm. In: Panigrahi, B.K., Suganthan, P.N., Das, S., Satapathy, S.C. (eds.) SEMCCO 2011, Part II. LNCS, vol. 7077, pp. 79–88. Springer, Heidelberg (2011)
17. Changsheng, Z., Dantong, O., Jiaxu, N.: An artificial bee colony approach for clustering. Expert Systems with Applications 37, 4761–4767 (2010)
18. Yau, K.L., Tsang, P.W.M., Leung, C.S.: PSO-based K-means clustering with enhanced cluster matching for gene expression data. Neural Computing and Application 22, 1349–1355 (2013)
19. Kao, Y., Cheng, K.: An ACO-Based Clustering Algorithm. In: Dorigo, M., Gambardella, L.M., Birattari, M., Martinoli, A., Poli, R., Stützle, T. (eds.) ANTS 2006. LNCS, vol. 4150, pp. 340–347. Springer, Heidelberg (2006)
20. Sandro, V.P., José, R.S.: A Survey of Clustering Ensemble Algorithms. International Journal of Pattern Recognition and Artificial Intelligence 25, 337–372 (2011)
21. Filkov, V.: Integrating microarray data by consensus clustering. IEEE International Conference on Tools with Artificial Intelligence 15, 418–426 (2003)
22. Mimaroglu, S., Erdil, E.: Obtaining Better quality final clustering by Merging a Collection of Clusterings. Bioinformatics 26, 2645–2646 (2010)
23. Fred, A., Jain, A.: Combining Multiple Clusterings Using Evidence Accumulation. IEEE Tran. Pattern Analysis and Machine Intelligence 27, 835–850 (2005)
24. Natthakan, I.O., Tossapon, B., Simon, G.: LCE: A Link-Based Cluster Ensemble Method for Improved Gene Expression Data Analysis. Bioinformatics 26, 1513–1519 (2010)
25. Yu, Z., Wong, H., Wang, H.: Graph-Based Consensus Clustering for Class Discovery from Gene Expression Data. Bioinformatics 33, 2888–2896 (2007)
26. Selim, M., Emin, A.: DICLEANS: Divisive Clustering Ensemble With Automatic Cluster Number. IEEE/ACM Tran. Computational Biology and Bioinformatics 9, 408–420 (2012)
27. Souto, M., Costa, I., de Araujo, D., Ludermir, T., Schliep, A.: Clustering Cancer Gene Expression Data: A Comparative Study. BMC Bioinformatics 9, 497 (2008)

Unimodular Loop Transformations
with Source-to-Source Translation for GPUs

Pasquale Cantiello[1], Beniamino Di Martino[1], and Francesco Piccolo[1]

Second University of Naples, Italy
pasquale.cantiello@unina2.it, beniamino.dimartino@unina.it,
piccolo.francesco@gmail.com

Abstract. Heterogeneous computing architectures offer the opportunity to exploit the extremely high performances of systems which are composed of different subsystems, assuring at the same time low energy consumption and accessible costs. In order to benefit from all these advantages, each computing unit should be programmed by using a specific model with properly optimized code to process its workload at best.

In the path of building a source-to-source transformer tool to automate the translation of code for heterogeneous architectures made by a combination of several CPUs and GPUs, a series of translator building blocks on top of ROSE compiler infrastructure have been built. In this work is presented the module that performs unimodular loop transformations and that provides output for GPUs.

Transformers can be used in the tool either manually according to user preference, or automatically driven by knowledge based techniques, e. g. algorithmic concept recognition. A chain of code transformations can produce parallel code, relieving accelerators and multicore programming hardness.

1 Introduction

The demand for increased heterogeneity in computing systems is partially due to the need for high performance and low power consuming systems. Less advances in technology and frequency scaling since the last decade, have advised the community to start looking at heterogeneous solutions as the primary method of gaining extra performance. Contemporary GPUs are massively parallel processors that have outpaced CPUs in terms of floating point operations per second, and so GPUs have become interesting hardware platform for solving parallel compute-intensive tasks.

Despite these advantages, accelerators present a serious challenge: several programming models and languages are available to develop applications for this kind of architectures, but developers are just beginning to explore programming for heterogeneous systems [5]. Compilers for automatic parallelization of sequential code have been investigated by researchers for several decades. Code generation for hardware accelerators has gained in popularity between majority of research or industrial compilers since the appearance of GPGPUs.

J. Kołodziej et al. (Eds.): ICA3PP 2013, Part I, LNCS 8285, pp. 186–195, 2013.
© Springer International Publishing Switzerland 2013

In this work is presented a source to source compiler transformer that have been implemented to run loop transformations and to do code mapping on parallel architectures as GPUs. The transformer has been built on top of ROSE [10] compiler infrastructure and is part of a project [3] to automatically offload computations between several heterogeneous cores (CPUs and GPUs), by compounding a series of transformations.

Typically source code passes through a series of transformers which are driven by user preferences, static analysis results and knowledge-based techniques eventually powered by algorithmic concept recognition [4]. A series of loop transformations are performed to expose the desired grade of parallelism, laying to CUDA mapping, OpenMP pragma generation or code factorization. The selection of the transformation chain permits to achieve a particular goal.

After the whole transformation, the intermediate representation can be unparsed back to source code ready to be processed by a native compiler.

After this introduction, the paper continues with a related works analysis in section 2. In section 3 a brief remind on unimodular loop transformation is presented along with the implementation of the loop transformer in ROSE. In section 4 is shown the CUDA mapping with sample output code. As a test case, a series of transformation over a matrix product are shown in section 5. Conclusions and future work directions are summarized in section 6.

2   Related Works

The compiler design for automatic parallelization of sequential code is an old but still very active field of investigation by scientist and engineers. The recent research works: PAR4ALL [11] and PIPS [1] are focused on automatic parallelization and mapping to accelerators, using a polyhedral model for analysis. The first one is able to automatically map a parallel loop nest to CUDA code. Many works have ventured in this field: in [2] is introduced an automatic C to CUDA code transformation system, for affine programs; hiCUDA [7] is an high-level directive-based language for CUDA programming; R-Stream compiler [8] a source to source mapping from a high-level annotated C to GPU. There are also several commercial compilers able to produce GPU code, including PGI Accelerator [13] and CAPS HMPP [6]. Both use a directive approach to split portions of the code between CPU and GPU.

The work presented here combines both source to source transformation for loop optimization and source code generation for CUDA enabled GPUs. The transformer can emit also OpenMP (not showed here) for multicore architectures. Furthermore, its modular nature permits combinations of similar transformers to create complex chains.

3   Loop Transformations

Unimodular loop transformation theory [12], is based on matrix transformations and it has been used for an important subset of loop nests. This technique can be applied to programs whose loop nests have two main characteristic: first, data dependences between loop iterations should be represented by a set of integer vectors, known as distance vectors; second, loop must be perfectly nested.

Unimodular loop transformations such as *interchange, reversal,* and *skewing* can be modelled as linear transformations in the iteration space. The effectiveness of this method lies on its formalism, where transformations are modelled by an unimodular matrix, and a compound transformation is still a unimodular matrix.

Transformation legality check can be run directly using a transformation matrix and dependence vectors. The entire process can be split in two parts: transformation matrix generation, and loop nest restructuring. The first problem is easy to apply, due to the simplicity of the transformation composition. On the other hand harder is the generation of the executable code. Two steps must be conducted: rewriting the loop body and rewriting the loop bounds. Also for each part there are two phases: calculating new expressions by using the transformation matrix and replacing the abstract syntax tree nodes with the new calculated one.

3.1   Loop Restructuring for Unimodular Transformations

Suppose having the loop nest in Fig. 1.

```
for(I_1=2; I_1<=N_1-1; I_1++) {
  for(I_2=2; I_2<=N_2-1; I_2++) {
    a[I_1][I_2] = a[I_1-1][I_2] + a[I_1][I_2-1] + a[I_1+1][I_2-1];
  }
}
```

Fig. 1. A loop nest

For a two dimension loop nest a transformation matrix T can be:

$$T = \begin{bmatrix} 2 & 1 \\ 1 & 0 \end{bmatrix}$$

It results from the composition of a skewing transformation of loop I_2 by loop I_1 with factor 2 and an interchange transformation between loops I_2 and I_1.

$$T = T_{inter}T_{skew} \qquad T_{skew} = \begin{bmatrix} 1 & 0 \\ 2 & 1 \end{bmatrix} \qquad T_{inter} = \begin{bmatrix} 0 & 1 \\ 1 & 0 \end{bmatrix}$$

In general loop body transformation only requires each iteration variable I_j to be replaced by the appropriate linear combination of I's, where the I's are the indexes for the transformed loop nest:

$$\begin{bmatrix} I_1 \\ I_2 \\ \vdots \\ I_n \end{bmatrix} = T^{-1} \begin{bmatrix} I'_1 \\ I'_2 \\ \vdots \\ I'_n \end{bmatrix}$$

Vector I' has the new loop body variable references.

The loop body update in our work has been done with ROSE by replacing all variable reference nodes met while traversing the loop body of the nesting, with new expressions. At first have been built new expression nodes map compounding add and multiply operations according to the inverse transformation matrix T^{-1}. A map is used to match old and new expressions for a particular variable reference symbol. Later a loop body rewrite traversal replaces old variable reference expressions with new expressions according to the map. A `SageBuilder::replaceExpression` has been used to the purpose.

The next step in the process of applying unimodular loop transformation is the more complex task of updating the loop bounds for each loop in the nesting.

A parametrized convex polyhedron can be used to represent the iteration space of a loop nest when the loop bounds of the nest are affine expressions of outer loop indices and symbolic constants. In this case loop bounds can be expressed by a system of inequalities as in Fig. 2 shown in Fig. 3. This holds the data representation of all the loop bounds in the nesting.

$$I_1 \geq 2$$
$$I_1 \leq N_1 - 1$$
$$I_2 \geq 2$$
$$I_2 \leq N_2 - 1$$

constants	N_1	N_2	I_1	I_2
-2	0	0	1	0
-1	1	0	1	0
-2	0	0	0	1
-1	0	1	0	-1

Fig. 2. Inequalities   **Fig. 3.** Inequalities matrix

Original loop bound expressions are extracted searching for init and test expressions to calculate the inequality matrix coefficients. The inequality matrix is filled by traversing these expressions searching for `SgIntVal` nodes and `SgVarRefExpressions` and separating iteration variables from the others.

Next step is the calculation of the absolute minimum and maximum for each loop index variable to determine loop bounds. Later updating of inequalities matrix by unimodular transformation matrix T is done by multiplying the transposed matrix T' with an extract of the inequality matrix. This extracted matrix must be set to the inequalities matrix columns from I_1 to I_n. After loop transformation the loop nest inequalities matrix 1 is shown in Fig. 4.

This changes the loop nest index expression. After changing inequalities defining the original loop bounds, new global maximum and minimum must be recomputed.

The last step consists in finding the new loop nesting bounds using inequalities matrix and the min and max lists calculated in the previous step.

constants	N_1	N_2	I_1	I_2
-2	0	0	0	1
-1	1	0	0	-1
-2	0	0	1	-2
-1	0	1	-1	2

Fig. 4. Inequalities matrix in Fig. 3 after transformation

Loop bounds can be expressed as a series of inequalities of the form $I_i \geq L_i^j$ and $I_i \leq U_i^j$. The lower bound of I_i is the $max_j(L_i^j)$, the smallest possible value for I_i is the maximum of the smallest possible values of L_i. The upper bound of I_i is the $min_j(U_i^j)$, the biggest possible value for I_i is the biggest possible value of U_i. To extract the lower and upper bounds of the loop I_2, at first is necessary to get all inequality involving the loop I_2; than must be separated lower bound inequality from upper bound inequality.

constants	N_1	N_2	I_1	I_2
-2	0	0	0	1
-1	0	1	-1	2

constants	N_1	N_2	I_1	I_2
-1	1	0	0	-1
-2	0	0	1	-2

Fig. 5. Upper and lower bound Inequalities extracted from code

If the current inequality contains a coefficient related to an innermost loop variable, its value must be replaced with the global min or the global max expression of that loop, according to the coefficient sign and the bound type (lower or upper bound). Now the inequality can be solved in I_2. If more than one inequality hold for a certain bound, the new bound will be the minimum of these (in case of upper bound) or the maximum of these (in case of lower bound). In the case of code in Fig.1 the lower bounds and upper bounds lists are shown in Fig. 6.

loop	LB expression
1	6
2	max(2,ceil((1 + -1 * N_2 + I_1) / 2))

loop	UB expression
1	-1 + N_2 + 2 * (-1 + N_1)
2	min(-1 + N_1,floor((-2 + I_1) / -2))

Fig. 6. Loop upper and lower bounds expressions

For loop 1, the lower bound is a constant, so a `SgIntVal` node type is used, while the upper bound requires the use of a `SgExpression`. Loop 2 can be processed with a `SgFunctionCallExp`. At the end of the transformation process, for each loop in the nesting, the initialization statement and the test expressions are replaced by calculated bounds.

4   Loop Nest CUDA Mapping

CUDA [9] adopts low level programming approaches that requires users to handle details about parallelism, data handlers and movement across levels of memory hierarchy. The automated technique in our work has been developed to create an equivalent CUDA code starting from its sequential C version after the transformation shown in previous section. The mapping of a parallel loop nest to CUDA code consists of several steps: parallel loops extraction from the nesting, data transfer generation, kernel function creation and kernel launch.

4.1   Generate Data Transfer Directives

In CUDA, the host (CPU) and device (GPU) have separate memory spaces. In order to execute a kernel on a device, it is necessary to allocate memory on the device by calling `cudaMalloc()` function of the framework. Then the data can be transferred from the host memory to the allocated device memory with calls to `cudaMemcpy()` function. Similarly, after kernel's execution, result data from the device needs to be copied back to the host's memory and no longer used device memory must be unallocated with `cudaFree()`.

To implement this transformation pass it has been traversed the program intermediate representation used by ROSE, searching for variables array references `SgVariableArrayRef`, included in the loop nest body candidate to be offloaded to the GPU. After that, arrays have been classified as *data-in*, *data-out* or *data-inout*, depending on their use (only read, only write, read and write). This affects the way data is allocated and copied to and from device.

In our work the intermediate representation is updated by inserting in the scope out of the parallelizable loop nest the declarations of, an error handler `cudaError_t`, a `cudaExtent` with the computation of array dimension and a call to `cudaMalloc()`. After that, parameters are calculated with the source array pointer, the destination pointer and the direction of the copy. A `cudaMemcpy()` function call insertion finalizes the data transfer arrays. The ROSE node build and insertion process is iterated for all arrays referenced into the code nesting that have to be included in a CUDA kernel. All this has been done by building proper ROSE `SgExpression` and putting them into the intermediate representation.

4.2   Create the CUDA Kernel

In CUDA, a kernel function specifies the code to be executed by all threads during a parallel phase. Mapping a loop nest into a CUDA kernel can be done by two passes: statements extraction from loop nest body and kernel function declaration creation.

A kernel function code is executed by a single CUDA thread, and than a single thread will execute all the statements included into the innermost loop of the parallelizable nesting. This organization of threads is specified upon kernel launching with a statement like `f<<<P,B>>>()`. This will launch P blocks of B threads each, for a total of $P * B$ parallel threads across the entire kernel. Every thread block is given a unique integral coordinate that is accessible within the device program via the special variable `blockIdx`. The threads of a given block are also given unique coordinates, whose components are accessible via `threadIdx`.

The loop nest to CUDA kernel translation process has been made first by creating a function definition and a function body for the future kernel and later by invoking SAGE builder facilities. Later, the function body is filled with all the statements nodes from loop nest body. After copying these statements nodes into the kernel function, all references to the previous loop iteration variables needs to be updated. A set of statements must be inserted in the function kernel in order to calculate, upon runtime, an index similar to the old iteration variable. Once a kernel body is outlined into the so created function, accesses to scalars and arrays inside have been redirected to their corresponding GPU memory variables.

4.3 Kernel Launch

Each CUDA thread executes the same kernel code on a grid of blocks of threads. The number of threads per block and the number of blocks per grid are specified with the chevron syntax <<<...>>>, already supported by ROSE compiler.

A cudaKernelCallExpression has been built using SAGE III build function. Arguments have been set using a kernel configurator.

5 Put It All Together: A Test Case

As a test case the source code performing a matrix matrix product shown in Fig. 7 is used. The resulting code after interchanging and tiling loop I_1 and loop I_2, is shown in Fig. 8. After loop transformations, each two dimensional tile (3 innermost loops) of the nest in Fig. 8 are mapped to CUDA code. In Fig. 9 is shown the generated code implementing data transfer between host and device (only for first matrix for brevity).

```
for (j = 0; j < nyc; j++) {
    for (i = 0; i < nxc; i++) {
        prod = 0;
        for (k = 0; k < nya; k++) {
            prod += A[k * nxa + i] * B[j * nxb + k];
        }
        C[j * nxc + i] = alpha * prod + beta * C[j * nxc + i];
    }
}
```

Fig. 7. Matrix multiply test code

```
for (_var_0 = 0; _var_0 <= nxc-1; _var_0 += tile_size_0) {
    for (_var_1 = 0; _var_1 <= nyc-1; _var_1 += tile_size_1) {
        // tiles loops
        for (i = _var_0; i <= min(nxc-1, _var_0 + tile_size_0-1); i+=1) {
            for (j = _var_1; j <= min(nyc-1, _var_1 + tile_size_1-1); j+=1) {
                prod = 0;
                for (k = 0; k <= nya-1; k+=1) {
                    prod += A[k * nxa + i] * B[j * nxb + k];
                }
                C[j * nxc + i] = alpha * prod + beta * C[j * nxc + i];
            }
        }
    }
}
```

Fig. 8. Matrix product after interchange and tiling loops I_1 and I_2

```
cudaError_t stat_dev_1_A;
cudaExtent ext_dev_1_A = make_cudaExtent((nxa*nya) * sizeof(float ),(1),(1));
/* Malloc on the device */
cudaPitchedPtr dev_1_A;
stat_dev_1_A = cudaMalloc3D(&dev_1_A,ext_dev_1_A);
if (stat_dev_1_A != cudaSuccess)
  fprintf(stderr,"%s\n",cudaGetErrorString(stat_dev_1_A));
/* Copy host to device */
cudaMemcpy3DParms param_1_dev_1_A = {0};
param_1_dev_1_A.srcPtr = make_cudaPitchedPtr(((void *)A),(nxa*nya) * sizeof(float ),(nxa*
    nya),(1));
param_1_dev_1_A.dstPtr = dev_1_A;
param_1_dev_1_A.extent = ext_dev_1_A;
param_1_dev_1_A.kind = cudaMemcpyHostToDevice;
stat_dev_1_A = cudaMemcpy3D(&param_1_dev_1_A);
if (stat_dev_1_A != cudaSuccess)
    fprintf(stderr,"%s\n",cudaGetErrorString(stat_dev_1_A));
```

Fig. 9. CUDA Data transfer code for matrix product

```
__global__ void kernel_1_1527(cudaPitchedPtr dev_1_A,int nxa,int nya,
    cudaPitchedPtr dev_2_B,int nxb,cudaPitchedPtr dev_3_C,
    int nxc,int nyc, int _var_0, int _var_1,int alpha,int beta) {
float *A = (float *)dev_1_A.ptr;
int widthA = dev_1_A.pitch / sizeof(float );
int sliceA = dev_1_A.ysize * widthA;
float *B = (float *)dev_2_B.ptr;
int widthB = dev_2_B.pitch / sizeof(float );
int sliceB = dev_2_B.ysize * widthB;
float *C = (float *)dev_3_C.ptr;
int widthC = dev_3_C.pitch / sizeof(float );
int sliceC = dev_3_C.ysize * widthC;
int _p_i, _p_j, _p_k;
int _upperb_y = (min(nyc-1, _var_1 + tile_size_1-1) - _var_1 - 1);
int _upperb_x = (min(nxc-1, _var_0 + tile_size_0-1) - _var_0 - 1);
int _idx = threadIdx.x + _var_0;
int _gidx = _idx + blockDim.x * blockIdx.x;
int _idy = threadIdx.y + _var_1;
int _gidy = _idy + blockDim.y * 1 * blockIdx.y;
if (_gidy >= _var_1 && _gidy <= (nxc - 1)) {
  if (_gidx >= _var_0 && _gidx <= (nyc - 1)) {
    float prod = 0;
      for (_p_k = 0; _p_k <= ((-1) + nya); _p_k += 1) {
      prod += (A[(_p_k * nxa) + _gidy] * B[(_gidx * nxb) + _p_k]);
      }
      C[(_gidx * nxc) + _gidy] = ((alpha * prod) + (beta * C[(_gidx * nxc) + _gidy]));
  }
 }
}
```

Fig. 10. CUDA mapping - kernel

In Fig. 10 is shown the source code section with kernel code to be executed
on device. In Fig. 11 is shown the generated code to be performed on the host
that invokes kernel execution on device.

```
for (_var_0 = 0; _var_0 <= nxc-1; _var_0 += tile_size_0) {
  for (_var_1 = 0; _var_1 <= nyc-1; _var_1 += tile_size_1) {
int num2blockDim_1_1527 = (min(nxc-1, _var_0 + tile_size_0-1) - _var_0 + 1) % 16 == 0?
        (min(nxc-1, _var_0 + tile_size_0-1) - _var_0 + 1) / 16 :
        (min(nxc-1, _var_0 + tile_size_0-1) - _var_0 + 1) / 16 + 1;
int num1blockDim_1_1527 = (min(nyc-1, _var_1 + tile_size_1-1) - _var_1 + 1) % 16 == 0?
        (min(nyc-1, _var_1 + tile_size_1-1) - _var_1 + 1) / 16 :
        (min(nyc-1, _var_1 + tile_size_1-1) - _var_1 + 1) / 16 + 1;
dim3 blockDim_1_1527(16,16,1);
dim3 gridDim_1_1527(num1blockDim_1_1527,num2blockDim_1_1527);
kernel_1_1527<<<gridDim_1_1527,blockDim_1_1527>>>
        (dev_1_A,nxa,nya,dev_2_B,nxb,dev_3_C,nxc,nyc,alpha,beta);
cudaThreadSynchronize();
cudaError_t err_kernel_1_1527 = cudaGetLastError();
if (err_kernel_1_1527)
  fprintf(stderr,"In %s, %s\n","kernel_1_1527",cudaGetErrorString(err_kernel_1_1527));
  }
}
```

Fig. 11. CUDA mapping - kernel launch

6   Conclusion and Future Work

In this paper has been presented a source to source transformer that performs unimodular loop transformations giving as output both a sequential code and a CUDA code. The transformer has been built on ROSE infrastructure and its process can be driven at present by user preferences or by external analyzers, as an algorithmic recognizer.

First tests were conducted on applying tiling and interchanging for loop nests to give both sequential and CUDA code. The module is also able to emit OpenMP code for multicore architectures.

Future works directions will be related to: implement more complex transformations, provide output for different parallel architectures, integrate transformers and analyzers into a common framework.

References

1. Amini, M., Ancourt, C., Coelho, F., Irigoin, F., Jouvelot, P., Keryell, R., Villalon, P., Creusillet, B., Guelton, S.: PIPS Is not (just) Polyhedral Software. In: International Workshop on Polyhedral Compilation Techniques (IMPACT 2011) (April 2011)
2. Baskaran, M., Ramanujam, J., Sadayappan, P.: Automatic C-to-CUDA code generation for affine programs. In: Gupta, R. (ed.) CC 2010. LNCS, vol. 6011, pp. 244–263. Springer, Heidelberg (2010)
3. Cantiello, P., Di Martino, B.: Software porting support with component based and language neutral source code analysis. International Journal of Computational Science and Engineering (IJCSE) (to appear)
4. Cantiello, P., Di Martino, B.: Automatic source code transformation for gpus based on program comprehension. In: Alexander, M., et al. (eds.) Euro-Par 2011, Part II. LNCS, vol. 7156, pp. 188–197. Springer, Heidelberg (2012)

5. Cantiello, P., Di Martino, B., Moscato, F.: Compilers, Techniques and Tools for Supporting Programming Heterogeneous Many/Multicore Systems, pp. 31–50. John Wiley and Sons Inc. (2014)
6. Dolbeau, R.: HMPP: A hybrid multi-core parallel. In: First Workshop on General Purpose Processing on Graphics Processing Units, pp. 1–5 (2007)
7. Han, T.D., Abdelrahman, T.S.: hicuda: High-level gpgpu programming. IEEE Trans. Parallel Distrib. Syst. 22(1), 78–90 (2011)
8. Leung, A., Vasilache, N., Meister, B., Baskaran, M., Wohlford, D., Bastoul, C., Lethin, R.: A mapping path for multi-gpgpu accelerated computers from a portable high level programming abstraction. In: Proceedings of the 3rd Workshop on General-Purpose Computation on Graphics Processing Units, GPGPU 2010, pp. 51–61. ACM Press, New York (2010)
9. NVIDIA. CUDA: Compute Unified Device Architecture., http://www.nvidia.com/cuda/
10. Quinlan, D.: ROSE Compiler project., http://www.rosecompiler.org/
11. Torquati, M., Vanneschi, M., Amini, M., Guelton, S., Keryell, R., Lanore, V., Pasquier, F.-X., Barreteau, M., Barrère, R., Petrisor, C.-T., Lenormand, É., Cantini, C., De Stefani, F.: An innovative compilation tool-chain for embedded multi-core architectures. In: Embedded World Conference (February 2012)
12. Wolf, M.E., Lam, M.S.: A loop transformation theory and an algorithm to maximize parallelism. IEEE Trans. Parallel Distrib. Syst. 2(4), 452–471 (1991)
13. Wolfe, M.: Implementing the pgi accelerator model. In: Proceedings of the 3rd Workshop on General-Purpose Computation on Graphics Processing Units, GPGPU 2010, pp. 43–50. ACM, New York (2010)

HMHS: Hybrid Multistage Heuristic Scheduling Algorithm for Heterogeneous MapReduce System

Heng Chen, Yao Shen, Quan Chen, and Minyi Guo

Department of Computer Science and Engineering,
Shanghai Jiao Tong University Shanghai, China
{chenheng417,quanchen1986}@gmail.com, {yshen,guo-my}@cs.sjtu.edu.cn

Abstract. The scale of data in a MapReduce system is increasing quickly. Thus how to efficiently schedule a set of production jobs has become increasingly important. For a given set of jobs, a well-designed scheduling algorithm can significantly reduce makespan and increase the utilization of clusters. However, there exists very few studies that aim to construct a scheduler that minimizes the makespan of batch jobs in a heterogeneous environment. This paper proposes a heuristic scheduling algorithm called Hybrid Multistage Heuristic Scheduling (HMHS), which tries to solve the scheduling problem by breaking down it into two-subproblems: sequencing and dispatching. For sequencing, we develop a heuristic based on *Pri*(the modified Johnson's algorithm). For dispatching, we offer two heuristics *Min-Min* and *Dynamic-Min-Min*. Our simulation results on two kinds of workloads demonstrate that every heuristic employed in HMHS contributes to reducing the makespan. As a whole, HMHS improves the performance ranging from 51% to 77% compared to FIFO.

Keywords: task scheduling, MapReduce, makespan, heterogeneous system, heuristic algorithm.

1 Introduction

Large scale of data has been generated daily. To handle such huge amount of data quickly, large companies (e.g. Google) group large number of commodity computers together to construct a distributed cloud system for data processing. Parallel programming model MapReduce which is popularized by Google [5] is widely used in these systems for handling data.

Empirically, a typical MapReduce system is usually used for running thousands of jobs periodically for data processing(e.g. 10,000 jobs are processed daily by Facebook's data center [15]). Obviously, for a given set of independent MapReduce jobs in a heterogeneous environment, the less time the clusters cost to execute these jobs, the earlier the resources of clusters can be released. However, the processing time is affected by several factors, such as the precedence constraints between map and reduce tasks. Therefore, a study on how to schedule a given

J. Kołodziej et al. (Eds.): ICA3PP 2013, Part I, LNCS 8285, pp. 196–205, 2013.

set of independent MapReduce jobs in a heterogeneous environment to minimize
the makespan is of great value.

Many researchers have proposed delicate job scheduling algorithms to improve
the system performance of MapReduce. Chang et al. [2] abstracted the scheduling problem as a novel optimization problem. They focused on constructing an
optimal scheduling algorithm that minimizes the weighted sum of the job completion times. However, they ignored the precedence relationships between map
and reduce tasks. Verma et al. [17] proposed a heuristic algorithm to organize
the order in which jobs are executed to minimize the completion time of a given
set of MapReduce jobs in a homogeneous environment. Since heterogeneous environment will greatly affect the performance of the scheduling algorithm, a algorithm works well in a homogeneous environment may have poor performance
in a heterogeneous environment.

In general, none of existing works design a scheduling algorithm to minimize
the makespan of a given set of independent MapReduce jobs in a heterogeneous
environment. To address this problem, we propose a Hybrid Multistage Heuristic
Scheduling (HMHS) algorithm, which tries to solve the scheduling problem by
dividing it into two sub-problems: sequencing and dispatching. For sequencing,
we consider the precedence constraints of map and reduce, and then design a
Pri based heuristic to get the order of jobs. (Here, *Pri* stands for the priority of
a MapReduce job which is defined in section 3.1.) Meanwhile, for dispatching,
we offer two heuristics: *Min-Min* and *Dynamic-Min-Min* to balance the load of
machines in a heterogeneous environment. We compare performance benefits of
HMHS with three scheduling strategies via simulation. The results demonstrate
HMHS outperforms FIFO by reducing up to 51%-77% makespan. We also study
how system heterogeneity will affect the performance of HMHS.

2   Problem Description

In this paper, we study how to schedule a set of independent MapReduce jobs in
a heterogeneous system to minimize the makespan. A real MapReduce system
is usually complex and affected by many factors. In this paper, we make several
assumptions to simplify the scheduling problem. We discuss some of assumptions
here. (1)We assume that all map (reduce) tasks of a given job are uniform. Thus,
the processing times of these map (reduce) tasks are same. Meanwhile, we assume
the processing times of tasks of a given job is known. This is not available in a
real system at present, but some researchers [16] try to approximately estimate
the processing time based on historical logs and job profiles. (2)We assume that
one map (reduce) machine contains one map (reduce) slot. In real MapReduce
system (e.g. Hadoop), each machine will contain a specified number of map slots
and reduce slots, and each map (reduce) slot can be used to execute one map
(reduce) task. Tasks executed at the same machine will preempt resources and
affect the processing time of each other. As mentioned in 1, the processing time
is supposed to be known and from statistical results. Thus, the assumption that
each machine owns one slot will not have a significant impact on our scheduling

problem. (3) We ignore the shuffle phase between map and reduce, and then assume that, for a given job, reduce tasks can only be launched when all map tasks have been finished. This assumption is widely used in literatures [2],[11],[17] to simplify the scheduling problem.

According to above assumptions and the setting of real MapReduce systems, the scheduling problem considered in this paper will satisfy the following conditions: Precedence relationships exist between map and reduce stage; Each job contains a specified number of map and reduce tasks; The processing times of map tasks of a given job are same, as well as the processing times of reduce tasks; Multiple map machines and reduce machines exist; All jobs arrive at zero; Task processing time is deterministic and given in advance; Each machine can process only one task at a time and processing tasks can not be interrupted; All MapReduce jobs are independent.

2.1 Definitions

To describe the problem more clearly, we give the following definitions, which are used throughout the paper.

N: Number of MapReduce jobs.

M^m (M^r): Number of alternative machines at map(reduce) stage.

T_i^m (T_i^r): Number of map(reduce) tasks of ith job.

P_i^m (P_i^r): Normal task processing time of ith job at map(reduce) stage.

V_{ij}^m (V_{ij}^r): Speed factor of any map(reduce) task of ith job on jth machine.

$\overline{P}_i^m$ ($\overline{P}_i^r$) : Average total processing time of map(reduce) tasks of ith job.

$$\overline{P}_i^m = P_i^m * \left(\sum_{j=1}^{M^m} V_{ij}^m \right) / M^m * T_i^m \ , \ \ \overline{P}_i^r = P_i^r * \left(\sum_{j=1}^{M^r} V_{ij}^r \right) / M^r * T_i^r \ . \tag{1}$$

FM_{ij}: Finish time of jth map task of ith job.

A_i: Arriving time of ith job's reduce tasks.

$$A_i = \max_{1 \leq j \leq T_i^m} (FM_{ij}) \ . \tag{2}$$

FR_{ij}: Finish time of jth reduce task of ith job.

C : The completion time of all jobs, which can also be called makespan.

$$C = \max_{1 \leq i \leq N} \max_{1 \leq j \leq T_i^r} (FR_{ij}) \ . \tag{3}$$

2.2 Hardness of Our Scheduling Problem

Two-stage flexible flow shop scheduling problem (2-FFS) is similar to our scheduling problem. The main difference is that each job in 2-FFS only contains one task at each stage, while each job considered in our work contains multiple tasks. Gupta [7] proved that the 2-FFS is NP-complete even if the number of machines at one of the two stages is one. Obviously, the scheduling problem in our paper is also NP-hard according to [7].

3   Hybrid Multistage Heuristic Scheduling Algorithm

As discussed above (section 2.2), the scheduling problem of the MapReduce system is NP-hard. Thus, we intend to simplify the problem. It is common to break down the scheduling problem into smaller pieces. This enlightens us to divide the problem into two sub-problems: (a) sequencing the tasks allocated to each machine; (b) dispatching tasks of jobs to heterogeneous machines at map and reduce stages.

We show the details of sequencing and dispatching problems in section 3.1 and section 3.2, respectively.

3.1   Sequencing

During map and reduce stage, each machine will be allocated multiple tasks. Precedence relationships between map and reduce tasks may block the jobs' execution. A well-designed sequencing algorithm can help to organize map tasks to decrease waiting time of reduce tasks.

Johnson [9] proposed an classical optimal algorithm for the two flow shop problem (only one machine is available at each stage and each job contains only one task at each stage), which is similar to our scheduling problem. In Johnson's algorithm, each job contains three attributes M_i, R_i and V_i. M_i stands for the task processing time at map stage. R_i stands for the task processing time at reduce stage. $V_i = \min (M_i, R_i)$. For a job List L with N jobs, the steps of Johnson's algorithm are:

Step 1. Define two output lists L1= {}, L2 = {}.
Step 2. Order all jobs in List L by V_i in nondecreasing order.
Step 3. Process the ordered list from the beginning. For each job, if $M_i \leq R_i$, place it at end of L1; otherwise, place it at the beginning of L2.
Step 4. Add list L2 to the end of list L1. L1 is the ordered list.

We approximately evaluate the sum of processing times of map (reduce) tasks of a given job, indicated by $\overline{P}_i^m$ ($\overline{P}_i^r$), by combining the average processing time of a map (reduce) task and the number of map (reduce) tasks. Hence, we can replace the task processing times M_i and R_i in Johnson's algorithm by $\overline{P}_i^m$ and $\overline{P}_i^r$, respectively. This enables us to apply Johnson's algorithm to sequence jobs.

In order to describe the sequencing algorithm, we define the priority Pri which takes advantage of Johnson's algorithm to indicate the processing order of a job. The smaller Pri a job has, the earlier it will be executed during map stage. The expression is modified from Gupta [7]. For each job i,

$$Pri^i = Sgn\left(\overline{P}_i^m - \overline{P}_i^r\right) / min\left(\overline{P}_i^m, \overline{P}_i^r\right)$$

$$where \quad Sgn = \begin{cases} 1, & if \ \overline{P}_i^m > \overline{P}_i^r \\ -1, & otherwise. \end{cases} \tag{4}$$

We can easily obtain the ordered list of jobs by sorting the Pri in nondecreasing order.

3.2 Dispatching

The basic intention of dispatching tasks is to balance the work load of all machines. Since the dispatching exists at both map and reduce stage, we discuss it in two cases:Assigning map tasks to map machines and assigning reduce tasks to reduce machines.

Algorithm 1. Dynamic-Min-Min heuristic

The set of N MapReduce jobs, U; Selected jobs to be dispatched, Jw; Available time of the earliest free machine, EAT; The execution time of reduce tasks of ith job on machine m_j, E_{ij}; The minimum completion time of reduce task of ith job if it is mapped to m_j, C_{ij}; The time that ith reduce machine finishes all tasks assigned to it, Ava_i;

1: **while** $U \neq \varnothing$ or $Jw \neq \varnothing$ **do**
2:    $EAT \longleftarrow min(Ava_i)$;
3:    **for** each $j_i \in U$ **do**
4:        **if** $A_i \leq EAT$ **then**
5:            add j_i to Jw, remove j_i from U;
6:        **end if**
7:    **end for**
8:    **if** $Jw == \varnothing$ **then**
9:        add the job with minimum A_i to Jw, remove it from U;
10:   **end if**
11:   **for** each $j_i \in Jw$ **do**
12:       **for** each machine m_j **do**
13:           $C_{ij} \longleftarrow E_{ij} + max(Ava_j, A_i)$;
14:       **end for**
15:   **end for**
16:   $C_{pq} \longleftarrow min(C_{ij})$;
17:   assign one reduce task of j_p to m_q;
18:   $Ava_q \longleftarrow C_{pq}$;
19:   **if** all reduce tasks of j_p are assigned **then**
20:       remove j_p from Jw;
21:   **end if**
22: **end while**

Dispatching Heuristic of Map Stage. During map stage, we try to select a heuristic to make the whole map stage finished as soon as possible. We employ Min-Min as the dispatching rule, which outperforms most heuristics on dispatching a set of independent tasks onto heterogeneous systems [1]. The key steps of Min-Min are: In each cycle, for each unassigned map task, Min-Min calculates its minimum completion time by comparing the completion times of it on different map machines. Then, the map task with the minimum completion time is assigned to corresponding map machine. Therefore, the possibility of the tasks assigned to their best matched machines is relatively high. The more tasks that are assigned to their best matched machines, the smaller makespan our scheduler can obtain.

Dispatching Heuristic of Reduce Stage. As mentioned above, our algorithm is designed to obtain an optimized batch scheduling policy for a large number of jobs. Multiple jobs with similar $\overline{P}_i^m$ will be launched at approximately the same time according to our sequencing algorithm. Thus, reduce tasks of these jobs will have similar arriving time. Under such assumption, we propose a new heuristic Dynamic-Min-Min, which takes advantage of the idea of Min-Min to dispatch arrived reduce tasks to balance the work load of reduce machines. Dynamic-Min-Min works as follows: At each round of task assignment, it firstly updates the job set Jw which contains all jobs to be dispatched, and then dispatchs a reduce task. Algorithm 1 shows the pseudocode of Dynamic-Min-Min. (Some definitions are explained in section 2.1.)

3.3 Hybrid Multistage Heuristic Scheduling Algorithm

By combining the solutions for sequencing and dispatching together, we can draw the outline of Hybrid Multistage Heuristic Scheduling Algorithm.
1) Dispatch map tasks of all jobs into map machines by heuristic Min-Min.
2) Define T_i as the set of tasks assigned to map machine i. For each T_i, sequence tasks by Pri in nondecreasing order.
3) Dispatch reduce tasks of all jobs into reduce machines by heuristic Dynamic-Min-Min.

4   Evaluation

In this section, we evaluate the benefits of our algorithm via simulations. We compare HMHS with the following three scheduling strategies.
Default FIFO Scheduler: FIFO is the default scheduler used by Hadoop (a widely used MapReduce system). Once a job arrives, FIFO scheduler partitions it into individual tasks and then assigns tasks to free machines.
FIFO-Pri Scheduler: To investigate the effect of our Min-Min and Dynamic-Min-Min dispatching strategies, we combine FIFO Scheduler and modified Johnson's algorithm together. The FIFO-Pri sorts all jobs by priority Pri first, and then uses FIFO Scheduler to assign tasks to free machines in order.
Reverse-Hybrid Multistage Heuristic Scheduler (R-HMHS): R-HMHS is designed to analyze how deeply the priority Pri affects HMHS. The R-HMHS reverses the sequencing result of HMHS. In other words, tasks are sorted by Pri in descending order.

4.1   Simulation Setup

Since building a large distributed system with thousands of machines is beyond the scope of our ability, to evaluate the performance of HMHS, we design a simulator and generate some synthetic workloads according to statistical results in [10],[19].

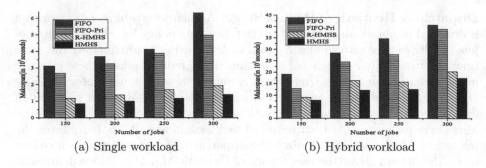

(a) Single workload (b) Hybrid workload

Fig. 1. Effect of heuristics

In our simulations, a single job is constructed from two aspects: task duration and job size. We generate two types of workloads.(1) Single workload: for each job, P_i^m and P_i^r are drawn from uniform distributions U[5, 45] and U[15, 135] respectively. T_i^m and T_i^r are drawn from U[1, 300] and U[1, 40]. (2) Hybrid workload: in real industry system, a small number of large and long jobs exist [13]. Thus, we generate the hybrid workload in the following way. Normal jobs(80%) are constructed in the same way of jobs of single workload. For long(15%) jobs, P_i^m and P_i^r are drawn from U[100, 2000] and U[300, 6000]. T_i^m and T_i^r are drawn from U[1, 300] and U[1, 40]. For large(5%) jobs, P_i^m and P_i^r are drawn from U[5, 45] and U[15, 135]. T_i^m and T_i^r are drawn from U[2000, 5000] and U[100, 400].

Besides the parameters used to represent workload, the speed factors(V_{ij}^m and V_{ij}^r) are generated to indicate the heterogeneous system. V_{ij}^m and V_{ij}^r are drawn from uniform distribution U[0.1, 1.0].

4.2 Simulation Results

A. Comparison with Other Heuristics. In our first simulation, to evaluate the benefits of our algorithm, we compare the makespan of our scheduler with FIFO, FIFO-Pri and R-HMHS. We generate multiply workloads with different job sizes under Single and Hybrid distributions respectively. We also create a heterogeneous system of 100 map and 100 reduce machines. From Fig. 1, we can see that HMHS works the best among all other strategies. Compared to FIFO, HMHS decreases up to 77% of makespan. We also observe that there is a slightly upward trend of makespan improvements with the increase of number of jobs.

Effect of dispatching heuristics: To investigate the effect of dispatching heuristics Min-Min and Dynamic-Min-Min, we analyze the results of FIFO-Pri and HMHS. By observing the result of FIFO-Pri in Fig. 1, we can find that HMHS decreases up to 72% makespan of FIFO-Pri for single workload and 55% for hybrid workload. This results clearly illustrate that our dispatching heuristics achieve significant makespan improvements.

Effect of sequencing heuristic: As mentioned above, R-HMHS is designed to test the effect of our sequencing algorithm. Fig. 1 illustrates that, compared to R-HMHS, HMHS exhibits 10%-30% makespan improvements. We can see that

Table 1. Configuration of heterogeneous systems

	Cluster 1	Cluster 2	Cluster 3	Cluster 4	Cluster 5	Cluster 6
slow slot(0.9-1)	0%	20%	40%	60%	80%	100%
random slot(0.1-1)	100%	80%	60%	40%	20%	0%

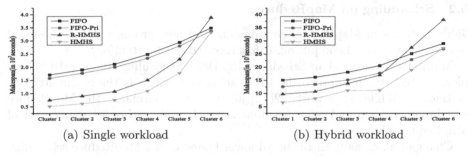

(a) Single workload   (b) Hybrid workload

Fig. 2. Impact of heterogeneity

there is no strong association between the effect of our sequencing algorithm and the job sizes. From the view point of workload sets, single workload gets about 7% more performance benefits than hybrid workload.

The above results fully demonstrate that each of our heuristics is effective in reducing the makespan of a given set of independent MapReduce jobs in a heterogeneous environment.

B. Impact of Heterogeneity

In practice, a cloud system is usually combined by heterogenous machines. By changing the percentage of slow machines in the system, we create six kinds of heterogeneous systems as shown in Table 1. Meanwhile, We suppose slow machines' speed factors are drawn from U[0.9, 1.0] and the rest machines' speed factors are drawn from U[0.1, 1.0] randomly. We generate two kinds of workloads with 100 jobs as the test workloads. Each heterogeneous system contains 100 map machines and 100 reduce machines. Fig. 2 shows that the performance of HMHS is close to FIFO when the system is dominated by slow machines. One major conclusion from Fig. 2 is that the less slow machines the cluster has, the more improvements our algorithm gains.

5 Related Work

5.1 Foundational Work on Job Scheduling Problem

Job Scheduling is not a new problem. Indeed, a lot of foundational works exist in the literature [12]. However, the problem discussed in this paper can not be corresponded to any classical problem. To the best of our knowledge, the classical two-stage flexible flow shop (2-FFS) scheduling problem has the closest model to ours.

The 2-FFS has been studied extensively [12], [14]. Gupta [7] proved the 2-FFS with parallel processors to minimize makespan is NP-Complete and developed an efficient heuristic algorithm for constructing an approximate solution. Haouari et al. [8] studied the 2-FFS with identical parallel machines at each stage. A tabu search heuristic and a simulated annealing algorithm are presented in their work.

5.2   Scheduling on MapReduce

Job scheduling in MapReduce environment is a new problem. With the rapid development of cloud computing, it has received much attention.

Many efforts(such as Fair Scheduler [18], Delay Scheduling [19], SAMR Scheduler [4] etc.) try to improve the FIFO scheduler, which is the origin strategy of Hadoop. While other works [2] [3] [6] [11] try to formalize the MapReduce scheduling problem and offer an offline scheduling algorithm for a given set of MapReduce jobs.

Chang et al. [2] gave an LP based lower bound of the MapReduce scheduling problem. Meanwhile, they designed a 3-approximation algorithm to minimize the sum of job completion times for offline case. However, they ignored the precedence relationships between map and reduce tasks. To improve Chang's work, Chen et al. [3] not only considered the precedence constraints, but also added the shuffle phase of MapReduce into their model. Similarly, they provided LP based lower bound and constant factor approximation algorithms to minimize the sum of job completion times, which is different from our goal.

The closest work to ours is by Verma et al. [17]. They offered an abstraction of the scheduling problem which is similar to ours in homogeneous system and aimed to minimize the completion time of a set of MapReduce jobs. They designed a heuristic, which extends the classical Johnson's algorithm [9]. In our work, we consider the scheduling problem in a heterogeneous environment. This encourages us to explore new algorithms to minimize the makespan.

6   Conclusion and Future Work

In this paper, we propose a novel algorithm, Hybrid Multistage Heuristic Scheduling(HMHS), which aims at minimizing the makespan of a given set of independent MapReduce jobs in a heterogeneous system. The simulation results show that the heuristics used in our algorithm exhibit significant makespan improvements. In the future, we plan to examine the performance of our algorithm by running the experiment in a real MapReduce cluster with larger input data. On the other hand, we plan to compare our algorithm with some advanced Hadoop schedulers, such as Fair Scheduler [18] and Delay Scheduling [19].

Acknowledgments. This work is supported by the 863 Program of China (No. 2011AA01A202), the Doctoral Fund of Ministry of Education of China (No. 20100073120022), Natural Science Foundation of China (No.61202025), Shanghai Excellent Academic Leaders Plan(No. 11XD1402900), the Program for Changjiang Scholars and Innovative Research Team in University of China (IRT1158, PCSIRT). Yao Shen is the corresponding author.

References

1. Braun, T.D., Siegel, H.J., et al.: A comparison of eleven static heuristics for mapping a class of independent tasks onto heterogeneous distributed computing systems. Journal of Parallel and Distributed Computing 61(6), 810–837 (2001)
2. Chang, H., Kodialam, M., Kompella, R.R., Lakshman, T., Lee, M., Mukherjee, S.: Scheduling in mapreduce-like systems for fast completion time. In: 2011 Proceedings IEEE INFOCOM. IEEE (2011)
3. Chen, F., Kodialam, M., Lakshman, T.: Joint scheduling of processing and shuffle phases in mapreduce systems. In: 2012 Proceedings IEEE INFOCOM. IEEE (2012)
4. Chen, Q., Zhang, D., Guo, M., Deng, Q., Guo, S.: Samr: A self-adaptive mapreduce scheduling algorithm in heterogeneous environment. In: 2010 IEEE 10th CIT. IEEE (2010)
5. Dean, J., Ghemawat, S.: Mapreduce: simplified data processing on large clusters. Communications of the ACM 51(1), 107–113 (2008)
6. Fischer, M.J., Su, X., Yin, Y.: Assigning tasks for efficiency in hadoop. In: Proceedings of the 22nd ACM Symposium on Parallelism in Algorithms and Architectures. ACM (2010)
7. Gupta, J.N.: Two-stage, hybrid flowshop scheduling problem. Journal of the Operational Research Society, 359–364 (1988)
8. Haouari, M., M'Hallah, R.: Heuristic algorithms for the two-stage hybrid flowshop problem. Operations Research Letters 21(1), 43–53 (1997)
9. Johnson, S.M.: Optimal two-and three-stage production schedules with setup times included. Naval research logistics quarterly 1(1), 61–68 (1954)
10. Kavulya, S., Tan, J., Gandhi, R., Narasimhan, P.: An analysis of traces from a production mapreduce cluster. In: 2010 10th CCGrid. IEEE (2010)
11. Moseley, B., Dasgupta, A., Kumar, R., Sarlós, T.: On scheduling in map-reduce and flow-shops. In: Proceedings of the 23rd ACM Symposium on Parallelism in Algorithms and Architectures. ACM (2011)
12. Pinedo, M.: Scheduling: theory, algorithms, and systems. Springer (2012)
13. Reiss, C., Tumanov, A., Ganger, G.R., Katz, R.H., Kozuch, M.A.: Heterogeneity and dynamicity of clouds at scale: Google trace analysis. In: Proceedings of the Third ACM Symposium on Cloud Computing. ACM (2012)
14. Ruiz, R., Vázquez-Rodríguez, J.A.: The hybrid flow shop scheduling problem. European Journal of Operational Research 205(1), 1–18 (2010)
15. Thusoo, A., Shao, Z., Anthony, S., Borthakur, D., Jain, N., Sen Sarma, J., Murthy, R., Liu, H.: Data warehousing and analytics infrastructure at facebook. In: The 2010 SIGMOD. ACM (2010)
16. Verma, A., Cherkasova, L., Campbell, R.H.: Aria: automatic resource inference and allocation for mapreduce environments. In: Proceedings of the 8th ACM International Conference on Autonomic Computing. ACM (2011)
17. Verma, A., Cherkasova, L., Campbell, R.H.: Two sides of a coin: Optimizing the schedule of mapreduce jobs to minimize their makespan and improve cluster performance. In: 2012 20th MASCOTS. IEEE (2012)
18. Zaharia, M., Borthakur, D., Sarma, J.S., Elmeleegy, K., Shenker, S., Stoica, I.: Job scheduling for multi-user mapreduce clusters. EECS Department, University of California, Berkeley, Tech. Rep. USB/EECS-2009-55 (2009)
19. Zaharia, M., Borthakur, D.: et al.: Delay scheduling: a simple technique for achieving locality and fairness in cluster scheduling. In: Proceedings of the 5th European Conference on Computer Systems. ACM (2010)

Dynamic Resource Management in a HPC
and Cloud Hybrid Environment

Miao Chen, Fang Dong, and Junzhou Luo

School of Computer Science and Engineering, Southeast University
Nanjing, China
{chenmiao,fdong,jluo}@seu.edu.cn

Abstract. Recently, the large-scale cluster of data center is usually constructed to support both HPC and Cloud computing. It can be explained from two aspects: (1) The data center is typically a sharing environment for all the users, users may submit different types of jobs (HPC and Cloud computing) for processing currently; (2) Some applications can be divided into two parts of subtasks which are suitable to HPC and Cloud computing respectively, e.g. the AMS (Alpha Magnetic Spectrometer) experiment is such a typical application. Thus in order to provide good service for both computing models, it is needed to construct a HPC and Cloud hybrid environment. An existing management mechanism is to allocate fixed proportions of resources for different application environments. However, this approach has a significant performance drawback that is the low resource utilization. In order to overcome this drawback, we propose a dynamic resource management framework and mechanism to satisfy the requirements of both HPC and Cloud computing. Firstly we present a prediction model that is used to predict the arrival rate of all kinds of jobs (HPC types and Cloud types). Based on the prediction results, we propose a dynamic resource allocation algorithm, which manages dynamic resources allocation by using queuing theory. Finally, we evaluate our mechanism by real data sets from AMS experiment and Cloud tasks running on the HPC center in Southeast University. The results show that the proposed mechanism can effectively improve resource utilization at least 30% in this hybrid environment.

1 Introduction

Growing expertise with clusters of commodity computers has enabled a number of institutions to harness petaflops of computation power in a cost-efficient manner. The large-scale cluster is typically a sharing environment, which usually needs to support different kinds of computing models in the same time, such as the HPC (High Performance Computing) and Cloud Computing, etc. This fact can be explained by two major reasons:

(1) There exists a certain application, which contains the subtasks that belong to multiple computing models. We take the actual scenario of SEU HPC Data Center as an example. Note that, the AMS experiment is a typically running application, in which there are three major tasks, data reconstruction, Monte Carlo simulations and physical analysis. The first two tasks have three obviously characteristics, that are

J. Kołodziej et al. (Eds.): ICA3PP 2013, Part I, LNCS 8285, pp. 206–215, 2013.

large number of data, high requirement of parallelism and sensitivity to network latency. Thus the first two tasks are typical HPC applications. However physical analysis has different requirements of operating system, software, speed of execution and so on, thus there is a need of elastic customizable resource to support. Thus cloud computing is good enough for the third task.

(2) Multiple dedicated applications which are deployed and running based on their own computing models respectively. There are many experiment tasks from different colleges and schools of SEU submitted by the researchers of the whole university. Among these dedicated applications, we note that the High Throughput Sequencing Data Analysis and Molecular Dynamics Simulation Experiment are experiment tasks which are suitable to HPC, since these experiments with large number of data need high computing speed. While Nano Particle Optical Properties Simulation and other virtual machine management requests are much more suitable to cloud computing due to diversity of operating system and elastic resource requirement.

Above all, we find that different computing models have different requirements on hardware resources. HPC needs strong parallel capacity and computing power, while cloud needs elastic resource adjustment. Thus running multiple applications in a single computing environment cannot achieve good performance. There is a need of hybrid environment which is composed of HPC and Cloud environment to meet the different kinds of application requirements.

To satisfy varied requirements of different kinds of application, the existing method is to allocate fixed proportions of the resources for different application environments [5][7]. However, this naive approach has significant performance drawbacks: (1) Over-provisioning resources based on worst case workload estimates can result in potential underutilization of resources. (2) Since the number of arriving jobs is dynamic, transient overload leads to system instability and bad system performance.

Based on the above discussion, we conclude that a static allocation strategy cannot satisfy the actual requirements of hybrid clusters environment. Then the key issue is how to dynamically allocate resources for HPC and cloud applications in a hybrid clusters environment legitimately to increase the resource utilization as well as guaranteeing the performance constraints.

Our experimental results from the hybrid environment performance confirm that this hybrid environment is stable and efficient. In particular, we compare it to the pure HPC environment. The utilization of resources in excess of 30% is observed.

2   HPC and Cloud Hybrid Framework

In the hybrid environment presented in this paper, the HPC and Cloud can be in fact consolidated effectively inside a common cluster infrastructure. Figure 1 (a) shows the architecture of our proposed hybrid environment. This hybrid environment is composed of HPC system, Cloud system and some reserved resources which are used for dynamic allocation. And there is a unified dynamic resource management module that is in charge of arrival rate prediction and dynamic resources allocation.

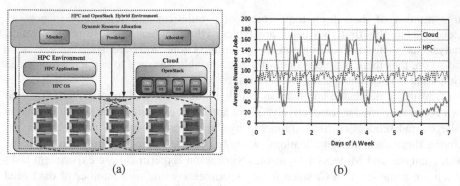

(a)   (b)

Fig. 1. (a)Architecture of HPC and Cloud hybrid environment; (b)Average number of jobs for HPC applications and Cloud tasks during one week

2.1   Prediction Model of Arrival Rate

Our observations are based on the analysis of real applications log files from SEU HPC Data Center within one year. Data are collected at a one-hour interval, for a total of 24 intervals each day. Figure 1 (b) shows that, for each workday morning, the cloud tasks arriving as people arrive at work. And the arriving cloud tasks peaks and remains there for most of the day. In late afternoon and weekdays, the values stay in a low level. However, since HPC applications are submitted automatically, there is a steady trend of the average number of arrival jobs during a week.

Since workload history arrival rate of HPC applications is almost stable, we predict the arrival rate of HPC applications based on AR(2) model. It has been demonstrated that lag 2 usually provides a good model due to the high prediction accuracy and low computation overhead within large-scale computing.

We are given historical data of workload in a form of time series x_i, where $i=1,2,\ldots, I$ is a measurement interval index. Precisely, the model is:

$$\hat{x}_i = \varphi_1 x_{i-1} + \varphi_2 x_{i-2} + \varepsilon_i \tag{1}$$

where φ_i and ε_i are autocorrelation function and   white noise component respectively.

On the other hand, for cloud tasks, from Figure 2, we can find that the trend of them is non-stationary and shows periodicity. Thus we suppose an AR based Periodic Decomposition (PD) prediction model for cloud workload prediction. We decompose the workload of cloud tasks time series x_i into a sum of x^j which is periodic components. So $x^j_{i+n*p_j} = x^j_i$ where n is an integer and p_j is a period. Specifically,

$$X_i = \sum_{j=1}^{p} x^j_i + r_i, \quad i = 0,1,\ldots \tag{2}$$

where P is the number of periodic components and r_i is residual components of the workload time series. Then, we model r_i using AR(2) model:

$$\hat{r}_i = \varphi_1 r_{i-1} + \varphi_2 r_{i-2} + \varepsilon_i \quad \text{for } i=0,1\ldots \tag{3}$$

Thus we get $\hat{x}_{HPC}$ and $\hat{x}_{Cloud}$ which are predicted whole workload of HPC applications and Cloud tasks respectively during interval I.

2.2   Dynamic Resource Allocation

In this part, jobs arrive into the hybrid system with arrival rate λ which is predicted in previous subsection. Service times at each server are assumed to be i.i.d. Random variables distributed exponentially with service rate μ. Thus dynamic resource allocation can be modeled as a G/M/n queuing system, and we regard response time R as the QoS requirement. Finally, we summarize the notation in the paper in Table 1.

Table 1. A Summary of Notation is Provided for Reference

Symbol	Definition
$\overline{x}$	Mean service time of servers
$\overline{t}$	Mean jobs interarrival time
μ	The service rate of servers in hybrid environment
σ_a^2	The variance of interarrival time
σ_b^2	The variance of service time

In [1], the defined of arrival rate of arriving jobs is $\lambda = \mu\rho$, where ρ denotes the utilization factor of the system server which is defined as follows:

$$\rho = \frac{\overline{x}}{n\overline{t}}, \rho < 1 \tag{4}$$

The waiting time for jobs in hybrid environment is represented by

$$W \cong \frac{1}{n\mu(1-\sigma)} \tag{5}$$

We must solve for the value of σ, which is given as the appropriate root by [1]:

$$\sigma = A * \left(n\mu - n\mu\sigma\right) \tag{6}$$

Making the change of variable $\alpha = n\mu(1-\sigma)$ and expand $A*(\alpha)$ in a power series, meanwhile we may neglect the higher-order terms and solving for α, we may finally get the approximate mean wait time in hybrid environment. In this G/M/n queuing system, the response time of jobs is the sum of waiting time and computing time, thus we have

$$R = \frac{X}{T} + \frac{\sigma_a^2 + (1/n^2)\sigma_b^2}{2\overline{t}(1-\rho)} \tag{7}$$

where X is the number of jobs completions in the previous measurement interval and T is the total time for computing completions in the previous interval.

Our objective is to minimize workload response time R subject to the constraint of $n<C$, where C is total resource capacity of hybrid environment and $\overline{x}<T'$, where T'

is required computing time from user's QoS requirement. The dynamic resource allocation problem can be formulated as follows:

$$OPT_p \quad \min \sum_{i=1}^{k} R_i \tag{8}$$

$$\text{Subject to: } \begin{cases} n < C \\ \overline{x} < T', \text{ where } \overline{x} = np\overline{t} \end{cases} \tag{9}$$

The optimization problem OPT_P is a nonlinear constrained integer optimization problem.

2.3   Procedure of Dynamic Resource Management

In this subsection, we bring out a heuristic algorithm to represent this procedure of Dynamic Resources Management (DRM) in hybrid environment. The DRM algorithm efficiently allocates the resource with the goal of guaranteeing application QoS.

Algorithm 1. DRM for dynamic resource management in hybrid environment
Input: jobs arrival rate of HPC applications λ_1 and Cloud tasks λ_2, QoS requirements for jobs like response time R and computing time T'
Output: plan to allocate proper computing resources to jobs

---

1 λ_1, λ_2: the job arrival rate of HPC applications and Cloud tasks
    J: set of the arrival jobs; T: history arrival rate dataset
    Scur: current resource status of hybrid system;
    Time: required jobs response time function
2 $RA \leftarrow$ initial resource allocation plan
3   **While** $\lambda_1 > 0$ **or** $\lambda_2 > 0$ **do**
4 T.add (λ_1, λ_2) //Put the λ_1, λ_2 into history arrival
    rate dataset T
5 $\hat{x}_i = \varphi_1 x_{i-1} + \varphi_2 x_{i-2} + \varepsilon_i$ //predict $\hat{\lambda}_1$ using AR(2) model
6 $r_i =$ getResidualValue (J) //break down time series get residual component
7 $\hat{r}_i = \varphi_1 r_{i-1} + \varphi_2 r_{i-2} + \varepsilon_i$ //predict residual component using AR(2) model
8 $\hat{\lambda}_2$ =add $(J, \hat{r}_i)$
9 RA=minimize$Time$ $(\hat{\lambda}_1, \hat{\lambda}_2, \overline{x})$ //solve OPT_P optimization problem
10 If (!isSatisfy $(RA, Scur)$)
11 adjustAllocation$(RA, Scur)$ //change resource allocation
12 **END**

---

3   Experimental Evaluation

3.1   Experimental Setup

Hardware and Software. We build a HPC and Cloud hybrid environment in SEU (Southeast University) HPC center which consists of a computing system and a storage system. Figure 2 illustrates that computing system contains 252 IBM H22 Blade servers while the storage is set up by 16 IBM X3650 M3 servers.

Note that, there are 20 IBM H22 Blade servers of SEU HPC center are used to construct the HPC environment of our hybrid system. Meanwhile, we use 14 IBM H22 Blade servers to construct a cloud environment which is managed by Openstack platform. One blade server is control node while the other 13 blade servers are computing nodes. In addition, there are 10 IBM H22 Blade servers deployed as a reserved resources pool which is prepared for elastic resources allocation.

HPC and Cloud Workload. Data reconstruction and MC simulations of AMS experiment are used to represent HPC workload of hybrid environment. We provide Cloud environment to the other colleges of SEU as experiments platform. The tested cloud workload is composed of the whole experiments of Southeast University.

3.2   Performance Evaluation

Prediction Accuracy of Arrival Rate. In this experiment, we make a comparison between the predicted jobs arrival rate $\hat{\lambda}$ and the real jobs arrival rate λ to evaluate our prediction mechanism. We implement two prediction methods for the cloud workload, that are: (1) AR based Periodic Decomposition (PD) is the presented prediction mechanism which extends the existing AR method with periodic decomposition, and (2) AR(2) is the traditional AR method without periodic decomposition. And for the HPC workload, that are: (1) AR (2) and (2) EP (32) (Extracted- based Prediction that is proposed by Wu [2]).

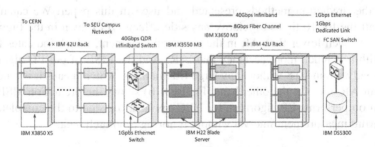

Fig. 2. The hardware archritecture of SEU HPC center

From Figure 3(a), we can find that our PD algorithm outperforms AR(2) in predicting cloud workload arrival rate, this is because the prediction error can be effectively corrected by the periodic decomposition mechanism. While in the Figure 3(b), we note that the AR-based prediction has the better accuracy than the EP method

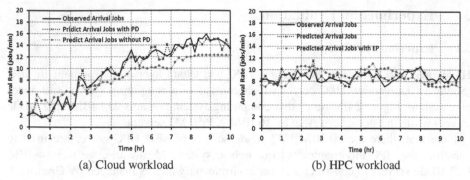

(a) Cloud workload   (b) HPC workload

Fig. 3. The prediction accuracy analysis

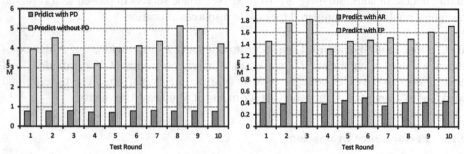

(a) AR based Periodic Decomposition (PD) and AR algorithms for cloud tasks (b) AR and EP algorithms for HPC applications

Fig. 4. The prediction MSE

in predicting HPC workload arrival rate. For EP algorithm, as many useful load data among a monitor period are ignored when reconstructing the new load series based on the original trace, it cannot obtain a good result.

On the other hand, we set the MSE (mean square error) as a performance metric to evaluate the prediction methods presented and used in this paper. We calculate the MSE of all the for 10 times to remove any side effects. As shown in the Figure 4(a), the MSE is much lower than AR in the cloud environment, which indicates that our PD algorithm is much more accuracy than AR. And the MSE of our PD algorithm is always steady around 0.8 without any large fluctuations, which means it is much more stable than AR, too. On the other hand, Figure 4(b) shows the prediction MSE of AR algorithm outperforms EP algorithm for HPC applications due to the complete monitoring during measurement interval without ignoring too much data.

Dynamic Resource Allocation Performance/ Hybrid Environment Performance. Based on the accurate prediction of jobs arrival rate generated form the last experiment (Figure 3,4), we evaluate our dynamic resource allocation techniques by comparing with static allocation techniques (the initial configuration of static allocation is set be 0.6:0.4) in this part.

Figure 5 (a) shows that the hybrid system resource utilization increases for both dynamic and static resource allocation technique firstly. When the number of incoming jobs is continuously increasing, the system resource utilization of static resource allocation becomes stable and steady around at 62%. This is because the relatively stable HPC workload becomes the only determination factor that affects the resource utilization when the resources of cloud environment cannot satisfy the incoming job requests, leading to the much more stable resource utilization. While in the case of dynamic one, we note that the system resource utilization is keep growing along with the increment of incoming jobs of cloud environment, this is expected as the freedom resources of HPC environment can be reallocated to the cloud environment in a real-time, satisfying the mutative job requests of cloud workload.

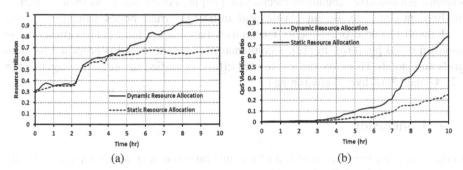

(a)   (b)

Fig. 5. (a) The resource utilization of dynamic and static resource allocation; (b) The QoS violation ratio of dynamic and static resource allocation

Figure 5 (b) shows that the QoS violation ratio increases when the number of arriving jobs increases. We can figure out that when the number of arriving jobs is low, the QoS requirements almost always can be met. When increasing number of arriving jobs, QoS violation ratio becomes higher. And the QoS violation ratio of static resource allocation is nearly 200% higher than that of dynamic resource allocation in general. This is because the fact that the job processing time and waiting time is increasing along with the increment of incoming jobs, since the insufficient resource affects the processing time of the running jobs (most jobs need to be processed in a parallel way) and extends the waiting time of the other concurrent jobs (jobs need to wait for the resource release). However, our dynamic resource allocation has a better performance than static one due to the flexible resource reallocation between HPC and cloud environment through the reserved resource pool, which can relieve the computation pressure of the cloud environment to a certain extent.

4   Related Work

Much research has been done on investigating the possibility of constructing HPC and Cloud together. References [3] and [4], present an environment that constructs HPC on the cloud. However cloud platform is unable to provide a completely satisfactory

HPC environment, particularly for communication-intensive applications, due to high network delay and lack of a high speed interconnect.

Some work have considered a hybrid computing environment which integrate clusters with clouds [6], [8]. Kim et.al. [6] discuss challenges to integrate clouds with cluster computing platforms and data centers, as well as develop and manage applications to utilize the cluster platform. Assuncao et.al. [8] demonstrate an approach of extending a local cluster to cloud resources using schedulers by applying different strategies. Their approach is simulated, and not executed on production runs on cloud resources.

There are models for resources scheduling on HPC and Cloud respectively. A cost model based on economic scheduling heuristics [9] is investigated for cloud based streams. An adaptive scheduling mechanism [10] uses economic tools such as market, bidding, pricing, etc. on an elastic grid utilizing virtual nodes from clouds. An on-demand resource provisioning mechanism based upon load [11] is presented in Amazon cloud platform. In [12], a combinatorial auction model is proposed for both grids and clouds. However there is limited effort on unified resources management in a HPC and Cloud hybrid environments.

5   Conclusion

In this paper, we study the problem of low utilization of data center resources. Firstly we present a HPC and Cloud hybrid environment to enhance the utilization of cluster of hardware resource in data center. Then, we use an AR based periodic decomposition algorithm to improve the prediction accuracy of jobs arrival rate. Based on it, we propose a G/M/n queuing model and present a heuristic algorithm to make dynamic resource allocation to meet the QoS requirements. Finally we have evaluated hybrid environment based on SEU HPC center, and the results demonstrate the efficiency and effectiveness of our approach.

The result shows that this hybrid environment enhances at least 30% utilization of system resources than the system with static resource allocation technique. It also demonstrates a well performance of hybrid environment to meet user's QoS requirement.

Acknowledgments. This work is supported by National Key Basic Research Program of China under Grants No. 2010CB328104, National Natural Science Foundation of China under Grants No. 61320106007, No. 61070161, No. 61202449, China National High Technology Research and Development Program under Grants No. 2013AA013503, China Specialized Research Fund for the Doctoral Program of Higher Education under Grants No. 20110092130002, Jiangsu research prospective joint research project under Grants No. BY2012202, BY2013073-01. Jiangsu Provincial Key Laboratory of Network and Information Security under Grants No.BM2003201, Key Laboratory of Computer Network and Information Integration of Ministry of Education of China under Grants No. 93K-9, and Shanghai Key Laboratory of Scalable Computing and Systems(2010DS680095).

References

1. Kleinrack, L.: Queueing Systems, Volume 11: Computer Applications. Wiley (1976)
2. Yongwei, W., Yulai, Y.: Load Prediction Using Hybrid Model for Computational Grid. In: 8th Grid Computing Conference, pp. 235–242 (2008)
3. He, Q., Zhou, S., Kobler, B., Duffy, D., McGlynn, T.: Case Study for Running HPC Applications in Public Clouds. In: Proc. 19th ACM International Symposium on High Performance Distributed Computing (HPDC), pp. 395–401 (2010)
4. Rehr, J.J., Vila, F.D., Gardner, J.P., Svec, L., Prange, M.: Scientic Computing in the Cloud. Computing in Science & Engineering 12, 34–43 (2010)
5. Chen, L., Agrawal, G.: A static resource allocation framework for Grid-based streaming applications. Concurrency and Computation: Practice and Experience, 653–666 (2006)
6. Kim, H., El-Khamra, Y., Jha, S., Parashar, M.: Exploring application and infrastructure adaptation on hybrid grid-cloud infrastructure. In: Proceedings of the 19th ACM International Symposium on High Performance Distributed Computing, June 21-25, 2010, pp. 402–412 (2010)
7. Braun, T.D., Siegel, H.J., Maciejewski, A., Hong, Y.: Static resource allocation for heterogeneous computing environments with tasks having dependencies, priorities, deadlines, and multiple versions. Journal of Parallel and Distributed Computing, 1504–1516 (2008)
8. Assuncao, M.D., Costanzo, A., Buyya, R.: Evaluating the cost-benefit of using cloud computing to extend the capacity of clusters. In: Pro. the 18th ACM International Symposium on High Performance Distributed Computing, pp. 141–150. ACM, New York (2009)
9. Martinaitis, P., Patten, C., Wendelborn, A.: Remote interaction and scheduling aspects of cloud based streams. In: 2009 5th IEEE International Conference on E-Science Workshops, pp. 39–47 (December 2009)
10. Nie, L., Xu, Z.: An adaptive scheduling mechanism for elastic grid computing. In: International Conference on Semantics, Knowledge and Grid, pp. 184–191 (2009)
11. Dornemann, T., Juhnke, E., Freisleben, B.: On-demand resource provisioning for bpel workflows using amazon's elastic compute cloud. In: The 2009 9th IEEE/ACM International Symposium on Cluster Computing and the Grid, pp. 140–147. IEEE Computer Society, Washington, DC (2009)
12. Ozer, A., Ozturan, C.: An auction based mathematical model and heuristics for resource co-allocation problem in grids and clouds. In: Fifth International Conference on Soft Computing, Computing with Words and Perceptions in System Analysis, Decision and Control, ICSCCW 2009, pp. 1–4 (September 2009)

Candidate Set Parallelization Strategies
for Ant Colony Optimization on the GPU

Laurence Dawson and Iain A. Stewart

School of Engineering and Computing Sciences,
Durham University, Durham, United Kingdom
{l.j.dawson,i.a.stewart}@durham.ac.uk

Abstract. For solving large instances of the Travelling Salesman Problem (TSP), the use of a candidate set (or candidate list) is essential to limit the search space and reduce the overall execution time when using heuristic search methods such as Ant Colony Optimisation (ACO). Recent contributions have implemented ACO in parallel on the Graphics Processing Unit (GPU) using NVIDIA CUDA but struggle to maintain speedups against sequential implementations using candidate sets. In this paper we present three candidate set parallelization strategies for solving the TSP using ACO on the GPU. Extending our past contribution, we implement both the tour construction and pheromone update stages of ACO using a data parallel approach. The results show that against their sequential counterparts, our parallel implementations achieve speedups of up to 18x whilst preserving tour quality.

Keywords: Ant Colony Optimization, Graphics Processing Unit, CUDA, Travelling Salesman.

1 Introduction

Ant algorithms model the behaviour of real ants to solve a variety of optimization and distributed control problems. Ant Colony Optimization (ACO) [7] is a population-based metaheuristic that has proven to be the most successful ant algorithm for modelling discrete optimization problems. One of these problems is the Travelling Salesman Problem (TSP) in which the goal is to find the shortest tour around a set of cities. Dorigo and Stützle note [7] that the TSP is often the standard problem to model as algorithms that perform well when modelling the TSP will translate with similiar success to other problems. Dorigo and Stützle also remark [7] that ACO can be applied to the TSP easily as the problem can be directly mapped to ACO. For this reason, solving the TSP using ACO has attracted significant research effort and many approaches have been proposed.

The simplest of these approaches is known as Ant System (AS) and consists of two main stages: *tour construction*; and *pheromone update*. An optional additional local search stage may also be applied once the tours have been constructed so as to attempt to improve the quality of the tours before performing the pheromone update stage. The process of tour construction and pheromone

J. Kołodziej et al. (Eds.): ICA3PP 2013, Part I, LNCS 8285, pp. 216–225, 2013.

update is applied successively until a termination condition is met (such as a set number of iterations or minimum solution quality is attained). Through a process known as *stigmergy*, ants are able to communicate indirectly through *pheromone trails*. These trails are updated once each ant has constructed a new tour and will influence successive iterations of the algorithm. As the number of cities to visit increases, so does the computational effort and thus time required for AS to construct and improve tours. The search effort can be reduced through use of a *candidate set* (or *candidate list*). In the case of the TSP a candidate set provides a list of nearest cities for each city to visit. During the tour construction phase these closest cities will first be considered and only when the list has been exhausted will visiting other cities be permitted.

As both the tour construction and pheromone update stages can be performed independently for each ant in the colony and this makes ACO particularly suited to parallelization. There are two main approaches to implementing ACO in parallel which are known as fine and coarse grained. The fine grained approach maps each ant to an individual processing element. The coarse grained approach maps an entire colony to a processing element [7].

NVIDIA CUDA is a parallel programming architecture for developing general purpose applications for direct execution on the GPU [8] for potential speed increases. Although CUDA abstracts the underlying architecture of the GPU, fully utilising and scheduling the GPU is non-trivial.

This paper builds upon our past improvements to existing parallel ACO implementations on the GPU using NVIDIA CUDA [3]. We observed that parallel implementations of ACO on the GPU fail to maintain their speedup against their sequential counterparts that use candidate sets. This paper addresses this problem and explores three candidate set parallelization strategies for execution on the GPU. The first adopts a naive ant-to-thread mapping to examine if the use of a candidate set can increase the performance; this naive approach (in the absence of candidate sets) has previously been shown to perform poorly [2]. The second approach extends our previous data parallel approach (as pioneered by Cecilia et al. [2] and Delévacq et al. [4]), mapping each ant to a thread block. Through the use of warp level primitives we manipulate the block execution to first restrict the search to the candidate set and then expand to all available cities dynamically and without excessive thread serialization. Our third approach also uses a data parallel mapping but compresses the list of potential cities outside of the candidate set in an attempt to further decrease execution time.

We find that our data parallel GPU candidate set mappings reduce the computation required and significantly decrease the execution time against the sequential counterpart when using candidate sets. By adopting a data parallel approach we are able to achieve speedups of up to 18x faster than the CPU implementation whilst preserving tour quality and show that candidate sets can be used efficiently in parallel on the GPU. As candidate sets are not unique to ACO, we predict that our parallel mappings may also be appropriate for other heuristic problem-solving algorithms such as *Genetic Algorithms*.

2   Background

In order to solve the TSP we aim to find the shortest tour around a set of cities. An instance of the problem is a set of cities where for each city we are given the distances from that city to every other city. Throughout this paper we only ever consider *symmetric* instances of the TSP where $d_{i,j} = d_{j,i}$, for every edge (i,j). For a more detail on the TSP we direct readers to [3].

The AS algorithm consists of two main stages: ant solution construction; and pheromone update [7] and are repeated until a termination condition is met. To begin, each ant is placed on a randomly chosen start city. The ants then repeatedly apply the random proportional rule, which gives the probability of ant k moving from its current city i to some other city j, in order to construct a tour (the next city to visit is chosen by ant k according to these probabilities). At any point in the tour construction, ant k will already have visited some cities. The set of legitimate cities to which it may visit next is denoted N^k and changes as the tour progresses. Suppose that at some point in time, ant k is at city i and the set of legitimate cities is N^k. The *random proportional rule* for ant k moving from city i to some city $j \in N^k$ is defined via the probability:

$$p_{ij}^k = \frac{[\tau_{ij}]^\alpha [\eta_{ij}]^\beta}{\sum_{l \in N^k} [\tau_{il}]^\alpha [\eta_{il}]^\beta}, \tag{1}$$

where: τ_{il} is the amount of pheromone currently deposited on the edge from city i to city l; η_{il} is a parameter relating to the distance from city i to city l and which is usually set at $1/d_{il}$; and α and β are user-defined parameters to control the influence of τ_{il} and η_{il}, respectively. Dorigo and Stützle [7] suggest the following parameters when using AS: $\alpha = 1$; $2 \leq \beta \leq 5$; and $m = |N|$ (that is, the number of cities), i.e., one ant for each city. The probability p_{ij}^k is such that edges with a smaller distance value are favoured. Once all of the ants have constructed their tours, the pheromone level of every edge is evaporated according to the user-defined *evaporation rate* ρ (which, as advised by Dorigo and Stützle [7], we take as 0.5). So, each pheromone level τ_{ij} becomes:

$$\tau_{ij} \leftarrow (1 - \rho)\tau_{ij}. \tag{2}$$

This allows edges that are seldom selected to be forgotten. After evaporation, each ant k deposits an amount of pheromone on the edges of their particular tour T^k so that each pheromone level τ_{ij} becomes:

$$\tau_{ij} \leftarrow \tau_{ij} + \sum_{k=1}^{m} \Delta \tau_{ij}^k, \tag{3}$$

where the amount of pheromone ant k deposits, that is, $\Delta \tau_{ij}^k$, is defined as:

$$\Delta \tau_{ij}^k = \begin{cases} 1/C^k, & \text{if edge } (i,j) \text{ belongs to } T^k \\ 0, & \text{otherwise,} \end{cases} \tag{4}$$

where C^k is the length of ant k's tour T^k. Depositing pheromone increases the chances of one of the shorter edges being selected by an ant in a subsequent tour.

2.1   Candidate Sets

For larger instances of the TSP, the computational time required for the tour construction phase of the algorithm increases significantly. A common solution to this problem is to limit the number of available cities which we refer to as a candidate set. In the tour construction phase the ant will first consider all closely neighbouring cities. If one or more of the cities in the candidate set has not yet been visited, the ant will apply proportional selection on the closely neighbouring cities to determine which city to visit next. If no valid cities remain in the candidate set, the ant then applies an arbitrary selection technique to pick from the remaining unvisited cities. Dorigo and Stützle [7] utilise greedy selection to pick a city with the highest pheromone value. Randall and Montgomery [10] propose several new dynamic candidate set strategies, however, for this paper we will only focus on static candidate sets.

2.2   CUDA and the GPU

NVIDIA CUDA is a parallel architecture designed for executing applications on both the CPU and GPU. CUDA allows developers to run blocks of code, known as kernels, on the GPU for potential speed increases. A CUDA GPU consists of an array of streaming multiprocessors (SM), each containing a subset of streaming processors (SP). When a kernel method is executed, the execution is distributed over a grid of blocks each with their own subset of parallel threads.

CUDA exposes a set of memory types each with unique properties that must be exploited in order to maximize performance. The first type registers, are the fastest form of storage and each thread within a block has access to a set of fast local registers that exist on-chip. However, each thread can only access it's own registers and as the number of registers is limited per block. For inter-thread communication within a block, shared memory must be used. Shared memory also exists on-chip and is accessible to all threads within the block but is slower than register memory. For inter-block communication and larger data sets, threads have access to *global, constant* and *texture memory*.

3   Related Work

In this section we will briefly cover our past parallel ACO contribution and detail a new parallel ACO implementation. For a comprehensive review of all ACO GPU literature to date we direct readers to [3].

In our previous contribution [3] we presented a highly parallel GPU implementation of ACO for solving the TSP using CUDA. By extending the work of Cecilia et al. [2] and Delévacq et al. [4] we adopted a data parallel approach mapping individual ants to thread blocks. Roulette wheel selection was replaced by a new parallel proportionate selection algorithm we called Double-Spin Roulette (DS-Roulette) which significantly reduced the running time of tour construction. Our solution executed up to 82x faster than the sequential counterpart and up to 8.5x faster than the best existing parallel GPU implementation.

Uchida et al. [11] implement a GPU implementation of AS and also use a data parallel approach mapping each ant to a thread block. Four different tour construction kernels are detailed and a novel city compression method is presented. This method compresses the list of remaining cities to dynamically reduce the number of cities to check in future iterations of tour construction. The speedup reported for their hybrid approach is around 43x faster than the sequential implementation (see [6]). Uchida et al. conclude that further work should be put into nearest neighbour techniques (candidate sets) to further reduce the execution times (as their sequential implementation does not use candidate sets).

We can observe that the fastest speedups are obtained when using a data parallel approach; however none of the current implementations ([3],[2],[4],[11]) use candidate sets and as a result fail to maintain speedups for large instances of the TSP. In conclusion, although there has been considerable effort put into improving candidate set algorithms (e.g. [5],[10],[9],[1]), there has been little research into developing parallel GPU implementations.

4   Implementation

In this section we present three parallel AS algorithms utilising candidate sets for execution on the GPU. The first uses a simple ant-to-thread mapping to check if this approach is suitable for use with candidate sets. The second and third implementations use a data parallel approach. The following implementations will only focus on the tour construction phase of the algorithm as we have previously shown how to implement the pheromone update efficiently on the GPU [3].

City data is first loaded into memory and stored in an $n \times n$ matrix. Ant memory is allocated to store each ant's current tour and tour length. A *pheromone matrix* is initialized on the GPU to store pheromone levels and a secondary structure called *choice_info* is used to store the product of the denominator of Equation 1. The candidate set is then generated and transferred to the GPU. For each city we save the closest 20 cities (as recommended by Dorigo and Stützle [7]) into an array. After initialization the pheromone matrix is artificially seeded with a tour generated using a greedy search as recommended in [7].

4.1   Tour Construction Using a Candidate Set

In Fig. 1 we give the pseudo-code for iteratively generating a tour using a candidate set based upon the implementation by Dorigo and Stützle [7]. First, an ant is placed on a random initial city; this city is then marked as visited in a *tabu* list. Then for $n - 2$ iterations (where n is the size of the TSP instance) we select the next city to visit. The candidate set is first queried and a probability of visiting each closely neighbouring city is calculated. If a city has previously been visited, the probability of visiting that city in future is 0. If the total probability of visiting any of the candidate set cities is greater than 0, we perform roulette wheel selection on the set and pick the next city to visit. Otherwise we pick the best city out of all the remaining cities (where we define the best as having the largest pheromone value).

```
procedure ConstructSolutionsCandidateSet
    tour[1] ← place the ant on a random initial city
    tabu[1] ← visited
    for j = 2 to n − 1 do
        for l = 1 to 20 do
            probability[l] ← CalcProb(tour[1 ... j − 1],l)
        end-for
        if probability > 0 do
            tour[j] ← RouletteWheelSelection(probability)
            tabu[tour[j]] ← true
        else
            tour[j] ← SelectBest(tabu)
            tabu[tour[j]] ← true
        end-if
    end-for
    tour[n] ← remaining city
    tour_cost ← CalcTourCost(tour)
end
```

Fig. 1. Overview of an ant's tour construction using a candidate set

4.2 Task Parallelism

Although it has previously been shown that using a data parallel approach yields the best results ([3],[2],[4],[11]), it has not yet been established that this holds when using a candidate set. Therefore our first parallelization strategy considers this simple mapping of one ant per thread (*task parallelism*). Each thread (ant) in the colony executes the tour construction method shown in Fig. 1. There is little sophistication in this simple mapping, however we include it for completeness. Cecilia et al. [2] note that implementing ACO using task parallelism is not suited to the GPU. From our experiments we can observe that these observations still persist when using a candidate set and as a result yield inadequate results which were significantly worse than those obtained by the CPU implementation. We can therefore conclude that the observations made by Cecilia et al. [2] hold when using candidate sets.

4.3 Data Parallelism

Our second approach uses a data parallel mapping (one ant per thread block). Based on the previous observations made when implementing a parallel roulette wheel selection algorithm [3] we found that using warp level primitives to avoid branching lead to the largest speedups. In DS-Roulette each warp independently calculates the probabilities of visiting a set of cities. These probabilities are then saved to shared memory and one warp performs roulette wheel selection to select the best set of cities. Roulette wheel selection is then performed again on the subset of cities to select which city to visit next [3]. This process is fast as we no longer perform reduction across the whole block and avoid waiting for other warps to finish executing. As we no longer need to perform roulette wheel selection across all cities, DS-Roulette is unsuitable for use with a candidate set. However, if we reverse the execution path of DS-Roulette we can adapt the algorithm to fit tour selection using a candidate set (see Fig. 2). Instead of funnelling down all potential cities to perform roulette wheel on one warp of potential cities, we first perform roulette wheel selection across the candidate set and scale up to all available cities if no neighbouring cities are available. Our new data parallel tour selection algorithm consists of three main stages.

The first stage uses one warp to calculate the probability of visiting each city in the candidate set. An optimisation we apply when checking the candidate set is to perform a warp ballot. Each thread in the warp checks the city against the tabu list and submits this value to the CUDA operation __ballot(). The result of the ballot is a 32-bit integer delivered to each thread where bit n corresponds to the input for thread n. If the integer is greater than zero then unvisited cities remain in the candidate set and we proceed to perform roulette wheel selection on the candidate set. Using the same warp-reduce method we previously used in [3] we are able to quickly normalize the probability values across the candidate set warp, generate a random number and select the next city to visit without communication between threads in the warp. We found experimentally that using a candidate set with less than 32 cities (1 warp) was actually detrimental to the performance of the algorithm. Scaling the candidate set up from 20 cities to 32 cities allows all threads within the warp to follow the same execution path.

In stage two the aim is to narrow down the number of remaining available cities. We limit the number of threads per block to 128 and perform tiling across the block to match the number of cities. Each warp then performs a modified version of warp-reduce [3] to find the city with the best pheromone value using warp-max. As each warp tiles it saves the current best city and pheromone value to shared memory. Using this approach we can quickly find four candidates (1 best candidate for each of the warps and as there are 128 threads with 32 threads per warp) for the city with the maximum pheromone value for the final stage of the algorithm using limited shared memory and without block synchronisation.

Finally we use one thread to check which of the four previously selected cities has the largest pheromone value, visit this city and save the value to global memory. The three stages of the algorithm are illustrated in Fig. 2.

4.4   Data Parallelism with Tabu List Compression

Section 3 details the recent work of Uchida et al. [11] presenting a novel tabu list compresssion technique. A tabu list can be represented as an array of integers with size n. When city i is chosen, the algorithm replaces city tabu$[i]$ with city tabu$[n-1]$ and decrements the list size n by 1. Cities that have previously been visited will not be considered in future iterations thus reducing the search space. By adding tabu list compression to our data parallel tour construction kernel we aim to further reduce the execution time. However, as a complete tabu list is stil required for checking against the candidate set we must use two tabu lists. The second list maintains the positions of each city within the first candidate list.

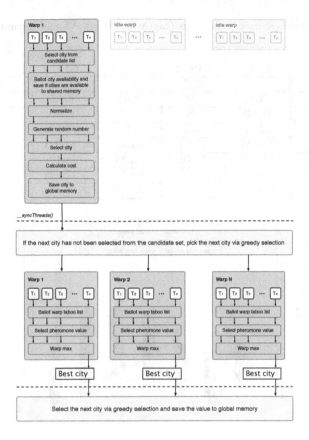

Fig. 2. An overview of the data parallel candidate set tour construction algorithm

5 Results

In this section we present the results of executing various instances of the TSP on our two data parallel candidate set implementations and compare the results to the sequential counterpart and our previous GPU implementation. We use the standard ACO parameters but increase the candidate set size from 20 to 32 (see Section 4). The solution quality obtained by our implementations was able match and often beat the quality obtained by the sequential implementation. Our test setup consists of a GTX 580 GPU and an i7 950 CPU. Timing results are averaged over 100 iterations of the algorithm with 10 independant runs.

In Table. 1 we present the execution times (for a single iteration) of the tour construction algorithm using a candidate set for various instances of the TSP. Columns 5 and 6 show the speedup of the two data parallel implementations over the CPU implementation using a candidate set. The CPU results are based on the standard sequential implementation ACOTSP (source available at [6]) and the two GPU columns correspond to the two proposed data parallel candidate set implementations in Section 4.

Table 1. Average execution times (ms) when using AS and a candidate set

Instance	CPU	GPU 1	GPU 2	Speedup GPU 1	Speedup GPU 2
d198	6.39	0.77	0.85	8.31x	7.53x
a280	13.44	1.59	2.04	8.42x	6.59x
lin318	18.60	1.90	2.07	9.74x	8.99x
pcb442	42.37	3.67	3.96	11.55x	10.69x
rat783	168.90	12.13	14.49	13.92x	11.66x
pr1002	278.85	19.76	26.34	14.10x	10.58x
nrw1379	745.59	42.37	68.78	17.60x	10.84x
pr2392	2468.40	131.85	393.98	18.72x	6.27x

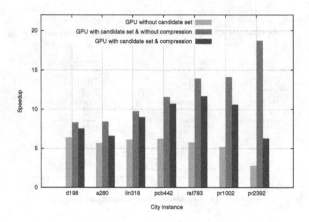

Fig. 3. Execution speedup using multiple GPU and CPU instances

Our results show the first data parallel GPU implementation achieves the best speedups across all instances of the TSP. Both data parallel approaches consistently beat the results obtained for the sequential implementation. The speedup obtained by the first data parallel implementation increased as the tour sizes increased. This is in contrast to our previous GPU implementation [3] in which the speedup reduced due to shared memory constraints and failed to maintain speedups against the sequential implementation when using a candidate set.

The results attained for the second data parallel implementation using tabu list compression show the implementation was not able to beat the simpler method without compression. As mentioned in Section 4 to implement tabu list compression, a second tabu list must be used to keep the index of each city in the first list. We observed the process of updating the second list for each iteration (for both the greedy search stage and proportionate selection on the candidate set stage) outweighed the benefits of not checking the tabu values for previously visited cities. We also observed that the increased shared memory requirements for larger instances reduced the performance of the solution.

In Fig. 3 we compare the speedup of our previous GPU implementation [3] without a candidate set against our data parallel GPU solutions. We can observe that for large instances, the speedup obtained from our GPU implementation with a candidate set increases as opposed to instances without a candidate set.

6   Conclusions

In this paper we have presented three candidate set parallelization strategies and shown that candidate sets can be used efficiently in parallel on the GPU. Our results show that a data parallel approach must be used over a task parallel approach to maximize performance. Tabu list compression was shown to be ineffective when implemented as part of the tour construction method and was beaten by the simpler method without compression. Our future work will aim to implement alternative candidate set strategies including dynamically changing the candidate list contents and size.

References

1. Blazinskas, A., Misevicius, A.: Generating high quality candidate sets by tour merging for the traveling salesman problem. In: Skersys, T., Butleris, R., Butkiene, R. (eds.) ICIST 2012. CCIS, vol. 319, pp. 62–73. Springer, Heidelberg (2012)
2. Cecilia, J.M., García, J.M., Nisbet, A., Amos, M., Ujaldon, M.: Enhancing data parallelism for ant colony optimization on GPUs. J. Parallel Distrib. Comput. 73(1), 42–51 (2013)
3. Dawson, L., Stewart, I.: Improving Ant Colony Optimization performance on the GPU using CUDA. In: 2013 IEEE Congress on Evolutionary Computation (CEC), pp. 1901–1908 (2013)
4. Delèvacq, A., Delisle, P., Gravel, M., Krajecki, M.: Parallel ant colony optimization on graphics processing units. J. Parallel Distrib. Comput. 73(1), 52–61 (2013)
5. Deng, M., Zhang, J., Liang, Y., Lin, G., Liu, W.: A novel simple candidate set method for symmetric tsp and its application in max-min ant system. In: Advances in Swarm Intelligence, pp. 173–181. Springer (2012)
6. Dorigo, M.: Ant Colony Optimization - Public Software,
   http://iridia.ulb.ac.be/~mdorigo/ACO/aco-code/public-software.html
   (last accessed July 31, 2013)
7. Dorigo, M., Stützle, T.: Ant Colony Optimization. MIT Press (2004)
8. NVIDIA: CUDA C Programming Guide, http://docs.nvidia.com/cuda/
   cuda-c-programming-guide/index.html
   (last accessed July 31, 2013)
9. Rais, H.M., Othman, Z.A., Hamdan, A.R.: Reducing iteration using candidate list. In: International Symposium on Information Technology, ITSim 2008, vol. 3, pp. 1–8. IEEE (2008)
10. Randall, M., Montgomery, J.: Candidate set strategies for ant colony optimisation. In: Proceedings of the Third International Workshop on Ant Algorithms, ANTS 2002, pp. 243–249. Springer, London (2002)
11. Uchida, A., Ito, Y., Nakano, K.: An efficient gpu implementation of ant colony optimization for the traveling salesman problem. In: 2012 Third International Conference on Networking and Computing (ICNC), pp. 94–102 (2012)

Synchronization-Reducing Variants of the Biconjugate Gradient and the Quasi-Minimal Residual Methods

Stefan Feuerriegel[1] and H. Martin Bücker[2]

[1] University of Freiburg, 79098 Freiburg, Germany
[2] Friedrich Schiller University Jena, 07743 Jena, Germany

Abstract. The Biconjugate Gradient (BiCG) and the Quasi-Minimal Residual (QMR) method are among the popular iterative methods for the solution of large, sparse, non-symmetric systems of linear equations. When these methods are implemented on large-scale parallel computers, their scalability is limited by the synchronization caused when carrying out inner product-like operations. Therefore, we propose two new synchronization-reducing variants of BiCG and QMR in an attempt to mitigate these negative performance effects. The idea behind these new s-step variants is to group several dot products for joint execution. Although these new algorithms still reveal numerical instabilities, they are shown to keep the cost of inner product-like operations almost independent of the number of processes, thus improving scalability significantly.

Keywords: s-step BiCG, s-step QMR, synchronization-reducing.

1 The Need for Rethinking of Algorithm Design

Current large-scale computer systems are sophisticated architectures based on multi- or manycore technology with deep memory hierarchies and, possibly, heterogeneity in the form of graphic or other coprocessors. For scientific and engineering applications, it is therefore currently challenging to get high-performance on these systems. Unfortunately, future extreme-scale computer systems are likely to be even more complex and it will become increasingly harder to get a sustained performance that is somewhere near their peak performance.

It is widely recognized that there are various intricate challenges for future large-scale computing. Rather than summarizing this ongoing discussion, the purpose of this paper is to focus on novel algorithmic techniques that will be required to fully exploit current large-scale and future exascale systems. Today, there is only a vague idea of how these future platforms will actually be built and how they will be programmed efficiently. Existing technology trends, however, strongly indicate that algorithm designers will have to pay crucial attention to reduce data movement at various memory levels and to reduce synchronization at various system levels. While communication cost associated with data movement has become an important issue in today's parallel algorithm design, the cost associated with synchronization is currently not receiving adequate consideration.

J. Kołodziej et al. (Eds.): ICA3PP 2013, Part I, LNCS 8285, pp. 226–235, 2013.

However, synchronization cost will soon outweigh communication cost as the degree of parallelism is increasing further. In fact, synchronization dictates the overall performance of various algorithms on current large-scale systems. Therefore, we here focus on synchronization-reducing variants of two Krylov methods for the solution of large sparse non-symmetric systems of linear equations. The new contributions of this paper are the design of new variants of the Biconjugate Gradient method (BiCG) [1] and the Quasi-Minimal Residual method (QMR) [2] as well as an assessment of their numerical stability and their parallel scalability.

In Sect. 2, we review related approaches for parallel Krylov methods. The generation of the underlying basis by an s-step Lanczos variant is summarized in Sect. 3. We also sketch in that section how this variant can be used to solve linear systems. In Sect. 4 and 5, we derive new variants of BiCG and QMR. In Sect. 6, these new variants are compared to their classical versions in terms of both numerical stability and parallel performance.

2   Related Work on Parallel Krylov Subspace Methods

There is a long history of parallel Krylov subspace methods [3–7]. Taking a serial algorithm and parallelizing each kernel operation is an option that does not change the long tradition of successful serial algorithm design. However, rather than considering parallelized implementations of serial algorithms, we focus on making these algorithms "more parallel" in some suitable way.

Typically, vector updates and matrix-by-vector products perform communication between nearby processors. In contrast, due to the underlying reduction operation, an inner product enforces a *global synchronization point*. It is defined as a location of an algorithm at which all local information has to be globally available in order to continue [8]. There have been early attempts to eliminate inner product-like operations [9]. Another class of algorithms tries to reduce the number of global synchronization points per iteration. This was advocated for the Conjugate Gradient method [10, 11], BiCG [8, 12], and QMR [13]. When only one global synchronization point is enforced for s iterations of the corresponding classical algorithm, this is called an s-step method [14–18]. The term "s-step" was also used in different settings. In [19], for instance, s iterations are grouped together without the intention to enforce a single global synchronization point. The communication-avoiding algorithms [20–22] are sometimes also referred to as s-step methods. However, these methods are different from our approach in that they typically rely on blocking to reduce the communication volume. Another class of techniques is based on communication overlapping aimed at reducing the impact of a communication event by overlapping it with computation and/or other communication. For instance, reduction operations are carried out while the Krylov basis is being generated in [23, 24]. There is also further research on handling synchronization hierarchically [25] or using non-blocking allreduce operations. Throughout this paper, we use the term "s-step" in the sense of [14–18] and derive new s-step variants of both BiCG and QMR. These algorithms are built on top of the following s-step Lanczos algorithm.

3 Solving Linear Systems Using the Lanczos Basis

For a non-symmetric matrix $A \in \mathbb{R}^{N \times N}$, the classical Lanczos algorithm [26] returns, after N steps, matrices $T, V, W \in \mathbb{R}^{N \times N}$ such that $W^T V$ equals the identity and that $AV = VT$ and $A^T W = WT^T$ where T is tridiagonal. However, the process typically converges in fewer than N steps. This classical algorithm unfolds an intrinsic dependence; computing the i-th basis vector v_i requires the preceding vector v_{i-1} which in turn requires v_{i-2}, and so forth. This is relaxed by the s-step Lanczos method [17, 18] which determines matrices $\ddot{T}, \ddot{V}$ and $\ddot{W}$ such that $\ddot{W}^T \ddot{V}$ is almost everywhere zero except for $s \times s$ blocks on the diagonal. Furthermore, $A\ddot{V} = \ddot{V}\ddot{T}$ and $A^T \ddot{W} = \ddot{W}\ddot{T}$ hold where the upper Hessenberg matrix $\ddot{T}$ is block tridiagonal. Compared to [17, 18], an s-step Lanczos algorithm with additional normalization is derived in [27]. Although the variant [27] slightly raises the computational cost for vector updates and matrix-by-vector products, it reduces numerical instabilities and global synchronization.

To solve $Ax = b$ where $x, b \in \mathbb{R}^N$, we use the Lanczos basis $V_n = [v_1 \ldots v_n] \in \mathbb{R}^{N \times n}$ whose i-th column is the Lanczos vector v_i. Let T_n denote the upper left $(n+1) \times n$ submatrix of T. The LU factorization of the tridiagonal matrix

$$T_n := \begin{bmatrix} \alpha_1 & \beta_2 & & \\ \gamma_2 & \alpha_2 & \ddots & \\ & \ddots & \ddots & \beta_n \\ & & \gamma_n & \alpha_n \\ \hline & & & \gamma_{n+1} \end{bmatrix} \text{ into } L_n U_n = \begin{bmatrix} \tau_1 & & & \\ \omega_2 & \tau_2 & & \\ & \ddots & \ddots & \\ & & \omega_n & \tau_n \\ \hline & & & \omega_{n+1} \end{bmatrix} \times \begin{bmatrix} 1 & \mu_2 & & \\ & 1 & \ddots & \\ & & \ddots & \mu_n \\ & & & 1 \end{bmatrix} \quad (1)$$

is computed via

$$\omega_n = \gamma_n, \quad \mu_n = \beta_n / \tau_{n-1}, \quad \tau_n = \alpha_n - \omega_n \mu_n, \quad \text{for } n \geq 2, \quad \text{with } \tau_1 := \alpha_1 .$$

Given an initial guess x_0 to the exact solution x, the current approximation is given by $x_n = x_0 + V_n z_n$ using the Lanczos basis. We will also use another basis $P_n = [p_1 \ldots p_n]$ defined by $V_n = P_n U_n$. From the structure of U_n according to (1), we find $p_n = v_n - \mu_n p_{n-1}$. Furthermore, the relation to the classical Lanczos algorithm is given by $AP_n = V_{n+1} L_n$. Introducing $y_n := U_n z_n$, we yield $x_n = x_0 + P_n y_n$. The residual $r_n := b - Ax_n$ is then

$$r_n = r_0 - AP_n y_n = \omega_1 v_1 - V_{n+1} L_n y_n = V_{n+1} \left([\omega_1, 0, \ldots, 0]^T - L_n y_n \right) , \quad (2)$$

where we choose $v_1 := r_0 / \omega_1$ with a scaling factor ω_1 set to $\|r_0\|_2$.

4 The s-Step Biconjugate Gradient Algorithm

The idea of BiCG [1] is to determine y_n by zeroing out the first n entries of the vector in parentheses in (2). More precisely, if $\bullet$ denotes an arbitrary value in the $(n+1)$-th component of that vector, we require

$$[\omega_1, 0, \ldots, 0]^T - L_n y_n = [0, \ldots, 0, \bullet]^T . \quad (3)$$

Let $\boldsymbol{y}_n = [\kappa_1, \ldots, \kappa_n]^T$. Inserting the above ansatz into the residual $\boldsymbol{r}_n$ gives

$$\boldsymbol{r}_n = V_{n+1}[0, \ldots, 0, -\omega_{n+1}\kappa_n]^T = -\omega_{n+1}\kappa_n \boldsymbol{v}_{n+1} .$$

Assuming that (3) is fulfilled in the first $(n-1)$ components, we find that $0 = -\omega_n\kappa_{n-1} - \tau_n\kappa_n$. Hence, $\kappa_n = -\omega_n\kappa_{n-1}/\tau_n$ with $\kappa_0 := -1$. The process of fixing $\boldsymbol{y}_n$ is easily updated in each iteration step because $\boldsymbol{y}_{n-1}$ coincides with the first $n-1$ components of $\boldsymbol{y}_n$. Therefore, the n-th approximation is obtained via

$$\boldsymbol{x}_n = \boldsymbol{x}_0 + P_{n-1}\boldsymbol{y}_{n-1} + \kappa_n\boldsymbol{p}_n = \boldsymbol{x}_{n-1} + \kappa_n\boldsymbol{p}_n .$$

The k-th block iteration of the s-step BiCG algorithm computes s Lanczos vectors and updates the LU decomposition of T_n from (1) with $n = sk$:

1: Initialize vectors $\boldsymbol{r}_0 \leftarrow \boldsymbol{b} - A\boldsymbol{x}_0$, $\boldsymbol{v}_1 \leftarrow \boldsymbol{r}_0/\|\boldsymbol{r}_0\|_2$, $\boldsymbol{p}_1 \leftarrow \boldsymbol{v}_1$
   and set $\kappa_0 \leftarrow -1$, $\omega_1 \leftarrow \|\boldsymbol{r}_0\|_2$, $\mu_1 \leftarrow 0$, $\tau_1 \leftarrow \alpha_1$.
2: **for** $k = 1$ **until** Convergence **do**
3:     Compute next s Lanczos vectors $\boldsymbol{v}_{s(k-1)+1}, \ldots, \boldsymbol{v}_{sk}$ as well as next entries
       in T_{sk}, i.e., $\alpha_{s(k-1)+1}, \ldots, \alpha_{sk}$, $\beta_{s(k-1)+1}, \ldots, \beta_{sk}$, $\gamma_{s(k-1)+1}, \ldots, \gamma_{sk}$.
4:     **for** $n = s(k-1)+1$ **to** sk **do**
5:         Update LU of T_{sk} via $\omega_n \leftarrow \gamma_n$, $\mu_n \leftarrow \beta_n/\tau_{n-1}$, $\tau_n \leftarrow \alpha_n - \omega_n\mu_n$.
6:         Compute vector $\boldsymbol{p}_n \leftarrow \boldsymbol{v}_n - \mu_n\boldsymbol{p}_{n-1}$.
7:         Set $\kappa_n \leftarrow -\omega_n\kappa_{n-1}/\tau_n$ and compute approximation $\boldsymbol{x}_n \leftarrow \boldsymbol{x}_{n-1} + \kappa_n\boldsymbol{p}_n$.
8:     **end for**
9: **end for**

Throughout the s-step BiCG algorithm, the call to the s-step Lanczos method in Step 3 introduces the only global synchronization point.

5   The s-Step Quasi-Minimal Residual Algorithm

The idea of QMR [2, 28] is to find $\boldsymbol{y}_n$ by minimizing the Euclidean norm of the vector in parentheses in (2). To solve these least-squares problems we follow [29]:

Theorem 1. *The unique solution of* $\boldsymbol{y}_n := \arg\min\limits_{\boldsymbol{y}\in\mathbb{R}^n} \left\|[\omega_1, 0, \ldots, 0]^T - L_n\boldsymbol{y}\right\|_2$ *is*

$$\boldsymbol{y}_n = \begin{bmatrix} \boldsymbol{y}_{n-1} \\ 0 \end{bmatrix} + \boldsymbol{g}_n, \qquad \boldsymbol{g}_n = \theta_n \begin{bmatrix} \boldsymbol{g}_{n-1} \\ 0 \end{bmatrix} + [0, \ldots, 0, \xi_n]^T, \qquad n \geq 2 ,$$

with $\boldsymbol{y}_1 = \boldsymbol{g}_1 = [\xi_1]$, *where*

$$\theta_n = \frac{|\tau_n|^2 (1 - \sigma_n)}{\sigma_n |\tau_n|^2 + |\omega_{n+1}|^2},$$

$$\xi_n = -\frac{\omega_n \overline{\tau}_n \xi_{n-1}}{\sigma_n |\tau_n|^2 + |\omega_{n+1}|^2}, \qquad \xi_0 = -1,$$

$$\sigma_{n+1} = \frac{\sigma_n |\tau_n|^2}{\sigma_n |\tau_n|^2 + |\omega_{n+1}|^2}, \qquad \sigma_1 = 1.$$

The approximation $\boldsymbol{x}_n$ *is derived from* $\boldsymbol{d}_n = \theta_n\boldsymbol{d}_{n-1} + \xi_n\boldsymbol{p}_n$ *and* $\boldsymbol{x}_n = \boldsymbol{x}_{n-1} + \boldsymbol{d}_n$.

The s-step QMR algorithm is given by the following pseudo-code:

1: Initialize vectors $r_0 \leftarrow b - Ax_0$, $\quad v_1 \leftarrow r_0/\|r_0\|_2$, $\quad p_1 \leftarrow v_1$, $\quad d_0 \leftarrow 0_N$
   and set $\xi_0 \leftarrow -1$, $\quad \sigma_1 \leftarrow 1$, $\quad \omega_1 \leftarrow \|r_0\|_2$, $\quad \mu_1 \leftarrow 0$, $\quad \tau_1 \leftarrow \alpha_1$.
2: **for** $k = 1$ **until** Convergence **do**
3:     Compute next s Lanczos vectors $v_{s(k-1)+1}, \ldots, v_{sk}$ as well as next entries
       in T_{sk}, i.e., $\alpha_{s(k-1)+1}, \ldots, \alpha_{sk}$, $\quad \beta_{s(k-1)+1}, \ldots, \beta_{sk}$, $\quad \gamma_{s(k-1)+1}, \ldots, \gamma_{sk}$.
4:     **for** $n = s(k-1) + 1$ **to** sk **do**
5:         Update LU of T_{sk} via $\omega_n \leftarrow \gamma_n$, $\quad \mu_n \leftarrow \beta_n/\tau_{n-1}$, $\quad \tau_n \leftarrow \alpha_n - \omega_n\mu_n$.
6:         Compute vector $p_n \leftarrow v_n - \mu_n p_{n-1}$.
7:         $\theta_n \leftarrow \dfrac{|\tau_n|^2(1-\sigma_n)}{\sigma_n|\tau_n|^2+|\omega_{n+1}|^2}$, $\quad \xi_n \leftarrow -\dfrac{\omega_n\bar{\tau}_n\xi_{n-1}}{\sigma_n|\tau_n|^2+|\omega_{n+1}|^2}$, $\quad \sigma_{n+1} \leftarrow \dfrac{\sigma_n|\tau_n|^2}{\sigma_n|\tau_n|^2+|\omega_{n+1}|^2}$.
8:         Compute $d_n \leftarrow \theta_n d_{n-1} + \xi_n p_n$ and approximation $x_n \leftarrow x_{n-1} + d_n$.
9:     **end for**
10: **end for**

Once more, the invocation of the s-step Lanczos subroutine in Step 3 represents the only synchronization point.

6 Numerical Experiments

We compare classical and s-step variants of BiCG and QMR in terms of numerical accuracy and parallel performance using an example from [28]. We consider the differential equation $-\Delta u + 40\,(xu_x + yu_y + zu_z) - 250\,u = f$ on $\Omega = (0,1) \times (0,1) \times (0,1)$ with $u = 0$ on the boundary. Using first-order centered differences and $\sqrt[3]{N}$ discretization points in each direction, we arrive at a linear system of order N. The right-hand side $f(x,y,z)$ is determined such that the vector of all ones is the exact solution. The initial guess is set to $x_0 := [0, \ldots, 0]^T$.

Both s-step BiCG and QMR are implemented in parallel using PETSc 3.0 and compared to their classical variants implemented in PETSc. We use a block Jacobi preconditioner and chose $N = 2^{24}$ since PETSc recommends at least 10 000 to 20 000 unknowns per process. All computations are performed on a *Nehalem*-based cluster[1] whose barrier times measured via PETSc are given in Figure 1. A synchronization with a reduction operation accounts for 5.97×10^{-4} s with 256 processes and 7.26×10^{-4} s with 512 processes.

The s-step variants can yield identical results as the classical methods. In exact arithmetic, s-step variants and their classical counterparts are mathematically equivalent. The iteration number is plotted against the relative residual norm in Figures 2 and 3. The findings are as follows: (1) The relative residual norms for classical and s-step algorithms are similar. (2) An increasing iteration index n augments the numerical discrepancy between s-step and classical solvers.

---

[1] Each node of this cluster at RWTH Aachen University, Germany, consists of 2 sockets, each equipped with Intel Xeon X5570 quadcore processors running at 2.93 GHz. Each core has a separate L1 and L2 cache; while 4 cores share an L3 cache of size 8 MB. So, each node of this cluster is made up of 8 cores called processes hereafter. The nodes are connected by a quad data rate InfiniBand network.

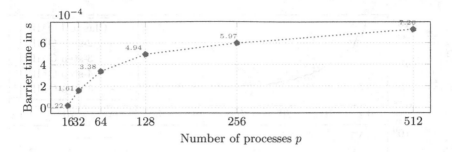

Fig. 1. Barrier time versus number of processes on the *Nehalem*-based cluster

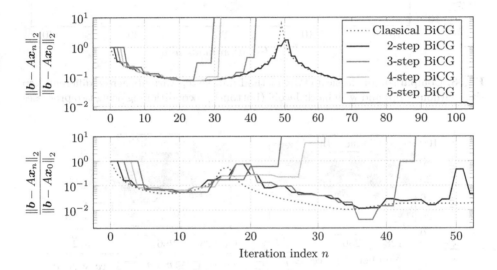

Fig. 2. Comparison of classical BiCG method and s-step variants across different step sizes without (top) and with block Jacobi (bottom) preconditioning using two processes

(3) Numerical instabilities grow with increasing step size s as the s-step Lanczos basis becomes more instable, causing even the possibility of breakdowns.

Figure 4 compares the ratio out of the total time that is spent in linear algebra operations. Due to barrier operations arising from global synchronization points, there is a gradual increase in the proportional influence of inner products. For the classical BiCG, the percentage of the total time resulting from inner products grows from around 12 % for 64 processes to almost 47 % for 512 processes. For the 2-step BiCG, however, there is only a moderate rise from around 8 % to about 13 % when varying the processes from 64 to 512. As almost half of the total computation time for the classical BiCG is spent within the evaluation of inner products, the scalability for a large number of processes is limited.

Figure 5 compares various linear algebra operations in terms of their absolute time consumption. The overall runtime of the classical BiCG is affected by inner

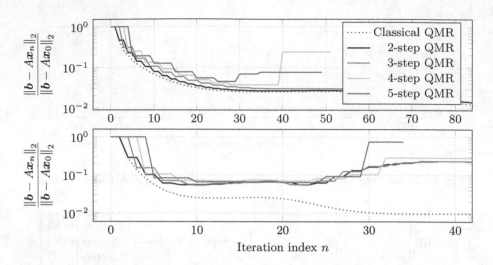

Fig. 3. Comparison of classical QMR method and s-step variants across different step sizes without (top) and with block Jacobi (bottom) preconditioning using two processes

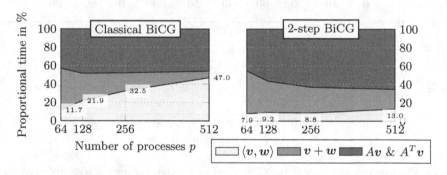

Fig. 4. Proportional time spent in linear algebra operations measured across 200 iterations including initialization for classical BiCG (left) and s-step BiCG method (right)

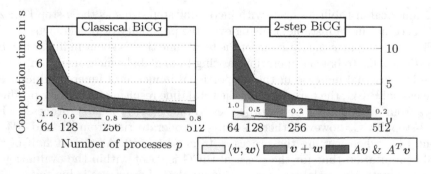

Fig. 5. Total time spent in linear algebra operations measured across 200 iterations including initialization for classical BiCG (left) and s-step BiCG method (right)

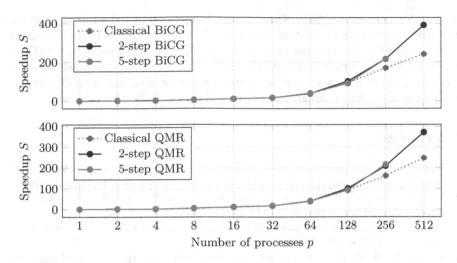

Fig. 6. Average speedup $S = T_{\text{par}}(1)/T_{\text{par}}(p)$ for a single loop iteration of BiCG (top) and QMR (bottom) measured across 200 iterations excluding initialization time

products to a large extent. In contrast, the 2-step BiCG computes all inner products in less time. With 512 processes, the classical BiCG needs 0.76 s for computing all inner products, whereas the 2-step BiCG needs only 0.17 s.

In Figure 6, the average speedup for a single loop iteration is depicted. With increasing number of processes, the speedup of the s-step solvers ascends more linearly compared to the classical variants that start to flatten out. Measurements for step sizes $s > 2$ are unavailable for more than 256 processes due to breakdowns. As a trend however, we conclude that, given a network with a relatively time-consuming barrier operation, the scalability of the new s-step variants is improved significantly, as compared to the classical algorithms.

7   Conclusions and Directions for Future Research

We derive s-step variants of BiCG and QMR by restructuring the original algorithms in such a way that multiple inner products are grouped for joint execution. So, we successfully reduce the number of global synchronization points. This offers a possible path of how sparse, non-symmetric systems of linear equations might be solved on current large-scale and future extreme-scale systems with significant improvements in scalability. However, there is still a long way to go. Most importantly, we observe severe numerical instabilities when increasing the step size s that requires further investigation. One option is to replace the monomial basis by Newton or Chebyshev bases [22]. Another viable alternative is to introduce residual replacement strategies [30, 31]. The techniques addressed in [32] might also improve the numerical stability further. Also, look-ahead techniques [2, 28, 33, 34] are advantageous to prevent breakdowns.

Acknowledgements. Parts of this research were conducted while the authors were in residence at the Institute for Scientific Computing, the Center for Computational Engineering Science, and the Aachen Institute for Advanced Study in Computational Engineering Science at RWTH Aachen University, D-52056 Aachen, Germany. Financial support from the Deutsche Forschungsgemeinschaft (German Research Foundation) through grant GSC 111 is gratefully acknowledged.

References

1. Fletcher, R.: Conjugate gradient methods for indefinite systems. In: Watson, G. (ed.) Numerical Analysis. LNM, vol. 506, pp. 73–89. Springer, Heidelberg (1976)
2. Freund, R.W., Nachtigal, N.M.: An implementation of the QMR method based on coupled two-term recurrences. SIAM J. Sci. Comput. 15(2), 313–337 (1994)
3. Saad, Y.: Krylov subspace methods on supercomputers. SIAM J. Sci. Stat. Comput. 10(6), 1200–1232 (1989)
4. van der Vorst, H.: Iterative methods for the solution of large systems of equations on supercomputers. Advances in Water Resources 13(3), 137–146 (1990)
5. Demmel, J., Heath, M., van der Vorst, H.: Parallel numerical linear algebra. Acta Numerica 2(1), 111–197 (1993)
6. Duff, I.S., van der Vorst, H.A.: Developments and trends in the parallel solution of linear systems. Parallel Computing 25(13-14), 1931–1970 (1999)
7. Bücker, H.M.: Iteratively solving large sparse linear systems on parallel computers. NIC Serices, John Von Neumann Institute f. Computing. Jülich 10, 521–548 (2002)
8. Bücker, H.M., Sauren, M.: Reducing global synchronization in the biconjugate gradient method. In: Yang, T. (ed.) Parallel numerical computations with applications, pp. 63–76. Kluwer Academic Publishers, Norwell (1999)
9. Fischer, B., Freund, R.: An inner product-free conjugate gradient-like algorithm for Hermitian positive definite systems. In: Brown, J., et al. (eds.) Proc. Cornelius Lanczos Intern. Centenary Conf., pp. 288–290. SIAM (1994)
10. Meurant, G.: The conjugate gradient method on supercomputers. Supercomputer 13, 9–17 (1986)
11. Van Rosendale, J.: Minimizing inner product data dependencies in conjugate gradient iteration. NASA Contractor Report NASA–CR–172178, NASA Langley Research Center, Center, Hampton, VA (1983)
12. Bücker, H.M., Sauren, M.: A Variant of the Biconjugate Gradient Method Suitable for Massively Parallel Computing. In: Bilardi, G., Ferreira, A., Lüling, R., Rolim, J. (eds.) IRREGULAR 1997. LNCS, vol. 1253, pp. 72–79. Springer, Heidelberg (1997)
13. Bücker, H.M., Sauren, M.: A Parallel Version of the Quasi-Minimal Residual Method Based on Coupled Two-Term Recurrences. In: Waśniewski, J., Dongarra, J., Madsen, K., Olesen, D. (eds.) PARA 1996. LNCS, vol. 1184, pp. 157–165. Springer, Heidelberg (1996)
14. Chronopoulos, A.T.: A Class of Parallel Iterative Methods Implemented on Multiprocessors. Technical report UIUCDCS–R–86–1267, Department of Computer Science, University of Illinois, Urbana, Illinois (1986)
15. Chronopoulos, A.T., Gear, C.W.: S-step iterative methods for symmetric linear systems. J. Comput. Appl. Math. 25(2), 153–168 (1989)
16. Chronopoulos, A.T., Swanson, C.D.: Parallel iterative s-step methods for unsymmetric linear systems. Parallel Computing 22(5), 623–641 (1996)

17. Kim, S.K., Chronopoulos, A.: A class of Lanczos-like algorithms implemented on parallel computers. Parallel Computing 17(6-7), 763–778 (1991)
18. Kim, S.K., Chronopoulos, A.T.: An efficient nonsymmetric Lanczos method on parallel vector computers. J. Comput. Appl. Math. 42(3), 357–374 (1992)
19. Alvarez-Dios, J.A., Cabaleiro, J.C., Casal, G.: A generalization of s-step variants of gradient methods. J. Comput. Appl. Math. 236(12), 2938–2953 (2012)
20. Mohiyuddin, M., Hoemmen, M., Demmel, J., Yelick, K.: Minimizing communication in sparse matrix solvers. In: Proc. Conf. High Perf. Comput. Networking, Storage and Analysis, SC 2009, pp. 36:1–36:12. ACM, New York (2009)
21. Hoemmen, M.F.: Communication-avoiding Krylov subspace methods. PhD thesis, EECS Department, University of California, Berkeley (2010)
22. Carson, E., Knight, N., Demmel, J.: Avoiding communication in two-sided Krylov subspace methods. SIAM J. Sci. Comput. 35(5), S42–S61 (2013)
23. Ghysels, P., Ashby, T.J., Meerbergen, K., Vanroose, W.: Hiding global communication latency in the GMRES algorithm on massively parallel machines. SIAM J. Sci. Comput. 35(1), 48–71 (2013)
24. Ghysels, P., Vanroose, W.: Hiding global synchronization latency in the preconditioned Conjugate Gradient algorithm. In: Parallel Computing (in press, 2013)
25. Curfmann McInnes, L., Smith, B., Zhang, H., Mills, R.T.: Hierarchical and nested Krylov methods for extreme-scale computing. In: Parallel Computing (in press, 2013)
26. Lanczos, C.: An iteration method for the solution of the eigenvalue problem of linear differential and integral operators. J. Res. Nat. Bur. Stand. 45(4), 255–282 (1950)
27. Feuerriegel, S., Bücker, H.M.: A normalization scheme for the non-symmetric s-Step Lanczos algorithm. In: Kołodziej, J., Aversa, R., Zhang, J., Amato, F., Fortino, G. (eds.) ICA3PP 2013, Part II. LNCS, vol. 8286, pp. 30–39. Springer, Heidelberg (2013)
28. Freund, R., Nachtigal, N.: QMR: a quasi-minimal residual method for non-Hermitian linear systems. Num. Math. 60(1), 315–339 (1991)
29. Sauren, M., Bücker, H.M.: On deriving the quasi-minimal residual method. SIAM Review 40(4), 922–926 (1998)
30. van der Vorst, H.A., Ye, Q.: Residual replacement strategies for Krylov subspace iterative methods for the convergence of true residuals. SIAM J. Sci. Comput. 22(3), 835–852 (2000)
31. Carson, E., Demmel, J.: A residual replacement strategy for improving the maximum attainable accuracy of s-step Krylov subspace methods. Technical Report UCB/EECS–2012–197, University of California, Berkeley (2012)
32. Gustafsson, M., Demmel, J., Holmgren, S.: Numerical evaluation of the communication-avoiding Lanczos algorithm. Technical Report 2012–001, Department of Information Technology, Uppsala University (January 2012)
33. Freund, R.W., Hochbruck, M.: A biconjugate gradient type algorithm on massively parallel architectures. In: Vichnevetsky, R., Miller, J.J.H. (eds.) IMACS 1991 Proc. 13th World Congress Comput. Appl. Math, pp. 720–721. Criterion Press, Dublin (1991)
34. Freund, R.W., Hochbruck, M.: A biconjugate gradient-type algorithm for the iterative solution of non-Hermitian linear systems on massively parallel architectures. In: Brezinski, C., Kulisch, U. (eds.) IMACS 1991, Proc. 13th World Congress Comput. Appl. Math. I, pp. 169–178. Elsevier Science Publishers (1992)

Memory Efficient Multi-Swarm PSO Algorithm in OpenCL on an APU

Wayne Franz, Parimala Thulasiraman, and Ruppa K. Thulasiram

University of Manitoba
{umfranzw,thulasir,tulsi}@cs.umanitoba.ca

Abstract. Multi-Swarm PSO (MPSO) is an extension of the PSO algorithm that incorporates multiple, collaborating swarms. Although embarrassingly parallel in appearance, MPSO is memory bound, introducing challenges for GPU-based architectures. In this paper, we use device-utilization metrics to drive the development and optimization of an MPSO algorithm applied to the task matching problem. Our hardware architecture is the AMD Accelerated Processing Unit (APU), which fuses the CPU and GPU together on a single chip. We make effective use of features such as the hierarchical memory structure on the APU, the 4-way very long instruction word (VLIW) feature for vectorization, and DMA transfer features for asynchronous transfer of data between global memory and local memory. The resulting algorithm provides a 29% decrease in overall execution time over our baseline implementation.

Keywords: PSO, Parallel Evolutionary Computing, APU, OpenCL.

1 Introduction

Particle Swarm Optimization (PSO) [1] is a meta-heuristic optimization algorithm that simulates a group of particles as they interact within a solution space.

Meta-heuristic algorithms like PSO have become increasingly popular techniques for approaching NP-complete optimization problems. Recent literature has demonstrated the effectiveness of mapping PSO variants to the GPU [2,3], and its application to task-matching [4]. Notably, Cagnoni et al. [5] implemented an asynchronous PSO algorithm in OpenCL and used it to compare the performances of a multi-core CPU and a GPU (however, this algorithm was not designed for the task matching problem). In general, the feasibility of mapping PSO to parallel GPU hardware is demonstrated through discussion of thread-to-data mappings, exploitation of different memory types, and speedup results. This work seeks to point out the importance of additional performance trade-offs centred around device occupancy and memory access patterns.

Solomon et al. [3] developed a collaborative multi-swarm PSO algorithm (MPSO) for the task matching problem on a discrete Nvidia GPU. The MPSO algorithm provides tremendous amounts of parallelism [6,7] and is well-suited for execution on parallel hardware.

J. Kołodziej et al. (Eds.): ICA3PP 2013, Part I, LNCS 8285, pp. 236–246, 2013.

Our MPSO variant [8] maintains several independent swarms, stopping periodically to migrate particles between them. Migrated particles maintain the memories of their personal best positions, and their current velocities. This creates an implicit form of communication between the swarms.

We apply MPSO to the task matching problem, which seeks to map a set of tasks to a set of distributed machines in such a way the time to complete all tasks (*makespan*) is minimized. This problem is NP-complete [9].

Task matching introduces some irregular memory accesses when updating particle fitnesses. These accesses degrade performance on Single Instruction Multiple Thread (SIMT) architectures such as the GPU, which are suited for applications with regular memory accesses. Also, the position, velocity, and fitness data is too large to fit entirely in smaller, faster GPU memories. Instead, we must rely on global memory, which has a significant latency period. Overlapping this latency period with computation is therefore a goal in increasing performance.

Our core performance metric is *kernel occupancy* [10]. Kernel occupancy is the ratio of the number of active wavefronts per Compute Unite (CU) to the maximum number of wavefronts supported per CU. This provides a simple indication of the proportion of GPU resources that a kernel is utilizing. *Estimated Kernel Occupancy* (EKO) refers to kernel occupancy as calculated by AMD profiling tools, which are able to determine the number of active wavefronts for a given executing kernel.

2   Algorithm and Implementation

We define the following symbols: let n be the user-defined maximum number of iterations, s be the number of swarms, p be the number of particles per swarm, $d = |T|$ be the number of dimensions (tasks), e be the number of particles exchanged between swarms, and $m = |M|$ be the number of machines.

This section illustrates optimizations using $s = 60$ and $p = 128$ for a total of $n = 1000$ iterations. The remaining MPSO parameters are taken from the work of Solomon *et al.* [3]. We set $d = 80$, $m = 8$, $e = 24$, $c1 = 2.0$, $c2 = 1.4$, $\omega = 1.0$, and exchange particles every 10 iterations. Execution times are averaged over 30 trials of 1000 iterations each.

Vectorized kernels use four-element vector data types, while *unvectorized* kernels use scalar data types. Pseudo-code is presented in unvectorized format.

2.1   Algorithm

Each particle k maintains three pieces of information: a position vector X_k, a personal-best position vector $\acute{X}_k$, and a velocity vector V_k. Each swarm j maintains the position of the best solution seen so far by any particle, $\hat{X}_j$. Position is used to compute fitness, f_k. We also maintain $\acute{f}_k$ and $\hat{f}_j$, the particle-best and swarm-best fitnesses, respectively. Velocity is modified at each iteration i according to the following equation [11]:

$$V_k^{i+1} = \omega * V_k^i + c_1 * R_1 * (\acute{X}_k - X_k^i) + c_2 * R_2 * (\hat{X}_j - X_k^i) \qquad (1)$$

Position is then updated using:

$$X_k^{i+1} = X_k^i + V_k^{i+1} \tag{2}$$

R_1 and R_2 are vectors of random numbers between 0 and 1 (selected from a uniform distribution), while c_1, c_2, and ω are user-defined weighting parameters used to balance the forces exerted by each of the three terms in (1).

We arrange swarms in a ring topology. Every given number of iterations, the e best particles from each swarm replace the e worst particles of its neighbour.

Data Storage. An *Estimated Time to Complete* (ETC) matrix [3] is used to prevent redundant makespan calculations. We store this data structure in constant memory. An ETC matrix value at row i, column j records the amount of time machine i requires to execute task j. We generate the matrix using the CPU, while the initial random number generation and particle initialization kernels are running on the device.

Position, velocity, and fitness data are stored in global memory arrays. Values are ordered by dimension first (in groups of four for the VLIW Processing Elements (PEs)), and particle index second. As threads iterate through a particle's dimensions (four elements at a time), collectively they will access contiguous chunks of memory.

Random Number Generation. Salmon *et al.* [12] recently proposed a counter-based parallel pseudo random number generator that is well-suited for the GPU. The only state storage requirements are simple counter values that are incremented before each call. We create a kernel that uses this library to fill a large 142 MB buffer (launched on demand). We alter the granularity of the parallelism by causing each thread to loop and place multiple calls. After determining the optimal number of loop iterations, we unroll the loop. Our completed kernel consumes 8 registers per CU, yielding an 87.5% EKO.

Particle Initialization. This kernel uses one thread per particle dimension ($s{*}p{*}d$ threads) to initialize particle positions and velocities in parallel. Since the thread-to-data mapping is one-to-one, it is easy to use four-way vector data types, reducing the number of required threads by a factor of four.

We assign position values in the range $[0, m-1]$, and velocity values in the range $[0, 2m]$. In addition, we initialize the particle-best and swarm-best fitnesses so as to ensure an update on the first fitness calculation. Register usage is low, since few calculations are performed. This is desirable because there is a pool of registers allocated to each CU. The fewer registers we use, the more wavefronts can be run simultaneously on the CU [10]. This kernel achieves 100% EKO.

Table 1. Particle Initialization Kernels (FU:Fetch Unit, T:Avg. time)

Kernel	T (ms)	ALU:Fetch	FU Busy (%)
unvec	0.988	7.52	22.65
vec	0.980	9.03	6.85

Table 2. Update Fitness Kernel Results (T: Avg. time)

Opt.	T (ms)	MPSO (sec)
uncached	0.313	15.835
cached	0.324	15.867

Table 1 shows statistics for vectorized and unvectorized kernels. The table shows two effects of vectorization. First, it significantly decreases the percentage of time that the fetch unit is busy by generating fewer, larger accesses. Second, the *ALU-op-to-fetch-op ratio* grows slightly as we move to a vectorized kernel. If this ratio is low, the kernel is more memory-bound, and context-switching provides little benefit. If it is high, the kernel is more compute-bound, allowing alternate wavefronts to cover a larger portion of a global memory latency period.

In this case, the small increase for the vectorized kernel is due to an increase in the number of calculations performed per thread. However, 9.03 ALU ops is still not nearly enough to cover the latency period of 300-600 cycles incurred by a single fetch. Overall, it appears that in spite of the fact that memory system can keep up with our requests, and we have 100% EKO, execution time is still limited by the memory-bounded characteristics of the kernel.

Update Fitness. This kernel is our objective function. We assign one thread per particle to calculate f_k^{i+1}, then write it to global memory. The makespan calculation uses a local memory array, allocating chunks of size m for each thread.

This kernel requires a large number of registers, severely limiting the number of wavefronts we can launch, and resulting in an EKO of 50%. The low number of active wavefronts per CU will also limit the benefit of context switching.

For kernels that use local memory, we incorporate as many swarms into one workgroup as possible. This improves kernel occupancy, since it increases the number of wavefronts executing on each CU. However, it is important to note that there is a corresponding increase in the amount of local memory used per CU. If memory usage becomes too high it will limit occupancy (there is a fixed amount per CU) [10]. For this kernel, profiling tools indicate that packing multiple swarms is worthwhile, as register usage is the factor limiting occupancy.

The makespan computation incurs a large number of irregular local memory accesses, introducing bank conflicts. There is no way to resolve these conflicts deterministically because we do not know in advance which machine each task will map to. This complicates the task of vectorization. If each thread handles four dimensions at once, then four local writes must be done atomically, since multiple tasks could map to the same machine.

One avenue for optimization is to "cache" the four previously read local memory values in registers. If subsequent tasks map to the same machine (the same array location), we can skip a read, grabbing the data from the register. However, this introduces several branch statements, which are a bottleneck for SIMT hardware. The results are shown in table 2. Unfortunately, the number of "cache hits" is not high enough to offset the overhead. Since this optimization does not affect kernel occupancy, overall execution time remains relatively unchanged.

Update Bests. In this kernel, we update the particle-best and swarm-best fitnesses and positions, launching one thread per particle. The kernel operates in two phases. The first involves a comparison between the f_k^i and f_k^{i+1}. Each thread replaces the former with the latter if necessary. If an update is required, each thread also overwrites $\acute{X}_k^i$ with X_k^{i+1}. Phase two performs a parallel reduction

```
1: if id < s * p then
2:     new_val = -1
3:     if f[id] < f̂[id] then
4:         f̂[id] = f[id]
5:         new_val = f[id]
6:     end if
7:     local_mem[id] = new_val
8: end if
9: barrier(local_mem)
10: if id < s * p then
11:     if local_mem[id] ≥ 0 then
12:         Update all components of X́_id
13:     end if
14: end if
15: Parallel reduction on local_mem (Skip values < 0)
16: barrier(local_mem)
17: if id = 0 then
18:     swarm_update = reduction produced a value ? 1 : 0
19:     if swarm_update && local_mem[0] < f̂[group_id] then
20:         f̂[group_id] = local_mem[0]
21:     end if
22:     local_mem[1] = swarm_update && (reduct. produced a value)
23: end if
24: barrier(local_mem)
25: if local_mem[1] && new_val = local_mem[0] then
26:     local_mem[2] = id
27: end if
28: barrier(local_mem)
29: if swarm_update && id < d then
30:     Read local_mem[2] and compute position offset
31:     Write chunk of X_{local_mem[2]} to X̂_{group_id}
32: end if
```

Fig. 1. Update Bests pseudo-code

using half of the threads allocated to each swarm. One thread per swarm then updates $\hat{f}_j$, if necessary. Finally, threads cooperate to update $\hat{X}_j$, if necessary.

There is a relationship between these two phases that we can exploit: each updated $\hat{f}_j$ is set to an updated $\acute{f}_k^{i+1}$ value (for some particle k in swarm j). The second phase requires local memory buffers for the parallel reduction. We re-use these buffers during the first phase to store information about which particles' best values were updated. The kernel proceeds as shown in figure 1.

Phase 1 comprises lines 1 through 14. Phase 2 (beginning on line 15) performs a reduction, storing the result in local_mem[0]. This reduction skips over any values that are less than zero (indicating that the personal best fitness has not changed, and therefore this value cannot be a new swarm-best fitness). Lines 17-23 update the swarm-best fitnesses, if necessary. We store a boolean value to local memory index one (line 22) indicating whether or not this was the case.

Next, if there was an update, we must determine which thread has the new swarm-best fitness value (lines 25-27) so that we can locate the corresponding position data to copy into the swarm-best positions global memory array. We use a race condition to identify one thread with the new swarm-best fitness (there may be multiple). It writes its particle index to local_mem[2]. Finally, (if necessary) threads read local_mem[2] and cooperate to copy the new position data to global memory in the swarm-best positions array (lines 29-32).

As we move from the unvectorized to the vectorized kernel, register usage forces a 25% decrease in EKO (see table 3). However, this is more than compensated for by the increase in the ALU-to-fetch ratio.

Table 3. Update Bests Kernels (T:Avg.time, R:Registers)

Kernel	T (ms)	R	EKO (%)	ALU:Fetch
unvec	0.224	6	100	76.5
vec	0.081	9	75	194.5

Table 4. Update Position/Velocity Kernels (T:Avg.time, R:Registers)

Kernel	T (ms)	R	EKO (%)	MPSO (sec)
unvec	1.209	6	75	2.749
vec	1.005	9	75	1.981
async copy	1.127	8	87.5	2.087
combined	1.177	10	75	2.124

Update Position/Velocity. In this kernel, we set V_k^{i+1} using (1), and then X_k^{i+1} using (2), for each particle k. Since (1) allows each dimension to be calculated independently, we can launch a full $s * p * d$ threads. As the same $\hat{X}_j$ is read by all threads operating on swarm j, we place $\hat{X}$ in constant memory.

Table 4 shows the effect of vectorization (each thread handles 4 dimensions) on average run time. EKO is limited to 75%, due to the number of registers required for the calculation of (1). One option to reduce register usage is to break to kernel into multiple pieces, one for each term in (1). However, intermediate kernels would have to store their partial results back to global memory. In addition, the position X_k^i would need to be read from global memory by two kernels, whereas previously it could be read once and stored in a register. Finally, the small independent kernels could not provide enough ALU operations to cover the combined latency of these global memory accesses.

A second option is to use local memory in place of one or more registers. OpenCL provides functions that asynchronously copy data from global to local memory (DMA transfer) within a kernel. We were able to replace a single register using this call. As table 4 shows, this was enough to raise the EKO. However, overall MPSO execution time also rises, since the bandwidth of local memory is less than that of register file. In order to support the four-way vectorization of the kernel, each thread must read four (rather than the optimal two) values from local memory, causing bank conflicts. This further increases execution time.

A third option involves combining this kernel with an adjacently launched kernel. This should allow the compiler to re-use registers between what was previously separated kernel code. The update bests kernel is launched immediately before this kernel, and is our only practical candidate for a merger (the following kernel is only invoked on iterations when particle swapping occurs).

One problem here is that the update bests kernel requires $s*p$ threads, while the update position/velocity kernel requires $s*p*d$ threads. Ordinarily, we could simply launch $s*p*d$ threads, and restrict the parallelism for the update bests code using a branch statement. However, there is a problem.

Threads in the update position/velocity kernel operate independently. So, the kernel may split the work for one swarm across multiple workgroups. Threads in the update bests kernel must cooperate using local memory. Since local memory cannot be used for inter-workgroup communication (only intra-workgroup), all threads operating on a swarm must be members of the same workgroup.

With this in mind, we launch $s*p$ threads, and use a loop that iterates through the update position/velocity kernel code d times. While this will increase the individual execution time of a kernel instance, it has little effect on occupancy. Table 4 shows the results of this strategy. The register usage of the combined kernel is less than the sum for the individual kernels. Unfortunately, this is not enough to increase the EKO. The loop pushes the combined kernel execution time just above the combined durations of the original kernels.

Find Best/Worst Particles. This kernel determines the indices of the particles with the e best and e worst fitnesses in each swarm. This information is stored in global memory buffers so that the exchange can be done later.

We begin by mapping one thread to each particle, employing an algorithm used by Solomon *et. al* [3]. This involves copying fitness data to local memory and performing e parallel reductions. Tracking the particle-indices of these particles requires additional local buffers. In total, five buffers of size p are used.

Four-way vectorization causes each thread to operate on four values, quadrupling the local memory requirements for each CU. Instead, we opt for a two-way vectorized kernel. This also provides a more efficient local memory access pattern. Table 5 shows statistics for this kernel. In spite of our efforts, local memory usage drops the EKO to 25%. With this in mind, we consider an alternative algorithm that requires less local memory (see figure 2).

This algorithm works by performing an all-to-all comparison and recording the number of comparisons each element wins. The ids of the threads with the highest (lowest) e win counts are the indices of the e best (worst) particles.

This approach is complicated by the fact that it is possible to have multiple identical fitness values. The loop (lines 11-27) works out the conflicts between elements that have the same loss count using a race condition. In the event of a conflict, one thread increments its count by one, and the loop is repeated.

The loop stops when all threads read back the expected value from the local memory array (lines 19-21). Using a separate local memory variable to record the stopping condition increases our local memory usage, limiting occupancy. Instead, we re-use array location zero for this purpose (lines 23-26, 12-14).

A two-way vectorized implementation of this algorithm uses only p space, lifting the limitation on EKO (see table 5).

Swap Particles. Our final task is to perform the actual particle exchange between swarms. Here we launch one thread for each dimension of each particle to be exchanged ($s*e*d$ threads). The e best particles in each swarm overwrite

```
 1: local_mem[id] = f[id]
 2: win_count = 0
 3: for i = 1 to p − 1 do
 4:    if f[id] > f[(id + i) mod p] then
 5:       counts += 1
 6:    end if
 7: end for
 8: done = False
 9: cmp = False
10: repeat
11:    if id == 0 then
12:       local_mem[0] = 1
13:    end if
14:    if !done and cmp then
15:       local_mem[win_count] = id
16:    end if
17:    if !done then
18:       test_val = cmp ? local_mem[win_count] : id
19:       cmp = (test_val != thread_index)
20:       done = !cmp
21:    end if
22:    if !done then
23:       win_count += cmp
24:       local_mem[0] = -1
25:    end if
26: until local_mem[0] ≥ 0
```

Fig. 2. Alternative Find Best/Worst Pseudocode

the e worst particles in the next. Specifically, positions, velocities, particle-best positions, and particle-best fitnesses are overwritten. Fitnesses are not overwritten, as they will be recalculated on the next iteration before they are needed again.

This kernel makes a large number of global memory accesses. A vectorized algorithm makes fewer, larger accesses, reducing the average time (see table 5). However, a large number of index calculations are needed to move the array values between swarms. Vectorization drives up register usage, limiting EKO.

We could attempt to replace registers that deal with best and worst particle indices with local memory. The asynchronous copy function must be called with the same arguments for all threads in a workgroup. For the best indices, this is not a problem. But for the worst indices, we must retrieve the next swarm's value (an offset of one). This means that there will be wrap-around in the global memory array we are reading from. As there are multiple swarms per workgroup, this leads to different values for different threads in the same workgroup. We therefore manually copy the worst indices to local memory using a loop.

The asynchronous copy call also forces us to move the best and worst indices from constant memory to global memory (constant to local asynchronous copies are not supported in OpenCL). This actually allows the compiler to reuse more

Table 5. Find Best/Worst Kernels (T: Avg. Time, LM:local memory

Kernel	T (ms)	LM (bytes)	EKO (%)
unvec	1.850	6144	62.5
vec	1.658	12288	25
vec (alt)	0.269	2048	100

Table 6. Swap Particles Kernels (T: Avg. Time, R: Registers)

Kernel	T (ms)	R	EKO (%)
unvec	2.463	7	100
vec	0.048	20	37.5
vec (local)	0.646	8	87.5

registers (see table 5) Unfortunately, the lower bandwidth of local memory, and the inability of global memory to broadcast, result in a larger execution time.

3 Results

Our test system uses an AMD A8-3530MX APU. This device incorporates a quad core CPU at 1.90 GHz with 6GB of RAM, and an on-die Radeon HD 6620G graphics processor. All experiments were compiled using OpenCL 1.2.

Optimizations that alter kernel occupancy tend to perform better with larger input sizes. We present the results of a simple scaling experiment below. We fix s at 60 and scale up p in the range $[4, 256]$. Figure 3 shows the effect that scaling p has on execution time. The gap between unvectorized and vectorized algorithms widens as p increases. This is true in spite of the fact that unvectorized kernels generally have a higher occupancy level. This trend reveals multiple levels of parallelism at work. In addition to parallelism at the work-item level (corresponding to kernel occupancy), there is also parallelism at the ALU level (corresponding to vectorization). In this case, the latter outweighs the former and we see the widening gap in the graph.

The slight rises and falls in the slopes of the lines result from the placement of multiple swarms into the same workgroups. In cases where the mapping works out evenly, we see a lower execution time due to an increase in parallel efficiency. But if an extra swarm narrowly fails to fit into a workgroup, the hardware scheduler my need to launch an extra round of workgroups on the CUs.

The update fitness caching optimization exhibits no improvement over the vectorized algorithm. Combining the update position/velocity and update bests kernels ultimately results in a higher execution time than the plain vectorized algorithm. This line does not quickly diverge from the vectorized series because the EKO of the combined kernel remains identical to both separate versions. However, the combined kernel suffers from lower parallelism at the work-item level, since it must iterate for the position/velocity section.

Moving the position/velocity kernel to local memory significantly increases execution time (though it increased occupancy) due to the lower bandwidth. On the other hand, moving the swap kernel to local memory has only a small effect. We attribute this to the fact that the local swap kernel uses much less local memory than the local position/velocity kernel. Finally, our alternative find best/worst algorithm decreases execution time slightly.

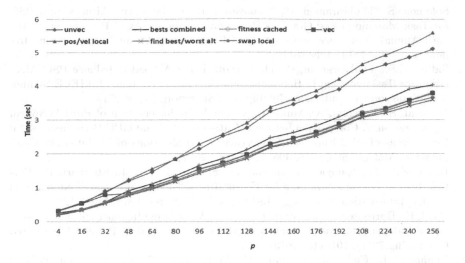

Fig. 3. Execution time as the number of particles per swarm increases

Moving from the unvectorized to the best-performing algorithm (find best/worst alt), at $p = 256$, execution time drops by approximately 29% (1.51 sec).

4 Conclusion

This work has traced the optimization process of an MPSO algorithm on an APU architecture. We have investigated optimizations to increase kernel occupancy, leverage vectorization, optimize memory access, and reduce register usage.

Nearly all of the ideas presented here may be directly applied to other parallel population-based algorithms. It is worth noting that even those techniques that did not consistently provide benefit to us may well prove worthwhile in other contexts or on other devices.

Acknowledgment. The authors acknowledge NSERC for partial funding support in conducting this research. The first author acknowledges the University of Manitoba for their funding support through the GETS program.

References

1. Kennedy, J., Eberhart, R.: Particle Swarm Optimization. In: IEEE International Conference on Neural Networks, Perth, Australia, vol. 4, pp. 1942–1948 (1995)
2. Cardenas-Montes, M., Vega-Rodriguez, M., Rodriguez-Vazquez, J., Gomez-Iglesias, A.: Accelerating Particle Swarm Algorithm with GPGPU. In: 2011 19th Euromicro International Conference on Parallel, Distributed and Network-Based Processing, Ayia Napa, Cyprus, pp. 560–564 (February 2011)

3. Solomon, S., Thulasiraman, P., Thulasiram, R.: Collaborative Multi-swarm PSO for Task Matching using Graphics Processing Units. In: ACM Proceedings of the 13th Annual Conference on Genetic and Evolutionary Computation, Dublin, Ireland, pp. 1563–1570 (July 2011)
4. Sidhu, M.S., Thulasiraman, P., Thulasiram, R.K.: A Load-Rebalance PSO Algorithm for Taskmatching in Heterogeneous Computing Systems. In: IEEE Symposium Series on Computational Intelligence, Singapore (April 2013)
5. Cagnoni, S., Bacchini, A., Mussi, L.: OpenCL Implementation of Particle Swarm Optimization: A Comparison between Multi-core CPU and GPU Performances. In: Proceedings of 2012 European Conference on Applications of Evolutionary Computation, Málaga, Spain, pp. 406–415 (April 2012)
6. Rabinovich, M., Kainga, P., Johnson, D., Shafer, B., Lee, J., Eberhart, R.: Particle Swarm Optimization on a GPU. In: 2012 IEEE International Conference on Electro/Information Technology, Indianapolis, USA, pp. 1–6 (May 2012)
7. Pinel, F., Dorronsoro, B., Bouvry, P.: Solving Very Large Instances of the Scheduling of Independent Tasks Problem on the GPU. Journal of Parallel Distributed Computing 73(1), 101–110 (2013)
8. Vanneschi, L., Codecasa, D., Mauri, G.: An Empirical Comparison of Parallel and Distributed Particle Swarm Optimization Methods. In: Proceedings of 12th Annual Conference on Genetic and Evolutionary Computation, Portland, USA, pp. 15–22 (July 2010)
9. Fernandez-Baca, D.: Allocating modules to processors in a distributed system. IEEE Transactions on Software Engineering 15(11), 1427–1436 (1989), doi:10.1109/32.41334
10. Advanced Micro Devices: AMD Accelerated Parallel Processing OpenCL Programming Guide (July 2012)
11. Shi, Y., Eberhart, R.: A Modified Particle Swarm Optimizer. In: IEEE World Congress on Computational Intelligence Evolutionary Computation Proceedings, Anchorage, Alaska, USA, pp. 69–73 (May 1998)
12. Salmon, J., Moraes, M., Dror, R., Shaw, D.: Parallel random numbers: as easy as 1, 2, 3. In: Proceedings of 2011 International Conference for High Performance Computing, Networking, Storage and Analysis, Seattle, Washington, USA, pp. 16:1–16:12 (November 2011)

Multi-objective Parallel Machines Scheduling for Fault-Tolerant Cloud Systems

Jakub Gąsior[1] and Franciszek Seredyński[2]

[1] Systems Research Institute, Polish Academy of Sciences, Warsaw, Poland
[2] Cardinal Stefan Wyszynski University, Warsaw, Poland

Abstract. We present in this paper a security-driven solution for scheduling of N independent jobs on M parallel machines that minimizes three different objectives simultaneously, namely the failure probability, the total completion time of the jobs and their respective tardiness. As this problem is NP-hard in the strong sense, a meta-heuristic method NSGA-II is proposed to solve it. This approach is based on the Pareto dominance relationship, providing no single optimal solution, but a set of solutions which are not dominated by each other. Thus, it was necessary to provide decision-making mechanisms selecting the best strategy from the Pareto frontier. The performance of the presented model and the applied GA is verified by a number of numerical experiments. The related results show the effectiveness of the proposed model and GA for small and medium-sized scheduling problems.

Keywords: Multi-objective optimization, Genetic algorithm, Risk resilience.

1 Introduction

A simple concept that has emerged out of the conceptions of heterogeneous distributed computing is that of the Cloud Computing (CC), where customers do not own any part of the infrastructure. It reduces the concept of computational power to a set of services, which can be rent from specialized organizations. However, after an initial enthusiastic reception, new issues concerning CC have been formulated. Beside problems in domains such as scheduling, CC highlights complementary needs in the area of fault-tolerance, results checking and software confidentiality such that novel approaches should be evaluated.

Truly secured environment for distributed execution should cover the problematics of confidentiality of both application code and user data, integrity, fault-tolerance and finally trust management. While the range of problems to be solved is wide, we focus on two key issues here. One is to provide a reasonable level of security-aware and robust computation in distributed systems. To obtain this, our approach proposes combination of generic methods of monitoring and discovery of anomalies, leading to defining a security-assurance condition during the job mapping process.

J. Kołodziej et al. (Eds.): ICA3PP 2013, Part I, LNCS 8285, pp. 247–256, 2013.

Another issue is providing efficient resource management. Such problems in their general form are known to be NP-hard, which means that a time complexity of exact algorithms delivering solutions will be at least exponential, and a provider of a system must rely on approximate solutions offered in an acceptable time using heuristic or meta-heuristics approaches. One of the distinctive features of this paper is an attempt to work out a class of load balancing and scheduling algorithms which, while maintaining performance criteria, will also provide security mechanisms enabling to work in untrusted or fault-tolerant environments.

Obviously, the conflict between achieving good performance and high security-assurance introduces new challenges in CC scheduling. Scheduling performance is affected by the heterogeneities of security and computational power of resources. Different jobs may have varied security requirement and even the same security requirements may exhibit different security overhead on different computational nodes. The aim of our study is to propose an efficient algorithm which effectively handles the multi-criteria parallel job scheduling problem, taking into account not only the job completion time but also the security constraints existing in a CC system.

The remainder of this paper is organized as follows. Section 2 presents the related work. In Section 3 we describe our system model. Section 4 briefs the NSGA-II algorithm and its application. Section 5 demonstrates the performance metrics, the input parameters and experimental results. Finally, Section 6 concludes the paper.

2   State of the Art and Our Approach

Recently, a great interest of researchers in Cloud and Grid Computing domains has been focused on the secure scheduling, which aims to achieve an efficient assignment of tasks to trustful resources. Due to the NP-hardness of the job scheduling problem, finding the exact solutions to solve the large-scale task scheduling problem in the dynamic environments is not always feasible. Therefore, the approximation methods providing a near optimal solution are more promising approaches. Heuristics and meta-heuristics have shown to be useful for solving a wide variety of combinatorial and multi-objective optimization problems.

One such a solution was presented in [5], where authors proposed a failure detection and handling service as a mechanism providing risk-resilience in Grid environment. In [4] authors proposed a solution capable of meeting diverse security requirements of multiple users simultaneously, while minimizing the number of jobs aborted due to resource limitations. Insecure conditions in on-line job scheduling in Grids caused by the software vulnerabilities were further analyzed in [7, 9, 10]. Their results were extended in [12] by considering the heterogeneity of the fault-tolerance in a security-assured job scheduling.

In [2, 8] authors applied *Genetic Algorithms (GA)* for solving job scheduling problem in Grid environments, optimizing both the makespan and total flowtime of proposed solutions. In [6] four genetic-based hybrid meta-heuristics have been proposed and evaluated as a non-cooperative non-zero sum game of the Grid users in order to address the security requirements. These works proved the GAs can be useful in the design of effective schedulers mapping a large number of jobs to the available resources. Similarly, in [14] two implementations of cellular *Memetic Algorithms (MA)* were proposed to solve the job scheduling problem. MA is a relatively new class of population-based heuristic methods in which the concepts of genetic algorithm (evolutionary search) and local search are combined [13].

Our approach provides the solution for parallel job scheduling problem in distributed CC environment, while taking into account the security constraints of both users and the system. We define our solution as a Pareto-based evaluation instead of a more common practice of converting the multi-objective problem into a single-objective by combining the various criteria into a single scalar value or alternating them in order to optimize one criterion at a time while imposing constraints on the others. In our approach a vector containing all the objective values representing the solution fitness and the concept of dominance is used to establish preference between multiple solutions.

3   System Model

In this section we formally define basic elements of the model and provide corresponding notation, characteristics of the model and the type of jobs to be scheduled. The system model is an extension of the work introduced in [11]. A system consists of a set of m parallel machines $M_1, M_2, ..., M_m$. Each machine M_i is described by a parameter m_i, which denotes the number of identical processors P_i, called also the size of machine M_i. Figure 1(a) shows a set of parallel machines in the CC system.

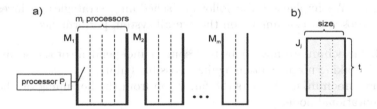

Fig. 1. Example of the Cloud Computing system. A set of parallel machines (a) and the multi-threaded job model (b).

Users $(U_1, U_2, ..., U_n)$ submit jobs to the system, expecting their completion before required deadline. Thus, in the system there is a set of n jobs $J_1, J_2, ..., J_n$. A job J_j is described by a tuple $(r_j, size_j, t_j, d_j)$. The release time r_j can be defined as the earliest time when the job can be processed. A $size_j$ is referred to as the processor requirements. It specifies a number of processors required to run the job J_j within assigned machine. We assume that job J_j can only run on machine M_i if $size_j \leq m_i$ holds, that is, we do not allow multi-site execution and co-allocation of processors from different machines. Finally, t_j, defines required number of instructions of job J_j and d_j is the required deadline of the job. Figure 1(b) shows an example of the multi-threaded job model.

3.1 Security Model

We consider a security-driven scheduling scheme, to address the reliability issues in a computational Cloud environment. We apply the approach presented in [10] to match job's security requirements submitted by the user with security index defined for each Cloud site. While a job is submitted, users define a *Security Demand* (SD) dependent on the job sensitivity and access control. On the other hand, the defense capability of a resource can be attributed to intrusion detection mechanisms and its attack response capacity. This capability is modeled by a *Security Level* (SL) factor.

Both are real fractions in the range [0,1] with 0 representing the lowest and 1 the highest security requirement/capability. A *Job Failure Model* is defined as a function of the difference between the job's demand and machine's security. The Formula (1) presented below expresses the failure probability regarding a scheduling of a job J_j with a specific SD_j value, to the machine M_i with Security Level value SL_i:

$$
P_{Failure} = \begin{cases} 0, & if\, SD_j \leq SL_i, \\ 1 - exp^{-(SD_j - SL_i)}, & if\, SD_j > SL_i. \end{cases} \tag{1}
$$

In a case of a typical scheduler, failed job would be aborted and returned to the queue for rescheduling. Such a failure may occur at any time during the job execution and scheduler does not have any *a priori* knowledge about the exact moment of failure. Thus, scheduler needs to react pro-actively to any failure occurrences. We implement the following scheduling strategies to investigate such scenarios and their impact on the overall system performance:

- **Risky mechanism** maps jobs to resources independent of the security demands, taking no precaution against possible failures;
- **Retry mechanism** restarts the failed job from the beginning on the same computational node;
- **Migration mechanism** reschedules the failed job on another computational node defined as its backup site;
- **Replication mechanism** allocates the job to be executed at multiple sites simultaneously. Replicas will stop execution once one of them is successfully completed;
- **Checkpoint mechanism** records the state of the job periodically at runtime. If the job fails, it is moved to another node and resumed from the last saved state.

4   GA-Based Multi Objective Scheduling Framework

We propose to apply a Multi Objective Genetic Algorithm (MOGA) to solve the studied problem. GA is a meta-heuristic search technique that allows large solution space to be heuristically searched, by applying evolutionary techniques from nature. It maintains a population of possible solutions to a problem, encoded as chromosomes based on a particular representation scheme. In this study we use the structure presented in Figure 2, where each gene is a pair of values (J_n, M_m), indicating that job J_n is assigned to machine M_m. The execution order of jobs allocated to the same machine is given by the positions of the corresponding genes in the chromosome on *First-Come-First-Serve* basis.

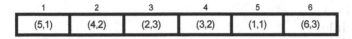

1	2	3	4	5	6
(5,1)	(4,2)	(2,3)	(3,2)	(1,1)	(6,3)

Fig. 2. Chromosome encoding schema. Upper numbers define allocation sequence. A job is first scheduled to the site identified by the leftmost (J_n, M_m) pair.

Each solution is associated with a fitness value, which measures the quality of a particular chromosome. Typical way of assessing system's performance is measuring the completion time of submitted jobs. Let us denote S as a schedule. The completion time of jobs on machine M_i in the schedule S_i is denoted by $C_i(S_i)$. Three different objectives are considered in this work:

- The minimization of the **Maximum Completion Time**, defined as $C_{max} = max_i\{C_i(S_i)\}$, which means the expected duration of all the processes;
- The minimization of the **Mean Failure Probability**, $\overline{P_{Failure}}$, defined as a mean failure probability of each allocation;
- The minimization of the **Total Tardiness**, ΣT_J, where T_j is the tardiness of job j, defined as $T_j = max(0, C_j - d_j)$.

Thus, the problem can be formulated as $Minimize\ (C_{max}, \overline{P_{Failure}}, \Sigma T_J)$. To solve it, we apply the second version of a Non-dominated Sorting Genetic Algorithm (NSGA-II) [3]. The overall structure of the NSGA-II is presented in Algorithm 1. An initial population P_0 is first randomly generated. In each generation t, the following processes are executed. The population of children Q_t (all the offspring chromosomes) is created with the operations of evaluation, selection, crossover and mutation. After that, all the individuals from P_t and Q_t are ranked in different fronts. The non-dominated front of Level 1 is constituted and includes all the non dominated solutions. In order to find the solutions in the next front, the solutions of previous fronts are discarded. This process is repeated until all the solutions are ranked and assigned to several fronts. Then, the best solutions (in the best front and with the best value of the crowding distance) are chosen for the new population P_{t+1}. This process is repeated until the stopping criterion is satisfied.

Algorithm 1. NSGA-II Algorithm

  Initialize Population P_0 of size N;
  Evaluate Objective Values;
  Assign Rank Based on Pareto dominance;
  while *stopping criterion is not satisfied* **do**
    Generate the Offspring Population Q_t of size N;
    Compose the populations of Parents and the Offspring in $R_t = P_t \cup Q_t$;
    Assign Rank Based on Pareto dominance in the combined population R_t;
    $P_{t+1} = 0$;
    $i = 1$;
    while $|P_{t+1}| + |F_i| < N$ **do**
      $P_{t+1} \leftarrow P_{t+1} \cup F_i$;
      $i = i + 1$;
    end while
    Rank the solutions of F_i by the crowding distance and add $N - |P_{t+1}|$
    solutions in P_{t+1} by descending order of the crowding distance.
  end while

4.1 Selection of the Pareto-efficient Strategy

We wish to further restrict the search space to Pareto-efficient strategies, from among which the user can then make an educated choice and select whatever solutions are best suited to the one's preferences [1]. However, the user does not know the failure probability-completion time trade-off, or if the selection of a strategy will accomplish execution of all submitted jobs in a required time. With that end in mind, we propose four simple scheduling policies defining basic goals and requirements. We depict in Figure 3 an exemplary Pareto frontier with highlighted strategies corresponding to those scheduling polices:

- **Maximum speed policy** selects a strategy from Pareto frontier yielding the shortest possible completion time;
- **Maximum reliability policy** selects a strategy from Pareto frontier yielding the minimal mean probability of execution failure;
- **Maximum reliability with deadline policy** selects a strategy from Pareto frontier yielding the minimal mean probability of execution failure while meeting the deadline required by the user;
- **Optimum policy** selects a strategy from Pareto frontier minimizing the weighted average of three objectives, that is $Min(0.33*C_{max}+0.33*\overline{P_{Failure}}+0.33*\Sigma T_J)$.

5 Performance Evaluation

In this section we analyze the performance of the NSGA-II based scheduling algorithms for the problem defined in this paper. We studied and compared the performance of previously described fault-tolerant scheduling mechanisms

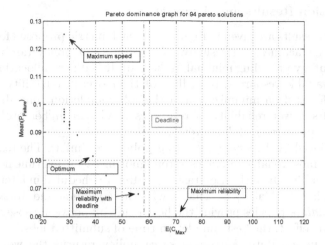

Fig. 3. Pareto Frontier and examples of strategies selected by four scheduling polices: Maximum speed, Maximum reliability, Maximum reliability with deadline and Optimum policy

and Pareto-efficient strategy selection policies. An open queuing network model is considered in this work. Arriving jobs are stored in a queue and they are dispatched to nodes at the end of predefined allocation intervals. We used in our experiments a set of randomly generated job instances with $n = 100$, 150 and 200 jobs and $m = 4$, 8 and 16 machines. The set was generated with the following parameters: the average execution time of a job $\overline{t_J}$ was set to 5, the average number of threads $\overline{size_J}$ was set to 4 and the average number of cores $\overline{m_i}$ was set to 6. 100 independent runs per configuration have been carried out to guarantee statistical significance and construct an approximate Pareto frontier by gathering non-dominated solutions in all executions.

5.1   Performance Metrics

To comprehensively evaluate the scheduling performance, we have used the following metrics:

- **Makespan:** the total running time of all jobs, defined as $max\{C_i, i = 1, 2, ..., N\}$;
- **Scheduling success rate:** the percentage of jobs successfully completed in the system;
- **System utilization:** the percentage of processing power allocated to successfully executed jobs;
- **Average response time:** let us denote the completion time for a job J_i as C_i, the arrival time as r_i, and the average response time is defined as $\frac{\sum_{i=1}^{N}(c_i - r_i)}{N}$.

5.2   Simulation Results and Analysis

The simulation results are given in Figure 4 for each metric proposed for 200 jobs scheduled on 4 machines. Surprisingly, *Maximum speed* policy rarely selects a scheduling strategy providing minimal Makespan. It is due to allocation of tasks to the first available resources, regardless of their overall reliability. Although optimization focused on minimization of the job completion time should yield the best results, lower reliability of resources results in higher probability of failures and frequent rescheduling events.

Results achieved by *Maximum reliability* policy are similar. The reason is the selection of the most reliable resources, often ignoring execution time not meeting the required deadline. In such cases, tasks are often rescheduled in later intervals, further increasing the Makespan. That is why the *Optimum* and *Maximum reliability with deadline* policies provide the best trade-off between those two objectives, and in the effect, the best completion time of submitted jobs.

As to the Success Rate, *Maximum speed* policy returns the worst results. Once again, selection of resources with lower reliability results in higher probability of failures and rescheduling events, thus leading to a worse performance.

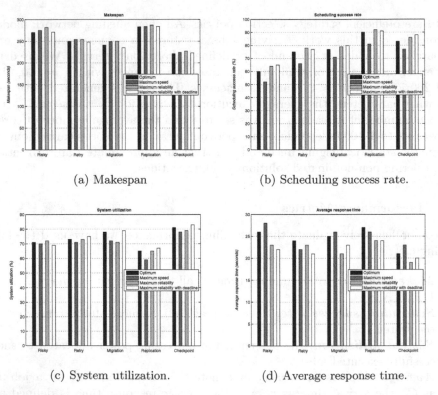

(a) Makespan

(b) Scheduling success rate.

(c) System utilization.

(d) Average response time.

Fig. 4. Performance results of using fault-tolerant scheduling strategies with various selection policies for 200 jobs scheduled on 4 machines. (a) Makespan. (b) Scheduling success rate. (c) System utilization. (d) Average response time.

Results yielded by other polices are comparable. Similar results can be observed for the System Utilization, with slightly lower utilization achieved by *Maximum speed* policy. Polices trying to achieve compromise between both optimization objectives yield better results than those focusing on a single objective. The Average Response Time results are highly correlated with the Makespan results, however the overall trend is more difficult to describe. In most cases, best results are returned by polices favoring reliability.

The scheduling strategies employing the fault-tolerant mechanisms clearly outperform the classic *Risky* scheduler except for the *Replication* mechanism, which has longer Makespan due to reservation of multiple machines no matter if a job fails or not. The Average Response Time results are usually shorter than the *Risky* mechanism. Utilization rates of the fault-tolerant mechanisms are fairly comparable, which suggest that they cannot necessarily save computational resources.

The *Checkpoint* mechanism achieved high performance for almost all metrics. The Utilization Rate can be kept at an acceptable level, while enhancing the overall performance. As to the *Success Rate*, a *Replication* scheduling approach may expect a higher success rate due to redundancy applied. However, the *Checkpoint* mechanism exhibits resilient behaviors with a moderate level of failures, which does not necessarily lead to a worse performance.

6   Conclusions and Future Work

Security-driven job scheduling is crucial to achieving high performance in a Cloud computing environment. However, existing scheduling algorithms largely ignore the security induced risks involved in dispatching jobs to untrustworthy resources. The paper proposes a paradigm of MOGA-based scheduling taking into account the security constraints of the system. Thus, the proposed solution makes efforts to incorporate security into job scheduling and aims to minimize both job completion time and possible security risks. Due to its very nature, it is capable of exploiting and exploring in the whole range of solution search space globally and picking near optimal scheduling solution.

Our future research will be oriented on enhancing the decision-making mechanisms to select the best Pareto-efficient strategy without further input from the end user. Additionally, we wish to define this issue as a game theoretical resource allocation mechanisms such as 1) the non-cooperative bid method where tasks are auctioned off to the highest bidder, 2) the semi-cooperative bid method in which each site delegate its work to others if it cannot execute it itself, and finally 3) the cooperative method in which all of the sites deliberate with one another to execute all the tasks as efficiently as possible.

Acknowledgment. This contribution is supported by the Foundation for Polish Science under International PhD Projects in Intelligent Computing. Project financed from The European Union within the Innovative Economy Operational Programme 2007-2013 and European Regional Development Fund (ERDF).

References

[1] Ben-Yehuda, O.A., Schuster, A., Sharov, A., Silberstein, M., Iosup, A.: Expert: Pareto-efficient task replication on grids and a cloud. In: IPDPS, pp. 167–178. IEEE Computer Society (2012)

[2] Carretero, J., Xhafa, F.: Using genetic algorithms for scheduling jobs in large scale grid applications. Journal of Technological and Economic Development 12, 11–17 (2006)

[3] Deb, K., Agrawal, S., Pratap, A., Meyarivan, T.: A fast elitist non-dominated sorting genetic algorithm for multi-objective optimisation: Nsga-ii. In: Deb, K., Rudolph, G., Lutton, E., Merelo, J.J., Schoenauer, M., Schwefel, H.-P., Yao, X. (eds.) PPSN 2000. LNCS, vol. 1917, pp. 849–858. Springer, Heidelberg (2000)

[4] Dogan, A., Özgüner, F.: On qos-based scheduling of a meta-task with multiple qos demands in heterogeneous computing. In: Proceedings of the 16th International Parallel and Distributed Processing Symposium, IPDPS 2002, pp. 227–234. IEEE Computer Society Press, Washington, DC (2002)

[5] Hwang, S., Kesselman, C.: A flexible framework for fault tolerance in the grid. Journal of Grid Computing 1, 251–272 (2003)

[6] Kolodziej, J., Xhafa, F.: Meeting security and user behavior requirements in grid scheduling. Simulation Modelling Practice and Theory 19(1), 213–226 (2011)

[7] Kwok, Y.-K., Hwang, K., Song, S.: Selfish grids: Game-theoretic modeling and nas/psa benchmark evaluation. IEEE Trans. Parallel Distrib. Syst. 18(5), 621–636 (2007)

[8] Martino, V.D., Mililotti, M.: Sub optimal scheduling in a grid using genetic algorithms. Parallel Comput. 30(5-6), 553–565 (2004)

[9] Song, S., Hwang, K., Kwok, Y.-K.: Trusted grid computing with security binding and trust integration. J. Grid Comput., 53–73 (2005)

[10] Song, S., Hwang, K., Kwok, Y.-K.: Risk-resilient heuristics and genetic algorithms for security-assured grid job scheduling. IEEE Trans. Comput. 55(6), 703–719 (2006)

[11] Tchernykh, A., Ramírez, J.M., Avetisyan, A.I., Kuzjurin, N.N., Grushin, D., Zhuk, S.: Two level job-scheduling strategies for a computational grid. In: Wyrzykowski, R., Dongarra, J., Meyer, N., Waśniewski, J. (eds.) PPAM 2005. LNCS, vol. 3911, pp. 774–781. Springer, Heidelberg (2006)

[12] Wu, C.-C., Sun, R.-Y.: An integrated security-aware job scheduling strategy for large-scale computational grids. Future Gener. Comput. Syst. 26(2), 198–206 (2010)

[13] Xhafa, F., Abraham, A.: Computational models and heuristic methods for grid scheduling problems. Future Generation Computer Systems 26(4), 608–621 (2010)

[14] Xhafa, F., Alba, E., Dorronsoro, B., Duran, B.: Efficient batch job scheduling in grids using cellular memetic algorithms. Journal of Mathematical Modelling and Algorithms 7, 217–236 (2008)

Exploring Irregular Reduction Support
in Transactional Memory

Miguel A. Gonzalez-Mesa, Ricardo Quislant, Eladio Gutierrez, and Oscar Plata

Dept. Computer Architecture
University of Malaga, 29071 Malaga, Spain
magonzalez@ac.uma.es, {quislant,eladio,oplata}@uma.es

Abstract. Transactional memory (TM) has emerged as an alternative to the lock-based parallel programming model offering an effective and optimistic management of concurrency. Recently, TM is being experimented in the context of high performance computing. Many applications in that area spent a large amount of computing time in irregular reduction operations, so their efficient parallelization is of utmost importance. This paper explores how to address irregular reductions in the TM model, analyzing which support needs to be added to the TM system to deal with reductions as a special case of conflicting memory accesses.

1 Introduction

Driven by the rise of modern shared-memory multicore architectures, Transactional memory (TM) has emerged as an alternative to the traditional lock-based parallel model with the aim of allowing an effective and optimistic management of concurrency [8]. In the current landscape, this model is receiving support from manufacturers, as evidenced by the inclusion of some TM features at hardware level in recent architectures, such as Intel Haswell [10]. In addition to hardware-based TM implementations (HTM), TM can be found also implemented in software (STM) or even in hybrid approaches [12].

TM is based in the concept of transaction, a piece of code that is executed isolated and with atomicity, being a replacement of a critical section but without the disadvantage of forcing a mandatory serialization. TM systems execute transactions in parallel while tracking all memory accesses (read-set and write-set). If two concurrent transactions conflict (write/write, read/write the same shared memory location), one of them must abort: it restores its initial state and it retries its execution. When a transaction concludes its execution without conflicts, it commits, making definitive its changes in memory. It is said that version management is eager if changes are immediately translated into memory and an undo-log is used to restore the state of aborted transactions. By contrast, in a lazy version management, changes are stored in a write-buffer and not written in memory until commit takes place. As well, a transaction can abort just when the conflict is detected (eager conflict detection), or postpone the conflict checks until its end (lazy conflict detection).

J. Kołodziej et al. (Eds.): ICA3PP 2013, Part I, LNCS 8285, pp. 257–266, 2013.

Parallel programming based on the TM model is a relatively new concept in the context of high performance computing. Only recently some authors are experimenting with the model for parallelizing their own scientific applications (for instance, [2]). Many scientific and engineering applications contains (irregular) reduction operations in their core and, frequently, they are responsible of an important fraction of the overall computing time. Parallelizing effciently such operations is of paramount importance. This paper explores the use of transactions in the implementation of parallel irregular reductions. We analyze how specific support for reductions can be added to a TM system, basically by adapting the data versioning mechanism and the commit phase. With the proposed reduction-aware TM (R-TM) design all conflicts due to reductions are avoided, reducing drastically the abort rate. Besides, R-TM allows programmers to use a new design dimension, the size of the transaction, that permits a finer control over the tradeoff between the frequency of thread synchronization and the implicit memory privatization associated to the TM mechanism. R-TM has been implemented in a simplified scenario, and compared with a base TM system. Its evaluation has proved the benefits of the approach.

2   Motivation

A reduction statement is a pattern of the form $O = O \oplus \xi$, where $\oplus$ is a commutative and associative operator applied to the memory object O, and ξ is an expression computed using objects different from O. A reduction loop is a computational pattern that includes one or several reduction statements with the same or different memory objects but with the same operator for each object. In addition, no references to those memory objects can occur in other parts of the loop outside the reduction statements [11].

Reductions are found in the core of many scientific and engineering applications such as sparse matrix computations, finite element solvers and molecular dynamics, and they are frequently associated with irregular access patterns. Examples of reduction loops are shown in Fig. 1. A reduction operator $\oplus$ (+, ×, max, min ...) is applied to a scalar variable A or the elements of a reduction array A[]. In this last case, the irregular nature of the operation comes from the access through the indirection arrays, f1 ... fn, acting as subscripts of the reduction array, which, in turn, are subscripted by the loop index.

From the data dependence viewpoint, accesses to the reduction object could give rise to loop-carried dependencies. In general, these memory conflicts can not be detected until run–time as the references (indirections) to the memory object are not known before execution. Moreover, the loop may include other true cross-iteration dependencies apart from the reduction statements. Nevertheless, the situation is more optimistic when the only true dependencies are caused by the reduction statements. In such a case, the iterations of the loop can be arbitrarily reordered without altering the final result, as a consequence of the commutativity and associativity of the reduction operator. Hence the loop can be executed in parallel in spite of the reduction dependencies.

```
float A;
for (i=0; i<N; i++){
    Calculate ξ;
    A = A ⊕ ξ;
}
```

```
int f1[fDim], f2[fDim], ..., fn[fDim];
float A[ADim];
for (i=0; i<fDim; i++){
    Calculate ξ1, ξ2, ..., ξn;
    A[f1[i]] = A[f1[i]] ⊕ ξ1;
    A[f2[i]] = A[f2[i]] ⊕ ξ2;
    ...
    A[fn[i]] = A[fn[i]] ⊕ ξn;
}
```

(a) Single scalar reduction statement   (b) Multiple irregular reduction statements

Fig. 1. Examples of reduction loops

Table 1. Techniques for parallelizing reduction loops

	Mutual exclusion	Privatization of the reduction array	Partitioning of the reduction array
Implementations	Critical sections Fine grain locks Atomic operations	Pure privatization Array Expansion Selective privatization	LOCALWRITE (LW) SYNCHWRITE (SW)
Advantages	Low programming effort	Low programming effort High concurrency	Reference locatity exploitation Low memory requirements
Disadvantages	Potential serialization High synchronization cost No locality exploitation	High memory overhead No locality exploitation	Inspection phase required Computation replication (LW) Workload imbalance (SW)

Transactional memory can be useful to extract optimistic parallelism from loops in the above situations, as TM has native support for tracking all memory accesses and detecting memory conflicts in runtime. This support can help to determine when the reduction conditions are met. As a first step to achieve this goal, this paper deals with fully parallel irregular reduction loops, and study how to support efficiently the parallel execution of those loops using TM. That is, our main interest is to deal with the reduction statements with no interference of other kind of dependence sources.

3 Reduction Parallelization Techniques

Solutions to parallelize irregular reduction loops can be classified into three groups based on: mutual exclusion, privatization of the reduction array and partitioning of the reduction array (see Table 1).

The first group involves a low programming effort as the loop can be executed in parallel by just enclosing the accesses to the reduction array in a critical section, solving all possible dependencies. Drawbacks of these techniques are the degree of serialization and the cost of synchronization in typical multicore processors. The degree of serialization is basically determined by the number of conflicting iterations but also by the particular implementation. In this regard, a pure critical section can yield to a high degree of serialization, which can be improved by using fine-grain locks, although this would require a lock array with as many positions as the reduction array. Notwithstanding, the use of atomic operations can be a more efficient alternative when available in hardware, with no need of additional data structures.

The second group of solutions distributes the iteration space into threads, each of which performs its reductions over a local reduction space. A preamble is necessary in order to initialize the private reduction space to the identity (neutral) element of the reduction operator. Similarly, a final reduction phase must accumulate all private reduction values into the (global) reduction array. Two representative examples in this class are *Replicated Buffer* [6] and *Array Expansion* [3]. The main drawback of privatization-based techniques is the memory overhead because the reduction memory space is multiplied by the number of threads. As a consequence, optimizations aimed at reducing the memory overhead have been proposed, such as *Selective Privatization/Reduction Table* [14]. These techniques try to minimize memory overhead by replicating selectively only those elements of the reduction array that are written by several threads, but at the cost of complex implementations.

Techniques in the third group avoid the privatization by partitioning the reduction array. They need an inspection phase that is in charge of determining the computation assigned to each thread. In this group we find methods like LOCALWRITE [7] and SYNCHWRITE [5].

4   Supporting Irregular Reductions in TM

This paper is not focused on proposing TM as an alternative to parallelize irregular reduction loops because, in general, classic methods performs well enough. In contrast, this work explores which mechanisms must be added to a TM system to support efficiently the execution of reduction statements, by taking advantage of the commutative and associative properties of the reduction operator to relax the transactional conflict management. This study can be considered as a starting point to extract optimistic concurrency from those loops that cannot be recognized statically as reduction loops. This section considers the simplified scenario where all memory conflicts come only from reduction statements, in such a way that the loop iterations can be safely reordered.

Our proposal of the reduction-aware TM (R-TM) requires only light modifications in the data versioning mechanism and in the commit phase, that can be implemented in any base TM system. It should be considered as an optimized TM system designed to improve the performance of parallel reduction loops.

Hereinafter it is assumed a base TM system with lazy data versioning, that is, all writes inside a transaction are buffered in a private storage, making the updates to shared memory at commit time. Lazy versioning simplifies the additional mechanisms required for privatizing reduction operations. On the other hand, conflict detection can be eager or lazy. This fact is not critical because in the simplified scenario we are assuming, all conflicts coming from reduction statements will be ignored.

Considering such a base system, the modifications required by R-TM are described as follows:

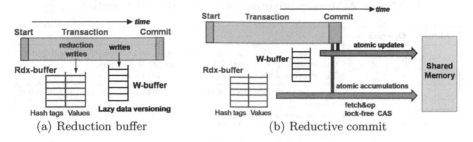

Fig. 2. Support for R-TM

- **Rdx-buffer:** A new private storage, the *reduction buffer* (*Rdx-buffer*) is added (see Fig. 2 (a)). This buffer stores all write operations on the reduction object made within a transaction. These writes are separated from the other transactional writes (that use the write buffer) because they are used during the commit phase to update correctly the reduction global data. The *Rdx-buffer* can be implemented as a table that stores all writes to reduction locations together with the corresponding memory addresses. For each write, the *Rdx-buffer* is searched for the memory address. If it is there, the corresponding stored valued is updated according to the reduction operator. Otherwise, a new entry is allocated in the buffer to insert the new pair (address, value).

  Note that it is required a specific reduction buffer for each considered reduction operator ($+$, $\times$, $max()$ ...), and that every new allocated entry on these buffers must be initialized to the identity element of the corresponding operator.

- **Reduction reads/writes:** All reads and writes of shared reduction data within a transaction must be instrumented in some way. Software TM (STM) systems or explicitly transactional hardware TM (HTM) systems [8] already provide special primitives/instructions to specify transactional memory operations. In implicitly transactional HTM systems, on the other hand, only the boundaries of the transactions are specified, and all memory accesses within these boundaries are considered transactional. In such systems, we may define special ISA instructions in order to distinguish between reduction reads/writes from the rest of transactional operations. A similar approach is followed in [13] for optional instructions useful for performance optimizations.

  Table 2 shows a description of the proposed reduction memory primitives. A reduction read (`tmrload`) does not read the global memory. Instead, it searches the *Rdx-buffer* for the memory address and takes the associated value if it is found. If the memory address is not located in the *Rdx-buffer*, a new entry, initialized to the identity element, is allocated in the buffer, and the reduction read returns that default value. This occurs only for the first read of a reduction address in the transaction. In addition, `tmrload` does not add the address to the current transaction read-set.

Table 2. Memory primitives needed for the R-TM system

Memory Operation	Description
Reduction read tmrload	Looks for memory address in the *Rdx-buffer* and returns the value if found. Otherwise a default value (identity element) is returned. The memory address is not added to the read set.
Reduction write tmrstore	Looks for memory address in the *Rdx-buffer* and accumulates the new value if found. The memory address is not added to the write set.

Table 3. Reduction-aware TM vs. OpenMP parallel reductions

	Reduction-aware TM		OMP Reduction		OMP Critical	OMP Atomic	
Reduc. Var. Type	Int	Float	Int	Float	Int/Float	Int	Float
Privatization	Yes		Yes		No	No	
Thread Synchronization	Atomic Op.	Lock Free	Lock / Atomic Op.	Lock / Lock Free	Lock	Atomic Op.	Lock Free
Privatization Overhead	$<\mathcal{O}(\#\text{Threads}\times\text{xactSize})$		$\mathcal{O}(\#\text{Threads}\times N)$		0	0	
Synchronization Overhead	$\mathcal{O}(\#\text{Transactions})$		$\mathcal{O}(\#\text{Threads})$		$\mathcal{O}(\#\text{Iterations})$	$\mathcal{O}(\#\text{Iterations})$	

A reduction write (`tmrstore`) works similarly to a transactional write but accumulating (according to the reduction operator) the new value in the *Rdx-buffer*, instead of simply storing the value in the write buffer. Besides, `tmrstore` does not add the address to the current transaction write-set.

- **Commit phase**: Not inserting the reduction addresses into the read and write sets allows to avoid conflicts when accessing such data within transactions. This behavior is valid in our simplified scenario because the reduction object can be privatized safely. Indeed, the use of the described *Rdx-buffer* is equivalent to a selective privatization of the reductive accesses inside the transaction. Consequently, when the transaction reaches the commit point, all these selectively privatized values must be properly accumulated into the reduction object in global memory. In order to accomplish this, the commit phase must include a process to atomically update shared memory with the contents of the *Rdx-buffer* (see Fig. 2 (b)).

The mutually exclusive access to shared reduction data can be assured by using locks. However, there are other options, like atomic operations, if they are supported in hardware by the processor architecture. These operations are usually implemented by locking the memory bus or the cache [9]. A third alternative is the use of lock-free algorithms, based on an atomic *compare-and-swap* (CAS) type operation. This last option is usual when reducing floating-point data, as atomic native hardware support is not common.

The execution model of R-TM results in a dynamic and selective privatization of the reduction object: The *Rdx-buffer* allocates a new entry only when required (due to reduction writes), and it releases the used space every time the transaction commits. The extra memory overhead due to the privatization is thus

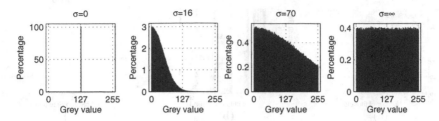

Fig. 3. Probability density for the tested images used in the histogram benchmark

limited by the transaction size. On the other hand, the accumulations in global memory carried out during commits are protected by locks or atomic operations, which introduce some synchronization overhead among threads. The number of thread synchronizations is the number of transaction commits. Observe that this corresponds to a intermediate situation between reduction parallelization using locks (or atomic operations) and full privatization. The tradeoff between privatization and synchronization overheads depends on the transaction size, a parameter that can be selected by the programmer/compiler. Table 3 summarizes the above discussion.

5   Experimental Evaluation

The proposed modifications introduced by R-TM were implemented in a light-weight software TM implementation, TinySTM [4], used as the base TM system. The experimental evaluation of this implementation was conducted on a server with quad Intel Xeon X7550 processors (32 cores in total) at 2GHz running Linux Kernel 2.6.32 (64-bits). The C-based benchmark code and the STM runtime were compiled with gcc v4.3.4. In all executions, only one thread was mapped to a core (hyperthreading was disabled). Experimental data correspond to the average of several dozens executions, in order to avoid random effects associated to transactional executions.

R-TM was evaluated using a synthetic benchmark code that computes the histogram of a grayscale image. The program (*Histogram*) comprises only one irregular reduction statement (accumulation in the histogram array of the number of pixels for each gray value) with no additional computational workload. We run experiments for four input images defined for testing different contention areas in the histogram array. The images were generated as a random set of 4M pixels within a range of 256 gray levels. Histogram contention areas were obtained by selecting different truncated Gaussian distributions of the gray values. Fig. 3 shows the probability density function for the tested images. All distributions were defined in the range [0,255] with the mean located in 0, except for the first image whose mean was located in 127. The images differ in the standard deviation (σ), ranging from 0 (uniform gray image, with maximum contention in one location of the histogram array) to infinite (uniform random image, with

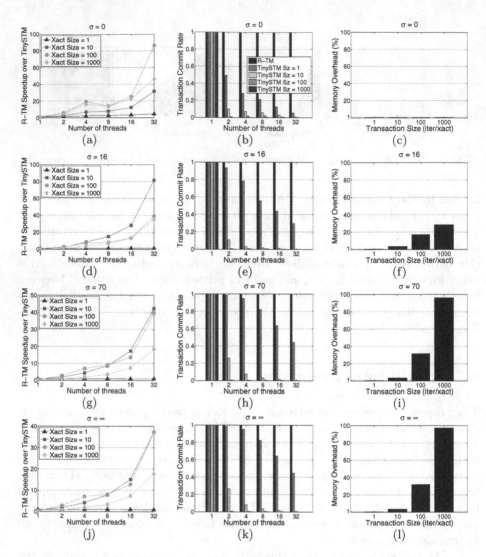

Fig. 4. Experimental results for the *Histogram* benchmark

no contention area). Two other standard deviation values were chosen, 16 and 70, that introduce narrow and wide contention areas, respectively.

Experimental results of R-TM for the *Histogram* benchmark are shown in Fig. 4, in terms of speedup with respect to the base TinySTM (without reduction support), *Transaction Commit Rate* (TCR) [1] and memory overhead involved by the *Rdx-buffer* during the execution of transactions. TCR is a suitable metric for the exploited concurrency and it measures the percentage of committed transactions in relation to the number of all launched transactions. Regarding the memory overhead, the percentage with respect to full privatization of the reduction array has been considered.

The speedup of R-TM with respect to the base TinySTM version (Fig. 4(a,d,g,j), for different input matrices) is particularly interesting. The high values for the relative speedup are basically caused by the large disparities exhibited in the abort rates. While R-TM exhibits a null abort rate (as all conflicts are originated in the reduction statement, so they are ignored), TinySTM experiments a high abort rate, that increases with the number of threads. In fact, in the highest-contention case ($\sigma = 0$), R-TM is almost 90 times faster than TinySTM for 32 threads and transactions of 100 (reduction) loop iterations. This relative speedup decreases when σ increases, as the contention area in the histogram array widens. As a result, the abort rate for TinySTM is lower (conflict pattern is spread across transactions) and the commit overhead for R-TM is higher (more values in the *Rdx-buffer* to merge with those in shared memory). Note that, in general, R-TM performs best for transaction sizes between 10 and 100 reduction loop iterations.

TCR measurements for *Histogram* is shown in Fig. 4(b,e,h,k) for different input matrices. As R-TM is carrying out an implicit selective privatization, in practice, this eliminates all aborts due to conflicts on the reduction array. This fact does not happen in the base TM system, resulting in an important loss of concurrency. In addition, the exploited concurrency for TinySTM decreases with the size of the transaction, as a large transaction aborts several times until succeeds to commit. Observe that the base system does not have good scalability, neither with the number of threads nor with the transaction size. While for 32 threads, TCR drops down 35% in average, a transaction size of 10 iterations makes the concurrency fall down about 70% in average because both parameters increase the number of data conflicts.

Finally, Fig. 4(c,f,i,l) shows the memory space (per thread) required for the *Rdx-buffer* for different input matrices. 100% memory overhead represents that of full privatization. As expected, the worst situation occurs for large transactions. In this benchmark, the memory overhead for the largest tested transaction (1000 loop iterations) is basically equivalent to the full privatization method. However, for smaller transactions, R-TM allows saving a great amount of memory space as the *Rdx-buffer* grows up dynamically acting as an effective selective privatization. In the case of transaction sizes with the best relative speedup (between 10 and 100 iterations), the memory overhead due to *Rdx-buffer* is between 5% and 35% of the full privatization case.

6   Conclusions

This work has explored how a specific support for irregular reductions can be added to a TM system. Such a reduction-aware TM (R-TM) approach can be regarded as a tradeoff between memory privatization overhead and thread synchronization effort. With this purpose the reduction accesses are handled in a special way, eluding all these conflicts, and introducing a specific write buffer (reduction buffer) to achieve a dynamic and selective privatization. Although the approach can be generalized, the study has been simplified by considering the case where all dependencies come from the reduction objects. The discussed

R-TM approach has been implemented on top of a lightweight STM, tinySTM, although it could be translated into other existing TM systems. The evaluation of the proposed solution has shown a high concurrency exploitation, compared to the base TM system, and a low extra memory overhead, compared to the full-privatization solution. Additionally, on being integrated into the transactional mechanism, no extra effort is required from the programmer, while it also provides control over the tradeoff between privatization and synchronization.

References

1. Ansari, M., Kotselidis, C., Jarvis, K., Luján, M., Kirkham, C., Watson, I.: Advanced concurrency control for transactional memory using transaction commit rate. In: Luque, E., Margalef, T., Benítez, D. (eds.) Euro-Par 2008. LNCS, vol. 5168, pp. 719–728. Springer, Heidelberg (2008)
2. Bihari, B.L.: Transactional memory for unstructured mesh simulations. J. Scientific Computing 54(2-3), 311–332 (2013)
3. Feautrier, P.: Array expansion. In: 2nd Int'l Conf. on Supercomputing (ICS 1988), pp. 429–441 (1988)
4. Felber, P., Fetzer, C., Marlier, P., Riegel, T.: Time-based software transactional memory. IEEE Trans. on Parallel and Distributed Systems 21(12), 1793–1807 (2010)
5. Gutiérrez, E., Plata, O., Zapata, E.: A compiler method for the parallel execution of irregular reductions in scalable shared memory multiprocessors. In: 14th Int. Conf. on Supercomputing (ICS 2000), pp. 78–87 (2000)
6. Hall, M., Anderson, J., Amarasinghe, S., Murphy, B., Liao, S., Bu, E.: Maximizing multiprocessor performance with the suif compiler. IEEE Computer 29(12), 84–89 (1996)
7. Han, H., Tseng, C.: Exploiting locality for irregular scientific codes. IEEE Trans. on Parallel and Distributed Systems 17(7), 606–618 (2006)
8. Harris, T., Larus, J.R., Rajwar, R.: Transactional Memory, 2nd edn. Morgan & Claypool Publishers, USA (2010)
9. Intel: Intel 64 and IA-32 Architectures Software Developer's Manual – Volume 3: System Programming Guide. Intel Corporation, Santa Clara, CA, USA (2013)
10. Jain, T., Agrawal, T.: The Haswell microarchitecture – 4th generation processor. International Journal of Computer Science and Information Technologies 4(3), 477–480 (2013)
11. Johnson, N.P., Kim, H., Prabhu, P., Zaks, A., August, D.I.: Speculative separation for privatization and reductions. In: 33rd ACM SIGPLAN Conf. on Programming Language Design and Implementation (PLDI 2012), pp. 359–370 (2012)
12. Larus, J., Kozyrakis, C.: Transactional memory. Communications of the ACM 51(7), 80–88 (2008)
13. McDonald, A., Chung, J., Carlstrom, B.D., Minh, C.C., Chafi, H., Kozyrakis, C., Olukotun, K.: Architectural semantics for practical transactional memory. In: 33rd Int'l. Symp. on Computer Architecture (ISCA 2006), pp. 53–65 (2006)
14. Yu, H., Rauchwerger, L.: An adaptive algorithm selection framework for reduction parallelization. IEEE Trans. on Parallel and Distributed Systems 17(10), 1084–1096 (2006)

Coordinate Task and Memory Management
for Improving Power Efficiency

Gangyong Jia[1,2], Xi Li[2], Jian Wan[1], Chao Wang[2], Dong Dai[3], and Congfeng Jiang[1]

[1] School of Computer Science, Hangzhou Dianzi University
Hangzhou, 310018, China
[2] School of Computer Science, University of Science and Technology of China
Hefei, 230027, China
[3] School of Computer Science, Texas Tech University
Lubbock TX 79409, USA
ganyong@mail.ustc.edu.cn

Abstract. As multicore systems are requiring increasing main memory bandwidth and capacity, the processor is no longer the unique dominating energy consumption component, in contrast, main memory is responsible for a large and increasing fraction of the energy consumed by systems. Therefore, improving power efficiency of processor and memory has received a lot of attention. However, most existing solutions concentrate on processor or memory separately and cannot combine well to simultaneously improve both. This paper presents a solution to improve both processor and memory power efficiency simultaneously through coordinating task and memory management (CTMM). The main idea is to adopt the concept of group which contains thread group and memory rank group. According group management, simultaneously scale CPU frequency and control memory power mode to reduce both CPU and memory power. Experimental results demonstrate our CTMM is more power efficient than some state-of-the-art solutions both in CPU and memory while improving system performance.

1 Introduction

Reducing power consumption has become a critical design issue not just for battery-operated mobile devices but also for high end systems due to the reliability issue and cooling/packaging cost. Historically, within the system, the processor has dominated energy consumption. However, as processors have become more energy-efficient and more effective at managing their own power consumption, their contribution has been decreasing. In contrast, main memory energy consumption has been growing [1, 2], as multi-core systems are requiring increasing main memory bandwidth and capacity [3, 4]. Today, main memory accounts for roughly 40% of system energy [5], which is comparable to or slightly higher than processor energy [13, 14]. So, to achieve an energy-efficiency design, all system components, especially processors and memory [2, 6], need to be considered simultaneously [1].

And simply supporting separate processor and memory energy management techniques is insufficient, as independent control policies often conflict, leading to oscillations, unstable behavior, or sub-optimal power/performance trade-offs. To see an example of such behavior, consider a scenario in which a chip multiprocessor's cores are stalled

J. Kołodziej et al. (Eds.): ICA3PP 2013, Part I, LNCS 8285, pp. 267–278, 2013.
© Springer International Publishing Switzerland 2013

waiting for memory a significant fraction of the time. In this situation, the CPU power manager might predict that lowering voltage/frequency will improve energy efficiency while still keeping performance within a pre-selected performance degradation bound and effect the change. The lower core frequency would reduce traffic to the memory subsystem, which in turn could cause its (independent) power manager to lower the memory power mode. After this latter mode change, the performance of the server as a whole may dip below the CPU power manager's projections, potentially violating the target performance bound. So, at its next opportunity, the CPU manager might start increasing the core frequency [12], inducing a similar response from the memory subsystem manager. Such oscillations waste energy. These unintended behaviors suggest that it is essential to coordinate power-performance management techniques across system components to ensure that the system is balanced to yield maximal energy savings [7].

To accomplish this coordinated control, however, faces several major challenges. First, the components of CPU and memory are heterogeneous. Thus, we cannot simply adopt power control policy of one component to widespread the whole system. Second, workloads in different components in a system are usually synergetic. For example, processor frequency downscaling may decrease the number of memory requests so that the memory power consumption decreases accordingly. Therefore, the synergy among components should be carefully addressed. Third, the workloads of different components are unpredictable at design time and may vary significantly at runtime. As a result, power control algorithms cannot rely on static power models or open-loop estimations. They must be self-adaptive to workload variations for improved server performance.

To tackle these issues, in this paper, we propose the framework of coordinating task and memory management (CTMM) to improve system power efficiency in multi-core systems. CTMM combines page allocation, task scheduling, dynamic voltage and frequency scaling (DVFS) and dynamic power management (DPM) policies according to thread group. CTMM features a four-phase design. First, partition threads and DRAM memory into thread groups and memory rank group respectively according to threads' behavior and memory characteristic. Threads in the same group are sharing memory address space and having similar behavior. Second, allocate memory page for thread based on group to achieve memory of the same group threads is in the same memory rank group. Third, adjust scheduler to achieve group scheduling which threads in the same group are scheduled simultaneously. Finally, scale frequency of CPU and adjust the power mode of memory ranks according to running thread group to simultaneously improve CPU and memory power efficiency. As a result, our solution can improve system power efficiency while improving system performance.

Specifically, this paper makes the following major contributions:

1) Through coordinating task and memory management, improve both CPU and memory power efficiency;

2) Through combining page allocation with thread group scheduling, prolong memory idleness, which creates more idleness without excessively degrading performance;

3) According running thread group to manage both CPU frequency and memory rank power modes, reduce the both frequency of CPU and all rank power modes transition;

4) Based on sharing memory address space to partition threads, decrease switch overhead between two threads in the same group.

We compare the proposed CTMM with two power aware policies, DVFS-based policy and PPT [9] policy. The DVFS-based policy scales frequency of CPU according to thread behavior, and PPT policy periodically shutdown hardly request memory modules. The experimental results show that compared to the DVFS-based policy, CTMM reduces memory power consumption by 49.2% and delivers comparable CPU power; while PPT policy achieves 47.4% power reduction for memory at the cost of CPU power increasing 23.5%. So, our CMTT reduces 24.6% and 11.9% system power comparing DVFS-based policy and PPT policy respectively. From the performance, CMTT is better than both two policies.

2 Background and Related Work

2.1 DRAM System

We describe DRAM memory systems and OS memory management mechanism.

DRAM Organization: modern memory system is usually packaged as DIMMs, each of which usually contains 1 or 2 ranks and 8 banks. A memory system can contain multiple channels, and each channel is associated with 1 or 2 DIMMs. A rank is the smallest physical unit for power management. Banks can be accessed parallel, hence, memory requests to different banks can be served concurrently [8]. Figure 1 demonstrates one organization of a modern memory subsystem. Memory device can be in four states – *active standby, precharge standby, active power-down and precharge power-down* – listed in a decreasing order of power dissipation [9].

OS Memory Management: Nowadays, Linux kernel's memory management system uses a buddy system to manage physical memory pages. In the buddy system, the continuous 2^{order} pages (called a block) are organized in the free list with the corresponding order, which ranges from 0 to a specific upper limit. When a program accesses an unmapped virtual address, a page fault occurs and OS kernel takes over the following execution wherein the buddy system identifies the right order free list and allocates on block (2^{order} physical pages) for that program. Usually the first block of a free list is selected but the corresponding physical pages are undetermined [10].

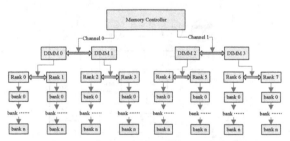

Fig. 1. Organization of a modern memory subsystem

3 CTMM Framework

The main idea of the proposed CTMM framework is to orchestrate page allocation, task scheduling, DVFS policy for CPU and DPM policy for memory to improve power efficiency. Figure 1 shows our memory configuration for a 2-channel memory system where each channel contains four ranks. In this paper, threads and ranks are partitioned into 4 groups, all kernel threads partitioned into one group, and all others partitioned into 3. Each group uses two ranks associated with two different channels. Threads of the same group are scheduled simultaneously. Threads in different groups are scheduled in round-robin fashion. Only two rank groups are active at each scheduling interval, one for kernel group and the other for running user group. The memory ranks of non-active groups could be turned into the low-power mode to save memory energy. In our CPU configuration, four frequencies can scale. So, each thread group is partitioned into 4 child-groups. Each child-group maintains the same CPU frequency. Threads of the same child-group are scheduled simultaneously. Threads in different groups are scheduled in round-robin fashion. Switch between different child-groups is the chance to scale CPU frequency, which simultaneously reduces CPU power and frequency scaling overhead.

Different DRAM organization affects the power and performance of the system. When the memory system is partitioned into more groups, ranks and channels allocated to each group are fewer; that means more memory ranks could be shut down to achieve more power savings, which in turn reduces available bandwidth. Also, the number of frequencies can be scaled affects the power and performance. The more numbers, the better performance and power efficiency, but more overhead.

Figure 2 demonstrates the description of four-phase power control framework:

In the first phase, all threads are partitioned into thread group according to their memory address space and load balance, and each thread group is partitioned into child-group according thread's behavior. Also, DRAM memory is partitioned into groups according to memory rank.

In the second phase, allocate memory according to thread group, threads in the same group are allocated memory in the same memory group. So memory of threads in the same thread group are aggregated into the same memory group.

In the third phase, based on partitioned thread group and child-group, modifying default scheduler to group scheduler.

In the final phase, based on DVFS and DPM to scale frequency for CPU and control power mode for memory according the running child-group/group to improve power efficiency.

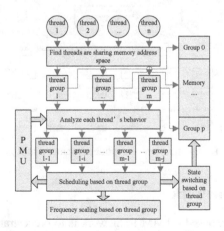

Fig. 2. The whole framework of our CTMM

3.1   Thread and Memory Rank Group Partition

Because of the 4 memory rank groups, we partition all threads into a two-layer group, first layer is a 4 thread groups based on sharing memory address space and load balance, second layer is each thread group partitioned into 4 child-groups based on thead behavior.

In the first layer, we find threads belonging to the same process are sharing memory address space and the CFS which is the default scheduler in current Linux operating system does not utilize this feature. We partition threads into the same thread group if they sharing memory address space. Specially, we partition all kernel threads into a unique group. And the two ranks allocating to kernel group is active all the time. Because only based on sharing memory address space partitioned groups are much more than 3, we partition them into 3 groups according load balance. So, all threads are partitioned into 4 groups, which one group contains all kernel threads, all non-kernel threads are divided into other 3 groups.

In the second layer, we analyze thread's behavior, in this paper we mainly take memory accessing into consideration when partition threads into different child-groups. We define the sensitive metric *Sen* to represent each thread's need of the CPU frequency.

$$Sen = \frac{I_{on}}{I} \tag{1}$$

I_{on} and I represents the on-chip instructions and total instructions respectively. And define three constant values C_1, C_2, C_3. All $0 \leq Sen \leq C_1$, $C_1 < Sen \leq C_2$, $C_2 < Sen \leq C_3$, and $C_3 < Sen \leq 1$ threads are partitioned into child-group 1, 2, 3 and 4 respectively.

3.2   Page Allocate

In Linux operating system, the default page allocation is using buddy algorithm, which allocates the first block of a free list to the request thread. So, a thread's occupying memory may cover all ranks of the memory. Buddy algorithm takes advantage of parallelism to improve performance. However, the necessary amount of banks one program requires is limited [15].

In contrast, our page allocation focuses specifically on maximizing energy efficiency. Considering the smallest power management unit rank, our algorithm allocates physical memory page to a thread based on belonging group, threads of the same group occupy the same rank group. So, a thread's pages aggregate in two ranks, spreading all banks of these two ranks, which improves power efficiency and prevents performance degradation simultaneously.

Figure 3 demonstrates our organization of physical memory page. The difference between ours with the default is our organization adds the rank information. Each rank group has free block lists, which likes whole memory partitioning into 4 in this paper. Every time requiring a free block, firstly determine the rank group, and then allocate corresponding free block.

3.3   Scheduling Based on Thread Group

After all threads are partitioned into two-layer groups, we rearrange these threads according two-layer groups, showing in figure 4. Threads in each child-group are organized into an *rb-tree* according each thread's *vruntime*, which is the same with the default Completely Fair Schedule (CFS) of Linux. 4 child-groups and 4 groups are also organized into an *rb-tree*, and their respective location is based on child-group/group *vruntime*. We define the child-group/group *vruntime* is the sum of all its threads' *vruntime*.

$$CG_{vruntime} = \sum_{i=1}^{m} vruntime_i \tag{2}$$

$$G_{vruntime} = \sum_{i=1}^{n} vruntime_i \tag{3}$$

$CG_{vruntime}$ and $G_{vruntime}$ represents the *vruntime* of child-group and group respectively. *vruntime$_i$* represents the *vruntime* of thread *i*. Our rearrangement forms a three-level *rb-tree*.

After getting each child-group and group's *vruntime*, group is becoming the unit of getting CPU time in our scheduling. When a group running more time than obtained, switch to the next group. Also, child-groups obtain CPU time within a group according child-group's *vruntime*. And threads obtain CPU time within a child-group according thread's *vruntime*. Therefore, our CTMM forms a three-level scheduler. The first level is group schedule, which is the smallest unit seen in the operating system. The second level is child-group schedule within group, which uses CFS policy among child-group. And the third level is thread schedule within child-group, which also uses CFS policy.

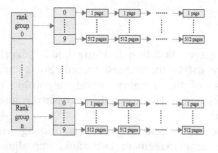

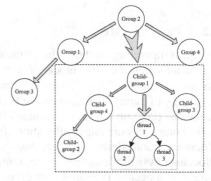

Fig. 3. Our organization of physical memory page

Fig. 4. Arrange all threads according two-layer groups

3.4 CPU Frequency Scale and Memory Mode Control Policies

CPU frequency scale and Memory mode control in the CTMM framework are archieved through child-group and group swtiching respectively.

Matching to the periodically scheduling threads in different child-groups, CPU frequency also periodically up and down. Because it takes several microseconds to scale up and down, which consumes power and time, therefore, in order to maximize energy efficiency, it must prevents scaling frequently. So, the question remains to be answered is how long the child-group switch interval should be. As we know, the shortest scheduling period (*sum_runtime*) is 20ms in Linux, and so the shortest switch interval is 20/12 ms (because we only partition 3 non-kernel groups and each has 4 child-groups). Even 20/12 ms is much longer than microseconds, so the cost of frequency scaling is negligible. Therefore, scaling CPU frequency according to child-group switch could achieve power savings while preventing high overhead from frequently switch. The more threads in the system, the more CPU frequency can keep.

Similarly, matching to the periodically scheduling threads in different groups, memory rank groups also periodically active and power down. And the shortest group switch interval is 20/3 ms (because we only partition 3 non-kernel groups). So the cost of rank mode switching is negligible. Therefore, setting rank mode switch according to thread group switch also could achieve power savings while better preventing high overhead from frequently switch. Also, the more threads in the system, the more memory rank idleness can prolong.

4   Experimental Setup

We use MARSSX86 [16] as the base full-system architectural simulator to run Linux 2.6.31 and extend its memory part with DRAMSim simulator to simulate DDRx DRAM systems in the details. Table 1 shows the major simulation parameters. To estimate the power consumption of CPU, each core has 4 DVFS levels normalized to the maximum frequency (i.e. 1, 0.85, 0.7, 0.55). The power of the core reported by Wattch [17]. And to estimate the power consumption of DRAM devices, the DRAMSim simulator keeps tracking the states of each memory channel, rank and bank. It follows the Micron power calculation methodology by default [18]. The parameters used to calculate the DRAM power and energy are the same with [3].

Table 1. Processor and memory configurations

Feature	value
CPU cores	Quad core
L1 I/D cache (per core)	16KB, 2-way
L2 cache (shared)	64KB
Cache block size	64bytes
Memory configuration	2 GB, 2 channels, 8 ranks, 8banks per rank

In order to evaluate our CTMM, we simultaneously run different combinations of selected from sysbench [19], SPEC2000 and SPEC2006. In table 2, the *number-appname* notation is the number of threads of the application with the name of *appname* for sysbench; for SPEC2000 and SPEC2006 workload, it is the number of copies of the application with the name of *appname*.

However, to analyze the effect of thread number, we classify the workloads into three categories: mix1, 2, 3 are 24 threads; mix4, 5, 6 are 48 threads, and mix7, 8, 9 are 96 threads. Similarly, we classify the workloads into three categories for analyzing the effect of thread's behavior: computation-intensive workloads (mix1, 4, 7), memory-intensive workloads (mix3, 6, 9) and balanced workloads (mix2, 5, 8).

Table 2. Workload description

mix	Sysbench, SPEC2000 and SPEC2006
mix1	12-sysbench cpu, 3-vortex, 3-gcc, 3-sixtrack, 3-mesa
mix2	6-sysbench cpu, 6-sysbench memory, 3-ammp, 3-gap, 3-wupwise, 3-vpr
mix3	12-sysbench memory, 3-swim, 3-applu, 3-art, 3-lucas
mix4	24-sysbench cpu, 6-vortex, 6-gcc, 6-sixtrack, 6-mesa
mix5	12-sysbench cpu, 12-sysbench memory, 6-ammp, 6-gap, 6-wupwise, 6-vpr
mix6	24-sysbench memory, 6-swim, 6-applu, 6-art, 6-lucas
mix7	48-sysbench cpu, 12-vortex, 12-gcc, 12-sixtrack, 12-mesa
mix8	24-sysbench cpu, 24-sysbench memory, 12-ammp, 12-gap,12- wupwise, 12-vpr
mix9	48-sysbench memory, 12-swim, 12-applu, 12-art, 12-lucas

5   Experimental Results

5.1   Memory Idleness Evaluation of CTMM

One of the most important thing to reduce memory power consumption is to create enough memory idleness. But they are difficult because of either causing excessively overhead or degrading performance for recent works. In order to evaluate our CTMM in prolonging how much idleness, we propose a metric *ior* (idleness time of each rank), which represents the average idle time of each rank after entering into low power mode.

$$ior = \frac{\sum_{i=1}^{n} ior_i}{n} \qquad (4)$$

ior_i represents the average idle time of rank i after entering into low power mode.

$$ior_i = \frac{\sum_{i=1}^{m} Ti_k}{m} \qquad (5)$$

Ti_k represents each idleness time of rank i. The bigger of the *ior* metric, the more idleness are created.

Figure 5 demonstates the normalized ior value to non-optimization. In this figure, *CFS, DVFS-based, PPT* [10] and *CPM* [20] represents the Linux default policy which non-optimization both in CPU and memory power efficiency, non-optimization policy in memory power efficiency but CPU, state of art policy in reducing memory power through scheduling, and one policy reducing both CPU and memory power simultaneously respectively. From this figure, we can find PPT and CPM are creating more idleness than CFS, and our CTMM is better than them. Also, along with the more threads (mix1, 2, 3 are 24 threads, mix4, 5, 6 are 48, and mix7, 8, 9 are 96), the *ior* value are bigger, and means the more idleness are created. More threads in the system means each group has more threads, which also means each group has more time in each period. Therefore, less switching will happen.

DVFS-based policy do nothing better in creating idleness than CFS, so they are the same in the *ior* value. Both PPT and CPM try to aggregate the memory access into the active ranks for a period time, so the *ior* value is better than CFS, but some times the memory access exceeds the active ranks, activating the low power ranks. But our CTMM hardly exceeds, so CTMM is better both PPT and CPM in creating memory idleness.

Both PPT and CPM are worse of the *ior* value as the workloads are more memory-intensive, mix3 is more memory-intensive, but worse in *ior* value than mix2 and mix1, the same circumstances are among mix4, 5, 6 and mix7, 8, 9. This is mainly from the reason of the more memory access the more possiblily exceeding the active ranks. But our CTMM is insensitive to the behavior, but to the thread number. Allocating the pages to thread according group and coordinating the group scheduling, CTMM prevents the exceeding circumstance.

5.2   Power Efficiency Improvement of the CTMM

Memory Power Efficiency Improvement. Through prolonging more idleness time, figure 6 demonstrates our CTMM reduces more memory power under using our group based mode control policy. Similarly, along with the more threads, more power is reduced for more idleness time prolonged. In 24 threads circumstances, our CTMM saves more 4% power than PPT and 9% than CPM on average; in 48 threads circumstances, more 10% than PPT and 16% than CPM; in 96 threads circumstances, more 14% than PPT and 19% than CPM.

From the figure, we can find the more computation-intensive the better in reducing memory power among the same number threads for both PPT and CPM. The reason is also the more memory access the more possiblily exceeding the active ranks to frequently activate the low power ranks. CTMM not only prevents disturbing low power ranks but also reducing power in more threads for creating more idleness.

CPU Power Efficiency Improvement. Figure 7 demonstrates different policies improve CPU power efficiency normalized to CFS. All DVFS-based, CPM and CTMM allocate CPU frequency according thread's behavior, so they almost improve the same power. But our CTMM is better although weakly. And the better is moslty from our CTMM scales frequency based on child-group which reduces the scaling times. Our results show the scaling times of our CTMM is almost 45% of DVFS-based, and the more threads the smaller precent is. Figure 8 explains the processor's frequency scaling in real time using DVFS-based and CTMM in 48 threads circumstance. The horizontal axis is the execution time slot, while the vertical index refers to the frequency. So, CTMM reduces more scaling times than DVFS-based.

System Power Efficiency Improvement. Figure 9 demonstrates different polices improve system power efficiency normalized to CFS. Obviously, CTMM is better than all other policies. CPM is better than both DVFS-based and PPT for they only improving one component. And CTMM saves more 3% system power than CPM on average in 24 threads circumstance, 6.6% in 48 threads, and 8.3% in 96 threads.

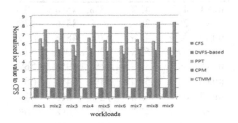

Fig. 5. Normalized ior value to CFS

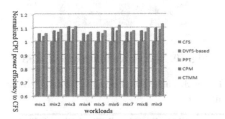

Fig. 7. CPU power efficiency

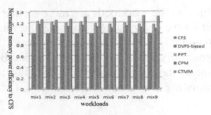

Fig. 6. Memory power efficiency

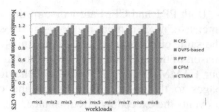

Fig. 9. System power efficiency

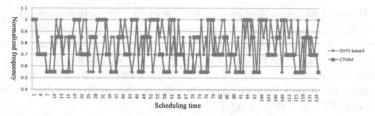

Fig. 8. Situation of the frequency scaling

5.3   Performance Analysis of CTMM

Figure 10 demonstrates the finish time of all policies normalized to default. The longer the finish time, the more performance declined. From this figure, our CTMM has better performance than CPS obviously, almost as well as DVFS-based and PPT, and the more threads, the better performance our CTMM is.

Table 3 and table 4 demonstrate the ratio switch between sharing memory address space and each thread occupies average bank number of four policies respectively, which explain the reason for more threads better performance of our CTMM. The more ratio of switching between sharing memory address space, the better performance it is. And also the more each thread occupies average bank number, the more parallelism it is, and the more performance will be. From table 3 and 4, we can easily to know the reason of our better performance than CPM.

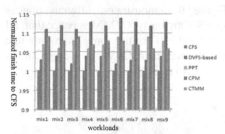

Fig. 10. Normalized finish time to CFS

Table 3. each thread occupies average bank number

	CFS	DVFS-based	PPT	CPM	CTMM
mix	19.5	19.5	7.8	6.6	14.2

Table 4. Ratio of switching between sharing memory

	CFS	DVFS-based	PPT	CPM	CTMM
mix1	42%	42%	53%	45%	58%
mix2	28%	28%	46%	34%	47%
mix3	43%	43%	57%	48%	60%
mix4	57%	57%	63%	60%	67%
mix5	39%	39%	51%	49%	58%
mix6	54%	54%	64%	64%	68%
mix7	65%	65%	72%	70%	82%
mix8	47%	47%	65%	56%	76%
mix9	66%	66%	77%	72%	85%

6   Conclusion

In this paper, we have presented a solution to improve both processor and memory power efficiency simultaneously through coordinating task and memory management (CTMM). Combining group partition, page allocation, group scheduling and group based frequency scale and mode control, our CTMM reduces CPU frequency scaling times and creating more memory idleness preventing frequently switching rank mode while reducing as much as CPU and memory power simultaneously. Experimental results show that CTMM can well reduce CPU and memory power simultaneously.

Acknowledgments. This work is supported by the National Science Foundation of China under grants (No. 61272131, No. 61202053, No. 61003077, No. 61202094), Jiangsu provincial Natural Science Foundation (No. SBK201240198), Jiangsu production-teaching-research joint innovation project (No.BY2009128). We also gratefully acknowledge the support of our industrial sponsor, SAMSUNG (CHINA) R&D CENTER.

References

1. Barroso, L.A., Hölzle, U.: The Datacenter as a Computer: An Introduction to the Design of Warehouse-Scale Machines. Synthesis Lectures on Computer Architecture (January 2009)
2. Lim, K., Chang, J., Mudge, T., Ranganathan, P., Reinhardt, S.K., Wenisch, T.F.: Disaggregated Memory for Expansion and Sharing in Blade Servers. In: ISCA 2009: International Symposium on Computer Architecture (2009)
3. Deng, Q., Meisner, D., Ramos, L., Wenisch, T.F., Bianchini, R.: MemScale: Active Low-Power Modes for Main Memory. In: ASPLOS (2011)
4. David, H., Fallin, C., Gorbatov, E., Hanebutte, U.R., Mutlu, O.: Memory Power Management via Dynamic Voltage/Frequency Scaling. In: ICAC (2011)
5. Ware, M., Rajamani, K., Floyd, M., Brock, B., Rubio, J., Rawson, F., Carter, J.: Architecting for Power Management: The IBM POWER7 Approach. In: HPCA (2010)
6. Lefurgy, C., Rajamani, K., Rawson, F., Felter, W., Kistler, M., Keller, T.W.: Energy Management for Commercial Servers. IEEE Computer 36(12) (December 2003)
7. Deng, Q., Meisner, D., Bhattacharjee, A., Wenisch, T.F.: CoScale: Coordinating CPU and Memory System DVFS in Server Systems. In: MICRO (2012)
8. Mutlu, O., Moscibroda, T.: Parallelism-aware batch scheduling: Enhancing both performance and fairness of shared DRAM system. In: ISCA-35 (2008)
9. Lin, C.-H., Yang, C.-L., King, K.-J.: PPT: Joint performance/power/thermal management of dram memory for multi-core systems. In: ISLPED, pp. 93–98 (2009)
10. Cho, S., Jin, L.: Managing Distributed, shared L2 Caches through OS-Level page Allocation. In: MICRO-39 (2006)
11. Meisner, D., Gold, B.T., Wenisch, T.F.: PowerNap: Eliminating Server Idle Power. In: ASPLOS (2009)
12. Jia, G., Li, X., Wang, C., Zhou, X., Zhu, Z.: Frequency Affinity: Analyzing and Maximizing Power Efficiency in Multi-core System. In: IEEE 20th International Symposium on Modeling, Analysis and Simulation of Computer and Telecommunication Systems, MASCOTS (2012)

13. Jia, G., Li, X., Wang, C., Zhou, X., Zhu, Z.: Memory Affinity: Balancing Performance, Power, Thermal and Fairness for Multi-core Systems. In: IEEE Conference on Cluster Computing, Beijing, China (2012)
14. Li, X., Jia, G., Chen, Y., Zhu, Z., Zhou, X.: Share Memory Aware Scheduler: Balancing Performance and Fairness. In: ACM/IEEE The 22th Great Lakes Symposium on VLSI, GLSVLSI (2012)
15. Liu, L., Cui, Z., Xing, M., Bao, Y., Chen, M., Wu, C.: A Software Memory Partition Approach for Eliminating Bank-level Interference in Multicore Systems. In: PACT (2012)
16. Patel, A., et al.: MARSSx86: a full system simulator for x86 CPUs. In: DAC (2011)
17. Brooks, D., et al.: Wattch: a framework for architectural-level power analysis and optimizations. In: ISCA (2000)
18. Micron. Calculating Memory System Power for DDR3 (July 2007)
19. Kopytov, A.: SysBench: a system performance benchmark (2004), http://sysbench.sourceforge.net/index.html
20. Chen, M., Wang, X., Li, X.: Coordinating Processor and Main Memory for Efficient Server Power Control. In: ICS 2011 (2011)

Deconvolution of Huge 3-D Images: Parallelization Strategies on a Multi-GPU System

Pavel Karas, Michal Kuderjavý, and David Svoboda

Centre for Biomedical Image Analysis, Faculty of Informatics, Botanická 68a,
602 00 Brno, Czech Republic
http://cbia.fi.muni.cz

Abstract. In this paper, we discuss strategies to parallelize selected deconvolution methods on a multi-GPU system. We provide a comparison of several approaches to split the deconvolution into subtasks while keeping the amount of costly data transfers as low as possible, and propose own implementation of three deconvolution methods which achieves up to 65× speedup over the CPU one. In the experimental part, we analyse how the individual stages of the computation contribute to the overall computation time as well as how the multi-GPU implementation scales in various setups. Finally, we identify bottlenecks of the system.

1 Introduction

Three-dimensional imaging is being increasingly used in various biomedical modalities, such as fluorescence microscopy, magnetic resonance imaging (MRI), computational tomography (CT) or ultrasound imaging. It allows scientists to visualise and study structures, from individual genes to whole organs, inside human body as well as their spatial organization.

The quality of the observed image is strongly affected by the properties of imaging system, in particular, it contains blurring and noise. This image corruption can be partially eliminated by so-called deconvolution, an inverted process that tries to restore the original image. It is an ill-posed problem because the impulse response (also denoted as point-spread function, PSF) does in general not have an inverse [24]. Therefore, a mathematical model describing the relation between original (ideal) image, observed image, PSF and noise is created; an optimal solution to this model can be found using appropriate numerical methods.

Respecting the fact, that the iterative methods produce better results than the direct approaches, the deconvolution appears to be a challenging task for high-performance computing—in practise, dozens of iterations are performed until a desired quality criterion is met. Furthermore, in a typical biomedical experiment, dozens of huge 3-D images (of size up to 100 million voxels) are acquired. The whole processing task can hence last hours.

During past years, deconvolution has been parallelized on various architectures, including a multi-core CPU [19, 26], a cluster of computers [18], graphics hardware [4, 8, 20], or multi-GPU and heterogeneous platforms [6, 7].

J. Kołodziej et al. (Eds.): ICA3PP 2013, Part I, LNCS 8285, pp. 279–290, 2013.
© Springer International Publishing Switzerland 2013

Our contribution is (i) to study several approaches to split the problem into subtasks—besides a popular overlap-save method, a frequency-based approach is considered, (ii) to analyse the individual phases of the computation, (iii) to assess the practical speedup on examples from the field of fluorescence microscopy, and (iv) to identify bottlenecks of the system. As a practical result, we implement deconvolution on a system with multiple GPUs. Using multiple GPUs allows us not only to shorten the computation time from hours to minutes, but also to process huge 3-D images which cannot fit in the GPU memory at once.

The paper is organized as follows: Firstly, we provide the necessary theoretical background and review the prior work on the parallelization of deconvolution. Secondly, we present the proposed method to split deconvolution into parallel subtasks and to implement it on a multi-GPU system. Thirdly, we show and discuss results of experiments conducted to test performance of our implementation. Finally, we conclude our work and achieved results.

2   Formulation of the Problem

The general mathematical model of the imaging process [24] is given by

$$\mathbf{g} = N(\mathbf{Hf} + \mathbf{b}), \tag{1}$$

where $\mathbf{f}$, $\mathbf{g}$, and $\mathbf{b}$ is the original image, the observed image, and the known background, respectively, denoted by vectors of length M, $N(\cdot)$ is the noise process, and H is the sampled PSF expressed by a blurring matrix $M \times M$.

In practical applications, the model is often simplified to a spatially-invariant PSF which means that $\mathbf{H}$ has a block-circulant form. This simplification is followed in this paper. In such case, we can formulate (1) using convolution:

$$g = N(h \otimes f + b), \tag{2}$$

where $\otimes$ is the convolution operator. For general 3-D convolution kernels, the most efficient approach is the so-called fast convolution which replaces the convolution with the point-wise multiplication in the Fourier domain [10, 14]. The Fourier transform can be efficiently computed in $O(M \log M)$ using the fast Fourier transform (FFT) algorithm [2, 12].

The *blind deconvolution* is the process of finding the optimal estimate of f, further denoted as $\hat{f}$, with the knowledge of functions g, b and the noise distribution N—usually, the Poisson or the Gaussian distribution are considered. In this paper, we further assume that h is known—this problem is commonly known as the *non-blind deconvolution*.

2.1   Selected Deconvolution Methods

Wiener deconvolution is an example of a linear non-iterative method [3]. In the Fourier domain, it is given by

$$\hat{F} = G \frac{H^*}{|H|^2 + \frac{\sigma_O^2}{\sigma_N^2}}, \tag{3}$$

where H^* is the complex conjugate of the Fourier transform of the PSF and σ_O, σ_N are the variance of the object and the noise, respectively.

Iterative Constrained Tikhonov-Miller (ICTM) is a non-linear iterative method [25]. The estimation of $\hat{f}$ in the $(k+1)$-th iteration can be computed as follows:

$$f^{k+1} = \mathcal{P}\left(f^k + \alpha^k d^k\right), \tag{4}$$

where $\mathcal{P}(\cdot)$ is the projection operator which cuts off the negative values and the initial estimate f^0 is usually set to g. For details about the estimation of the *step size* α^k and the *search direction* d^k, refer to [24].

Expectation Maximization-Maximum Likelihood Estimation (EM-MLE): this iterative method [5, 21] maximizes the likelihood of $\hat{f}$ for Poisson noise. The estimation of $\hat{f}$ in the $(k+1)$-th iteration is given by

$$f^{k+1} = \left[\frac{g}{h \otimes f^k} \otimes h^T\right] f^k, \tag{5}$$

and can be further restricted to non-negative values by $\mathcal{P}(\cdot)$.

There exist many other approaches for deconvolution but the parallelization principles we propose in our paper can simply be adopted for the most of those methods as they are based on the same class of fundamental operators, such as convolution, mapping (e.g. point-wise operations) and reduction [19].

2.2   Parallelization of Deconvolution

Coarse-grained. For the parallelization on multi-core CPU [26] or a small cluster [18], a sectioned approach based on a popular overlap-save method [23] is used. Here, input image is simply split into sections, each convolved separately with the input PSF. The sections must hence overlap, the size of overlap is equal to the size of PSF. After the computation, the overlaps are discarded if the computation is complete, or exchanged between nodes if another iteration is required. Extensive communication is hence the main drawback of the method.

Fine-grained. Many successful attempts [4, 8, 19, 20] proved the massively-parallel graphics hardware to be suitable for the deconvolution problem. Implementations are often based on the popular CUDA framework [16] with the CUFFT library [15]. However, the size of the GPU memory may be insufficient in applications where large images are processed [11, 13].

Hybrid approaches. On a multi-GPU system or a heterogeneous CPU-GPU platform, one has to consider both coarse-grained and fine-grained parallelization methods. Domanski et al. [6, 7] implemented the 3-D Richardson-Lucy deconvolution on both architectures. On a coarse-grained level, the sectioned approach with no overlaying image segments exchange was used, in order to avoid a communication overhead. However, this simplification was possible due to fact that only small PSF ($19 \times 19 \times 16$ pixels) was tested.

Other approaches. Out of the three fundamental operators (convolution, mapping and reduction), convolution is the most difficult task in a parallel implementation of deconvolution, because it requires extensive communication between nodes. Besides the aforementioned overlap-save method, other approaches can be considered, such as the overlap-add method and the combination of the two [22]. Furthermore, the decimation-in-frequency algorithm [11, 13] can be employed. In the following section, we discuss the optimal choice of the decomposition approach and present our implementation on a multi-GPU system.

3   Proposed Method

3.1   Choice of the Optimal Decomposition Method

In order to achieve an optimal performance of a coarse-grained or a hybrid parallel implementations, one has to select an appropriate method to decompose the deconvolution. We will show that the optimal choice depends on a chosen deconvolution algorithm and also on the size of the deconvolved image and the PSF. There are basically two groups of the decomposition methods.

Spatial-based methods. The overlap-save and overlap-add methods [17] are based on the image division in the spatial domain. Svoboda [22] implemented the convolution of 3-D microscopy images on a cluster using the former to split the image and the latter to split the PSF. In the paper, it is referred to as signal and kernel tiling, respectively. It was shown that the signal tiling is the optimal approach for the division of the image until the image sections are smaller than the PSF. At that point, a combination with the kernel tiling should be used so that the size of image and PSF sections are equal.

Frequency-based methods. The decimation in frequency (DIF) and decimation in time (DIT) [17] provide the division in the frequency domain. They are the cornerstone of the popular FFT algorithm. Karas et al. [11, 13] showed that the DIF algorithm is suitable for the convolution of 3-D microscopy images on one and multiple GPUs and that the DIT algorithm is not appropriate as it would require the extensive data transfers between the nodes.

In [12], authors provide a detailed comparison of overlap-save, overlap-add, DIF and DIT methods—refer to Table 1. In terms of the communication overhead, the DIF algorithm is the most efficient method for the decomposition of the convolution, it is hence the optimal choice for the linear deconvolution methods including the Wiener deconvolution. On the other hand, the non-linear deconvolution methods consist of a sequence of operations. Besides convolution, reduction and point-wise operations are required. These operations cannot be performed separately in individual image sections if the decomposition is performed in the frequency domain. Here, the usage of the DIF is hence not optimal and spatial-based approach should be used instead.

Table 1. Comparison of methods for the parallel fast convolution
The size of input image g and PSF h is denoted as $M^g = M_x^g \cdot M_y^g \cdot M_z^g$ and $M^h = M_x^h \cdot M_y^h \cdot M_z^h$, respectively. For the convolution in the Fourier domain, both image and PSF have to be padded to the size $M = M_x \cdot M_y \cdot M_z$ where $M_* = M_*^g + M_*^h - 1$. O^h, O^g denote sizes of overlapping regions which are proportional to M^h and M^g, respectively. The number of the computation nodes is denoted by d. In the 2nd and 3rd column, we omit the size of the used datatype.

Method	# of operations	Data transfers	Memory per node
DIF	$M \left[\frac{9}{2} \log_2 M + 1 \right]$	$3M$	$2M/d$
DIT	$M \left[\frac{9}{2} \log_2 M + 2 \right]$	$(d+1)M$	$4M/d$
Signal tiling	$dM \left[\frac{9}{2} \log_2 (\frac{M}{d}) + 1 \right]$	$3M + dO^h$	$2M/d + O^h$
Kernel tiling	$dM \left[\frac{9}{2} \log_2 (\frac{M}{d}) + 1 \right]$	$3M + 2(d-1)O^g$	$2M/d + O^g$

3.2 Wiener Deconvolution

Our implementation consists of seven stages. For details, refer to Alg. 1:

1. The input image g and PSF h are padded to size (M_x, M_y, M_z) where $M_* = M_*^g + M_*^h - 1$. We choose M_* to be the nearest larger integer which fulfils additional constraints: (i) for the computation on d GPUs, M_z must be divisible by d; (ii) M_x must be even because we use an optimization for real (non-complex) images [13]; (iii) in order to achieve a better performance of FFT, we choose M_* to have the small prime factors, namely 2, 3, 5 and 7.
2. The DIF-based decomposition, optimized for real images [13], is performed on CPU. Both the image and the PSF are split into sub-parts which are stored in whole separate segments of the host memory.
3. The individual sub-parts are transferred from CPU to individual GPU nodes.
4. In each node, the Wiener deconvolution is performed according to Eq. (3).
5. The filtered sub-parts are transferred back to CPU. In order to achieve better performace, the stages 3–5 may be overlapped.
6. The inverse operation to the decomposition is computed on CPU.
7. The resulting image is cropped to the original size.

3.3 ICTM and EM-MLE

The implementation consists of six stages. For the sake of brevity, we provide details on the EM-MLE method only (Alg. 1), ICTM is implemented analogously.

1. Before the filtering, the input image g and PSF h are padded in the same manner as in the previous case. Subsequently, they are split into sections.
2. The individual sections are copied from CPU to individual GPU nodes.
3. In each node, a single iteration is computed according to Eq. (5).
4. The overlapping regions are exchanged between the nodes.
5. After finishing all the iterations, output data are copied back to CPU.
6. The resulting image is merged and cropped to the original size.

Algorithm 1. Deconvolution on a multi-GPU system
Wiener: g and h are input/output image and PSF, respectively, d denotes the number of GPU nodes, and $e = \sigma_O^2/\sigma_N^2$ is the noise estimate—refer to Eq. (3).
EM-MLE: g, f and h are input and output image and PSF, respectively, d denotes the number of GPU nodes, and n is the number of iterations.

---

procedure WIENERDECONVOLUTION(g, h, d, e)
    $g' \leftarrow$ **MirrorPad**(g, M_x, M_y, M_z)   ▷ mirror padding of image
    $h' \leftarrow$ **ZeroPad**(h, M_x, M_y, M_z)   ▷ zero padding of PSF
    if $d \leq 2$ **then**
        $g' \leftarrow$ **Decompose**(g', d)   ▷ DIF-based decomposition
        $h' \leftarrow$ **Decompose**(h', d)
        for $k \leftarrow 0, d-1$ **do**
            Copy g'_k, h_k from host to k−th device
            $g'_k \leftarrow$ **Wiener**(g'_k, h'_k, e)   ▷ evaluates Eq. (3) in the Fourier domain
            Copy g'_k from k−th device to host
        end for
        $g' \leftarrow$ **Compose**(g', d)   ▷ DIF-based composition
    else   ▷ if $d > 2$, the alternative function **WienerAlt** is used as the
                    result of convolution $g \otimes w$ depends on the recombination
                    of the sub-parts g_k, h_k with g_{d-k}, h_{d-k} [13]
        $g' \leftarrow$ **Decompose**($g', 2d$)
        $h' \leftarrow$ **Decompose**($h', 2d$)
        for $k \leftarrow 0, d-1$ **do**
            Copy $g'_k, h_k, g'_{2d-k}, h'_{2d-k}$ from host to k−th device
            $(g'_k, g'_{2d-k}) \leftarrow$ **WienerAlt**($g'_k, h'_k, g'_{2d-k}, h'_{2d-k}, e$)
            Copy g'_k, g'_{2d-k} from k−th device to host
        end for
        $g' \leftarrow$ **Compose**($g', 2d$)
    end if
    $g \leftarrow$ **RemovePad**(g', M_x^g, M_y^g, M_z^g)   ▷ removes padding
end procedure

---

procedure EM_MLE(g, h, d, n)
    $g' \leftarrow$ **MirrorPad**(g, M_x, M_y, M_z)   ▷ mirror padding of image
    $h' \leftarrow$ **ZeroPad**(h, M_x, M_y, M_z)   ▷ zero padding of PSF
    $\{g'_k\} \leftarrow$ **SignalTiling**(g', d)   ▷ splits image into sections
    for $k \leftarrow 0, d-1$ **do**
        Copy g'_k, h' from host to k−th device ▷ g is split using signal tiling [22]
        $f'_k \leftarrow g'_k$
        for $i \leftarrow 0, n-1$ **do**
            $f'_k \leftarrow$ **EM_MLEIter**(f'_k, g'_k, h')   ▷ evaluates Eq. (5)
            Synchronize   ▷ exchanges regions of overlap between GPU nodes
        end for
        Copy f'_k from k−th device to host
    end for
    $f' \leftarrow$ **Merge**(f'_k, d)   ▷ merges image from sections
    $f \leftarrow$ **RemovePad**(f', M_x^g, M_y^g, M_z^g)   ▷ removes padding
    return f
end procedure

4   Experimental Results

All experiments were conducted on the computer described in Tab. 2. For FFT, the FFTW library [9] and the CUFFT library [15] were used. The decomposition and composition in the Wiener deconvolution were performed on CPU and improved with SSE/SSE2 intrinsics and multi-threading for a better performance.

Table 2. Machine used for experiments

| CPU/GPU | Nodes | Cores | Parameters of a single node | | |
			Clock speed	RAM size	Bandwidth
Intel Xeon E5620	2	8	2.40 GHz	48 GB	25.6 GB/s
NVIDIA Tesla M2090	4	512	1.30 GHz	6 GB	177.4 GB/s

4.1   Wiener Deconvolution

We measure the performance of the Wiener deconvolution for various precisions and system configurations, on randomly generated images. For the global comparison, refer to Fig. 1(a),(b). The results show overall computation times including data transfers. We can conclude that the GPU implementation is in average 7.9× and 4.6× faster than the CPU one in the single and double precision, respectively.

The results also show that using more than one GPU does not bring any further speedup. This is due to the fact that only a small portion of the time is spent by the computation of the Wiener deconvolution itself which can be performed in parallel on all nodes whereas the most of the time is spent by padding and cropping of the images, in accordance with the well-known Amdahl's law [1]. Moreover, with larger number of GPU nodes, the time spent by the DIF stages on CPU is longer. The overall time can be expressed as follows:

$$T = \sum_{i=1}^{n_s} s_i + \frac{1}{d} \sum_{i=1}^{n_p} p_i, \tag{6}$$

where s_i, p_i is the time spent in a serial and a parallel stage, respectively, n_* refers to their numbers, and d is the number of GPU nodes. In our case, s_i is represented by steps 1–3 and 5–7 described in Section 3.2 and p_i by step 4 only. To compare Eq. (6) with empirical results, refer to Fig. 1(c).

Despite the above reservations, we note that the benefit of the decomposition is the fact that the maximum size of the image that can be processed is no longer limited by the memory size of the GPU node. In our case, it enables single-GPU processing of the 128-Mpx image in the single precision and the 64- and 128-Mpx images in the double precision, with a negligible performance decrease.

4.2   ICTM and EM-MLE

In the second experiment, we analysed the non-linear iterative methods using the same approach as in the previous section. For the sake of brevity, we tested the single precision only. The results are shown in Fig. 2.

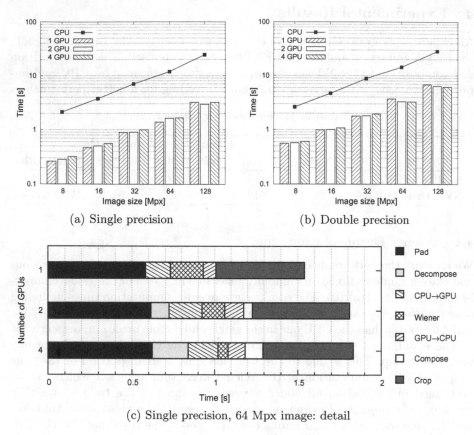

(a) Single precision

(b) Double precision

(c) Single precision, 64 Mpx image: detail

Fig. 1. Computation time of the Wiener deconvolution. As input, various image sizes and a fixed PSF size of $65 \times 65 \times 65$ voxels were used.

Depending on the image size, the speedup of the multi-GPU system over CPU is 17–$31\times$ and 41–$44\times$ for the EM-MLE and the ICTM method, respectively. We note that some data are missing due to insufficient GPU memory. It is not straightforward to extend the implementation in order to process larger images as it would require excessive data transfers after each iteration.

For iterative methods, the overall time is given by

$$T = \sum_{i=1}^{n_s} s_i + \frac{1}{d} \sum_{i=1}^{n_p} p_i + n \left(\sum_{i=1}^{n_{s'}} s_i' + \frac{1}{d} \sum_{i=1}^{n_{p'}} p_i' \right), \qquad (7)$$

where n is the number of iterations, s_i, p_i refer to serial and parallel stages performed once only, and s_i', p_i' relate to serial and parallel stages of each iteration. For both the ICTM and the EM-MLE method, s_i is represented by steps 1, 2, 5 and 6 described in Section 3.3, s_i' by step 4, and p_i' by step 3. Refer to Fig. 2(c),(d) to compare Eq. (7) with empirical results.

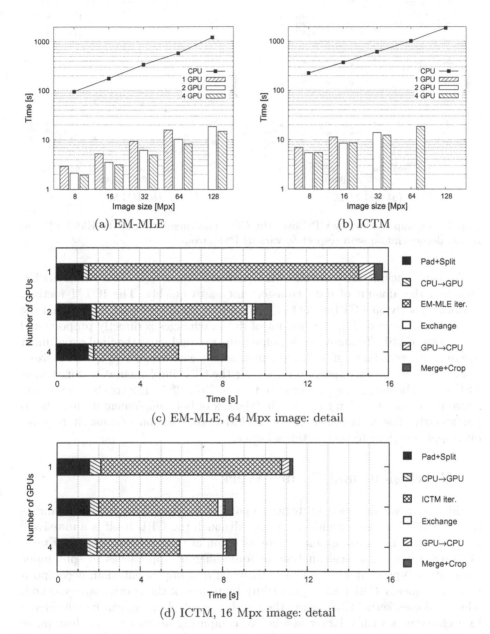

Fig. 2. Computation time of the EM-MLE and ICTM deconvolution. As input, various image sizes and a fixed PSF size of $65 \times 65 \times 65$ voxels were used. For the sake of simplicity, we provide the overall times for the EM-MLE/ICTM iteration and the Exchange phase in the detailed view, instead of displaying each individual iteration.

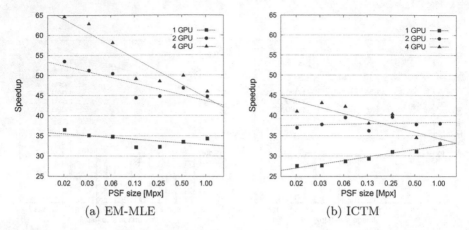

(a) EM-MLE　　　　　　　　　　　(b) ICTM

Fig. 3. Speedup reached by GPU over the CPU implementation of the EM-MLE and ICTM deconvolution with respect to various PSF sizes.

We can conclude that the EM-MLE method scales well for 2 and 4 GPUs, although the amount of data transfers increases quickly. The ICTM method performs poorly on 4 GPUs due to the communication overhead. As we used the signal tiling method [22], the amount of data exchanges is directly proportional to the size of PSF. To analyse this behaviour, we conducted the final experiment to study the scalability of both implementations with respect to the PSF size.

In Fig. 3, we provide speedup rates over the CPU implementation for various PSF sizes. The image size was fixed and set to $257 \times 257 \times 129$ voxels. The results prove the communication to be the bottleneck of both implementations. This is particularly true in the case of the ICTM deconvolution because it requires overlapping regions to be two times larger.

5　Conclusions and Future Work

In this paper, we discussed strategies to parallelize selected deconvolution methods on a platform with multiple GPUs. Although the GPU itself is a massively parallel unit, the coarse-grained decomposition of the problem is the key task. We provided a theoretical analysis of four different approaches to split input data into sub-parts and chose two of them for own implementation: decomposition in frequency (DIF) and signal tiling by means of the overlap-save method. The third one, kernel tiling using the overlap-add technique, can be considered in architectures with a larger number of computing nodes such as clusters, as explained in Section 3.1.

The first approach was used for the linear Wiener deconvolution. Despite the efficiency of the DIF decomposition, the speedup achieved by multiple GPUs was negligible as the most of the time was spent by serial steps, such as image padding/cropping and data transfers. Thus, the bandwidth of the CPU memory and of the communication bus (PCI-Express) are the major bottlenecks in the system. We assume that iterative linear methods could be more suitable for the multi-GPU implementation. This will be the subject of our future work. On the other hand, we show that the decomposition allows to process even large images that cannot fit in the GPU memory with a negligible loss of performance.

The second technique was chosen for the non-linear ICTM and EM-MLE methods. In this case, we achieved a significant speedup over the CPU implementation (up to 65× for EM-MLE and 43× for ICTM). We showed that the performance strongly depends on the size of the PSF which influences the amount of data transfer. Here, the system is bottlenecked by the bandwidth of the PCI-Express bus. We also demonstrated that the usability of the implementation is determined by the size of the GPU memory which poses limits on the maximum size of input images. This is a serious issue for biomedical applications which we would like to deal with in our future work.

Finally, we note that although the results and conclusions presented in this paper were achieved on the multi-GPU platform, they can also be applied to other similar architectures such as small clusters.

Source Code. The source code of the program along with test images is available at http://sourceforge.net/projects/multigpudeconvolution/.

Acknowledgments. This work has been supported by the Grant Agency of the Czech Republic (Grant No. P302/12/G157).

References

[1] Amdahl, G.: Validity of the single processor approach to achieving large scale computing capabilities. In: Proceedings of the Spring Joint Computer Conference, April 18-20, pp. 483–485. ACM (1967)

[2] Brigham, E., Morrow, R.: The fast Fourier transform. IEEE Spectrum 4(12), 63–70 (1967)

[3] Castleman, K.R.: Digital Image Processing. Prentice Hall (1996)

[4] D'Amore, L., Marcellino, L., Mele, V., Romano, D.: Deconvolution of 3D Fluorescence Microscopy Images Using Graphics Processing Units. In: Wyrzykowski, R., Dongarra, J., Karczewski, K., Waśniewski, J. (eds.) PPAM 2011, Part I. LNCS, vol. 7203, pp. 690–699. Springer, Heidelberg (2012)

[5] Dempster, A.P., Laird, N.M., Rubin, D.B.: Maximum likelihood from incomplete data via the em algorithm. Journal of the Royal Statistical Society. Series B (Methodological), 1–38 (1977)

[6] Domanski, L., Bednarz, T., Vallotton, P., Taylor, J.: Heterogeneous parallel 3D image deconvolution on a cluster of GPUs and CPUs. In: 19th Int'l Congress on Modelling and Simulation, Perth, Australia (December 2011), http://mssanz.org.au/modsim2011/A8/domanski.pdf (cited August 1, 2013)

[7] Domanski, L., Bednarz, T., Gureyev, T.E., Murray, L., Huang, E., Taylor, J.A.: Applications of Heterogeneous Computing in Computational and Simulation Science. In: 2011 Fourth IEEE International Conference on Utility and Cloud Computing (UCC), pp. 382–389. IEEE (2011)

[8] Domanski, L., Vallotton, P., Wang, D.: Two and three-dimensional image deconvolution on graphics hardware. In: Proceedings of the 18th World IMACS/MODSIM Congress, Cairns, Australia, pp. 13–17 (July 2009)

[9] Frigo, M., Johnson, S.G.: The design and implementation of FFTW3. Proceedings of the IEEE 93(2), 216–231 (2005); Special Issue on Program Generation, Optimization, and Platform Adaptation

[10] Gonzales, R.C., Woods, R.E.: Digital Image Processing, 3rd edn. Prentice-Hall (2007)

[11] Karas, P., Svoboda, D.: Convolution of large 3D images on GPU and its decomposition. EURASIP Journal on Advances in Signal Processing 2011(1), 120 (2011)

[12] Karas, P., Svoboda, D.: Algorithms for Efficient Computation of Convolution. In: Design and Architectures for Digital Signal Processing, 1st edn., pp. 179–208. InTech, Rijeka (2013)

[13] Karas, P., Svoboda, D., Zemčík, P.: GPU optimization of convolution for large 3-D real images. In: Blanc-Talon, J., Philips, W., Popescu, D., Scheunders, P., Zemčík, P. (eds.) ACIVS 2012. LNCS, vol. 7517, pp. 59–71. Springer, Heidelberg (2012)

[14] Nussbaumer, H.: Fast Fourier transform and convolution algorithms. Springer Series in Information Sciences 2 (1982)

[15] NVIDIA Corporation: CUFFT Library (2012), http://docs.nvidia.com/cuda/pdf/CUDA_CUFFT_Users_Guide.pdf (cited August 1, 2013)

[16] NVIDIA Corporation: NVIDIA Developer Zone (2012), http://developer.nvidia.com/category/zone/cuda-zone (cited August 1, 2013)

[17] Oppenheim, A., Schafer, R., Buck, J., et al.: Discrete-time signal processing, vol. 2. Prentice Hall, Upper Saddle River (1989)

[18] Pawliczek, P., Romanowska-Pawliczek, A., Soltys, Z.: Parallel deconvolution of large 3D images obtained by confocal laser scanning microscopy. Microscopy Research and Technique 73(3), 187–194 (2010)

[19] Quammen, C.W., Feng, D., Taylor II, R.M.: Performance of 3D Deconvolution Algorithms on Multi-Core and Many-Core Architectures. University of North Carolina at Chapel Hill, Dpt. of Computer Science, Tech. Rep. (2009)

[20] Serafini, T., Zanella, R., Zanni, L.: Gradient projection methods for image deblurring and denoising on graphics processors. In: Int. Conf. on Parallel Computing ParCo 2009. Advances in Parallel Computing, vol. 19, pp. 59–66 (2010)

[21] Shepp, L.A., Vardi, Y.: Maximum likelihood reconstruction for emission tomography. IEEE Transactions on Medical Imaging 1(2), 113–122 (1982)

[22] Svoboda, D.: Efficient computation of convolution of huge images. In: Maino, G., Foresti, G.L. (eds.) ICIAP 2011, Part I. LNCS, vol. 6978, pp. 453–462. Springer, Heidelberg (2011)

[23] Trussell, H., Hunt, B.: Image restoration of space variant blurs by sectioned methods. In: IEEE International Conference on Acoustics, Speech, and Signal Processing, ICASSP 1978, vol. 3, pp. 196–198. IEEE (1978)

[24] Verveer, P.J.: Computational and optical methods for improving resolution and signal quality in fluorescence microscopy. Ph.D. thesis, Delft TU (1998)

[25] Voort, H., Strasters, K.: Restoration of confocal images for quantitative image analysis. Journal of Microscopy 178(2), 165–181 (1995)

[26] Wendykier, P., Nagy, J.G.: Image processing on modern CPUs and GPUs. Tech. rep., Emory University TR-2008-023 (2009)

Hardware-Assisted Intrusion Detection by Preserving Reference Information Integrity

Junghee Lee[1], Chrysostomos Nicopoulos[2], Gi Hwan Oh[3], Sang-Won Lee[3], and Jongman Kim[1]

[1] Georgia Institute of Technology, Atlanta, USA
junghee.lee@gatech.edu, jkim@ece.gatech.edu
[2] University of Cyprus, Nicosia, Cyprus
nicopoulos@ucy.ac.cy
[3] Sungkyunkwan University, Suwon, South Korea
{wurikiji,swlee}@skku.edu

Abstract. Malware detectors and integrity checkers detect malicious activities by comparing against reference data. To ensure their trustworthy operation, it is crucial to protect the reference data from unauthorized modification. This paper proposes the Soteria Security Card (SSC), an append-only storage. To the best of our knowledge, this work is the first to introduce the concept of an append-only storage and its application to information security. The SSC framework allows only read and append operations, and forbids over-write and erase operations. By exploiting this trait, we can protect the reference data that must be updated constantly. It is demonstrated how SSC facilitates log protection and file integrity checking.

Keywords: log, hardware, protection, security.

1 Introduction

There are numerous software tools that prevent or detect malicious activities in a computer system by comparing against reference data. For example, anti-virus programs detect malware by matching files or snapshots of memory against signature databases. A signature database contains measurable characteristics of known malware. On the other hand, integrity checkers validate their target by comparing against the target's integrity information. For example, file integrity checkers validate files by checking if their checksum matches an a priori measured one. Additionally, log information – which is a trace of various server activities – also constitutes very important reference data when an attack is investigated. Thus, protecting reference data is critical for the above-mentioned techniques, because they would become useless once the reference data is contaminated.

Since reference data is constantly updated, we cannot protect it by enforcing a read-only property on it. Encryption can effectively protect data, as long as the key is not revealed. However, according to a recent report [1], 76% of data breaches occurring in 2012 exploited weak or stolen credentials. It is not a trivial

J. Kołodziej et al. (Eds.): ICA3PP 2013, Part I, LNCS 8285, pp. 291–300, 2013.

task to keep the key itself secret. Using a virtual machine is also an effective way to protect or monitor important reference data. The host operating system (OS) can serve as the protector of reference data in the guest OSes. In a virtual machine environment, the integrity of the host OS becomes even more critical, because all the guest OSes are threatened once the host OS is compromised. There should be a mechanism to protect the reference data of the *host* OS.

Toward this end, this paper proposes the *Soteria*[1] *Security Card*, or SSC. SSC is a card that attaches to the host machine through a standard interface, such as Serial AT Attachment (SATA). The purpose of SSC is to protect reference data from unauthorized modification. SSC allows only read and append operations. Overwriting and erasing stored data is physically impossible. Therefore, it can be a secure foundation for storing important reference data. To the best of our knowledge, this work is the first attempt to introduce the concept of append-only storage and to apply it to information security. Note that write-once-read-many (WORM) devices can also be considered as append-only storage; compact disks (CD) and digital versatile disks (DVD) are typical examples. However, these devices are significantly slower than hard-disk drives and their media should be replaced once they become full. Instead, SSC offers better performance than WORM devices and has the necessary intelligence to sweep old data. Log protection and file integrity checking will be presented as two proof-of-concept examples of the capabilities of SSC.

The rest of this paper is organized as follows: the Soteria Security Card is presented in Section 2, followed by the two case-study examples of log protection and file integrity checking in Sections 3 and 4, respectively. Section 5 discusses related work, while Section 6 concludes this paper.

2   The Soteria Security Card: An Append-Only Storage Solution

To implement append-only storage, we have developed specialized hardware in the form of (a) an add-on card that can be attached to the host machine, (b) firmware running on the hardware, and (c) a device driver that provides an interface to the host OS. The architecture of the Soteria Security Card is explained in sub-section 2.1, followed by its implementation and performance evaluation results in sub-section 2.2.

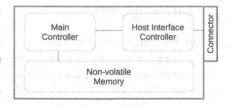

Fig. 1. The high-level block diagram of the developed *Soteria Security Card*

2.1   The SSC Architecture

The *Soteria Security Card (SSC)* consists of an interface controller to the host system, non-volatile memory, and a main controller. A high-level block diagram of the SSC is illustrated in Figure 1.

---

[1] In ancient Greek mythology, Soteria was the goddess of safety and recovery from harm.

The interface controller to the host system connects the SSC to the host system through a standard system bus, such as Peripheral Component Interconnect (PCI), Serial AT Attachment (SATA), and Small Computer System Interface (SCSI). In our specific implementation, the SATA interface is employed. The interface controller handles the protocol of the system bus. The non-volatile memory is used to store the log files. The memory could be of any non-volatile type, such as NAND flash, NOR flash, Phase-Change Memory (PCM), or Spin-Transfer Torque Memory (STT-RAM). In this implementation, we adopted NAND flash memory. The main controller is an embedded processor where the firmware runs. An ARM7 microprocessor is used in the current implementation.

Figure 2 depicts the architecture of the firmware running on the SSC. The layers shown in the grey box are part of the firmware. The heart of the firmware is the file management layer. It manages files according to commands issued through the host interface. Through the host interface, the firmware accepts only read and append commands. The file management layer is a simple file system. It maintains a file descriptor table that keeps meta data for files, such as file name, file size, and position pointer. It maintains a main data region that stores data. Whenever an append command is issued, it appends data to the end of the data region and updates the meta data accordingly.

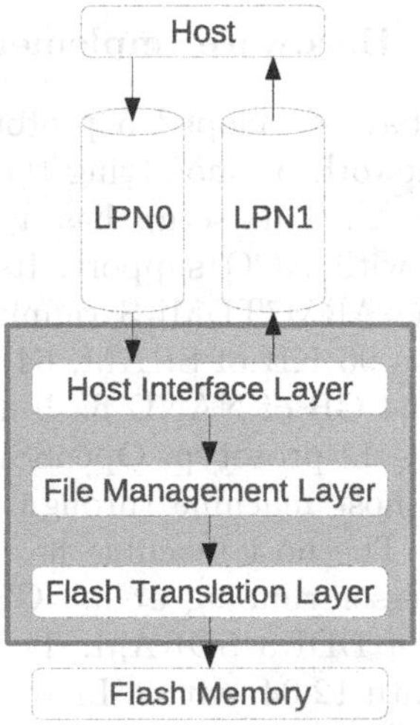

Since the capacity of NAND flash memory is limited, the data region eventually becomes full. The file management layer then deletes the oldest data to make space for new data. This is the only situation where the stored data are deleted. If this attribute is known to attackers, it could be exploited. However, var-

Fig. 2. The firmware architecture of the *Soteria Security Card*. The layers in the grey box are part of the firmware. The term "LPN" stands for Logical Page Number.

ious defense mechanism are possible, which depend on the application. Details of some defense mechanisms will be presented through the examples in the following sections.

The file management layer operates based on commands. The commands are given through the host interface. The host interface interprets the SATA protocol. One way to implement the commands to the file management layer is to modify the SATA protocol, because the SATA protocol also operates based on commands. For example, we may extend the SATA protocol using unused SATA commands. However, this requires modifications to the SATA device driver in the host OS. To minimize modifications, we implement the commands on top of the SATA protocol.

We introduce two logical pipes on top of the SATA protocol, as illustrated in the upper half of Figure 2. Logical page number 0 (LPN0) is always written by the host and LPN1 is written by the SSC. Under normal SATA protocol, writing to LPN0 means writing data to a physical page associated with LPN0. In SSC, this is interpreted as a command. Similarly, writing data to LPN1 is interpreted by the SSC as a response. From the perspective of the host, it is not required to modify the SATA device driver. Since there are many variations of SATA device drivers, depending on the manufacturer, modifying the entire SATA device driver is impractical. Instead, using two logical pipes requires only a simple device driver for the SSC. The SSC driver is, thus, independent of the manufacturer and platform, because it works over existing SATA device drivers.

2.2 Hardware Implementation

We have developed a prototype of the SSC framework by modifying the OpenSSD platform [2]. This setup has a SATA 2.0 interface with NCQ support. Its microcontroller is the ARM7TDMI-S running at 87.5 MHz. It has 96 KB of SRAM, 64 MB of SDRAM, and 64 GB of NAND flash memory. Figure 3 shows the prototype OpenSSD board attached to a host machine through the SATA interface. The host machine has an Intel Core i3 processor running at 3.3 GHz and having 4 GB of DDR3 SDRAM. The OS installed is Ubuntu 12.04, with a Linux kernel version of 3.9.2. The measured throughput of SSC in this environment is 100.71 KB/s.

Fig. 3. The Soteria Security Card implemented on an OpenSSD board and attached to a host machine through the SATA interface

3   Log Protection Through the Use of the SSC Framework

3.1   Problem Statement

The primary target of log protection is any server generating logs. When the administrator detects or suspects an attack, he/she usually investigates it by examining the logs. If the logs are contaminated or removed, it is extremely difficult for the administrator to deal with the attacks [3–6]. Even worse, the administrator may not even be aware of the attack(s) if the logs are fabricated. If the attacker manages to obtain root privileges, they can make changes to every file, including the logs.

This paper assumes the strongest adversary, i.e., one that can obtain root privileges and make changes to anything they want, including the OS, device drivers, file systems, and applications. Our goal is to prevent the attacker from modifying or removing the logs, even if they obtain root privileges. The ultimate goal of the proposed mechanism is to prevent an attacker from modifying *existing* logs. Of course, if the intruder obtains root privileges, they can stop logging, or they can start generating forged logs *after* the intrusion. However, they cannot make changes to *existing* logs that have been generated *before* the intrusion. If the attacker obtains root privileges by using some sort of hacking tool, the history of using the tool will be recorded in the logs and the logs would not be modifiable. Additionally, the location where the attack originated from will also be traced in the log file. Therefore, the logs would still hold valuable information for the administrator to investigate, even if the attacker obtains all-encompassing root privileges.

In summary, the scope of the proposed technique is as follows:

- **Target system:** Servers generating logs.
- **Threat model:** Attackers may have root privileges to modify or remove logs.
- **Goal:** Prevent attackers from modifying and removing existing logs.

3.2 Employing SSC for Log Protection

Since SSC is an append-only storage solution, it is very well suited to applications that maintain log information, whereby new data is constantly added, but existing data is not supposed to be overwritten. Figure 4 illustrates how SSC may be used to protect logs.

We do not change the existing path to store logs. When a server needs to generate logs, it uses Application Programming Interfaces (APIs) provided by a file system, such as open, write, and close. The file system updates meta data and log data. These are actually stored on a hard drive through a block device driver.

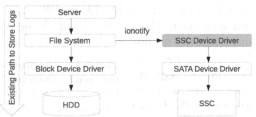

Fig. 4. High-level system overview of how SSC may be used to store and protect log information

To snoop logs from the existing path, we exploit the `ionotify` capability that is supported by modern file systems. Users can be notified when an event occurs to any file. The SSC device driver can be notified when new log data is written to a log file. In the case of Linux, the shell command "`tail -F`" works using `ionotify`.

It should also be noted that the "`tail -F`" command does not incur significant performance overhead. This is because it does not keep monitoring (polling) the file, but, instead, the file system issues a notification when an event occurs. Also, this command runs in a separate process, independently from the server that generates logs. Since the write operation to the SSC is performed by a separate process – and not by the server itself – the access latency to the SSC does not affect the performance of the server.

The intruder may generate a huge amount of dummy logs, so that the old logs would be erased from the SSC memory. We call this a *log flooding attack*.

To cope with log flooding attacks, we first need to detect them. To do so, we employ a threshold-based mechanism. If the rate of incoming logs, in terms of events per second (eps), exceeds a pre-defined threshold for longer than a pre-defined period of time, a log flooding attack is declared. Since the range of normal logging rates varies with the system, the threshold should be determined by the administrator. When an attack is detected (or suspected), an alarm is sent to the administrator. Upon notification, the firmware intentionally delays any responses, so as to reduce the logging rate. If the responses from the SSC are slowed down, the storing of logs is delayed, which, in turn, slows down the generation of dummy logs. This reaction gives time to the administrator to find a way to handle the attack. The administrator may shut down the network, or copy existing protected logs to a safe place before valid logs are deleted. Each file is identified by its associated minor number. When SSC is installed, the administrator sets which minor number will store log files, so that the defense mechanism can be enabled only for the log files. After initialization is performed, the setting cannot be modified, unless SSC is physically re-installed.

3.3   Performance Evaluation

To evaluate the performance degradation incurred by the SSC, we measured the response time of the Apache 2.2.22 Web Server by using the Apache Benchmark [7]. When the SSC technique is adopted, logs generated from the web server – as well as those from the Linux OS – are recorded by the SSC. When SSC is not employed, all logs are stored as regular files on the hard drive. Table 1 summarizes the results.

The average response time (time per request) increases by a near-negligible 0.88%. In fact, the chosen settings correspond to a very pessimistic worst-case scenario for the SSC, because the response time is unrealistically small due to the very small size of the requested document (only

Table 1. Comparison of Apache Web Server response times between an unprotected system and a system employing the SSC engine. Note that the average response time (time per request) increases by a near-negligible 0.88%.

Item	No Log Protection	SSC
Document length	117 bytes	117 bytes
Number of requests	10000	10000
Time per request	0.113 msec	0.114 msec
	100.00 %	100.88 %
Transfer rate	3.812 MB/sec	3.794 MB/sec
	100.00 %	99.51 %

117 bytes). Moreover, we ran the Apache Benchmark on the same machine where the web server was running. In other words, the reported response time did not include any network delay. In real situations, the size of the request is usually much larger than 117 bytes, and requests are made remotely over the network. Thus, the absolute value of the response time is much larger than that of this experiment. In such situations, the overhead incurred by the SSC would be imperceptible.

The SSC framework aims to minimize its impact on the process(es) running on the server whose operations are being logged, by employing a separate process for storing the logs. Of course, the maximum logging rate supported by SSC is limited by the maximum attainable throughput of the card itself. The measured throughput of the SSC prototype used in this work is 100.71 KB/s. Assuming the log size of one event is 50 bytes, the SSC throughput can support up to 2062.54 events per second (eps). Obviously, the current SSC incarnation cannot be used in a server generating logs at a higher rate than this. However, according to a recent report [8], the average logging rate of various benchmarked devices is lower than 50 eps, and even the average *peak* rate is less than 2000 eps, except in one device (2414 eps). Therefore, even the throughput of the current prototype SSC is enough to support the logging needs of most modern servers. We envision the throughput of future SSC implementations to increase to levels well above the maximum peak logging rates of most (if not all) servers available on the market. The current implementation of the SSC has 64 GB NAND flash memory. Assuming 20 eps and 50 bytes per event, this capacity can accommodate 795 days (2.18 years) worth of logs. This is a sufficiently long time to retain logs, because 96% of data breaches are discovered within a few months [1].

4   File Integrity Checking by the SSC

4.1   Problem Statement

File modification is usually (if not always) a prerequisite or a result of malware. In order for malware to be installed, an existing file is modified, or a new file is secretly placed in the system. Some malware tries to hide itself by replacing existing software utilities, which results in file modification. Therefore, file integrity checking is a powerful tool to find out the cause of attacks and malware. The threat model is that the attacker may modify or install files. Further, our threat model assumes that the attacker may be able to contaminate the reference data.

The scope of the proposed technique is summarized as follows:

- **Target system:** Any type of server.
- **Threat model:** Attackers may modify or install files, and they may be able to update reference data in an authentic way.
- **Goal:** Detect file modification even if the reference data is contaminated.

4.2   Employing the SSC for File Integrity Checking

SSC is employed as storage for the reference data. The a priori measured integrity information is added to SSC in the following format: (*timestamp, comment, reference data*). The timestamp is the time the integrity information is measured. The timestamp is provided by the SSC. The comment is a short description that can be recognized by the administrator. The reference data is the actual integrity information.

Let us consider an example to illustrate how SSC works for integrity checking. The administrator wants to protect the `netstat` utility from unauthorized modification, right after a kernel upgrade. Its checksum is measured and stored to the

SSC with a timestamp "2013-09-12 09:11:11" and a comment saying "upgraded kernel to 3.10.11". When netstat has not been modified further, the integrity checker displays a message "The current file is matched to version 2013-09-12 09:11:11" when the administrator runs the checker. If netstat has been modified by an attacker, but the reference data has *not* been breached, the current file cannot be matched with any record in the reference data. If netstat and the reference data have been modified, a new record is added to SSC with a different timestamp. Note that the timestamp is given by the SSC and *cannot be modified, nor erased under any circumstances.* If the timestamp and the comment are not recognizable to the administrator, the administrator can detect the file modification. Note that if the reference data is modifiable, the attacker may also modify the date of the data file, so that the data file may look unmodified. Detecting unauthorized modification of the timestamp can be automated. When the administrator runs the integrity checker, they specify a certain date when the last authorized modification was made. The integrity checker reports any file whose modification date is later than the given date, or whose integrity information does not match.

The performance of an integrity checker that employs the SSC is compared with an unprotected one in Table 2. The unprotected integrity checker stores reference data as a regular file on a hard-disk drive. Unlike the case of log protection, in this application the SSC af-

Table 2. Comparison of response times between an unprotected integrity checker and an integrity checker employing SSC.

Item	No protection	SSC
Number of files checked	1000	1000
Average file size	108 KB	108 KB
Checksum	MD5	MD5
Response time per file	1.59 msec	1.89 msec

fects the overall system performance, because a separate process is not employed. However, since the integrity checker is an off-line utility and runs in the background, the performance impact on foreground processes can be minimized by assigning a low priority.

5 Related Work

Traditionally, hardware-assisted approaches for information security are involved in encryption (authentication) or monitoring.

The Trusted Platform Module (TPM) [9] is a hardware-assisted approach that offers secure generation of encryption keys. It can also encrypt data using the TPM endorsement key, which is burnt in the hardware during manufacturing. As mentioned in the introduction, once the key is revealed, or the software associated with the TPM is compromised, the encrypted data is not secure any longer. Instead of keeping keys, a security protocol using Physically Uncloneable Functions (PUFs) [10, 11] is an alternative way to provide authentication. PUF is a disordered physical system that cannot be reproduced exactly [10]. TrustZone [12], provided by ARM, enables the implementation of a secure execution environment, by separating the *secure world* from the *normal world.*

The separation is facilitated by hardware. While the proposed SSC aims to protect data from unauthorized modification, the aforementioned approaches can protect data from both unauthorized modification and breaches. SSC can easily accommodate existing encryption techniques, if deemed necessary.

Another category of hardware-assisted security is monitoring. A separate hardware keeps monitoring the main system to check for attacks. This approach is especially useful for detecting rootkits, which compromise the OS kernel. Since rootkits reside within the kernel, it is hard to detect by software-only approaches. Copilot [13], RKRD [14], and KI-Mon [15] are typical examples.

Since logs contain essential information to detect and analyze intrusion, there have been many *software-based* techniques that provide log protection [3–6]. All of these techniques employ cryptography to prevent unauthorized access to logs. However, encryption-based approaches only make it harder to access logs, but not impossible. As described in Section 3, our threat model assumes that the attacker can obtain root privileges and make changes to any software component. In an extreme case, the attacker may delete everything on the hard drive in an unrecoverable manner. In this extreme case, the above-mentioned software-based techniques cannot protect logs from removal, even if the logs are encrypted. This problem still exists in the hardware-assisted log protection technique proposed by Boeck et al. [16], because the hardware is used only for authentication, but the log files are still stored on the hard disk.

File integrity checkers are usually part of Host-based Intrusion Detection Systems (HIDS). Zhang et. al [17] discuss the feasibility of implementing HIDS on a co-processor. In their implementation, the co-processor is attached to a Peripheral Component Interconnect (PCI) bus, whereby the device can issue commands to the main memory. The file integrity monitor can be secured by a virtual machine [18]. The monitor in the host OS checks the integrity of the guest OS.

6   Conclusion

Many software-based security solutions rely on reference data to prevent or detect malicious activities. It is crucial for such approaches to protect the reference data from unauthorized modification in order to guarantee their trustworthy operation. In this paper, we propose the Soteria Security Card, which is a hardware-based append-only storage solution for securing the reference data. SSC is a card attachable to the host machine through a standard bus interface. Since SSC allows only read and append operations, over-write and erase operations are physically impossible. Owing to its attributes, the SSC framework can facilitate efficient log protection and file integrity checking. Experimental results demonstrate that the performance degradation caused by the add-on hardware is negligible. The two example case studies presented in this paper (i.e., log protection and file integrity checking) merely serve as proof-of-concept. The SSC framework may be employed to protect any type of reference data.

Acknowledgement. This research was partly supported by Basic Science Research Program through the National Research Foundation of Korea(NRF) funded by the Ministry of Education, Science and Technology(2012R1A1A2A10044300) and the IT R&D program of MKE/KEIT [10041244, SmartTV 2.0 Software Platform].

References

1. Verison: 2013 data breach investigations report (2013)
2. Chung, H.: Barefoot SSD controller technical reference manual (2011)
3. Takada, T., Koike, H.: NIGELOG: protecting logging information by hiding multiple backups in directories. In: Proceedings of Tenth International Workshop on Database and Expert Systems Applications, pp. 874–878 (1999)
4. Waters, B., Waters, B.R., Balfanz, D., Balfanz, D., Durfee, G., Durfee, G., Smetters, D.K., Smetters, D.K.: Building an encrypted and searchable audit log. In: The 11th Annual Network and Distributed System Security Symposium (2004)
5. Schneier, B., Kelsey, J.: Secure audit logs to support computer forensics. ACM Trans. Inf. Syst. Secur. 2(2), 159–176 (1999)
6. Kawaguchi, N., Ueda, S., Obata, N., Miyaji, R., Kaneko, S., Shigeno, H., Okada, K.: A secure logging scheme for forensic computing. In: Proceedings from the Fifth Annual IEEE SMC Information Assurance Workshop, pp. 386–393 (2004)
7. Foundation, A.S.: Apache HTTP server
8. Butler, J.M.: Benchmarking security information event management (SIEM) (2009)
9. Group, T.C.: Trusted platform module (TPM) specifications (2011)
10. Ruhrmair, U., van Dijk, M.: Pufs in security protocols: Attack models and security evaluations. In: 2013 IEEE Symposium on Security and Privacy (SP), pp. 286–300 (2013)
11. Brzuska, C., Fischlin, M., Schröder, H., Katzenbeisser, S.: Physically uncloneable functions in the universal composition framework. In: Rogaway, P. (ed.) CRYPTO 2011. LNCS, vol. 6841, pp. 51–70. Springer, Heidelberg (2011)
12. ARM: ARM security technology (2009)
13. Petroni Jr., N.L., Fraser, T., Molina, J., Arbaugh, W.A.: Copilot - a coprocessor-based kernel runtime integrity monitor. In: Proceedings of the 13th Conference on USENIX Security Symposium, vol. 13 (2004)
14. Grover, S., Khosravi, H., Kolar, D., Moffat, S., Kounavis, M.: Rkrd: Runtime kernel rootkit detection 48, 224–236 (2009)
15. Lee, H., Moon, H., Jang, D., Kim, K., Lee, J., Paek, Y., ByungHoon, K.B.: KI-Mon: a hardware-assisted event-triggered monitoring platform for mutable kernel object. In: Proceedings of 22nd USENIX Security Symposium (2013)
16. Boeck, B., Huemer, D., Tjoa, A.M.: Towards more trustable log files for digital forensics by means of "trusted computing". In: 24th IEEE International Conference on Advanced Information Networking and Applications, pp. 1020–1027 (2010)
17. Zhang, X., van Doorn, L., Jaeger, T., Perez, R., Sailer, R.: Secure coprocessor-based intrusion detection. In: Proceedings of the 10th Workshop on ACM SIGOPS European Workshop, EW 2010, pp. 239–242. ACM, New York (2002)
18. Quynh, N.A., Takefuji, Y.: A novel approach for a file-system integrity monitor tool of xen virtual machine. In: Proceedings of the 2nd ACM Symposium on Information, Computer and Communications Security, pp. 194–202 (2007)

A DNA Computing System of Modular-Multiplication over Finite Field GF(2^n)

Yongnan Li[1,2], Limin Xiao[1,2], Li Ruan[1,2], Zhenzhong Zhang[1,2], and Deguo Li[1,2]

[1] State Key Laboratory of Software Development Environment,
Beihang University,
Beijing, 100191, China
[2] School of Computer Science and Engineering,
Beihang University,
Beijing, 100191, China
liyongnan.buaa@gmail.com, {xiaolm,ruanli}@buaa.edu.cn,
{zzzhang,lideguo}@cse.buaa.edu.cn

Abstract. The enormous parallel computing ability and high memory density of DNA computing bring potential challenges and opportunities to traditional cryptography. Finite field GF(2^n) is one of the most commonly used mathematic sets for cryptography. It is an open problem that how to implement the arithmetic operations over finite field GF(2^n) based on DNA computing. Existing research has the problem that the lengths of parameters in the DNA tile assembly process could not match each other strictly. This paper proposes a parallel molecular computing system to compute the modular-multiplication, an operation combining multiplication and reduction over finite field GF(2^n). The multiplication and the reduction are executed simultaneously in this system. One concrete example of $1100 \cdot 1001$ *mod* 10011 is proposed to show the details of our tile assembly system. The time complexity of this system is $\Theta(n)$ and the space complexity is $\Theta(n^2)$. This system requires 210 types of computation tiles and 17 types of boundary tiles.

Keywords: Modular-multiplication, Tile assembly model, Tile assembly system, Finite field GF(2^n), DNA tile.

1 Introduction

The field of DNA based computing, creatively proposed by Leonard Adleman [1], is a new calculation method that used biological molecule DNA as calculation medium and biochemical reaction as calculation tool. Two major advantages of DNA computing lie in huge memory capacity and high parallelism, which — in data processing — leads molecule computing procedures to solve many combinatorial optimization problems (such as maximal clique problem [2], satisfiability problem [3], 0-1 integer knapsack problem [4], graph isomorphism problem [5], set-partition problem [6], etc). Several researches have also proved that the molecular computer is possible to perform parallel computation in the future [7]. The tile assembly model [8–10] is a commonly used DNA computing model. It is an extension of the model presented by Wang [11]. Tile assembly system is a concept of the computation through self-assembly process of the DNA tiles

J. Kołodziej et al. (Eds.): ICA3PP 2013, Part I, LNCS 8285, pp. 301–311, 2013.

based on the theoretical underpinnings of tile assembly model. The implementation of tile assembly system is a process of folding a single long scaffold strand into an arbitrary shape by using small helper strands [12–14].

Finite field $GF(2^n)$, in which carry bits do not need to be propagated, is one of the most commonly used mathematic sets for error-correcting codes [15] and cryptography [16–18]. There is very little research that has been proposed to compute the arithmetic over finite field $GF(2^n)$. A few studies proposed parallel tile assembly models for basic operations over finite field $GF(2^n)$[19, 20]. However, the polynomials, the length of which were not constant, were defined as the basic computing units, so the lengths of parameters in the assembly process could not match each other strictly. Our previous works[21–23], in which the basic parameters were coded as single bits, have discussed the square, the modular-square and the modular-multiplication over finite field $GF(2^n)$.

This paper proposes one parallel tile assembly system which could compute the modular-multiplication over finite field $GF(2^n)$. Differing our previous research in [23], two operations — multiplication and reduction — are executed simultaneously to obtained the final result over finite field $GF(2^n)$. In order to verify the correctness of the tile assembly system, rigorous theoretical proofs are described and a specific computing instance is given after defining the basic tiles and the assembly rules. This DNA computing system could complete process of parallel computing within linear assembly time, and it cost less tile assembly steps compared with [23]. The modular-multiplication is one of the fundamental operations over finite field $GF(2^n)$. Many researches have been proposed to deal with parallel computation of these basic operations as part of elliptic curves cryptosystem over this specific finite field. These studies mainly focus on reducing computing unit [24, 25], accelerating computing speed [26, 27] and lowering power consumption [28, 29]. Our work, differing from these researches, contributes on figuring out the result in linear assembly time, and it is supposed to obtain the solution space within as less tile assembly steps as possible.

The rest of this paper is organized as follows. Next section will introduce the tile assembly model. Section 3 will describe our tile assembly system that computes the modular-multiplication over finite field $GF(2^n)$. Section 4 will provide a conclusion of the contributions.

2   Tile Assembly Model

The tile assembly model [30, 31] will be introduced in this section. Σ is a four-tuple $\{\sigma_N, \sigma_S, \sigma_W, \sigma_E\} \in \Sigma^4$, including the binding domains on the north, south, west and east. The set of directions $D = \{N, S, W, E\}$ is a set of four functions from positions to positions i.e. $\mathbb{Z}^2$ to $\mathbb{Z}^2$.

The positions (x, y) and (x', y') are neighbors if $\exists d \in D$ such that $d(x, y) = (x', y')$. For a tile t, for $d \in D$, $bd_d(t)$ is referred as the binding domain of tile t on d's side. A special tile $empty = <null, null, null, null>$ represents the absence of all other tiles. The position relationships are listed as follows:

$$\begin{cases} E(x,y) = (x+1,y) \\ W(x,y) = (x-1,y) \\ S(x,y) = (x,y-1) \\ N(x,y) = (x,y+1) \end{cases} \tag{1}$$

A strength function $g : \Sigma \times \Sigma \to \mathbb{R}$, where g is commutative and $\forall \sigma \in \Sigma$, $g(null, \sigma) = 0$, denotes the strength of the binding domains, the value of which may be 0, 1 or 2 (called *null*, *weak*, *strong* bonds, respectively). It is common to assume that $g(\sigma, \sigma') = 0 \Longleftrightarrow \sigma \neq \sigma'$. The binding domains determine the interaction between tiles when two tiles attach to each other. Finally, a tile system $\mathbb{S}$ is a triple $< T, g, \tau >$, where T is a finite set of tiles containing *empty* tile, g is a strength function, and $\tau \geq 0$ is a parameter about the temperature. This paper uses $g = 1$ to denote $\forall \sigma \in \Sigma$, $g(\sigma, \sigma) = 1$ and $\forall \sigma \neq \sigma'$, $g(\sigma, \sigma') = 0$.

If A is a configuration, then within $\mathbb{S}$, a tile t can attach to A at position (x,y) and produce a new configuration A'. The conditions are listed as follows:

$$\begin{cases} A(x,y) = empty \\ \Sigma_{d \in D}\, g(bd_d(t), bd_{d-1}(A(d(x,y)))) \geq \tau \\ \forall (u,v) \in \mathbb{Z}^2, (u,v) \neq (x,y) \Rightarrow A'(u,v) = A(u,v) \\ A'(x,y) = t \end{cases} \tag{2}$$

Given a tile system $\mathbb{S} =< T, g, \tau >$, a set of seed tiles Γ, and a seed configuration $S : \mathbb{Z}^2 \leftarrow \Gamma$, one may attach tiles of T to S if the above conditions are satisfied. A tile can attach to a configuration only in empty positions and only if the appropriate binding domains match the tiles in neighboring positions.

Configuration produced by $\mathbb{S}$ on S is the process of attaching tiles from T to S. If this process terminates, the final configuration with no more attachments could be produced. If all possible final configurations are identical for every sequence of tile attachment, then $\mathbb{S}$ is said to produce a unique final configuration on S.

3 Modular-Multiplication

In this section, a tile assembly system will be presented to compute the modular-multiplication over finite field GF(2^n). According to the characteristic of finite field GF(2^n), carry bits do not need to be propagated in the process of mathematic computation.

Fig. 1 shows the concept tile, with two input sides (west and south) and two output sides (east and north), of the tile assembly system of modular-multiplication.

Theorem 1. Let $\Sigma = \{$ ###, #11, #10, 000, 001, 010, 011, 100, 101, 110, 111, 0'00, 0'01, 0'10, 0'11, 1'00, 1'01, 1'10, 1'11, 200, 201, 210, 211, 300, 301, 310, 311, 0##, 1##, 0'##, 1'##, 2##, 3##, 01#, 11#, 0'1#, 1'1#, 21#, 31# $\}$, $g = 1, \tau = 2$, and T be a set of tiles over Σ as described in Fig. 2. Then $\mathbb{S} =< T, g, \tau >$ computes the function $c(x) = a(x)b(x) \bmod f(x)$ over finite field GF(2^n). $1'$ only denotes the different case from 1 in the assembly process, and they represent the same value in the coding principle.

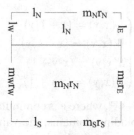

Fig. 1. The concept tile. The tile has two input sides (west and south) and two output sides (east and north). The l_N bit is the value of the tile. In every computation tile, $m_N r_N = m_W r_W$, $m_E r_E = m_S r_S$. The values of l_N and l_E depend on different input cases.

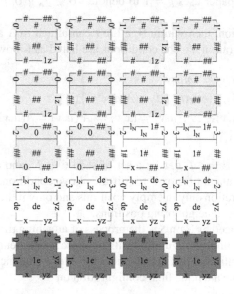

Fig. 2. The computation tiles. The parameters $d, e, x, y, z \in \{0, 1\}$. The total number of computation tiles is 210.

So is the encoding way of $0'$. Let the actual values of $1'$ and $0'$ be equal to 1 and 0, respectively.

As shown in Fig. 2, the l_W bit of the west side has six different values. Once the m_W bit of the west side is f_n while the l_W bit of the west side is 1 or 0, the value of l_E will be assigned as another value, which is different from l_W, to determine different cases. Fig. 3 shows the boundary tiles that are used to construct the seed configuration. Fig. 4 shows the encoding principle of the common seed configuration.

Fig. 5 shows the final configuration of one example, with the solution 110 encoded on the top row. The yellow tiles of the seed configuration are encoded by the four input parameters. The gray tiles are only used for passing the parameter b_i ($0 \leq i \leq n - 1$) from left tile to right tile or performing the operation of a right-shift for the module $f(x)$ and parameter $a(x)$. Magenta tiles identify that what kind of operation this assembly

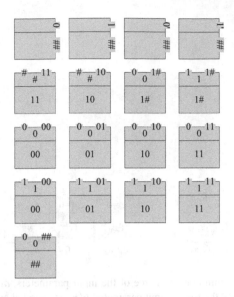

Fig. 3. The boundary tiles. The total number of boundary tiles is 17.

row would execute by assigning its l_E bit as 3 or 2 or $1'$ or $0'$. In the magenta tiles, the value of l_E is not equal to l_W. The white tiles are the actual computation tiles used in the process of self-assembly. Fig. 6 shows the assembly order of this example.

The tile identification conditions are listed as follows:

- Magenta tile: $l_W \in \{0,1\}$ and $m_W r_W \neq$ ##,
- White tile: $l_W \in \{0', 1', 2, 3\}$ and $m_W r_W \neq$ ##,
- Gray tile: $m_W r_W =$ ##.

Proof of Theorem 1. Consider the tile system $\mathbb{S}$. Let $a(x)$ and $b(x)$ be the numbers to multiply over finite field GF(2^n). Let $f(x)$ and $c(x)$ be the module and the result. The sizes, in bits, of $a(x), b(x), f(x)$ and $c(x)$, are $n, n, n+1$ and $2n-1$, respectively. For all $i \in \mathbb{N}$, let $a_i, b_i, f_i, c_i \in \{0,1\}$ be such that $a(x) = a_{n-1} \ldots a_0$, $b(x) = b_{n-1} \ldots b_0$, $f(x) = f_n \ldots f_0$ and $c(x) = c_{2n-2} \ldots c_0$. In this tile assembly system, we define that $\forall u \in \{0,1\}$, $xor(\#, u) = u$, $xor(u, \#) = u$ and $xor(\#, \#) = \#$.

Let $\Gamma = \{ \alpha_{\#11} = <$ #11, *null, null, null* $>$, $\alpha_{\#10} = <$ #10, *null, null, null* $>$, α_{000} $= <$ 000, *null, null, null* $>$, $\alpha_{001} = <$ 001, *null, null, null* $>$, $\alpha_{010} = <$ 010, *null, null,* $null >$, $\alpha_{011} = <$ 011, *null, null, null* $>$, $\alpha_{100} = <$ 100, *null, null, null* $>$, $\alpha_{101} = <$ 101, *null, null, null* $>$, $\alpha_{110} = <$ 110, *null, null, null* $>$, $\alpha_{111} = <$ 111, *null, null, null* $>$, $\alpha_{01\#} = <$ 01#, *null, null, null* $>$, $\alpha_{11\#} = <$ 11#, *null, null, null* $>$, $\alpha_{0\#\#} = <$ 0##, *null,* $null, null >$, $\beta_{0\#\#} = <$ *null, null, null,* 0## $>$, $\beta_{1\#\#} = <$ *null, null, null,* 1## $>$, $\beta_{0'\#\#}$ $= <$ *null, null, null,* 0'## $>$, $\beta_{1'\#\#} = <$ *null, null, null,* 1'## $> \}$.

In finite field GF(2^n), f_n and f_0 — the highest bit and the lowest bit of the module — would always be 1. Then the seed configuration $S : \mathbb{Z}^2 \rightarrow \Gamma$ is such that

- $S(0, -1) = \alpha_{\# f_n a_{n-1}}$,
- $\forall i \in \{1, \ldots, n-1\}, S(i, -1) = \alpha_{0 f_{n-i} a_{n-1-i}}$,
- $S(n, -1) = \alpha_{0 f_0 \#}$,

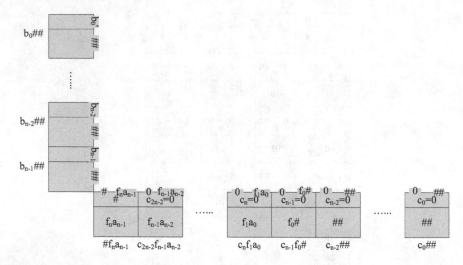

Fig. 4. The common seed configuration. Three of the input parameters, $a(x), f(x)$ and $c(x)$, are coded on the bottom row and the fourth input parameter, $b(x)$, is encoded on the leftmost column. As the length of $c(x)$ would be already smaller than $f(x)$ on the top row, b_0, the lowest bit of $b(x)$, have to be encoded as $1'$ or $0'$ — representing 1 or 0, respectively — to avoid executing one reduction operation.

- $\forall i \in \{n+1, \ldots, 2n-1\}, S(i, -1) = \alpha_{0\#\#}$,
- $\forall j \in \{0, \ldots, n-2\}, S(-1, j) = \beta_{b_{n-1-j}\#\#}$,
- $S(-1, n-1) = \begin{cases} \beta_{0'\#\#}, & \text{if } b_0 = 0 \\ \beta_{1'\#\#}, & \text{if } b_0 = 1 \end{cases}$.

Σ has 210 computation tiles with the west side and the south side as the input sides, and the east side and the north side as the output sides. There would be only one single position where a tile may attach to S since its west neighbor tile and south neighbor tile are fixed. Obviously, the self-assembly process begins from the position $(0,0)$. For $\forall t \in T$, the two-tuple $< bd_S(t), bd_W(t) >$ is unique. It is certain that $\mathbb{S}$ produces a unique final configuration on S. The abutting binding domains of two tiles have to match each other when a tile attaches to S.

Let the final configuration be F. For all $0 \le i \le 2n-1, 0 \le j \le n-1$, S and F agree on $S(i, -1)$ and $S(-1, j)$. For $0 \le i \le 2n-1, 0 \le j \le n-1$, let $t = F(i, j)$. Since t binds with two neighbor tiles, $bd_S(t) = bd_N(F(i, j-1)), bd_W(t) = bd_E(F(i-1, j))$. For those tiles with three-bit binding domains bd, let $l(bd)$ be the first bit, $m(bd)$ be the second bit, and $r(bd)$ be the third bit. Then, $mr(bd)$ represents the second bit and the third bit. For all $t \in T$, let $v(t) = l(bd_N(t))$. Thus, the initial inputs of all binding domains are

- $l(bd_S(F(0,0))) = \#$,
- $\forall 1 \le i \le 2n-1, l(bd_S(F(i,0))) = 0$,
- $\forall 0 \le i \le n, m(bd_S(F(i,0))) = f_{n-i}$,
- $\forall n+1 \le i \le 2n-1, m(bd_S(F(i,0))) = \#$,

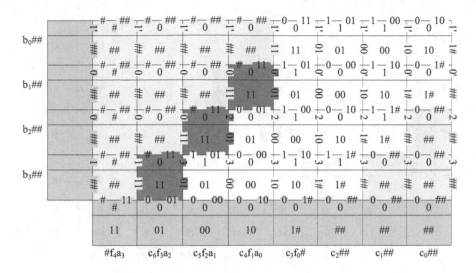

Fig. 5. The final configuration of one sample input of $a(x) = 1100$, $b(x) = 1001$, $f(x) = 10011$ and $c(x) = 0000000$. The top row reads the solution:110. Note that the colors are only used for a better understanding, the tiles themselves have no sense of color.

- $\forall 0 \le i \le n-1, r(bd_S(F(i,0))) = a_{n-1-i}$,
- $\forall n \le i \le 2n-1, r(bd_S(F(i,0))) = \#$,
- $\forall 0 \le j \le n-2, l(bd_W(F(0,j))) = b_{n-1-j}$,
- $l(bd_W(F(0,n-1))) = \begin{cases} 0', & \text{if } b_0 = 0 \\ 1', & \text{if } b_0 = 1 \end{cases}$,
- $\forall 0 \le j \le n-1, mr(bd_W(F(0,j))) = \#\#$.

For all computation tiles, the tile color determines which operation this tile would perform. All cases are listed as follows:

- Gray tile: Only data transfer is performed in this tile. $l_N = l_S$, $l_E = l_W$.
- Magenta tile: The l_N bit is assigned as #. The value of l_E would be different from l_W. If $l(bd_W(t)) = 1$ and $xor(l(bd_S(t)), r(bd_W(t))) = 1$, which means that the highest bit of the dividend $c(x)$ is 1, one reduction would be needed to decrease the power of the index. Therefore, the value of $l(bd_E(t))$ would be assigned as 3 to compute $xor(l(bd_S(t)), m(bd_W(t)), r(bd_W(t)))$ — bitwise XOR operation between $c(x)$, $a(x)$ and $f(x)$ — for the rest of the tiles on that row; If $l(bd_W(t)) = 1$ and $xor(l(bd_S(t)), r(bd_W(t))) = 0$, the highest bit of the dividend $c(x)$ would be 0. Thus, $l(bd_E(t))$ would be assigned as $1'$ and the rest tiles on that row only need to compute the operation of $xor(l(bd_S(t)), r(bd_W(t)))$, one bitwise addition between $c(x)$ and $a(x)$ over finite field GF(2^n); If $l(bd_W(t)) = 0$ and $l(bd_S(t)) = 1$, which means the highest bit of the dividend $c(x)$ is 1, one reduction has to be executed to decrease the power of the index, and the operation of $xor(l(bd_S(t)), m(bd_W(t)))$ — bitwise XOR operation between $c(x)$ and $f(x)$ — would be calculated by encoding $l(bd_E(t))$ as 2 on that row; If $l(bd_W(t)) = 0$ and $l(bd_S(t)) = 0$, only the operation of a right-shift is needed on that row, so $l(bd_E(t))$ is assigned as $0'$.

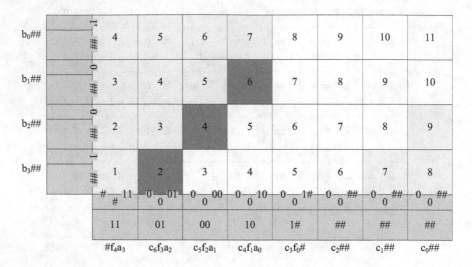

Fig. 6. The assembly order of this example. It costs 11 DNA assembly steps.

- White tile: The value of l_E is assigned as l_W. The value of l_N is computed according to l_W. If $l(bd_W(t)) = 0'$, $l_N = l_S$; If $l(bd_W(t)) = 2$, the operation of $xor(l(bd_S(t)), m(bd_W(t)))$ would be calculated to decrease the power of the index; If $l(bd_W(t)) = 1'$, only bitwise addition over finite field $GF(2^n)$ is needed to perform $xor(l(bd_S(t)), r(bd_W(t)))$; If $l(bd_W(t)) = 3'$, both bitwise addition and decreasing the power of the index are needed, so $xor(l(bd_S(t)), m(bd_W(t)), r(bd_W(t)))$ is performed.

For $\forall 0 \leq i \leq 2n - 1$, $\forall 0 \leq j \leq n - 1$, the followings expressions are the tile assembly rules:

$$- \; l(bd_N(t)) = \begin{cases} xor(l(bd_S(t)), m(bd_W(t)), r(bd_W(t))), \\ \qquad \text{if } l(bd_W(t)) = 3 \\ xor(l(bd_S(t)), r(bd_W(t))), \\ \qquad \text{if } l(bd_W(t)) = 1' \\ xor(l(bd_S(t)), m(bd_W(t))), \\ \qquad \text{if } l(bd_W(t)) = 2 \\ \#, \qquad \text{if } l(bd_W(t)) = 0 \text{ and} \\ \qquad \quad mr(bd_W(t)) \neq \#\# \\ \#, \qquad \text{if } l(bd_W(t)) = 1 \text{ and} \\ \qquad \quad mr(bd_W(t)) \neq \#\# \\ l(bd_S(t)), \qquad \text{else cases} \end{cases}$$

$- \; mr(bd_N(t)) = mr(bd_W(t))$

$$- \ l(bd_E(t)) = \begin{cases} 1', & \text{if } l(bd_W(t)) = 1 \text{ and} \\ & mr(bd_W(t)) \neq \#\# \text{ and} \\ & xor(l(bd_S(t)), r(bd_W(t))) \\ & = 0 \\ 3, & \text{if } l(bd_W(t)) = 1 \text{ and} \\ & mr(bd_W(t)) \neq \#\# \text{ and} \\ & xor(l(bd_S(t)), r(bd_W(t))) \\ & = 1 \\ 0', & \text{if } l(bd_W(t)) = 0 \text{ and} \\ & mr(bd_W(t)) \neq \#\# \text{ and} \\ & l(bd_S(t)) = 0 \\ 2, & \text{if } l(bd_W(t)) = 0 \text{ and} \\ & mr(bd_W(t)) \neq \#\# \text{ and} \\ & l(bd_S(t)) = 1 \\ l(bd_W(t)), & \text{else cases} \end{cases}$$

$- \ mr(bd_E(t)) = mr(bd_S(t))$

The concrete process of tile self-assembly in Fig. 5 is listed as follows:

- the 0th row: $b_3 = 1$, $xor(l(bd_S(F(1,0)))$, $r(bd_W(F(1,0)))) = 1$, then, for $2 \leq i \leq 7$, $l(bd_W(F(i, 0))) = 3$, $l(bd_N(F(i, 0))) = xor(l(bd_S(F(i,0)))$, $m(bd_W(F(i,0)))$, $r(bd_W(F(i, 0))))$, $c(x) = 101100$,
- the 1st row: $b_2 = 0$, $l(bd_S(F(2,1))) = 1$, then, for $3 \leq i \leq 7$, $l(bd_W(F(i, 1))) = 2$, $l(bd_N(F(i, 1))) = xor(l(bd_S(F \ (i, 1)))$, $m(bd_W(F(i, 1))))$, $c(x) = 01010$,
- the 2nd row: $b_1 = 0$, $l(bd_S(F(3,2))) = 0$, then, for $4 \leq i \leq 7$, $l(bd_W(F(i, 2))) = 0'$, $l(bd_N(F(i, 2))) = l(bd_S(F(i, 2)))$, $c(x) = 1010$,
- the 3rd row: $b_0 = 1'$, then, for $4 \leq i \leq 7$, $l(bd_N(F(i, 3))) = xor(l(bd_S(F(i, 3)))$, $r(bd_W(F(i, 3))))$, $c(x) = 0110$.

As $\tau = 2$, only one tile with two neighbors may attach at any time in this system. Therefore, no tile could attach to the configuration unless its west neighbor and south neighbor have already existed. When $F(2n-1, n-1)$ tile attaches to the position $(2n-1, n-1)$, this parallel molecular computation of modular-multiplication will terminate. Obviously, the assembly time of this system is $T(n) = 2n + n - 1 = 3n - 1 = \Theta(n)$ and the space complexity is $S(n) = 2n \cdot n = \Theta(n^2)$. This system of modular-multiplication over finite field GF(2^n) requires a constant number of different tile types: 210 types of computation tiles and 17 types of boundary tiles.

4 Conclusions

This paper proposes a tile assembly system to compute the modular-multiplication over finite field GF(2^n). This tile assembly system was extended from the methods of implementing arithmetic computations used by Brun for binary addition and multiplication [30]. One example over finite field GF(2^4) was provided to show the details of our system. This system could fulfill the process of self-assembly and figure out the solution in linear assembly time. The assembly time of this system is $T(n) = \Theta(n)$ and the space complexity is $S(n) = \Theta(n^2)$. This system requires 210 types of computation tiles and 17 types of boundary tiles.

Acknowledgments. This study is sponsored by the fund of the State Key Laboratory of Software Development Environment under Grant No. SKLSDE-2012ZX-06, the Hitech Research and Development Program of China (863 Program) under Grant No. 2011AA01A205, Beijing Natural Science Foundation under Grant No. 4122042, the National Natural Science Foundation of China under Grant No. 61232009, the National Natural Science Foundation of China under Grant No. 61003015 and the National Natural Science Foundation of China under Grant No. 61370059.

References

1. Adleman, L.M.: Molecular computation of solutions to combinatorial problems. Science 266, 1021–1024 (1994)
2. Ouyang, Q., Kaplan, P.D., Liu, S., Libchaber, A.: Dna solution of the maximal clique problem. Science 278, 446–449 (1997)
3. Lipton, R.J.: Dna solution of hard computational problems. Science 268(5210), 542–545 (1995)
4. Darehmiraki, M., Mishmast Nehi, H.: Molecular solution to the 0-1 knapsack problem based on dna computing. Applied Mathematics and Computation 187(2), 1033–1037 (2007)
5. Hsieh, S.Y., Chen, M.Y.: A dna-based solution to the graph isomorphism problem using adleman-lipton model with stickers. Applied Mathematics and Computation 197(2), 672–686 (2008)
6. Chang, W.L.: Fast parallel dna-based algorithms for molecular computation: The set-partition problem. IEEE Transactions on Nanobioscience 6(4), 346–353 (2007)
7. Benenson, Y., Paz-Elizur, T., Adar, R., Keinan, E., Llvneh, Z., Shapiro, E.: Programmable and autonomous computing machine made of biomolecules. Nature 414(6862), 430–434 (2001)
8. Schulman, R., Winfree, E.: Programmable control of nucleation for algorithmic self-assembly. In: Ferretti, C., Mauri, G., Zandron, C. (eds.) DNA 2004. LNCS, vol. 3384, pp. 319–328. Springer, Heidelberg (2005)
9. Rothemund, P.W., Winfree, E.: Program-size complexity of self-assembled squares. In: Proceedings of the Annual ACM Symposium on Theory of Computing, Portland, OR, USA, pp. 459–468 (2000)
10. Winfree, E.: Algorithmic self-assembly of dna. In: Proceedings of 2006 International Conference on Microtechnologies in Medicine and Biology, Okinawa, Japan (2006)
11. Wang, H.: Proving theorems by pattern recognition i. Bell System Technical Journal 40, 1–42 (1961)
12. Rothemund, P.W.: Folding dna to create nanoscale shapes and patterns. Nature 440(7082), 297–302 (2006)
13. Rothemund, P.W.: Design of dna origami. In: Proceedings of IEEE/ACM International Conference on Computer-Aided Design, Digest of Technical Papers (ICCAD 2005), San Jose, CA, United states, pp. 470–477 (2005)
14. Rothemund, P.W.: Beyond watson and crick: Programming dna self-assembly for nanofabrication. In: Proceedings of 2012 7th IEEE International Conference on Nano/Micro Engineered and Molecular Systems, NEMS 2012, Kyoto, Japan, pp. 1–2 (2012)

15. Blahut, R.E.: Theory and practice of error control codes, vol. 126. Addison-Wesley, Reading (1983)
16. Koblitz, N.: Elliptic curve cryptosystems. Mathematics of Computation 48, 203–209 (1987)
17. Miller, V.S.: Use of elliptic curves in cryptography. In: Williams, H.C. (ed.) CRYPTO 1985. LNCS, vol. 218, pp. 417–426. Springer, Heidelberg (1986)
18. Chen, Z.-G., Song, X.-X.: A public-key cryptosystem scheme on conic curves over zn. In: Proceedings of the Sixth International Conference on Machine Learning and Cybernetics, ICMLC 2007, Hong Kong, China, vol. 4, pp. 2183–2187 (2007)
19. Cheng, Z.: Computation of multiplicative inversion and division in gf(2(n)) by self-assembly of dna tiles. Journal of Computational and Theoretical Nanoscience 9(3), 336–346 (2012)
20. Barua, R., Das, S.: Finite field arithmetic using self-assembly of dna tilings. In: Proceeding of the 2003 Congress on Evolutionary Computation (CEC 2003), vol. 4, pp. 2529–2536. IEEE (2003)
21. Li, Y., Xiao, L., Ruan, L., Xie, K., Yao, G.: Square over finite field GF(2n) using self-assembly of DNA tiles. International Journal of Hybrid Information Technology 6(4), 63–70 (2013)
22. Li, Y., Xiao, L., Ruan, L., Liang, A.: Arithmetic computation using self-assembly of DNA tiles: modular-square over finite field GF(2n). In: Proceeding of the 15th IEEE International Conference on High Performance Computing and Communications (HPCC 2013), Zhangjiajie, China. IEEE Computer Society (in press, 2013)
23. Li, Y., Xiao, L., Ruan, L.: Parallel molecular computation of modular-multiplication based on tile assembly model. In: Proceeding of the 19th IEEE International Conference on Parallel and Distributed Systems Workshops (ICPADS 2013 Workshops), Seoul, Korea. IEEE Computer Society (in press, 2013)
24. Hassan, M.N., Benaissa, M., Kanakis, A.: Flexible hardware/software co-design for scalable elliptic curve cryptography for low-resource applications. In: Proceedings of the International Conference on Application-Specific Systems, Architectures and Processors, Rennes, France, pp. 285–288 (2010)
25. Hassan, M.N., Benaissa, M.: A scalable hardware/software co-design for elliptic curve cryptography on picoblaze microcontroller. In: Proceedings of 2010 IEEE International Symposium on Circuits and Systems: Nano-Bio Circuit Fabrics and Systems, Paris, France, pp. 2111–2114 (2010)
26. Cohen, A.E., Parhi, K.K.: Fast reconfigurable elliptic curve cryptography acceleration for gf(2 m) on 32 bit processors. Journal of Signal Processing Systems 60(1), 31–45 (2010)
27. Li, Y., Xiao, L.: Parallelization of two arithmetic operations over finite field gf(2n). International Journal of Security and its Applications 6(2), 223–228 (2012)
28. Seo, S.C., Han, D.G., Kim, H.C., Hong, S.: Tinyecck: Efficient elliptic curve cryptography implementation over gf(2m) on 8-bit micaz mote. IEICE Transactions on Information and Systems E91-D(5), 1338–1347 (2008)
29. Seo, S.C., Han, D.-G., Hong, S.: Tinyecck16: An efficient field multiplication algorithm on 16-bit environment and its application to tmote sky sensor motes. IEICE Transactions on Information and Systems E92-D(5), 918 (2009)
30. Yuriy, B.: Arithmetic computation in the tile assembly model: Addition and multiplication. Theoretical Computer Science 378(1), 17–31 (2007)
31. Yuriy, B.: Nondeterministic polynomial time factoring in the tile assembly model. Theoretical Computer Science 395(1), 3–23 (2008)

A Message Logging Protocol
Based on User Level Failure Mitigation

Xunyun Liu, Xinhai Xu, Xiaoguang Ren, Yuhua Tang, and Ziqing Dai

State Key Laboratory of High Performance Computing
National University of Defense Technology, Changsha, China
xuxinhai@nudt.edu.cn

Abstract. Fault-tolerance and its associated overheads are of great concern for current high performance computing systems and future exascale systems. In such systems, message logging is an important transparent rollback recovery technique considering its beneficial feature of avoiding global restoration process. Most previous work designed and implemented message logging at the library level or even lower software hierarchy. In this paper, we propose a new message logging protocol, which elevates payload copy, failure handling and recovery procedure to the user level to present a better handling of sender-based logging for collective operations and guarantee a certain level of portability. The proposed approach does not record collective communications as a set of point-to-point messages in MPI library; instead, we preserve application data related to the communications to ensure that there exists a process which can serve the original result in case of failure. We implement our protocol in Open MPI and evaluate it by NPB benchmarks on a subsystem of Tianhe-1A. Experimental results outline a improvement on failure free performance and recovery time reduction.

Keywords: Fault tolerance, Message logging, Checkpointing, User Level, Rollback-recovery.

1 Introduction

In a constant effort to deliver steady performance improvements, the size of High Performance Computing (HPC) systems, as observed by the Top 500 ranking, has grown tremendously over the last decade [1]. Unfortunately, the rise in size has been accompanied by an overall decrease in the mean time between failures (MTBF) [2]. In order to make large-scale parallel applications simultaneously survive crashes and mitigate the reliability-wall effects [3] in such systems, we need efficient and reliable fault tolerance mechanisms.

The Message Passing Interface (MPI) has become a de facto standard used to build high-performance applications [4], and fault tolerance for message passing applications is usually achieved by Checkpoint/Restart approach because of its simplicity of implementation and recovery [5]. However its recovery procedure is relatively time-consuming since the failure of one process makes all application

J. Kołodziej et al. (Eds.): ICA3PP 2013, Part I, LNCS 8285, pp. 312–323, 2013.

processes rollback to the last coordinated checkpoint. Message logging protocols present a promising alternative to Checkpoint/Restart, as they do not require coordinated checkpointing and globally rollback. Instead, only the crashed processor is brought back to the previous checkpoint, while the other processors may keep making progress or wait for the recovering processor in a low-power state [2].

To be more precise, message logging is a family of algorithms that attempt to provide a consistent recovery set from checkpoints taken at independent dates [6]. In message logging protocols, message exchanges between application processes are logged during failure free execution to be able to replay them in the same order after a failure, this is the so-called payload copy mechanism [7]. Also, the event logging mechanism is used to correct the inconsistencies induced by orphan messages and nondeterministic events, by adding the outcome of nondeterministic events to the recovery set, so it can be forced to a deterministic outcome (identical to the initial execution) during recovery.

Mainly due to the lack of support from the programming model, most of the previous implementations of message logging are located at the MPI library level, thus recent advances in message logging mostly focused on reducing the overhead of payload copy and event logging in the MPI library and had indeed achieved a reasonable fault tolerance cost [7–9]. But there are still few drawbacks in those researches: firstly, MPI itself has several different implementations (MPICH, Open MPI, etc.), thus it would take effort to transplant a message logging protocol designed for a specific MPI library to another environment. Secondly, fault tolerance ability for collective communications is provided by recording fine-grained point-to-point communications in the MPI library, which results in the inefficiency of the handling of collective operations in payload copy and recovery procedure.

In this paper, we adapt a message-logging protocol to run at the user level, rather than the MPI library level by building it on top of the User Level Failure Mitigation (ULFM) proposal [1]. Imposing a fault tolerance layer above ULFM certainly guarantees a level of portability, and recording the collective communication result into the sender's message logger as a whole alleviates the fault tolerant overhead for collective communications.

The rest of the paper is organized as follows. Section 2 introduces the basic idea behind the User Level Message Logging (ULML) by an example. Section 3 describes our fault-tolerance framework and the implementation. Section 4 discusses our evaluation methodology and demonstrates the superiority of our protocol over the classical method by benchmarking. Then section 5 reviews the related work, and finally, Section 6 concludes the paper.

2 Motivation and Basic Idea

This section starts by analyzing the drawbacks of classical library level message logging when handling collective operations. Afterwards, we introduce the motivation and basic idea behind the user level message logging (ULML).

As with most previous researches on message logging, we assume that the process execution is piecewise deterministic, and communications channels between processes are reliable and FIFO. Therefore, we will concentrate on the faults of computing processes with the assumption of fail-stop fault model.

2.1 Message Logging at Library Level

A parallel program with checkpointing is illustrated in the table below, its execution is constituted by 2 processes, denoted by P_0, P_1, which have been checkpointed to disk before executing any code.

```
1 --CKPT_HERE--
2 int a, int b;
3 MPI_Barrier(MPI_COMM_WORLD);
4 if(my_rank == 0)
5 {
6     a=4;
7   MPI_Send(&a,1,MPI_INT,1,0,MPI_COMM_WORLD);
8 }
9 if(my_rank == 1)
10 {
11   a=5;
12   MPI_Recv(&b,1,MPI_INT,0,0,MPI_COMM_WORLD);
13 }
14 MPI_Allreduce(&a,&b,1,MPI_INT,MPI_MAX,MPI_COMM_WORLD);
```

The pessimistic message logging cited from [2] is chosen to illustrate the classical protocol at MPI library level. It is worth noting that even the recent advances have further refined the logging scheme to record only important events and messages at library level [8–10], they still confront with the same drawback as the original approach does when handling collective operations.

In this approach, a process, before sending a message, has to ask the receiver for a *ticket* (the Reception Sequence Number) to compose the determinant for that message. The determinant and the message are stored in the memory of the sender, and at that point the message can be actually sent to the receiver. Messages at the receiver are processed according to their assigned ticket number, and on recovery ticket numbers can be used to recreate the reception order of all messages. Furthermore, a collective communication should be divided into two point-to-point communications at library level, for the reason that the MPI library of a process must receive the ready signal of the opposing process to finish the implementation. Fig.1 demonstrates the communication procedure at the library level.

After executing this program, message m_1, m_2, m_3, m_4, m_5 and their assigned tickets will be recorded, which indicates that recording fine-grained point-to-point messages for one collective operation induces multiple payload overhead. If a process error occurs at this moment, the substitution needs to replay all the receptions in order of their tickets, thus the performance of recovery will be also remarkably slowed down when the scale of application rises.

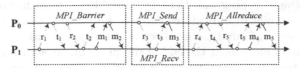

Fig. 1. The communication procedure of the example program with pessimistic message logging at library level, r_i represent requests, t_i represent tickets and m_i represent messages

2.2   Our Approach: Message Logging at User Level

Rabenseifner presented A five-year profiling study of applications running in production mode on the Cray T3E 900 at the University of Stuttgart, and it revealed that more than 40% of the time spent in MPI functions was spent in the two functions MPI_Allreduce and MPI_Reduce [11]. That implies collective communications account for a substantial percentage of total communication cost. Because of performing collectives frequently, scientific computing parallel programs magnify the drawbacks of library level message logging markedly, impelling us to explore an alternative solution at user level.

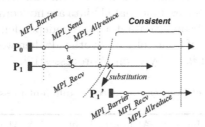

Fig. 2. The communication procedure of the example program with message logging at user level, P_1' is the substitution of P_1, and the system states are denoted by dashed lines

Our approach elevates the checkpointing/rollback mechanism, payload copy mechanism and recovery mechanism to user level, allowing us to record communication as a whole statement without splitting it into implementation details, so that we can re-transmit the result of collectives instead of individual point-to-point messages. For the same example program, Fig.2 presents all the communications at user level, and the payload copy mechanism is detailed below:

- MPI_Barrier: after finishing MPI_Barrier, each process increases a local variable representing the number of barrier operations executed by 1.
- MPI_Send/MPI_Recv: P_0 simply preserves the variable a into the message logger after sending the message to P_1.
- MPI_Allreduce: each process increases a local variable representing the number of all-reduce operations by 1, and then it logs the local variable b which is the result of the operation, into the message logger separately.

After executing this program, P_0 stores variables a, b in the volatile memory as message logs, while P_1 only stores variable b into the message logger. Meanwhile, the statistics information of collective communications is updated in each process. If P_1 malfunctions at the end of the program, as shown in Fig.2, a new incarnation of the failed process denoted by P_1' is recovered from the checkpoint. By exchanging information between process P_0 and P_1', P_0 is informed that variable a needs to be resent and P_1' learns that there are a barrier operation and an all-reduce operation in the coming recovery procedure. So during recovery, P_1' skips the barrier operation, replays reception in MPI_Recv, and when executing MPI_Allreduce, P_1' does not replay the collective communication, instead, it receives the original operation result variable b from P_0 with MPI_Recv statement. Finally, the recovery system reaches a consistent global state after a failure.

2.3   Comparison of Overhead

The user level message logging significantly reduces the overhead of fault-tolerance for collective communications. taking MPI_Allreduce as an example: the all-reduce operation combines values from all processes and distributes the results to all processes, so it is often used when calculating and determining whether the computational accuracy meets the requirement or not at the end of the iteration in scientific computing programs. If we assume that (1)data are not compressed during the all-reduce operation and (2)source data items are independent of one another, table 1 shows the comparison of fault-tolerant overhead when we perform an all-reduce operation of X items of *itsize* bytes on P processes[12].

Table 1. Comparison of overhead induced by different message logging protocols

Message logging	At library level	At user level
Log number	$2 \times (P-1)$	P
Maximum size of each message log	$2 \times \frac{P-1}{P} \times X \times itsize$	$X \times itsize$
Fault free execution time-consumption	$\lceil \lg P \rceil (\alpha + n\beta + n\gamma + n\delta)$	$\lceil \lg P \rceil (\alpha + n\beta + n\gamma) + n\delta$
Minimum recovery time-consumption	$\alpha + n\beta$	$\alpha + n\beta$
Maximum recovery time-consumption	$\lceil \lg P \rceil (\alpha + n\beta)$	$\alpha + n\beta$

In the table above, a simple cost model is used to estimate the cost of the algorithm in terms of latency and bandwidth use. To be specific, α is the latency (or startup time) per message, independent of message size, β is the transfer time per byte, and n is the number of bytes transferred. In the case of reduction operations, we assume that γ is the computation cost per byte for performing the reduction operation locally on any process, and δ is the preservation cost per byte for storing the message into memory.

3   Framework of the Protocol and Its Implementation

Our framework consists of three mechanisms: the **sender based payload copy mechanism** saves exchanged messages into volatile memory; the **communicator maintenance mechanism** is responsible for updating communicator when a process fails; once the improper communicator is updated, the **recovery mechanism** will resend logged messages to the substitution process and ensure the consistency of the system.

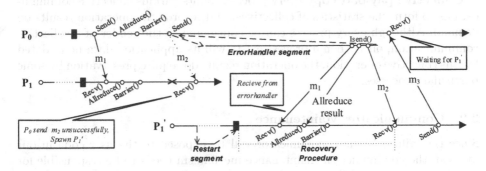

Fig. 3. Example execution of the user level message logging framework, the ErrorHandler segment and the Restart segment are highlighted in bold, and words in bubbles explain the actions of processes

The flow of the framework is illustrated in Fig.3 by an example. At first the application executes normally, P_0 sends a message m_1 to P_1 via MPI_Send and then records m_1 as a message log. When executing the all-reduce operation, both P_0 and P_1 preserve the operation result into memory. After finishing the barrier operation, P_1 fails unexpectedly. P_0 detects the communicator failure when it is trying to send m_2 to P_1, so it moves into the Error Handler segment automatically, then it spawns P_1' as a substitution process, re-transmits the logged message to help P_1' recover. After that, P_0 jumps out of the Error Handler, continues execution or waits for message m_3 from the opposite. On the other side, P_1' takes the place of P_1 in the communicator, jumps to the checkpoint address, reads the live variables and enters the recovery procedure by means of the execution of the Restart segment. During P_1''s recovery, all the external message it needs will be resent by P_0, and it will not replay any collective communication until the recovery completes successfully.

Next, we discuss in further detail about how these three mechanisms work.

3.1   Sender Based Payload Copy

Sender based payload copy rules can be classified into two categories: point-to-point payload copy and collective payload copy, which correspond to the two types of MPI communications.

Point-to-point payload copy for senders, messages sent to the different destinations are kept in different log queues, and those messages are sorted by the assigned Send Sequence Number (SSN) according to the transmission sequence. Also, the length and tag of the message need be recorded alongside in order to rewrite the send statement on demand. In preparation for the transmission, each message will be packed into a flat format with the SSN appended at the end.

For receivers, they need to resolve the SSN after receiving a message, and preserve it into the Highest Sequence number Received (HSR) array representing the latest message received from the sending end. Any message that has a smaller SSN is supposed to have been handled correctly according to our assumption.

Collective payload copy every process counts various collective communications to form the statistics of collectives, and records the operation results on demand. Although every process can be considered as the sender of a collective communication, only when a process exists will its application data be updated by this collective operation, the operation results do require preservation by some particular processes.

3.2   Communicator Maintenance

Since the failure of the communicator will be exposed to the user code in our method, the communicator maintenance mechanism needs to be responsible for the detection of the failure and the restoration of the communicator with the help of the ULFM support.

The communicator could be modified for the purpose of fault tolerance in three cases: process initialization, communicator fault, and the substitution process restart. Thus the maintenance can be divided into three parts, and its work requires the mutual cooperation between processes, as shown in Fig.4.

Communicator maintenance in process initialization for all processes, process initialization is the procedure following the initialization of MPI environment. The maintenance duplicates the communicator from MPI_COMM_WORLD to a globally defined symbol, and attaches our Errorhandler function to the communicator as the default error handling procedure.

Communicator maintenance in Errorhandler the Errorhandler function will be automatically called whenever a process detects the failure on the communicator and returns the error code. In this function, surviving processes revoke the original communicator so that any subsequent operation on the original communicator will eventually fail. Afterwards, they create a new communicator from the revoked one by excluding its failed process. Then the failed processes is discovered by comparing the group of processes in the shrunken communicator with the group of processes in the original communicator. After that, a substitution will be spawned and the inter communicator generated will be merged into an intra-one. Finally the substitution will replace the failure process by reordering the ranks on the new communicator.

Communicator maintenance in Restart segment the Restart segment is a procedure where the substitution operates in collaboration with the surviving processes to merge and reorder the communicator after the MPI environment is initialized. Afterwards, it also attaches our Errorhandler function to the new communicator.

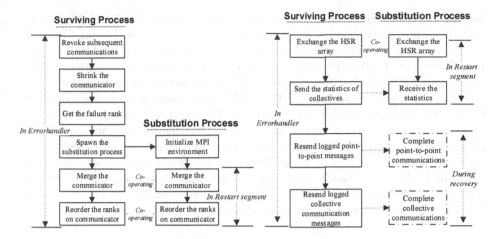

Fig. 4. The flow of the communicator maintenance once a failure occurs

Fig. 5. The flow of the recovery, operations which are dashed may be performed multiple times

3.3   Recovery

Recovery mechanism ensures the consistency of the system by means of operations at user level. There are two key problems that need to be solved: (1) determine which messages need to be re-issued, and (2) guide the substitution process to jump over collective communications correctly during recovery. Therefore the recovery mechanism should exchange the records of reception between processes, and inform the substitution of the number of collective communications which have already been executed. The flow of the recovery mechanism is illustrated in Fig.5.

Recovery mechanism in Errorhandler firstly, each process obtains the Highest Sequence number Received (HSR) arrays which are kept in the other processes' memory, and forms the Highest Sequence number Delivered (HSD) array to determine whether a point-to-point message has been delivered successfully. After that, the logged messages whose SSN is bigger than HSD stored will be resent in order. For the logged collective messages, one of the surviving processes sends the statistics of collective communications to the substitution, Then all the logged collective operation results should be sent successively.

Recovery mechanism in the Restart segment the substitution gets the information it needs (HSR arrays and statistics of collective communication) by the execution of the Restart segment. When entering the recovery procedure, all the point-to-point receptions could be replayed by their original receive statements, and the collective communications will turn into receptions of the logged messages or even empty operations.

3.4   Implementation of User Level Message Logging

User level message logging (ULML) encapsulates the default MPI communication functions (including point-to-point and collective), thereby integrating message logging fault tolerance capabilities in Open MPI. Each of the ULML MPI functions is an implementation of a particular fault tolerant algorithm, and its goal is to extend the communication with message logging features. ULML does not modify any core Open MPI component or the communication semantics, it calls the default MPI interface functions to perform the actual communications.

In order to implement the ULML in MPI programs, programmers need to follow these steps detailed below: 1. Analyze the communication features of the program, and insert user level checkpoints into the original programs with compiler directive $\#CKPT_i$. The method of choosing the positions of checkpoints has already been discussed in [4]. 2. Replace the original error handler function with our ULML error handler to bring in the communication maintenance and recovery mechanism. 3. Replace the original MPI communication functions with ULFM functions, in order to introduce the payload copy mechanism.

4   Experiments

4.1   Evaluation Methodology

Our computer platform is a subsystem of Tianhe-1A, located in Tianjin, China. Each node of the computer is equipped with two 2.93G Intel Xeon X5670 CPUs (12 cores per node) and 24 GB RAM. The interconnection is the same as described in [4], and the simplex point-to-point bandwidth is 80 Gb/s. All the experiments are executed in Redhat 5.5, and the results presented are mean values over 5 executions of each test.

To investigate application performance we use the NAS Parallel Benchmark suite. The CG benchmark presents heavy point-to-point latency driven communications, while the FT benchmark presents a collective communication pattern by performing all-to-all operations. Thus the class C problem of those benchmarks are tested in order to evaluate the performance of point-to-point payload copy and collective payload copy respectively.

Moreover, we choose the naive pessimistic message logging approach from [2] and the active optimistic message logging protocol (O2P) from [10] as comparative methods at library level.

4.2   Fault Free Performance Evaluation on NAS Benchmarks

In Fig.6, we plot the normalized execution time of CG according to a growing number of processors to evaluate the comparative scalability, the standard execution time of coordinated application-level checkpointing/restart equals 1. Notice that only the performance penalty associated with message logging is presented since no checkpoints and faults are imposed. Fig.6 shows that the performance of the ULML and O2P is comparable, the executions of the two protocols are very similar and exhibit the same scalability with the overhead stays under 5%. Conversely pessimistic approach experiences a severe performance degradation topping at 17% increase in execution time, the increasing point-to-point communication rate (19988 times at 64 cores to 25992 times at 128 cores for example) greatly affects the overhead induced by pessimistic message logging. But our ULML is immune to this defect by avoiding any bandwidth consumption, except for appending the SSN which has a negligible influence on the message size. Overall, considering its simplicity of implementation, the ULML presents a salutary alternative to refined message logging protocols at library level.

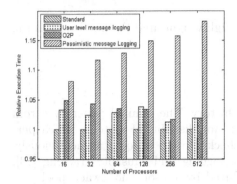
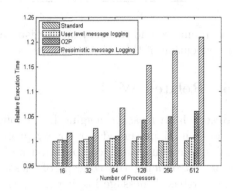

Fig. 6. Scalability of CG Class C   **Fig. 7.** Scalability of FT Class C

Fig.7 presents the execution time of FT with processor numbers ranging from 16 to 512, normalized to each benchmark with standard execution. For up to 512 cores, the scalability of the proposed message logging approach is excellent since the overhead is solely due to sender-based payload logging. Also, O2P works quite well up to 64 processes, but when the amount of data piggybacked continues to increase because the event logger is overloaded and does not manage to log the determinants in time, O2P eventually suffers from at most a 6% slowdown in our test case. The performance superiority is mainly imputed to the better handling of collectives in the ULML, and the overhead induced by it is very close to the error margin of measurements.

4.3   Recovery Performance Evaluation

We simulate a fault on a processor by sending SIGKILL to a process, CG Class C running on 8 processes is chosen as our test case. First we checkpoint the system at iteration 10, then introduce a failure to process 3 at iteration 70. Table 2 presents the elapsed wall clock time and CPU time consumed to recover the system. We find that the ULML reduces the wall clock time by 26.9% and saving CPU time by 22.1%. Also, different phases of the recovery procedure are timed to measure the factors limiting the speed of our restart protocol. Take process 1 as an example: it spends 0.1253 seconds on communicator maintenance in Errorhandler, and 0.002924 seconds on recovery mechanism in Errorhandler to resend 4741 messages (these two time statistics are not stable, but will not exceed 0.2 seconds). After finishing the Errorhandler segment, process 1 enters a suspended state for 59.761 seconds. Therefore, we believe that our communicator

Table 2. Comparison of recovery time-consumption (Seconds)

	Checkpoint/Restart		User level message logging	
	Failure free	Failure occurred	Failure free	Failure occurred
Wall time	2.78	5.24	2.83	3.83
CPU time	21.33	38.54	22.12	30.01

maintenance and recovery mechanism are lightweight, and the bottleneck is the re-execution of the substitution process.

5   Related Work

Research on message logging has a long history. The seminal paper by Strom and Yemini presented a recovery protocol for distributed systems which permits communication, computation and checkpoint to proceed asynchronously, thus introducing the concept of message logging and causality tracking [13]. Sender-based message logging was introduced by Johson and Zwaenepoel [14], by describing how to secure the correctness of the protocol with the Send Sequence Number and the messages logged in sender's volatile memory. Alvisi and Marzullo presented a classification of the different message logging schemes into three families: pessimistic, optimistic, and causal, according to the different methods of logging reception orders [6]. Recently, Bouteiller used determinism in MPI applications to reduce the number of determinants to log [8]. Guermouche proposed an uncoordinated checkpointing protocol for send-deterministic MPI applications and achieved a satisfying overhead [9]. But all the researches above rely on modifying the MPI library, thus they will face portability issues and induce multiple overhead for collectives in all cases.

The User-Level Failure Mitigation proposal was put forward to improve the resilience of application from programming model in 2012. This proposal allows libraries and applications to increase the fault tolerance capabilities by supporting additional types of failures, and build other desired strategies and consistency models to tolerate faults. The ULFM proposal makes it possible to elevate the message logging layer and guarantee the portability.

6   Conclusion

In this article, we introduce the user level message logging protocol, a new kind of portable fault tolerance method for MPI programs. The new methodology proposed is simple yet effective, particularly suited for collective communication intensive programs. Overall, our work facilitates the adoption of message logging in large-scale scientific computing programs.

Acknowledgment. This work is supported by the National Natural Science Foundation of China under Grant No.61303071 and 61120106005, and funds (No.124200011) from Guangzhou Science and Information Technology Bureau.

References

1. Bland, W.: User level failure mitigation in mpi. In: Caragiannis, I., Alexander, M., Badia, R.M., Cannataro, M., Costan, A., Danelutto, M., Desprez, F., Krammer, B., Sahuquillo, J., Scott, S.L., Weidendorfer, J. (eds.) Euro-Par Workshops 2012. LNCS, vol. 7640, pp. 499–504. Springer, Heidelberg (2013)
2. Meneses, E., Bronevetsky, G., Kale, L.V.: Evaluation of simple causal message logging for large-scale fault tolerant hpc systems. In: Proceedings of the 2011 IEEE International Symposium on Parallel and Distributed Processing Workshops and PhD Forum, IPDPSW 2011, pp. 1533–1540. IEEE Computer Society (2011)
3. Yang, X., Wang, Z., Xue, J., Zhou, Y.: The reliability wall for exascale supercomputing. IEEE Transactions on Computers 61, 767–779 (2012)
4. Xu, X., Yang, X., Lin, Y.: Wbc-alc: A weak blocking coordinated application-level checkpointing for mpi programs. IEICE Transactions, 786–796 (2012)
5. Chakravorty, S., Kale, L.: A fault tolerance protocol with fast fault recovery. In: IEEE International Parallel and Distributed Processing Symposium, IPDPS 2007, pp. 1–10 (2007)
6. Alvisi, L., Marzullo, K.: Message logging: Pessimistic, optimistic, causal, and optimal. IEEE Trans. Softw. Eng. 24, 149–159 (1998)
7. Bouteiller, A., Herault, T., Bosilca, G., Dongarra, J.J.: Correlated set coordination in fault tolerant message logging protocols. In: Jeannot, E., Namyst, R., Roman, J. (eds.) Euro-Par 2011, Part II. LNCS, vol. 6853, pp. 51–64. Springer, Heidelberg (2011)
8. Bouteiller, A., Bosilca, G., Dongarra, J.: Redesigning the message logging model for high performance. Concurr. Comput.: Pract. Exper. 22, 2196–2211 (2010)
9. Guermouche, A., Ropars, T., Brunet, E., Snir, M., Cappello, F.: Uncoordinated checkpointing without domino effect for send-deterministic mpi applications. In: 2011 IEEE International Parallel Distributed Processing Symposium (IPDPS), pp. 989–1000 (2011)
10. Bouteiller, A., Ropars, T., Bosilca, G., Morin, C., Dongarra, J.: Reasons for a pessimistic or optimistic message logging protocol in mpi uncoordinated failure recovery. In: IEEE International Conference on Cluster Computing (Cluster 2009), New Orleans, États-Unis, pp. 1–9 (2009)
11. Rabenseifner, R.: Automatic mpi counter profiling of all users: First results on a cray t3e 900-512. In: Proceedings of the Message Passing Interface Developer's and User's Conference(MPIDC 1999), pp. 77–85 (1999)
12. Patarasuk, P., Yuan, X.: Bandwidth efficient allreduce operation on tree topologies. In: IEEE IPDPS Workshop on High-Level Parallel Programming Models and Supportive Environments, pp. 1–8 (2007)
13. Strom, R., Yemini, S.: Optimistic recovery in distributed systems. ACM Trans. Comput. Syst. 3, 204–226 (1985)
14. Zwaenepoel, W., Johnson, D.: Sender-Based Message Logging. In: Proceedings of the Seventeenth International Symposium on Fault-Tolerant Computing, pp. 49–66 (1987)

H-DB: Yet Another Big Data Hybrid System of Hadoop and DBMS

Tao Luo[1], Guoliang Chen[1], and Yunquan Zhang[2]

[1] School of Computer Science and Technology,
University of Science and Technology of China
230027 Hefei, China
luotao1@mail.ustc.edu.cn,
glchen@ustc.edu.cn
[2] State Key Laboratory of Computer Architecture,
Institute of Computing Technology, CAS
100190 Beijing, China
yunquan.cas@gmail.com

Abstract. With the explosion of the amount of data, analytics applications require much higher performance and scalability. However, traditional DBMS encounters the tough obstacle of scalability, and could not handle big data easily. In the meantime, due to the complex relational data model, the large amount of historical data and the independent demand of subsystems, it is not suitable to use either shared-nothing MPP architecture (e.g. Hadoop) or existing hybrid architecture (e.g. HadoopDB) to replace completely. In this paper, considering the feasibility and versatility of building a hybrid system, we propose a novel prototype H-DB which takes DBMSs as the underlying storage and execution units, and Hadoop as an index layer and a cache. H-DB not only retains the analytical DBMS, but also could handle the demands of rapidly exploding data applications. The experiments show that H-DB meets the demand, outperforms original system and would be appropriate for analogous big data applications.

1 Introduction

In many areas such as science, internet and e-commerce etc, the volumn of data to be analyzed grows rapidly [1]. For example, the Large Hadron Collider near Geneva, Switzerland, produced about 15PB of data per year [2]. Petabyte datasets are increasingly the norm today, so do requirements for efficiently extracting value. Yet our ability to store data is fast overwhelming that to process what we store, even read back is distressing. Given the tendency for multi-terabyte and petabyte analytic data repositories, performance and scalability problems become increasingly severe [3].

Google File System (GFS) [4] and MapReduce [5, 6] are developed by Google for large-scale dataset storage and processing. Hadoop [7] is an open source system for distributed computing and big data processing, and is best known for MapReduce and its distributed file system (HDFS) [8, 9]. However, Hadoop yields an order of magnitude slower performance than parallel databases on structured data analysis

J. Kołodziej et al. (Eds.): ICA3PP 2013, Part I, LNCS 8285, pp. 324–335, 2013.
© Springer International Publishing Switzerland 2013

workloads [10]. It lacks many of features that have proven effective, thus, traditional data analytical processing, especially the standard reports and repeated queries, is poorly suited for this one-time query processing model.

Database management system, by comparison, has optimized implementation to improve the efficiency. However, though parallel databases have been proven to scale well into tens of nodes, there exists no published deployment of a parallel database with nodes numbering into thousands.

It is now clear that neither Hadoop nor parallel databases are ideal solutions for big data analytics applications [11,12]. HadoopDB [13] is therefore a hybrid system that combines the scalability advantages of Hadoop with the performance advantages of parallel databases. However, this method uses a data loader to dump the data out of the database and replicate them to some other nodes before processing, which causes loading to be the bottleneck of whole system and one node related to others.

In this paper, we propose our approach to integrate DBMS and Hadoop for performing big data analytics. Similar to HadoopDB, we also take DBMSs as the underlying storage and execution units, and uses Hadoop as the task coordinator and network communication layer. Yet, we add a cache layer and a global index layer in HDFS to further improve the query performance. In our architecture, the following benefits are obtained:

- The cache layer in HDFS is used to store tables with high frequency access but relatively small amount of data from the underlying DBMS nodes. The high concurrency of HDFS avoids the failure of DBMS due to the limit numbers of database connection when multi-user access.
- The DBMS engine executes the sub-queries in parallel with the efficiency advantage as is the case for HadoopDB. The global index layer in HDFS is able to co-operate with the DBMS engines, and significantly improves the performance for certain queries.
- Only few tables and indexes are loaded into HDFS, loading is no longer the bottleneck of whole system. And the underlying DBMS changed nothing to maintain the independence of the original system.

The remainder of the paper is organized as follows: Section 2 introduces the related work; Section 3 analyzes the application requirements and existing systems, and then positions the desired solution; Section 4 describes our proposed system H-DB; Section 5 gives experiment results; and Section 6 concludes the paper.

2   Related Work

There has been some recent work on bringing MapReduce together with DBMS, mainly divided into two categories. The first one focuses on language and interface issues. Yahoo's Pig [14] offers SQL-style high-level data manipulation constructs, which can be assembled in an explicit dataflow and interleaved with custom Map- and Recude- style functions or executables. Hive [15] supports queries expressed in a SQL-like declarative language-HiveQL, which are compiled into map-reduce jobs executed on Hadoop.

The second one focuses on hybrid solution at the system level. HadoopDB means Hadoop database, is the first, as we know, to try to merge parallel DBMS and Hadoop. While DBEHadoop [16] means database Hadoop, integrates modified DBMS engines as a read-only execution layer into Hadoop, where DBMS plays a role of providing efficient read-only operators rather than managing the data. EMC's Greenplum [17] is a unified engine for RDBMS and MapReduce, leverages a shared-nothing architecture using commodity hardware. It is a database system provides both high performance of query processing for OLAP and scalability and fault-tolerance.

3   Systems for Big Data Analytics

3.1   Application Requirements

Our case is the *"Chinese Earthquake Precursor Network Data Management Program"*. Fig. 1 shows the architecture of this network. It is a three-layer structure from bottom to top. There are hundreds of station nodes in bottom layer, tens of regional nodes in middle layer, and only one national node in top layer. One regional node manages several corresponding station nodes, and the national node manages all regional nodes. Each node is an independence DBMS, and establishes connection to others through network. All data stored in the lower-layer node have a replica in the corresponding upper-layer node, i.e. each data has three replicas in whole system. The national node has all the data, and provides analytics service for people.

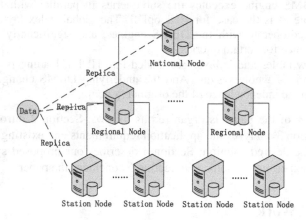

Fig. 1. Architecture of Earthquake Precursor Network

Large-Scale Multi-user Parallel Processing. The data that we should analyze on National node is growing very fast, 2TB daily now. And the system should provide data processing services to at least hundreds of users simultaneously. Thus the National node built on DBMS always fails and we have an urgent need for infrastructure that could deal with large-scale multi-user parallel processing.

High Query Performance. Our application is to do ad-hoc analytic queries over long existing dataset. It is worthwhile to take some optimized data structures, execution mechanism and advantages of system itself to improve the query performance. For example, a) Queries on the same data set often exist, so the cache is usable. b) Some queries are always with predicates on certain attributes, for which using index can reduce the execution time and get benefit to repeated usage. c) The characteristic of existed data replicas in our system can be used in parallel querying.

Independent Original System. Our program is not a completely new development. Each station or regional node is an integral and independent subsystem where engineers do jobs on it. Thus, the previous DBMS-based system can't be changed, and we should find a suitable way to solve the difficulties for new demands of the program.

3.2   HadoopDB Discussed

HadoopDB [23] is an important work to integrate MapReduce and DBMS. The basic idea behind HadoopDB is to take DBMS as the storage and execution units, and Hadoop as a coordination layer that manages task execution and network communication.

However, HadoopDB uses batched approach to dump the data out of each DBMS and replicate them to others before data processing, which causes two troubles: a) It's too stressful for HadoopDB's loader to partition and load the big data, loading would be the bottleneck of system. b) Data movement from one node to another would destroy the integrity and independence of underlying DBMSs. c) Since all DBMSs are single-node database with local index only, and there lacks any global structure mechanism in HadoopDB, it is unable to further improve the query performance when query is with predicates of high selectivity.

4   H-DB System

4.1   Overview

There are two types of tables in our application: one is metadata table with high frequency access but relatively small amount of data, while the other is data table with low frequency access but large amount of data and usually a Blob or Clob attribute to store big objects like files or photos.

The system consists of four parts as shown in Fig. 2. The bottom is the storage layer DBMSs. On top of DBMSs is HDFS, which not only stores the system metadata and result set of query like that in HadoopDB, but also adds a cache layer for metadata tables and a global index layer for data tables. The top is MapReduce system responsible for parallelization and fault tolerance. The middleware contains the

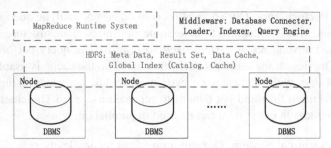

Fig. 2. Architecture of H-DB

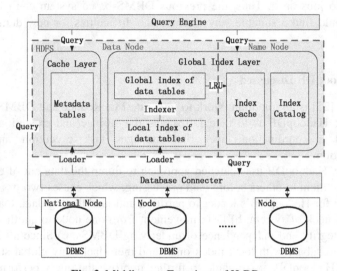

Fig. 3. Middleware Functions of H-DB

database connector, loader, indexer and query engine, and their functions are shown in Fig.3.

Database Connector. The connector is the interface between original DBMSs residing on nodes and Hadoop. It uses DBInputFormat provided by Hadoop to access JDBC-compliant database, and TextOutputFormat to return result into HDFS.

Loader. The loader loads metadata tables and local index of data tables from the underlying DBMS nodes to HDFS. The former are permanently stored in cache layer, while the latter are temporarily lay in global index layer. Only few tables and indexes are loaded into HDFS, thus loading is no longer the bottleneck of system.

Indexer. The indexer creates global index on the loaded local index of data tables. It uses MapReduce paradigm to join the separated local index to be a global index, and delete the local index after success. If global index is too big to search, the indexer would automatically partition it into proper-size files. Besides, the index catalog in HDFS maintains the locations of global index, and is an XML file stored in the local disk of Hadoop's name node. The index cache is also in the same position, where LRU (Least Recently Used) algorithm is adopted as usual to store the index file. The detailed index structure and access method will be presented in Section 4.2.

Query Engine. The query engine provides different execution methods for different input query. For query on metadata tables or data tables without predicate, it directly accesses the cache layer on HDFS or DBMS on National node. Yet, for query on data tables with predicate, it first accesses the global index layer on HDFS to obtain which underlying DBMSs should be sub-queried, then executes sub-queries in each desired DBMSs in parallel. The detailed execution method will be presented in Section 4.3.

4.2   Global Index Mechanism

In order to take advantage of data replicas in our system, we implement a global index mechanism which indexes the data across the whole underlying DBMSs. Using this mechanism, not only national node, but also other nodes with data replica will be accessed. Sub-queries are executed by these nodes in parallel, making performance more efficient.

Index Creation
Since many popular databases provide a pseudo column to locate the physical address of a row in a table, which is generally considered as the fastest way to search for a given row in the database, we use this existing pseudo column to achieve our goal. As a running example, we choose *rowid* (the representation of pseudo column in Oracle) to illustrate the algorithm *index creation* as follows.

1) Load local indexes of all DBMSs into HDFS.

- Do in parallel for each DBMS: load the < *composite primary key, rowid*> pairs from all the records in DBMS to the local index file in HDFS using MapReduce paradigm.

2) Create global index of all local indexes in HDFS.

- Join the local index files on *predicate attribute* (one of *composite primary key*) to be the global index using MapReduce paradigm. The joint-format of global index is < *predicate attribute, rowid$_1$, node$_1$, rowid$_2$, node$_2$, ..., rowid$_n$, node$_n$*>. (n is the number of replicas, and *node$_i$* represents which node the replicas is in)

- If the file size of global index is bigger than a threshold, partition the global index file into proper-size on *predicate attribute*, and update the index catalog.

Considering simplicity, consistency and space utilization, we discuss the improved joint-format of global index in our scenario. Note that there are three data replicas in our application, one replica one layer (see Fig.1). We orderly write the < *rowid$_i$, node$_i$* > (i=1, 2, 3) pairs based on the layer (from top to bottom) of node, while emit the column *node$_1$* due to the only one node (the national node) in top layer. Thus, the improved joint-format of global index in our scenario is < *predicate attribute, rowid$_1$, rowid$_2$, node$_2$, rowid$_3$, node$_3$* >.

Index Access

When the query is with predicate of high selectivity on the attribute, the index access method can be adopted. Before the introduction of algorithm *index access*, we give the definition of *index-tree* which will be used in the algorithm. The *index-tree* is a subset of precursor network mentioned in Section 3.1. Each node of tree contains a list of *rowid* values, and each *rowid* value locates the desired record of this node. Thus, algorithm *index access* can be considered as the construction of *index-tree* as follows.

1) Insert leaf node to index-tree.

- Scan the entire global index file. Mark the row where the value of *predicate attribute* satisfies the predicate. Every different node appeared in the column $node_3$ of these rows is the leaf node.

- Create pointers for every marked row. Each pointer consists of an identifier of this (partition) global index file and an offset within the file to identify the given row. Assign them to the corresponding leaf node based on the value in column $node_3$ of their pointed row.

2) Insert non-leaf node to index-tree.

- Insert the internal nodes and root node to index-tree based on the topological relationship of precursor network. Each non-leaf node contains an empty list of pointers temporarily.

3) Update the list for each node in index-tree.

- Let N be the number of nodes in *index-tree*, and P is the number of pointers of leaf nodes. Then each node should have $P' = \lceil P/N \rceil$ pointers in average.

- Do in parallel for each leaf node: If a node has more than P' pointers, remains the first P' pointers, and moves the rest to the list of its parent internal node.

- Do in parallel for each internal node: If a node has more than P' pointers, remains the first P' pointers, and move the rest to the list of root node.

- Do in parallel for each node: For each pointer in list, find the given row in global index file based on their identifier and offset, get the *rowid* value based on the layer of node (i.e. if node is in layer i, then get the value in column $rowid_i$). Thus, a list of *rowid* values is obtained.

4.3   Query Execution

The algorithm *query execution* provides different execution methods for different input query as follows.

1) Query on metadata tables

- Query the table in HDFS using MapReduce paradigm.

2) Query on data tables without predicate

- Query the table in DBMS of national node.

3) Query on data tables with predicate

- Based on index catalog and predicate, load the desired (partition) global index file from data node of HDFS to index cache in local disk of name node. If the file is existed already, skip this step.

- Call algorithm *index access* on loaded global index file to obtain an *index-tree*.

- Do in parallel for each node of *index-tree*: Based on the *rowid* value of node's list, query the table of corresponding DBMS directly one by one.

4.4   Summary and Analysis

So far we have proposed a hybrid system H-DB integrating DBMS and Hadoop. H-DB uses different optimization strategies for different types of table. For tables with high frequency access but relatively small amount of data (i.e. metadata table), H-DB loads all of them from underlying DBMS nodes to HDFS, and takes advantage of high concurrency of HDFS to guarantee the multi-user accesses. For tables with big data set (i.e. data table), H-DB concentrates on parallelization of query processing. Its global index mechanism makes the underlying DBMS engines execute the sub-queries in parallel for certain queries.

5   Experiments

5.1   Configurations

The experiments are conducted in a cluster consisting of four nodes connected by a gigabit Ethernet. Each node has two quad-core Intel x5550 2.6 GHZ processors, 16GB Memory, and a 2TB RAID level 0 disk. The kernel of operating system is Ubuntu 11.04 x86_64. Hadoop 0.20.203 is set up on the cluster, and Oracle 10201 x86_64 is running on each data node.

The benchmark is from our application. Despite the specific Earthquake Precursor domain, the data schema is common to other applications. It contains two metadata table *stations* and *stationpoints*, and one data table *data*: table *stations* has 1 integer and 1 string attributes, which are *stationid* (key) and *stationname*; table *stationpoints* has 2 integer attributes, which are *stationid* (key) and *pointid*; table data has 1 string, 3 integer and 1 blob attributes, which are *startdate, stationid, pointid, itemid* and *obsvalue*, and its composite primary key is the union of the first four attributes.

Besides, *stationid, pointid* and *itemid* are respectively uniformly distributed in the integer range [1, 10000), [1, 10), and [1, 100); *starttdate* starts from 01-Jan-12, and increases by 1 day every 40000 records; *stationname* is a 20 character random string; and *obsvalue* is a binary sequence with 8.7KB average size. Table *data, stations* and *stationpoints* respectively have about 10,000,000, 1,000, 10,000 records, and their space occupancy are 95GB, 0.0625MB, 0.25MB correspondingly.

For ease of testing, we assume that the Precursor Network contains 7 nodes, i.e. 1 national node, 2 regional nodes, and 4 station nodes. Each regional node manages 2 station nodes, and the national node manages all regional nodes. Considering that there are only 4 machines in our cluster, we deploy the nodes within the same layer on one machine, and regard the remaining one machine as the name node in Hadoop.

A data generator is designed to produce records. It yields all the same metadata table per node, while only 25% records (2.5 million) of data table per station nodes. An uploading of data records will be done from lower-layer node to upper-layer node next, and finally, each regional node contains 50% data records (5 million), and the national node contains the whole 10 million data records.

The queries we use are as follows. The first query joins two metadata tables on *stationid* attribute. And the second query finds the records in table *data* by *stationid* and *pointid* attributes with a predicate on *stationid* attribute, where the *where* clause varies in different experiments.

SELECT *a.stationid, a.stationname, b.pointid*

FROM *stations a, stationpoints b*

WHERE *a.stationid=b.stationid*;

SELECT *startdate, stationid, pointid, itemid, samplerate, obsvalue*

FROM *data*

WHERE *stationid* IN (*stationid_list*) [and *pointid* IN (*pointid_list*)];

5.2   Initialization

We report the initialization of H-DB, including loading metadata tables into HDFS and creating global index on *stationid* attribute of table *data*. Table I gives the result. The loading takes 0.9 minute for two metadata tables. This overhead is mainly due to the startup of MapReduce. The creation time of global index takes 16.1 minutes, and the entire global index files occupy 877.4MB. In summary, H-DB required as little as 17 minute to completely initialize the whole 95GB dataset, and only few tables and indexes (0.9%) are loaded into HDFS, loading is not the bottleneck of H-DB.

Table 1. Initialization of H-DB

	Metadata table	
	Table *stations*	28
Loading time (s)	Table *stationpoints*	26
	Total time	54
	Data table	
Index creation	Local index creation	493.5
time (s)	Global index creation	473.7
	Total time	967.2
Index size (MB)	Each partition size	97.6
	Total size	877.4

5.3   Query with Multi-user

This experiment tests whether system supports multi-user doing join operation on two metadata table simultaneously. Table 2 shows the elapsed time of two systems on join operation with multi-user. H-DB is slower than Oracle when there are fewer users, since its performance is affected by completely scanning all two tables in HDFS. However, with the exponential growth of the users, Oracle fails due to its limit number of database connection, while H-DB behaves well since it takes advantage of high concurrency of HDFS. In addition, the elapsed time of H-DB almost grows linearly with the number of users, namely that we can accommodate more users simply by adding more machines, yet without reducing the performance to existing users.

Table 2. Elapsed Time of the Query with Multi-user

Number of users	1	10	100	1000	10000
Oracle (ms)	333	819	9338	crash	crash
H-DB (ms)	9813	10606	19599	95808	924763

5.4   Query with Predicate

We now test the query with predicate. These queries are to find records in data table with *stationid* value in *stationid_list* and sometimes with *pointid* value in *pointid_list* simultaneously. When the predicate is under high selectivity, for example, *stationid*=50000 [and *pointid*=5], or *stationid* ∈[50000,50010], it is worth using our global index mechanism to improve the performance.

Fig. 6 illustrates the power of using our hybrid system H-DB. The elapsed time of H-DB (both cache miss and cache hit) are much shorter than that of Oracle. H-DB (cache miss) represents that the desired global index file is not existed in index cache and should be loaded from data node of HDFS to local disk of name node first. Though the overhead of this loading is 270ms per 100MB, it takes an average increase of 81.2% in elapsed time than Oracle. And H-DB (cache hit), without this overhead of loading, takes a further increase of 76.2% on average than H-DB (cache miss).

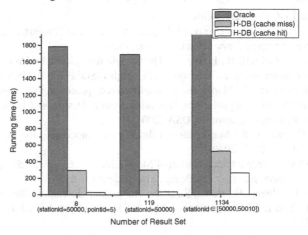

Fig. 4. An Example of Index-Tree

In a word, H-DB (cache hit) only spends an average 5% elapsed time of Oracle's. This significant performance improvement is because H-DB partitions a query among multiple DBMSs, executes the sub-queries in parallel and uses pseudo column *rowid* to directly locate the record. However, one thing to note: with the growth in the number of query result set (from 8 to 1134 in Fig.4), since Oracle does query optimization in choosing the lightest SQL plan, the performance improvement of H-DB decline.

6   Conclusion

DBMS and Hadoop are not ideal for big data analytics. HadoopDB as a hybrid system bringing their ideas together is prospective, but still limited due to some causes which are hard to conquer. Thus, we propose a novel hybrid system H-DB which takes DBMSs as the underlying storage and execution units, and Hadoop as an index layer and a cache. Though H-DB is similar to HadoopDB to some extent, it solves some limitations posed by HadoopDB: a) Only few tables and indexes are loaded from DBMS to HDFS, which solves the problem in loading bottleneck. b) The cache layer in HDFS is used to store tables with high frequency access but relatively small amount of data, which benefits for the multi-user accesses. c) The global index mechanism is adapted for certain queries, which shows much better performance than Oracle. All above make H-DB not only meets the demands of our application, but also would be appropriate for analogous big data applications.

Acknowledgment. This research was supported by the National Natural Science Foundation of China (Grant No.61033009, No. 61133005 and No. 61303047).

References

1. Gantz, J., Chute, C., Manfrediz, A.: The diverse and exploding digital universe. IDC White Paper (2008)
2. Worldwide LHC Computing Grid,
   http://public.web.cern.ch/public/en/LHC/Computing-en.html
3. WinterCorp., http://www.wintercorp.com/
4. Ghemawat, S., Gobioff, H., Leung, S.: The Google file system. In: Proceedings of the 19th ACM Symposium on Operationg System Principles (SOSP 2003), USA (2003)
5. Dean, J., Ghemawat, S.: MapReduce: Simplified data processing on large clusters. In: Proceedings of the 6th Symposium on Operating System Design and Implementation (OSDI 2004), San Francisco, California, USA (2004)
6. Dean, J., Ghemawat, S.: MapReduce: a flexible data processing tool. Communications of the ACM 53(1), 72–77 (2010)
7. Hadoop: Open-source implementation of MapReduce, http://hadoop.apache.org
8. The HDFS Project, http://hadoop.apche.org/hdfs
9. Shvachko, K., Huang, H., Radia, S., et al.: The hadoop distributed filesystem. In: Proceedings of the 26th IEEE Symposium on Massive Storage Systems and Technologies, MSST 2010 (2010)

10. Xu, Y., Kostamaa, P., Gao, L.: Integrating hadoop and parallel DBMS. In: Proceedings of the 2010 International Conference on Management of Data (SIGMOD 2010), Indianapolis, Indiana (2010)
11. Stonebraker, M., Abadi, D., DeWitt, D.J., et al.: MapReduce and parallel DBMSs: friends or foes? Communications of the ACM 53(1), 64–71 (2010)
12. Loebman, S., Nunley, D., Kwon, Y., et al.: Analyzing Massive Astrophysical Datasets: Can Pig/Hadoop or a Relational DBMS Help? In: IEEE International Conference on Cluster Computing and Workshops (CLUSTER 2009). New Orleans, Louisiana, USA (2009)
13. Abouzeid, A., Bajda-Pawlikowski, K., Abadi, D., et al.: HadoopDB: An Architectural Hybrid of MapReduce and DBMS Technologies for Analytical Workloads. In: Proceedings of the Conference on Very Large Databases (VLDB 2009), Lyon, France (2009)
14. The Pig Project, http://hadoop.apache.org/pig
15. The Hive Project, http://hadoop.apache.org/hive
16. An, M., Wang, Y., Wang, W., et al.: Integrating DBMSs as a Read-Only Execution Layer into Hadoop. In: Proceedings of the 2010 International Conference on Parallel and Distributed Computing, Applications and Technologies, PDCAT 2010 (2010)
17. Greenplum is driving the future of Big Data analytics, http://www.greenplum.com/

Sequential and Parallelized FPGA Implementation of Spectrum Sensing Detector Based on Kolmogorov-Smirnov Test

Roman Marsalek[1], Martin Pospisil[1], Tomas Fryza[1], and Martin Simandl[2]

[1] Department of Radio Electronics
Brno University of Technology, Czech Republic
Technicka 12, Brno, Czech Republic
{marsaler,fryza}@feec.vutbr.cz,xpospi29@stud.feec.vutbr.cz
[2] TESLA a.s.
Podebradska 56/186,
Prague 9 - Hloubetin, Czech Republic
simandl.martin@tesla.cz

Abstract. This paper deals with the implementation of the spectrum sensing detector based on the Kolmogorov-Smirnov (K-S) statistical test in the FPGA-based software defined radio system. After a brief introduction and the literature survey on the similar up-to-date implementation works, the principle of K-S test is briefly reviewed. The core of the paper describes the principles of two different algorithm implementations in the Xilinx Spartan-3A DSP device. First implementation is straightforward sequential solution, with low requirements on FPGA resources. Afterwards a new parallel solution with simpler structure and faster sensing time is presented. Both approaches have been verified using both the behavioral and the post place and route simulation. The integration of the detector into the complete target software defined radio transceiver - Universal Software Radio Peripheral (USRP N200) is also briefly discussed at the end of the paper.

1 Introduction

The cognitive radio (CR) approach is a potential enabler to overcome the spectrum scarcity and increased throughput problems for future wireless communication systems. From the first theoretical concepts defined by Mitola in [1] in 1999, the CR technologies evolved to the stage of real-time implementations and evaluation. The software defined radios, e.g. the Universal Software Radio Peripheral (USRP) family are very suitable for testing of the cognitive radio technologies. One of them is spectrum sensing - the process to detect the presence of primary (licensed) users in the radio frequency spectrum.

One of the FPGA-based cognitive radio systems is presented in [2]. This system is able to sense IEEE802.11a, IEEE802.11b and W-CDMA signals with sensing times of 7056, 7056, and 8703 ms., respectively. The VHDL simulation of the autocorrelation-based feature spectrum sensing detector was presented

J. Kołodziej et al. (Eds.): ICA3PP 2013, Part I, LNCS 8285, pp. 336–345, 2013.
© Springer International Publishing Switzerland 2013

in [3]. The presented model consumes around 1000 LUT flip-flop pairs and is suitable for detection of OFDM signals. In [4] we presented the implementation of energy detector designed in the System Generator software targeted to Xilinx Virtex 4 FPGA device and evaluated its performance on DVB-T broadcasting signals. Besides the universal FPGA boards, some implementations were done using the specialized hardware like the WARP system in [5] based on a Xilinx Virtex 2 Pro device. In this paper the energy detector with double thresholding has been proposed. Recently a demo has been presented and described in [12] making use of a CRUSH platform - the Xilinx ML605 FPGA Development board connected to the USRP N210 radio. Again, the energy detector is used for its low complexity, standard-independence and ease of implementation.

If the dedicated hardware is not available, the FPGA board with the hardware-in-the-loop simulation can be used, similarly as to [6] where the energy and cyclo-stationary detectors were simulated. The System generator in Simulink was used for the implementation of the progressive decimation filter bank spectrum sensing detector in [7] with 300,000 gates necessary in the Virtex 2 device. The same Simulink environment was used for the multitaper method implementation [11] in Virtex 5 device. For the correctness of the spectrum sensing device utilization, the proper setting of decision threshold has to be ensured. This aspect has been treated for example in [8]. Several spectrum sensing detectors have been implemented with the use of the USRP, similarly to our case. As the example we can mention the paper [9] and the master thesis [13], describing the implementation of energy detector using the USRP2 radio. From the theoretical point of view the closest to our approach is the master thesis [14] describing the Kolmogorov-Smirnov (K-S) and Anderson-Darling tests implementation in the USRP2. But although this work uses the same theoretical background as our presented contribution, the both works differ in the implementation point of view - we perform an implementation in the VHDL to be built-in directly in the FPGA inside the USRP, while the authors of [14] used the GNU radio environment.

This paper follows up our approach presented in [10] in which two options for the application of the K-S test for spectrum sensing have been proposed and evaluated in MATLAB. The rest of the paper is structured as follows: The section 2 briefly revises the principle of K-S test and its application in spectrum sensing. Then the main principles and results of two distinct implementations of K-S test (fully sequential and parallelized) are described in sections 3,4 and the integration in the USRP N200 in section 5.

2   K-S Test as the Spectrum Sensing Technique

In the spectrum sensing problem, the goal is to distinguish between two hypothesis - whether a received signal $r(n)$ contains only a noise component $w(n)$ (H_0), or whether also the primary signal $s(n)$ is present (H_1):

$$H_0 : r(n) = w(n), H_1 : r(n) = s(n) + w(n). \tag{1}$$

Note that in our case we considered discrete time signals with sample index n. The K-S test belongs to the goodness-of-fit tests (these test are based on the estimation and comparison of distribution functions) family. A null hypothesis H_0 corresponds to the case that the two probability distributions (one measured from the received signal, second of the expected noise in the communication channel) are not significantly different. The alternative hypothesis H_1 corresponds to the case that the measured (empirical) distribution $F(r)$ differs with respect to the expected theoretical distribution $G(r)$ of the noise component.

Following three equations represent the three general steps of the K-S test implementation. First the cumulative distribution function of the received signal has to be estimated from its N samples. This formula can be used for that reason, [10]

$$F(r) = \frac{1}{N} \sum_{n=1}^{N} \Gamma\left(r(n) \leq r\right), \tag{2}$$

with Γ denoting the indicator function, which is equal to one if its argument is true, and equal to zero otherwise.

Subsequently, the supremum of the difference between the sampled versions (at r_i) of measured $F(r_i)$ and theoretical $G(r_i)$ distribution functions is approximated with the test statistics T_{KS}:

$$T_{KS} = \max_{i} \{F(r_i) - G(r_i)\} \tag{3}$$

The null hypothesis is rejected at the significance level α when the value of test statistic is higher than a critical value $k(\alpha, N)$. In the case of $N \geq 50$, the critical values can be approximated as $k(\alpha, N) = \sqrt{\frac{1}{2N} \ln\left(\frac{2}{\alpha}\right)}$.

3   Algorithm Implementation

The K-S test algorithm has been implemented in VHDL in the Xilinx ISE 13.4 software with the use of Xilinx IP core library to ease of the implementation of blocks as memories or arithmetic operators.

3.1   Sequential Solution

In the first step, the sequential solution has been designed. A simplified schematic of the system for cumulative distribution function estimation from the measured data is shown on the left part of Fig. 1. The data are stored in the RAM memory DATA. Another RAM memory (in schematic denoted as $F()$) is used to store the values of estimated CDF sampled at point $r(ADRESS)$ approximated by the sum (number of cases with non-zero indicator function) according to eq. 2. For each data sample (consisting of baseband I and Q sample pair), its absolute value is computed first. Then it is compared with the intervals spanning from $r = 0$ to the maximal value of independent axis of CDF (r). If the output of the indicator function from eg. 2 is equal to one (comparator is used), the corresponding entry in RAM $F()$ is increased by 1. Otherwise the RAM entry remains unchanged.

Subsequently, the address for RAM $F()$ is incremented and the process is repeated for the next address until the whole range of CDF is passed through. As soon as the indicator function becomes equal to 0 (all remaining indicator functions for higher r are equal to 0 too), the counter of addresses is initialized to zero. This process is repeated for all input data samples. In order to control the

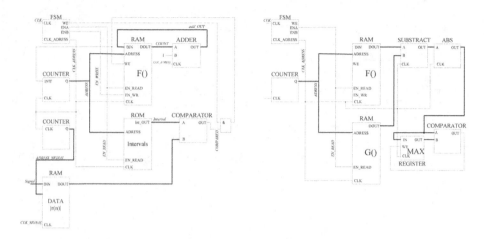

Fig. 1. Simplified schematic of circuit for CDF estimation (left) and maximum search (right) -sequential solution

read and write operation of memory $F()$ of CDF values, a simple Finite State Machine (FSM) has been created, In the first state, the valid address is present at the RAM $F()$ address buss, second state is used for CDF entry read, third for indicator function computation. In the final state the corresponding RAM entry is increased by 1 (or let unchanged if the indicator function is equal to 0).

Once the CDF of the input data is estimated, the maximum according to eq. 3 is searched for with the use of circuit shown in the simplified form on the right part of Fig. 1. All entries of the CDF RAM are subtracted with the corresponding entries of RAM $G()$ defining the values of theoretical CDF of the noise in the channel. Subsequently the maximal difference between the two distributions is stored in the register MAX. Final decision is done by comparison of the maximal difference with the precomputed critical value $k(\alpha, N)$.

3.2   Parallelized Solution

The sequential solution presented above is advantageous (as will be confirmed numerically below) from the point of view of FPGA resource utilization. For each input sample, the indicator function is computed successively for all values of CDF abscissa. On the other hand, such sequential approach is time consuming if the goal is to estimate the CDF precisely (i.e. for fine abscissa resolution).

The parallelized solution for CDF estimation is based on the parallel computation of CDF samples for all points on the abscissa. The input sample is compared with a set of M comparators, as depicted on the left part of Fig. 2. The comparator directly works as a indicator function generating unit, see equation 2. The summation from this equation is implemented in the set of M accumulators.

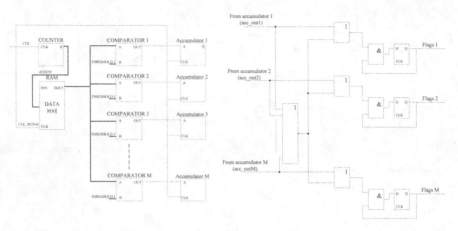

Fig. 2. Simplified schematic of circuit for CDF estimation (left) and maximum search (right) - parallelized solution

Also the algorithm for searching the maximal difference between two CDF's (equation 3) can be implemented in more clever way than is the pure sequential solution. The sequential solution described above requires number of comparisons (and thus corresponding number of clock cycles) equal to number of estimated CDF points. This can be a drawback if the fast sensing time is required. The proposed solution is based on the comparison at bit level rather than on the sample level. Imagine we compare the differences between two CDF's that are represented in unsigned 16-bit format and are stored in M accumulators. The algorithm to search for the maximal number stored in the accumulator can be described (in simplified form) as:

1. At the begining, all $m = 1..M$ numbers $data_1, data_2, \ldots data_M$ are candidates for the maximum. The set of candidates for maximum is initialized as $S_c = \{data_1, data_2, \ldots data_M\}$
   The membership of one particular $data_m$ in S_c is indicated with variables $Flags_m$ equal to 1 ($data_m \in S_c$) or equal to 0 ($data_m \notin S_c$). The variables $Flags_m$, $m = 1..M$ are initialized to ones.
2. The data are processed from the MSB down to LSB.
   FOR u=1:U   ($u = 1$ corresponds to MSB, $u = U$ corresponds to LSB)
   $\forall$ $data_v \in S_c$:

IF (u-th bit of data$_v$ is equal to 1) OR (u-th bits of all data$_v \in S_c$ are equal to 0)

THEN

data$_v$ remains to be candidate for the maximum (variable $Flags_v=1$)

ELSE

data$_v$ is certainly not the maximum (set the variable $Flags_v=0$). The data$_v$ is removed from the set of candidates $S_c = S_c - \{$data$_v\}$

3. continue in 2) with the next bit (until the LSB is reached)
4. At the end, the value of $Flags=1$ at corresponding m-th position indicates the maximum.

This parallelized solution requires the number of clock cycles to be equal to bit resolution used for the representation of CDF's difference only(e.g. in our case only 16 clock cycles), even if the CDF is estimated in fine abscissa resolution of e.g. 100 points. The method can be easily implemented using a set of registers (D type) and OR/AND gates, see Fig.2.

4 Verification by Simulation

4.1 Sequential Solution

The results of post-place and route simulation of the sequential way of CDF estimation blocks are shown on figure 3. This figure shows the timing of all corresponding signals for the example case of indicator function equal to 1 (i.e. CDF RAM write enabled). Note that for the sake of easy graphical representation, the CDF is approximated for 16 input entries only (address width of 4 bits). The 16 bits precision for data is used, as corresponds to the USRP devices signal format. Both time plots starts at the instant when the input signal RAM entry is read after the tick of clock CLK_signal. The address $ADRESS$ is then successively incremented from the starting point 0000 in order to go through the whole CDF. If the input data $signal$ is below the limit of $interval\ r$ (see eq. 2), the signal $COMPARED$ (indicator function) is equal to 1 and the update of RAM $F()$ is enabled.

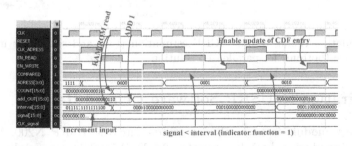

Fig. 3. Post place and route simulation results - CDF estimation (sequential solution), indicator function equal to 1

4.2   Parallelized Solution

Similarly to the sequential case, the parallelized solution has been verified by the VHDL post place and route simulation. The results for the CDF estimation and maximum search are shown in figure 4. The top part shows the results for CDF estimation. The input signal samples (SIGNAL) are successively read from the memory and compared with a set of comparators. For sake of clarity only five comparators have been used in the simulation to create this figure. The corresponding thresholds were set (Q5 format) to 000001, 000010, 000100, 001000 and 001100. It is possible to verify that the corresponding accumulators are incremented only if the input sample is above the threshold.

The procedure for searching the maximum is illustrated in the bottom part. Again, in order to provide easy interpretation of the results, only the four unsigned numbers (1001,1001,1100 and 1101) represented in 4 bit format have been used for the simulation. Note that a variable *accumbits* represents successively the i-th bits of all numbers compared, i.e. first sample of *accumbits* represents MSB's of all four numbers, second sample of *accumbits* represents MSB-1's etc. As the numbers are compared starting from MSB to LSB, the variables *Flags* are changed. At the end only the 4-th bit of *Flags* is equal to 1 indicating the 4th number (with a value of 1101) is the maximum.

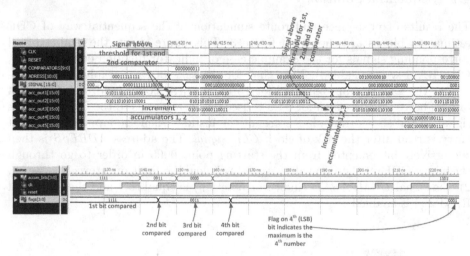

Fig. 4. Simulation timing results - CDF estimation (top) and search for maximum CDF difference (bottom) for parallelized solution

5   Integration to USRP Software Defined Radio

The K-S test module is currently integrated into the USRP N200. Its main board is equipped with the Xilinx Spartan 3A-DSP 1800 device and dual 14 bits

A/D converters with 100 MS/s. sampling rate. The USRP can be used in connection with various different front-end modules ranging from DC to 6 GHz frequency.

The simplified schematic of USRP N200 receiver chain is shown on top part of the Fig. 5. Data from the antenna are received by the front-end, converted to digital domain by the A/D converters and subsequently Digitally Down-Converted (DDC) to baseband. The USRP source code is ready to be modified by the custom Verilog code to be included in several positions of the transceiver chain. In the receiver, the user can access data from the front-end (position 1 in Fig. 5), input to the DDC (position 2 in Fig. 5), output of the DDC (position 3) or baseband data (position 4). In standard configuration, the custom blocks are bypassed, i.e. the position 1 is connected to 2 and position 3 is connected to position 4. From the I and Q samples of the received signal at the DDC output we computed the signal absolute value and stored into the RAM $F()$, see section 3.

The device utilization summaries for CDF estimation and MAX search for both sequential and parallelized solutions are shown in Table 1, together with the summary for the standard configuration of USRP N200 and total available resources of in-built FPGA. It is possible to see that the number of resources required by the spectrum sensing algorithm is very low in comparison with the resources occupied by the standard configuration of USRP. The implementation complexity is compared with the several state-of-the-art methods in Table 2 in term of number of used FPGA slices. Note that this table presents only rough comparison, as various authors used different FPGA devices and the slices are not the only FPGA blocks. Most of the benchmark implementations from table 2 are slightly disadvantaged over our implementation, as the authors often used Simulink-based development environment System Generator and not the VHDL implementation.

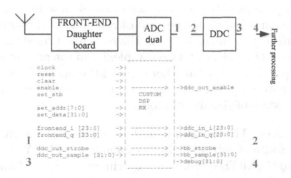

Fig. 5. USRP receiver chain (top) and custom module

Table 1. Device utilization summary - Post Place and Route reports for sequential (seq.) and parallel(par.) implementations, resources consumed by the USRP itself and total available resources for the specific FPGA device

	CDF estimation (seq./par.)	Max search (seq./par.)	USRP alone	Available
Slices	59/688	64/135	16529	16640
SliceMs	0	0	2182	8320
RAM16s	4/2	0	42	84
DSP48As	0	0	34	84
DCMs	0	0	1	8

Table 2. Comparison of resource utilization of several state-of-the-art spectrum sensing implementations in term of number of slices

Reference	Algorithm type	Device family	No. of Slices
[3]	autocorrelation	Virtex 5	993
[5]	energy, double threshold	Virtex 2 Pro	6600
[6]	cyclostationary	Virtex 2	1315
[6]	energy detector	Virtex 2	350-827
[11]	multitaper energy	Virtex 5	9954

6   Conclusions

This paper presents our work dealing with the implementation of spectrum sensing device in the FPGA and its integration into the software defined radio USRP N200. The used algorithm is the statistical test comparing the distribution of received signal with a distribution of the expected channel noise. This approach is advantageous from the point of view of easy implementation and low resources requirements. The consumed resources of the sequential spectrum sensing detector are around 1 percent of the total device available resources, while the parallelized version requires less than 5 percent of resources of the same device. Both methods can thus be implemented also in the software defined radio systems like the USRP family. The implementation complexity of the presented methods was also briefly compared with several other state-of-the-art implementations. It can be noticed that both proposed implementations require low amount of resources compared to the state-of-the-art solutions.

Acknowledgments. The research described is a part of ENIAC JU European project no. 270683-2 and corresponding national project MEYS of the Czech Republic no. 7H11097 (ARTEMOS). The experiments were performed in the laboratories of the SIX research center, reg. no. CZ.1.05/2.1.00/03.0072 built with the initial support of the project CZ.1.07/2.3.00/20.0007 WICOMT. Thanks also to the internal project FEKT-S-11-12. The participation in the collaborative COST IC1004 action was made possible through the MEYS of the Czech Republic project LD12006 (CEEC).

References

1. Mitola, J., Maguire, G.Q.: Cognitive radio: making software radios more personal. IEEE Personal Communications 6(4), 13–18 (1999)
2. Harada, H.: A Small-size Software Defined Cognitive Radio Prototype. In: Proceedings of IEEE 19th International Symposium on Personal, Indoor and Mobile Radio Communications, pp. 1–4 (2008)
3. Kokkinen, K., et al.: On the Implementation of Autocorrelation-based Feature Detector. In: Proceedings of the 4th International Symposium on Communications, Control and Signal Processing, ISCCSP 2010, Limassol, Cyprus (2010)
4. Povalac, K., et al.: Real-Time Implementation of Periodogram Based Spectrum Sensing Detector in TV Bands. In: Proceedings of International Conference Radioelektronika 2010, Brno, Czech Republic, pp. 1–4 (2010)
5. Hanninen, T., et al.: Implementation of spectrum sensing on wireless open-access research platform. In: Proceedings of 3rd International Symposium on Applied Sciences in Biomedical and Communication Technologies (ISABEL), pp. 1–5 (2010)
6. Sabat, S.L.: FPGA realization of Spectrum Sensing techniques for Cognitive Radio Network. In: Proceedings of 2010 International Workshop on Cognitive Radio (IWCR), pp. 1–5 (2010)
7. Lin, M., Vinod, A.P.: Implementation of a Low Area and High-Speed Spectrum Sensor with Reconfigurable Sensing Resolution for Cognitive Radios. In: Proceedings of IEEE 9th International New Circuits and Systems Conference (NEWCAS), pp. 303–304
8. Song, C., et al.: Proposal and Hardware Implementation of Smart Threshold Setting Methods for Spectrum Sensing. In: Proceedings of IEEE International Workshop on Recent Advances in Cognitive Communications and Networking, pp. 918–923 (2011)
9. Chaitanya, G.V.: Real Time Hardware Implementable Spectrum Sensor for Cognitive Radio Applications. In: Proceedings of International Conference on Signal Processing and Communications (SPCOM), pp. 1–5 (2012)
10. Marsalek, R., Povalac, K.: Kolmogorov – Smirnov test for spectrum sensing: from the statistical test to energy detection. In: Proceedings of 2012 IEEE Workshop on Signal Processing Systems, pp. 97–102 (2012)
11. Kyperountas, S.: A MultiTaper Hardware Core for Spectrum Sensing. In: Proceedings of 2012 IEEE International Symposium on Dynamic Spectrum Access Networks, pp. 42–46 (2012)
12. Eichinger, G.: Cognitive Radio Universal Software Hardware. In: Proceedings of 2012 IEEE International Symposium on Dynamic Spectrum Access Networks (DySPAN)- Demos, pp. 270–271 (2012)
13. Aftab, A., Mufti, M.N.: Spectrum Sensing Through Implementation of USRP2, Master thesis, Blekinge Institute of Technology (2012)
14. Hu, Q.: Radio spectrum sensing: theory, algorithms, implementation, and testing, Master thesis, University of York (2011)

A Reconfigurable Ray-Tracing Multi-Processor SoC with Hardware Replication-Aware Instruction Set Extension

Alexandre S. Nery[1,3], Nadia Nedjah[2], Felipe M.G. França[1],
Lech Jozwiak[3], and Henk Corporaal[3]

[1] LAM – Computer Architecture and Microeletronics Laboratory
Systems Engineering and Computer Science Program, COPPE
Federal University of Rio de Janeiro
[2] Department of Electronics Engineering and Telecommunications
Faculty of Engineering, State University of Rio de Janeiro
[3] Department of Electrical Engineering – Electronic Systems
Eindhoven University of Technology, The Netherlands

Abstract. Application code and processor parallelization, together with instruction set customization, are the most common and effective ways to enhance the performance and efficiency of application-specific processors (ASIPs). Both the effective code parallelization and data/task parallelism exploitation, as well as effective instruction set customization, enable an ASIP to achieve a significant performance improvement using limited extra hardware resources. However, a naive parallelization or instruction set customization may not result in the required performance improvement, leading to a waste of computing and energy resources. Therefore, when performing parallelization or custom instruction selection, complex tradeoffs between processing speed, circuit area and power consumption must be closely observed. In this paper, we propose and discuss an efficient ASIP-based Multi-Processor System-on-a-Chip (MP-SoC) design for ray-tracing, exploiting application parallelism and hardware replication-aware instruction set customization. Without hardware sharing among the custom instructions units, the proposed parallel ray-tracer MPSoC design with custom instructions achieves 77% speed up in comparison to a single microprocessor design with the default instruction set. However, with the replication-aware instruction set customization, the speed up increases to 81%.

1 Introduction

Application-specific processors and hardware accelerators have become an attractive alternative to general purpose processors [4,3], as they can be tailored in order to better satisfy the requirements of modern highly-demanding applications. Specifically, communications and multimedia applications are often very demanding regarding throughput and energy consumption, requiring sophisticated application-specific (co-)processor implementations. For instance, a set of operation patterns that are frequently executed by an application or a class of applications can be implemented as a hardware accelerator or as a set of custom

J. Kołodziej et al. (Eds.): ICA3PP 2013, Part I, LNCS 8285, pp. 346–356, 2013.
© Springer International Publishing Switzerland 2013

instructions in an ASIP datapath, resulting in a possible substantial increase of the execution speed [12].

The ray-tracing algorithm is an example of a multimedia application highly-demanding in terms of throughput, circuit-area and energy consumption [6,8]. First of all, the algorithm performance can be considerably improved by means of code and processor architecture parallelization [2]. Secondly, the algorithm may compute several ray-object intersection tests for every ray vector, which requires specific intersection computations/routines for each 3-D object of the whole 3-D scene [1]. Thus, in an ASIP design process, each intersection computation may be implemented as a specialized function unit in hardware, contributing to further speed up the overall execution. However, the more processing elements and specialized function units are added to the design, the higher becomes the overall system circuit area and energy consumption [6,8].

Hardware sharing (or more generally resource sharing) [10,13], is a well-known optimization approach, traditionally employed for saving circuit area, in which two or more equivalent hardware parts (e.g. functional units) that are never used at the same time during an application execution (unless they are pipelined [9]) are replaced by a single part. For instance, in a class of similar applications, there is usually large sets of equivalent operation patterns that can be identified, evaluated and finally selected for extending an existing instruction set. The instruction set extension may increase the processor performance, but it may also significantly increase the processor circuit area. The increase of the circuit area can be limited through hardware re-use. Thus, hardware sharing represents an important optimization problem. While many hardware synthesis tools provide some resource sharing transformations, their results are often far from ideal [11].

This paper presents a parallelization strategy of the ray-tracing algorithm to be implemented in a Reconfigurable Multi-Processor System-on-a-Chip, as well as, hardware replication-aware instruction set extension based on the identification of equivalent computation patterns that are frequently executed in the ray-tracing application. Based on the information collected during the application profiling, which is performed using the LLVM compiler framework [7], candidates for instruction set extension are decided and implemented as specialized function units in the ASIP-based MPSoC to further speed up the ray-tracing execution time. Such extensions may substantially increase the circuit-area. To mitigate the impact on the area, the resource sharing maximal common subgraphs based on maximal cliques [5] is used.

The rest of this paper is organized as follows: Section 2 briefly describes the ray-tracing algorithm. Section 3 introduces and discusses the automatic instruction set extension tool based on the LLVM compiler framework. Subsequently, Section 4 presents the MPSoC macro-architecture synthesis with Instruction Set Extension. Section 5 discusses speed up and area results for the ray-tracing MPSoC, comparing the instruction set extension with and without hardware sharing. Finally, Section 6 draws some conclusions and ideas for future work.

2   Ray Tracing

In contrast to traditional 3-D rendering algorithms [1], the ray tracing algorithm produces a higher fidelity image representation of a 3-D scene. For every primary ray (e.g. light vector), the ray tracing algorithm usually computes intersection tests against all the 3-D primitives (a.k.a. objects) of the scene, looking for the objects that are visible from a virtual camera's perspective. If an intersection is encountered, the object properties are used to determine wether the ray will be reflected, refracted or completely absorbed. For instance, if the ray is reflected or refracted, the algorithm is recursively executed to determine the objects that are visible from the previous intersection point perspective, which is why the algorithm can naturally produce mirror like effects in the final image. On the other hand, if the ray is absorbed, the processing ends and all the information that has been gathered until that point is merged to compose the color of the corresponding pixel of the viewplane. The program main entry is presented in Algorithm 1, in which the primary rays are being traced. The *trace* procedure in Algorithm 1 is responsible for determining the closest intersection point. Such procedure is recursively executed until a maximum reflection/refraction threshold is reached. Further details on ray tracing can be found in [1].

Algorithm 1. Ray Tracing primary rays

```
1  3-D scene = load3DScene(file);
2  viewplane = setupViewplane(width,height);
3  camera = setupCamera(viewplane,eye,view_direction);
4  depth = 0;
5  for i = 1 to viewplane's width do
6  |    for j = 1 to viewplane's height do
7  |    |    ray = getPrimaryRay(i,j,camera);
8  |    |    image[i][j] = trace(3-D scene, ray, depth);
```

---

3   Automatic Instruction Set Extension

Instruction-set extension (ISE) is a well-known technique often used to improve the performance of reconfigurable instruction-set processors and application-specific instruction-set processors. In other words, such processors are optimized to the execution of a specific application or class of applications through the implementation of dedicated hardware (custom instructions) based on an extensive profiling of the application for which the processor is being designed for.

Usually, the customization process involves three main steps: *pattern identification, pattern selection* and *code transformation*. Using the LLVM compiler framework [7], an instruction set extension tool has been developed that automatically generates a library of custom instructions. Code transformation is out of the scope of this work. Therefore, custom instructions must be manually identified and tagged in the source code to force the compiler to use their custom hardware units. Otherwise, a retargetable compiler should be used.

3.1   Pattern Identification

The pattern identification step is usually the most complex. First, it compiles the application specification (written in a high level language such as C or C++) and produces an equivalent Control-Flow Graph (CFG) representation. Such graph-based representation of the application is then optimized and partitioned into Data-Flow Graphs (DFG), which are based on the application's basic blocks partitions. Each DFG is a Directed Acyclic Graph (DAG) that is analyzed to identify patterns (set of basic operations) that are common to several basic blocks. Our LLVM-based instruction set extension tool uses the LLVM-operation code of each basic operation to appropriately color a node in its corresponding data-flow graph representation, as depicted in Fig. 1.

Finding the maximal common subgraphs is equivalent to finding the maximal clique in an edge product or vertex product graph (a.k.a compatibility graph) [5,10]. For example, when applied to the graphs depicted in Fig. 1, the tool identified the common patterns shown in Fig. 1c.

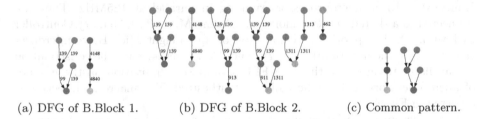

(a) DFG of B.Block 1.   (b) DFG of B.Block 2.   (c) Common pattern.

Fig. 1. Data-flow Graph representation of two different basic blocks of the ray-tracing application and their common pattern

3.2   Pattern Selection

Once the common patterns (maximal common subgraphs) are identified, they are evaluated regarding their frequency of execution in the application and their frequency of occurrence. Also, the simple arithmetic average of every basic block execution frequency can indicate, for instance, the basic blocks that are more frequently executed in comparison to the rest. In the chart of Fig. 2, the execution average is 0.645 (in normalized logarithm scale), indicated by the dot line. Thus, the pattern selection step can ignore the patterns that are not as frequently executed as dictated by the average frequency.

The frequency of pattern occurrence is extracted together with the pattern identification step, which also produces a histogram chart that shows how many times each common pattern was identified in every basic block, as shown in Fig. 3. For the ray-tracing application, 26 patterns were identified. The average can also indicate which patterns are good candidates for hardware implementation, i.e. the ones that have appeared more often in all the basic blocks.

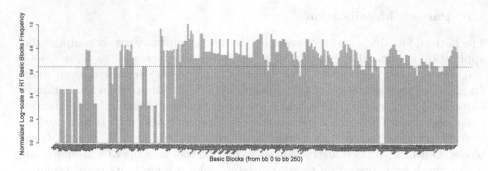

Fig. 2. Ray-Tracing basic blocks frequency of execution histogram (in normalized logarithm scale)

4   Ray-Tracing MPSoC Macro-Architecture

The ray-tracing reconfigurable MPSoC macro-architecture consists of several Xilinx MicroBlaze microprocessors running in parallel at 125MHz. They are connected to a shared DDR memory via a Xilinx Multi-Port Memory Controller (MPMC), which supports the connection of up to eight MicroBlaze microprocessors. Thus, the multi-port memory controller, together with the constraint on the available resources in the used FPGA, impose a limitation on the number of microprocessors that can actually be synthesized. The macro-architecture is depicted in Fig. 4.

Each microprocessor's instruction set can be extended with up to 16 custom instructions, implemented as co-processors through the Xilinx Fast Simplex Link (FSL) bus. Thus, in the ray-tracing MPSoC, each custom instruction works as a special floating-point co-processor.

4.1   Parallel Ray-Tracing in MPSoC

The parallel ray-tracing implementation is presented in Algorithm 2, where iterations of the external *for loop* are split across the microprocessors, as shown in

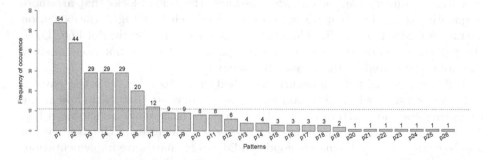

Fig. 3. Frequency of pattern occurence among all basic blocks of the ray-tracing application

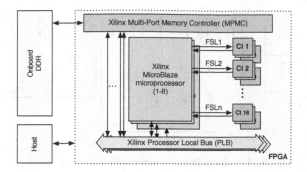

Fig. 4. The Ray-Tracing Reconfigurable MPSoC Macro-Architecture

line 5. Therefore, in Algorithm 2, groups of rays are assigned to different microprocessors, because every ray can be processed independently from the others.

Each microprocessor will produce different columns of the final rendered image. Every microprocessor knows which data to read and to write, according to its own identification number (MB_ID = $0, 1, 2, ..., n-1$) and also according to the total number of enabled microprocessors (NUM_OF_MB = $1, 2, ..., n$), as shown in lines 5 and 9 of Algorithm 2. Observe that, at each inner-loop iteration, an image pixel is produced, as shown in line 8. There are no memory write conflicts, because the pixels produced by different microprocessors are always written at different memory addresses. Due to the memory controller limitation of eight ports, the total number n of MicroBlaze microprocessors is currently limited to eight.

Algorithm 2. Parallel Ray Tracer in MPSoC

---

1 3-D scene = load3DScene(file);
2 view = setupViewplane(width,height);
3 cam = setupCamera(viewplane,eye,view_direction);
4 u24 * image = (u24 *) XPAR_DDR2_SDRAM_MPMC_BASEADDR;
5 **for** $i = MB\_ID$ **to** *viewplane's width* **do**
6   **for** $j = 0$ **to** *viewplane's height* **do**
7   ray = getPrimaryRay(i,j,cam);
8   image[j + i * cam.view.height] = trace(3-D scene, ray);
9   i = i + NUM_OF_MB;

4.2   Ray-Tracing Instruction Set Extension

Using our LLVM-based instruction set extension tool, presented in Section 3, three floating-point custom instructions were added to each microprocessor instruction set, as shown in Fig. 5. The instruction extensions were selected from the most frequently executed operation patterns and accounting for the most common pattern occurrences found between the basic blocks during the profiling of the ray-tracing application. Finally, the custom instructions were manually mapped into the application source code.

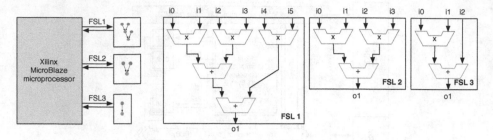

Fig. 5. The Ray-Tracing instruction set extensions

5   Experimental Results

In this section, the MPSoC-based macro-architecture, as described in Section 4, was synthesized using Xilinx EDK 14.4 for a Virtex-5 XC5VFX70T FPGA and the parallel algorithm implementation was compiled using MicroBlaze GCC compiler, without optimizations. Two implementations and experimental results are presented: the first one (Section 5.1) without ISE hardware sharing and the second (Section 5.2) with ISE hardware sharing.

5.1   Results of ISE without Hardware Sharing

The results are based on the ISE without hardware sharing exploration. In this ISE configuration, up to 4 MicroBlaze microprocessors were synthesized. The execution time results, shown in Fig. 6a, are given in seconds and the speed up in comparison to a single microprocessor implementation is presented in Fig. 6b. It is easy to observe that the speed up grows linearly with using more processing elements in parallel. Moreover, if the instruction set extensions are enabled, the speedup grows in the direction of the linear parallel speed up. Whenever they were enabled, the instruction set extensions provided altogether 8.2% speedup

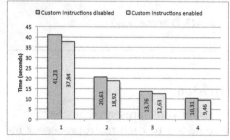

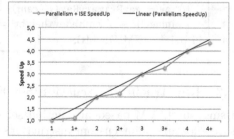

(a) Execution time results, varying from 1 to 4 microprocessors.

(b) Parallel ray-tracer speed up, varying from 1 to 4 microprocessors. A plus signal (+) indicates usage of ISE.

Fig. 6. Parallel ray-tracer execution time results

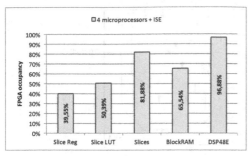

(a) FPGA resources usage for 4 microproces-   (b) Ray-tracer output image (800 ×
sors and peripherals.   600 pixels).

Fig. 7. MPSoC FPGA area occupancy and the final output image

in any configuration of microprocessors. Four microprocessors with enabled instruction set extensions achieved 77% speedup in comparison to the standard
single-processor solution.

In the MPSoC design, almost all the FPGA slices are used (80%), as well
as the available DSP48Es (81%), which are essential to lower the delay of the
floating-point units in FPGA. Therefore, we could only fit in 4 microprocessors
running in parallel with their instruction set extensions, as shown in Fig. 7a.
The resultant ray-traced image is presented in Fig. 7b.

Furthermore, in order to better evaluate the impact/improvement due to the
instruction set extensions, the complexity of the 3-D scene has been increased.
Namely, we included 100 extra spheres in the 3-D scene. In this way, the number
of required floating-point computations (during the intersection tests) has also
increased. In this case, the instruction set extensions provided 10% speedup.
Thus, the more data is fed into the custom instructions, the higher the speedup.

5.2   Results of ISE with Hardware Sharing

Observe in Fig. 5 that each custom instruction presents a few function units
in common. This is the same problem of maximal common subgraph identification (common pattern identification), as discussed in Section 3.1. Therefore, we
analyzed the proposed instruction set extension regarding its hardware sharing
possibilities. Our instruction set extension tool was able to merge the common
patterns and produce a compact function unit hardware that can still compute
the custom instructions one at a time, as depicted in Fig. 8.

The instruction set extensions with hardware sharing saved enough circuit
area to enable the inclusion of an additional microprocessor with custom instructions along to the other 4 microprocessors. Thus, using the same Virtex
5 XC5VFX70T FPGA, up to 5 MicroBlaze microprocessors were included and
synthesized. All the execution time results, shown in Fig. 9a, are given in seconds
and the speed up is in reference to a single microprocessor implementation is
presented in Fig. 9b.

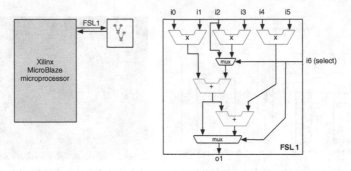

Fig. 8. Instruction set extensions with Hardware Sharing

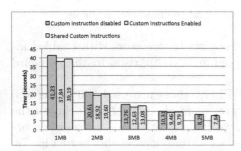

(a) Execution time results, varying from 1 to 5 microprocessors with hardware sharing.

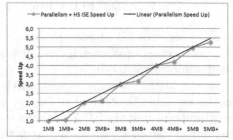

(b) Parallel ray-tracer speed up, varying from 1 to 5 microprocessors. A plus signal (+) indicates usage of ISE with HS.

Fig. 9. MPSoC parallel ray-tracer execution time comparison, with hardware sharing

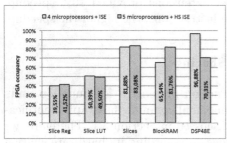

(a) FPGA resources usage for 5 microprocessors with Hardware Sharing (HS).

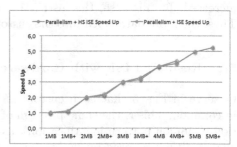

(b) Speed up comparison, varying from 1 to 5 microprocessors. A plus signal (+) indicates usage of ISE.

Fig. 10. MPSoC FPGA area occupancy and speedup results, with hardware sharing and without it

The design with hardware sharing presented a better FPGA occupancy efficiency, as shown in Fig. 10a. As expected, there is a very small loss of performance in the version of ISEs with hardware sharing, because the selection hardware requires an additional operation control signal to select which data-path should be followed at each time. Thus, altogether, the instruction set extensions with hardware sharing provided 5% speedup when enabled. The speedup is almost the same as that achieved by the ISEs with no hardware sharing, as shown in the comparison depicted in Fig. 10b. Furthermore, the fifth microprocessor further improved the overall speedup to 81%, in comparison to the standard single-processor solution.

6   Conclusion

In this paper, we presented a Reconfigurable MPSoC with processors equipped with custom instructions for speeding up the parallel ray-tracing algorithm. With the MPSoC implementation on a single Virtex-5 XC5VFX70T FPGA we were able to explore the usage of up to five MicroBlaze microprocessors in parallel, running at 125MHz. The speed up is almost linear with increasing the number of processing elements (microprocessors) employed in the parallel algorithm execution. Although the interactive performance is not yet achieved, an Application-Specific Integrated Circuit (ASIC) implementation of such an application-specific MPSoC design, instead of FPGA, could most probably run substantially faster, while resulting in a much lower area and power consumption. Such ASIC-based implementation is in our plans for future work.

Moreover, we introduced and discussed an automatic instruction set extension tool, that is able to identify the most promising operation patterns (sets of basic operations) throughout performing an application data-flow graph analysis. We researched the problem of hardware sharing in the instruction set extension of the ray-tracing MPSoC design. It is possible to observe that adequate optimization techniques involving hardware sharing are of primary importance for the design of ASIPs and hardware accelerators. For instance, after hardware sharing optimizations in the proposed instruction set extensions, the saved circuit-area enabled the inclusion of an extra microprocessor with its custom instructions, further increasing the parallel capabilities of the MPSoC design. This is of extreme importance for the ray-tracing speedup, because the algorithm strongly benefits from the parallel processing of the ray vectors. Therefore, the overall achieved speedup with 4 microprocessors is 77%, while with with 5 microprocessors the overall achieved speedup is 81%, in both cases with custom instructions enabled. In the future, the automatic instruction set extension tool will also consider circuit-area and power consumption information during the selection of a given custom instruction.

References

1. Akenine-Möller, T., Haines, E., Hoffman, N.: Real-Time Rendering, 3rd edn. A. K. Peters, Ltd., Natick (2008)
2. Gribble, C., Fisher, J., Eby, D., Quigley, E., Ludwig, G.: Ray tracing visualization toolkit. In: Proceedings of the ACM SIGGRAPH Symposium on Interactive 3D Graphics and Games, I3D 2012, pp. 71–78. ACM, New York (2012)

3. Jówiak, L., Nedjah, N., Figueroa, M.: Modern development methods and tools for embedded reconfigurable systems: A survey. Integr. VLSI J. 43, 1–33 (2010)
4. Józwiak, L., Nedjah, N.: Modern architectures for embedded reconfigurable systems - a survey. Journal of Circuits, Systems, and Computers 18(2), 209–254 (2009)
5. Koch, I.: Enumerating all connected maximal common subgraphs in two graphs. Theoretical Computer Science 250(1), 1–30 (2001)
6. Kopta, D., Shkurko, K., Spjut, J., Brunvand, E., Davis, A.: An energy and bandwidth efficient ray tracing architecture. In: Proceedings of the 5th High-Performance Graphics Conference, HPG 2013, pp. 121–128. ACM, New York (2013)
7. Lattner, C., Adve, V.: Llvm: A compilation framework for lifelong program analysis & transformation. In: Proceedings of the International Symposium on Code Generation and Optimization: Feedback-Directed and Runtime Optimization, CGO 2004, p. 75. IEEE Computer Society, Washington, DC (2004)
8. Lee, W.-J., Shin, Y., Lee, J., Kim, J.-W., Nah, J.-H., Jung, S., Lee, S., Park, H.-S., Han, T.-D.: Sgrt: a mobile gpu architecture for real-time ray tracing. In: Proceedings of the 5th High-Performance Graphics Conference, HPG 2013, pp. 109–119. ACM, New York (2013)
9. Lin, H., Fei, Y.: Resource sharing of pipelined custom hardware extension for energy-efficient application-specific instruction set processor design. ACM Transactions on Design Automation of Electronic Systems (TODAES) 17(4), 39 (2012)
10. Moreano, N., Borin, E., de Souza, C., Araujo, G.: Efficient datapath merging for partially reconfigurable architectures. IEEE Transactions on Computer-Aided Design of Integrated Circuits and Systems 24(7), 969–980 (2005)
11. Nery, A.S., Jozwiak, L., Lindwer, M., Cocco, M., Nedjah, N., Franca, F.M.G.: Hardware reuse in modern application-specific processors and accelerators. In: 2011 14th Euromicro Conference on Digital System Design (DSD), August 31-September 2, pp. 140–147 (2011)
12. Xiao, C., Casseau, E.: An efficient algorithm for custom instruction enumeration. In: Proceedings of the 21st of the Great Lakes Symposium on Great Lakes Symposium on VLSI, pp. 187–192. ACM (2011)
13. Zuluaga, M., Topham, N.: Exploring the unified design-space of custom-instruction selection and resource sharing. In: 2010 International Conference on Embedded Computer Systems (SAMOS), pp. 282–291 (July 2010)

Demand-Based Scheduling Priorities for Performance Optimisation of Stream Programs on Parallel Platforms

Vu Thien Nga Nguyen and Raimund Kirner

University of Hertfordshire
{v.t.nguyen,r.kirner}@herts.ac.uk

Abstract. This paper introduces a heuristic-based scheduler to optimise the throughput and latency of stream programs with dynamic network structure. The novelty is the utilisation of positive and negative demands of the stream communications. It is a centralised approach to provide load balancing for stream programs with dynamic network structures. The approach is designed for shared-memory multi-core platforms. The experiments show that our scheduler performs significantly better than the reference implementation without demand considerations.

1 Introduction

Programming models based on stream programming have become an active research topic, as stream programming has some nice benefits for parallel programming. For example, it makes some forms of parallelism explicit and the communication over streams facilitates implicit synchronisation. Because of this advantage, several research projects have introduced stream programming frameworks such as StreamIt [18], Brook [2], S-Net [9], and CnC [3] to name a few.

For a parallel programming model to gain practical acceptance, it has to be possible to produce efficient code for parallel platforms. The idling time of individual physical resources has to be minimised in order to use the parallel platform efficiently. Efficient code in general depends on the combination of compilation techniques and resource management strategies by the runtime system. There are rather static approaches like StreamIt [18], which assume constant message arrival rates, and more dynamic approaches like S-Net [9], which do not make any assumptions on the message arrival rate and also support dynamically changing streaming-network structures.

In this paper we present a novel heuristics-based scheduler to optimise both throughput and latency of streaming programs with dynamic stream program structures. The scheduler uses a heuristic based on data demand of stream communications. As we address dynamic structures of stream programs, the particular challenge is that static scheduling based on formal constraints or probabilities is not applicable.

The context of our scheduling problem is described in more detail in Section 2, which includes the stream execution model we assume and also the performance metrics we are interested in. Section 3 provides guidelines to design a stream scheduler targeting throughput and latency optimisation. Based on these guidelines, the proposed scheduler is presented in Section 4. In Section 5 we give technical implementation details including a pointer to the *Light-weight Parallel Execution Layer* (LPEL) [15], where

J. Kołodziej et al. (Eds.): ICA3PP 2013, Part I, LNCS 8285, pp. 357–369, 2013.
© Springer International Publishing Switzerland 2013

we deployed our scheduler. In Section 6 we study the influence of some design parameters of our scheduling policy and present some performance comparisons, showing that the new scheduler gives significant performance improvements compared to the original LPEL scheduler. Section 7 discusses related work, followed by a conclusion in Section 8.

2   Background

2.1   Stream Programs

Stream programming is a paradigm that allows concurrency to be expressed by decoupling computations and communications [18,2,9]. The structure of stream programs can be illustrated as a graph whose vertices are computation nodes and edges are communication channels called streams. In this paper we refer to computation nodes simply as nodes. Streams connect nodes in different ways, e.g., pipeline, parallel, feedback, etc.

Stream programs are classified by different properties of computation nodes and communication streams [16]. In general, streams can be uni-directional or bi-directional, while within this paper we limit ourselves to uni-directional streams. A node's behaviour can be deterministic or non-deterministic. The program structure can be dynamic or static.

2.2   Data in Stream Programs

Data arrives to a stream program as a virtually infinite sequence of messages. Input messages coming from the external environment are called *external input messages*. Similarly output messages sent to the external environment are called *external output messages*. Execution of a node consumes n input messages from its input streams and produces m output messages to its output streams. An external input message is **completed** when all the associated external output messages are produced.

2.3   Stream Execution Model

Conceptually the stream execution model includes two layers: a runtime system (RTS) and a scheduler. At the RTS layer, each stream is represented as a FIFO buffer for storing messages and each node of the stream program is transformed into one task. A task is an iterating process that reads messages from its input streams, performs the associated node's computations, and writes output messages to its output streams. Tasks consuming external input messages are *entry tasks*, and tasks producing external output messages are *exit tasks*. All other tasks are called *middle tasks*.

The RTS controls the state of tasks, i.e., it controls when a task is ready to be scheduled. A task is *ready* to be executed if all required messages are available on their input streams. Otherwise the task is *blocked*.

The scheduler, which is the layer below the RTS, employs a policy to distribute ready tasks to physical resources. The scheduler's policy decides: i) which ready task will be processed; ii) which physical resource will process the ready task; and iii) the length of the scheduling cycle, i.e., the processing count of a task before re-scheduling.

2.4 Performance of Stream Programs

Similar to communication networks, stream programs transfer messages from an entry to an exit via interconnected nodes. Thus, their performance is evaluated by the same metrics: throughput and latency.

Throughput. The throughput of stream programs is measured as the number of external input messages that are completed per time unit.

Latency. In stream programs the latency of an external input message is the time interval from when it is consumed by the program to when it is completed. The stream programs is evaluated by the average latency as the arithmetic mean of the latency of all observed external messages. In the context of this paper, latency is used to indicate the average latency unless it is explicitly mentioned as latency of a specific message.

3 Guidelines for Scheduler Design

In this section we present guidelines to design a scheduler aiming for performance optimisation. As unidirectional streams can be considered as queues of messages which are required to pass through connected nodes, a stream program can be considered as a queuing system. We consider here only stable queuing system where the arrival rate does not exceed the maximum throughput and the number of external messages inside the stream program $\overline{M_{cp}}$ is bounded [13].

3.1 Guidelines for Throughput Optimisation

Consider a stream program deployed on a platform of N homogeneous physical resources for a time period $P = [0, t]$. After the period P, M external messages have been completed and M_{cp} external messages are partly processed. Let the average computational time required to complete one external message be $\overline{C}$. The total computational time required to complete these M messages is $C_M = M \cdot \overline{C}$. The total computational time for partly processing these messages is C_{Mcp}. Since $\overline{M_{cp}}$ is bounded, M_{cp} is bounded and so is C_{Mcp}.

During the period P, the total processing time of the N resources is $T = N \cdot t$. The total idling time of the N resources is W and the total overhead time is O. The relative idling time of the system is defined as $\widetilde{W} = \frac{W}{t}$ and similarly the relative overhead time is $\widetilde{O} = \frac{O}{t}$. During the period P, the N resources contribute to the computations of M completed messages; the computations of M_{cp} partly processed messages; and idling time. We therefore have:

$$T = N \cdot t = C_M + C_{Mcp} + W + O = M \cdot \overline{C} + C_{Mcp} + \widetilde{W} \cdot t + \widetilde{O} \cdot t$$

Therefore,

$$M = \frac{N \cdot t - C_{Mcp} - (\widetilde{W} + \widetilde{O}) \cdot t}{\overline{C}} \tag{1}$$

The throughput over the period P is:

$$\text{TP} = \frac{M}{t} = \frac{N \cdot t - C_{Mcp} - (\widetilde{W} + \widetilde{O}) \cdot t}{\overline{C} \cdot t} = \frac{1}{\overline{C}} \cdot \left(N - \frac{C_{Mcp}}{t} - (\widetilde{W} + \widetilde{O}) \right) \tag{2}$$

When the stream program processes infinite external input messages, the overall throughput is obtained when $t \rightarrow +\infty$. As C_{Mcp} is bounded, $\lim_{x \rightarrow +\infty} \frac{C_{Mcp}}{t} = 0$. Therefore, the overall throughput is:

$$\text{TP}_{t \rightarrow \infty} = \frac{(N - \widetilde{W} - \widetilde{O})}{\overline{C}} \tag{3}$$

As $\overline{C}$ varies on the implementation and the underlying hardware, it is not under the sphere of control of the scheduler.

Therefore, to optimise the throughput the scheduler should: i) keep $\overline{M_{cp}}$ bounded and ii) reduce $\widetilde{W}$ and $\widetilde{O}$.

3.2 Guidelines for Latency Optimisation

According to Little's law [13], the latency is equal to the average number of external messages in the stream program, decided by the message consumption rate of the stream program:

$$L = \frac{\overline{M_{cp}}}{\lambda_{consumption}} \tag{4}$$

Where L is the latency and $\lambda_{consumption}$ is the rate at which the stream program consumes external messages. It is also called the consumption rate. To reduce the latency, the scheduler needs to increase the consumption rate and at the same time keep $\overline{M_{cp}}$ low. Within stable systems, the consumption rate is equivalent to the throughput, therefore to maximise throughput is also to contribute in minimising the latency.

4 A Heuristic Stream Scheduler for Performance Optimisation

Generally, a scheduler consists of two sub-schedulers: a space scheduler which decides on which resource a task should be executed; and a time scheduler which decides when a task is executed and for how long. This section presents a scheduler based on the above guidelines to optimise both the throughput and latency by minimising $\widetilde{W}$ and $\overline{M_{cp}}$.

4.1 Space Scheduler

In the proposed scheduler, we can consider one CPU core as a worker. The terms core and worker are used interchangeably in the rest of the paper. The space scheduler does not mapped permanently tasks to any worker. Instead ready tasks are stored in a central queue (CTQ). A task is assigned to a worker whenever it is free. Dynamic network structures are well supported by using the CTQ with its dynamic scheduling of tasks to available resources. That helps to reduce the $\widetilde{W}$ but does not guarantee to minimise it. This depends on the time scheduler which controls the availability of ready tasks. This design of the space scheduler allows flexibility for the time scheduler to controls the ready task availability as well as $\overline{M_{cp}}$.

4.2 Time Scheduler

One responsibility of the time scheduler is to choose a relevant ready task from the CTQ to be executed by a free worker, i.e. to define the task priority. Another responsibility is to decide for how long a worker should execute the assigned task, i.e. to define the scheduling cycle. In stream programming, it is hard to derive an exact scheduling policy providing the best performance because of the dynamic properties of stream programs.

Task Priority. The time scheduler on one side has to activate enough ready tasks and on the other side controls $\overline{M_{cp}}$. Note that the availability of ready tasks is also the availability of messages in side the stream program. We propose a demand-based heuristic strategy for the task priority function which decides when a task should get executed. Tasks with higher priorities will be executed first.

This heuristic is based on the positive demand S_I and the negative demand S_O, where S_I is the total number of messages in the input streams and and S_O is the total number of messages in the output streams. The heuristic is proposed as follows.

- **The priority of an entry task should have a negative correlation with its S_O.** Entry tasks are ready as soon as there are external messages. Their execution makes following tasks ready. This heuristic helps entry tasks to be executed when the potential of ready tasks is low. Once executed, their priority is reduced and after a certain time they have to release resources for other tasks keeping $\overline{M_{cp}}$ bounded.
- **The priority of exit tasks should be higher than other types of tasks.** This is because exit tasks send messages to the external environment, they should be executed as soon as possible to keep $\overline{M_{cp}}$ as low as possible.
- **The priority of a middle task should have a positive correlation with S_I and negative correlation with S_O.** Exit tasks should be executed as soon as possible, however they become ready only when messages are transferred over the stream program passing other middle tasks. A middle task T_0 while performing the associated node's computations consumes n messages from its input streams and produces m messages to its output streams which are read by other tasks $T_i|1{\le}i{\le}n$. The task's S_I is reduced by n and its S_O is increased by m. With this heuristic, T_0's priority is reduced and its chance to hold physical resources is reduced. Meanwhile the S_I values of tasks $T_i|1{\le}i{\le}n$ are increased. That means tasks $T_i|1{\le}i{\le}n$ will have a higher chance to be scheduled and the newly created messages are likely to move forward to the output.

Scheduling Cycle. Ideally each task after performing one node execution should be returned so that other higher priority tasks can proceed. However, task switching can cause overhead and locality loss. Therefore the worker should run a task long enough so that the task switching overhead becomes negligible. We propose a heuristic strategy to define the scheduling cycle based on a timeout value E_{sc}. Once assigned to a worker, a task is executed until it is blocked or the timeout value has been reached. The timeout value E_{sc} can be defined based on the number of node executions, the number of produced output messages or a time period. It is hard to analytically derive the value of E_{sc}. We therefore propose to derive this value through practical experiments.

5   Implementation of the Heuristic Stream Scheduler

The proposed stream scheduler is implemented as a new scheduler for the execution layer LPEL [15] to support S-Net stream programs [9]. LPEL was chosen for supporting

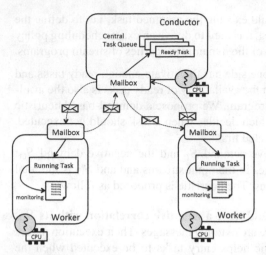

Fig. 1. The heuristic stream scheduler for performance optimisation

Table 1. Priority functions of the middle tasks

Priority Function	T_{Middle}
PF_1	$\frac{S_I+1}{S_O+1}$
PF_2	$\frac{(S_I+1)^2}{S_O+1}$
PF_3	$\frac{S_I+1}{(S_O+1)^2}$
PF_4	$S_I - S_O$

At the first three priority functions, '1' is added to S_O to avoid division-by-zero. '1' is also added to S_I to have a fair proportion against S_O.

task reallocation among CPU cores on a shared memory platform without extra cost; and for providing a sufficient mailbox implementation for core-to-core communications.

The implementation of the proposed scheduler is demonstrated in Figure 1. As the task priority is dynamically changing over time, one worker is dedicated as the **conductor** to keep track of the task priority. The conductor also arranges ready tasks according to their priorities by using a heap structure. Once a worker is free, it requests a new task from the conductor. The conductor then chooses the ready task with the highest priority from the CTQ and sends to the requesting worker. All the communications between the conductor and workers are exercised via mailboxes.

In this implementation, workers do not have to search through the CTQ for the highest priority task. Workers also do not need locks for accessing the shared CTQ. This way of implementing minimises the overhead and waiting time on workers. Although the dedicated conductor can be considered as scheduling overhead, this overhead can be paid off with a large number of cores.

Table 1 lists some priority functions for middle tasks according to the proposed heuristic in Section 4. Functions PF_1 and PF_4 are simple and typical for functions with the same significance of S_I and S_O. Function PF_2 is an example for which S_I has higher significance and function PF_3 is an example for which S_O has higher significance. The priority function for entry tasks is the same for middle tasks but with S_I being zero. As an exit task (with $S_O = 0$) should have higher priority than other tasks, there are 2 choices. The first is to use the priority function of middle tasks but with S_O is zero; this makes an exit task a higher priority compared to a middle task with the same S_I value. The second is to set the priority of exit tasks to infinity ($+\infty$).

We did experiments with all the combinations of these priority functions for entry, exit and middle tasks. None of them has shown superior performance compared to the others. In fact, the variation coefficient is relatively small, about 2~3%. For its simplicity, we choose to use the priority function PF_4 for middle tasks, for entry tasks with $S_I = 0$, and for exit task with $S_O = 0$.

To obtain instant values of S_I and S_O during the runtime, the scheduler is supported by the stream monitoring framework presented in [14]. This monitoring framework allows us to observe the fill level of streams (i.e., the number of messages currently in the stream). As the program structure is dynamic, a task's input and output streams are dynamic. This monitoring framework also allows us to keep track of this information. From the listed monitoring information, the S_I and S_O values of each task can be derived. In addition, the monitoring framework provides other required information to analyse the throughput and latency of stream programs [14]. In the current implementation, the user can define the scheduling cycle based on the number of produced output messages.

6 Evaluation

In this section we compare the performance between our new centralised scheduler with heuristic task priority and LPEL's default scheduler. We compare the peak throughput and the corresponding processing latency when the peak throughput is achieved. The default scheduler of LPEL has one global mapper that distributes generated tasks to workers. Each worker employs a round-robin policy for time-scheduling of ready tasks.

We also evaluate the heuristic priority function by comparing it with random priority. For convenience, we denote DS as the default scheduler of LPEL; CS-HP as the centralised scheduler with heuristic priority; and CS-RP as the centralised scheduler with random priority.

The experiments were performed on a shared memory machine with 48 cores AMD Opteron™ Processor 6174 and 256GB of shared memory. 2 cores are used to imitate the source producing external input messages, and the sink consuming external output messages. The experiments are performed with 5 different applications implemented in the S-Net language:

- DES: performs DES encryption on 32KB-size messages
- FFT: computes FFT algorithm on messages of 2^{20} discrete complex values
- HIST: calculates histogram of images with average size of 5342 x 3371
- IMF: applies a series of filters on images with average size of 4658 x 3083
- OBD: detects 4 different types of objects from 1920 x 1080 images

These applications are chosen for their common usages in stream processing. DES is used for stream encryption and FFT is used in signal processing. HIST is used for thresholding in image processing. Also IMF and OBD are commonly used in image processing. The stream structure of each application is cloned into several copies connected in parallel in order to increase concurrency. The number of copies is varied depending on the number of cores.

We derived the scheduling timeout value E_{sc} by experiments on these five applications with different values of E_{sc} from 1 to 30. The observed difference in throughput and latency has been relatively small. This shows that the task-switching overhead in LPEL is negligible. Thus, for the further experiments we decided to just use an arbitrary value for E_{sc} in the range of 1 to 30.

6.1 Performance Comparison

Figure 2 demonstrates the comparison in performance and throughput scalability between CS-HP and DS. We dedicate one worker as the conductor, we only measure CS-HP with 2 or more cores. For a small number of cores the relative overhead of the conductor is high, the peak throughput therefore is better in DS. When the number of cores increases, this overhead is reduced and the peak throughput of CS-HP is improved. In the case of 46 cores, the peak throughput of CS-HP is significantly higher than DS. In particular, the peak throughput of the DES, FFT, HIST, IMF and OBD are respectively 1.8, 1.8, 2.7, 2.0 and 2.3 times higher with CS-HP.

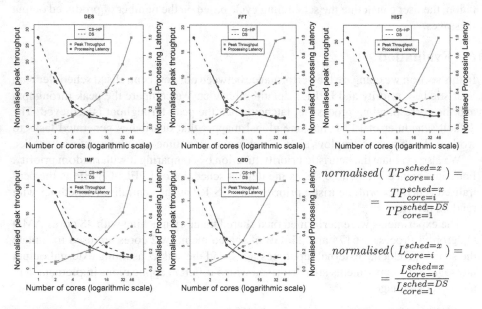

$$normalised\left(TP_{core=i}^{sched=x} \right) =$$
$$= \frac{TP_{core=i}^{sched=x}}{TP_{core=1}^{sched=DS}}$$

$$normalised\left(L_{core=i}^{sched=x} \right) =$$
$$= \frac{L_{core=i}^{sched=x}}{L_{core=1}^{sched=DS}}$$

Fig. 2. Normalised peak throughput and processing latency (with $\lambda = TP_{peak}$) of CS-HP and DS on various applications

The processing latency of CS-HP and 2 cores is better than DS for IMF and the same for FFT despite the higher overhead of CS-HP. Starting from 4 cores, the processing latency of CS-HP is better than or equal to DS for all applications. Note that the processing latency is measured when the peak throughput is achieved. CS-HP provides higher peak throughput than DS in most of the cases, i.e., the applications can cope with a higher arrival rate. Furthermore, if the arrival rate for CS-HP gets reduced down to the peak throughput of DS, then CS-HP will exercise a significantly lower processing latency. Figure 3 demonstrates this for the OBD application. With $\lambda = TP_{peak}$, i.e., when two schedulers are compared with their own peak throughput, the processing of CS-HP is 1.5 to 2.4 times lower than DS. With $\lambda = TP_{peak}^{DS}$, i.e., when two schedulers are compared with the same arrival rate, the processing of CS-HP is 7.7 to 12.4 times lower than DS. The cases of 2 and 4 cores are not shown because the peak throughput of CS-HP is smaller or equivalent to DS, as mentioned above.

6.2 Scalability Comparison

The processing latency depends on the concurrency level of the stream program which is reflected in the structure of the program. For this reason, the comparison in the latency scalability between 2 schedulers is not so appropriate. We therefore focus on the throughput scalability. The results in Figure 2 shows that CS-HP has a better throughput scalability than DS.

For the DES application, CS-HP and DS scales at the same rate from 2 to 16 cores. DES is a special application where the stream program structure consist of multiple pipelines. Each pipeline has 16 tasks with the same amount of computations. As DS uses a round-robin approach to map tasks to cores, it creates a load balanced mapping when the number of tasks is a multiple of the number of cores. In this case, the idling time is minimal and therefore the best throughput is achieved. With 32 and especially 46 cores, the number of tasks is not a multiple of the number of cores, the round-robin mapper of DS does not provide load balance. Consequently the throughput is not well scaled for DS. In contrast, the scalability of CS-HP is not affected and overtakes DS.

6.3 Priority Function Evaluation

To evaluate the proposed priority function, we compare the performance of CS-HP and CS-RP. The behaviour of all applications are quite similar. We thus present here one illustrated case of the HIST application in Figure 4. As explained in Section 4, with bounded $\overline{M_{cp}}$ the throughput is maximised when the idling and overhead time is minimised. As $\overline{M_{cp}}$ is controlled by entry and exit tasks, the random task priority cannot be guaranteed to have bounded $\overline{M_{cp}}$ though the unbounded chance is low. Using the centralised approach, the CS-RP has minimised idling time $\overline{W}$. CS-RP has less time overhead $\overline{O}$ than CS-HP because it does not need to monitor the stream fill level and keep track of the task-stream relationship. Therefore when $\overline{M_{cp}}$ is bounded the peak throughput of CS-RP is better than CS-HP.

Since the stream structure of the program is cloned into more copies for more cores, the number of tasks and streams is increased according to the number of cores. The overhead for monitoring tasks and streams in CS-HP increases when the the number of cores increases. The difference in throughput between CS-HP and CS-RP is higher for the higher numbers of cores.

In contrast, the processing latency of CS-HP is significantly better than CS-RP for all numbers of cores. This shows that the proposed priority function has a meaningful influence on the processing latency. However, the overhead of calculating the priority function at the same time reduces the maximum throughput.

7 Related Work

Maximising Throughput. The fundamental technique for maximising throughput is balancing load among physical resources. There is a significant volume of prior works dealing with load balancing. Here we list major work of load balancing in stream programming and conceptually similar models.

Gordon et al. propose a static strategy using iterative greedy heuristic to partition a *StreamIt* program into a set of balanced partitions and assign to tile processors of the

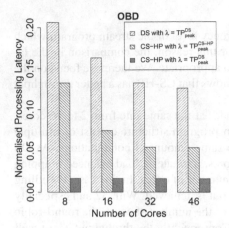

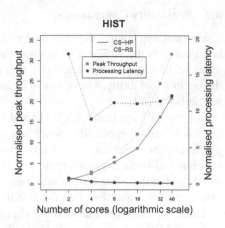

Fig. 3. Processing latency comparison with different arrival rates

Fig. 4. Performance of HIST using CS-HP and CS-RP

Raw architecture [8,7]. Instead of using iterative heuristics, two successor approaches have been introduced using ILP solvers [12] and approximative algorithms [6]. With the assumption that the programmer has a prior knowledge of the expected load, Chen et al. establishes a static user-specified load balance [4]. Another approach of statically partitioning StreamIt programs is to use machine learning [19]. The approach first uses supervised machine learning to predict the ideal structure of the partitioned program and then selects from all partition possibilities the nearest one to the ideal structure.

Taking advantage of *StreamIt* filters (which are computation nodes in our terminology) being stateless, the work in [5] proposes a dynamic load balance approach based on the back pressure implications from the bounded streams. Another dynamic load balance approach is proposed for the DIAMOND distributed search system [10]. This system is similar to the stream programming model because data arrive in DIAMOND as an infinite sequence of objects. The difference is that each object needs to independently pass a fixed set of filters in a fixed order. The approach aims to efficiently distribute the processing of these filters to the set of computing nodes. This approach is similar to ours as it uses the state of upstream and downstream queues to avoid overfull and under-full queues.

To maximise throughput for both predictable and unpredictable *StreamIt* programs, Zhang et al. combine static and dynamic strategies [21]. For predictable stream programs, static software pipeline techniques from previous work [7] are used. For unpredictable stream programs, a central scheduler is used to maintain the state of the program to maximising only the throughput.

Another example of scheduling methods for fixed-structure networks, which is a more specific problem than ours, is given by Tassiulas et al. [17]. This approach it is actually more related to our work than the SDF-based scheduling work of StreamIt. In [17] the authors are able to prove that their derived task execution leads to maximal throughput for any input arrival rate where a stable schedule (bounded message queues) is possible. However, as soon as dynamic network structures are involved, their formal optimality proof would not be valid any more. In case of dynamic network structures the authors would have to, like we did, switch to a heuristic scheduling approach for which they would need to experimentally show its effectiveness.

Minimising Latency. Work on latency optimisation focuses mostly on the processing latency. In this direction there is not as much research available on stream programming literature as is on throughput maximisation. Karczmarek et al. introduced the concept of *phase scheduling* for StreamIt programs, exploiting the static nature of the streaming graph [11]. The goal of phase scheduling is to address the trade-off between code size and buffer size [1]. When the buffer size is zero, the phased schedule has an unlimited number of phases and is referred as the minimum latency schedule. In this case the entrance filter is not executed until the exit node has not been finished. That guarantees that the processing latency is minimal, though the throughput is worst. Xing et al. introduce a dynamic load distribution strategy for the Borealis stream processor [20]. Although it is not clearly explained, the strategy is based on the assertion that minimising the end-to-end processing latency can be achieved by minimising the load variance or maximising the load correlation between processing nodes.

To the best of our knowledge, our approach is the first heuristic scheduler for stream programs with dynamic network structures. Our heuristics with entry tasks having their own priority function is novel as well, allowing for a stable schedule when the arrival rate is higher than the peak throughput.

8 Conclusion and Future Work

In this paper we have presented a novel heuristics-based scheduler to optimise in terms of throughput and latency the performance of stream programs with dynamic network structures. The scheduler deploys a centralised approach with a demand-based heuristics for task selection, which is geared towards optimising throughput and latency.

In contrast to the new scheduler, the default scheduler of the reference system does not deploy knowledge about the structure and state of the streaming network. The experimental results show that the new scheduler offers significant improvements of throughput compared to the default scheduler. For 46 cores the throughput showed improvements by a factor of 1.6 to 2.7. When limiting the arrival rate of the new scheduler down to the maximum throughput of the default scheduler, we observed at the same time improvements of the latency by a factor of 7.7 to 12.4 for the OBD application on 8 and more cores.

As future work we plan to extend our approach with a hierarchical scheduler to support distributed platforms. For this we will explore techniques to efficiently divide the stream program into subprograms to be distributed.

Acknowledgements. We would like to thank Hugh Leather for discussions at a HiPEAC summer school ACACES 2012, resulting in useful ideas. The research leading to these results has received funding from the IST FP7 research project *"Asynchronous and Dynamic Virtualization through performance ANalysis to support Concurrency Engineering* (ADVANCE)", contract no IST-2010-248828, and the FP7 ARTEMIS-JU research project *"ConstRaint and Application driven Framework for Tailoring Embedded Real-time Systems"* (CRAFTERS), contract no 295371.

References

1. Bhattacharyya, S.S.: Optimization trade-offs in the synthesis of software for embedded dsp. In: IN CASES (1999)
2. Buck, I., Foley, T., Horn, D., Sugerman, J., Fatahalian, K., Houston, M., Hanrahan, P.: Brook for GPUs: stream computing on graphics hardware. ACM Trans. Graph. 23(3) (August 2004)
3. Burke, M.G., Knobe, K., Newton, R., Sarkar, V.: Concurrent Collections programming model. In: Padua, D. (ed.) Encyclopedia of Parallel Computing. Springer US (2011)
4. Chen, J., Gordon, M.I., Thies, W., Zwicker, M., Pulli, K., Durand, F.: A reconfigurable architecture for load-balanced rendering. In: Proceedings of the ACM SIGGRAPH/EUROGRAPHICS Conference on Graphics Hardware, HWWS 2005. ACM, New York (2005)
5. Collins, R.L., Carloni, L.P.: Flexible filters: load balancing through backpressure for stream programs. In: Proceedings of the Seventh ACM International Conference on Embedded Software, EMSOFT 2009. ACM, New York (2009)
6. Farhad, S.M., Ko, Y., Burgstaller, B., Scholz, B.: Orchestration by approximation: mapping stream programs onto multicore architectures. In: Proc. 16th International Conference on Architectural Support for Programming Languages and Operating Systems (ASPLOS 2011), New Port Beach, CA, USA, pp. 357–368 (March 2011)
7. Gordon, M.I., Thies, W., Amarasinghe, S.: Exploiting coarse-grained task, data, and pipeline parallelism in stream programs. SIGARCH Comput. Archit. News 34(5) (October 2006)
8. Gordon, M.I., Thies, W., Karczmarek, M., Lin, J., Meli, A.S., Lamb, A.A., Leger, C., Wong, J., Hoffmann, H., Maze, D., Amarasinghe, S.: A stream compiler for communication-exposed architectures. SIGOPS Oper. Syst. Rev. 36(5) (October 2002)
9. Grelck, C., Scholz, S.-B., Shafarenko, A.: A Gentle Introduction to S-Net: Typed Stream Processing and Declarative Coordination of Asynchronous Components. Parallel Processing Letters 18(2) (2008)
10. Huston, L., Nizhner, A., Pillai, P., Sukthankar, R., Steenkiste, P., Zhang, J.: Dynamic load balancing for distributed search. In: Proceedings of the High Performance Distributed Computing, HPDC 2005. IEEE Computer Society, Washington, DC (2005)
11. Karczmarek, M., Thies, W., Amarasinghe, S.: Phased scheduling of stream programs. SIGPLAN Not. 38(7) (June 2003)
12. Kudlur, M., Mahlke, S.: Orchestrating the execution of stream programs on multicore platforms. SIGPLAN Not. 43(6) (June 2008)
13. Little, J.D.C.: A Proof for the Queuing Formula: L= W. Operations Research 9(3), 383–387 (1961)
14. Nguyen, V.T.N., Kirner, R., Penczek, F.: A multi-level monitoring framework for stream-based coordination programs. In: Xiang, Y., Stojmenovic, I., Apduhan, B.O., Wang, G., Nakano, K., Zomaya, A. (eds.) ICA3PP 2012, Part I. LNCS, vol. 7439, pp. 83–98. Springer, Heidelberg (2012)
15. Prokesch, D.: A light-weight parallel execution layer for shared-memory stream processing. Master's thesis, Technische Universität Wien, Vienna, Austria (February 2010)
16. Stephens, R.: A survey of stream processing. Acta Informatica, 34 (1997)
17. Tassiulas, L., Ephremides, A.: Stability properties of constrained queuing systems and scheduling policies for maximum throughput in multihop radio networks. IEEE Transaction on Automatic Control 37(12), 1936–1948 (1992)
18. Thies, W., Karczmarek, M., Amarasinghe, S.: StreamIt: A language for streaming applications. In: Nigel Horspool, R. (ed.) CC 2002. LNCS, vol. 2304, p. 179. Springer, Heidelberg (2002)

19. Wang, Z., O'Boyle, M.F.: Partitioning streaming parallelism for multi-cores: a machine learning based approach. In: Proceedings of the 19th International Conference on Parallel Architectures and Compilation Techniques, PACT 2010. ACM, New York (2010)
20. Xing, Y., Zdonik, S., Hwang, J.-H.: Dynamic load distribution in the borealis stream processor. In: Proceedings of the 21st International Conference on Data Engineering, ICDE 2005. IEEE Computer Society, Washington, DC (2005)
21. Zhang, D., Li, Q.J., Rabbah, R., Amarasinghe, S.: A lightweight streaming layer for multi-core execution. SIGARCH Comput. Archit. News, 36(2) (May 2008)

A Novel Architecture for Financial Investment Services on a Private Cloud

Ranjan Saha, Bhanu Sharma, Ruppa K. Thulasiram*,
and Parimala Thulasiraman

Department of Computer Science
University of Manitoba
Winnipeg, Canada
{rksaha,bsharma,tulsi,thulasir}@cs.umanitoba.ca

Abstract. One of the important paradigms in Cloud computing is Software as a Service (SaaS). Saas has been provided by many cloud vendors for different applications. One of the application that has not been explored is financial investment. In this work, we propose an architecture for a SaaS model that provides service to financial investors who are not familiar with various mathematical models. Such finance models are used to evaluate financial instruments, for example, to price a derivative that is currently being traded before entering into a contract. An we consider a situation of an investor approaches the Cloud Service Provider (CSP) to price a particular derivative and specify the time, budget, and accuracy constraints. Based on these constraints specified by investors, the service provider will be able to compute the option value using our model proposed in this study. To evaluate our proposed model, we compared pricing results with the classical model that provides a closed-form solution for option pricing. After establishing the accuracy of our pricing results, we further ensure that the Service Level Agreement (SLA) between the Financial SaaS Provider (FSP) and the investors is honoured by meeting the constraints put forth by the investors.

Keywords: Financial SaaS, Financial Derivatives, Investment Decision Making, Option Pricing, and Financial Service Architecture.

1   Introduction and Motivation

Different sectors such as IT, business, manufacturing, travel, medical, and security are benefitting from Cloud services.

Often clients would like to use an application a few times. For example, in finance, an investor would like to modify the current portfolio by selling part of his portfolio such as stocks and buying new assets. To buy new asset, an investor is interested in finding the benefits of investing in a company in near future. To verify if the asking price of the stock (asset) at a future date is worth for that asset, the investor has to speculate price path of the assets performance towards

---

* Corresponding author.

J. Kołodziej et al. (Eds.): ICA3PP 2013, Part I, LNCS 8285, pp. 370–379, 2013.

the date of purchase in the future. There are many ways to create various price paths using various finance models, which are highly mathematical and beyond the comprehension of an average investor. These financial models can be provided as *Software as a Service (SaaS)* on Cloud to potential investors.

The financial instrument that allows investors to decide over a period of time (known as contract period) before buying/selling an asset is known as *financial option* or *financial derivative* [1]. This contract does not obligate the investor to buy/sell through the contract. To find the price of an option, we can use different algorithmic approaches [2], [3], [4] [5]. The computations involved in finding the price of an option is difficult for an average investor to understand without having fundamental knowledge of how the algorithms work and hence financial software as a service would be an attractive way to expand the customer base for a cloud service provider.

In this study we develop a novel architecture that integrates a SaaS model in Cloud with financial algorithms that enables providing services to ordinary investors who are neither familiar with financial models to compute the price of an option before deciding to invest nor do they have resources to do the computation. To the best of our knowledge, no real financial SaaS model has been developed that uses Cloud to compute option price and help making decisions that best matches the investor's need satisfying quality and time constraints.

1.1 Option Pricing

An option [1] is a contract between two parties where one party called holder of the option gets the right to exercise (that is, buy or sell) the option at his/her will during the contract period (T) whereas the other party called writer of the option, is obliged to the decisions of the holder. Options are of two types: Call option and Put option. A Call (Put) option gives holder the right to buy (sell) the assets underlying the option contract at a pre-specified price called strike price (K). Option contract can be exercised in many different styles. A European option allows the holder to exercise the option only at the expiration date whereas an American option allows the holder to exercise the option on or before the expiration date.

There are many fundamental algorithmic techniques available in the literature for calculating option pricing. Some important techniques include are: binomial lattice (BL) [4], [7] fast Fourier transform (FFT) [2], finite-difference (FD) technique [8], [5] and Monte-Carlo (MC) simulation [3], [9]. We refer the reader to [1] for details of these techniques.

2 Related Work and Contribution

SaaS model in Cloud computing can be one of the choices that can be adopted by investors to compute option prices.

Garg et al. [12] have developed a SaaS model for ordinary investors who want to evaluate price of an option. The researchers implemented different HPC algorithms [2], [4], [9], [5] in a Cloud simulator [13] to compute the option price. Our objective in the current study is to develop an architecture that integrates financial algorithms that compute option values and to provide service to cloud clients who have a little or no knowledge on finance models.

In our SaaS model, we have implemented several algorithms based on the service requested by the customer. The CSP implements all option pricing algorithms in advance and the customer who wants to know the worthiness of investing in a particular financial option request for a service. The CSP speculates the price path of the underlying asset using any or all of these algorithms. The CSP collects few parameters from investors such as time budget and accuracy constraints to use as inputs to the algorithms in addition to the name of the asset. Then, CSP collects other data on the underlying asset from reliable on-line sources and determines an algorithm that is better suited for a customer based on the accuracy and time constraint proposed by the customer. We assume that the CSP also owns the infrastructure that is used to implement the model. However, the algorithm is constrained with the demands of time over accuracy.

Prime contribution in this study is to build a FSM architecture that can be used by CSP, to provide financial computing services and optimize the user requests to meet the time, budget and accuracy constraints.

3   Financial SaaS Architecture

Initially, the investors will access the FSM to compute the price of a particular option written on some underlying asset. The FSP will provide the investor with a set of questionnaire to collect basic information such as name of the stock, the constraints on the service and so on. While it is generally expected that the investors would require high accuracy in the option pricing results, many times the investors would like to get a feel for the trend in the price of underlying asset by noting the option pricing result. Hence, accuracy is also treated as a parameter. Based on three main parameters (time, budget contraints and accuracy), one of the techniques [2], [3], [4] [5], [6] will be selected by our FSM model to compute the option price.

To develop FSM for option pricing application, our study has four different components/models. First, we develop a private Cloud using Eucalyptus open source Cloud software [14] which will dynamically scale up or down the Cloud resources depending on the application workload for financial services. It will allow users to acquire and release required resources on-demand. In addition, this Cloud system also has the ability to be used by multiple users simultaneously where they will share resources based on the customer demand. Eucalyptus also has very reliable security system which supports WS-Security policies and features such as authentication, authorization, network and machine isolation that prevents network trafficking from hackers.

Second, to support multiple customers, we have developed a unified and innovative multi-layered customization model that supports and manages the variability of SaaS applications and customer-specific requirements.

Third, our model incorporates a recommendation engine to support requirements of new customers based on the inputs given by them. This engine will explore the financial needs of the customer and additional results on option price based on a slightly different scenario (such as additional price path, different expiration date, and different initial asset price) than requested by the customer. The recommendation engine will compute option values for various parametric conditions around the initial values provided by the customer. This is a value added service that further helps the customer in deciding to buy/sell options confidently.

Fourth, we have implemented three option pricing algorithms (binomial lattice, Monte Carlo simulation and finite-difference technique) on the back end server to execute as and when needed for individual customers - .

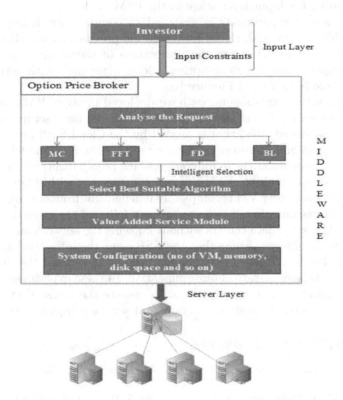

Fig. 1. Proposed FSM model to compute option value

We have illustrated the proposed multilayered FSM in figure 1. The model consists of three different layers: input layer, middleware, and server layer. The input and server layer form the foundation of FSM model. The input layer takes inputs from investors and provide the information to the middleware. The server layer is the actual back end Cloud server which computes the option price and returns the best suitable result back to the investor. The middleware decides on the particular algorithm based on the input parameter. In addition it includes a recommendation system that helps the FSP to provide value added service.

To provide the required service, the middleware would undergo customization based on the option pricing algorithms. Each of the algorithms has specific strengths and weaknesses that match the investor's requirements. Also, each algorithm possesses different accuracy level.

4   Experiments and Results

Our evaluation methodology is based on the perspective of both customer satisfaction as well as FSP. Deadline is one of the key performance measures in the FSM model. Initially, at the input layer, the FSP enters into a SLA with the investors during the input layer stage in the FSM model.

Our first set of experiments is designed to compare our European option pricing algorithms [15] with closed-form solution provided by the Black-Scholes-Merton [1] model to determine the correctness of the algorithms. Moreover, we have compared our American option pricing algorithms with actual market values available from Yahoo! Finance [16].

In another set of experiments, we have deployed multiple VMs into the Eucalyptus open source Cloud system. Furthermore, we have setup the required software (as presented later) that is needed by the Cloud SaaS provider. Multiple VMs can start and shutdown on-demand so that the FSM model can provide maximum available resources to different specific requirements of the service requests. In addition, multiple VMs can run concurrently with different software environments since every VM is completely independent from one another on the same physical machine. In our experiments, we followed the general approach of deploying VMs on the data centers without knowing the network and application requirements though we assume that the FSP owns the infrastructure.

Finally in the fourth set of experiments, we have evaluated the SLA policies to determine the success rate of our application. In these experiments, the FSM engine dynamically selects an algorithm to execute the investor's request. The selection depends on the desired accuracy and service completion time.

	High (70-100%)	Medium (50-70%)	Low (0-50%)
Finite Difference	1	3	3
Monte-Carlo	3	2	2
Binomial	2	1	1

	Immediate (0-50%)	Moderate (50-70%)	Slow (70-100%)
Binomial	1	2	3
Monte-Carlo	2	1	2
Finite-Difference	3	3	1

Fig. 2. Rank of Techniques for Accuracy Requirements

Fig. 3. Rank of algorithms for various response types

For accuracy, the FSM model selects the option pricing algorithm based on a pre-computed table designed using the benchmark results [15] of the option price algorithms. The Table in Figure 2 designates a rank for each option pricing algorithm used in our experimental study. We have classified accuracy into three distinct levels (high, medium and low) to serve various clients' needs better and an algorithm gets a rank for each of these classification. Often an investor would like to get a feel of the market pulse without worrying about the accuracy of the option values for an initial decision making. The last two columns on this table are meant to be used for providing service for such clients. However, we note that the FSM will not compromise on the the accuracy of the results for a serious client. Likewise, the service completion time presented in the Table in figure 3 ranks each option pricing algorithm based on three distinct response type categories: immediate, moderate and slow. In our model, we have combined the ranking of the algorithms in these two figures before selecting an algorithm as per the request of the client on accuracy and timing. For example, if a client requests for immediate response and moderate accuracy, then the model will select binomial lattice for pricing the option. However, if an investor requests for both high accuracy as well as immediate response time, then such a request is declined as there is no algorithm that can help FSP to provide the service. This can be seen as our admission control policy in the FSM for the stream of jobs that are taken up for service.

For our experiments, we have considered a window of 90 seconds response time. This response time window comprises of the entire workflow from the start of the user interaction with FSM until the user receives the desires service.

4.1   FSM Implementation

We ran our experiments in two different environments: 1) on a local machine, 2) on multiple Cloud VMs where each VM work as an independent computational machine. The virtual machines each have 1 CPU core, 512 MB of RAM. Figure 4 illustrates the characteristics of the machines we used in our experiments.

Type of Machine	Processor Type	# of Core	Architecture	Memory	Disk Space	Network
Local Machine	AMD, 1.9Ghz	4	64 bit	4GB	250GB	10 Gb Ethernet
VM	AMD 1.9Ghz	1	64 bit	512MB	15GB	1 Gb Ethernet

Fig. 4. Type of machine used in the study

To run experiment in our FSM model, we have collected the required set of option pricing data from Yahoo! Finance [16] for companies such as IBM, Apple, Amazon, Chevron, Walmart, Google, Johnson & Johnson and Toyota with expiration time of three, six and nine months.

4.2   Analysis of Results

Correctness of Option Pricing Algorithms. Initially, the investor enters his/her trade details and requirements in input layer. This input layer of the FSM model includes the name of the underlying (asset) stock, time of maturity, accuracy and type of response. Then, the FSM model analyzes the accuracy and response type requirements by the investor and dynamically selects the best-suited algorithm to compute the option price.

We carried out several experiments to verify the correctness of the option pricing algorithms that we have developed.

Figure 5 and Figure 6 compare the Call and Put option price results obtained from Monte-Carlo, binomial lattice, and finite-difference methods [15]. Moreover, we have executed all our experiments based on the expiration time of the option price. As Black-Scholes [1] option pricing algorithm is considered to be a benchmark for the European option pricing model, the aim of these experiments is to evaluate the accuracy of the option values returned from our algorithms in comparison to Black-Scholes closed-form solution.

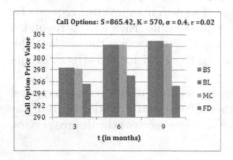

Fig. 5. Comparison of European Call Option Prices using various models for different expiration dates

Fig. 6. Comparison of European Put Option Prices using various models for different expiration dates

We have ensured that our option pricing algorithms provide option price close to the Black-Scholes model for both Call as well as Put options for various expiration dates.

We have also compared our American Call and Put option pricing results against the option values obtained from Yahoo Finance [16]. Figure 7 and Figure 8 show that the option value returned from various algorithms is slightly more than the ask value for both Call as well as the Put options by 0.37% ((298.3-297.2)/297.2) to 2.37% ((302-295)/295).

S = 865.42, K = 570, σ = 0.4, r = 0.02					
t (in months)	Ask	Bid	Binomial Lattice	Monte Carlo	Finite Difference
3	297.2	294.5	298.3316957	298.3577	294.935
6	298.4	296	302.2807118	303.1442	297.1528
9	295.3	292.4	302.8866654	302.6053	300.6465

S = 72.23, K = 80, σ = 0.4, r = 0.02					
t (in months)	Ask	Bid	Binomial Lattice	Monte Carlo	Finite Difference
3	6.85	6.75	8.448557287	8.421458	7.059314
6	7.7	7.6	9.864749481	9.937963	8.913536
9	8.45	8.35	10.9621752	11.01055	10.99489

Fig. 7. Comparison of real data versus American option pricing for Call Option

Fig. 8. Comparison of real data versus American option pricing for Put Option

The FSM model also acts as a recommendation engine and computes option values by altering the strike price K to provide the investors with further opportunity to decide whether to invest into a particular option. This is achieved by altering the strike price to return an option value between ask and bid price. That is, the asking price in Yahoo! finance would only be good for the new strike price indicating that asking price would be too high for the unaltered strike price. Figure 9 depicts the valued added service provided by the FSM model for Johnson & Johnson European Call option for 3 months expiration time period using the finite-difference algorithm.

Initially, the finite-difference algorithm returned the option value as \$41.9247085 for strike price of \$50, which did not lie between ask and bid price range. When the recommendation engine of the FSM model is called, the strike price is altered to \$52.5 to recompute the option value as \$39.4317737, which lies between the expected posted ask and bid prices. Therefore, the recommendation engine of the FSM identifies profitable opportunities for the investor.

To support multitenancy, we have launched eight VMs instances in Eucalyptus Cloud system.

The biggest advantage of multitenancy is that it is a cost-effective solution that provides optimum usage of resources. In our multitenancy configuration, each of the eight Eucalyptus instances are running on the same software and hardware and yet providing service to eight different investors simultaneously with specific requirements. In addition, the multitenancy environment also provides security to the investor data by customizing the application design so that one investor cannot see data from another investor or cannot share data with others.

Call Options: S = 89.18, σ = 0.4, r = 0.02			
Strike Price (K)	Ask	Bid	Output from Algorithm
50	39.5	39	41.9247085
52.5	39.5	39	39.43717737

Fig. 9. Value added service

SLA Agreement Table								
Service Completion Time (in seconds)	Customer 1	Customer 2	Customer 3	Customer 4	Customer 5	Customer 6	Customer 7	Customer 8
Between 0 and till 45 (0-50%)	10.9	6.569			8.016	6.308		
Above 45 and till 63 (50-70%)			53.008					
Above 63 and till 90 (70-100%)				74.348			81.705	89.974
Above 90								

Fig. 10. Service completion time

Fig. 11. Comparing the SLA between investor request and service provided based on service completion time

The success rate of a SLA is measured for the service provided against the investor's request based on desired accuracy and service completion time. Our FSM model always selects the best-suited option pricing algorithm based on accuracy and service completion time to calculate the option value as discussed above. Figure 10 lists the service completion time obtained by each of eight

# of Customer	1	2	3	4	5	6	7	8
Expection on Service Completion Time	Low	Moderate	Moderate	Low	Immediate	Immediate	Low	Low
Result Achieved (Success/ Failure)	Success	Success	Success	Success	Success	Success	Success	Success

Fig. 12. Success/Failure Result on SLA for customer based on service completion time

investors for each service request. The graph depicted in Figure 11 clearly marks the service completion time category to which each request belongs. In addition, Figure 12 shows the requested response type and calculates success or failure using the response type obtained based on Figure 3 and Figure 10. We observed from Figure 10 that our algorithm results in 0 failures out of 8 times, which accounts for 100% success rate.

5   Conclusions

In this study we have developed a SaaS Architecture for financial investors called FSM that will provide service to the ordinary investors who are not familiar with complex financial algorithms that are used to compute the price of an option. The Architecture has three different layers, namely input, middleware, and server layer. The FSM computes the pricing of an option based on the input (time, accuracy, and budget) given by the financial investors. The middleware includes a recommendation engine which selects the best suitable algorithm to be executed into the server layer and provides additional results than the requested result to help the client make better decision. We have evaluated the SLA between the investors and the FSP and show that the FSP provide required Quality of Service (QoS) to meet the SLA. We have also measured the performance of our FSM model based on several parameters such as time, budget and accuracy constraints. There are three key contributions in this work. (1) Determine which option pricing algorithm best meets the user's requirements and constraints. (2) Provide the option pricing results from this algorithm as well as more results to capture variation in the market trend to help the investor decide better. This is a value added service to the client. (3) Satisfying investor's constraints on time, accuracy and budget.

Acknowledgments. The first author acknowledges the Computer Science scholarship. The second author acknowledges the University of Manitoba Graduate Fellowship (UMGF) and the Department of Computer Science Merit Scholarship for partial financial support for his graduate studies. The third and fourth authors acknowledge partial financial support from Discovery Grants of the Natural Sciences and Engineering Research Council (NSERC) Canada.

References

1. Hull, J.: Options, futures, and other derivatives. Pearson (2009)
2. Barua, S., Thulasiram, R., Thulasiraman, P.: High performance computing for a financial application using fast fourier transform. Accepted in Quality Technology and Quantitative Management (QTQN), ISSN 1684-3703

3. Boyle, P.P.: Options: A monte carlo approach. Journal of Financial Economics 4(3), 323–338 (1977)
4. Cox, J.C., Ross, S.A., Rubinstein, M.: Option pricing: A simplified approach. Journal of Financial Economics 7(3), 229–263 (1979)
5. Thulasiram, R., Zhen, C., Chhabra, A., Thulasiraman, P.: A second order L0 stable algorithm for evaluating european options. International Journal of High Performance Computing and Networking 4(5), 311–320 (2006)
6. Haug, E.G.: The complete guide to option pricing formulas, vol. 2. McGraw-Hill, New York (1998)
7. Solomon, S., Thulasiram, R., Thulasiraman, P.: Option pricing on the gpu. In: Proceedings of 12th IEEE International Conference on High Performance Computing and Communications (HPCC 2010), Melbourne, Australia, pp. 289–296 (September 2009)
8. Carr, P., Madan, D.: Option valuation using the fast fourier transform. Journal of Computational Finance 2(4), 61–73 (1999)
9. Rahmail, S., Shiller, I., Thulasiram, R.: Different estimators of the underlying assets volatility and option pricing errors: parallel monte carlo simulation. In: Proceeding of International Conference on Computational Finance and its Applications, pp. 121–131. WIT Press, Bologna (2004)
10. Zhang, N., Lim, E., Man, K., Lei, C.: Cpu-gpu hybrid parallel binomial american option pricing. In: Proceedings of the International MultiConference of Engineers and Computer Scientists (IMECS 2012), Hong Kong, vol. 2 (2012)
11. Zhang, J., Bandyopadhyay, S., Piramuthu, S.: Real option valuation on grid computing. Decision Support Systems 46(1), 333–343 (2008)
12. Garg, S.K., Sharma, B., Calheiros, R.N., Thulasiram, R.K., Thulasiraman, P., Buyya, R.: Financial application as a software service on cloud. In: Parashar, M., Kaushik, D., Rana, O.F., Samtaney, R., Yang, Y., Zomaya, A. (eds.) IC3 2012. CCIS, vol. 306, pp. 141–151. Springer, Heidelberg (2012)
13. Calheiros, R., Ranjan, R., Rose, C.A.F.D., Buyya, R.: Cloudsim: A novel framework for modeling and simulation of cloud computing infrastructures and services. Computing Research Repository abs/0903.2525 (2009)
14. Eucalyptus.: Open source cloud software, http://www.eucalyptus.com/ (accessed on December 25, 2012)
15. Sharma, B., Thulasiram, R.K., Thulasiraman, P.: Technical Memo CFD058-W10, Computational Financial Derivatives Lab, Department of Computer Science, University of Manitoba (2010), http://www.cs.umanitoba.ca/tulsi
16. Yahoo-Finance!: Option price data, http://ca.finance.yahoo.com/ (accessed on July 5, 2013)

Building Platform as a Service for High Performance Computing over an Opportunistic Cloud Computing

German A. Sotelo[1], Cesar O. Diaz[2], Mario Villamizar[1], Harold Castro[1], Johnatan E. Pecero[2], and Pascal Bouvry[2]

[1] Universidad de los Andes, Bogota D.C., Colombia
{ga.sotelo69,mj.villamizar24,hcastro}@uniandes.edu.co
[2] University of Luxembourg, L-1359 Luxembourg-Kirchberg, Luxembourg
{cesar.diaz,johnatan.pecero,pascal.bouvry}@uni.lu

Abstract. Platform as a Service providers deliver development and runtime environments for applications that are hosted on the Cloud. In this paper, we present a Platform as a Service model constructed over a desktop-based Cloud infrastructure for developing high performance computing applications taking advantage of unused resources opportunistically. We highlight the key concepts and features of the platform, as well as its innovation on an opportunistic computing and we present the results of several tests showing the performance of the proposed model.

Keywords: IaaS, PaaS, Cloud Computing, High Performance Computing, Opportunistic Computing.

1 Introduction

Opportunistic computing is a very successful and mature concept in the field of high performance computing (HPC). It is a sustainable alternative to satisfy the growing demand of computing resources. In this paper, we introduce a novel cloud platform for developing high performance computing applications over an opportunistic environment. We consider a cloud-based opportunistic infrastructure called UnaCloud [1] over this, the new platform as a service has being developed (UnaCloud PaaS). UnaCloud PaaS is a cloud computing platform oriented to use of opportunistic IaaS to deploy high performance applications. UnaCloud PaaS offers multipurpose platforms for low IT knowledge HPC users, that wants to use an opportunistic infrastructures to deploy and run specific applications. It is created to facilitate the complexity of opportunistic desktop based infrastructures to run applications.

Taking advantage of unused resources opportunistically, we present the main characteristics of UnaCloud PaaS as well as each of its components defined. UnaCloud PaaS can be deploy two platform types: Condor and MPI. Each platform is specified by a set of roles. A role is a set of homogenous machines regarding software, operating system and configuration.

J. Kołodziej et al. (Eds.): ICA3PP 2013, Part I, LNCS 8285, pp. 380–389, 2013.
© Springer International Publishing Switzerland 2013

To show the performance of the platforms, we conduct several experiments, measuring system response time and execution time of running platforms as well as one sample application execution called Gromacs. Furthermore a set of test, using a well know benchmark, were made in one of the platforms. Our experimental settings reflect the need of an opportunistic aware PaaS for the execution of successful platforms over opportunistic infrastructures. This paper is organized as follows: Section 2 presents related work. The definition, features, and components of UnaCloud PaaS are described in Section 3. Section 4 presents the implementation and the evaluation performance of UnaCloud PaaS is described in Section 5. Section 6 concludes the paper and presents future work.

2   Related Work

On the field of PaaS implementations for HPC we can find many solutions. Manjrasoft©presents Aneka [2], a solution to develop .NET applications using multiple programming models, and run them over hybrid infrastructures. Microsoft Windows Azure [3] offers an entire set of services on a platform for application development and deployment over Microsoft datacenters. It provides APIs, libraries and services for solving specific application problems like storage, cache, application synchronization, scalability and resource acquisition. MagosCloud [4] offers an opportunistic PaaS for web 2.0 services. It is focused on developers and offers a declarative way to express platforms and requirements over a XML schema. Amazon offers special HPC cloud VMs [5] with high performance hardware instances in their data centers. Amazon also [6] offers an Elastic Map Reduce service to execute Map Reduce workflows over a managed and scalable infrastructure. The FEFF Project [7] makes an offer to deploy and manage platforms for spectroscopy analysis and material science software. These clusters are deployed over Amazon EC2.

Sabalcore [8] is a commercial solution for HPC that allows to deploy custom virtual clusters over their specialized infrastructures. It offers solutions stacks and software for engineering modeling, financial simulations, energy computations and more. ViteraaS [9] propose a PaaS model for running HPC programs. ViteraaS is a virtual cluster management tool, which allows users to deploy on-demand virtual clusters of various sizes. The objective of ViteraaS is to simplify the creation/deletion of virtual HPC clusters and job submission.

Unlike the commercial and academic PaaS models implementations, Una-Cloud PaaS is specially designed to use opportunistic infrastructures to deploy managed platforms for scientific computations. UnaCloud PaaS makes use of UnaCloud IaaS opportunistic infrastructure to deploy customized virtual clusters (CVC) over it. Once this CVCs are deployed, UnaCloud PaaS configures them to execute and manage user applications.

3   UnaCloud Platform Architecture for HPC

UnaCloud PaaS is a Platform-as-a-Service implementation that provides managed and scalable platforms to deploy HPC applications over opportunistic infrastructures. It uses UnaCloud IaaS services to deploy and manage virtual clusters over the available infrastructure. Once these clusters are deployed, UnaCloud PaaS configure and installs all software and configuration requirements to build platforms for user program executions. Each execution is accomplished, managed and monitored. Each platform execution runs on a virtualized environment that is completely isolated from other executions.

A platform, in UnaCloud PaaS, is defined as a set of machines that are configured at hardware, operating system, network and software levels, and they are offered as a scalable and managed service for application executions. UnaCloud PaaS uses the concept of *role*. Each role is defined by its main module (which identifies the platform type), its size and a set of software modules. A software module is a collection of configurations and programs that are applied and installed on a virtual machine to satisfy a requirement. Each module have a set of input parameters, whose values are established by the system and users. For example, currently at UnaCloud PaaS there are two main modules: Condor and OpenMPI. Those modules are used by two platform types that can be deployed: Condor (BoT) and MPI. Also, there is a set of software modules that can be applied to a platform role before its execution. For example a user can choose to add Gromacs [10] to a MPI platform. Across these modules, an user can add software dependencies required by its application or program. An user can also add files to a platform execution. A file can be chosen from the local machine where the user is consuming the PaaS services.

Finally a platform execution has a list of commands that are executed on specific environments. The content and environment of a command is defined by the user. The environment refers to the shared folder where the command is executed and the multiplicity of the command.

3.1   UnaCloud PaaS Cloud Features

The characteristics of UnaCloud PaaS are summarized below:

- *Fault tolerance:* One of the most important feature needed to successful deploy platforms and applications over opportunistic infrastructures is the fault tolerance. UnaCloud PaaS provides a component that led the failures of the platform called *Failure manager* and it is described later.
- *Efficiency:* Through the opportunistic environment, UnaCloud PaaS provides a framework for developing distributed application taking advantage of the share utilization of the machine by its service oriented architecture.
- *Usability:* UnaCloud PaaS provides Web interfaces, whose operation is almost intuitive for a basic IT knowledge. Additionally it provides an API to access UnaCloud PaaS services from other applications.
- *self-service:* The design of UnaCloud PaaS permits to users consumes unilaterally platform resources by a self-service model.
- *Broad Network Access:* UnaCloud PaaS provides platform executions services that are available over internet and are consumed through standard secure remote access mechanisms like https and ssh.

- *On-demand services customization:* UnaCloud PaaS provides ways to cus-tomize execution environments required on demand by end-users using the *API Client* component defined in the following sections. This customization is able to meet large scale computational requirements.
- *Scalability:* UnaCloud PaaS uses an opportunistic commodity horizontal scal-ing infrastructure service that is based on a private cloud deployment model.
- *Interoperability:* UnaCloud PaaS is based in loose coupling and interoper-ability services operating over highly heterogeneous, distributed and non-dedicated infrastructures.
- *Extensiblity:* Based on open source tools, UnaCloud PaaS is broadly diffused in order to facilitate its extensibility.
- *Security:* UnaCloud uses authentication, authorization, confidentiality and non-repudiation mechanisms to secure the PaaS model deployment. Also, each platform runs on an isolated virtualized environment.
- *Measured service:* UnaCloud PaaS records and reports, by logs, all events regarding platform executions. It also takes traceability of used resources and the operations over them.

3.2   UnaCloud PaaS Components

Figure 1 shows the component structure of UnaCloud PaaS. It is divided in three major layers. IaaS layer, which provides infrastructure services. Currently the IaaS layer is provided by UnaCloud IaaS. API layer, that provides a specification to implement a web service client and it is connected to one of the two interfaces of PaaS layer. And finally, a PaaS layer, it is the main module of UnaCloud PaaS. It provides services to deploy and manage platforms from two interfaces: a web user interface and web services. The web services are consumed by an

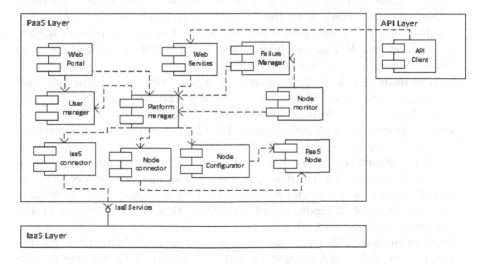

Fig. 1. UnaCloud PaaS component diagram

API layer as above mentioned. This provides abstract access to UnaCloud PaaS features due of its service oriented architecture.

Each UnaCloud PaaS component is described below.

+ **Web Portal:** is the main way of access to UnaCloud PaaS services. It provides a set of pages and web forms to manage all system entities. It also provides a set of forms to deploy and manage platform executions.
+ **Web Services:** is a component that exposes the platform execution services and operations through Web Services. This component only exposes services to start, manage and stop platform executions. System administration should be done through web portal.
+ **API Client:** it is a component specification that offers an abstraction to web services. It facilitates the complexity of the use of web services, so the user can consume UnaCloud PaaS operations in terms of objects and methods, and not by complex web services.
+ **User manager:** It is in charge of user account management. It includes passwords, user permissions and user traceability. This component is used by other components to check user permissions and limits before any resource or security related action.
+ **Node connector:** It allows the server to connect to the PaaS nodes. It uses standard mechanisms like SSH as tunnel to execute remote commands on each node. The main purpose of this component is to execute remote commands on deployed clusters.
+ **Platform manager:** This is the main component of the system. It is in charge of coordinate and orchestrate all other component to deploy cloud platforms. It has the logic to deploy, manage and control the platform executions. It is also in charge of storing a historic log of all deployed platforms.
+ **Node monitor:** This component is in charge of monitoring all node instances of all running platforms to determine if there is a node with a hardware failure. If so, it reports it to the Failure manager. The monitoring process involves taking running commands SO ids and check for process health. When a running VM cannot be accessed, it is marked as failed and sent to Failure Manager
+ **Failure manager:** It is the component which have the algorithms and business logic to recover a platform execution after a failure on one of its components. It uses the platform manager to orchestrate this process. The recovery process depends on deployed platform. It include checkpointing and platform restart thecniques.
+ **Node Configurator:** This component configures and manage configuration settings for the platform nodes. It implements an interface between the external configuration manager and UnaCloud PaaS. A node configuration is specified by a set of modules and parameters that are used to install and configure software and tools.
+ **IaaS connector:** This component connects to the underlying infrastructure provider to deploy and manage virtual machines. This component get the information of VM deployment retrieved after a cluster start operation on

the underlying IaaS system and transform it into a UnaCloud PaaS managed object.

+ **PaaS node:** This last component is mounted on every virtual machine used by UnaCloud PaaS. It contains some basic configurations to be compatible with Node connector and Configurator components. It is composed by an SSH server and a configurator manager client.

4   Implementation

The implementation takes the design and architectural decisions of UnaCloud to provide the following services to end users:

1. *Platform deployments:* Two platforms are offered to end users: Condor and OpenMPI. These platforms can be consumed by a web interface that allows the customization of each platform. Some software modules are offered to be added to the platforms: Gromacs, Blast, High Performance Linpack and Java.
2. *Platform execution monitoring:* Platform executions are monitored, so it is restored in failure cases. Also, the program execution is checked so, at successful termination the user is notified about the results.
3. *Platform execution management:* The user can stop and pause running executions.
4. *User folder management:* The user can manage its user folder to add, move and delete files that can be used on platform deployments.
5. *PaaS management:* Finally, the implementation offers a way to manage all configurations, entities and services of UnaCloud PaaS. It can add and delete software modules, platforms, files, users and more.

4.1   Parameter Tunning

To achieve the implementation, it was used UnaCloud IaaS infrastructure. UnaCloud IaaS has been deployed in three computer laboratories at Universidad de los Andes. Each laboratory has 35 computers with Intel Core i5 (3.01GHz) processors, 8GB of RAM and Windows 7 as their main operating system. In addition, UnaCloud Servers (PaaS and IaaS) were deployed on virtual machines running on a server, which is located in the data center (for availability reasons).

A set of tests was made to measure system response time and execution time of running platforms varying the number of virtual machines for each platform software. For each configuration, we ran an executable with an exact duration of 60 seconds.

UnaCloud PaaS was tested using an MPI application with production dataset inputs provided by the Department of Chemical Engineering at University of Los Andes. The application executes a Molecular Dynamics simulation using the GROMACS [10] package of the transmembrane domain from the Outer membrane protein A (OmpA) of *Escherichia coli.* The purpose of the simulation is to calculate the annihilation free energy of the transmembrane domain by coupling the intramolecular interactions of the protein in vacuo. The same simulation is executed varying the number of virtual machines and the number of cores per VM.

5   Testing and Results

A set of tests was made to evaluate the performance of the proposed PaaS solution according to the objectives of the present work.

5.1   System Response and Run Times

As aforementioned, several platform executions were launched varying the number of virtual machines of the main role and the platform software modules.

Table 1. System Response Times

Platform	Modules	VMs	VM Start time (s)	Config. time (s)	Run time (s)
MPI	-	1	60	90	83
MPI	-	2	60	100	104
MPI	-	4	61	111	81
MPI	-	8	61	137	99
MPI	-	16	60	208	99
MPI	-	32	60	271	99
MPI	Gromacs	1	55	330	89
MPI	Gromacs	2	60	325	100
MPI	Gromacs	4	60	352	85
MPI	Gromacs	8	80	414	110
MPI	Gromacs	16	70	463	90
MPI	Gromacs	32	61	518	105
Condor	-	1	90	111	136
Condor	-	2	110	137	116
Condor	-	4	120	156	151
Condor	-	8	121	163	151
Condor	-	16	120	207	131
Condor	-	32	121	298	144

In Table 1 we can see the virtual machines start time, configuration time and run time, in seconds, of different platforms varying its total size. We can see that virtual machines starts in the same time, independently of the size. However, condor platforms take about the double to start its VMs. It is because this platform has two roles (master/slave), in contrast to MPI platforms that have one (exec). On MPI cases it has a mean error of +30 seconds, it was due the fact that each 60 seconds the platforms are inquired to determine if the executables have finished. On condor cases the error is about +60 seconds because there is a time expended on queue management.

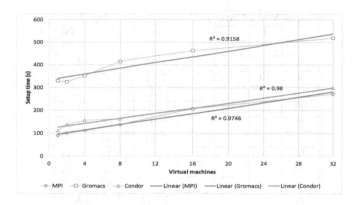

Fig. 2. Configuration time of different platforms varying the amount of VMs

In Figure 2 we present the configuration time for each platform setup as the number of VMs is increased. A linear regression and the Pearson product-moment correlation coefficient (R2) is shown for each setup. We can conclude that configuration time is linear dependent with the size of the platform.

5.2 Sample Application Execution

Several executions were made varying the amount of VMs and cores per VM. It was measured the execution time (T) in hours, the amount of nanoseconds of simulation per day and the Gflops obtained from each test. Every test was executed 3 times, the mean values are presented on Table 2. In total, the tests takes 12 days of human execution time and more than 374 days of machine time. Without a system to manage those platform executions it could be impossible to run all these tests. Thank to our failure recovery algorithms and strategies, these test could be executed on a reasonable time.

5.3 Benchmarking

Finally a set of tests were made to measure the performance of one of the platforms, MPI platform. We use the High-Performance Linpack Benchmark implementation provided by the Innovative Computing Laboratory of the University of Tennessee. We use OpenMPI to run it in parallel. As implementation of the Basic Linear Algebra Subprograms is was used GotoBLAS2 [11] provided by the Texas Advanced Computing Center.

Several tests were made varying the number of VMs and the amount of cores per VM. Figure 3 shows the result. As we can see, there is not a despicable potential that can be farmed from UnaCloud opportunistic infrastructure.

Table 2. Gromacs Simulation Results

Cores	VMs	Cores/VM	Gflops	ns/day	T(h)
1	1	1	4.84	0.89	8.06
2	2	1	5.39	1.00	7.30
5	5	1	8.52	1.58	4.59
10	10	1	7.97	1.47	4.88
15	15	1	11.12	2.06	3.61
20	20	1	11.18	2.07	3.65
2	1	2	9.02	1.67	4.31
4	2	2	7.41	1.37	5.27
10	5	2	11.84	2.19	3.34
20	10	2	10.9	2.2	3.59
30	15	2	9.93	1.84	3.93
40	20	2	10.02	1.85	3.99
4	1	4	11.19	2.07	3.48
8	2	4	7.58	1.40	5.26
20	5	4	770	1.43	5.07
40	10	4	5.27	0.98	8.00
60	15	4	5.07	0.94	9.15
80	20	4	5.79	1.07	17.15

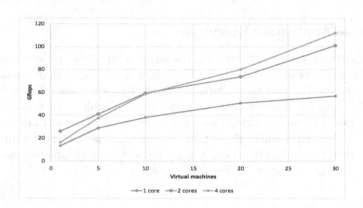

Fig. 3. Cluster Gflops varying the number of VMs and the cores per VM

6   Conclusions and Future Work

We presented UnaCloud PaaS, a novel implementation of the cloud computing PaaS model that can be deployed over opportunistic infrastructure for the
execution of HPC platforms. Our PaaS implementation offers a convergence between cloud computing paradigm and the opportunistic trend. It probes that
it is possible (and necessary) an opportunistic aware PaaS for the execution of
successful platforms over opportunistic infrastructures. UnaCloud PaaS represents a next step on opportunistic use of unused infrastructures. As future work

we will increase the amount of platforms and software modules [12] offered on UnaCloud PaaS. Additionally, we are planning to implement UnaCloud SaaS model to complete the service level offer of UnaCloud Suite [13].

References

1. Rosales, E., Castro, H., Villamizar, M.: Unacloud: Opportunistic cloud computing infrastructure as a service. In: Cloud Computing 2011, IARIA, pp. 187–194 (2011)
2. Vecchiola, C., Chu, X., Buyya, R.: Aneka: A software platform for .net-based cloud computing. CoRR abs/0907.4622 (2009)
3. Microsoft.: Windows Azure (2013), http://www.windowsazure.com/ (Online, accessed January 21, 2013)
4. De la Pava Torres, J.Y., Jimenez-Guarin, C.: Magoscloud secure: A secure, highly scalable platform for services in an opportunistic environment. In: 2012 Intl. Conf. on High Performance Computing and Simulation (HPCS), pp. 53–59 (2012)
5. Amazon.: High Performance Computing on AWS (2013), http://aws.amazon.com/hpc-applications/ (online accessed July 2013)
6. Iordache, A., Morin, C., Parlavantzas, N., Feller, E., Riteau, P.: Resilin: Elastic mapreduce over multiple clouds. In: 13th IEEE/ACM CCGrid, pp. 261–268 (2013)
7. Rehr, J.J., Kas, J.J., Vila, F.D., Prange, M.P., Jorissen, K.: Parameter-free calculations of x-ray spectra with feff9. Phys. Chem. Chem. Phys. 12, 5503–5513 (2010)
8. SabalcoreComputing.: Sabalcore Home (2013), http://www.sabalcore.com/ (accessed January 21, 2013)
9. Doelitzscher, F., Held, M., Reich, C., Sulistio, A.: Viteraas: Virtual cluster as a service. In: IEEE Int. Conf (CloudCom), pp. 652–657 (2011)
10. Berendsen, H., van der Spoel, D., van Drunen, R.: Gromacs: A message-passing parallel molecular dynamics implementation. Computer Physics Communications 91(1-3), 43–56 (1995)
11. Texas-Advanced-Computer-Center: GotoBLAS2 (2013), http://www.tacc.utexas.edu/tacc-projects/gotoblas2 (accessed January 28, 2013)
12. Wang, L., Tao, J., Ma, Y., Khan, S.U., Kolodziej, J., Chen, D.: Software design and implementation for mapreduce across distributed data centers. Appl. Math. Inf. Sci. 7, 85–90 (2013)
13. Kolodziej, J., Khan, S.U.: Multi-level hierarchic genetic-based scheduling of independent jobs in dynamic heterogeneous grid environment. Inf. Sci. 214, 1–19 (2012)

A Buffering Method for Parallelized Loop with Non-Uniform Dependencies in High-Level Synthesis

Akihiro Suda, Hideki Takase, Kazuyoshi Takagi, and Naofumi Takagi

Kyoto University,
Yoshida-Hommachi, Sakyo-ku, Kyoto, Japan
suda.akihiro.82s@st.kyoto-u.ac.jp,
{takase,ktakagi,takagi}@i.kyoto-u.ac.jp

Abstract. Recently, polyhedral optimization has become focused as a parallelization method for nested loop kernels. However, access conflicts to an off-chip RAM have been the performance bottleneck when applying polyhedral optimization to high-level synthesis. In this paper, we propose a method to accelerate synthesized circuits by buffering off-chip RAM accesses. The buffers are constructed of on-chip RAM blocks that are placed on each of processing elements (PEs) and can be accessed in less cycles than the off-chip RAM. Our method differs from related works in support for non-uniform data dependencies that cannot be represented by constant vectors. The experimental result with practical kernels shows that the buffered circuits with 8 PEs are on average 5.21 times faster than the original ones.

Keywords: On-Chip Memory, Buffering, Polyhedral Optimization, High-Level Synthesis.

1 Introduction

In the field of parallel computation, hardware implementations using high-level synthesis (HLS) have been popular because of its high performance and productivity. In this context, HLS means a method to compile high-level language descriptions that are friendly to software engineers into descriptions for FPGA/ASIC circuit designing. Most of languages used in HLS (e.g., Handel-C[1], LegUp[2]) are designed to be similar to orthodox C language, although some special syntaxes are usually added to describe parallelism. Thus HLS can eliminate costs to implement parallel computation programs as hardwares.

However, the effect of parallel computation cannot be exploited when the multiple processing elements (PEs) access the global off-chip RAM concurrently. Therefore, an appropriate memory management method should be introduced in designing of such a circuit, so as to eliminate waiting time for acquisition of access permission to the off-chip RAM.

In this paper, we propose a new method to construct on-chip buffers for parallelized nested loop kernels. Parallelization of nested loop kernels can be done by

J. Kołodziej et al. (Eds.): ICA3PP 2013, Part I, LNCS 8285, pp. 390–401, 2013.

using a state-of-the-art technology called *polyhedral optimization*[3,4] that splits the iteration space of kernel into tiles. Our method uses this tiling information and builds an appropriate *buffer map* that denotes how the off-chip RAM data will be copied to the on-chip buffers. Although there have been some works for applying polyhedral optimization into HLS[5,6], these works do not cover kernels with complicated dependencies, e.g., a non-uniform data dependency that cannot be represented by a constant vector. Our buffering method for non-uniform dependencies has the following advantages:

Avoidance of Access Conflict. In our method, each of the multiple buffers can be accessed by its owner PE at the same time. Hence the buffers contribute to elimination of access conflicts to the off-chip RAM, which cannot be concurrently accessed by multiple PEs.

Burst Access. When the *word size* (the size of an array element) is less than the bus width of the off-chip RAM, multiple consecutive words can be accessed at a single RAM access (*burst access*). Our method performs burst read accesses for array elements, and then copies the read data into the buffer before they are processed. After the data processing, burst write accesses are also performed. This burst access contributes to elimination of the number of access times to the off-chip RAM.

Data Reuse. In our method, the buffers keep data that can be reused for several iterations. This data reuse contributes to elimination of wasteful repeated accesses to the same data on the off-chip RAM.

Fig. 1 shows the overview of our method. Threading means conversion of an OpenMP directive that is generated by the polyhedral optimizer into a description for HLS. Buffering means building a buffer map and insertion of a buffer management code into the description for HLS. In the synthesized circuit, the global controller manages requests from the PEs for access to the off-chip RAM, and synchronization of the PEs. Each of the PEs handles its own independent on-chip buffer so as to reduce accesses to the off-chip RAM.

This paper is organized as the following. In Section 2, we present a brief look at polyhedral optimization theory. Some related works in the field of HLS are introduced in Section 3. In Section 4, we present the overview of our buffering method. We present the compilation-time flow of our method in Section 5, and then present the run-time flow in Section 6. We discuss an experimental result of the proposed method in Section 7. We summarize the paper in Section 8.

2 Polyhedral Optimization

Polyhedral optimization is the general term for algorithms that perform parallelization and locality improvement on nested loop kernels by applying several linear algebra computations. In this section, we introduce an existing polyhedral optimizer called PLUTO and its usage briefly.

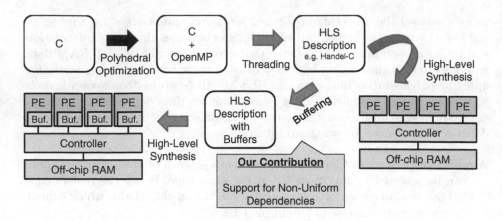

Fig. 1. Overview of our method

```
/* 8-bit unsigned integer */
uint8_t a[N][N];
#pragma scop
for (i=0; i<N; i++)
  for (j=1; j<N; j++)
    a[i][j] = a[j][i] + a[i][j-1];
#pragma endscop
```

(a) pluto_template

```
/* 32-bit fixed-point num (16:16) */
fix16_t a[N][N];
for (k=0; k<N; k++) {
#pragma scop /* scop 1 */
  for (j=k+1; j<N; j++)
    a[k][j] /= a[k][k];
#pragma endscop
#pragma scop /* scop 2 */
  for(i=k+1; i<N; i++)
    for (j=k+1; j<N; j++)
      a[i][j] -= a[i][k] * a[k][j];
#pragma endscop
}
```

(b) lu

```
/* 32-bit fixed-point num (16:16) */
fix16_t a[N][N]
fix16_t b[N][N];
for (i=0; i<N; i++)
#pragma scop
  for (j=0; j<N; j++)
    for (k=i+1; k<N; k++) {
      if (k == i+1)
        b[j][i] /= a[i][i];
      b[j][k] -= a[i][k] * b[j][i];
    }
#pragma endscop
```

(c) strsm

Fig. 2. Example of input SCoP codes for PLUTO

2.1   PLUTO

PLUTO [3,4] is the de facto standard polyhedral source-to-source C compilation algorithm and its implementation. Variants of PLUTO have been adopted in several practical compilers such as GCC [7] or clang[8]. We adopt PLUTO due to its wide applicable scope including kernels with non-uniform dependencies. PLUTO transforms a C source code description of what is called SCoP (Static Control Parts) into parallelized C source code with OpenMP directives. SCoP is a nested loop structure of which all loop boundaries, branch conditions, and array indices can be represented by affine expressions of iteration variables. Fig. 2 (a), (b), and (c) are examples of SCoP.

After applying PLUTO, the iteration space of input loop is split into parallelogram-shaped tiles. The tiling is done by computation of *space* direction vector and *time* direction vector. The space direction vector is used to assign tiles into threads, and the time direction vector is used to represent execution order of tiles within a thread.

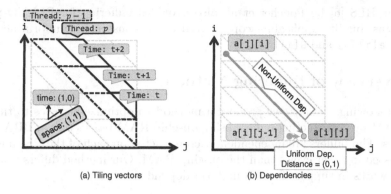

Fig. 3. Visual representation of pluto_template kernel (Fig. 2 (a))

2.2 Example

The pluto_template kernel (Fig. 2(a)) is an example of nested loop kernel with non-uniform dependency, which is focused in several works [4,9]. Further details of PLUTO and this example kernels are explained in [4].

By applying PLUTO, the tiling vectors of this kernel can be computed as: $(1, 1)$ for the space direction, $(1, 0)$ for the time direction (Fig. 3 (a)).

Although we do not explain in here due to the limitation of the paper space, PLUTO also analyzes dependency information. For the example kernel, there is a uniform dependency across the space direction and a non-uniform one across the time direction (Fig. 3 (b)).

2.3 Application into HLS

An OpenMP directive (#pragma omp parallel for) generated by PLUTO can be easily converted to a description for HLS. In our method, a chunk of multiple consecutive *logical threads* (iterations marked as parallel) is assigned to a PE. Each of the PEs is synchronized using barrier functions that are provided by HLS tools.

3 Related Works

In HLS, just parallelized circuits cannot achieve much better performance than the original circuit due to access conflicts to the off-chip RAM. Although some existing related works [5,6] handle this problem by copying array elements into on-chip buffers, these works do not cover non-uniform dependencies such as the one between a[i][j] and a[j][i] appeared in pluto_template. Wu et al.'s work [5] is the first work that integrated PLUTO into the field of HLS with buffering capability. However, this work has been evaluated with only simple kernels: matrix-matrix multiplication(MM) and matrix-vector multiplication(MV).

PolyOpt/HLS [6] by Pouchet et al. also provides buffering for PLUTO-based toolchains, but its applicable scope is limited to consecutive uniform accesses such as a[i][j] and a[i][j-1].

4   Overview of Buffering Method

In the following sections, we propose a method to optimize accesses to the off-chip RAM by constructing buffers using on-chip RAM blocks (a.k.a. BRAM) or registers. The buffers are independently constructed on each of the PEs and can be accessed in fewer cycles than the off-chip RAM. Our method differs from the related works in support for non-uniform dependencies.

4.1   Applicable Scope

Our method can be applied to SCoP kernels which satisfies the following conditions.

1. The kernel has up to two-dimensional iteration space. If the kernel has three or more dimensional iteration space, our method can be applied to the inner two-dimensional part. Currently we do not handle such a many-dimensional iteration space directly, because the parallelized codes generated by PLUTO tend to be too complicated for humans to debug manually.
2. The data array is up to two-dimensional.
3. The kernel has no irregular access (data-dependent access) such as a[b[i]].

We applied our method to three kernels shown in Fig. 2 (a), (b), and (c). The pluto_template kernel (a) is the example kernel that we referred in the previous section. We assume that the bus width of off-chip RAM is 64-bit and the word size of pluto_template is 8-bit, i.e., 8 words can be accessed at once.

The lu kernel (b) (LU decomposer) and strsm kernel (c) (triangular matrix solver) are adopted as practical examples for algebraic kernels. A branch condition k==i+1 appeared in strsm is treated as constantly true while applying the compilation-time flow of our method. The word size of these kernels is 32-bit, i.e., 2 words can be accessed at once. The tiling vectors of lu are $(i, j) = (1, 0)$ for space direction and $(0, 1)$ for time direction. The tiling vectors of strsm are $(j, k) = (1, 0)$ for space direction and $(0, 1)$ for time direction.

4.2   Overall Flow

Our method is composed of the compilation-time flow and the run-time flow.

On compilation-time, our method builds a *buffer map* that denotes how the data will be copied to the buffers in a two-dimensional rectangular shape. The buffer map is used to generate synthesizable codes.

On run-time, each of the PEs on the synthesized circuit copies the off-chip RAM contents to its own on-chip buffer, and then processes the buffered data. The buffered data are written back to the off-chip RAM with a careful consideration for data consistencies.

INPUT: data access statement set S and tile size (t_h, t_w) of the given SCoP
OUTPUT: buffer map $M = \{M_u, M_n\}$

Initialize the empty buffer map M:
    $M_u = M_n = \phi$.
for all data access statement $s \in S$ **do**
    Construct a uniform part m_u for the write access (i.e., left-hand side) expression a_w appeared
    in s:
        $m_u = \{LLCoord, RUCoord, Reusability\} = \{(0,0), (t_h, t_w), NotReusable\}$.
    for all uniform dependent read access expression a_{r_u} appeared in s **do**
        Extend m_u using a distance vector $d_u = |a_{r_u} - a_w|$:
            $m_u = \{\dots, RUCoord(m_u) + d_u, \dots\}$.
    end for
    Align up coordinates of m_u to the off-chip RAM bus width.
    Add m_u to M_u:
        $M_u = M_u \cup m_u$.
    for all non-uniform dependent read access expression a_{r_n} appeared in s **do**
        if the first index of a_{r_n} is constant and the second one is uniform **then**
            Construct a new non-uniform part m_n along the uniform index. The size of m_n is $(1, t_w)$
            before performing alignment:
                $m_n = \{MostLUCoord(M), MostRUCoord(M) + (1,0), NotReusable\}$.
        else if the first array access index of a_{r_n} is uniform and the second one is constant **then**
            Construct a new non-uniform part m_n along the uniform index. The size is $(t_h, 1)$:
                $m_n = \{MostRLCoord(M), MostRUCoord(M) + (0,1), InnerReusable\}$.
        else if all the indices of a_{r_n} are constant **then**
            Construct a new non-uniform part m_n and put on the odd place. The size is $(1,1)$:
                $m_n = \{\dots, \dots, OuterReusable\}$.
        else
            Construct a new non-uniform part m_n. The size is the domain of the non-uniform access
            vector (aligned to (t_h, t_w)).:
                $z_n = AlignUp(DomainOf(a_{r_n}), (t_h, t_w))$.
                $m_n = \{MostLUCoord(M), MostRUCoord(M) + z_n, NotReusable\}$.
        end if
        Align up coordinates of m_n to the off-chip RAM bus width.
        Add m_n to M_n:
            $M_n = M_n \cup m_n$.
    end for
end for

Fig. 4. Compilation-time buffer mapping algorithm for a SCoP

5 Compilation-Time Flow

The compilation-time buffer mapping flow is summarized as Fig. 4. The buffer map M is constructed from uniform parts M_u and non-uniform parts M_n. A uniform part $m_u \in M_u$ is allocated for a write access and uniform dependent read accesses appeared in a statement. A non-uniform part $m_n \in M_n$ is allocated for a non-uniform dependent read access with special consideration for particular access patterns.

Before buffer mapping flow, the iteration space of logical thread is classified as uniform parts and non-uniform parts as in Fig. 5 (a). Then the iteration space is distorted to the rectangular buffer map as in Fig. 5 (b).

In this section, we present details of how data access expressions are classified and used to construct the buffer map.

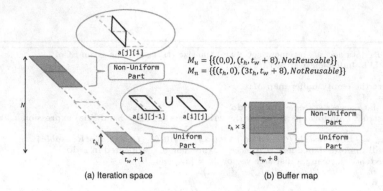

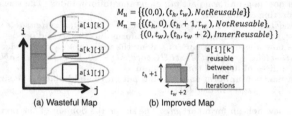

Fig. 5. Iteration space and buffer map for `pluto_template` kernel (Fig. 2 (a))

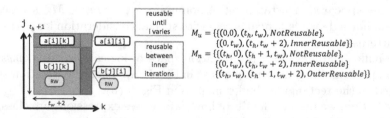

Fig. 6. Buffer map for `lu` kernel (Fig. 2 (b))

5.1 Representation of Buffer Map

As shown in Fig. 4, an element m of the buffer map M ($m \in \{M_u \cup M_n\}$) can be represented as a tuple of *LLCoord*, *RUCoord* and *Reusability*. The *LLCoord* and *RUCoord* components are left-lower and right-upper coordinates of the corresponding part in the buffer addressing space.

The *Reusability* $= \{NotReusable | InnerReusable | OuterUsable\}$ component is used to indicate the reusability of the corresponding part (Section 6). Fig. 5, 6, and 7 represents the buffer maps for the example kernels graphically.

Fig. 7. Improved buffer map for `strsm` kernel (Fig. 2 (c))

The buffer map does not include an attribute that denotes *ReadWrite* or *ReadOnly*, as all the uniform parts are defined as *ReadWrite* and all the non-uniform ones are *ReadOnly*. This is because a write acccess expression (the left-hand side of a data access statement) is just used for allocation of the uniform parts. However, the uniform parts and the non-uniform parts may have common element as in Fig. 7. How to handle such a case is explained in Section 6.

5.2   Uniform Parts

A uniform part is the union of the domain of the write access and the domains of its uniform dependent read accesses when the iteration vector moves within one tile shape. For `pluto_template`, the uniform part is a union of the domain of `a[i][j]` and the domain of `a[i][j-1]` as in Fig. 5 (a).

Suppose that the size of the original tile shape is (t_h, t_w) and the set of the distance vectors of uniform dependencies is D_u. Then the size of the uniform part in the iteration space (t'_h, t'_w) can be computed as : $(t'_h, t'_w) = (t_h, t_w) + \sum_{d_u \in D_u} d_u$. For `pluto_template`, $d_u = (0,1)$. According to [6], components of d_u are up to 1 in most cases.

In the buffer map, the actual size of the uniform part (t''_h, t''_w) is aligned to the off-chip RAM bus width. For `pluto_template`, t''_w is set to $t_w + 8$ when t_w is multiplicand of 8 (Fig. 5 (b)). For `lu` and `strsm`, t''_w is set to just t_w when t_w is multiplicand of 2 (Fig. 6 (b) and Fig. 7).

5.3   Non-Uniform Parts

A non-uniform part encloses the domain of a non-uniform dependent read access when the iteration vector moves within one tile shape. A non-uniform part exists per one non-uniform access expression, although a uniform part exists per one statement.

In the buffer map, a non-uniform part is aligned to the size of uniform tiling shape (t''_{u_h}, t''_{u_w}). For `pluto_example`, the non-uniform part of its buffer map is as large as two uniform tiles (Fig. 5 (b)). This alignment limitation enables the burst read access for the whole domain of `a[j][i]` before processing it.

5.4   Special Non-Uniform Parts

The above generic method produces too wasteful buffer map for two-dimensional non-uniform read accesses of which an array index is constant and the other index is uniform. Therefore we handle such a non-uniform access separately to improve actual usage of buffer mapping space. In the improved buffer map, non-uniform parts for such a access are jointed to the uniform part along their uniform array indices.

For `lu`, `a[i][k]` and `a[k][j]` are treated as such special accesses because k is considered to be constant in the two-dimensional SCoP kernel. Fig. 6 (a) shows that almost two tile shapes are wasted when the generic method is applied. In the improved buffer map (Fig. 6 (b)), the a[i][k] part is jointed along a[i][*] and the a[k][j] part is jointed along a[*][j]. Note that the a[i][k] part is reusable between inner iterations as it is considered to be constant until the outer iteration variable i varies.

For the b[j][k] uniform part of strsm, b[j][i] and a[i][k] are respectively jointed along b[j][*] and b[*][k], as i is considered to be constant. Then the fully constant part a[i][i] is placed in the left over area. The b[j][i] part is usable between inner iterations and the a[i][i] part is so until i varies (Fig. 7). Note that the b[j][i] part is also attributed as a uniform part because b[j][i] is updated when the value of expression (k == i+1) is true.

6 Run-Time Flow

Fig. 8 shows the run-time buffer management flow of each of the PEs. An access to the off-chip RAM must be done exclusively so that a single PE can acquire access rights at a time. In this section, we present some run-time data consistency issues and solutions for them.

6.1 Consistency between a Uniform Part and a Non-Uniform Part

A uniform part and a non-uniform part may contain common buffer chunks. In this context, a buffer chunk means a chunk of consecutive words that are accessible at a single RAM access, e.g., 8 words for pluto_template, 2 words for lu and strsm. When such a common buffer chunk is accessed by one of the PEs, the instance in the uniform part should be used, because the contents of the uniform part may be updated while the non-uniform part is defined as read-only.

6.2 Consistency between Uniform Parts

The consistency problem also exists between multiple uniform parts. In our method, when a write access to a common buffer chunk in a uniform part is performed, the instances in the succeeding uniform parts are also updated. Furthermore, the updated chunk is also written through to the off-chip RAM immediately. Therefore the *burst access* advantage of buffering (Section 1) cannot be exploited for writing back of such an overlapping uniform part content.

For strsm, this consistency problem happens between the "preceding" uniform part b[j][i] and the "succeeding" uniform part b[j][k] because b[j][i] and b[j][k] are loaded to the same buffer chunk when ((k == i+1) && (i % 2 == 0)) is true.

7 Evaluation

We applied our proposal method to the three example kernels (Fig. 2) and evaluated its effectiveness. The array size parameter N is set to 256. We evaluated

---

INPUT: buffer map $M = \{M_u, M_n\}$

Load the outer reusable non-uniform parts using M_n to the buffer.
for the first iteration variable moves in the original tile **do**
    Load the inner reusable non-uniform parts using M_n.
    for the second iteration variable moves in the original tile **do**
        Load the rest of the non-uniform parts using M_n.
        Load the uniform part using M_u.
        for all data access statement s **do**
            for all read access expression a_r appeared in s **do**
                if the accessed buffer chunk exist in both of $m_u \in M_u$ and $m_n \in M_n$ (Section 6.1)
                then
                    Fetch the instance from the uniform part of the buffer into a register.
                else
                    Fetch the instance from the buffer into a register.
                end if
            end for
            Execute the operator of s using registers, and store the result to the buffer.
            if the write access expression a_w appeared in s overlaps the "succeeding" uniform part
            (Section 6.2) **then**
                Write through the updated buffer chunk to the off-chip RAM.
            end if
        end for
    end for
end for
Write back the uniform part of the buffer if not yet fully written through.
Perform barrier synchronization between the PEs.

Fig. 8. Run-time buffer management flow of a PE

the execution cycles and the number of NAND gates of the synthesized circuit for both of the non-buffered versions and the buffered versions. We used Mentor Graphics Handel-C 5.1 as the HLS and simulation tool.

In the simulated environment, an access for the off-chip RAM needs 8 cycles and on the other hand on-chip buffers can be accessed in only one cycle. The bus width of the off-chip RAM is set to 64-bit as in Section 4. We validated correctness of the synthesized circuit by calculating a checksum of the array after all write accesses to the off-chip RAM have finished.

As shown in Fig. 9(a), the speed-ups (ratios of the execution cycles) from the original sequential versions can be estimated using the Handel-C simulator. The execution cycles of the original versions are shown in Table. 1. The non-buffered versions stay at the almost same performances as the original versions even with 8 PEs. On the other hand, the buffered versions can achieve on average 5.21 times speed-up with 8 PEs. Even with just a single PE, the buffered versions can achieve on average 2.22 times speed-up. This result is not strange because our buffering method can exploit its advantages of *burst access* and *data reuse* (Section 1) even for just a single PE.

How the speed-ups vary when the tile size varies can be estimated as in Fig. 9(b). The best tile sizes are 16×16 for `pluto_template`, 16×16 for `lu`, and 32×32 for `strsm`. The result indicates that too small tile size leads

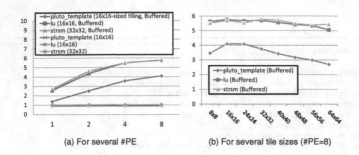

Fig. 9. Estimated speed-ups from the original versions

Table 1. Estimated performances and circuit areas of the original versions

Kernel	Execution Cycles	NAND gates
pluto_template	$2,415,874$	$1,278,264$
lu	$329,588,610$	$4,726,396$
strsm	$496,063,746$	$4,728,309$

Table 2. Buffer sizes (in # array elements) for tile size (t_h, t_w)

Kernel	Buffer Size
pluto_template	$(3t_h) \times (t_w + 8)$
lu	$(t_h + 1) \times (t_w + 2)$
strsm	$(t_h + 1) \times (t_w + 2)$

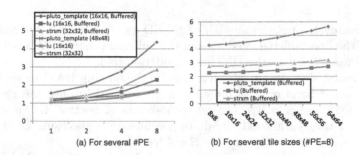

Fig. 10. Estimated increase of the number of NAND gates

to poor performance because of small buffers. In contrast, too large tile size also leads to poor performance. This seems to be caused by the waiting time of each of the PEs to acquire rights to access the off-chip RAM.

When the tile size (t_h, t_w) varies, the buffer sizes also varies as shown in Table 2. These buffer sizes are independent from the array size e.g., N in Fig. 2.

The increases of the number of NAND gates (including controller/validator circuits other than the kernel) can be estimated as in Fig. 10 (a) and (b). The actual numbers of NAND gates of the original versions are shown in Table. 1. The increases are almost linear to the number of the PEs. Although the increases of the buffer sizes (Table 2) are polynomial to the tile sizes, the increases of the number of NAND gates are narrow. Therefore the tile sizes can be virtually determined without consideration for the number of available gates.

8   Conclusions

We proposed a new buffering method to accelerate nested loop kernel with non-uniform dependencies in HLS. Our method achieved on average 5.21 times speed-up with 8 PEs. To the best of our knowledge, this is the first work to handle non-uniform dependencies in the field of polyhedral optimization for HLS with buffering.

We are planning to formulate an optimization method for the tile size and the number of the PEs, with considerations for both of the performance and the resource limitation.

Acknowledgements. This work is supported by VLSI Design and Education Center(VDEC), The University of Tokyo with the collaboration with Mentor Graphics Corporation.

References

1. Mentor-Graphics: Handel-c synthesis methodology,
   http://www.mentor.com/products/fpga/handel-c/
2. Canis, A., Choi, J., Aldham, M., Zhang, V., Kammoona, A., Anderson, J.H., Brown, S., Czajkowski, T.: Legup: high-level synthesis for fpga-based processor/accelerator systems. In: Proc. of the Int'l Symp. on FPGAs, pp. 33–36. ACM (2011)
3. Bondhugula, U., Hartono, A., Ramanujam, J., Sadayappan, P.: A practical automatic polyhedral parallelizer and locality optimizer. In: Proc. of PLDI (2008)
4. Bondhugula, U.K.R.: Effective Automatic Parallelization and Locality Optimization Using the Polyhedral Model. PhD thesis, Ohio State University (2008)
5. Wu, G., Dou, Y., Wang, M.: Automatic synthesis of processor arrays with local memories on fpgas. In: Proc. of the Int'l Conf. on FPT, pp. 249–252. IEEE (2010)
6. Pouchet, L.N., Zhang, P., Sadayappan, P., Cong, J.: Polyhedral-based data reuse optimization for configurable computing. In: Proc. of the Int'l Symp. on FPGAs, pp. 29–38. ACM (2013)
7. Pop, S., Cohen, A., Bastoul, C., Girbal, S., Silber, G.A., Vasilache, N.: Graphite: Polyhedral analyses and optimizations for gcc. In: Proc. of the GCC Developers Summit (2006)
8. Grosser, T., Zheng, H., Raghesh, A., Simbürger, A., Grösslinger, A., Pouchet, L.N.: Polly - polyhedral optimization in llvm. In: Proc. of the First International Workshop on Polyhedral Compilation Techniques, IMPACT (2011)
9. Darte, A., Vivien, F.: Optimal fine and medium grain parallelism detection in polyhedral reduced dependence graphs. Int'l Journal of Parallel Programming 25(6), 447–496 (1997)

Character of Graph Analysis Workloads and Recommended Solutions on Future Parallel Systems*

Noboru Tanabe[1], Sonoko Tomimori[2], Masami Takata[2], and Kazuki Joe[2]

[1] Toshiba Research and Development Center,
Kawasaki, Kanagawa 212-8582, Japan
noboru.tanabe@toshiba.co.jp
[2] Nara Women's University, Nara, Nara, 630-8506, Japan

Abstract. Graph500 is a benchmark suite for big data analysis. Matrices used for Graph500 inherit the properties of graph analysis such as breadth first search for SNS and PageRank for web searching engine. Especially power saving is very important for its execution on future massively parallel processors and clouds. The spatial locality of sparse matrices used for Graph500 and its behaviors on cache memory are investigated. The experimental results show the spatial locality of sparse matrices used for Graph500 is very low. It is very difficult to solve the problem by just software approach because of the huge size and the randomness of their accesses. Therefore, we recommend hardwired scatter/gather functions at memory side. They improve the processing speed in an order of magnitude. For achieving both of low power and high throughput of random access, we recommend implementing hardwired scatter/gather functions on logic-base in Hybrid Memory Cube (HMC). We also describe brief considerations of the power saving in the case of low cache hit rate application such as graph500. For example, when the hit rate is 15%, the power saving ratio of memory access is about 30-fold.

1 Introduction

In recent years, graph analysis meets real social needs as explosive growth of Web and SNS. The characteristics of graph analysis workloads such as PageRank[1] and Graph500[2] are essentially equivalent to large scale irregular sparse matrix operations. It is known as an application area that is not effectively performed by existing computer systems. Moreover the memory wall is getting higher year after year. However, such kind of application should be well executed on high-end computers, and it is regarded as an important demand for future high-end computers. The final goal of this research is establishing green computer architectures for large sparse matrix operations that are important both in HPC and graph analysis. Dally[3] pointed out the importance of elimination of data movements through long wires and controlling granularity for power efficient exascale computers.

* A part of this work is supported by the Ministry of Internal Affairs and Communications (Soumu-sho).

J. Kołodziej et al. (Eds.): ICA3PP 2013, Part I, LNCS 8285, pp. 402–415, 2013.
© Springer International Publishing Switzerland 2013

The first contribution of this paper is showing the character of matrices used in Graph500[2] and its behavior on cache memory with experiments. The second contribution of this paper is showing a recommended solution and its big potential of the effects on power saving and performance of graph processing.

In the rest of the paper, the problem from random accesses in graph processing is shown in Section 2. We introduce a metric for the spatial locality in Section 3. The evaluations on the above metric of graph processing workloads , and its behavior on cache memory are presented in Section 4. The recommended memory system is presented in Section 5. The brief considerations of processing speed and power consumption are shown in Section 6. We show related work in Section 7, and conclusion and future works in Section 8.

2   Problem from Random Accesses in Graph Processing

2.1   Data Block Size and Access Granularity

Table 1 shows various data block sizes for well-known memory systems. Even a 1-bit access may trigger the movement of a large data block. Namely, frequent data block movements directly increase the power consumption. When the target platform has the bottleneck of memory bandwidth, such a tiny access may deteriorate the system performance.

Table 1. Data Block Size for Various Memory Systems

Name of block	Block size	Ratio
TLB (Large page)	2MB-256MB	512K - 128M
HDFS[4] (block)	64MB -128MB	16MB - 32MB
memcached[5](slab)	2MB	512K
memcached[5](chunk)	80B - 1MB	20 - 256K
TLB (Normal page)	4KB - 8KB	1K - 2K
HDD (Sector)	512B	128
NAND flash (Page)	512B	128
GPU (cacheline)	128B	32
CPU (cacheline)	64B - 128B	16 - 32
Conventional HMC[7][8]	32B - 128B	8 - 32
Recomended HMC[9][10]	4B	1

Table 2 shows access granularities in some applications with random accesses. It is observed that there is a large gap between the grain sizes and the block sizes shown in Table 1. It means that the larger the gap is, the worse performance the platform has. For example, a large graph processing package Pegasus[6] included in Microsoft® Windows® Azure™ provides scalable sparse matrix-vector multiplication implemented on Hadoop[4] to easily support PageRank[1],etc. With more computing nodes, the processing speed of Pegasus may be sufficient. However, there is a considerable gap between Pegasus' granularity and the access block size of the target platform. If the gap was controllable, the target platform with a single computing node would achieve significant speed-up that means significant reduction of power consumption. Since Pegasus is implemented on Hadoop, the huge gap between the access granularity of Pegasus and the data block size of HDFS degrades the execution performance. It is possible to cache the HDFS accesses on the main memory by memcached[5], but the accesses are converted to be issued by chunkand the gap still remains.

Table 2. Access Granularities of Random Access Applications

Application	Kernel	Access granularity
PageRank[1]	SpMV	4B
Graph500[2]	BFS	1bit - 8B
FEM	SpMV	4B - 8B

2.2 Gap Problem on Cache Memory

In general, cache memory has the performance degradation problem when it receives non contiguous data accesses such as indirect array accesses. Since graph analysis applications tend to have sparse matrices with randomly located non-zero elements, the above mentioned problem of indirect memory accesses occurs considerably for conventional cache based memory systems with CPUs and/or GPUs as shown in Fig. 1.

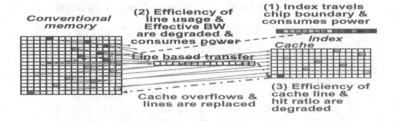

Fig. 1. Problems caused by indirect accesses on conventional systems

Three of main problems caused by fine grained random accesses are shown below. (1) Index array which is a kind of address trace has to make a round trip between processor and memory through long wire. Therefore, power and memory bandwidth are consumed. (2) Since the effective data on a cache line decreases, efficiency of using long wire between chips and effective bandwidth. Therefore, the power for transmission increases. (3) Since the effective data on a cache line decreases, many cache lines are consumed. Therefore, the cache hit rate decreases.

3   Spatial Locality Metric for Sparse Matrices

In this section, we introduce a metric[11] for the suitability of sparse matrices to cache memory using the characteristics of sparse matrices. The metric is used for classifying sparse matrices to decide appropriate cache organizations, and obtained as the spatial locality of sequences of row indices. Fig. 2 illustrates the concept of the proposed metric in [11]. The definition of the characteristics of sparse matrices is given below. Just non-zero elements of a given sparse matrix are stored in the CSR format. When reading index arrays sequentially from the beginning to obtain row vector x, we count the number of the non-zero elements while their page addresses are the same except the lower 5 bits. When a different page address is detected, the count value is recorded and the counter is reset. We define the spatial locality of sequences of row indices as the average of the recorded count values. Assume a cache memory module with just a single cache line, when sparse matrix-vector multiplications are performed to a sparse matrix in the CSR format, row vectors are accessed through the cache memory. The spatial locality presents the average number of valid elements in the single cache line. The reciprocal of the spatial locality represents the deterioration of the memory bandwidth for the above described accesses. Note that the above average values do not strictly represent the characteristics of real cache memory but approximations because real cache memory provides a lot of cache lines to increase the temporal locality. So the spatial locality index explains a part of characteristics of cache memory and sparse matrices. In the above definition, the meaning of 5 bits is as follows. Provided with 128 byte cache line (a typical cache line size for GPUs), there are 32 (2^5) four byte data in the cache line and an access to some of them corresponds to a cache hit.

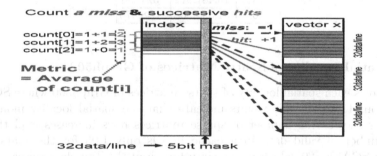

Fig. 2. Definition of Spatial locality of the sequences of row indices of sparse matrix[11]

4   Evaluation

4.1   Experimental Setup

Table 3 shows the evaluation environment[1]. We evaluate the suitability of memory access sequences in a graph of Graph500 to a cache memory system from the view point of spatial locality. The problem size in Graph500 is expressed as a parameter SCALE where the number of target graph nodes is 2^{SCALE} [2].

The experimented sparse matrices are shown in Table 4. To generate the sparse matrices, we use kronecker_generator.m and kernel_1.m that are Octave

---

[1] Intel, Xeon are trademarks of Intel Corporation in the U.S. and/or other countries.

Table 3. Experimental Environment

Host	Intel®Xeon®CPU X5670 @ 2.93GHz
GPU	Nvidia Tesla C2050 (448cores,3GB,144GB/s)
Host I/F	PCI express x16 Gen.2(8GB/s)
OS	RedHat Enterprise Linux Client release5.5 + Cuda3.2

programs included in Graph500 Reference code2.1.4. We convert the sparse matrices generated by kernel_1.m to the mtx form, and each spatial locality metric shown in Fig.2 is calculated for the evaluation.

Table 4. Experimental matrices

SCALE	# of Non-0	# of row
11	45,536	2,048
12	97,010	4,095
13	203,826	8,192
14	426,578	16,384
15	883,126	32,768
16	1,818,824	65,536
17	3,730,586	131,072
18	7,609,740	262,144
19	15,481,872	524,287
20	31,398,208	1,048,576

4.2 Spatial Locality of Sparse Matrices of Graph500

Fig. 3 shows each spatial locality of sparse matrices of Graph500 where SCALE varies from 11 to 20. The results indicate that the spatial locality monotonically decreases as the number of sparse matrices rows increases, and the average number of valid data in a cache line is only 1.03 for the sparse matrix with SCALE=20, which is one sixty-fourth of the Toy class sparse matrix (SCALE=26). This means that there is almost no spatial locality for sparse matrices of Graph500.

4.3 Cache Hit Rate of Graph500

It is known that L1 cache hit rates are strongly affected by the performance of sparse matrix-vector multiplications. Fig.4 shows the cache hit rates of sparse matrix-vector multiplications on a GPU Nvidia C2050. The L1 cache hit rate monotonically decreases as the number of sparse matrix rows increases, and the L1 cache hit rate for the sparse matrix with SCALE=20 is only 5.8%. The hit rate includes contiguous accesses to the target array elements as well as indirect memory accesses. The reason of the saturation of cache hit rate is that the sparse

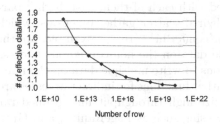

Fig. 3. Spatial locality of the sequence of row indices for matrix of Graph500

matrix-vector multiplications include a fixed amount of contiguous accesses to the target array elements. The average number of valid data in a cache line is about one while the capacity of cache line is 128 bytes for the most cases. When the data type of vectors is 8 bytes, one indirect data access to the 8 bytes data type vectors get just 8 byte valid data remaining other 120 bytes in the same cache line wasted. 90% of memory accesses of the sparse matrix-vector multiplication are performed as indirect memory accesses with extremely poor bandwidth.

A hit ratio of a virtual cache combining L1 and L2 probably has a similar shape as the shape of Fig.4(a). Therefore, the hit ratio has to be decreased as the SCALE increases. According to Fig.4(a) and (b), a L2 hit ratio has not completely gone down in SCALE20. Although the size of SCALE20 fits a device memory on the GPU, a Graph500 has actually a large matrix size which is from 64-fold to 128-fold even though it is a single node. Thus, we expect that an effect of cache is decreasing since L2 hit ratio degrades if a capacity of the device memory is able to include the data for the SCALE.

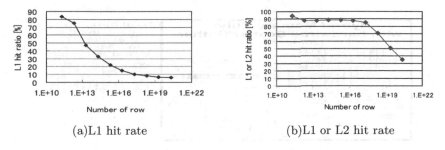

(a)L1 hit rate   (b)L1 or L2 hit rate

Fig. 4. Cache hit rate on executing SpMV for Graph500 sparse matrix on GPU

5   Recommended Solution

The problems in Fig. 1 and very low spatial locality for graph analysis workload presented in section 4 can be solved by using the hardwired scatter/gather function on Hybrid Memory Cube(HMC)[9][10]as shown in Fig.5 HMC[7][8] is consisted in several DRAM chips and another chip called logic-base which are stacked and connected with each of them with highly parallel Through Silicon Viahole(TSV)s. Hardwired scatter/gather functions, which are implemented in every cores of Intel®Xeon®Phi™[16] for example, are the vector load instructions to read multiple data on the non-contiguous addresses (Gather) and the vector store instructions to write multiple data on the non-contiguous addresses (Scatter). Scatter/Gather functions for indirect accesses are important for graph processing. They realize high throughput fine grained random accesses which appear in graph processing such as PageRank[1] and Graph500[2]. We propose implementing hardwired scatter/gather functions on logic-base of HMC. Vector registers, which hold vector data, and command registers, which hold control information to be executed, are implemented in logic-base of HMC. They are mapped to the special region in user virtual memory space which is separated to the normal paged region. Normal paged region on the HMC can be accessed with the compatibility of HMC standard.

HMC realizes low power and high bandwidth transfer between DRAMs and a logic base by using many TSV with short length. In the proposed memory system, we can make interleaved memory system with highly parallel banks by using HMC. In this way, both of low power consumption and high random access throughput can be satisfied.

Since HMC includes a chip called logic-base in the package for the structural reason, it is easy to implement hardwired scatter/gather functions on it. This improves not only processing speed but also power efficiency which is important for Green Graph500[2].The improvement of power efficiency is highly expected for the following reasons: (i) Index information does not pass through wired logic lines between packages, (ii) fine grain data accesses for gather operation passes through highly parallel very short TSV between multi-layered memory chips, and (iii) any data that is not used does not pass through wired logic lines between packages.

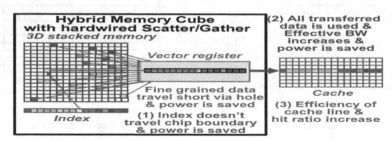

Fig. 5. Recommended solution using HMC with hardwired scatter/gather

6   Consideration on Performance and Power Consumption

In this section, we would like to show the processing speed of sparse matrix-vector product and the power consumption modeling related to memory access, which are for the cases that operating with cache architecture and the recommended memory system with Scatter/Gather functions.

6.1 Performance

A modeling in this section targets for the processing speed of sparse matrix-vector product $y = Ax$. We define some values as follows for creating a formula of a required bandwidth per one FLOPS.

hit_xFA hit ratio of accessing to column vector x

SFSpatial locality metric (the number of effective data of 32 in the line)

IFA data size per one index[B]

The sum of three values as follows shows a required bandwidth per one FLOPS on a processor based on a cache.

$$BPF_{cache} = \alpha + \beta + \gamma = 2 + I/2 + (1 - hit_x) * 128/S \qquad (1)$$

α : A required bandwidth to get an indexF$I/2$[B/FLOP] (continuous & no reuse)

β : A required bandwidth to get a matrix AF2[B/FLOP] (continuous & no reuse)

γ : A required bandwidth to get a column vector x: A required bandwidth to get 2[B/FLOP], the same as A, only with effective data

We assume that A is as a single precision real number (4 byte) to decide a performance when it uses mixed precision which is improved the precision. In addition, a column vector x is much larger than a capacity of a cache. It is taken by the cache in the replacement operation of a cache miss.

The above γ corresponds to a bandwidth which is consumed while it brings x of 0.5 pieces (2B) by the replacement. Moving 128B twice needs x(4B) of S pieces only one miss by the replacement. Moving $0.5 * 256/S$[B] needs x of 0.5 pieces by the replacement when the miss rate is 1. It means that it moves $128/S$[B] per one FLOPS. Also it moves $\gamma = (1 - hit_x) * 128/S$[B] per one FLOPS when the miss rate is $1 - hit_x$. Therefore a processing speed for a main memory bandwidth W_{cache}[B/s] is as follows.

$$F_{cache} = W_{cache}/(2 + I/2 + (1 - hit_x) * 128/S) \qquad (2)$$

In the case of a recommended memory system, Scatter/Gather is operated on the memory. Index does not move from the memory side. Therefore bandwidth consumption corresponding to α is included in Gather throughput W_{gather}[B/s]. β is 2[B/s] in the same rate as the case of cache. γ is 2[B/s] in the same rate as β since Gather in memory side keeps x continuous as well as A. Overall, a formula as follow shows required memory bandwidth per one FLOPS on a recommended memory system.

$$BPF_{gather} = 4 \qquad (3)$$

The processing speed for the case of Gather throughput W_{gather}[B/s] shows as follow.

$$F_{gather} = W_{gather}/BPF_{gather} = W_{gather}/4 \qquad (4)$$

We can observe an acceleration ratio by Gather function in memory against the cache for fixed parameter setting with a real GPU environment. In order to validate above performance model, we made an additional experiment.

In this experiment, performance for Gather function in memory is measured using pre-gathered x on the device memory. In this setting, array data A and pre-gathered x are sequentially and simultaneously accessed by GPU in the same access rate. Therefore, the performance is equivalent with that for the case of Gather throughput W_{gather} is half bandwidth of a device memory bandwidth of the GPU. In this experiment, a program which simulates the recommended memory completes Gather on a device memory outside of measuerd part in advance. In order not to add noise by Not-a-Number (NaN) interrupting, the value is properly initialized. Then it is organized to be able to measure correctly not the result but computation time. The program is applied Fold-method[17] as preprocessing and zero padding for GPU. Zero padding was needed to avoid large overhead of conditional branching on GPU. In this measurement, the folding is executed at the folding point which is 1.5-fold of the average number of non-zero elements per line.

A Fig.6 shows that an acceleration ratio by Gather function against the cache when a sparse matrix vector product is running on the GPU. We change the SCALE of the sparse matrix Graph500 from 11 to 20. 5.76-fold acceleration ratio has been observed at $SCALE = 20$. As a result by using 0-padding, a total number of accessing has increased approximately doubled (from 2.13-fold to 2.25-fold). 0 should be read not from the main memory but from the register. It includes unnecessary memory access with the zero padding. On the other hand, the accesses for the zero padding in the program for the cache are counted as hit. In other words, the performance of the proposed method is set up a situation that the observed in half on this measurement program.

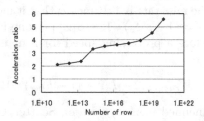

Fig. 6. The Scale of a sparse matrix Graph500 and acceleration ratio by Scatter/Gather function in memory against the cache(GPU : Nvidia C2050)

We try to assign values to the performance model mentioned above in order to validate it. Maximum device memory bandwidth W_{cache} in GPU is 144GB/s. The data type of index for SCALE20 can be 4B therefore it indicates as I = 4. A ratio hitting L1 or L2 is 35.1% in SCALE20, as shown in Figure 5. This is a hit rate "hit_{all}" that includes hit by sequence data and continuous access of index (31 times of hit in the 32 times of access). In order to get hit_x in a performance model formula (**2**), it needs to convert formula(**5**) with S, which is spatial locality metric, to formula(**6**).

$$hit_{all} = hit_x * 32/S + 31/32 * 2/(32/S + 2) \qquad (5)$$

$$hit_x = (32/S + 2) * hit_{all} - 31/32 * 2 * S/32 \qquad (6)$$

The result of Fig.3 leads that the value of a spatial locality index is $S = 1.03$ in SCALE20. A formula(6), S, and hit_{all} shows that $hit_x = 0.311$ in SCALE20. Substituting W_{cache} ,I, S, and hit_xinto a formula(2) indicates $F_{cache} = 1.61$[GFLOPS].

On the other hand, since it operates by means of dividing a device memory bandwidth in half with array data and the serialized x, Gather throughput is $W_{gather} = 72$GB/s. Then substituting this into a formula(4) leads to $F_{gather} = 18$[GFLOPS]. Therefore an acceleration ratio that F_{gather}/F_{cache}derived from performance model in SCALE20 is 11.2-fold. This value is about twice of 5.76-fold that the acceleration ratio has been observed. This fits the effect by zero padding, which we wrote before, observed value that is reduced to half. Then we got an evidence that a performance model is valid. A graph of an acceleration ratio in the measurement results of Fig.6 are bent in a zigzag shape. This phenomenon is occurred by the overflow of L1 cache and L2 cache. Thus, when the matrix size has been increased from SCALE 11 to SCALE14, a growth of an acceleration ratio is remarkable since L1 hit ratio dropped to more than half. When the matrix size has been increased from SCALE14 to SCALE17, a growth of an acceleration ratio slowed down since a change of a hit ratio of L1 cache goes worse and L2 cache hits. When the matrix size is increased from SCALE17 to SCALE20, L2 cache misses begin and then an acceleration ratio will begin to go up again. That is a combination of several factors has made a zigzag curve.

6.2   Power Consumption

In this section and next section, a power modeling is approximated that power for address calculation does not embed for the sake of simplicity. According to Dally[3], a long distance movement of closed to calculated data would consume much amounts of power in future semiconductor systems. That is the first basis that its approximation is correct. In the case of the cache, a software can handle the address calculation. A power of the processing is same as a processing by a dedicated hardware on a proposed memory or larger. Therefore, a configuration that the power for address calculation does not embed that does not have advantageous one for the proposed method. That is the second basis.

When it runs the sparse matrix vector product in cached-based, energy consumption E_{cache} of the memory access is modeled by the following formula (7). Besides, Cache line size is 128B (1024bit), Data matrix data size and Vector data size is 32bit and Index data size is 64bit. In addition, R_{hit} is the cache hit ratio, E_{miss} is the energy consumption for a 1-bit memory access when a cache hit occurs, and N_{access} is the total number of accesses and $b_{average}$ is the average number of access bits when it runs the sparse matrix vector product.

E_{hit} is dose of consumption energy E_{on}in 1-bit on-chip memory access and then E_{miss} is approximated to the sum of the dose of consumption energy E_{on} in 1-bit on-chip memory access and two doses of consumption energy E_{off} in 1-bit off-chip memory access. It would get the same number of times each 32bit in

Matrix value, 64bit in index value, and $128B/S$ (S is spatial locality) in vector value per one memory access. Thus, it would get the average $(32+64+1024/S)/3$ bit. N_{access} is three times of total number of non-zero elements N_{nz}. In the case of $E_{off} \gg E_{on}$ and $S \risingdotseq 1$, it shows a formula (10) that is approximated. In the Graph500, we can guess both S and R_{hit} are small therefore E_{cache} has a large consumed energy taken off-chip transfer of vector value.

$$E_{cache} = (R_{hit} * E_{hit} + (1 - R_{hit}) * E_{miss}) * N_{access} * b_{average} \tag{7}$$

$$\risingdotseq (R_{hit} * E_{on} + (1 - R_{hit}) * (E_{on} + 2E_{off})) * N_{access} * b_{average} \tag{8}$$

$$= R_{hit} * E_{on} + (1 - R_{hit}) * (E_{on} + 2E_{off})) * 3N_{nz} * (32 + 64 + 1024/S)/3 \tag{9}$$

$$= R_{hit} * E_{on} + (1 - R_{hit}) * (E_{on} + 2E_{off})) * N_{nz} * (32 + 64 + 1024/S) \tag{10}$$

$$\risingdotseq 2240(1 - R_{hit})N_{nz}E_{off} \quad (If \ E_{off} \gg E_{on}, S \risingdotseq 1) \tag{11}$$

On the other hand, in the case of performing prefetch with Hybrid Method Cube combined Gather function, consumption energy of memory access E_{gather} shows a formula (12) as follow when it runs the sparse matrix vector product. Besides, E_{array} is the matrix value(32 bit), E_{gather} is the index value(64 bit), and E_{vector} is the vector value(32 bit), which is an consumption energy to get one element.

All of the matrix value and the vector value, which are as burst data, are prefetched by the long distance transfer on the board and are on-chip accessed from the cache to the arithmetic unit. The consumption energy by each transfer is approximated that $32E_{on} + 32E_{off}$. Additionally the vector value in the process of Gather is transferred short distance in the Hybrid Memory Cube and then the consumption energy is approximated $32E_{on}$.

The index value is transferred not long distance on the board but all short distance by way of TSV in Hybrid Memory Cube. Thus, the consumption energy to get one index value is approximated $64E_{on}$.

In the case of $E_{off} \gg E_{on}$ a formula (14) is approximated like a formula (15). That is, it shows that Hybrid Memory Cube combined Gather function has much smaller consumption energy instead of cache compared to a formula (11).

In the case of $E_{off} \gg E_{on}$ and $S \risingdotseq 1$, a formula (16) shows the ratio of consumption energy by Hybrid Memory Cube combined Gather function instead of cache. It turns out to save electrical power of about thirty times when the cache hit rate is 15% and about seventeen times when the cache hit rate is 50%.

$$E_{gather} = N_{nz} * (E_{array} + E_{index} + E_{vector}) \tag{12}$$

$$\risingdotseq N_{nz} * ((32E_{on} + 32E_{off}) + 64E_{on} + (32E_{on} + 32E_{off} + 32E_{on})) \tag{13}$$

$$= N_{nz} * (160E_{on} + 64E_{off}) \tag{14}$$

$$\risingdotseq 64N_{nz}E_{off} \quad (If \ E_{off} \gg E_{on}) \tag{15}$$

$$E_{cache}/E_{gather} = 35(1 - R_{hit}) \tag{16}$$

In Fig.7, a hit ratio of L1 cache is nothing but 5.8% in SCALE20. A hit ratio of L1 cache or L2 cache is 35.1%. Substituting these above values into a power model formula(**16**) shows that a power ratio of memory access is the difference of 22.7-fold. It is considered that it is a matter of time that L2 cache does not hit like L1 cache increasing SCALE from 20 to much further. When a hit ratio hitting L1 cache or L2 cache is 15%, a power of memory access has a difference of 30-fold.

7   Related Works

Many efforts have been done for accelerating graph processing. Although Suzumura [14] analyzes a reference implementation of Graph500 from several points of view, there is no analysis about cache memory effect. Ueno[13] reported an implementation of Graph500 using 2D partitioning. They propose an optimization technique for cache named vertex sorting. However the resultant speedup gain is only 10%.

As for the PageRank[1] speedup works, Yang[12] reported for GPUs. PageRank on GPUs can be accelerated more effectively than on CPUs because the memory bandwidth of GPUs is higher than that of CPUs. PEGASUS[6] that is graph analysis processing framework represented in sparse matrix-vector multiplications are implemented with Hadoop. These works are aimed for scaling out using many nodes. There is no analysis for cache memory effect among these works, too.

Accelerating Scatter/Gather operations has long history. Vector supercomputers have vector load/store instructions since antiquity. Strided vector load/store instructions, Indexed (indirect reference) vector load/store instructions and Mask vector load/store instructions support Scatter/Gather operations. Convey HC-1[18] has hardwired Scatter/Gather functions on a memory controller on motherboard. There is very small effect of saving power in memory controller on motherboard based solution. DIMMnet-2[19] has them on a memory module (DIMM). Although this is the nearest the recommended HMC based solution[9][10], there is small effect of saving power in DIMM based solution.

Recently, the instructions executing Scatter/Gather have been implemented on processor such as Intel Larabee[15] and Intel®Xeon®Phi™[16] which is a commercial many core CPU. These approaches based on processor side Scatter/Gather invoke inefficient memory accesses, when the cache hit rate is low on executing some applications such as graph processing. Therefore, there is no effect of saving power and acceleration which are shown in this paper.

8   Conclusions

In this paper, the spatial locality of sparse matrices used for Graph500 and its behaviors on cache memory are investigated. The experimental results show the spatial locality of sparse matrices used for Graph500 is very low and there is about 1 or a little more valid data on a cache line for the memory accesses issued by SpMV in average. It is very difficult to solve the problem by just software approach because of the huge size of sparse matrices and the randomness of their accesses to degrade the optimization based on cache awareness. Therefore, we recommend hardwired scatter/gather functions at memory side. They are promising for taking advantage in the Graph500 lists. They improve the processing speed in an order of magnitude. For achieving both of low power and high throughput of random access, we recommend implementing hardwired scatter/gather functions on logic-base in Hybrid Memory Cube (HMC). We also describe brief considerations of the electrical power saving in the case of low cache hit rate application such as graph500. For example, when the hit rate is 15%, the power saving ratio of memory access is about 30-fold. Such effects cannot be realized with scatter/gather functions on processor side such as them on Xeon Phi. Our future work includes more precise simulator based performance and power evaluation, implementation of Graph500 using scatter/gather functions at memory side, etc.

References

1. Page, L., Brin, S., Motwani, R., Winograd, T.: The PageRank citation ranking: Bringing order to the Web. Technical Report Stanford Digital Library Working Paper SIDL-WP-1999-0120, Stanford University (1999)
2. Graph500, http://www.graph500.org/
3. Dally, W.J.: Power, Programmability, and Granularity: The Challenges of ExaScale Computing. In: IPDPS 2011 Keynote (2011), http://techtalks.tv/talks/keynote-power-programmability-and-granularity-the-challenges-of-exascale-computing/54110/
4. Hadoop, http://hadoop.apache.org/
5. Memcached, http://memcached.org/
6. Kang, U., Tsourakakis, C.E., Faloutsos, C.: PEGASUS: A Peta-Scale Graph Mining System - Implementation and Observations. In: International Conference on Data Mining, pp. 229–238 (2009)
7. Micron Technology, Hybrid Memory Cube: Breakthrough DRAM Performance with a Fundamentally Re-Architected DRAM Subsystem. HotChips 23 (2011)
8. Hybrid Memory Cube Consortium, http://hybridmemorycube.org/
9. Tanabe, N., Nuttapon, B., Nakajo, H., Ogawa, Y., Kogou, J., Takata, M., JoeF, K.: A memory accelerator with gather functions for bandwidth-bound irregular applications C. In: Proceedings of the First Workshop on Irregular Applications: Architectures and Algorithm (IAAA 2011) in Conjunction with SC 2011, pp. 35–42 (2011)
10. Tanabe, N., Kogou, J., Tomimori, S., Takata, M., Joe, K.: Future Irregular Computing with Memory Accelerators. In: FUTURE COMPUTING 2013, pp. 74–80 (2013)
11. Tanabe, N., Tomimori, S., Takata, M., Joe, K.: Locality Analysis for Characterizing Applications Based on Sparse Matrices. In: International Conference on Parallel and Distributed Processing Techniques and Applications, PDPTA 2013 (2013)
12. Yang, X., et al.: Fast sparse matrix-vector multiplication on GPUs: implications for graph mining. Proc. VLDB Endowment 4(4), 231–242 (2011)
13. Ueno, K., Suzumura, T.: Highly Scalable Graph Search for the Graph500 Benchmark. In: 21st International ACM Symposium on High-Performance Parallel and Distributed Computing (HPDC 2012), June 2012, pp. 149–160 (2012)

14. Suzumura, T., et al.: "Performance Evaluation of Graph500 on Large-Scale Distributed Environment. In: IEEE IISWC 2011 (November 2011)
15. Seiler, L., et al.: Larrabee: A Many.Core x86 Architecture for Visual Computing. ACM Trans. Graph. 27(3), Article 18 (August 2008)
16. Intel: Intel®Xeon®Phi™ Coprocessor Data sheet (November 2012)
17. Tanabe, N., Ogawa, C.Y., Takata, C.M., Joe, C.K.: Scaleable Sparse Matrix-Vector Multiplication with Functional Memory and GPUs. In: 19th Euromicro Conference on Parallel, Distributed and Network-Based Computing (PDP 2011), pp. 101–108 (2011)
18. Brewer, T.M.: Instruction Set Innovations for the Convey HC-1 Computer. IEEE Micro 30(2), 70–79 (2010)
19. Tanabe, N., Hakozaki, H., Dohi, Y., Luo, Z., Nakajo, H.: An enhancer of memory and network for applications with large-capacity data and non-continuous data accessing. The Journal of Supercomputing 51(3), 279–309 (2009)

HySARC²: Hybrid Scheduling Algorithm Based on Resource Clustering in Cloud Environments

Mihaela-Andreea Vasile, Florin Pop, Radu-Ioan Tutueanu,
and Valentin Cristea

University *Politehnica* of Bucharest
Computer Science Department, Faculty of Automatic Control and Computers
{mihaela.vasile,radu.tutueanu}@cti.pub.ro,
{florin.pop,valentin.cristea}@cs.pub.ro

Abstract. Cloud Computing is a fairly new paradigm but evolving very fast. Nowadays, business enterprise services and middle ware such as SAP or Oracle are integrated into a Cloud infrastructure. Also, Cloud services are used for computational or IO intensive applications from multiple science fields like physics, microbiology or weather forecast, due to the large amount of resources available. In this context, it must be paid attention to resource utilization in Cloud environments. Therefore, the scheduling of tasks on Cloud resources is a core issue, with impact for users and service providers. We proposed HySARC², a novel scheduling algorithm based on traditional approaches, which considers clustering of the available resources in the infrastructure in the phase of resource allocation. The resources clustering into groups is used by our proposed algorithm in a hierarchical way, executed in two phases. First, tasks are assigned to groups of resources and further, in a second phase, inside each group of resources a classical scheduling algorithm is executed. The proposed algorithm is suitable for heterogeneous systems and sets of applications with various requirements (both IO and computational intensive).

Keywords: Scheduling, Resource Allocation, Clustering, Cloud Computing.

1 Introduction

Cloud systems represent a significant choice for applications requiring intensive computations or big data processing, because the Cloud infrastructure provides a large amount of resources in terms of memory, disk and impressive processing power [1] [2]. Multiple research applications in different domains, like: medicine, weather forecasting, physics or national defense use the resources of a private, public or hybrid Cloud for the above reasons. As a response to the fast evolving of Cloud importance in nowadays activities, there were developed Cloud platforms (provided by companies like Amazon, Google, SAP or Microsoft), frameworks for evaluating Cloud platforms (OpenNebula, Eucalyptus or Nimbus [3]) and also simulation environments (CloudSim, GreenCloud or ICanCloud).

J. Kołodziej et al. (Eds.): ICA3PP 2013, Part I, LNCS 8285, pp. 416–425, 2013.

The applications that rely on the Cloud infrastructure are characterized by a number of requirements: estimated processing time, required memory, IO operations, a budget or a deadline. Given the previous arguments, the role of scheduling of tasks on resources is a key part of a Cloud infrastructure. The scheduling must take into account all tasks requirements, improve the utilization of the resources, load balancing or total execution time.

In this paper we propose HySARC², a scheduling algorithm that improves workload on the resources available into the Cloud and satisfies tasks requirements. The algorithm has three parts: (i) Analyse the available resources and group them into clusters (resource aware algorithm); (ii) Provision different groups of similar tasks to different clusters of resources; and (iii) Schedule the tasks in each cluster of resources. HySARC² is applied for Bag-of-Tasks (BaT) applications such as data mining algorithms or Monte Carlo simulations, having both IO and computational intensive phases.

The paper is structured as follows. Section 2 analyzes actual solution for task scheduling in a data-center and discuss the related work. The third Section describes in detail the proposed solution: architecture, the clustering algorithm and scheduling algorithm. The experimental methodology is covered in Section 4. For those we analyze the total execution time and scalability. Section 5 presents HySARC² integration in real Cloud platforms and in the last part, Section 6, are presented the conclusions and future research work.

2   Related Work

The paper aims to find a way of improving the resource allocation in a given Cloud environment. Therefore the execution of various tasks will be scheduled on adequate resources in order to satisfy both user requirements and service provider interests. In order to achieve this goal, we proposed an approach based on the clustering and labeling of resources .

Cloud service providers are interested in optimizing available resources, in order to being able to satisfy as many user requirements as possible and as a result improving the profit. Efficient energy management is a challenging research issue in resource management in Cloud [4] [5]. The HySARC² algorithm aims an efficient resource utilization: tasks assigned on suitable resources, having as effect energy saving because inadequate resources could be put in a hibernate state, in the limits of the Service Level Agreement (SLA). We will describe several solutions that take into consideration the resource allocation.

In [6] it is described a Resource Aware Scheduling Algorithm which stands on top of the analysis of two existing task scheduling algorithms: Min-min and Max-min. Both algorithms use an estimation of tasks completion time and resource execution time. Min-min algorithm selects the task with minimum completion time and schedules it on the resource with the minimum execution time. Max-min assigns the larger tasks first and after the smaller ones; in this case, a greater number of large tasks causes problem in scheduling efficiency. The algorithm alternates the two algorithms depending on input tasks.

An important feature for scheduling algorithms is to have a dynamic behaviour according to real environment evolution. Such an algorithm is described in [7]. The algorithm is suitable for arbitrary constraints tasks, their dependencies may be organized as a graph, having as nodes the tasks and as edges the constraints. It consists in to parts: first, the scheduling phase - select the first task in the list and then allocate it on the resource with earliest start time; next, follows the re-scheduling phase. For the second phase, the algorithm is treating separately different types of tasks: entry task (no tasks depend on the task that fails, then only the current task is re-scheduled) and inner task (all tasks depending on the failure node have to be rescheduled).

In [8] is presented an algorithm having good results on the compromise cost-execution time. The tests showed that the cost may descend with over 15% while the execution time satisfy users requirements or the execution time may be shorter with average 20% and the costs would remain almost the same. The main steps of the algorithm are: (i) Reschedule tasks from previous rounds with highest priority; (ii) Compute tasks sub-deadlines: latest completion time that cannot be exceeded; (iii) Compute execution time and cost for each task on each resource; (iv) Each task is distributed to the resource with lowest execution time and lowest cost; (v) Allow the user to view a graph with the relation time-cost and to choose desired compromise; (vi) Repeat for next scheduling round.

A heuristic genetic approach is described in [9] and [10], with a slight improve-ment of execution time. The proposed algorithm generates an initial schedule for tasks using a heuristic algorithm such as Min-min (described above in [6]); compute parameters like make span for the generated allocation; select nodes (scheduled resources) using the previous computed parameters; crossover and mutation of tasks scheduling on resources; test stop condition. Another strategy used as optimization method is co-allocation. Co-allocation provides a schedule for task with dependencies, having as main purpose the efficiency of the schedule, in terms of load balancing and minimum time for the execution of the tasks [11].

There are several scheduling algorithms and strategies adopted in private Clouds. The scheduling in *OpenStack* [12] framework is accomplished by the nova-scheduler. The main scheduling phases in the process are: 1. filtering avail-able resources according to users requirements; and 2. weighting phase - the filtered hosts are applied a cost function depending on the input tasks and then sorted from the best to the worst. When using *OpenNebula* framework [13], the default available scheduling is related to the allocation of VMs on hosts. It uses a Rank Policy for that purpose: the hosts not fulfilling VMs requirements (memory or CPU) are excluded; the remaining hosts are evaluated using a configurable rank function; VMs are allocated to hosts with higher rank.

The most used Cloud simulator is CloudSim [14]. In CloudSim there are avail-able default scheduling policies both for VMs allocation on hosts and for tasks allocation on processing elements. The simulator offers space-shared and time-shared policies for VMs and tasks provision and those two available policies may be used in every combination having different effects in tasks execution.

3   HySARC^2: Model, Architecture and Algorithm

Theoretical Model. A task represents a sequence of operations, needing a resource in order to execute its operations. A set of tasks may be independent or interdependent (having different types of constraints). In our model, the tasks received from the user are independent (similar to BoT model) [15]. We have a set of tasks $T = \{T_i\}$. A task is a set of four properties, $T_i = (P_1^T, P_2^T, P_3^T, P_4^T)$, where P_1^T is CPU processing time, P_2^T is IO time, P_3^T is pre-emption flag (pre-emptive or non-pre-emptive) and P_4^T is deadline. A resource is "anything that can be scheduled" or allocated from a physical machine or processors to a network. We have a set of resources $R = \{R_j\}$. A resource represents a physical processing element, having a set of properties. The characteristics used by the algorithm are $R_i = (P_1^R, P_2^R)$, where P_1^R is processing speed and P_2^R is IO speed. Other properties that can be considered as extensions are: parallel (single, uniform or unrelated processors) or dedicated processors, network topology.

Architecture. To describe HySARC^2 behavior, we consider as input a set of tasks grouped into clusters. We monitor the resources from Cloud environment, then classify them into clusters. We allocate tasks clusters on the available resources according to the scheduling algorithm for each cluster of resources. We consider four modules: Monitoring Service, Analyzer and Scheduler (Fig. 1).

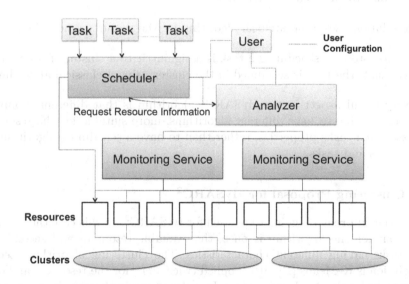

Fig. 1. Proposed Architecture used by HySARC^2

Monitoring Service. This module is used as a background process, starting at the system initialization. At start up, the Monitoring Service finds the available resources. Each time a resource is added to the system, it notifies the Monitoring Service. The role played is to be aware of the available resources and their characteristics. This list is used by the Scheduler and Analyzer without having to request information from the system each time an algorithm is ran.

The **Analyzer** is used for clustering the resources and tasks according to user configuration or default predefined settings. We proposed the following behavior: (a) the Analyzer supports user configuration. The user provides information about how many groups of tasks and resources should be created after the clustering phase. The default values are three clusters of tasks and three clusters of resources: CPU intensive, I/O intensive or mixed (both CPU and I/O intensive); (b) next, the Analyzer gets the list of resources and properties from the monitoring service, apply a clustering algorithm on the set of resources and labels each resource with the associated cluster; (c) the Analyzer receives the list of tasks and their properties from the scheduler and applies the clustering algorithm; (d) it provides the scheduler the list of clusters for the resources and tasks.

The **Scheduler** has the role of receiving input tasks and assign them to available resources. The work-flow for the Scheduler module is:

1. The Scheduler receives the input tasks.
2. Next, the Scheduler sends the tasks to the Analyzer for clustering.
3. Further, the Scheduler receives from the Analyzer the clusters of tasks and available cluster of resources.
4. Finally, the Scheduler applies a hierarchical scheduling algorithm and send each task to the identified resource.

The solution uses a hierarchical algorithm for the resource scheduling:

A. the first step for scheduling a task is assigning it to a cluster of resources.
B. after that, the task is scheduled in the cluster using a classical algorithm.

A very useful aspect in the HySARC^2 algorithm is that different groups of resources are able to have different algorithms, more suitable for the resources and associated tasks properties, rather than to have a scheduling algorithm for all resources and tasks.

3.1   Clustering Proposal for HySARC^2

A clustering approach is going to be used for HySARC^2. In this case the abstract data input for the algorithm is once, the available resources and second, the input tasks having different characteristics. The clustering algorithm used in this solution is K-Means [16]. It is applied twice, once for the resources and once for the tasks by the Analyzer module. In order to apply the algorithm, we must define the properties for tasks and resources taken into account by the clustering and also the "distance" between two elements in the set, as follow:

The properties are the ones defined at the beginning of this section:

Tasks : estimated CPU processing time (P_1^T) and I/O operations time (P_2^T)
Resources : CPU processing power (P_1^R) and I/O operations speed (P_2^R)

The "distance" between two tasks or resources is necessary for identifying the "closest" cluster center. The "distance" highlights the similarity between entities. We define the same distance for tasks and resources as follow:

1. normalize the values of parameters along the entire set of entities (E and K denote a task or a resource). We define the normalized value for property P_i^E, where $i = 1, 2$ as: $\tilde{P}_i^E = \frac{P_i^E}{\sum_K P_i^K}$.
2. the two normalized parameters are considered as coordinates, so the distance between entity E_a and entity E_b having the properties P_1 and P_2 is the Euclidean distance: $distance(E_a, E_b) = \sqrt{\left(\tilde{P}_1^{E_a} - \tilde{P}_1^{E_b}\right)^2 + \left(\tilde{P}_2^{E_a} - \tilde{P}_2^{E_b}\right)^2}$.

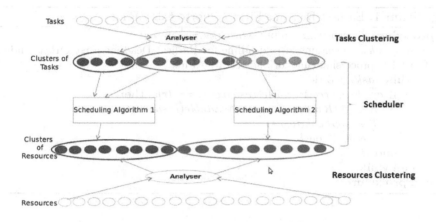

Fig. 2. Clustering Phase for HySARC²

After the clustering phase is completed, we follows the actual scheduling of the resources for the input tasks, now grouped into clusters (see Fig. 2).

3.2 HySARC² Scheduling Algorithm

The scheduling algorithm is applied by the Scheduler module in two steps:

STEP 1 : associate groups of tasks with groups resources, according to average parameters in tasks and resources groups. In other words, the clusters of tasks having a high average processing time required ("large" tasks) are assigned to resources with high computational capacity. The same reasoning applies to "small" tasks.

STEP 2 : inside each group of resources run a scheduling algorithm in order to allocate the tasks.

Scheduling Algorithms Used by HySARC². Given the fact that the tasks being processed by the scheduler are a set of independent tasks, we apply specific scheduling algorithms. The scheduler implements two scheduling algorithms for independent tasks: —Shortest Job First (SJF) and *Earliest Deadline First* (EDF), and alternates them in each cluster of resources, for analysis and comparison purposes. The SJF algorithm associates with a task, its estimated CPU processing time ("small" job means having a low processing time), and as soon a resource is available, it assigns on it the shortest task in the waiting list. In order to achieve this more efficiently, the list of tasks are sorted ascending after the CPU processing time (see Algorithm 1). The EDF algorithm associates with a task its deadline, and as soon a resource is available, it assigns on it the task with the nearest deadline in the waiting list. The tasks are kept into a priority list, the priorities are the inverse of the deadline, and the tasks with higher priority are scheduled sooner (see Algorithm 1).

Algorithm 1. Earliest Deadline First / Shortest Job First

1: **procedure** CLASSICAL_SCHEDULING(*tasks, resources*)
2:     *sort tasks*: descending after deadline for Earliest Deadline First **OR** ascending after CPU processing time for Shortest Job First.
3:         **while** *tasks* $\neq \phi$ **do**
4:             **if** *anyResourceAvailable(resources)* == *true* **then**
5:                 $R \leftarrow getRandomResourceAvailable(resources)$
6:                 $T \leftarrow popTask(tasks)$
7:                 execute T on R.
8:             **end if**
9:         **end while**
10: **end procedure**

We may observe that the difference between the two algorithms is how the tasks are being sorted in the waiting list. The list is being used as a stack.

4   Experimental Methodology and Results

For the test cases, we generated tasks with various random requirements. The same approach is also used for generating different resources. The characteristics of the processing elements are chosen randomly from the following values:

- MIPS : 200, 400, 500, 800, 1000, 2000, 4000, 5000, 8000, 10000;
- RAM dimension: 512, 1024, 2048, 4096, 8192, 16384;
- we vary also the total storage value, but the values are not relevant.

Using CloudSim [14], we generate a maximum number of 1000 tasks, 1000 Processing Elements (PE) and 10 Virtual Machines (VM) with different number of cores. In each simulation we vary the number of virtual machines from 1 to 10 and the number of processing elements from 10 to 1000, given 1000 tasks.

Tasks and Resources Clustering Phase. We analyze the Clustering Phase duration, along the above set of scenarios and for different grades of variability of the generated parameters (the parameters are in certain different grades similar or very different). In Fig. 3(left) we have the task clustering phase duration. In Fig. 3(right) we have the resource clustering phase duration. A large number of tasks produce an overhead and we can slit the set of submitted tasks into multiple requests. For resource clustering we have similar times, so we can run periodically this procedure without any inconvenient. The overhead observed justifies itself because it slightly reduces the execution time.

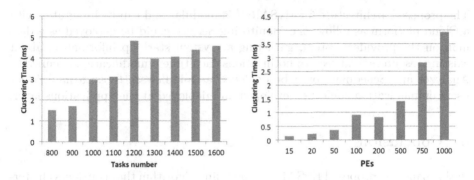

Fig. 3. (left) Task clustering duration; (right) Resource clustering duration

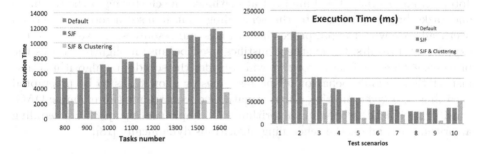

Fig. 4. (left) Execution time comparison (simulation time/steps); (right) Scalability

Execution Time. We analyze the average execution time of tasks along a combination of scenarios using a certain configuration (5 virtual machines and 100 processing elements): (i) we test by using or not the clustering algorithm; (ii) we also test with or without the default scheduling algorithm inside clusters; (iii) the tests are taken for three clusters of resources and three clusters of tasks or four clusters of resources and four clusters of tasks. In Fig. 4(left) we present the results for initial CloudSim Scheduling (2), only clustering (3), clustering and SJF algorithm (1). The conclusion is that the clustering phase add an overhead, but using a specialized scheduling algorithm we obtain a good improvement.

Scalability. We analyze the average execution time, along the entire above set of scenarios and for different grades of variability of the generated parameters (the parameters are in certain different grades similar or very different).

In Fig. 4(right) we have the average execution time for initial CloudSim scheduling, for clustering and any scheduling algorithm (SJF or EDF). We can conclude that by adding HySARC^2 in a specific Cloud environment the scalability is preserved.

5   HySARC^2 Integration in Real Cloud Platforms

The proposed architecture for HySARC^2 is modular and can be integrated with a Cloud platform as follow: the Monitoring Service could be deployed as a daemon on the provider system, gathering at system start up information about existing resources, and receive notifications each time a modification occurs; the Analyzer and Scheduler could be deployed as middleware tools; a module for user communication could be developed and deployed at the applications layer.

6   Conclusion

In this paper we proposed HySARC^2 scheduling algorithm that considers clustering of the available resources before the phase of resource allocation. HySARC^2 is based on traditional scheduling algorithm and we used in this paper the Shortest Job First and Earliest Deadline First algorithms. The clustering of the resources and tasks brings efficiency to the scheduling, but it also introduce a certain overhead once with the pre-processing of tasks and resources. As we seen in the experimental results, the overhead justifies itself because it slightly reduces the processing time. As future work we will consider the scheduling algorithms that inspect the dynamic behavior of the resources or allow tasks to be preempted according to a given priority, different natures of constraints (for example DAG, considering ICPDP scheduling algorithm [17]), implementing specific scheduling algorithms and adapt the scheduling algorithms dynamically [18].

Acknowledgment.   The research presented in this paper is supported by projects: *"SideSTEP - Scheduling Methods for Dynamic Distributed Systems: a self-* approach"*, ID: PN-II-CT-RO-FR-2012-1-0084; *"ERRIC - Empowering Romanian Research on Intelligent Information Technologies"*, FP7-REGPOT-2010-1, ID: 264207; and by CyberWater grant of the Romanian National Authority for Scientific Research, CNDI-UEFISCDI, project number 47/2012.

References

1. Fox, A., Griffith, R., Joseph, A., Katz, R., Konwinski, A., Lee, G., Patterson, D., Rabkin, A., Stoica, I.: Above the clouds: A berkeley view of cloud computing. Dept. Electrical Eng. and Comput. Sciences, University of California (2009)
2. Marinescu, D.C.: Cloud Computing: Theory and Practice, vol. 2014. Morgan Kaufmann (2013)

3. Sempolinski, P., Thain, D.: A comparison and critique of eucalyptus, opennebula and nimbus. In: Proc. of the 2010 IEEE Second Int. Conf. on Cloud Computing Technology and Science. IEEE Computer Society (2010)
4. Jing, S.Y., Ali, S., She, K., Zhong, Y.: State-of-the-art research study for green cloud computing. J. Supercomput (2013)
5. Kolodziej, J., Xhafa, F.: Modern approaches to modeling user requirements on resource and task allocation in hierarchical computational grids. Int. J. Appl. Math. Comput. Sci. 21(2), 243–257 (2011)
6. Parsa, S., Entezari-Maleki, R.: Rasa: A new task scheduling algorithm in grid environment. World Applied Sciences Journal (2009)
7. Olteanu, A., Pop, F., Dobre, C., Cristea, V.: A dynamic rescheduling algorithm for resource management in large scale dependable distributed systems. Comput. Math. Appl. (2012)
8. Liu, K., Jin, H., Chen, J., Liu, X., Yuan, D., Yang, Y.: A compromised-time-cost scheduling algorithm in swindew-c for instance-intensive cost-constrained work-flows on a cloud computing platform. Int. J. High Perform. Comput. Appl. (2010)
9. Kaur, K., Chhabra, A., Singh, G.: Heuristics based genetic algorithm for scheduling static tasks in homogeneous parallel system. Int. J. of Comp. Sci. and Sec. (2010)
10. Kolodziej, J., Xhafa, F.: Enhancing the genetic-based scheduling in computational grids by a structured hierarchical population. Future Gener. Comput. Syst. 27(8), 1035–1046 (2011)
11. Moise, D., Moise, E., Pop, F., Cristea, V.: Resource coallocation for scheduling tasks with dependencies, in grid. In: HiPerGRID Workshops Proceeding, Bucharest, Romania, pp. 2065–2701 (2008) ISSN: 2065-0701
12. Jackson, K.: OpenStack Cloud Computing Cookbook. Packt Publishing (2012)
13. Milojicic, D., Llorente, I.M., Montero, R.S.: Opennebula: A cloud management tool. IEEE Internet Computing (2011)
14. Calheiros, R.N., Ranjan, R., Beloglazov, A., De Rose, A.F., Buyya, R.: Cloudsim: a toolkit for modeling and simulation of cloud computing environments and evaluation of resource provisioning algorithms. Softw. Pract. Exper. 41(1) (2011)
15. Xhafa, F., Kolodziej, J., Barolli, L., Kolici, V., Miho, R., Takizawa, M.: Hybrid algorithms for independent batch scheduling in grids. Int. J. Web Grid Serv. 8(2), 134–152 (2012)
16. MacQueen, J.: et al.: Some methods for classification and analysis of multivariate observations. In: Proc. of the Fifth Berkeley Symp. on Math. Statistics and Probability, USA (1967)
17. Simion, B., Leordeanu, C., Pop, F., Cristea, V.: A hybrid algorithm for scheduling workflow applications in grid environments (icpdp). In: Meersman, R. (ed.) OTM 2007, Part II. LNCS, vol. 4804, pp. 1331–1348. Springer, Heidelberg (2007)
18. Bessis, N., Sotiriadis, S., Cristea, V., Pop, F.: Modelling requirements for enabling meta-scheduling in inter-clouds and inter-enterprises. In: Intelligent Networking and Collaborative Systems (INCoS), pp. 149–156 (2011)

M&C: A Software Solution to Reduce Errors Caused by Incoherent Caches on GPUs in Unstructured Graphic Algorithm

Kun Wang, Rui Wang, Zhongzhi Luan, and Depei Qian

Key Laboratory in Beijing of Network Technology,
School of Computer Science and Engineering, Beihang
University, 100191 Beijing, China
{Kun.wang,Rui.wang,Zhongzhi.luan}@jsi.buaa.edu.cn,
Depeiq@{xjtu.edu.cn,buaa.edu.cn}

Abstract. Recently, researchers have focused on addressing incoherent caches on GPUs as current GPUs lack hardware to support that. Moreover, the support for inter-block communication also lacks which limits the scalability of parallel programming especially in the unstructured algorithm in which program would share data between different threads. Barrier synchronization can be a solution but it becomes invalid because of incoherent caches. In this paper, we propose a set of rules for programming on current GPUs to avoid the errors caused by incoherent caches when applying barrier synchronization. We also leverage these rules into an unstructured graphic algorithm -- constrained Delaunay triangulation. In comparison with traditional ways such as (1) disabling L1 cache and (2) using keyword *volatile*, we find that when vertices is over 300K the error rate is lesser than (1) by 91.19% and than (2) by 84.2% on average.

1   Introduction

The graphics processing units (GPUs) have been widely used for parallel computing in recent years. A GPU has more streaming processors (SPs) than a traditional CPU and the bandwidth of memory is higher. Applications can be tremendously accelerated if they map well to GPU hardware, and it is cost-effective for those applications with plenty of data parallelism such as FFT, mesh generation, etc. But the bandwidth is still not enough. To get better performance, a multilevel cache hierarchy is introduced into GPUs to reduce the demand for bandwidth of global memory. Programmers can run their applications much faster ignoring the hardware details and paying attention to the algorithms instead of racking their brains to limit the access to global memory by data reuse.

However, GPUs have no mechanism for cache coherence which is necessary for some algorithms. Besides the cache coherence, the lack of inter-block communication also limits the effectiveness and scalability of parallel programming on GPUs. Many solutions [1] [2] [8-10] are proposed but only a few can be practical for programmers.

J. Kołodziej et al. (Eds.): ICA3PP 2013, Part I, LNCS 8285, pp. 426–435, 2013.

```
__global__ void kernel_function() {        __device__ function1() {
    __device__function1();                     ... ...
    __gpu_sync();//barrier synchronization     writeData();
    __device__funciton2();                     __threadfence();
    __gpu_sync();//barrier synchronization     ... ...
    ... ...                                 }
}
```

Fig. 1. GPU synchronization function call

Barrier synchronization is a practical option to solve the synchronization problem. Shucai Xiao [9] proposes a simple barrier synchronization by using functions like __gpusync() and threadfence() to synchronize all threads between SMs on a GPU. This method is friendly for the programmers because when they want to synchronize all threads on the GPU they just need to call those functions as shown in Fig. 1. These functions can synchronize program and coherent memory. But this synchronization does not provide a method to synchronize incoherent caches since the GPU had no caches at that time.

As NVIDIA introduces caches into GPUs from Fermi architecture while without cache coherence, programmers need to address coherence by their own way, or else errors may occur as showed in Fig. 2. Thread i and Thread j are two threads running on different SMs. In function 1, they read values from global memory, and cache them into their private caches. Then they write a new value back. After that they call a barrier synchronization function to synchronize threads between different SMs. In the function 2, threads want to read the new value which is modified by another thread, but would get the old value from their caches, rather than the new value from the global memory. Then cache incoherence occurs and runtime errors are raised.

Therefore, in this paper we propose three methods for programmers to address the cache coherence with barrier synchronization. The first method is to mark all the data needed by threads. The privileges to access data are determined by the thread id. One thread can only read and write its own data. The second method is to cluster those relative threads that are accessing same pieces of data and put these threads onto the same SM. Then the data can only have one copy in one SM and the coherence can be avoided. The third method called M&C which is short for *Mark&Cluster* is to combine these two methods together and take advantage of the benefits of both.

We also introduce these methods into a typical unstructured graphic algorithm, constrained Delaunay triangulation. We adjust this algorithm with barrier synchronization first. Then we write two programs which disable the L1 cache on the GPU and declare parameters as volatile respectively. As these two methods are commonly used to provide trivial coherence, we set these two methods as the baselines to test the performance of our own. Then we modify the algorithm with our methods and measure their execution time and error rates to compare with baselines. Our experiments show our best method, M&C, is 91.19% better than disabling the L1 cache and 84.2% than using keyword volatile when the vertices increase to 300K or more.

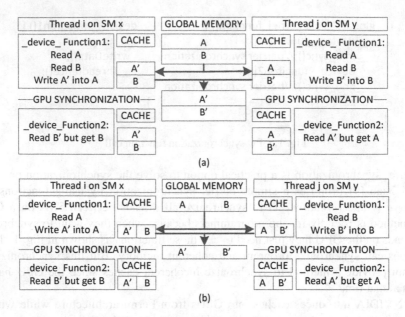

Fig. 2. Read errors caused by incoherent caches

The rest of the paper is organized as follows. Section 2 describes the traditional ways to avoid cache coherence and gives a brief introduction to constrained Delaunay triangulation algorithm. Section 3 discusses related work. Section 4 interprets our three methods in details. Section 5 and 6 presents our methodology and results, and Section 7 concludes.

2   Background

2.1   Traditional Solutions

Invalidation of the L1 Cache. Disabling L1 cache is a traditional way for the programmers to avoid the problems caused by cache coherence. Nowadays, GPUs have two hierarchical caches, L1 caches and L2 caches. L1 caches are private to each SM while L2 are shared by all SMs. L1 caches are incoherent while L2 caches are coherent. Besides L1 caches, each SM has its own registers, local memory and other memories which also have no mechanism to ensure the coherence with other SMs. So disabling L1 cache is not enough since there are some other incoherent resources in GPUs. Then disabling L1 caches cannot solve this problem perfectly. Our experiments show that disabling L1 cache is efficient when the dataset is small, but its performance decreases significantly as the dataset becomes larger.

```
__device__ void function1(volatile int* p,....) {
    ... ...
}
__global__ void kernel_function(int* p,....) {
    ... ...
    function1(p, ....);
    __gpu_sync();//barrier synchronization
    ... ...
}
```

Fig. 3. Pseudo code for using keyword *volatile*

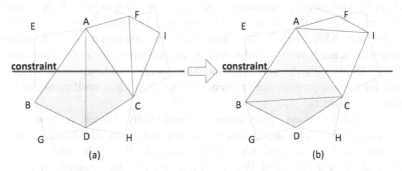

(a)   (b)

Fig. 4. Two triangle pairs (a) and two flipped triangle pairs (b)

Use of the keyword *Volatile*. Using keyword volatile is common in multithreads programming, programmers tell the compiler not to optimize code for memory access and read the value from the memory rather than the cache. Here we use the keyword *volatile* as prefix to the parameters of the functions called in kernel (Fig. 3). Then the program would bypass the caches and get the data directly from global memory.

2.2 Constrained Delaunay Triangulation

Delaunay triangulation is a popular method to produce unstructured meshes for finite element analysis in CFD [11]. Delaunay triangulation is to divide an input domain by triangles. Each triangle's circumcircle does not contain any vertices from other triangles. The domain could be non-convex and has prespecified constraints. Constructing a constrained Delaunay triangulation is the basis for Delaunay refinement. Chew et al. [12] proposed constrained Delaunay triangulation in 1989.

Inserting constraints is one phase of the entire algorithm. Edge flipping is a traditional method first introduced by Lawson [13]. In order to ensure all the triangles would not intersect with the constraints inserted, these triangles need to flip their edges to reduce the amount of intersected edges as Fig. 4 depicts.

In this paper, we take this algorithm as example because when flipping the edges, we need to update the triangle pairs' data about vertices, edges and neighbor triangles. Besides that, we also need to update their neighbor triangles' data (e.g. △ABE's data about neighbor is updated from △ABD to △ABC by △ABC). When we flip these edges in parallel, every single triangle pair is mapped to a single thread. Then one thread would change other threads' data. So if these threads are not on the same SM, cache coherence problems occur. Our algorithm is modified from the work by Meng Qi et al. [14], and detailed information can be found in that paper.

3   Related Work

Cache coherence has been studied on CPUs for dozens of years. Providing a hardware cache coherence mechanism into processors is one way to guarantee memory consistency on general-purpose chip multiprocessors (CMPs) [3]. Recently, researchers also introduce coherence protocol into the hardware of GPUs as what they do earlier to CPUs. Inderpreet et al. [1] propose a hardware coherence protocol on GPUs and get 85% performance improvement compared with disabling the incoherent L1 cache. However, Inderpreet et al. implement their work on simulators, such as GEMS [4], GPGPU-Sim [5], rather than in real machines. So it would take a long time for current programmers to benefit from their ideas until manufacturers put them into new products.

As for synchronization, programmers traditionally launch a new kernel to implement an implicit synchronization or call the function *cudaThreadSynchronize()* on host to synchronize explicitly. After that, all the code and data can be synchronized. Shucai Xiao and Wuchun Feng [8] [9] then implement a lock-free barrier synchronization on GPU and perform well for less-data-dependent algorithms because it takes less time in synchronization compared with the traditional ways. But it is invalidated on the current series of GPUs since coaches are introduced in while this mechanism cannot ensure that caches are coherent. Cederman et al. [10] also propose a dynamic load balancing queue by lock-free synchronization and performs better than Shucai's work. Yilmazer Ayse et al. [2] provide a synchronization mechanism for GPUs which gets better performance in the simulation than the synchronization implemented by Spin Locks with Atomic (SLA) instructions. Just like mechanisms for cache coherence, most of the solutions for synchronization are also based on simulation except Shucai's work which is easy for programmers to use into their algorithms.

4   M&C Software Solution

Since the incoherence is caused by data sharing between threads on different SMs, then here is our software solution: reduce the data shared and put relative threads on the same SM. We mark all the data that one thread dominates by thread id to reduce data sharing and make a task queue for every SM to process relative threads that scheduled to this SM. We merge these two methods together and get a better solution called M&C.

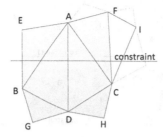

Fig. 5. Mark all the triangles needed by a triangle pair

4.1   Mark All: Reduction of Data Sharing

As shown in Fig. 2, the incoherent error occurs when one thread tries to write to the data that threads on the other SMs will read later. Then we can mark all the data with thread's id and only the thread with smallest/biggest id has the privilege to access that piece of data. Here we set an id array for all triangle pairs and use *atomicMin/ atomicMax* function to set thread id.

In the original constrained Delaunay triangulation algorithm, we only need to mark the flappable triangle pairs if all the caches are coherent (e.g. △ABD and △ACD or △ACF and △CFI) and then we flip edges as Fig. 4 shows.

But if the caches are incoherent, new flipped triangle would still see the old triangle as their neighbor, rather than the new one (e.g. △ABC still sees △ACF as its neighbor. △ACF still sees △ACD as its neighbor.) since it doesn't know what its neighbors' threads do. Although this thread's neighbors try to tell this thread its new neighbor triangles by update this thread's data about adjacent triangles, they can only alter the data in global memory while the old data in caches remain. So we mark all the triangles the triangle pairs needed (the triangle pair and all its neighbors) to avoid this problem. In Fig. 5, we mark these triangles in gray. Here we assume that triangle pair △ABD and △ACD has higher privilege and then the triangle pair △ACF and △CFI won't be processed at this time.

4.2   Cluster Threads: Relative Threads Cluster to a Same SM

For those threads that would access the same pieces of data, we can put those threads on the same SM. Then the data they shared would only have one copy in all caches.

Hence, our strategy is to put the triangles that intersect with the same constraint onto the same SM. Since triangle pair △ABD and △ACD and triangle pair △ACF and △CFI are intersected with the same constraint, we put these two triangle pairs into the same SM's task queue. Since Shucai's [9] synchronization mechanism limits that the blocks' quantity should not be more than the amount of SMs. Then the amount of blocks we use here is the same to SMs. So the SM that one block maps is ensured and the task queue that one SM processes is guaranteed.

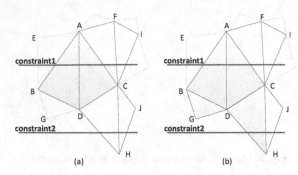

Fig. 6. Two triangle pairs intersecting with different constraints (a) and marked triangles (b)

4.3   Mark&Cluster: Combination of Two Methods Above

The weakness of the first method is that those adjacent triangle pairs cannot flip their edges in parallel. The shortcoming of the second method is that the incoherence still occurs when two adjacent triangle pairs intersect with different constraints and then they would map to threads on the different SMs as shown in Fig. 6 (a).

By combining these two methods together, we can put those triangle pairs intersecting with the same constraint onto the same SM. Besides that, we only mark those adjacent triangles that intersect with different constraints (only △BDG and △CDH, while △ABE and △ACF are not included) as shown in Fig 6 (b). Here we still assume that triangle pair △ABD and △ACD has higher privilege, and the triangle pair △ABD and △ACD can be processed with triangle pair △ACF and △CFI in parallel.

5   Methodology

We have tested our modified algorithms on an Intel Xeon E5620 2.4GHz PC with 24G DDR3 RAM and an NVIDIA Tesla C2070 with 5375MB DDR5 VRAM. Our GPU programs are written and compiled by NVIDIA CUDA 4.2. We disable the L1 cache by setting the *nvcc* compiler flag *-Xptxas -dlcm=cg* when compiling the program and use keyword *volatile* as shown in Fig. 3.

In order to verify the error rates and execution time of different methods, we use a 1000-round for loop and calculate the mean value of the execution time and error rates. For those methods that have high error rates, the programs encounter run-time errors before the loop breaks. When the program fails, we record the running time and the counter of the cycle as the times of execution, and then increase the error counter by 1 as the program crashes for incoherent caches last time. Then we recalculate the mean running time and mean error rate with the data we calculated last time. Then we rerun the program for another round. We do the work above many times until the mean execution time and the mean error rate become stable.

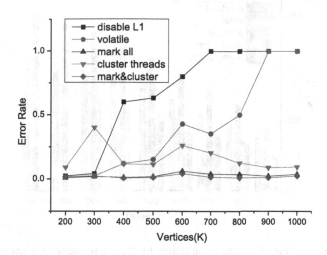

Fig. 7. The error rate of inserting constraints by these five methods when computing the constrained Delaunay triangulation, with 100K constraints and varying the number of vertices from 200K to 1M

6   Results

We present the performance of these methods by execution time and error rate as shown in Fig. 7 and Fig. 8.

In Fig. 7, we can see that the error rates are at a low level at the beginning when the amount of vertices is from 200K to 300K. The error rates of these five methods are 2.38%, 1.49%, 0.97%, 8.96% and 1.67% respectively. As the volume of vertices increase, the error rate of *disable L1* rises sharply. When the volume is up to 700K, the rate is up to 100% and *disable L1* is not available any more. *Volatile* is a little better than *disable L1*, but still useless when there are 900K vertices or more. *Cluster threads* is better than the above two baselines because it solves incoherent problems within one constraint. But it does nothing to avoid the incoherent caches between different constraints. The last two methods can solve the incoherence both inter-constraints and inner-constraints. So they can get the best performance. The mean error rate of *mark&cluster* (i.e. M&C) is only 1.8%. On average, when the amount of vertices is over 300K, M&C's the error rate is lesser than disabling L1 cache by 91.19% and lesser than using the keyword volatile by 84.2%. We also notice two peaks at 300K and 600K. It is because the error rate is also concerned with the condition of constraints. If many constraints are adjacent, the condition in Fig. would happen frequently and the error rate would be higher especially for *mark all* as it only cares about the coherence within one constraint.

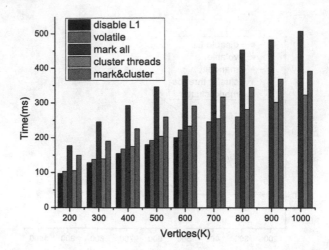

Fig. 8. The running time of inserting constraints by these five methods when computing the constrained Delaunay triangulation, with 100K constraints and varying the number of vertices from 200K to 1M

Fig. 8 shows the running times of these methods. As we only add new functions to avoid incoherent caches and do nothing to optimize the original algorithm, so our methods always execute longer. *Mark all* takes the longest time which is 188% of *disable L1* and 173% of *volatile* because it reduces the parallel degree and need more loops. *Cluster threads* takes less time which is only 112% of *disable L1* and 104% of *volatile* because storing the triangle id into task queue of the SM can be processed in parallel and it won't spend too much time. *Mark&cluster* approximately takes the time as the meaning value of the two methods before, which is 147% of *disable L1* and 134% of *volatile* as it is implemented by combining these two methods together.

7   Conclusion

In this paper, we propose three new methods to avoid incoherence caches and reduce the errors caused by that. These methods do not change the original algorithm's data structures. We implement these methods through a practical algorithm and evaluate their performance on a real machine. These three methods can be concluded into three rules: maximize the resources that one thread dominated, cluster those threads that share data and make a tradeoff to get a better performance. These rules could be useful for those programmers who also try to accelerate unstructured graphic algorithms on GPUs. Besides that, the experience about false sharing on CPUs would also be helpful. Programmers may need to redesign their algorithms' data structures but performance would be better. We would also put this into our future work.

Acknowledgements. This research is supported by the NSF of China under grant 61133004 and 61073011, and 863 Program of China under grant 2012AA010902.

References

1. Singh, I., et al.: Cache coherence for GPU architectures. In: HPCA (2013)
2. Yilmazer, A., Kaeli, D.: HQL: A Scalable Synchronization Mechanism for GPUs. In: 2013 IEEE 27th International Symposium on Parallel & Distributed Processing, IPDPS (2013)
3. Ros, A., Acacio, M.E., García, J.M.: DiCo-CMP: Efficient cache coherency in tiled CMP architectures. In: IPDPS 2008, IEEE International Symposium on Parallel and Distributed Processing. IEEE (2008)
4. Martin, M.M., et al.: Multifacet's general execution-driven multiprocessor simulator (GEMS) toolset. ACM SIGARCH Computer Architecture News 33(4), 92–99 (2005)
5. Bakhoda, A., et al.: Analyzing CUDA workloads using a detailed GPU simulator. In: IEEE International Symposium on Performance Analysis of Systems and Software, ISPASS 2009. IEEE (2009)
6. Zaspel, P., Griebel, M.: Solving incompressible two-phase flows on multi-GPU clusters. Computers & Fluids (2012)
7. Torres, Y., Gonzalez-Escribano, A., Llanos, D.R.: Understanding the impact of CUDA tuning techniques for Fermi. In: 2011 International Conference on High Performance Computing and Simulation (HPCS). IEEE (2011)
8. Feng, W.-C., Xiao, S.: To GPU synchronize or not GPU synchronize? In: Proceedings of 2010 IEEE International Symposium on Circuits and Systems (ISCAS). IEEE (2010)
9. Xiao, S., Feng, W.-C.: Inter-block GPU communication via fast barrier synchronization. In: 2010 IEEE International Symposium on Parallel & Distributed Processing (IPDPS). IEEE (2010)
10. Cederman, D., Tsigas, P.: On dynamic load balancing on graphics processors. In: Proceedings of the 23rd ACM SIGGRAPH/EUROGRAPHICS Symposium on Graphics Hardware. Eurographics Association (2008)
11. Rebay, S.: Efficient Unstructured Mesh Generation by Means of Delaunay Triangulation and Bowyer-Watson Algorithm. Journal of Computational Physics 106(1), 125–138 (1993)
12. Paul Chew, L.: Constrained delaunay triangulations. Algorithmica 4(1-4), 97–108 (1989)
13. Lawson, C.L.: Transforming triangulations. Discrete Mathematics 3(4), 365–372 (1972)
14. Qi, M., Cao, T.-T., Tan, T.-S.: Computing 2D constrained Delaunay triangulation using the GPU. In: Proceedings of the ACM SIGGRAPH Symposium on Interactive 3D Graphics and Games. ACM (2012)

Interference-Aware Program Scheduling for Multicore Processors

Lin Wang, Rui Wang, Cuijiao Fu, Zhongzhi Luan, and Depei Qian

Sino-German Joint Software Institute
School of Computer Science and Engineering, Beihang University
100191 Beijing, China
{lin.wang,rui.wang,cuijiao.fu,zhongzhi.luan}@jsi.buaa.edu.cn,
depeiq@buaa.edu.cn

Abstract. Running multiple application programs on a multicore processor can maximize processor resources utilization. However, contention to the shared resources may result in interference among co-running programs, and make the program performance unstable and unpredictable. In order to optimize the performance of co-running programs and ensure the QoS of latency-sensitive applications, we propose an interference-aware scheduling strategy IA for systems based on multicore processors. Our work begins with analysis of the behavior of a set of benchmark programs, after that we train a simple program classifier. We use this classifier to classify the benchmark programs into three categories according to their interference with each other. The interference-aware scheduler tries to schedule the programs with less interference to the same multicore processor. Experiments results show that our method improves system performance while maintaining reasonable resource utilization. It outperforms the previously published scheduling strategy in guaranteeing the QoS of latency-sensitive applications.

1 Introduction

Running multiple application programs on a multicore processor can maximize processor resources utilization. However, contention [1] to the shared resource may introduce performance interference among different programs and result in application performance degradation [2]. Also, many programs are latency-sensitive and require real-time response to the user. Running multiple programs at the same time on a multicore processor may affect the responsiveness of programs and lower the QoS of those real-time applications. One method to guarantee the performance of the latency-sensitive applications is to allocate dedicated resource for those programs. But the drawback is it will lower the resource utilization because some cores of the processor may be idle at most of the time. As a consequence, the resource utilization of data centers adopting this strategy is often low [3].

The program run-time behavior and the way of competing for the shared resources [4] determine the degree of performance interference [5-7]. Experiments on typical multicore processor-based servers have shown that applications running on the same

J. Kołodziej et al. (Eds.): ICA3PP 2013, Part I, LNCS 8285, pp. 436–445, 2013.

processor (socket) are prone to compete for the shared resource and tend to lead to performance degradation, while applications running on different sockets have less chance to interfere with each other. Our work is focused on the interference caused by contention to the shared LLC and memory [8]. The purpose of our work is to investigate how the contention to the shred resource and the execution behavior of the program influence the performance of the co-running programs [9,10]. we have developed an interference-aware scheduler IA which can schedule the programs having less interference with each other to the same socket so that the overall application performance as well as the resource utilization are optimized [5,11].

In order to implement the online interference-aware scheduling strategy, several steps are taken. First, we sample the relevant events during program execution and obtain a profile of the program. Then we analyze the behavior of the program using the profiling information [12,13]. Based on the criteria for distinguishing program behaviors we classify the set of programs in our experiments into three categories, each category has a particular pattern of accessing shared resources and shows a specific degree of interference to the co-running programs. Then the scheduler uses the program category information to determine the appropriate combination of the co-running programs and schedules the programs onto hardware resources for execution.

The rest of this paper is organized as the follows: In section 2 we give the motivation of our research. Section 3 discusses the way of analyzing the application behaviors. Section 4 presents the principle and implementation of an online interference-aware scheduler. The scheme for evaluating the interference-aware scheduling and the experiment results are presented in section 5. Related works are discussed in section 6. Finally we conclude in paper in section 7 by summarizing the work we have done and propose the future research topics.

2   Motivation

One of the metrics adopted by the modern OS in scheduling threads across resources is load balancing. The OS scheduler balances tasks across processors. But the OS scheduler does not take interference between threads into consideration. This kind of scheduling often results in the situation of resource contention, making applications performance unstable and unpredictable, and in some cases even seriously degraded [14-16]. Therefore, interference due to resource contention must be one of the important considerations in scheduling. For example, we try two scheduling strategies. We run four programs simultaneously on a two-way computing node with two programs on one socket. In the first scheduling strategy we execute 445 and 453 on one socket, and 470 and 482 on another socket. In the second scheduling setting we run 445 and 470 on one socket, and 453 and 482 on the other. In the system running the tests, programs executed on the same socket share LLC. The experiment results are shown in Fig. 1. We can see that the total execution time of the second scheduling strategy is better than the first one. The reason is that the interference between programs in the second scheduling is less severe than that in the first one.

Programs running together share a variety of resources, such as memory, memory controller, and LLC, etc. Which kind of contention to the shared resources exists and what is the main cause of interference? We find that when programs are executed on the different sockets of the node, the execution time is substantially the same compared to the one when the program executes solely on the node. This means that programs running on different sockets do not interfere with each other very much. On the other hand, the programs executing on the same socket suffer significant performance degradation. It can be inferred from this fact that the LLC and memory associated with the socket are the main shared resource to compete and usually result in performance degradation. With this observation we focus our study to the interference caused by LLC and memory accesses.

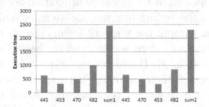

Fig. 1. Comparison of two scheduling stratrgies

3   Behavior Profiling and Program Classification

3.1   Co-running Program Behavior

Our experimental platform is IBM HS22 server implemented with Intel Xeon E5620 processor. The server has two sockets, on each of the socket is an eight-core Xeon E5620. Each socket is equipped with 12MB 16–way L3 shared cache and a IMC. Each core contains private L1 instruction and data cache and a private unified L2 cache. We repeatedly execute a set of benchmark programs on the server to investigate their run-time behavior. Ten programs listed in Table 1 (group 1) are selected from SPEC CPU2006 as the workload.

The programs are executed in group of two with every possible combination to see the interference between different programs. We can learn some facts from the experiment data. First, some programs, such as 416, 444, 445 and 453, have little influence to the performance of other programs running on the same socket, and are also not vulnerable to the execution of other co-running programs. Second, some programs, such as 429, 433, 450 and 482, tend to influence the performance of other programs running on the same socket, and are also prone to be affected by other co-running programs. Third, some programs such as 410 and 470 do seriously affect the performance of other co-running programs on the same socket, but are less influenced by the execution of other programs. These three categories cover the behaviors of the 10 programs and form a partition of the benchmark programs. With the above observation, we could characterize the program behavior with two attributes.

For the first attribute, i.e., the influence to other co-running programs, the programs can be classified as either "mild" or "aggressive". A mild program is a moderate program which hardly influences the performance of other co-running programs. An aggressive program, on the other hand, will significantly interfere the execution of programs running on the same socket. With this attribute, we can classify the 10 benchmark programs into to two types, with 416, 444, 445 and 453 as mild, and 410, 429, 433, 450, 470 and 482 as aggressive.

For the second attribute, the extent that a program is influenced by the co-running programs, the programs can be characterized as either "firm" or "fragile". A firm program is less sensitive to the co-execution of other programs, while a fragile program is vulnerable to interference. We can characterize 429, 433, 450 and 482 as fragile, and 410, 416, 444, 445, 453 and 470 as firm.

Table 1. Workloads used for experiments

Group	Workloads
1	410, 416, 429, 433, 444, 445, 450, 453, 470, and 482
2	416, 429, 433, 434, 458, 459,462, 464
3	435, 437,470,471

Table 2. Event profiling online

Event	Description
Instruction Retired	Instruction retired
Unhalted Core Cycles	Unhalted core cycles
LLC Reference	Last level cache reference
LLC Miss	Last level cache miss
UNC_DRAM_OPEN.CH0	Counts number of DRAM Channel 0 open commands issued either for read or write
UNC_DRAM_OPEN.CH1	Counts number of DRAM Channel 1 open commands issued either for read or write
UNC_DRAM_OPEN.CH2	Counts number of DRAM Channel 2 open commands issued either for read or write

3.2 Program Classification

We need to identify the parameters which can reflect the resource contention. We need to monitor events accessing those resources and quantitatively profile the program's behavior. Table 2 gives a summary of events we gather from program execution. We use perf [17] to access the built-in performance counters [18] in Intel Xeon E5620. In order to get enough information while still keep reasonable profiling, we carry out sampling during the execution of first 10^7 instructions of each program.

Mild and Aggressive Division

We know from our experience that memory access dominates program performance. The mild program has less interference to other co-running programs because it usually has fewer accesses to the shared LLC resources [19]. On the other hand, an aggressive program must have more intensive access to the shared LLC. Therefore, we consider two aspects in defining a mild or aggressive program: first, LLC occupancy, and second, sensitivity to the LLC size. We use the following formula to distinguish a program as either mild or aggressive.

Total LLC Reference < 30000 and Total LLC Miss <6000

The threshold values are determined by executing the 10^7-instructions. With these threshold values, programs are divided into mild and aggressive.

Firm and Fragile Division

A fragile program is vulnerable to interference from other programs. The literature [20] points out that memory-sensitive application has high bank parallelism. But we can't get events related to bank parallelism with our profiling tool. So we use memory channel access [21] instead. This decision is based on the concept that a fragile program with more memory channel accesses tends to have contention with other co-running programs. We set the threshold of being a fragile program as the follows:

$$Channel\ Access > 0.9 * 10^7$$

Non-fragile programs are classified into the firm category.

3.3   Training the Classifier

We use the above criteria to train a simple classifier for online classification of programs. 18 representative programs listed in Table 1 are selected from SPEC CPU 2006 benchmark SUITE to represent a wide range of program behavior. The ten programs in group 1 are the program mentioned in section 3.1 and used as the workload of offline training. The programs in group 2 and group 3 are the workloads for online classification and for evaluating the performance of our interference-aware scheduler. The program classification process is illustrated in Fig. 2.

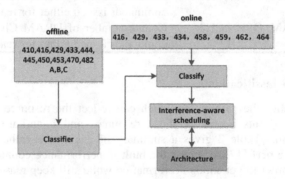

Fig. 2. Program classification for scheduling

With the above process, we can classify the programs in our study (group 1 in Table 1) into categories as shown in Table 3. Note, the programs in the category D (mild, fragile) are missing. Logically, with two classifying attributes and two values for each attribute, there must be four program categories. But in our experiments we did not find the program which is both "mild" and "fragile". It is because that a mild program is usually also "firm" since it has less LLC accesses and therefore less contention with the co-running program.

Table 3. Programs classification

Category	Behavior	Description	Benchmark Application
A	(mild, firm)	no significant impact to the performance of co-running program on the same socket, and less vulnerable to the interference introduced by co-running programs.	416,444,445,453
B	(aggressive, fragile)	significant impact to the performance other co-running programs on the same socket, and vulnerable to the interference introduced by co-running programs.	429,433,450,482
C	(aggressive, firm)	significant impact to the performance other co-running programs on the same socket, and less vulnerable to the interference introduced by co-running programs.	410,470
D	(mild, fragile)	no significant impact to the performance of co-running program on the same socket, and vulnerable to the interference introduced by co-running programs.	

4   Interference-Aware Scheduling

The concept of the interference-aware scheduling is to avoid bad combination of co-running programs on the same socket to ensure the program performance and improve resource utilization. We obtain the profiling information from execution of the first 107 instructions of the running program. The data is sent the input of the classifier, and the output from the classifier is the information indicating the category of the running program. This process is done online. So we profile as few parameters as possible to avoid heavy overhead. The scheduling policy is determined based on the knowledge of program categories. Table 4 shows the scheduling policies for scheduling two programs onto the same socket.

We implement the interference-aware scheduling strategy as a separate module and insert it into the current OS scheduling program. We identify online the category of programs and map them to the home environment for execution according to the scheduling policy. The interference-aware scheduler records the information about what kind of program is running on each socket and assigns the new coming program to an appropriate socket.

Table 4. Scheduling policies

Program pair	Co-run characteristic
A & B	Good
A & C	Good
B & C	Bad, should be avoid
A & A	Good, but less preferred
B & B	Very bad, never do it
C & C	Fair, can do it

5   Evaluation

5.1   Comparison with the Default Scheduling

We first compare the performance of the interference-aware scheduling (IA) and the DIO scheduler with the default OS scheduler. Fig. 3 shows the percentage of performance gain over the default OS scheduling. Eight programs execute in pairs on four sockets, "sum" in Fig. 3 is the total execution time of the eight programs. We note that both IA and DIO are better than the default scheduler. But compared with DIO, IA is slightly better, but not very much. Then what is the advantage of IA in improving programs performance? In the next experiment we can see another benefit of using IA in satisfying the QoS requirement of different workload sets.

5.2   QoS Guarantee

Fig. 4 depict the QoS degradation of the three above mentioned schedulers relative to the solo execution. The QoS requirement is defined as the follows: The execution time of programs co-running on one socket cannot be more than 5% longer than that of non-solo scheduling. We can see from the results both the default OS scheduler and DIO cannot satisfy the above QoS requirement. The reason is that they are more dependent on the characteristics of the workload than IA.

In the experiment shown by Fig. 4, the workload group 3 contains 4 programs, three of them are of large cache miss rate. DIO first matches the program 471 (with a high miss rate) with the program 435 (with a low miss rate), and assigns them to one socket. Then DIO is facing two programs left, 470 and 437, both having a high miss rate. DIO can do nothing but assign them to the same socket, resulting in serious interference and violation of the QoS requirement (prolong execution of program 437). But the IA scheduling can solve the problem. By obtaining programs behavior online, the IA scheduler knows that the program 435 is in category A and other three are in category B. The IA scheduler first schedules 470 to co-run with 435. Then two left programs, 437 and 471, are both in B category (aggressive, fragile). Instead of mapping them to one socket, the IA scheduler applies for another extra socket and makes the two programs executing separately on different socket. This approach can guarantee the QoS requirement but at the cost of extra resource.

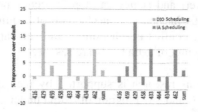

Fig. 3. Performance of DIO and IA relative to the default OS scheduling (workload group 2)

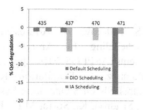

Fig. 4. QoS degradation relative to solo execution (workload group 3)

6   Related Work

Regarding to performance interference, there are generally two methods to reduce the interference between applications. The first method is called resource partition [22], most of the works in this strategy are to partition the cache among multiple programs by re-mapping programs' cache line. The second method is to re-map by scheduling. The approach in [1] re-maps programs by keeping the cache miss rate even on each socket. Reference [15,16] use a prediction model to predict program performance in different contention conditions.

For QoS control, the Google data center uses a sizeable test program "bubble" to predict contention on shared resources [3,4]. Strategy in [2] directly estimates performance of applications in different cache configurations. Reference [11] proposes a compilation approach that statically manipulates contentions among applications to enable the co-location of applications with varying QoS requirements.

There are some works done in understanding application behavior. One way is to characterize contentions among applications and to identify which resources is the cause of performance degradation [8]. Reference [20] reveals that the application behavior is closely related to the pattern of memory access. [19] shows that stabilization of application performance is relative to the last level cache sensibility.

7   Conclusion

In this paper, we propose an interference-aware scheduling for improving program execution performance and guaranteeing application's QoS. Compared with other scheduling strategies, our interference-aware scheduling IA is definitely better than the default OS scheduler, and achieve a slightly better performance than the DIO scheduler. In addition, IA introduces a mechanism of acquiring extra resources when encountering unsolvable conflict in scheduling, and can satisfy the QoS requirement at the cost of limited amount of extra hardware resources.

Acknowledgements. This research is supported by the NSF of China under grant 61133004 and 61073011, and 863 Program of China under grant 2012AA010902.

References

1. Zhuravlev, S., Blagodurov, S., Fedorova, A.: Addressing shared resource contention in multicore processors via scheduling. In: Architectural Support for Programming Languages and Operating Systems (ASPLOS 2010), pp. 129–141 (March 2010)
2. Moreto, M., Cazorla, F., Ramirez, A., Sakellariou, R., Valero, M.: Flexdcp: a qos framework for CMP architectures. SIGOPS Operating Systems Review 43(2) (April 2009)
3. Mars, J., Tang, L., Hundt, R., Skadron, K., Soffa, M.L.: Bubble-Up: increasing utilization in modern warehouse scale computers via sensible co-locations. In: Proceedings of the 44th Annual IEEE/ACM International Symposium on Microarchitecture, December 3-7 (2011)
4. Tang, L., Mars, J., Vachharajani, N., Hundt, R., Soffa, M.L.: The impact of memory subsystem resource sharing on data center applications. In: ISCA 2011, pp. 283–294. ACM Press, New York (2011)
5. Nathuji, R., Kansal, A., Ghaffarkhah, A.: Q-clouds: managing performance interference effects for qos-aware clouds. In: Proceedings of the 5th European Conference on Computer Systems, EuroSys 2010 (2010)
6. Govindan, S., Liu, J., Kansal, A., Sivasubramaniam, A.: Cuanta: quantifying effects of shared on-chip resource interference for consolidated virtual machines. In: Proceedings of the 2nd ACM Symposium on Cloud Computing, SOCC (2011)
7. Dwyer, T., Fedorova, A.: A Practical Method for Estimating Performance Degradation on Multicore Processors, and its Application to HPC Workloads, SC12
8. Dey, T., Wang, W., Davidson, J., Soffa, M.L.: Characterizing multi-threaded applications based on shared-resource contention. In: ISPASS (2011)
9. Pusukuri, K.K., Vengerov, D., Fedorova, A., Kalogeraki, V.: FACT: a Framework for Adaptive Contention-aware Thread Migrations. In: Computing Frontiers (2011)
10. Paolieri, M., Qui Andones, E., Cazorla, F., Davis, R., Valero, M.: Ia3: An interference aware allocation algorithm for multicore hard real-time systems. In: 2011 17th IEEE Real-Time and Embedded Technology and Applications Symposium (RTAS), pp. 280–290 (April 2011)
11. Tang, L., Mars, J., Soffa, M.L.: Compiling for niceness: Mitigating contention for QoS in warehouse scale computers. In: Proceedings of the 10th Annual IEEE/ACM International Symposium on Code Generation and Optimization. ACM, New York (2012)
12. Saez, J.C., Shelepov, D., Fedorova, A., Prieto, M.: Leveraging workload diversity through OS scheduling to maximize performance on single-ISA heterogeneous multicore systems. Journal of Parallel and Distributed Computing 71(1), 114–131 (2011)
13. Xie, Y., Loh, G.: Dynamic Classification of Program Memory Behaviors in CMPs. In: Proc. of CMP-MSI, Held in Conjunction with ISCA-35 (2008)

14. Chiang, R.C., Huang, H.H.: TRACON: Interference-Aware scheduling for data-intensive applications in virtualized environments. In: Proc. of the Int'l Conf. for High Performance Computing, Networking, Storage and Analysis (2011)
15. Xu, C., Chen, X., Dick, R., Mao, Z.: Cache contention and application performance prediction for multi-core systems. In: ISPASS 2010 (March 2010)
16. Chandra, D., Guo, F., Kim, S., Solihin, Y.: Predicting inter-thread cache contention on a chip multi-processor architecture. In: HPCA 2005, Washington, DC, USA, pp. 340–351 (2005)
17. https://perf.wiki.kernel.org/index.php/Main_Page
18. Azimi, R., Tam, D.K., Soares, L., Stumm, M.: Enhancing operating system support for multicore processors by using hardware performance monitoring. SIGOPS Oper. Syst. Rev. 43(2), 56–65 (2009)
19. Qureshi, M.K., Patt, Y.N.: Utility-based cache partitioning: A lowoverhead, high-performance, runtime mechanism to partition shared caches. In: MICRO 39: Proceedings of the 39th Annual IEEE/ACM International Symposium on Microarchitecture, pp. 423–432 (2006)
20. Kim, Y., Papamichael, M., Mutlu, O., Harchol-Balter, M.: Thread Cluster Memory Scheduling: Exploiting Differences in Memory Access Behavior. In: Proceedings of MICRO (2010)
21. Liu, F., Jiang, X., Solihin, Y.: Understanding how off-chip memory bandwidth partitioning in chip multiprocessors affects system performance. In: HPCA 2010, pp. 1–12 (2010)
22. Zhang, X., Dwarkadas, S., Shen, K.: Towards practical page coloring-based multicore cache management. In: Proceedings of the 4th ACM European Conference on Computer Systems (EuroSys 2009), pp. 89–102 (2009)

WABRM: A Work-Load Aware Balancing and Resource Management Framework for Swift on Cloud

Zhenhua Wang[1], Haopeng Chen[1], and Yunmeng Ban[2]

[1] Shanghai Jiao Tong University, Shanghai, China
[2] University of Massachusetts at Amherst, Amherst, USA
aspiration@foxmail.com, chen-hp@sjtu.edu.cn,
banyunmeng@gmail.com

Abstract. Fueled by increasing demand of big data processing, distributed storage systems have been more and more widely used by enterprises. However, in these systems, few storage nodes holding enormous amount of hotspot data could become bottlenecks. This stems from the fact that most typical distributed storage systems mainly provide data amount balancing mechanisms without considering the difference of access load between different storage nodes. To eliminate bottlenecks and tune the performance, there is a demand for such systems to employ a work-load aware balancing and resource management framework to optimize the performance and computation resource utilization.

In this paper, we propose WABRM, a load balancing and resource management framework for *Work-load Aware Balancing* and *Resource Management* in Swift, a typical distributed storage system. By designing such an optimization framework, it is possible to eliminate bottlenecks caused by hotspot data. Our experimental results show that the framework can achieve its goals.

Keywords: distributed storage system, Swift, work-load balancing, resource management.

1   Introduction

The distributed storage system significantly improves the capacity of big data storage, process and security. Swift [1], as a well-known and typical distributed storage system, is playing an important role in cloud storage. In Swift, there are mainly two kinds of nodes, including proxies and storage nodes. Data requests are sent to proxies and proxies fetch data stored in storage nodes to respond to users.

Concurrently, virtualization technology is making a significant impact on how resource are used and managed in a cloud computing platform. Several virtualization solutions (Xen [2], XenServer [3] and VirtualBox) are getting more and more mature in resource management.

Load balancing mechanisms for distributed system are also very important. There are mainly three default load balancing mechanisms in Swift. Firstly, scalable proxy mechanism allows users to set up more than one proxy to distribute requests from users to these proxies. Secondly, replica load balancing mechanism balances the work-load through responding with data replicas stored in different storage nodes.

J. Kołodziej et al. (Eds.): ICA3PP 2013, Part I, LNCS 8285, pp. 446–457, 2013.

Finally, data amount balancing mechanism tries to distribute data to all the storage nodes evenly. If the access load of each data is nearly the same, the work-load is balanced. In addition, there are also plenty of relative researches, such as research work [4, 5]. Their balancing targets are similar to the mechanisms' of Swift. However, almost all the previous researches remain the static data storage mechanism unmodified. And how to achieve the goal of load balancing dynamically in distributed storage systems has not been well studied. Hence we propose the framework named WABRM.

WABRM mainly contains three aspects, including discovery of work-load exception, algorithms of workload balancing and data migration method. Some relative work introductions are as follows.

Discovery of work-load exception is the basis of work-load aware balancing. Compare with the monitoring architecture of [6], in WABRM, each node monitors itself. Consequently, it is much easier to locate the hotspot data. In [7], for each chunk in MongoDB [8], its access-load is evaluated by the numbers of various operations on it. In WABRM, the access-load is evaluated by computation resource utilization, which can more objectively reflect its actual access-load. In [9], the exception of work-load is detected based on the predicted access load. It is good, but large amount of historical records is needed to guarantee its precision.

Algorithms of work-load balancing are the cores of work-load aware balancing framework. In [10], the files are divided into several zones according to the foreseen work-load in order to balance the access load. However, it is static since the location of a file will not be changed once it is stored into the zone. In [11], the data are dynamically re-partitioned to facilitate rapid data balancing by a graph theoretic way. Unfortunately, it is time consuming in some situations. In WABRM, we propose novel work-load balancing algorithms, which is dynamic and efficient.

Data migration is one way to achieve the goal of dynamic work-load balancing. In [12], a cost aware method is designed to minimize the interference between virtual machines. But the amount of data to be migrated is not reduced. In [13] and [14], a location-aware method is proposed to save energy when performing data migration in large-scale datacenters. Actually, we aim to balance access-load instead of storage amount. Thus, we can achieve this goal through virtual machine migration. WABRM adopts virtual machine live migration as its migration method.

In summary, work-load aware balancing is crucial for storage applications with hotspot data.

The contributions of this paper are summarized as follows. Firstly, we propose a work-load aware balancing and resource management framework based on the virtualization technology, which can be applied to Swift. WABRM is lightweight and requires no source code change in the guest OS and storage application. Secondly, we implement dynamic work-load balancing mechanisms for physical machines and virtual machines in WABRM. Finally, we conduct an experiment to demonstrate the effectiveness of WABRM in tuning the performance of Swift when hotspot data exist.

The rest of the paper is organized as follows. Section 2 describes motivating experiments to show the poor performance of the default load balancing mechanisms of Swift when hotspot data exist. Section 3 introduces the framework of WABRM as well as the design and implementation of the algorithms we integrated it. Section 4 presents the experimental results and analysis. Section 5 draws some conclusions.

2   Motivation

This section mainly describes the motivating experiment to show the poor work-load balancing performance of Swift when hotspot data exist as well as the analysis of the problem. We conduct the experiment on 15 virtual machines created by XenServer. They are represented by VM1, VM2…VM15 respectively. Storage nodes of Swift are deployed in these virtual machines. This experiment is simple but effective.

In this experiment, the number of replicas of a file is set to be 3, which is mostly accepted by the industry. Firstly, we upload some files to Swift. And we observe File A and its replicas are stored in VM1, VM9 and VM13 while File B and its replicas are stored in VM3, VM9 and VM14. We notice that VM9 stores both replicas of File A and File B. Through simulation of requests for File A and File B, we can observer the work-load difference of nodes. To simulate data access, Pylot [15], a web stress test tool is used to simulate clients. In this experiment, 100 clients and another 100 clients are simulated to fetch File A and File B respectively. The simulation of client requests is last for 15 minutes. During the 15 minutes, the concurrent 200 simulated users send their requests to Swift continuously and the interval between two requests is 100ms.

As Figure 1 shown, the work-load of VM1 and VM2 is significantly different and VM1 is much higher than VM2. The reasons are as follows. VM1 stores a replica of File A while VM2 stores no replicas of File A and File B, consequently, VM1 need more computation resource to respond to user requests and its work-load is much heavier. Even though there are three balancing mechanisms in Swift, they don't work in this scenario.

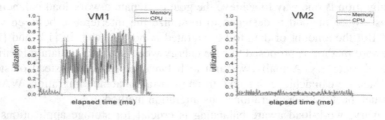

Fig. 1. Comparison of busy and free storage nodes

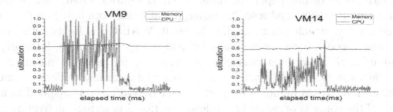

Fig. 2. Comparison of busy storage nodes

As Figure 2 shown, both VM9 and VM14 are busy, however, their work-load is obviously different. As mentioned before, VM9 stores replicas of File A and File B and VM14 only stores replica of File B, as a result, work-load of VM9 is obviously higher than VM14's. In Swift, this work-load imbalance is caused by its imperfect replica load balancing mechanism. Ideally, the storage system should first choose the replica in the storage node with the lightest work-load to respond. Actually, this imbalance can be resolved through rescheduling the response replica. To reduce the work-load, another solution is dynamic computation allocation, which is used in WABRM.

As Figure 1 and Figure 2 shown, the work-load of different storage nodes is different. So it is irrational to distribute computation resource to each storage node evenly. In WABRM, with Swift storage node deployed in virtual machines, we can allocate the resource to the storage nodes elastically. Further, a physical machine's resource utilization can be optimized through Split and Merge algorithms, which will be discussed in this paper.

Based on the aforementioned analysis, we try to optimize the work-load balancing of storage node in Swift through virtualization technology, a novel method. Through our method, the system performance is tuned and computation resource utilization is improved.

3   WABRM Architecture

This section mainly discusses the design of WABRM as well as the algorithms we have incorporated it. Before introducing WABRM architecture, we first present the work-load balancing model of WABRM.

3.1   Work-Load Balancing Model of WABRM

In traditional distributed storage systems, there is only one mapping of data to storage locations. Data are distributed and stored into different storage nodes according to some mapping rules, e.g. hash values. The mapping rule is static and difficult to change. To achieve the goal of dynamic work-load balancing, in WABRM, in addition to such mapping, there is a mapping of storage nodes to physical machines, which is dynamic and easy to modify. In this model, storage nodes are deployed in virtual machines and virtual machines reside in physical machines. By this way, data are divided into several much smaller subset, which improves the efficiency of locating hotspot data. Through dynamic changing the mapping of virtual machines to physical machines, work-load is balanced in physical machines.

As Figure 3 shown, WABRM is mainly composed of two layers, including physical layer and virtual layer. In this paper, a virtual machine with WABRM and Swift deployed is called a virtual node and a physical machine with WABRM and virtualization server deployed is called a physical node.

In virtual layer, WABRM is responsible for monitoring the work-load of a virtual node and scheduling the computation resource allocated to it according to its work-load through interacting with the WABRM in the physical node. And in physical layer, WABRM is responsible for monitoring the work-load of a physical node and regulating it through interacting with other physical nodes and virtual node migration.

To achieve the optimization goal, we implement algorithms for virtual layer and physical layer.

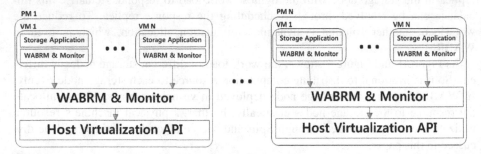

Fig. 3. WABRM Architecture

3.2 Work-Load Monitoring and Analysis

To achieve the goal of work-load aware balancing and resource management, work-load monitor is necessary in the framework. It provides a foundation for the algorithms we proposed. Through the monitor, work-load states of physical nodes and virtual nodes are collected and saved for further work-load analysis. In WABRM, there are two kinds of work-load monitors for different monitoring objectives. Work-load monitor for virtual node intermittently collects computation resource utilization information, including CPU and Memory utilization for the input of the algorithms for virtual layer. And Work-load monitor for physical node intermittently collects NetworkIO utilization in addition to the computation resource utilization information collected by work-load monitor for virtual node for the input of the algorithms for physical layer.

The goal of work-load analysis is to learn the work-load state of a node. To simplify the problem, in WABRM, we define three work-load types of a node, including underloaded, normal and overloaded. Generally, a node's work-load state can be represented by a computation resource utilization vector, which consists of CPU utilization, memory utilization, etc.

The current state vector of the node is calculated by historical monitoring states collected by work-load monitor of the node, since it is unreasonable to determine a node's state through single monitoring. Currently, in WABRM, computation resource utilizations in the state vector are the averages of their recent historical monitoring values. However, WABRM provides an interface for the realization of this node state calculation algorithm, any new algorithm, e.g. algorithms based on prediction can be integrated in to WABRM.

If the state vector is calculated, we use the following function to determine the load type of the node.

$$L(n) = \begin{cases} overloaded & \exists i, u_i > opt_i \\ underloaded & \sum_{i=1}^{n} \mu_i(opt_i - u_i) > t \\ normal & otherwise \end{cases} \quad (1)$$

In this function, u_i represents the utilization of Resource i, μ_i represents the weight of Resource i, opt_i represents the defined ideal utilization of Resource i and t represents the threshold of underloaded. Since excessive utilization of any resource can lead to poor system performance, the rule for determining overloaded is rational. And the rule for determining underloaded takes all kinds of resource utilization into consideration as well as provides weight for elastic configuration. Therefore, it is rational, too.

Apparently, excessive resource utilization can cause poor system performance. Based on this principle, WABRM optimizes the performance through regulation of the computation resource utilization. However, low resource utilization doesn't mean high performance, since critical resources may lead to low resource utilization. This problem is caused by the design of the native system. So WABRM may not improve the native system performance by this way, but it can tune the performance.

3.3   Algorithms

Currently, WABRM mainly integrates algorithms for physical layer and virtual layer. Other algorithms are applicable to WABRM architecture as well.

Resource Reallocate Algorithm
To regulate a virtual node, Resource Reallocate Algorithm (RRA) is invoked in the virtual node when it is determined to be overloaded or underloaded.

Because of the work-load difference between different storage nodes, it is irrational to distribute computation resource to each virtual node evenly. RRA reallocates the computation resource based on the load type of a virtual node. Generally, an overloaded node should be allocated more computation resource while an underloaded node's computation resource should be deallocated. Thus, RRA is designed to achieve this goal in virtual nodes.

To calculate the reallocation resource, we use the following function:

$$r_i = \frac{C_i * u_i}{opt_i} \quad (2)$$

In this function, C_i represents the capacity of original allocated Resource i, u_i represents the current utilization of Resource i and opt_i represents the ideal utilization of Resource i. Theoretically, the utilization of resource will reach ideal value after operation and the load type of the node will become normal. Thus, busy nodes will be allocated more computation resource while free nodes' resource will be deallocated. After calculation, the operation sends the request to the physical node in which the virtual node resides and the request is processed by the physical node.

If a physical node doesn't have enough computation resource to reallocate to an overloaded virtual node, it will allocate its resource to the virtual node as much as possible. Although it is possible that the virtual node remains overloaded after regulating, the physical node and virtual node will be further regulated by the follows algorithms for physical layer.

Split and Merge Algorithms

To regulate a physical node, Split Algorithm (SA) is invoked in the physical node when it is determined to be overloaded while Merge Algorithm (MA) is invoked when it is determined to be underloaded.

An overloaded physical node may be caused by the following reasons. 1. Numerous overloaded virtual nodes reside in it. 2. Some extremely overloaded virtual nodes reside in it. Thus, to regulate an overloaded physical node, it is rational to regulate the virtual nodes in it. SA is designed to achieve this goal. SA relieves an overloaded physical node's work-load through virtual node migration.

Before virtual node migration, SA decides the virtual node to be migrated. The policy meets two constraints: the number of virtual node to be removed is as little as possible and after migration, the physical node is not overloaded. To meet these constraints, SA figures out the nodes through backtracking. When the virtual nodes are selected, Pair Algorithm is invoked to pair another physical node as target for migration.

Correspondingly, when a physical node is determined to be underloaded, MA is invoked and tries to move all the virtual nodes in it to other physical nodes. However, MA is not executed immediately since there may be some overloaded physical nodes searching for underloaded nodes for SA. Therefore, it waits for a specified period and if there are no requests from overloaded nodes, MA continues and invokes PA to determine the virtual node migration program. If the migration is successful, the physical node is empty. Hence, it can go to sleep for energy saving.

Pair Algorithm

To regulate a physical node, Pair Algorithm (PA) is invoked in the physical node when it is determined to be overloaded or underloaded.

If the work-load exceptions of some physical nodes in the cluster are detected, we try to dispose of them through interaction with other physical nodes in the global cluster. PA is designed to achieve this goal.

To an overloaded physical node, PA tries to pair a physical node or boot up a new physical node for it. Through migration of some virtual nodes in it to the paired physical node, its work-load is reduced.

To an underloaded physical node, PA tries to pair one or more physical nodes for it. Through migration of all the virtual nodes in it to the paired physical node(s), the amount of physical nodes in service is reduced.

Considered the maturity and advantages of P2P, all the physical nodes are organized as P2P structure. Similar to unstructured P2P, a physical node is joined the P2P network and searches other physical nodes for pair. It has some obvious advantages, including robustness, avoidance of single point failure, etc.

Before virtual node migration, to determine the suitability of the searched physical node, we use the following function to estimate the computation resource utilization after migration:

$$u_{i,e} = \frac{u_i * C_i + u_{i,p} * C_{i,p}}{C_{i,p}} \tag{3}$$

In this function, u_i represents the utilization of computation Resource i of the migration virtual node, C_i represents the capacity of its Resource i, $u_{i,p}$ represents the utilization of computation Resource i of the searched physical node and $C_{i,p}$ represents the capacity of its Resource i. From this function, the computation resource utilization after virtual node migration can be estimated.

Through the computation resource utilization estimation, the load type of the searched physical node after virtual node migration can be estimated by the rule above. If the estimating load type is not overloaded, the searched physical node is selected as a suitable one and the virtual nodes will be migrated to it. Otherwise, PA will try to search another node. If none of the physical nodes within the P2P network of physical nodes can be paired, the algorithm will be cancelled.

4   Experiment and Evaluations

4.1   Experiment Configuration

To demonstrate the effectiveness of the proposed framework, we build an experiment environment with 4 physical nodes and 15 virtual nodes.

In the physical nodes, XenServer is set up as the virtualization server. And in each physical node, WABRM is deployed and interact with the API of XenServer.

In the virtual nodes, Ubuntu 12.04 Server is installed in each node. And Swift storage nodes are deployed in these virtual nodes.

The details of the physical machines used to set up the experiment environment are as follows. 4 physical machines with Intel i5 3.30GHz CPU, 4GB memory and 500GB disk are used as virtualization servers. There are another 4 physical machines with Intel i3 3.30GHz CPU, 4GB memory and 500GB disk. 2 of them are used as proxy nodes while the others are used as clients.

The details of the values of the parameters mentioned above for work-load analysis are as follows. To physical nodes, opts of CPU, memory and NetworkIO are 0.6, 0.95 and 0.95. And weights of CPU, memory and NetworkIO are 0.1, 0.2 and 0.2. Threshold of underloaded is 0.3. To virtual nodes, opts of CPU and memory are 0.7and 0.95. And weights of CPU and memory are 0.2 and 0.8. Threshold of underloaded is 0.3. The choice of the parameters should weight the costs and performance. Presently, we choose the parameters according to the performance priority principle to guarantee the storage system performance. And the method for determining the values of parameters will be presented by the later work.

Physical machine Clinet1 and Client2 are used to simulate clients for data access. 200 users are simulated by them respectively. At the beginning of the experiment, there is no user access to the storage system. It lasts for 1000s and the work-load of the entire system is quite light in the first 1000s. Then, the simulation of user access starts. The number of concurrent simulated users increases evenly in the first 1000s. Then it reaches steady state. The simulated users send their data requests continuously and the interval between two requests is 100ms. The state lasts for 5000s then the simulation stops.

4.2   Improvement of Computation Resource Utilization

As Figure 4 shown, the number of physical nodes is changed over the work-load of the entire system. At the beginning, since there is no user access to the system, the work-load is very light. Therefore, the virtual nodes can be integrated to 3 physical nodes and number of physical nodes in service is reduced from 4 to 3. With the increase of simulated concurrent user access, the work-load is getting heavier and heavier. Consequently, the number of physical nodes is increase from 3 to 4 to guarantee the performance of the entire system. At last, with the end of the simulation, the work-load is light again and the number of physical nodes is reduced from 4 to 3.

4.3   Improvement of Work-Load Balancing in Physical Machines

As Figure 5 shown, during the heavy work-load period, the work-load of P1 is extremely heavy at the beginning because of hotspot data. And its resource utilization exceeds the threshold, as shown in the yellow circle part. Fortunately, with the effect of WABRM, the work-load of the node is reduced. In addition, part of work-load is transferred to P3, another relatively light physical node. By this way, the work-load of the physical machines is balanced.

The work-load of P2 and P4 is displayed by Figure 6. Compared Figure 6 with Figure 5, the computation resource utilization of each physical machine is controlled under its defined threshold, thus the work-load is controlled. It demonstrates the effect of work-load regulation of WABRM.

4.4   Tuning of System Performance

As Figure 7 shown, the response times of Swift with WABRM and without WABRM are different. With WABRM, the response time is less as a whole.

However, WABRM can't always improve the system performance. Since we set the threshold of resource utilization for overload according to the performance priority principle in this experiment, the average response time is shortened. Practically, low resource utilization may cause high costs of hardware resources. And to different service providers, they should find the suitable compromise of the performance and the costs. WABRM provides the parameters for elastic configuration and they are intuitive. Anyhow, WABRM can eliminate the system bottlenecks caused by hotspot data and guarantee the basic performance of the entire system. In a word, WABRM can achieve its goal of tuning of the system performance.

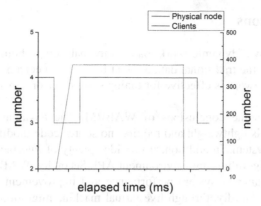

Fig. 4. Change of number of physical nodes over time

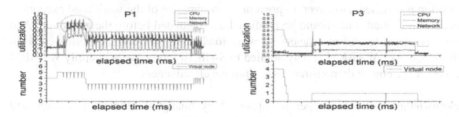

Fig. 5. Effect of work-load balancing

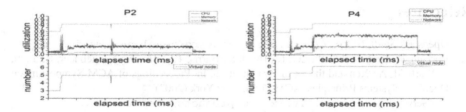

Fig. 6. Work-load of P2 and P4

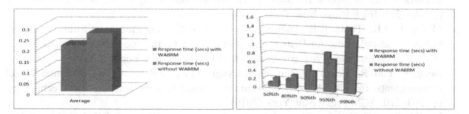

Fig. 7. Comparison of response times (secs) of Swift with and without WABRM

5   Conclusions

As discussed above, dynamic work-load aware balancing should be indispensably complementary to the traditional data amount balancing mechanisms. And WABRM, the proposed framework is effective for tuning system performance when hotspot data exist.

We can draw some conclusions of WABRM. The advantages are as follows. Firstly, WABRM is lightweight and requires no source code modification of the guest OS and storage system. In addition, it provides plenty of interfaces for different implementation of algorithms and environment API. Secondly, WABRM can achieve its design goal of tuning of system performance and improvement of computation resource utilization. Thirdly, through live virtual machine migration, during the regulation operations of WABRM, the service is almost not interrupted.

The disadvantages are as follows. WABRM regulates a node when its work-load exception is detected. However, to prevent the occurrence of the work-load exception, a node's work-load state should be predicted and regulated before the exception. And how to set the values of parameters for work-load analysis remains an unsolved problem. In addition, WABRM is only applied to Swift, in future, we will apply WABRM onto other systems to demonstrate its ubiquitous effectiveness.

Acknowledgement. This paper is supported by Shanghai Municipal Science and Technology Commission under Grant No.11dz1502500.

References

1. Openstack Swift, http://docs.openstack.org/developer/swift/
2. Barham, P., Dragovic, B., Fraser, K., Hand, S., Harris, T.L., Ho, A., Neugebauer, R., Pratt, I., Warfield, A.: Xen and the art of virtualization. In: Proceedings of ACM Symposium on Operating Systems Principles. ACM Press, New York (2003)
3. XenServer, http://www.citrix.com/products/xenserver/resources-and-support.html
4. Yamamoto, H., Maruta, D., Oie, Y.: Replication methods for load balancing on distributed storages in P2P networks. In: International Symposium on Applications and the Internet, pp. 264–271. IEEE Press, New York (2005)
5. Madathil, D.K., Thota, R.B., Paul, P., Xie, T.: A Static Data Placement Strategy towards Perfect Load-Balancing for Distributed Storage Clusters. In: International Symposium on Parallel and Distributed Processing, pp. 1–8. IEEE Press, New York (2008)
6. Deng, Y., Lau, R.: Heat Diffusion Based Dynamic Load Balancing for Distributed Virtual Environments. In: 17th ACM Symposium on Virtual Reality Software and Technology, pp. 203–210. ACM Press, New York (2010)
7. Liu, Y., Wan, Y., Jin, Y.: Research on The Improvement of MongoDB Auto-Sharding in Cloud Environment. In: 7th International Conference on Computer Science & Education, Melbourne, VIC, Australia, pp. 851–854 (2012)
8. MongoDB, http://www.mongodb.org/

9. Pearce, O., Gambliny, T., Supinskiy, B., et al.: Quantifying the Effectiveness of Load Balance Algorithms. In: 26th ACM International Conference on Supercomputing, pp. 185–194. ACM Press, New York (2012)

10. Zhu, Y., Yu, Y., Wang, W., et al.: A Balanced Allocation Strategy for File Assignment in Parallel I/O Systems. In: 5th IEEE International Conference on Networking, Architecture and Storage, pp. 257–266. IEEE Press, New York (2010)

11. Bui, T.N., Deng, X., Zrncic, C.M.: An Improved Ant-Based Algorithm for the DegreeConstrained Minimum SpanningTree Problem. J. IEEE Transactions on Evolutionary Computation 16, 266–278 (2012)

12. Qin, X., Zhang, W., Wang, W., et al.: Towards a Cost-Aware Data Migration Approach for Key-Value Stores. In: 2012 IEEE International Conference on Cluster Computing, pp. 551–556. IEEE Press, New York (2012)

13. Liu, Z., Lin, M., Wierman, A., et al.: Greening Geographical Load Balancing. In: Liu, Z., Lin, M., Wierman, A., et al. (eds.) 2011 ACM SIGMETRICS Joint International Conference on Measurement and Modeling of Computer Systems, pp. 233–244. ACM Press, New York (2011)

14. Lin, M., Wierman, A., Andrew, L.L.H., et al.: Dynamic Right-sizing for Powerproportional Data Centers. In: 2011 IEEE INFOCOM, pp. 1098–1106. IEEE Press, New York (2011)

15. Pylot, http://www.pylot.org/

Cache Optimizations of Distributed Storage for Software Streaming Services

Youhui Zhang[1,2], Peng Qu[1], Yanhua Li[1], Hongwei Wang[1],
and Weimin Zheng[1,2]

[1] Department of Computer Science and Technology, Tsinghua University
100084 Beijing, China
[2] Research Institute of Tsinghua University in Shenzhen
518057 Shenzhen, China
zyh02@tsinghua.edu.cn

Abstract. Software streaming is a form of on-demand software distribution services, which means a program need not be installed on the client for execution but parts of it can be delivered as needed. This paper has analyzed a collection of real traces of desktop applications from a production deployment, and located some opportunities for caching data: First, several local cache strategies have been compared and adjusted to fit the access pattern of data. Second, a special cooperative file caching mechanism is designed between clients and server(s). In detail, the cooperative caching mechanism employs the application-level semantics to trace cache status for each application rather than each file, which remarkably reduces the management overheads while the hint accuracy is still high. In addition, we present DES3, the DistributEd Storage for Software Streaming. It adopts the above optimizations; tests show that DES3 can greatly reduce the server load and give acceptable client latency.

Keywords: software as services, distributed storage, application virtualization.

1 Introduction

Software streaming, referred to as one type of software-as-a-service, is a delivery model in which software and associated data are centrally hosted and are available to clients over the network. From the aspects of virtualization technologies used, our work is based on application virtualization. This mode has the virtualization layer positioned between the operating system and applications. Microsofts SoftGrid [1] is such an instance in the LAN environment, which can convert applications into virtual services that are managed and hosted centrally but run on demand locally. Some other similar systems include VMwares ThinApp [2] and Citrixs XenApp [3] and so on. Fundamentally, application virtualization decouples software from OS and delivers it to client machines on demand.

J. Kołodziej et al. (Eds.): ICA3PP 2013, Part I, LNCS 8285, pp. 458–467, 2013.

The contributions of this paper contain three parts:

Firstly, we analyze a 7 day-long trace of desktop applications from a production deployment. We examine the breakdown of request workload and try to locate the opportunities for caching data both within and across client machines for optimizations. In addition, trace analysis shows that the characteristics of IO workloads are different from those of solutions based on VM (Virtual Machine) techniques.

Secondly, based on the trace analysis, we describe the design of corresponding optimizations to reduce the aggregate load on central storage, as well as access delays:

1. We design a segmented cache mechanism, which contains an extra victim cache to occupy the replaced data belonging to Top N applications. Tests show that, compared with the common LRU / LFU strategies, it performs best in most cases.
2. A cooperative caching mechanism is introduced to reduce the aggregate load on the central server(s) for scalability. Different from the traditional solution, the server records the status of whole software (instead of each file), which remarkably reduces the corresponding overheads and the hint accuracy is still high.

Lastly, DES3, DistributEd Storage for Software Streaming, is presented. DES3 adopts the above optimizations, which can gives acceptable latencies for clients.

In contrast, most existing storage solutions, like Capo [4], Collective [5], MokaFive [6], and Lithium [7] and so on are designed for VM. Compared with them, our application virtualization solution has the following features: (1) it works on the file-level so that application semantics can be grasped directly; (2) it only handles storage accesses issued by applications, which show different patterns from those issued by the whole VM.

2   Related Work

One early study is IBMs PDS [8]. PDS is a virtual execution environment and infrastructure designed specifically for deploying software on demand while enabling management from a central location. PDS uses a file-based delivery mechanism between clients and the central server. One local cache on every client is used to contain needed data to achieve low overhead, while no sophisticated optimization has been deployed.

Another similar work is FVM (Feather-weight Virtual Machine) [9]. In FVM, the streaming software is stored on the server and accessible to the client through the Common Internet File System (CIFS), because Windows supports CIFS inherently. Besides the default cache mechanism inside the OS, no optimization has been used.

CDE [10] is a tool implemented for Linux systems. It uses *sshfs* to stream uninstalled software from the server in a compatible way. CDE has implemented its own caching mechanism. The key point is to employ a deep-copy technology to copy a file-system entity from the server into the local entity while preserving its original structure.

In industry, some existing solutions are usually based on the single file system and common network sharing solutions; VMwares ThinApp [11] is such a typical case. It packages the whole application into a single file; the contents of this file are streamed to client computers in a block-based fashion over the network using some common file sharing protocols (like ftp, CIFS, etc.). Therefore, it also lacks some sophisticated optimizations for application virtualization. Similar solutions are used by Microsofts SoftGrid [1], Symantec Workspace Virtualization [12], and so on.

Furthermore, as we know, the only one dedicated to storage for streaming based on application-virtualization is [13]. It is implemented as a kernel file-system driver to redirect accesses to the remote server and uses the local file cache for optimizations.

3   Trace Analysis

3.1   Methodology

We record a 7 day-long trace of typical desktop applications from a production deployment of 20 Windows desktops (Windows 7) in a research laboratory.

Here we mainly pay attention to accesses to any file of desktop applications: after trace collection, we have picked up the information of *Part Install* and *Part Runtime*[1] of each desktop application involved and filtered out any unrelated logs. We collected 21GB of logs and in the rest of this section we present our analysis.

3.2   Analysis

1. Data vs. Metadata
At first we differentiate metadata operations from data, and then isolate reads from writes: About 30.1% of workloads' operations concern metadata accesses, which account for only 0.2% of the total data traffic. For data operations, reads account for large portion of the requests, about 68.1%, which account for 89.8% of the traffic. These findings contrast those from [4] whose study showed that 65% of workloads are writes. The reason lies in that we only focus on accesses to application files.

Another interesting fact is: a large portion of data is repeatedly read, which occupies more than 85% of the total read traffic.

2. Usage frequencies of applications
The analysis shows that there are averagely 42 kinds of applications used on a single machine. We list the top applications according to their access frequencies

---

[1] For any streaming software, Part Install contains what are created/modified/deleted by the installation process; Part Runtime is the data created/modified/deleted during the runtime.

(for any application, each visit to its files is regarded as one access) on each machine. Statistics show that the 10 top applications occupy the majority on each machine, from 51% to 98%, and the average value is 89.2%. In addition, Top 10 applications occupy 41% of the read traffic on average. For Top 20 applications, the ratio of request counts is higher than 94% averagely.

Furthermore, we consider the top applications across all machines and similar results have been drawn: such Top 10 applications occupy about 41.3% of the reads; for Top 30, the ratio is about 95.5%. Results also show that there is a high similarity of usage frequencies between users: on each machine, accesses of these 30 top applications (across all machines) occupy more than 85% of the amount.

3. Access pattern of a single application

Here we focus on the 30 top applications mentioned in the previous section. We compare the number of accessed files with the total file-number of each application; the average ratio is about 60%. From the aspect of data amount, the ratio is about 32%. It means that, compared with the whole space occupied by software, the amount of really-used data is limited.

Based on the analysis, we can see that access patterns of application virtualization are different from those of the whole VM: (1) For the latter (as mentioned by Capo [4]), the VM workload is write-heavy in IOps, and read-heavy in throughput, both by approximately two to one. In contrast, our analysis shows that read operations occupy the overwhelming majority. (2) Moreover, [4] disclaimed that directories typically managed by the OS are frequently accessed, including the OS Page files and the TEMP folders. In our case, because only software files have been considered, a large fraction of those accesses has been excluded.

Enlightened by the previous analysis, local caches (including the data cache and meta-data buffer) on the client are believed promising to satisfy a large portion of access requests. From the aspect of all machines, the set of frequently-used software is relatively fixed; thus some cooperative mechanism will be useful to share common software between clients.

4   Optimizations

For application virtualization, any resource of streaming software can be saved as files and the runtime environment redirects accesses to the real positions. Therefore, the equivalent problem is how to access files in the multi-layer system efficiently, as well as how to fully use application-level features for straightforward designs.

4.1   Local Caching

A persistent file cache is located on the client-side. When an application attempts to access any file, this local cache will be checked first. If the file is not already cached or the cached copy is not up to date, the client fetches a new version either from other clients (the cooperative cache) or directly from the server.

We design a particular caching mechanism that takes account of both the traditional LRU (Least Recently Used) and LFU (Least-Frequently Used) strategies. It can be regarded as a type of SLRU (Segmented LRU) caches [14]: The cache is divided into two segments, A and B; in each segment the LRU mechanism is used. B is a victim cache to occupy the replaced data belonging to Top N applications, while any other replaced data from A will be discarded directly. In addition, hits are removed from wherever they currently reside and added to the most recently accessed end of A. Cache data is identified by the software name (combined with the version no.), the file name and its aligned offset in the file. By replaying the collected traces using different local caching policies, we evaluate the efficiency of our cache design and compare it with the LRU and LFU strategies.

The evaluation process contains two phases: Phase 1 is the warming stage: We use the traces of the first day to fulfill the local cache; Phase 2 simulates the remaining data to give the evaluation miss-ratios of each day (from the second day to the seventh). We also assume that the N top applications have been identified based on the usage history before the simulation.

In the evaluation, the whole cache size is set to the following values respectively: 20%, 40%, 60% and 80% of the data traffic (redundant data has been excluded). In addition, there are other two configurations: the size of the victim cache and the value of N. If N is too large (for example, 20), most accesses would belong to the top set, which makes the segmentation meaningless. Thus, we set N as 10. Moreover, tests show that, to set the size as about 25% of the whole capacity has performed best.

On the other side, there are traces from 20 machines; thus we simulate the traces respectively and present the final weighted averages of miss rates of these six days: If the cache size is small (20% of the data amount), all of these strategies behave similarly; As the size is increasing, the SLRU-like strategy performs best in most cases and the LRU-based is the second. For example, as the cache size is set as 40% of the traffic, in the seventh day the miss rate of the SLRU-like strategy is 8.8% while the LRU is 12.3% and the LFU is 20%.

We know the LRU algorithm does not consider the usage-frequency entirely so that some data of frequently-used applications may be kicked out; the victim cache can remedy this situation. Similarly, the LFU cache may sacrifice those recently used data, which usually happens when the cache is close to the full and a new application is used. Therefore our hybrid design is a good tradeoff. In other words, if we set the local cache size as 40% of the amount of data amount without redundancies (about 800MB in our case averagely), the miss ratio can be as low as 8.8%.

4.2   Cooperative Caching

The local persistent cache goes a long way towards eliminating redundant read requests on individual machines. But as growing software deployments lead to larger numbers of physical hosts, redundant reads across these hosts place additional burden on the central server(s).

We introduce a cooperative caching mechanism to release the central burden because the analysis shows that there is a high similarity of usage frequencies between users.

Usually speaking, the cooperative cache is referred to as the layer in the storage hierarchy positioned between the local client and the server. Whenever a client misses data in its local cache, it attempts to fetch the data from the caches of other clients. Therefore, how to trace and locate data accurately is the focus.

A straight strategy is to trace status of each file. However, it will introduce more overheads on the server: In the trace, there are about 120 kinds of desktop applications used and the number of their files is more than 196000. Therefore, to record cache status of each application rather than each file will greatly reduce the amount of proxy information maintained on the server by several orders of magnitude, as well as the received request number for one application.

It is necessary to note that, the proxy list provided by the server is only a location hint: the needed files may be discarded or modified by the proxy. Thus the key point is the location accuracy of each file.

We have analyzed it using the same simulation method as described in the previous section: After the warming stage, we assume that one machine has lost all cached data (it can be also regarded as a new machine has joined), and then it has to fetch data from the network. For example, the second days trace of this machine shows that on average, about 82% of the requested applications have been used by other machines and 98.4% of these applications requested files will be found on those machines. It means that up to 80.6% of the requested data can be fetched from peers.

The second problem is how to identify the file gotten from other clients is valid. We have computed the hash value of each application file and embedded them into the meta-data package, which has been fetched at first. Thus, the client can check file content by comparing hash-values.

At last, to show the design validity, we replay trace on our prototype using different cache configurations and present the IOps observed at the server. The details will be presented in Section 5.2.

5   Implementation

We implement a distributed storage system for software streaming, DES3, which adopts the above optimizations and especially suitable for the enterprise environment. DES3 includes the following components:

1. A virtual file system on the client OS. It achieves access transparency for streaming software, which also acts as the local file cache to satisfy redundant reads.
2. The centralized storage server(s). In addition, it is the supervisor that manages all clients to form a cooperative file cache to reduce the load further.

The workflow of DES3 is: After connecting to the server for the first time, the client machine downloads the metadata package of all subscribed software from the server. For any software, the package contains its information of folder hierarchy and attributes of each file. Here attributes include a hash-value that identifies the file contents. This package is stored locally and updated as necessary during the runtime.

Next, when a client attempts to launch an application, it will connect the server for files if missed in the local cache. Under heavy load, the server will use the cooperative cache to provide the data.

5.1   The Client End

We use Dokan [15], an open-source framework of the user-space file system for Windows OSes, to implement the local virtual file system on each client machine. The file system is mounted as a local virtual drive and all streaming software looks like located in this drive. Dokan contains a virtual file system program and a kernel proxy driver. The latter can intercept requests targeted at the virtual file system, and redirect them to the former for real handling.

All operations work on the file-level: When a file is first read/write, the access will be redirected to the remote server to fetch the data and store it in the local. To conform to the streaming principle, the workflow of the virtual file system is:

The server storage is read-only; all modifications are done locally. To do so, any file or folder on the virtual file system is assigned one of three states: *remote, new, or deleted*. The first type means the file is located in the server (but may be cached locally); the second stands for any file created or modified during the runtime while the last means the file has been erased.

Correspondingly, three file lists are maintained for data consistency. When the file system is launched the first time, the new list and deleted list are both empty while all files/folders of the virtual file system are remote. During the runtime, the state of each file may change according to the concrete operations.

The organization of the local cache is straight: for any file that is cached, a corresponding local sparse file is created in a reserved folder on the local file system; the information of which range has been cached is recorded in a block bitmap. Then, after the name mapping and lookup phases, to access the cache is just as to read or write a common file.

The REST protocol is used as the transfer protocol between clients and the server. To simplify management, the offset and size of data access are set as 8KB-aligned. Therefore, any remote read during the runtime will be converted into an HTTP GET request with the size of an integer multiple of 8KB; the fetched data is stored in the local cache. In addition, some other key data-structures, including the three file lists and the necessary cache-related statistics, will be made persistent locally.

5.2   The Server End

An Apache WEB server is used as the storage server: all reads, including the metada-ta download, will be converted into HTTP requests. Of course, we can use any data delivery mechanism as the background: WEB server is only a choice of implementation, not an architectural requirement. Moreover, on the server side, the cooperative caching module is implemented by inserting hooks into the request-processing.

Moreover, DES3 is designed for the enterprise environment where a client usually accesses the server through its departments NAT gateway. Thus, the server can simply judge whether multiple clients are located on the same subnet; it is apt to redirect requests to proxies behind the same gateway with the requester.

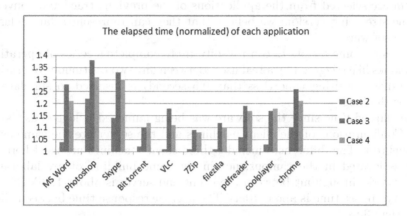

Fig. 1. Running performance of software on the client

5.3   Server Test

We evaluate the optimization effects on the server by replaying the collected I/O traces using three different caching policies: no cache, the SLRU cache without / with cooperative caching. On each machine, we set the cache size as 40% of the amount of data traffic (redundant data has been excluded).

The test environment consists of two PCs which serve as client machines to replay requests, and a server is used as the backend storage. Client machines are equipped with 4 GBytes DDR3 SDRAM, one Intel Core i5 CPU (2.53GHz). The server is a Windows server; equipped with one Intel Core 2 Duo E4500 CPU (2.2 GHz), 8 GBytes DDR3 SDRAM. All machines are connected by a 1Gb Ethernet switch.

We replay workload on the two client machines synchronously. Of course, it is impractical to replay all trace according to time stamps strictly, we select one peak region from each days trace and each region is of about 30 minutes. Therefore, after the warming phase (one days trace), six regions have been replayed strictly and loads observed by the server have been recorded. In addition, we recreated the state the local cache could be in at the start of each region by priming it from whole trace up to that point, as well as proxy-information on the server.

Tests show that the cooperative caching, combined with local caches, can reduce the access number of the server by about 94.6%; local caches themselves can reduce the number by 85.1%.

5.4   Client Test

Here we evaluate the running effects of 10 kinds of software on one client, including MS Office Word, Photoshop, Skype, Bittorrent, VLC, 7Zip and so on. All of them are selected from the applications of the previous trace and converted into the streaming version; we believe that they can represent a large class of desktop software.

We design some scripts to control software to complete a series of operations, which looks like triggered by a real user. Between any two continuous operations, some random waiting time (less than 0.5 second) is inserted to simulate the humans thinking.

The elapsed time since the software was being launched is logged as the run time. Configurations of the client machines and the server are the same as the previous test. The differences include: three client machines are used here; the server is located in the campus, not in the same building of my laboratory. The network throughput between the client and server is about 1.96MBps; the average response time is about 10ms. The average response time between clients is less than 3ms.

The following cases have been tested:

Case 1: All applications are installed locally. In this case, DES3 is not used; it is the baseline for the following comparisons.

Case 2: DES3 is employed, and the hit ratio of the local cache is set to 100%.

Case 3: DES3 is employed; the hit ratio of the local cache is set to 90% . All misses are handled by the server.

Case 4: DES3 is employed; the hit ratio of the local cache is set to 90%. All misses are handled by the other 2 clients.

Results (elapsed time of each application) are presented in Figure 1. Because the values have been normalized, only Case 2, 3, 4 are given. Compared with the baseline, DES3 with the perfect local cache will introduce about 6.8% extra running time; for the hit ratio of 90% (without cooperative caching), it is 21.6% on average; for the last case, the overhead is 14.6%.

6   Conclusion

After analyzing a real trace of desktop applications from a production deployment, we presented DES3, a network file system designed for the enterprise-scale desktop software deployment. DES3 uses the local disks on individual clients to cache software files and uses an application-granularity cooperative cache to reduce the server load further. Trace simulation has shown that the SLRU-like local-cache strategy performs better than the common LRU and LFU algorithms. Moreover, the simulation analysis also illustrates that the coarse-grained cooperative cache can locate target files accurately, as well as reducing the number of requests on the server remarkably. We have implemented the prototype of DES3 and test results have proven the designs efficiency.

Acknowledgement. The work is supported by the High Tech. R&D Program of China under Grant No. 2013AA01A215.

References

1. http://www.microsoft.com/systemcenter/softgrid/
2. VMware, ThinApp Users Guide, http://www.vmware.com/support
3. http://www.citrix.com/products/xenapp/overview.html
4. Shamma, M., Meyer, D.T., Wires, J., Ivanova, M., Hutchinson, N.C., Capo, A.W.: Recapitulating Storage for Virtual Desktops. In: Proceeding of: 9th USENIX Conference on File and Storage Technologies, San Jose, CA, USA (February 2011)
5. Chandra, R., Zeldovich, N., Sapuntzakis, C., Lam, M.S.: The Collective: A Cache-Based System Management Architecture. In: Proceedings of the Second Symposium on Networked Systems Design and Implementation (NSDI 2005) (May 2005)
6. http://www.mokafive.com/
7. Hansen, J., Jul Lithium, E.: virtual machine storage for the cloud. In: Proceedings of the 1st ACM Symposium on Cloud Computing, pp. 15-26. ACM (2010)
8. Alpern, B., Auerbach, J., et al.: PDS: a virtual execution environment for software deployment. In: Proceedings of the First ACM International Conference on Virtual execution Environments (March 2005)
9. Yu, Y., Guo, F., Nanda, S., et al.: A feather-weight virtual machine for windows applications. In: Proceedings of the 2nd ACM/ USENIX Conference on Virtual Execution Environments, VEE 2006 (2006)
10. Guo, P.: CDE: Run Any Linux Application On-Demand Without Installation. In: Proceedings of the USENIX Large Installation System Administration Conference. USENIX (2011)
11. VMWare. Virtual machine disk format (2010), http://www.vmware.com/technical-resources/interfaces/vmdk.html
12. http://www.symantec.com/workspace-virtualization
13. Cui, Y., Hu, C., Wo, T., Wang, H.: A virtual file system for streaming loading of virtual software on windows NT. In: Li, R., Cao, J., Bourgeois, J. (eds.) GPC 2012. LNCS, vol. 7296, pp. 231–243. Springer, Heidelberg (2012)
14. Karedla, R., Spencer Love, J., Wherry, B.G.: Caching Strategies to Improve Disk System Performance. In: Computer (1994)
15. Dokan, user mode file system for windows, http://code.google.com/p/dokan

AzureITS: A New Cloud Computing Intelligent Transportation System

Siamak Najjar Karimi

Department of Computer Engineering, Shabestar Branch,
Islamic Azad University, Shabestar, Iran
siyamak.karimi@gmail.com

Abstract. Intelligent Transportation Systems (ITS) use communications and new technology to increase road throughput and optimize the traffic control for increased safety of drivers. This enables people to find services and information which they need to drive more safely and comfortably. Cloud computing is a new technology which can solve many issues such as real-time problem of the urban traffic control system and enable the end users to access the required services on demand without worrying where they actually exist. It delivers everything as a service and is generally termed as XaaS. In this paper, we propose a new system for intelligent traffic systems to manage and improve traffic condition as well as to solve the limited resource issue of car device to monitor and analyze events happening in the way of car by using cloud computing. To achieve this purpose, we use the facilities of Windows Azure and Ajax to implement the system.

1 Introduction

Today, transportation research and development is no longer a field dominated by civil, mechanical, operations research, and other traditional engineering and management disciplines. Rather, computer sciences, control, communication, the Internet, and methods developed in artificial intelligence (AI), computational intelligence, web sciences, and many other emerging information sciences and engineering areas have formed the core of new ITS technology and become integral and important parts of modern transportation engineering [1][2]. The increase of traffic congestion and accidents causing million injuries and mortalities exist in different regions of the world and wastes fuel and time and increases the costs. These problems are major obstacles for the development of society and they are growing day by day. They could be solved easily by providing relevant information to the vehicles or the drivers. It makes roads safer and more efficient for drivers and forces lower costs to governments and in general it makes optimal efficiency of vehicles and their features [3].

Intelligent traffic systems use communication technology to manage traffic flow enabling drivers to select the best route. Furthermore, avoiding traffic congestion helps much time and fuel be saved and large modern cities be restored. In this paper, we propose a new system for ITS using the facilities of Windows Azure to announce vehicles related with an accident quickly. Moreover, this system, considering the type of incident like a simple vehicle accident or an incident with injured driver, informs the nearest police and emergency stations, automatically. After an event happens, this

J. Kołodziej et al. (Eds.): ICA3PP 2013, Part I, LNCS 8285, pp. 468–478, 2013.

system using a matrix based approach, finds all streets and lines joined to the road on which the incident or changing traffic condition has happened. Then it creates messages about the event and puts in Azure Service Bus Topics providing a highly scalable, durable, flexible, and cost-effective way to publish messages and deliver them to vehicles moving in finding lines, police and emergency station, asynchronously. So these vehicle's drivers can avoid passing through streets that are closed or have heavy traffic; besides, police and ambulance can arrive on time, which in turn clears the road quickly and saves injured people without any waste of urgent time. In addition, to help drivers who do not understand the language, this system demonstrates the occurrence of the accident and the traffic condition on that street by using the related symbol of the incident and changing the color of the street on the monitor of vehicle, Ajax carries out all mentioned operations rapidly. In addition, a key challenge in building the effective car device to analyze street events is the resource limitation. Existing solutions consume much resources for their operation, such as memory, storage, and CPU which lead to increase the price of them and drivers avoid such solutions. To solve this matter, we offer a flexible solution, Car Device Agent, to perform various powerful analysis by using Windows Azure Worker Role, while imposing little resource utilization on the car device.

The remainder of the article is organized as follows: Section 2 introduces the background of Vehicular Communication Networks, Cloud computing and Windows Azure. Section 3, provides the state of the art of ITS cloud computing. Section 4 shows an overall view of the proposed system. Section 5 shows the kinds of messages data formats used in our system. Section 6 describes symbols and streets colors related to an event. Section 7 describes the implementation of our proposed system and section 8 present the advantage of this system. Finally, conclusions are drawn in Section 9.

2   Background

2.1   Vehicular Communications Networks

Vehicular Communication Networks (VCNs) is a subcategory of Mobile Communications Networks that has the special characteristics of high node mobility and fast topology changes. It is a technology aim for improving traffic safety and efficiency in different road systems and networks that offer an efficient communication platform for intelligent transportation systems and related services, as well as multimedia and date services [4]. This will enable the formation of vehicular networks, commonly referred to as VANETs, an instance of mobile ad hoc networks with cars as the mobile nodes [5]. VANET is a special type of mobile ad-hoc network, utilizing vehicles as mobile nodes to create a network that provides safe aspects of roads [6].

The main goal of VANET is to provide the awareness to the vehicles about the safety measures and alert messages. The vehicular communication can be classified as vehicle to vehicle communication (V2V) and vehicle to infrastructure communication (V2I) [7]. Fig. 1 shows an example of a vehicular network.

2.2   Cloud Computing

Cloud computing is a model for enabling ubiquitous, convenient, on-demand network access to a shared pool of configurable computing resources that can be rapidly provisioned and released with minimal management effort or service provider interaction[10]. Cloud computing services are divided into three classes, namely: (1) Infrastructure as a Service (IaaS), (2) Platform as a Service (PaaS), and (3) Software as a Service (SaaS) [11].

IaaS offering virtualized resources on demand. A cloud infrastructure enables on-demand provisioning of servers running several choices of operating systems and a customized software stack[12] [13]. SaaS is a software delivery method that provides access to software and its functions remotely as a Web-based service [14]. PaaS offerings including facilities for application design, application development, testing, deployment and hosting [15].The Windows Azure platform fits best in the PaaS category, because it does not provide access to the underlying virtualization environment or operating system details [16].

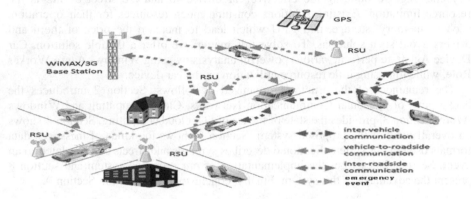

Fig. 1. An example of a vehicular network

2.3   Windows Azure

Windows Azure is an operating system for the cloud that completely abstracts the physical components of the system: the developer chooses the features, the components, and the level of Service Level Agreement (SLA) without the configuration of hardware or software on the assigned machines and can build massively scalable applications with lots and lots of users. [17].

2.3.1 Service Bus Topics

The Windows Azure Service Bus provides a hosted, secure, and widely available infrastructure for widespread communication, large-scale event distribution, naming, and service publishing. Moreover, it provides durable, asynchronous messaging components such as Queues, Topics, and Subscriptions [8]. Service Bus topics and subscriptions implement a publish/subscribe pattern that delivers a highly scalable, flexible, and cost-effective way to publish messages from an application and deliver them to multiple subscribers. Fig. 2 below shows the structure of a Service Bus topics that a sending application sends messages to a topic, these messages are then routed to zero, one or more subscriptions based on a set of rules[9].

Fig. 2. The structure of Service Bus topics

2.3.2   The Worker Role

A Worker Role is a type of service that, by default, is not exposed with an endpoint but is instead dedicated to performing process operations in the back end. Worker Role (back end) and Web Role (front end of a web application) instances can be adjusted independently. When there are more orders, the instances for the front-end can be increased. The queue will accept more orders without any problems, and the front-end thread that serves the user request can be placed in the pool to serve another incoming request. Similarly, if the queue length starts to increase, the number of Worker Role instances would rise accordingly.

2.3.3   Windows Azure Traffic Manager

This service reduces network latency by directing users to the nearest instance of an application running in the cloud. It maximize availability of cloud applications and can also detect whether an instance of a service has failed or is unreachable, automatically directing user requests to the next available service instance.

2.3.4   Autoscaling and Windows Azure

One of the key benefits that the Windows Azure delivers is the ability to rapidly scale application in the cloud in response to changes in demand. An autoscaling solution reduces the amount of manual work involved in dynamically scaling an application [19][20].

3   Related Works

In the current literature, most urban traffic problems are studied in algorithms or models about several intersections or control agents [21]. Agent-based control methods provide a reliable and flexible approach for intelligent, effective management of traffic and transportation systems in connected environments [22].There are some works using cloud computing based urban traffic control system that propose several frameworks and applications trying to use cloud to store data and access traffic knowledge from cloud as a service. In addition, some works propose solutions to solve issue like real-time problems. In [23] the authors propose the application that combines geographical addressing and cloud service discovery mechanisms for requesting routing. The authors in [3] put forward a new system that tries to improve the current systems and reduce their limitation by using Grid and Cloud technologies. In [24] the authors present the concept of autonomous vehicular cloud (AVC) with application scenarios that related research challenges and the set up process of AVC are explained.

In [25] the authors present three tier vehicle cloud architecture from device, communication and service level providing several customized cloud vehicle services like driver healthcare monitoring and in-car resource sharing services is proposed. In [26] some survey work about the platform-as-a-service of public cloud requirements with target application in a mobile and interactive environment like a car is provided. The authors in [2] propose a prototype urban-traffic management system using multi agent using cloud to handle the large amount of storage resources and mass transportation of data effectively and efficiently. However, all mentioned works did not offer a real economic ITS cloud application that is able to support a numerous requests asynchronously.

4   Proposed System Overview

In this proposed system, we use Windows Azure facilities to build massively scalable and cost effective ITS cloud application with numerous vehicles of a metropolis, which processes all events happened on different streets immediately. Azure Service Bus Topics is used between cloud application and both on-premises (such as police station) and mobile applications (vehicles), allowing them to exchange messages in a loosely coupled way for improved scale and resiliency. It sends asynchronously messages to mobile device of vehicles and stations related to events taking place on various streets and also there will not be any worries about delivery assurance, reliable messaging and scale.

By virtue of using multi-instances processing capability of windows Azure, our system is able to process several events happening in various parts of a metropolis on multiple instances simultaneously which leads to decrease the response time significantly. To accomplish it, the operators of program should increase the number of instance to deal with the rise of demands and then again reduce it to decline the cost. However, in our system, as it is explained in section VII, all mentioned operations are carried out automatically. Besides, the scalable and massive SQL Azure and Azure Storage are used to store the information of streets and some especial data such as videos and images provided by street cameras, respectively.

When an incident or changing traffic conditions like heavy (or semi) traffic happens on a street, proposed cloud application, using a matrix based approach, finds all related lines of streets; then messages, the topic of which is the id of every finding line, are created. In addition, a message for police station and, in case any injury, a message for emergency station is generated. Then all messages are put in Azure Service Bus Topics which are delivered to corresponding vehicles (figure 6), the nearest police and emergency stations (figure 7), asynchronously.

Fig. 3 shows a simple sample of using our proposed system in a part of a metropolis where the blue car is involved in a collision with a red car on which a tree has fallen, and not only is the driver of the red car injured, but also this line of the street is closed. Thus, messages for purple and yellow cars moving in related street, police and emergency stations are created and then put in Azure Service Bus Topics. For example, as you can see, after receiving the message of this incident, the purple car turns to right to pass from a parallel street and the yellow car avoids passing this street.

Another noticeable capability of system is that drivers can be aware of the latest condition of every street throughout the city in the form of animation immediately by proposed technique in section 6. Thus, after receiving a message revealing an event or congested condition on a street, driver can easily see the condition of other relevant streets and select the best one to go destination.

Additionally, by using this system vehicles can communicate with cloud directly which leads to no need to establish infrastructure communication along streets and also when V2V communication is impossible; the message of vehicles are sent to cloud application delivering it to corresponding cars via Service Bus Topics asynchronously.

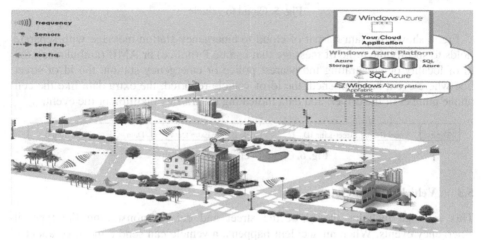

Fig. 3. A sample of our proposed system

5   Message Data Format

In this system several types of messages are used that include the following:

5.1   Vehicle to Cloud

This message has separate fields to specify the id of vehicle, the id of street's line where the accident has happened and Data determining the type of events like ordinary vehicle accident or injury vehicle accident. Fig. 4 shows its data format. For example, when a vehicle reports an injury vehicle accident, our system informs not only the police and emergency stations but also the cars moving on the streets joined to Street-Line ID, the street's line of this message.

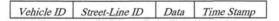

| Vehicle ID | Street-Line ID | Data | Time Stamp |

Fig. 4. Vehicle to cloud message data format

5.2   Cloud to Vehicles and Stations

When receiving a message about an accident or new traffic condition on a street, our cloud application creates response messages and puts them in Azure Service Bus topics. There are two types of response messages: cloud to vehicle and cloud to emergency stations. Fig. 5 exposes a cloud to vehicle message data format with separate fields to specify the id of finding (Target) Street line related to reported event and Data indicating the traffic condition or incident which has happened on the street. Target Street-Line ID is the topic of message that related vehicles can receive it from the Azure Service Bus topics.

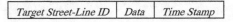

Target Street-Line ID	Data	Time Stamp

Fig. 5. Cloud to vehicle

Fig. 6 shows the data format of cloud to emergency station message with separate fields to specify the topic of message that can be P (police) or AMB (ambulance), the id of locality demonstrating the nearest police or emergency station, the id of street line where event has happened, the id of vehicle reported, the extra data like the cell phone number of the driver, and data indicating the traffic condition or the event.

Topic	Local ID	Street-Line ID	Vehicle ID	Extra Data	Data	Time Stamp

Fig. 6. Cloud to emergency station

5.3   Vehicle to Vehicle

This message includes the id of the street and data demonstrating the type of emergency events. When an accident happens, a vehicle can send a message about it so that other vehicles on the same street can receive it, by means of Street ID code.

Street ID	Data	Time Stamp

Fig. 7. Inter Vehicle communication

6   Symbols and Colors

For those who do not know the language, they can comprehend the pictorial representation easily. The event symbols and streets colors play a major role for understating things quickly. When an event happens or there is a changing traffic condition on a street, not only are the symbols of the event with related message shown but also the color of street is changed at monitor of vehicles. So this system helps drivers to understand the last condition of streets easily to select the best route. Table 1 shows corresponding color and symbol with each event which may take place on the streets.

In addition, it is rare to build a new web application today and not include Ajax features. Technically, Ajax stands for asynchronous JavaScript and XML. In practice, Ajax stands for all the techniques you use to build responsive web applications with a great user experience. ASP.NET MVC 4 is a modern web framework, and like every modern web framework there is support for Ajax right from the start [19]. Thus, Ajax is used to change the color of streets and appear the symbols of the event with a related text message on vehicles monitor, all of which are carried out rapidly.

Table 1. Symbols and color of street conditions

Color of Street	Condition of Street	symbols
Maroon	Street is closed	 Street is closed
Red	Heavy Traffic	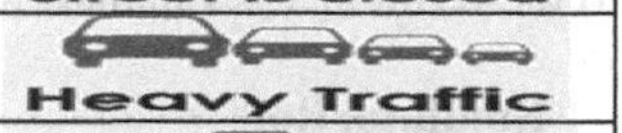 Heavy Traffic
Pink	Semi-Heavy Traffic	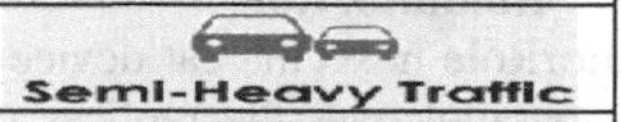 Semi-Heavy Traffic
Yellow	ordinary	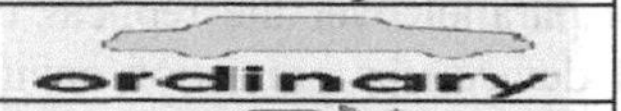 ordinary
Bronze	ordinary vehicle accident	 ordinary vehicle accident
Orange	injury vehicle accident	 injury vehicle accident

7   Implementation

To implement proposed cloud application, ASP.NET MVC 4 is used to utilize Windows Azure facilities like Service Bus Topics and Azure storage. This application is made up of cloud application code that Windows Azure deploys to every node and Configuration Settings files: ServiceDefinition and ServiceConfiguration.

The ServiceDefinition file contains the metadata that is required by the Windows Azure environment for the requirements of your application. This file also contains configuration settings that apply to all instances. These configuration settings can be read at runtime using the Windows Azure Service Hosting Runtime API.

The ServiceConfiguration file sets values for the configuration settings defined in the service definition file that can be updated while service is running in Windows Azure. Fig. 8 shows its simple form that Instances count (2) specifies the number of instances is required for each of application roles when developer first deploy the application to Windows Azure.

This system by using Enterprise Library Autoscaling Application Block ("Wasabi") of Windows Azure can automatically handle changes in the load levels that it might experience over time which leads to minimize its operational costs, while still providing excellent performance and availability to users. It also helps to reduce the number of manual tasks that operators must perform. To apply Wasabi we defined some rules in XML format stored in Windows Azure blob storage, and also we use Windows Azure Traffic Manager to maximize availability of proposed application.

```xml
<?xml version="1.0" encoding="utf-8"?>
<ServiceConfiguration serviceName="...">
  <Role name="AzureITSApp">
    <Instances count="2" />
    <ConfigurationSettings>
      ...
    </ConfigurationSettings>
  </Role>
</ServiceConfiguration>
```

Fig. 8. ServiceConfiguration.cscfg

7.1   Car Device Agent

Car Device Agent is a lightweight software that runs on the smartphones registered to use AzureITS service. It collects sensor inputs from the device's interfaces and sends them to the AzureITS 's EmulatorRole.

7.1.1   EmulatorRole

EmulatorRole hosts the car device replicas as well as different analyzing solution that run in parallel over the replicas corresponding to several actual devices. Unlike an actual device, the emulation environment is not resource-limited, and hence can be used to deploy multiple analysis and security solutions concurrently to monitor sensor inputs from the device's interfaces and device replicas for various types of likely compromises. Taking we use Windows Azure web Role and Worker Role to implement EmulatorRole into account, if there are more events to process, the instances for the front-end (Web Role) would increase to accept more event data. Subsequently, by increasing the queue length, the number of back-end (Worker Role) instances increase to process events.

8   Advantages of the Proposed System

Because of using cloud computing approach, Windows Azure facilities, and Ajax for implementation, our system has several advantages which can be summarized as following:

First of all, the scalability of application is automatic and network latency is low. Secondly, only related vehicles are informed, which is done at a very high speed, without any trouble in sending messages, and, of course, in a loosely coupled way. Thirdly, there is no limit: neither on the number of users nor on the amount of data stored. Last but not least, it contributes to solve some problems of VANET, improve traffic condition considerably and save much money.

9   Conclusion and Future Work

Nowadays the necessity of drivers' awareness of road conditions to avoid undesirable situation such as collision and traffic congestion which wastes time and money, is obvious. Cloud computing based on intelligent transportation systems (ITSs) concept is considered to solve these needs recently. In this paper, we proposed a new system based on cloud computing approach as well as Windows Azure facilities and Ajax which are used to implement it. So this system not only has all advantage of cloud computing that developers do not worry to support their application during peak demand time and the limitation of storages to store massive data increased every moment but also only vehicles and stations related to an event are informed. Moreover, because of using Azure Service Bus topics, this system can inform a lot of vehicles and stations related to an event asynchronously.

In the future we will gather the statistics of Urban Traffic Centre to evaluate efficiency, availability, scalability and load balancing of our proposed system as well as compare traffic congestion, the amount of using fuel and air pollution, the rate of vehicle accidents and drivers' opinions before and after using this system.

References

1. Buyyaa, R., Shin Yeoa, C., Venugopala, S., Broberga, J., Brandic, I.: Cloud Computing and Emerging IT Platforms: Vision, Hype, and Reality for Delivering Computing as the 5th Utility. Future Generation Computer Systems 25(6), 599–616 (2009)
2. Trivedi, P., Deshmukh, K., Shrivastava, M.: Cloud Computing for Intelligent Transportation System. International Journal of Soft Computing and Engineering, IJSCE (2012)
3. Alipour, B., Mohammad Khanli, L., Mahan, F.: KGIC-ITS, a new system in intelligent transport system with corporation knowledge grid & cloud technology. In: IEEE International Conference on Vehicular Electronics and Safety, Istanbul, Turkey (2012)
4. Daher, R., Vinel, A.: Roadside Networks for Vehicular Communications. IGI Global (2012) ISBN: 978-1-4666-2224-1
5. Padmavathi, K., Maneendhar, R.: A Surveying on Road Safety Using Vehicular Communication Networks, Journal of Computer Applications, EICA (2012)
6. Moustafa, H., Zhang, Y.: Vehicular Networks: Techniques, Standards, and Applications (2009) ISBN: 978-1420085716
7. Baby, D., Sabareesh, R.D., Saravanaguru, R.A.K., Thangavelu, A.: VCR: Vehicular cloud for road side scenarios. In: Meghanathan, N., Nagamalai, D., Chaki, N. (eds.) Advances in Computing & Inf. Technology. AISC, vol. 178, pp. 541–552. Springer, Heidelberg (2012)
8. Manheim, S., Squillace, R.: Windows Azure Service Bus Reference. Microsoft (2012)
9. Smith, A.: Windows Azure Service Bus Developer Guide (2011)
10. Mell. P., Grance, T.: The NIST Definition of Cloud Computing, National Institute of Standards and Technology, Information Technology Laboratory, Technical Report Version 15 (2009)
11. Buyya, R., Broberg, J., Goscinski, A.: CLOUD COMPUTING Principles and Paradigms. John Wiley & Sons (2011) ISBN 978-0-470-88799-8
12. Sotomayor, B., Montero, R., Llorente, I., Foster, I.: Virtual infrastructure management in private and hybrid clouds. IEEE Internet Computing, 14–22 (2009)
13. Nurmi, D., Wolski, R., Grzegorczyk, C., Obertelli, G., Soman, S., Youseff, L., Zagorodnov, D.: The Eucalyptus open-source cloud-computing system. In: Proceedings of IEEE/ACM International Symposium on Cluster Computing and the Grid (2009)
14. http://www.webopedia.com/TERM/S/SaaS.html
15. http://en.wikipedia.org/wiki/Platform_as_a_service
16. Brunetti, R.: Windows Azure™ Step by Step. O'Reilly Media, Microsoft, USA (2011) ISBN: 978-0-7356-4972-9
17. http://www.windowsazure.com
18. Densmore, S., Homer, A., Narumoto, M., Sharp, J., Zhang, H.: Building Hybrid Applications in the Cloud, Microsoft (2012)
19. http://msdn.microsoft.com/
   en-us/library/hh680945(v=pandp.50).aspx
20. http://msdn.microsoft.com/en-us/library/ff966483.aspx
21. Li, S.: A Survey of Urban Traffic Coordination Controls in Intelligent Transportation Systems. IEEE (2012)
22. Wang, F.: Agent-Based Control for Networked Traffic Management Systems. Intelligent Systems, 92–96 (2005)

23. Jaworski, P., Edwards, T., Moore, J., Burnham, K.: Cloud Computing Concept for Intelligent Transportation Systems. In: 14th International IEEE Conference on Intelligent Transportation Systems, Washington, DC, USA (2011)
24. Eltoweissy, M., Olariu, S., Younis, M.: Towards Autonomous Vehicular Clouds. In: Proc. AdHocNets, pp. 1–16 (2010)
25. Wang, J., Ma, T., Cho, J., Lee, S.: Real Time Services for Future Cloud Computing Enabled Vehicle Networks. WCSP (2011)
26. Bernstein, D., Vidovic, N., Modi, S.: A Cloud PAAS for High Scale, Function, and Velocity Mobile Applications. In: Proc. the Fifth International Conference on Systems and Networks Communications, pp. 117–123 (2010)

Author Index